2/23/12
$95.00

BUILDING SYSTEMS FOR INTERIOR DESIGNERS

SECOND EDITION

Corky Binggeli, A.S.I.D.

John Wiley & Sons, Inc.

Published by John Wiley & Sons, Inc., Hoboken, New Jersey
Published simultaneously in Canada

For general information about our other products and services, please contact our Customer Care
Department within the United States at (800) 762-2974, outside the United States at (317) 572-3993 or
fax (317) 572-4002.

Wiley also publishes its books in a variety of electronic formats. Some content that appears in print
may not be available in electronic books. For more information about Wiley products, visit our web site
at www.wiley.com.

Library of Congress Cataloging-in-Publication Data:
Binggeli, Corky.
    Building systems for interior designers / Corky Binggeli. — 2nd ed.
            p. cm.
        ISBN 978-0-470-22847-0 (cloth)
    1. Buildings—Environmental engineering. 2. Buildings—Mechanical equipment—Design and
construction. 3. Buildings—Electric equipment—Design and construction.
    I. Title.
TH6014.B56 2010
696—dc22   2008047057

Printed in the United States of America

10 9 8 7 6 5 4 3

To my mother, Genevieve Bingley,
who taught me to love learning, and
to my father, Walter Bingley,
who showed me how buildings are made.

To my father-in-law, Edward T. Kirkpatrick,
whose lifelong commitment to engineering education
continues to inspire me, and
to my mother-in-law, Barbara Kirkpatrick,
whose lessons in calm and loving acceptance are
the best antidotes to anxiety and stress.

CONTENTS

PREFACE

When the first edition of *Building Systems for Interior Designers* was published in 2003, it was the only textbook available that supported the special concerns of the interior designer, while connecting those issues to the work of the rest of the building design team. To the best of my knowledge, this remains true of the second edition as we go to press.

The experience of teaching from *Building Systems for Interior Designers* over the past few years has shown me where the first edition could be improved. The second edition has a great many more illustrations and explanatory captions. There are new tables that condense useful information into an easy-to-read format, along with bulleted lists. The chapter structure has been modified to simplify organization and make it easier to break up the text into reading assignments. Material has been reviewed for accuracy and updated to reflect current design trends. This is now an even better book than it was before.

The approach of building design professionals to building systems has changed dramatically in the past five years. The relationship of global climate change to the way buildings are heated and cooled is now a major concern of architects, engineers, and government officials. The political, economic, and environmental costs of using fossil fuels are internationally recognized, leading to a dramatic increase in interest in alternative fuels and energy conservation. The importance of good indoor air quality for the health of occupants is recognized by those who design, fund, build, and furnish buildings.

This second edition of *Building Systems for Interior Designers* addresses these issues by increasing information about sustainable building design, giving the interior designer the resources needed to participate as part of a sustainable design team. Part I: The Building and Its Environment has updated and new material relating to energy use and sustainable design.

An entirely new section, Part II: Structural Systems, has been added to provide interior designers with basic information about types of new and existing structures and how they affect building interior spaces. It completes the scope of building systems covered and provides a framework for discussions of other systems. Part II is written specifically to inform interior designers about possible structural issues that they might encounter in their work and to encourage them to work with architects, engineers, and other design professionals with advanced knowledge of structures.

Part III: Water Supply, Distribution, and Waste Systems has been updated to address solid waste and recycling issues in more detail. Part IV: Thermal Comfort: Heating and Cooling Systems streamlines the introduction of basic principles, indoor air quality issues, and equipment systems, with a focus on energy sources and conservation.

Part V: Electrical and Lighting Systems now includes both electrical and lighting systems, as well as electrical appliances and equipment. Once again, the focus is on energy conservation, including daylighting.

The information in Part VI: Fire Safety has been updated and checked for accuracy. The section on fire safety tests for interior materials is now clearer and easier to use.

The awareness of the role noise control plays in our interior environment continues to grow. Part VII: Acoustics gives interior designers the information needed to design spaces that protect speech privacy and block unwanted noise. These areas are especially appropriate for interior designers to address.

As interior designers continue to be integrated into the design/build team, their need to understand the work of other design professionals continues to grow. The expanding adoption of LEED certification of buildings relies on the close coordination of design team members. The introduction of BIM (building information management) software is changing the way buildings are designed and built and making teamwork an essential part of the process. Buildings are being designed not as isolated objects, but within the context of a global environment. *Building Systems for Interior Designers, Second Edition* is written to help interior designers contribute their special awareness of interior environments to this team effort.

ACKNOWLEDGMENTS

The second edition of *Building Systems for Interior Designers* has been improved by the availability of new publications and new editions of older ones, including the Tenth Edition of *Mechanical and Electrical Equipment for Buildings* by Benjamin Stein, John S. Reynolds, Walter T. Grondzik, and Alison G. Kwok (John Wiley & Sons, Inc., Hoboken, NJ, 2006). Its comprehensive and clear coverage of building systems is both a standard for excellence and a source for accurate information.

Since writing the First Edition of this book, I have developed a continuing and productive relationship with the staff at John Wiley & Sons, Inc., whose professionalism, support, and good advice continue to guide my efforts. I especially want to thank my editor, Paul Drougas, for his encouragement, feedback, and good humor. I would also like to thank Sadie Abuhoff, editorial assistant; Alda Trabucchi, senior production editor; Cindy Geist, designer and compositor; Liz Harvey, copy editor; and Catherine Bielitz and Shannon Egan, proofreaders.

This edition has benefitted greatly from the feedback of my students and faculty colleagues. They have contributed honest criticism and clear expressions of their needs that are reflected in improvements throughout the book.

Finally, I am as always deeply indebted to my husband, Keith Kirkpatrick. This book is a testament to his patience, insight, diligence, and steadfast support in a thousand small ways.

CORKY BINGGELI, A.S.I.D.

PART

I

· · · · · · · · · · · · · · · ·

THE BUILDING AND ITS ENVIRONMENT

Although interior designers are primarily concerned with the conditions inside buildings, they benefit from observing a building's site, climate, and geography. Interior spaces are increasingly blended with their natural settings. Wise energy use dictates awareness of how sun, wind, and cold affect the building's interior. Interior designers today are working as part of environmentally aware design teams.

Environmental Conditions and the Site

Like our skins, a building is the interface between our bodies and our environment. The **building envelope** is the point at which the inside comes into contact with the outside; it is the place where energy, materials, and living things pass in and out. The building's interwoven structural, mechanical, electrical, plumbing, and other systems create an interior environment that supports our needs and activities and responds to exterior weather and site conditions. In turn, the building itself and its site are affected by the earth's larger natural patterns.

THE OUTDOOR ENVIRONMENT

The sun acting on the earth's atmosphere creates climate and weather conditions. During the day, the sun's energy heats the atmosphere, the land, and the sea. At night, much of this heat is released back into space. The warmth of the sun moves air and moisture across the earth's surface and generates seasonal and daily weather patterns.

Solar energy is the source of almost all of our energy resources. **Ultraviolet (UV) radiation** from the sun triggers photosynthesis in green plants, producing the oxygen we breathe, the plants we eat, and the fuels we use for heat and power. UV wavelengths make up only about 1 percent of the sun's rays that reach sea level and are too short to be visible. About half of the energy in sunlight that reaches the earth arrives as visible wavelengths. The remaining energy is infrared (IR) radiation, with wavelengths longer than visible light that carry the sun's heat.

The distance that radiation must travel through the earth's atmosphere largely determines the amount of radiation that reaches the earth's surface. This distance varies with the angle of the earth's tilt toward or away from the sun; this tilt is responsible for the seasons.

The sun warms our bodies and our buildings both directly and indirectly by warming the air around us. We depend on the sun's heat for comfort, and our buildings are designed to admit sunlight for warmth. Passive and active solar design techniques also protect us from excessive heat and help keep our buildings comfortable in hot weather.

The sun's heat also powers the **hydrologic cycle** by evaporating water into the air and purifying it through distillation. The water vapor condenses as it rises, then precipitates as rain and snow, which clean the air as they fall to the earth. Heavier particles fall out of the air because of gravity, and the wind (driven by the sun's heat) dilutes and distributes any remaining contaminants when it stirs up the air.

The sun illuminates the indoors through windows and skylights during the day. Direct sunlight is often too bright for comfortable vision. When the atmosphere scatters visible light, the resulting shade offers an even, restful illumination. Under heavy clouds and at night, artificial light provides adequate illumination.

Sunlight disinfects surfaces that it touches, which is one reason the old-fashioned clothesline may be superior to the clothes dryer. UV radiation kills many harmful microorganisms, purifying the atmosphere and eliminating disease-causing bacteria from sunlit surfaces. It also creates vitamin D in our skin, which we need to utilize calcium.

However, sunlight can also be destructive. While most UV radiation is blocked by the high-altitude ozone layer, enough UV radiation gets through to burn our skin painfully, sometimes even fatally. Over the long term, exposure to UV radiation may result in skin cancer.

In addition to providing direct solar heat and light, the sun's energy is transferred, stored, and used by plants and animals.

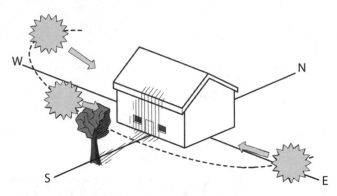

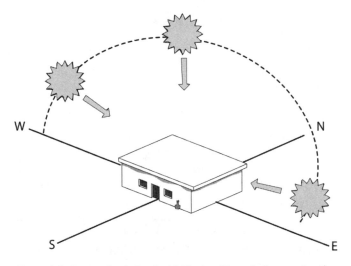

Figure 1-2 **Sun angles in northern latitudes.** In the northern hemisphere, direct solar radiation in midsummer strikes perpendicular to the earth's surface. In the winter, solar radiation travels a longer, lower-angled path through the atmosphere.

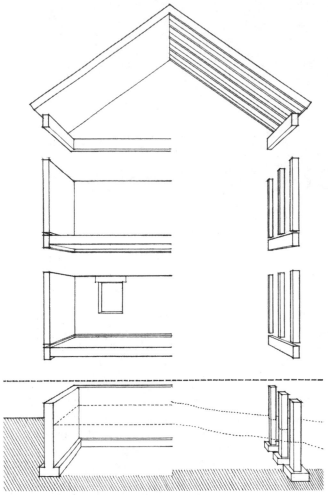

Figure 1-1 **Superstructure and foundation.** The underground part of the building is in direct contact with soil, rock, and groundwater. The aboveground superstructure is affected by wind, rain, snow, and sun. Building designs can blend into or shut out environmental conditions. Our design choices have a direct impact on our world.

Figure 1-3 **Sun angles in tropical latitudes.** Closer to the equator, the sun remains more directly overhead throughout the year.

Plants combine the sun's energy with water and turn it into sugars, starches, and proteins through photosynthesis. During this process, plants remove carbon dioxide from the air and return oxygen. Humans and other animals breathe in oxygen and exhale carbon dioxide, thereby completing the cycle.

Besides the roles photosynthesis plays in food supply and oxygen production, it is also instrumental in producing wood for construction, fibers for fabrics and paper, and landscape plantings for shade and beauty.

☑ **Sunlight contributes to the deterioration of paints, roofing, wood, and other building materials. Fabric dyes may fade, and many plastics decompose when exposed to direct sun. This is an issue that interior designers must consider when specifying materials.**

Plants transfer the sun's energy to us when we eat them, as well as when we eat plant-eating animals. This energy goes back into the environment when animal waste decomposes and releases nitrogen,

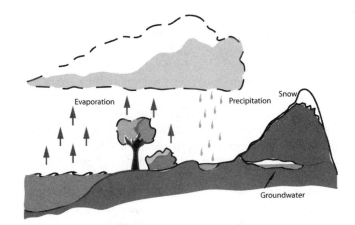

Figure 1-4 **Hydrologic cycle.** Changing climate conditions affect how much water evaporates from ice, snow, and surface bodies of water. When, where, and how much water precipitates back to the earth are also affected by climate, including wind and storm patterns. Warming temperatures influence how much water is stored as ice and snow.

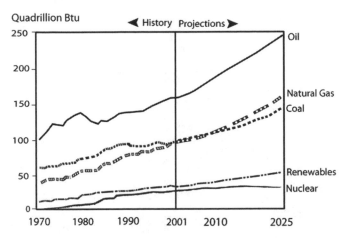

Quadrillion Btu
◀ History | Projections ▶

Oil
Natural Gas
Coal
Renewables
Nuclear

Figure 1-5 Graph of world energy use. This graph shows worldwide energy use.

phosphorus, potassium, carbon, and other elements into the soil and water. Animals or microorganisms break down dead animals and plants into basic chemical compounds, which then reenter the cycle to nourish plant life.

All of our energy sources are derived from the sun, with the exception of geothermal, nuclear, and tidal power.

- **Photovoltaic (PV)** technology converts solar energy directly into electricity at a building's site. PV collectors provide energy for heating water or for electrical power.
- Wind power derives from currents created when the sun heats the air and the ground.
- Hydroelectric power is made possible by the solar-driven cycle of evaporation and precipitation of water.
- Electricity produced by solar or wind energy can in turn be used to generate hydrogen, a high-grade fuel, from water.
- Photosynthesis provides the materials for biomass conversion, which is the combustion of firewood, crop waste, and even animal waste.

All of the above are considered to be renewable resources because they can be continually replenished, but our demand for energy may exceed the rate of replenishment.

Our most commonly used fuels—coal, oil, and gas—are fossil fuels. Huge quantities of decaying vegetation were compressed and subjected to the earth's heat over hundreds of millions of years, creating the fossilized solar energy we use today. Clearly, these resources are not renewable in the short term.

LIMITED ENERGY RESOURCES

According to the Department of Energy (DOE), 85 percent of the energy used in the United States comes from fossil fuels. With only 5 percent of the world's population, the United States consumes roughly 25 percent of the world's fossil fuel resources, of which buildings use 40 percent to operate.

The sun's energy arrives at the earth at a constant rate, and the supply of solar energy stored over millions of years in fossil fuels is limited. The population keeps growing, and people continue using more energy. We do not know exactly when we will run out of energy, but we do know that wasting the limited resources we have is dangerous. Through careful design, architects, interior designers, and building engineers can help make these finite resources last longer.

Historically, human societies have used a variety of energy sources. Before 1800, solar energy was the dominant source of heat and light, and wood was used for fuel. Wind was used for transportation and processing of grain. Early industries located along rivers and streams utilized waterpower.

Around the beginning of the nineteenth century, mineral discoveries introduced portable, convenient, and reliable coal, petroleum, and natural gas fuels to power the Industrial Revolution.

Figure 1-6 Medieval power sources. In 1556, Georg Bauer, known as Agricola, included this image of mining in Bohemia in *De re metallica*. A water wheel is the primary power source for a geared windlass (center) supplemented by horsepower (top) for smaller loads.

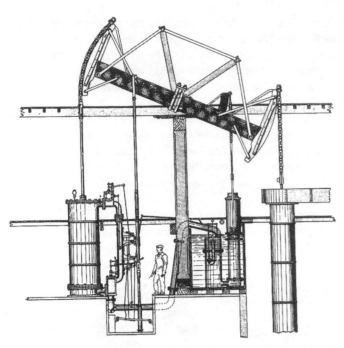

Figure 1-7 **Steam engine.** This early Boulton & Watt pumping engine was built in 1777 and remained in operation for more than 125 years.

Figure 1-8 **Gas chandelier.** *The Crystal Palace Exhibition Illustrated Catalog* of 1851 praises this work by Mr. Potts of Burlington as "a beautiful example of metallurgical manufacturing art."

In the 1830s, the earth's population, which was approximately one billion, depended on wood for heat and animals for transportation and work. Oil and gas were burned to illuminate interiors. By the 1900s, coal was the dominant fuel, followed by hydropower and natural gas.

By 1950, petroleum and natural gas split the energy market about evenly. The United States was completely energy self-sufficient because of relatively inexpensive and abundant domestic coal, oil, and natural gas. The introduction of nuclear power promised an energy source that used resources very slowly. Nuclear plants contain high pressures, temperatures, and radioactivity levels during operation and require long and expensive construction periods. The public has serious concerns over the release of low-level radiation over extended periods as well as the risks of high-level

Figure 1-9 **Bradley coal mine, Staffordshire.** In the early nineteenth century, women carried coal in wicker baskets up 100-foot-tall ladders. Trucks were hauled by women and children who could work in passages too low even for pit ponies. Miners worked in poor ventilation by handpick and crowbar, blasting without a safety fuse until its invention in 1831.

Figure 1-10 Pearl Street generating station, 1882. Thomas Edison's central generating station provided electrical energy for New York; widespread distribution remained a problem.

releases. Civilian use has been limited to research and the generation of electricity.

Since the 1950s, the United States has experienced steadily rising imports of crude oil and petroleum products. In 1973, political conditions in oil-producing countries led to wildly fluctuating oil prices, and high prices encouraged conservation and the development of alternative energy resources. The 1973 oil crisis had a major impact on building construction and operation. Between the late 1970s and 1982, the amount of oil imported by the United States dropped from more than 40 percent to 28 percent.

Since the 1990s, coal use in U.S. buildings has declined, with many large cities limiting its application. Currently, most coal is used for the generation of electricity and heavy industry, where fuel storage and air pollution problems can be treated centrally. Modern techniques scrub and filter out sulfur ash from coal combustion emissions, although some older coal-burning plants still contribute significant amounts of airborne pollution.

Today, buildings are heavily reliant on electricity because of its convenience and versatility. Consumption of electricity is expected to continue to rise significantly, especially in the developing economies of Asia.

• Electricity and daylight provide almost all illumination.
• Electric lighting produces heat, which, in turn, increases air conditioning use in warm weather, using even more electricity.
• Only one-third of the energy used to produce electricity for space heating actually becomes heat; most of the remaining energy is wasted at the production source.

World fossil fuel reserves are limited, with much of it expensive and environmentally objectionable to remove. Buildings under construction today could outlive fossil fuel supplies if use continues at current rates. Traditional off-site networks for natural gas and oil and the electric grid will continue to serve many buildings, often in combination with on-site sources.

As the world's supply of fossil fuels diminishes, buildings must use nonrenewable fuels conservatively if at all, and look to on-site resources, such as daylighting, passive solar heating, passive cooling, solar water heating, and PV electricity. On-site resources take up space locally, can be labor intensive, and sometimes have high initial costs that take years to recover. Owners and designers must look beyond these immediate obstacles and consider a building's impact on its larger environment throughout its life.

Building designers and owners now strive for energy efficiency to minimize costs and conserve resources. U.S. building codes include energy conservation standards, and public awareness of the need to conserve petroleum has risen dramatically. Even so, the quantity of imported oil remains at high levels, according to March 2008 data from the DOE:

• U.S. energy consumption rose 17.5 percent between 2002 and 2006.
• Fossil fuels made up just slightly less than 86 percent of energy consumed in 2006.
• Coal and petroleum use increased, while natural gas use decreased.
• Nuclear electric power increased.
• Renewable energy increased about 17 percent, with increases in biofuels as well as geothermal, hydroelectric, solar, PV, and wind power.

Today, the United States is regarding energy use and global climate change seriously. Time will tell whether the use of environmentally friendly energy sources will become standard practices in the future.

THE GREENHOUSE EFFECT

Human activities, including building construction and operation, are adding greenhouse gases—pollutants that trap the earth's heat—to the atmosphere at a faster rate than at any time over the past several thousand years. Today, we are witnessing global climate change at an unprecedented rate.

The following are some facts about the greenhouse effect:

- It is a natural phenomenon that helps regulate the temperature of the earth, protecting the earth's surface from extreme differences in daytime and nighttime temperatures.
- As greenhouse gases accumulate in the atmosphere, they absorb both sunlight and IR and prevent some of the heat from radiating back out into space, thereby trapping the sun's heat around the earth.
- If all of these greenhouse gases were to disappear suddenly, the earth would be 15.5°C (60°F) colder than it is currently—and uninhabitable.
- Human activities contribute significantly to the production of greenhouse gases, especially emissions of carbon dioxide from burning fossil fuels.
- Significant increases in the amount of these gases in the atmosphere cause global temperatures to rise.

☑ **Designers can reduce greenhouse gases caused by power plants and building fuel consumption by designing for energy conservation and using clean and renewable energy sources. Designers can specify materials and equipment that avoid fuel combustion and environmentally damaging refrigerants, as well as select insulation, upholstery, and other products made with environmentally benign materials.**

SUSTAINABLE DESIGN STRATEGIES

Sustainable architecture looks at human civilization as an integral part of the natural world and seeks to preserve nature through encouraging conservation in daily life. According to Design Ecology, a project sponsored by Chicago's International Interior Design Association (IIDA) and Collins & Aikman Floorcoverings, "Sustainability is a state or process that can be maintained indefinitely. The principles of sustainability integrate three closely intertwined elements—the environment, the economy, and the social system—into a system that can be maintained in a healthy state indefinitely."

Energy conservation in buildings is a complex issue that involves sensitivity to the building site, construction methods, the use and control of daylight, the selection of finishes and colors, and the design of artificial lighting. The choice of **heating, ventilating, and air conditioning (HVAC)** and other equipment can have a major effect on energy use.

The materials and methods used for building construction and finishing also have an impact on the larger world. The design of a building determines how much energy it will use throughout its life. The materials used in the building's interior are tied to the waste and pollution generated by their manufacture and eventual disposal. Increasing energy efficiency and using clean energy sources can limit greenhouse gases.

Environmentally conscious interior design is a practice that attempts to create indoor spaces that are environmentally sustainable and healthy for their occupants. Sustainable interiors address their impact on the global environment.

TABLE 1-1. GREENHOUSE GASES

Greenhouse Gas	Man-made Sources	Comments
Carbon dioxide (CO_2)	Burning fossil fuels, cement production, deforestation	Most potent greenhouse gas
Methane (CH)	Landfills, rice farming, cattle raising, burning fossil fuels	Second most potent greenhouse gas
Carbon monoxide (CO)	Industrial smokestacks, coal-fired electric utilities, tobacco smoke	Toxic to humans; eventually converts to carbon dioxide in atmosphere
Nitrous oxide (N_2O)	Nylon production, nitric-acid production, agriculture, automobile engines, biomass burning	Third most potent greenhouse gas
Hydrofluorocarbons (HFCs)	Fire suppressants, refrigerants	Replacement for CFCs; do not affect ozone layer but add carbon dioxide
Perfluorocarbons (PFCs)	Production of aluminum from alumina	Very potent, very long-lived
Chlorofluorocarbons (CFCs)	Refrigeration; air conditioning; blowing agents for foamed plastics for insulation, upholstery padding, packaging; propellants for fire extinguishers, aerosols	Man-made compounds banned by Montreal Protocol in 2000; very stable; last up to 50 years; destroy ozone in upper atmosphere
Sulfur hexafluoride (SF_6)	Electrical-equipment manufacturing, window-filling inert gas, magnesium casting	Extremely potent but low amount in atmosphere

☑ To achieve sustainable design, interior designers must collaborate with architects, developers, engineers, environmental consultants, facilities and building managers, and contractors. The professional ethics and responsibilities of the interior designer include the creation of healthy and safe indoor environments. An interior designer's choices can provide comfort for the building's occupants while benefiting the environment, an effort that often requires initial conceptual creativity rather than additional expense.

Setting Sustainability Goals

"Setting sustainability goals with your client is a great opportunity to educate them on sustainable design costs and benefits, and it is a great way to establish a trusting relationship with your client as you begin a project," according to Tom Hootman, American Institute of Architects (AIA), LEED AP (*ASID ICON*, January/February 2008, p. 38). He identifies two key types of sustainability goals: resource reduction and performance enhancement.

Resource-reduction goals include:
- Energy-use reductions
- Carbon-emission reductions
- Water-use reductions
- Materials reuse and recycled content
- Waste reduction

Performance-enhancement goals include:
- Air-quality improvements
- Thermal-comfort improvements
- Acoustical-performance enhancements
- Light- and visual-quality enhancements

It is often possible to use techniques that have multiple benefits, spreading the cost over several applications to achieve a better balance between initial costs and benefits. For example, a building designed for daylighting and natural ventilation also offers benefits for solar heating, indoor air quality, and lighting costs. This approach cuts across the usual building system categories and ties the building closely to its site. We will discuss many of these techniques in this book, crossing conventional barriers between building systems in the process.

Sustainable Design Strategy List

Sustainable design strategies include the following:
- Use alternative energy sources, waste control, water recycling, and control of building operations and maintenance.
- Limit greenhouse gas production by specifying energy-efficient lighting and appliances.
- Reduce energy use by employing natural light, natural ventilation, and adequate insulation.
- Specify materials that require less energy to manufacture and transport.
- Use products made of recycled materials that can, in turn, be recycled when they are replaced.
- Reduce energy use while improving conditions for the building's occupants with user-operated controls, such as low-tech shades or operable windows.
- Use natural on-site energy sources to reduce a building's fossil-fuel needs.
- Carefully site buildings to enhance daylighting as well as passive cooling by night ventilation, support opportunities for solar heating, improve indoor air quality, reduce use of electric lights, and add acoustic absorption.
- Employ rainwater retention for irrigation and flushing toilets.
- Use on-site wastewater recycling for irrigation.
- Reduce noise pollution through building siting, space planning, materials selections, and equipment selection.

Building designers can look at the building envelope, HVAC system, lighting, equipment and appliances, and renewable energy systems as a whole. **Energy loads**—the amount of energy a building uses to operate—are reduced by integration with the building site, the use of renewable resources, the design of the building envelope, and the selection of efficient lighting and appliances. Energy load reductions lead to smaller, less expensive, and more efficient HVAC systems that in turn use less energy.

Buildings as well as products can be designed for reuse and recycling. A building designed to easily adapt to changed uses reduces the amount of demolition and new construction and prolongs the building's life. Products that do not combine different materials allow easier separation and reuse or recycling of metals, plastics, and other constituents than products whose diverse materials are bonded together. The use of removable and reusable demountable building parts increases adaptability but may require a heavier structural system because floors are not integral with beams. In addition, mechanical and electrical systems must be well integrated to prevent leaks or cracks.

The LEED System

The U.S. Green Building Council, a nonprofit coalition that represents the building industry, has created a comprehensive system for building green known as **Leadership in Energy and Environmental Design**™ **(LEED)**. LEED provides investors, architects and designers, construction personnel, and building managers with information on green building techniques and strategies. LEED certifies buildings that meet the highest standards of economic and environmental performance and offers professional education, training, and accreditation. LEED programs cover new and renovation construction, commercial interiors, and residential projects.

☑ **LEED Professional Accreditation recognizes an individual's qualifications in sustainable building. Interior designers are among those who can become LEED-accredited professionals by passing the LEED Professional Accreditation examination, which establishes minimum competency in much the same way as the NCIDQ and other professional exams. Training workshops are available to those who are preparing for the exam.**

The LEED process for designing a green building starts with setting goals. Next, alternative strategies are evaluated. Finally, the design of the whole building is approached in a spirit of integration and inspiration.

Energy Star®

The **Energy Star**® label was created in conjunction with the U.S. Department of Energy and the U.S. Environmental Protection Agency to help consumers quickly and easily identify energy-efficient products, such as homes, appliances, and lighting. Energy Star products are also available in Canada.

Advances in Sustainable Design

An article in *Contract* (January 2008) discusses the plans put forth by the U.S. Green Building Council (USGBC) to revamp LEED into a system that better assesses the environmental impact of the built environment, and the collaboration between USGBC and Autodesk to develop software that could create a more integrated design process via a holistic approach to building systems. Article author Douglas Wittnebel of Gensler (p. 136) predicts that "most, if not all, planned and constructed projects will be ecologically fingerprinted (like a new identification and approval system for appropriating energy and materials for design and construction)." In the same article, Joe Rondinelli of Shepley Bulfinch Richardson Abbott forecasts that "sustainability will be well woven into the building process, eliminating a stand-alone rating system such as LEED."

"Imagine a highly sophisticated **building integrated modeling (BIM)** software capable of calculating real-time energy and water use levels, for example, and USGBC LEED points based upon evolving design decisions, as they're made." So begins an article by Barbara Horwitz-Bennett (*Contract*, January 2008, p. 48).

Conservation of limited resources is good, but it is possible to create beautiful buildings that generate more energy than they use and actually improve the health of their environments. Rather than reducing the amount of damage buildings do to the environment, which results in designs that do less—but still some—damage, designs can have a positive net effect. Buildings can model the abundance of nature, creating more and more riches safely and generating delight in the process.

This work has been pioneered by William McDonough of William McDonough + Partners and McDonough Braungart Design Chemistry, LLC, and Dr. David Orr, chairman of the Oberlin Environmental Studies Program. Their designs employ a myriad of techniques for efficient design.

Creative approaches to environmentally friendly design are in the news daily. In addition, people are looking to techniques used historically and in traditional societies throughout the world for ideas that are responsive to local conditions and respectful of resources.

Figure 1-11 Energy Star® label.

TABLE 1-2. ENERGY STAR® PRODUCTS

Product Category	Energy Star® Products
Appliances	Clothes washers, dishwashers, room air conditioners, room air cleaners, others
Heating and Cooling Equipment	Boilers, fans, central air conditioning, furnaces, thermostats, others
Home Envelope	Insulation, roofing products, windows, doors, skylights
Office Equipment	Computers, copiers, printers, scanners
Lighting	Compact fluorescent light bulbs, residential lighting fixtures, ceiling fans, exit signs
Commercial Equipment	Food-service equipment, vending machines, water coolers, others

BUILDING SITE CONDITIONS

Where and how a building is positioned on the earth affects its structure, supply and retention of water, collection and retention of heat from the sun and the earth, cooling and ventilation by winds, exposure to fire, and level of acoustic quiet or noise. Each of these conditions shapes the building's design; the result can reflect and communicate a sense of place.

Climates vary with the earth's position in relation to the sun and with latitude and longitude. The characteristics of a climate include the amount of sunlight, humidity and precipitation, and air temperature, motion, and quality. In addition, climates change over time; currently, we are experiencing a period of accelerated global climate change.

Local Climates

Local temperatures vary with the time of day and the season of the year. Because the earth stores heat and releases it at a later time (a phenomenon known as **thermal lag**), afternoon temperatures are generally warmer than morning temperatures. Typically, the lowest daily temperature is just before sunrise, when most of the previous day's heat has dissipated. Although June experiences the most solar radiation in the northern hemisphere, summer temperatures peak in July or August due to the long-term effects of thermal storage. Because of this residual stored heat, January and February—about one month past the winter solstice on December 21—are the coldest months. Temperatures are usually lower at higher latitudes, both north and south, as a result of shorter days and less solar radiation.

Sites may have microclimates, different from surrounding areas, that result from their elevation, proximity to large bodies of water, shading, and wind patterns. Cities sometimes create their own microclimates—heat islands—with relatively warm year-round temperatures produced by such heat sources as air conditioners, furnaces, electric lights, car engines, and building machinery. Energy released by urban vehicles and buildings warms the air 3°C to 6°C (5°F–11°F) above the surrounding countryside. The rain that runs off hard paved surfaces and buildings into storm sewers is not available for evaporative cooling. Wind is channeled between closely set buildings, which also block the sun's warmth in winter. The convective updrafts created by the large cities can affect the regional climate. Sunlight is absorbed and reradiated off massive surfaces, and less is given back to the obscured night sky.

Climate Types

Environmentally sensitive buildings are designed in response to the climate type of the site. Indigenous architecture, which has evolved over centuries of trial and error, provides models for building in the four basic climate types.

COLD CLIMATES

Cold climates feature long, cold winters with short, very hot periods occurring occasionally during the summer. Cold climates are generally found around 45 degrees latitude north or south; North Dakota is an example. Buildings designed for cold climates:

- emphasize heat retention
- offer protection from rain, snow, and winter wind
- often use passive solar heating to encourage heat retention without mechanical assistance

In cool regions, minimizing the surface area of a building reduces exposure to low temperatures. Buildings are oriented so that they absorb heat from the winter sun. Cold air collects in valley bottoms. North slopes get less winter sun and more winter wind, and hilltops lose heat to winter winds. Setting buildings into a protective south-facing hillside reduces the amount of heat loss and provides wind protection, as does setting buildings in earth. In cold climates, dark colors on south-facing surfaces increase the absorption of solar heat. Dark roofs with steep slopes collect heat. This effect is negated when the roofs are covered with snow; however, the snow itself insulates the buildings from heat loss.

TEMPERATE CLIMATES

Temperate climates, which have cold winters and hot summers, are found between 35 degrees and 45 degrees latitude. For example, Washington, DC, is in a temperate climate zone. Buildings in such zones generally require:

- winter heating and summer cooling, especially if it is humid
- south-facing walls exposed to winter sun
- summer shade for exposures on the east and west and over the roof

Deciduous shade trees that lose their leaves in the winter help protect buildings from the sun in hot weather and allow winter sunlight through. Temperate climates favor a design that encourages air movement in hot weather while protecting against cold winter winds.

Figure 1-12 Shading and ventilation. Building orientation and landscaping create shade, while window locations aid ventilation.

Figure 1-13 Design for temperate climate. This small 1930s house faces the sun, with shade trees sheltering its east and west sides. When the weather becomes colder and leaves fall, more sunlight warms and illuminates the building's interior.

HOT, ARID CLIMATES

Hot, arid climates have long, hot summers and short, sunny winters, and daily temperatures range widely between dawn and the warmest part of the afternoon. Arizona is an example of a location with such a climate. Buildings designed for hot, arid climates:

- feature heat and sun control
- often try to increase cooling and humidity by taking advantage of wind and rain
- make the most of the cool winter sun
- shade windows and outdoor spaces from the sun
- provide summer shade to the east and west and over the roof

Enclosed courtyards offer shade and encourage air movement, and the presence of a fountain or pool and plants increases humidity. Even small bodies of water produce a psychological and physical evaporative cooling effect. Sites in valleys near a watercourse keep cooler than poorly ventilated locations. In warm climates, sunlit surfaces should be a light color in order to reflect as much sunlight as possible.

HOT, HUMID CLIMATES

Hot, humid climates have very long summers with slight seasonal variations and relatively constant temperatures, as in New Orleans. Buildings designed for hot, humid climates:

- take advantage of cooling breezes and shading from the sun to reduce solar heat gain
- minimize east and west exposures to reduce solar heat gain, although some sun in winter may be desirable

Wall openings are directed away from major noise sources so that they can remain open to take advantage of natural ventilation. If possible, the floor is raised above the ground, with a crawl space under the building for good air circulation.

Figure 1-15 Deciduous shade tree in winter. Bare tree branches allow lower lower sun angles to penetrate to the building interior.

The Site

The climate of a particular building site is determined by the sun's angle and path; air temperature, motion, and quality; humidity; and precipitation. Building designers describe sites by type of soil, ground surface characteristics, and topography. The presence of water on the site affects the plants and animals found there. People living on the site are exposed to and alter its views, heat levels, noise, and other characteristics.

Subsoil and topsoil conditions, subsurface water levels, and rocks affect excavations, foundations, and landscaping of the site. Hills, valleys, and slopes determine how water drains during storms and whether soil erosion occurs. Site contours shape paths and roadway routes, shelter from the wind, and plant locations. Elevating a structure on poles or piers minimizes disturbance of the natural terrain and existing vegetation.

Building structures depend on the condition of the soil and rocks on the site. The construction of the building may remove or use earth and stone or other local materials. Construction can introduce utilities to the site, including water, electricity, and natural gas. Alterations destroy, alter, or establish habitats for native plants and animals.

The presence of people creates a major environmental impact. Buildings contribute to air pollution directly through fuel combustion and indirectly through the electric power plants that supply energy and the incinerators and landfills that receive waste.

- Coal-burning power plants are primary causes of acid rain (which contains sulfur oxides) and smog (which contains nitrogen oxides).
- Industrial smoke, gases, dust, and chemical particles pollute the air.
- Idling motors at drive-up windows and loading docks may introduce gases into building air intakes.
- Sewage and chemical pollutants damage surface water or groundwater.

Built-up areas upset natural drainage patterns. Other nearby buildings shade areas of the site and can divert wind. Close neighbors may limit visual or acoustic privacy. Weeds or soil erosion result from previous land use.

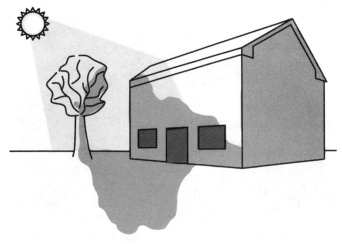

Figure 1-14 Deciduous shade tree in summer. Interior building temperatures benefit from seasonal changes in sun angles and plant growth.

Figure 1-16 On-site sound masking. Plants and water in the Dr. Sun Yat Sen Chinese Garden create a quiet oasis in the center of Vancouver, British Columbia. The placid, contemplative design feels miles away from the busy urban area nearby.

The interior of the building responds to these surrounding conditions by opening up to or turning away from views, noises, smells, and other disturbances. Interior spaces connect to existing on-site walks, driveways, parking areas, and gardens. The presence of wells, septic systems, and underground utilities influence the design of residential bathrooms, kitchens, and laundries as well as commercial buildings.

Traffic, industry, commerce, recreation, and residential uses all create noise. The hard surfaces and parallel walls in cities intensify noise. Mechanical systems of neighboring buildings may be quite noisy and are hard to mask without reducing air intake, although newer equipment is usually quieter. Plants only slightly reduce the sound level, but the visually softer appearance gives a perception of acoustic softness, and the sound of wind through the leaves helps to mask noise. Fountains also provide masking sounds.

BUILDING USE LAYERS

As you move up and down a site or within a multistory building, each level lends itself to certain types of uses. The sky layer is usually the most inaccessible and offers the most exposure to wind, sun, daylight, and rain. The near-surface layer is more accessible to people and activities. The surface layer encourages the most frequent public contact and the easiest access. The subsurface layer confers isolation by enclosure and provides privacy and thermal stability, but it may have groundwater problems.

WIND AND THE SITE

Winds are usually weakest in the early morning and strongest in the afternoon, and can change their effects and sometimes even their directions with the seasons. Evergreen shrubs, trees, and fences slow and diffuse winds near low-rise buildings; the more open a windbreak, the farther away its influence will be felt. Although dense windbreaks block wind in their immediate vicinity, the wind whips around them to ultimately cover an even greater area. Wind

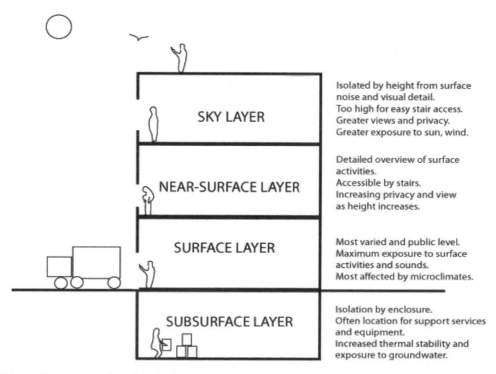

Figure 1-17 Building use layers. Multistory buildings are often layered in ways that reflect the relation to the ground in the placement of building functions.

speed may increase through gaps in a windbreak. Blocking winter winds may sometimes also block desirable summer breezes. Wind patterns around buildings are complex, and localized wind turbulence between buildings often increases wind speed and turbulence just outside building entryways.

Openings in the building are the source of light, sun, and fresh air. Building openings provide opportunities for wider personal choices of temperature and access to outdoor air. On the other hand, they limit control of humidity as well as permit the entry of dust and pollen. The desire for daylight and wind-driven ventilation affects the configuration and location of buildings.

Forests, trees, hills, and other buildings shape local wind patterns. The absorbency of the ground surface determines both how much heat will be retained to be released at night and how much will be reflected onto the building surface. Light-colored surfaces reflect solar radiation, while dark ones absorb and retain radiation. Plowed ground or dark pavement will be warmer than surrounding areas, radiating heat to nearby surfaces and creating small updrafts of air. Grass and other ground covers lower ground temperatures by absorbing solar radiation. They also aid cooling through evaporation.

WATER AND THE SITE

Water appears on the site in four forms:

- precipitation of rainwater or snow
- presence of groundwater and soil moisture
- availability of **potable** (drinkable) water
- treatment or removal of wastewater

Fountains, waterfalls, and trees tend to raise the humidity of a site and lower the temperature. Large bodies of water, which are generally cooler than land during the day and warmer than land at night, act as heat reservoirs that moderate variations in local temperatures and generate offshore breezes. Large water bodies are usually warmer than land in the winter and cooler than land in the summer.

Rainwater falling on steeply pitched roofs with overhangs is usually collected by gutters and downspouts to be carried away as surface runoff or underground through a storm sewer. Even flat roofs have a slight pitch, and the water collects into roof drains that pass through the interior of the building. **Drain leaders** are pipes that run vertically within partitions to carry water down through the structure to the storm drains. Interior drains are usually more expensive than exterior gutters and leaders.

Sites and buildings should be designed for maximum on-site rainfall retention. **Roof ponds** and **cisterns** hold water that falls on the roof, giving the ground below more time to absorb runoff. The evaporation from a roof pond also helps cool the building. Water collected on the roof for later use adds weight and increases structural requirements.

Porous pavement has a water-permeable pavement surface with a stone reservoir underneath. It may look like regular asphalt or concrete, but it is made without fine filler materials; the resulting void spaces allow water to infiltrate.

Incremental paving consists of small concrete or plastic paving units alternating with plants, so that rainwater can drain into the ground. Parking lots can also be made of open-celled pavers that allow grass or groundcover plants to grow in their cavities. Brick paving set on gravel with sand allows water to pass through to the soil below.

In some parts of North America, half of residential water is consumed outdoors, much of it for lawn sprinklers that lose water to evaporation and runoff. Sprinkler timing devices control the length of the watering cycle and the time when it begins, so that watering can be done at night when less water evaporates. Rain sensors shut off the system, and monitors check soil moisture content. Bubblers with very low flow rates lose less water to evaporation. With drip irrigation, which works well for individual shrubs and small trees, a plastic tube network slowly and steadily drips water onto the ground surface near plants, soaking them at a rate they prefer.

The use of recycled or reclaimed water, including **graywater** (wastewater that is not from toilets or urinals) and stored rain, is gradually being allowed by building codes in North America.

Animal and Plant Life

Building sites provide environments for a variety of plant and animal life forms. Grasses, weeds, flowers, shrubs, and trees trap precipitation, prevent soil erosion, provide shade, and deflect wind. They also play a major role in food and water cycles, and their growth and change through the seasons help us mark the passage of time.

Bacteria, mold, and fungi break down dead animal and vegetable matter into soil nutrients. Bees, wasps, butterflies, and birds pollinate useful plants but generally must be kept out of buildings. Termites may attack a building's structure. Building occupants may welcome cats, dogs, and other pets into the building, but usually they will want to exclude such nuisance animals as mice, raccoons, squirrels, lizards, and stray dogs.

PLANTS AND BUILDINGS

Plants near buildings foster privacy, provide wind protection, and reduce sun glare and heat. They frame or screen views, moderate noise, and visually connect a building to its site. Plants improve air quality by trapping particles on their leaves. Particles are then washed to the ground by rain; photosynthesis assimilates gases, fumes, and other pollutants.

Deciduous plants grow and drop their leaves on a schedule that responds more to the cycles of outdoor temperature than to the position of the sun. In the northern hemisphere, the sun reaches its maximum strength beween March 21 and September 21, while plants provide the most shade between June and October, when the days are warmest. A deciduous vine on a trellis over a south-facing window grows during the cooler spring, shades a building's interior during the hottest weather, and loses its leaves in time to welcome the winter sun. The vine also cools its immediate area through evaporation. Evergreens provide shade all year and help reduce snow glare in winter.

When selecting plants for use in the landscape, designers should consider their structure, shape, and mature height, as well as the spread of their foliage and the speed with which they grow. The density, texture, and color of foliage may change with the seasons. A plant's requirements for soil, water, sunlight, and temperature range as well as the depth and extent of the root structure need to be evaluated. Low-maintenance native or naturalized species have the best chances of success; they also encourage local wildlife. To support plant life, soil must be able to absorb moisture, supply appropriate nutrients, be aerated, and be free of concentrated salts.

Trees' ability to provide shade depends upon their orientation to the sun, proximity to a building or outdoor space, shape, height, and spread, and the density of their foliage and branch structure. In the northern hemisphere, the most effective shade is on the southeast in the morning and the southwest during the late afternoon, when the sun has a low angle and casts long shadows.

Air temperatures in the shade of a tree are about 3°C to 6°C (5°F–11°F) cooler than in the sun. A wall shaded by a large tree in direct sun may be between 11°C and 14°C (20°F–25°F) cooler. This temperature drop is caused by the shade plus cooling evaporation from the enormous surface area of the leaves. Shrubs located right next to a wall produce similar results, trapping cooled air and preventing drafts from infiltrating the building. Neighborhoods with large trees have maximum air temperatures up to 6°C (10°F) lower than those without such trees.

Remarkably, a moist lawn will be 6°C to 8°C (10°F–14°F) cooler than bare soil and 17°C (31°F) cooler than unshaded asphalt. Low-growing, low-maintenance groundcovers or paving blocks with holes are also cooler than asphalt.

As buildings are increasingly opened up to their sites, building occupants become more aware of their environment. Fresh air and sunlight enter the building and improve the health of those inside. In Chapter 2: Designing Building Functions for Human Health and Safety, we will explore how building codes and standards originally written to protect the health and safety of occupants have expanded to consider energy use and sustainable design.

2

....

Designing Building Functions for Human Health and Safety

The earliest shelters probably provided only a little shade or protection from rain and were warmed by a fire and enclosed by one or more walls. Today, we expect a lot from our buildings, beginning with the necessities for supporting human life. We must have clean air to breathe and clean water to drink, prepare food, wash our bodies and our belongings, and flush away wastes. We need facilities for food preparation and places to eat. Human body wastes, wash water, food wastes, and rubbish have to be removed or recycled.

As buildings become more complex, we expect less protection from our clothing and more from our shelters. We also expect to control air temperatures and the temperatures of surfaces and objects around us for **thermal comfort**. We control the humidity of the air and the flow of water vapor. We prevent rain, snow, and groundwater from entering buildings, and circulate the air in them.

Once these basic physical needs are met, we turn to creating conditions for sensory comfort, efficiency, and privacy. We need illumination to see and barriers to provide for visual privacy. We seek spaces where we can hear others speak clearly, yet where we have acoustic privacy.

The next group of functions supports social needs. We try to control the entry or exit of other people and of animals. Buildings facilitate communication and connection with the world outside through windows, telephones, mailboxes, and computer and video networks. Our buildings support our activities by distributing concentrated energy to convenient locations, primarily through electrical systems.

The structure of a building provides stable support for its architectural features and all of the people and objects inside it. The structure resists the forces of snow, wind, and earthquakes. Buildings protect their own structure, surfaces, internal mechanical and electrical systems, and other architectural features from water and precipitation. They also adjust to their own normal movements without damage to their structure or contents. They protect occupants, contents, and themselves from fire. Buildings support our comfort, safety, and productive activity with floors, walls, stairs, shelves, countertops, and other built-in elements.

Finally, a building capable of accomplishing all of these complex functions must be constructed without excessive expense or difficulty. Once built, it must be able to be operated, maintained, and changed in a useful, economical manner. Ideally, the building should be flexible enough to adapt to changing uses and priorities. Eventually, the building's components may be disassembled and returned to use in other construction.

THE BUILDING ENVELOPE

The **building envelope** is the transition between the outdoors and the interior of a building, consisting of windows, doors, floors, walls, and roofs. The envelope encloses and shelters space and protects against the sun, rain, wind, and harsh temperatures. Entries are the transition zone between the building's interior and the outside world.

Traditionally, the building envelope was regarded as a barrier separating the interior from the outdoor environment. Architects created an isolated environment, and engineers equipped it with energy-using devices to control conditions. Because of the need to conserve energy, we now consider the building envelope to be a dynamic boundary that interacts with the external natural energy forces and the internal building environment. The envelope is sensitively attuned to the resources of the site: sun, wind, and water.

16

Figure 2-1 Basic shelter. A stone wall built into the rock provides protection from the sun, wind, cold, and rain. This dramatic design is in the Serra da Estrela, Portugal.

Figure 2-2 Plains Indian tipi as dynamic boundary. Edward W. Curtis photographed Slow Bull in front of this Dakota tipi in 1907. The portable structure filters sunlight while keeping out rain and wind. The smoke flaps at the top vent smoke; the entire covering can be adjusted to the user's need.

The boundary is manipulated to balance the energy flows between inside and outside.

This dynamic approach leads the architect to support proper thermal and lighting conditions through the design of the building's form and structure. Engineers design mechanical and electrical support systems with passive control mechanisms that minimize energy consumption.

A building envelope can be an open frame or a closed shell. It can be dynamic and sensitive to changing conditions and needs, letting in or closing out breezes, sounds, and the sun's warmth and light. Openings and barriers may be static, like a wall; allow on-off operation, like a door; or offer adjustable control, like venetian blinds. The appropriate architectural solution depends on the range of options desired, the local materials available, and local style preferences.

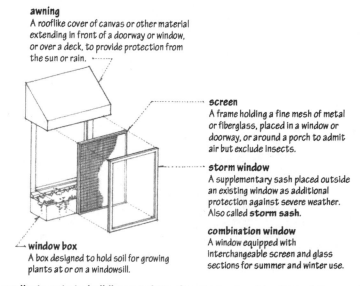

awning
A rooflike cover of canvas or other material extending in front of a doorway or window, or over a deck, to provide protection from the sun or rain.

screen
A frame holding a fine mesh of metal or fiberglass, placed in a window or doorway, or around a porch to admit air but exclude insects.

storm window
A supplementary sash placed outside an existing window as additional protection against severe weather. Also called **storm sash**.

combination window
A window equipped with interchangeable screen and glass sections for summer and winter use.

window box
A box designed to hold soil for growing plants at or on a windowsill.

Figure 2-3 User adjustments to building envelope. Occupants of residential buildings routinely modify the building envelope to accommodate changes in sun angle and outside temperature as well as to invite in breezes while excluding insects. Modifications are often made for both aesthetic and practical reasons.

A dynamic envelope demands that the user understand how, why, and when to make adjustments. The designer must ensure that people using the building have this information.

BUILDING FORM

Energy conservation has major implications for a building's form. The orientation, height, and width of a building determine how it will be shielded from excess heat or cold or open to ventilation or light. For example, the desire to provide daylight and natural ventilation to each room limits the width of multistory hotels.

Designing for Building Systems

At the initial conceptual design stage, the architect and interior designer group similar functions and spaces with similar needs close to the resources they require, thereby consolidating and minimizing distribution networks. The activities that attract the most frequent public participation belong at or near ground level. Closed offices and industrial activities with infrequent public contact can be located at higher levels and in remote locations. Spaces with isolated and closely controlled environments, such as lecture halls, auditoriums, and operating rooms, should be placed at interior or underground locations. Mechanical spaces that require acoustic isolation

and restricted public access or access to outside air should be placed close to related outdoor equipment, such as condensers and cooling towers, and must be accessible to enable easy repair and replacement.

Large buildings are divided into zones. Perimeter zones are immediately adjacent to the building envelope, usually extending 4.6 to 6 meters (15–20 ft) inside. Perimeter zones are affected by changes in weather and light and warmth from the sun. In small buildings, the perimeter zone conditions continue throughout the buildings. Interior zones are protected from weather extremes and generally require less heating because they maintain a stable temperature. Generally, interior zones require cooling and ventilation.

Between Floors and Ceilings

An enclosed portion of a building structure that is designed to allow the movement of air, forming part of an air distribution system, is commonly called a **plenum**. Although the term plenum is specifically used for the chamber at the top of a furnace, also called a bonnet, from which ducts emerge to conduct heated or conditioned air to the inhabited spaces of the building, it is also commonly used to refer to the open area between the bottom of a floor structure and the top of the ceiling assembly below. In some cases, air is carried

Figure 2-4 Mill building models. The width of nineteenth-century mill buildings was limited by the need for daylight and natural ventilation. This extensive Lego construction shows the mill buildings of Manchester, New Hampshire.

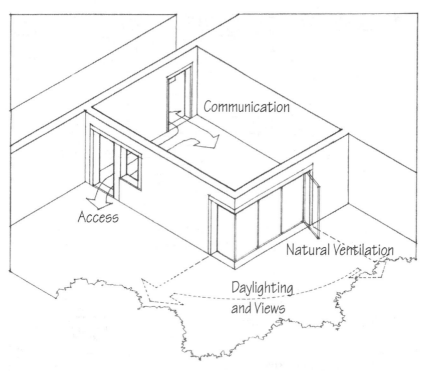

Figure 2-5 Grouping functions near required resources. Windows provide access to daylight and outdoor air for cooling and ventilation. Points of entry influence where interior functions are located.

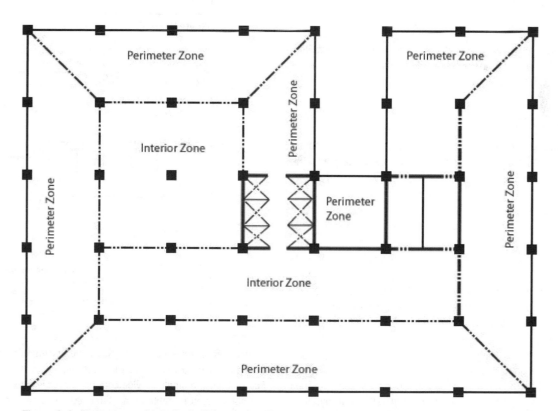

Figure 2-6 Perimeter and interior building zones. The spaces in a mixed-use building are divided between perimeter zones that are most affected by exterior conditions and interior zones that remain relatively stable. Varying uses as well as scheduling and internal heating and cooling loads within these zones could require subdivision into additional zones.

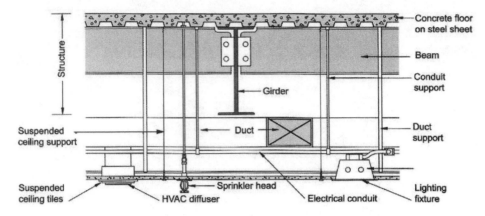

Figure 2-7 Space between floor and ceiling. The area between the floor above and the ceiling below is typically full of electrical, plumbing, heating, cooling, lighting, fire-suppression, and other equipment.

through this space without ducting; in these situations, it is called an open plenum.

Building codes limit where open plenum systems can run in a building, prohibit combustible materials in plenum spaces, and allow only certain types of wiring. Equipment in the plenum sometimes continues vertically down a structurally created shaft, called a **chase**. The open plenum must be isolated from other spaces so that debris in the plenum and vertical shaft is not drawn into a return air intake.

☑ **As an interior designer, you will often be concerned with how you can locate lighting or other design elements in relation to all of the equipment in the plenum.**

Service Cores

In most multistory buildings, the stairs, elevators, toilet rooms, and supply closets are grouped together in a **service core**. The mechanical, plumbing, and electrical chases, which carry wires and pipes vertically from one floor to the next, also use the service cores, along with the electrical and telephone closets, service closets, and fire protection equipment. Often, the plan of these areas varies little if at all from one floor to the next.

Service cores may have different ceiling heights and layouts than those of the rest of the floor. Mechanical equipment rooms may need higher ceilings for big pipes and ducts. Some spaces, including toilet rooms, stairs, and elevator waiting areas, benefit from daylight, fresh air, and views, so access to the building perimeter can be a priority.

Service cores can take up a considerable amount of space. Along with the entry lobby and loading docks, service areas may nearly fill the ground floor as well as the roof and basement. Their locations must be coordinated with a building's structural layout. In addition, they must coordinate with patterns of space use and activity. The clarity and distance of the circulation path from the farthest rentable area to the service core have a direct impact on the building's safety during a fire.

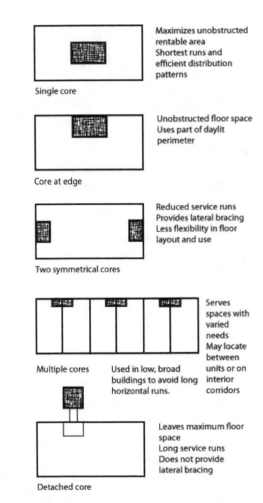

Figure 2-8 Service core layouts. Of the several common service-core layouts, central cores are the most frequent type. In high-rise office buildings, a single service core provides the maximum amount of unobstructed rentable area. Detached cores are located outside the body of a building to save usable floor space; however, these cores require long service runs. Multiple cores are used in apartment buildings and structures made of repetitive units, with the cores located between units along interior corridors.

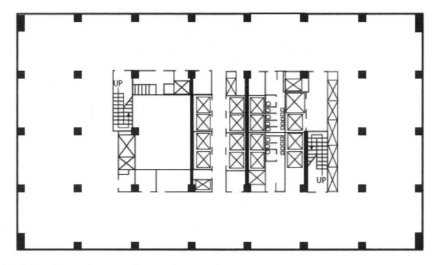

Figure 2-9 Plan with service core. The service core often contains stairs and elevators; toilet rooms; heating, ventilating, and air conditioning (HVAC) ductwork; and electrical and plumbing spaces.

EMBODIED ENERGY OF BUILDING MATERIALS

The selection of building materials affects both the quality of a building and the environment beyond the building. When we look at the energy efficiency of a building, we should also consider the **embodied energy** used to manufacture, transport, and dispose of the materials from which the building is made.

Power plants that supply electricity for buildings use very large quantities of water, which is returned at a warmer temperature, or as vapor. Mechanical and electrical systems use metals and plastics, along with some clay. These materials are selected for their strength, durability, and fire resistance as well as their electrical resistance or conductivity. Their environmental impact involves the energy cost to mine, fabricate, transport, and ultimately dispose of them.

THE DESIGN TEAM

In the past, architects were directly responsible for the design of an entire building. Heating and ventilation consisted primarily of steam radiators and operable windows. Lighting and power systems were also relatively uncomplicated. Some parts of buildings, such as sinks, bathtubs, cooking ranges, and dishwashers, were considered to be separate items in the past, but they are now less portable and more commonly viewed as fixed parts of a building. Portable oil lamps have been replaced by lighting fixtures that are an integral part of the building, tied into the electrical system.

Today, an architect typically serves as the leader and coordinator of a team of specialist consultants, including structural, mechanical, and electrical engineers, along with fire protection, acoustic, lighting, and elevator specialists. Energy-conscious design requires close coordination of the entire design team from the earliest design stages.

The design process establishes the design intent of a project by defining characteristics of a proposed building solution. These become focal points for the efforts of the design team. Example design intents include:

- providing outstanding comfort for occupants
- accommodating the latest in information technology
- focusing on indoor environmental quality and sustainable design
- using primarily passive systems to accomplish design goals through the building itself rather than through the addition of equipment
- providing a high degree of flexibility for occupants so that changes in use or other conditions are readily accommodated

The design team's success or failure to accomplish its design intent is measured by design criteria. The following are examples of criteria (Benjamin Stein et al., *Mechanical and Electrical Equipment for Buildings,* 10th Ed, John Wiley & Sons, pp. 7–8):

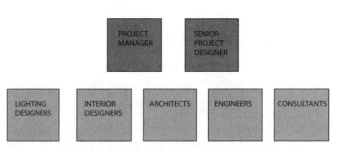

Figure 2-10 Project team. On larger projects, a design team may include a wide range of professionals. Interior designers work directly for the architect as part of the architectural team, serve as consultants to the architect, or work independently on building interiors.

- Thermal conditions will meet the requirements of ASHRAE Standard 55-2004.
- The power density of the lighting system will be no greater than 0.7 W per square foot.
- The building will achieve a Silver LEED rating.
- Fifty percent of building water consumption will be provided by rainwater capture.
- Background sound levels in classrooms will not exceed RC 35.

Building Information Modeling (BIM) is emerging as a major design and organizational tool for design and building construction. The traditional design process involves translating a design to two-dimensional architectural drawings, then checking and coordinating these with engineering drawings, followed by calculating quantities and costs, and eventually representing the final design in rendered three-dimensional drawings. BIM enables all of these steps to take place simultaneously, with changes continually recorded and coordinated. According to Guy Geier of FXFOWLE Architects (*Contract*, January 2008, p. 137):

> Building Information Modeling (BIM)… has the potential to revolutionize the [building design] process. As we design, the "smart" BIM databases will have attributes assigned to every element of the project including cost, availability, sustainability, and quantities.

Design becomes fully three-dimensional and interdisciplinary. BIM has caused "many cultural changes that will pervade almost all aspects of practice, from design, to staffing assignment, to fees, to construction administration services, and everything in between" (Glenn W. Birx, AIA, "BIM Evokes Revolutionary Changes to Architecture Practice at Ayers/Saint/Gross" *AIArchitect*, December 12, 2005. http://www.aia.org/aiarchitect/thisweek05/twl209/twl209 changeisnow.cfm)

THE HUMAN BODY AND THE BUILT ENVIRONMENT

Buildings provide environments in which people can feel comfortable and safe. To understand the ways building systems are designed to meet these needs, we must first look at how the human body perceives and reacts to interior environments.

Maintaining Thermal Equilibrium

Our perception that our surroundings are too cold or too hot is based on many factors beyond air temperature. The season, the clothes worn, the amount of humidity and air movement, and the presence of heat given off by objects in the space all influence our comfort. Contact with surfaces or moving air, or with heat radiating from an object, produces the sensation of heat or cold. A wide range of temperatures will be perceived as comfortable for one individual over time and in varying situations. We can regulate the body's heat loss with three layers of protection: the skin, clothing, and buildings.

HUMAN BODY HEAT PRODUCTION

The human body operates as an engine that produces heat. The fuel is the food we eat, in the form of proteins, carbohydrates, and fats. The digestive process uses chemicals, bacteria, and enzymes to break down food. Useful substances are pumped into the bloodstream and carried throughout the body. Waste products are filtered out during digestion, then stored for elimination.

The normal internal human body temperature is approximately 37°C (98.6°F). This temperature cannot vary by more than a few degrees without causing physical distress. The human body turns only about one-fifth of the food energy it consumes into mechanical work. The other four-fifths of this energy is given off as heat or stored as fat. The body requires continuous cooling to give off all of this excess heat. The amount of heat our bodies produce depends on what we are doing. This is why a room full of people doing aerobic exercise heats up pretty quickly.

An individual's metabolism sets the rate at which energy is used; it is based primarily on his or her level of muscular activity. What, when, and how much we eat influences our **metabolic rate**; it also follows a normal daily cycle. A person's metabolic rate varies with body surface area and weight, health, sex, and age. The amount of clothing a person is wearing and the surrounding thermal and atmospheric conditions also influence the metabolic rate. It increases when we have a fever, during continuous activity, and in cold conditions if we are not wearing warm clothes. Our metabolic rates are highest at age 10 and lowest in old age. The weight of heavy winter clothing may add 10 to 15 percent to the metabolic rate. Pregnancy and lactation increase the rate by about 10 percent.

The set of conditions that allows your body to stay at the normal body temperature with the minimal amount of bodily regulation is called **thermal equilibrium**. We feel uncomfortable when our bodies work too hard to maintain their thermal equilibrium. We experience thermal comfort when heat production equals heat loss. Our minds feel alert, our bodies operate at maximum efficiency, and we are at our most productive.

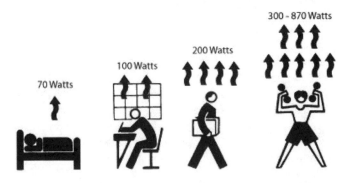

Figure 2-11 Activity and body heat generation. An average-size person at rest gives off about the same amount of heat as a 70-watt incandescent light bulb. This amount of heat rises to about 100 watts when an average-size person sits at a desk, 200 watts when the person walks, and more than 300 watts when the person exercises vigorously.

☑ As designers of interior spaces, our goal is to create environments where people are neither too hot nor too cold to function comfortably and efficiently.

Effects of Heat and Cold

Studies have shown that industrial accidents increase at higher- and lower-than-normal temperatures, when our bodies struggle to run properly. When we are cold, we lose too much heat too quickly, especially from the back of the neck, the head, the back, and the arms and legs. When our bodies lose too much heat, we become lethargic and mentally dull. The heart pumps an increased amount of blood directly to the skin and back to the heart, bypassing the brain and other organs, which puts an increased strain on the heart. Because we transfer heat from one part of the body to another through the bloodstream, it is sometimes difficult to figure out where heat loss is actually occurring. We may need to wear a hat to keep our feet warm!

Our skin surface provides a layer of insulation between the body's interior and the environment, which approximates putting on a light sweater. When the body loses more heat to a cold environment than it produces, it attempts to lower the heat loss by constricting the outer blood vessels, thereby reducing the blood flow to the outer surface of the skin. Goose bumps result when the skin tries to fluff up meager body hairs to provide more insulation. If excessive heat loss continues, involuntary muscle action causes us to shiver, which in turn increases heat production. We fold our arms and close our legs to reduce exposed area. When the level of heat loss is too great, muscle tension makes us hunch up—a strained posture that produces physical exhaustion. Ultimately, when deep body temperatures fall, we experience hypothermia, which can result in a coma or death. The slide toward hypothermia can be reversed by exercise to raise heat production, consuming hot food or drink, or taking a hot bath or sauna.

When we get too hot, the blood flow to the skin's surface increases, sweat glands secrete salt and water, and body heat is lost through evaporation of water from the skin. Water continually evaporates from our respiratory passages and lungs; the air we exhale is usually saturated with water. In high humidity,

evaporation is slow and the rate of perspiration increases as the body tries to compensate. When the surrounding air approaches body temperature, only evaporation by dry, moving air will lower body temperature.

Overheating, like being too cold, increases fatigue and decreases resistance to disease. If the body is not cooled, the deep-body temperature rises and impairs metabolic functions, which can result in heat stroke and death.

The surplus heat in our bodies is passed to the environment in four ways:

- **convection:** heat from the body is absorbed by air molecules
- **conduction:** heat is transferred through direct contact with cooler surfaces
- **radiation:** heat radiates to cooler surfaces without physical contact
- **evaporation:** heat is drawn from the body's surface to provide energy to turn liquid water into water vapor

We will look at each of these in detail in Chapter 9: Principles of Thermal Comfort.

Visual and Acoustic Comfort

Visual comfort covers a range of situations, including providing adequate illumination for the task at hand, controlling glare, and providing views and connections to the outdoors.

The eye focuses light on the light-sensitive rod and cone cells of the retina. Cones give the eye its ability to see detail sharply and to detect color. The clarity of our center of focus is the result of cone cells packed into a tiny area near the fovea. Rod cells are found farther from the fovea. They can operate at lower light levels than cones but are less sensitive to bright light; they help us see at night. Because rods lack the color sensitivity of cones, the eye perceives color poorly in dim light.

Our eyes can be damaged if we look even quickly at the sun or for too long at a bright snow landscape or light-colored sand. Direct glare from lighting fixtures can blind us momentarily. Low illumination levels reduce our ability to see well. Adjusting to moderately low light levels can take several minutes, an important consideration when entryways between the outdoors (which may be very bright or very dark) and the building's interior are designed.

☑ Interior designers should avoid strong contrasts that make vision difficult or painful, such as a very bright object against a very dark background or a dark object against a light background. Lighting levels and daylight contrasts are important parts of interior design.

The buildings we design should help us use our senses comfortably and efficiently. Loud sounds can damage our hearing, especially over time. We have trouble hearing sounds that are much less intense than the background noise. The art and science of acoustics addresses how these issues affect the built environment.

Figure 2-12 Body heat loss areas. People tend to lose heat most rapidly from the head, back, arms, legs, and the back of the neck.

OTHER HUMAN ENVIRONMENTAL REQUIREMENTS

We need a regular supply of water to move the products of food processing around the body. Water also helps cool the body. We need food and drinking water that are free from harmful microorganisms. Contaminated food and water spread hepatitis and typhoid. Building systems are designed to remove body and food wastes promptly for safe processing. We will look at these issues in Part III: Water Supply, Distribution, and Waste Systems.

We must have air to breathe for the oxygen it contains, which is the key to the chemical reactions that **combust** (burn) the food-derived fuels that maintain body functions. When we breathe air into our lungs, some oxygen dissolves into the bloodstream. We exhale air mixed with carbon dioxide and water, which are produced as wastes of combustion. Less than one-fifth of the air's oxygen is replaced by carbon dioxide with each lungful, but a constant supply of fresh air is required to prevent unconsciousness from oxygen depletion and carbon dioxide accumulation. Building ventilation systems ensure that the air we breathe indoors is fresh and clean.

The human body is attacked by a very large variety of bacteria, viruses, and fungi. The skin, respiratory system, and digestive tract offer a supportive environment for microorganisms. Some microorganisms are helpful or at least benign, but some cause disease and discomfort. Buildings provide facilities for washing food, dishes, skin, hair, and clothes in order to keep these other life-forms under control. Poorly designed or maintained buildings can be breeding grounds for microorganisms. These are issues for both the design of building sanitary waste systems and indoor air quality.

Buildings exclude disease-carrying rodents and insects. Pests spread typhus, yellow fever, malaria, sleeping sickness, encephalitis, plague, and various parasites. Inadequate ventilation encourages the spread of tuberculosis and other respiratory diseases. Adequate ventilation carries away airborne bacteria and excess moisture. Sunlight entering a building dries and sterilizes the environment.

Our soft tissues, organs, and bones need protection from hard and sharp objects. Level floor surfaces prevent trips and leg and foot injuries. Buildings help us move up and down from different levels, and they keep fire and hot objects away from the skin.

☑ **Interior designers must always be on the alert for aspects of a design that could cause harm from falling objects, explosions, poisons, corrosive chemicals, harmful radiation, and/or electric shocks. By designing spaces with safe surfaces, even and obvious level changes, and appropriately specified materials, interior designers protect people who use their buildings. Interior designs help prevent and suppress fires as well as facilitate escapes from burning buildings.**

Buildings give us space to move, work, and play. Our residential designs support family life with a place for rearing children, preparing and sharing food with family and friends, studying, and communicating verbally, manually, and electronically. We provide spaces and facilities to pursue hobbies and to clean and repair the home. Our designs create opportunities to display and store belongings, and many people now work at home, adding another level of complexity to these spaces. The spaces we design may be closed and private at times and open to the rest of the world at other times. We design buildings that are secure from intrusion and provide ways to communicate both within and beyond a building's interior. We provide stairways and mechanical means of conveyance from one level to another for people with different levels of mobility.

Our designs also support all of the social activities that occur outside of the home. We provide power to buildings so that people who work in warehouses, markets, offices, studios, workshops, barns, and laboratories can design, produce, and distribute goods. These workplaces require the same basic supports for life activities as our homes, along with accommodations for the tasks they house. We gather in groups to worship, exercise, play, entertain, govern, and educate as well as to study or observe objects of interest. Designing these communal spaces is even more challenging because they must satisfy the needs of many people at once.

BUILDING CODES

When people gather together for activities, building functions become more complex, and there is a greater chance that someone will be injured. Governments respond to safety concerns by developing building codes, which are government-mandated documents that establish minimum acceptable building practices. These codes dictate both the work of the interior designer and architect and the manner in which the building's mechanical, electrical, plumbing, and other systems are designed and installed.

The jurisdiction of a project is determined by a building's location. A **jurisdiction** is a geographical area that adheres to the same codes, standards, and regulations. A jurisdiction may be as small as a township or as large as a state. The **authority having jurisdiction** for a particular project location—for example, the building department or health department—enforces the code requirements; several authorities may oversee a single project.

☑ **Most jurisdictions have strict requirements about who can design a project and what types of drawings are required for an interior design project. Often, drawings must be stamped by a licensed architect or licensed engineer registered within the state. In some cases, interior designers are not permitted to be in charge of a project and may have to work as part of an architect's team. Some states may allow registered interior designers to stamp drawings for projects in buildings with three or fewer stories and below a certain number of square feet. Working out the proper relationships with the architects and engineers on your team is critical to meeting code requirements.**

The International Building Code (IBC) is a model building code that attempts to unify code requirements across geographic barriers. Introduced by the International Codes Council (ICC) in 2002, the ICC codes have been adopted by many states and other jurisdictions.

Spurred by the energy crisis in the 1970s, governments developed code requirements for energy efficiency. These mandated minimum levels of energy efficiency continue to evolve, but they may lag behind the optimal performance level.

The most generally used standard for commercial and institutional buildings in the United States is **ASHRAE** *Standard 90.1*. Some states also have their own energy codes. These codes cover almost every building system, including lighting and electrical distribution.

Codes and standards for residential energy efficiency include the *International Energy Code* and the *Model Energy Code*. Residential energy codes focus on minimum requirements for the building envelope (walls, floors, roofs, doors, windows) and for heating, cooling, and domestic hot water equipment efficiency.

Because most energy-efficiency standards consider only on-site energy usage, energy used, for example, to transport fuel oil or to generate electricity is not considered. As a result, requirements may take a short-sighted view of the energy costs of some fuel sources.

☑ **Interior designers must keep current on code requirements. Some states have statewide codes based on a model code, while others have local codes; sometimes, both state and local codes cover an area. Not every jurisdiction updates its codes on a regular basis, which means that in a particular jurisdiction, the code cited may not be the most current edition of that code. The interior designer must check with the local jurisdiction to determine which codes to follow. When codes are changed, one or more addenda are published annually with the changes and incorporated in the body of the code when the next full edition of the code is published. Professional organizations and government agencies offer continuing-education programs when major code changes are introduced.**

In addition to the basic building code, jurisdictions issue plumbing, mechanical, and electrical codes. Interior designers are not generally required to know or to research most plumbing or mechanical code issues. On projects with a significant amount of plumbing or mechanical work, registered engineers will take responsibility for design and code issues. On smaller projects, a licensed plumber or mechanical contractor will know the codes. However, the interior designer needs to be aware of some plumbing and mechanical requirements, such as how to determine the number of required plumbing fixtures.

Code Officials

The codes department is the local government agency that enforces the codes within a jurisdiction. The size of the codes department varies with the size of the jurisdiction it serves. A **code official** is an employee of the codes department with the authority to interpret and enforce codes, standards, and regulations within that jurisdiction.

The fire marshal usually represents the local fire department. The fire marshal examines drawings with the plans examiner during preliminary and final reviews, checking for fire code compliance.

Figure 2-13 Plans examiner. A plans examiner is a code official who checks plans and construction drawings at both the preliminary and the final permit-review stages of a project. The plans examiner checks for code and standards compliance and works most closely with the designer of the project.

The building inspector visits the project job site after the building permit is issued and ensures that all of the construction complies with the codes as specified in the construction drawings and in code publications.

Coordinating with Architects and Engineers

The interior designer often meets with the architect and engineers in the preliminary stages of the design process to coordinate the interior design with new and existing plumbing, mechanical, and electrical system components. The location of plumbing fixtures, sprinklers, fire extinguishers, air diffusers and returns, and other items covered by plumbing and mechanical codes must be coordinated with interior elements. The plumbing, mechanical, and electrical systems are often planned simultaneously, especially in large buildings. Vertical and horizontal chases are integrated into building cores and stairwells. Suspended ceiling and floor systems house mechanical, electrical, and plumbing components. Their locations affect the selection and placement of finished ceilings, walls, and floor systems. We will look at the details of this coordination throughout this book.

Standards and Organizations

Codes cite standards developed by government agencies, trade associations, and standards-writing organizations as references. A standard may consist of a definition, recommended practice, test method, classification, and/or required specification.

In 1896, the **National Fire Protection Association (NFPA)** was formed to develop standards for the early use of sprinklers to put out fires. The NFPA develops and publishes about 250 standards in booklet form. The *Life Safety Code* and the *National Electric Code* are both NFPA publications that provide guidelines for fire safety. The NFPA establishes testing requirements that cover everything from textiles to firefighting equipment to the design of means of egress.

The **American National Standards Institute (ANSI)** was formed in 1918 to coordinate the development of voluntary standards and approve standards developed by other organizations, with the goal of avoiding duplications and establishing priorities. ANSI standards were the first to focus on achieving independence for people with disabilities by emphasizing the need for accessible features in building design; they also provided a basis for the Americans with Disabilities Act (see below).

The **American Society for Testing and Materials (ASTM)** dates to 1898. ASTM standards are used to specify materials and ensure quality. ASTM methods integrate production processes, promote trade, and enhance safety. While ASTM's 69 volumes of standards include all types of products, a separate two-volume set of about 600 standards covers the building construction industry.

In 1959, the **American Society of Heating, Refrigeration, and Air-Conditioning Engineers (ASHRAE)** was formed to sponsor research projects and to develop performance level standards for HVAC and refrigeration systems. Mechanical engineers and refrigeration specialists and installers use ASHRAE standards.

☑ **As an interior designer, you will typically not need to refer to ASHRAE standards. However, provision *90A: Energy Conservation in New Building Design* is the basis of most building-code energy provisions in the United States and will affect the total amount of energy use permitted for lighting, heating, cooling, and other functions in the projects you design.**

Underwriters Laboratories (UL) is a testing agency that tests products, systems, and materials, and determines their relationship to life, fire, and casualty hazards as well as crime prevention. UL lists all of the products it tests and approves in product directories. Interior designers will find the *Building Materials, Fire Protection Equipment,* and *Fire Resistance* directories the most useful. Codes will require UL testing and approval for certain products, and interior designers should specify tested products when they are required.

Several sustainable design rating systems are widely recognized. These include the **U.S. Green Building Council's Leadership in Energy and Environmental Design (LEED)** system and an international evaluation methodology entitled GBTool. Similar rating systems are used in the United Kingdom and Canada.

Figure 2-14 UL label. UL tags appear on many household appliances as well as on lighting and other electrical fixtures.

Federal Regulations

The federal government regulates the building of federal facilities, including federal buildings, Veterans Administration hospitals, and military establishments. Typically, the construction of federal buildings is not subject to state or local building codes and regulations. The federal government issues regulations for government-built and -owned buildings, similar to the model codes. On particular projects, federal authorities may opt to comply with stricter local requirements, so interior designers must verify which codes apply.

Codes and Regulations

There are more than 1000 separate codes and a wide range of federal regulations. In an effort to limit federal regulation, the Consumer Product Safety Commission encourages industry self-regulation and standardization, and industry groups have formed hundreds of standards-writing organizations and trade associations that represent almost every industry.

Congress can pass laws that supersede all state and local codes and standards. The *Federal Register* publishes federal regulations daily. They are collected in the *Code of Federal Regulations*, which is revised annually. The Occupational Safety and Health Act (OSH Act), Fair Housing Act (FHA), and Americans with Disabilities Act (ADA) are examples of laws passed by Congress that have far-reaching implications for interior designers and architects.

OCCUPATIONAL SAFETY AND HEALTH ACT

In 1970, the **Occupational Safety and Health Act (OSH Act)** established the Occupational Safety and Health Administration (OSHA) as a branch of the Department of Labor to protect employees in the workplace. OSHA adds to code requirements by regulating the design of buildings and interior projects where people are employed to ensure the safety of employees in the workplace. Contractors and subcontractors on construction projects must strictly adhere to OSHA requirements, which stress safe installation of materials and equipment in order to create a safe work environment for construction workers and for future building occupants. Interior designers should be aware that these regulations exist and affect the process of building construction and installation of equipment and furnishings.

AMERICANS WITH DISABILITIES ACT

The term **accessible** in building codes refers to handicapped accessibility as required by codes, the **Americans with Disabilities Act (ADA)**, and other accessibility standards. The Departments of Justice and Transportation developed the provisions of the ADA, which was passed by Congress in 1990 and became enforceable in 1992 and 1993. In addition, some states also have their own accessibility standards.

The ADA is a comprehensive civil rights law with four sections. Title I protects individuals with disabilities in employment. Title II covers state and local government services and public transportation.

Title III covers all public accommodations, defined as any facility that offers food or services to the public. This section also applies to commercial facilities, which are nonresidential buildings that do business but are not open to the general public. Title IV deals with telecommunications services and requires telephone companies to provide telecommunications relay services for individuals with hearing and speech impairments.

☑ **Titles III and IV affect the work of interior designers most directly, and ADA provisions will be referred to throughout this book.**

The regulations included in Title III have been incorporated into the **Americans with Disabilities Act Accessibility Guidelines (ADAAG)**. The text of the ADAAG is law, but its appendix, which offers helpful information on interpretation and compliance, is not binding. The ADAAG discusses such architectural concerns as accessible routes and the design of restrooms for wheelchair access. Communications issues covered include alarms systems and signage for people with vision and hearing impairments.

All new buildings with public accommodations and/or commercial facilities must conform to specific ADAAG requirements, including lodging, restaurants, hotels, and theaters. Shopping centers and malls, retail stores, banks, places of public assembly, museums, and galleries also must comply, as must libraries, private schools, day-care centers, and professional offices. State and local government buildings and one- and two-family dwellings are not required to conform.

The ADA requirements are most stringent for new buildings or additions to existing buildings. The laws are not as clear concerning the renovation of existing buildings and interiors. When an existing building is renovated, specific areas of the building must be altered to conform to the ADA requirements. These alterations are limited to those deemed readily achievable in terms of structure and cost. Exemptions may be made for undue burden as a result of the difficulty or expense of an alteration. These situations are determined on a case-by-case basis by regulatory authorities or the courts and often involve difficult judgment calls.

For example, if a restaurant must add an elevator in order to expand into a second-floor space, will the added seating create enough income to offset the cost of the alterations? If the business expands but does not provide access for people who are unable to use stairs, they risk the bad publicity and embarrassment of a lawsuit and perhaps a public protest, and the even greater cost of retrofitting the space after the initial renovation. Sometimes there is no fair and easy answer.

FAIR HOUSING ACT

The Department of Housing and Urban Development (HUD) enforces the **Fair Housing Act (FHA)**, which prohibits discrimination and provides protection for people with disabilities and for families with children. It applies to housing with four or more units. Such buildings must have public and common areas accessible to people with disabilities. Minimally, the ground floor units must be accessible and must meet specific construction requirements. The FHA is essentially a residential version of the ADA.

While the **One and Two Family Dwelling Code (OTFDC)** is not a federal regulation, it has been adopted by many jurisdictions in the United States. The OTFDC is the main code used for construction of single and duplex family residences.

Chapters 1 and 2 have introduced the environmental and governmental criteria that affect the design of buildings. In Part II: Structural Systems, we will see how a building's structure supports, protects, and shapes its interior spaces.

PART

II

· · · · · · · · · · · · · · · ·

STRUCTURAL SYSTEMS

Although the work of interior designers is concerned with interior spaces, interior designers benefit from an understanding of the way buildings are constructed, why they stand up or fall down, and how different building techniques affect the shaping and utilization of interior space.

3

....

Basic Structural Principles and Elements

The **structural system** of a building is designed and constructed to support the loads applied to the building, as well as to transmit them safely to the ground without damaging the building. Some structural systems are based on a single material, such as heavy timber structures. Others combine materials. For example, structural steel–framed buildings often have horizontal steel beams and vertical steel columns, along with horizontal floor planes of steel and concrete. A building may have more than one structural system, such as when a concrete **foundation** supports a light wood-framed **superstructure**. In other buildings, what appears to be the structural material, such as brick, is actually only an exterior facing material, with the real **structural load** carried by a concrete structural system.

SUPERSTRUCTURE AND FOUNDATION

A building's vertical extension aboveground is called its superstructure, which includes the **columns, beams,** and **load-bearing walls** that support the floors and roof structures. A building's superstructure rests on its foundation.

The foundation, in turn, is supported by the earth below and surrounding it. Soil conditions, the presence of water below the surface, and the characteristics of bedrock below are all taken into account in the design of the foundation.

BUILDING LOADS

The term **building load** refers to any of the forces to which a structure is subjected. The weight of the building materials is part of the building load, as are any furnishings or equipment inside the building. Building loads also take into account people and objects that move into and out of the building. In addition, building structures are designed to accommodate winds (including storms), the weight of accumulated snow, and **seismic** forces (earthquakes).

Static and Dynamic Loads

A **static building load** is applied slowly and steadily to a structure until it reaches its maximum weight-bearing capacity. A structure responds slowly to a static load and is affected the most when the static force is at its greatest. Static loads include:

- the weight of the structure itself
- the weight of building elements, fixtures, and equipment permanently attached to it
- movable or moving **live loads**

Live loads change over time, but they generally do so gradually. They include:

- the weight of the building's occupants
- any mobile equipment and furnishings
- any collected snow and water

Dynamic loads are applied suddenly to a structure, often with rapid changes in the size of the force and the point to which it is applied. Earthquakes and the loads caused by winds are examples of dynamic loads.

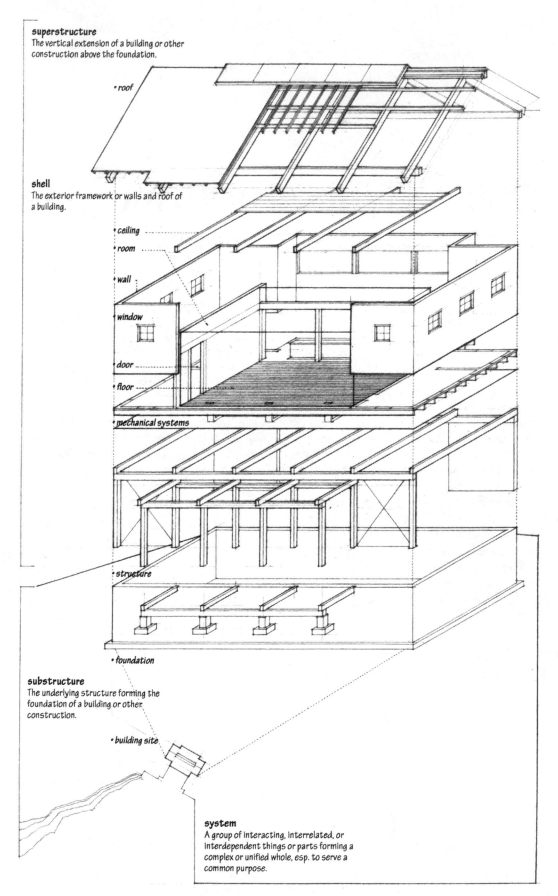

superstructure
The vertical extension of a building or other construction above the foundation.

• roof

shell
The exterior framework or walls and roof of a building.

• ceiling

• room

• wall

• window

• door

• floor

• mechanical systems

• structure

• foundation

substructure
The underlying structure forming the foundation of a building or other construction.

• building site

system
A group of interacting, interrelated, or interdependent things or parts forming a complex or unified whole, esp. to serve a common purpose.

Figure 3-1 Building structure. The components of a building structure protect the building's occupants and contents.

Compression, Deflection, and Tension

Compression is the shortening or pushing together of a material that results in a reduction in its size or volume. For example, if you press down on a firm cushion, the material inside is squeezed together. This squeezing may cause the shape of the cushion to deform and stretch the covering fabric in some places while pushing it together in others.

In a **beam**—a horizontal structural member that is longer than it is wide or deep— compression may cause the beam to bend downward. If the pressure (**load**) is applied at the center of a beam that is supported at both ends, the center will bend down from the horizontal. The distance between the beam's supports is called its **span**.

The perpendicular distance that a beam is bent down when a load is placed on it is called **deflection**. Deflection increases as the load becomes heavier and the span becomes longer. When a beam deflects under a load, the beam's material under the load at the top of the beam is pushed together (compressed). At the same time, the material at the bottom of the load is pulled apart.

Tension is the reaction of a material to stresses stretching or pulling on a material along the direction of its length. A beam that bends and deflects is subject to an internal combination of compressive and **tensile** (related to tension) stresses. Interestingly, the material that lies between the compressed and stretched areas is subject to relatively little stress. This is why steel beams, for example, can be designed with a wide top and bottom and a narrow middle.

Because the stresses from the loads are proportionally greater along the upper and lower parts of a beam's cross section, increasing the beam's depth and placing more material where stresses are greatest helps the beam carry loads more efficiently.

Structural loads are transferred through a building's structural system to the ground. Loads are transferred across openings by systems of beams and columns.

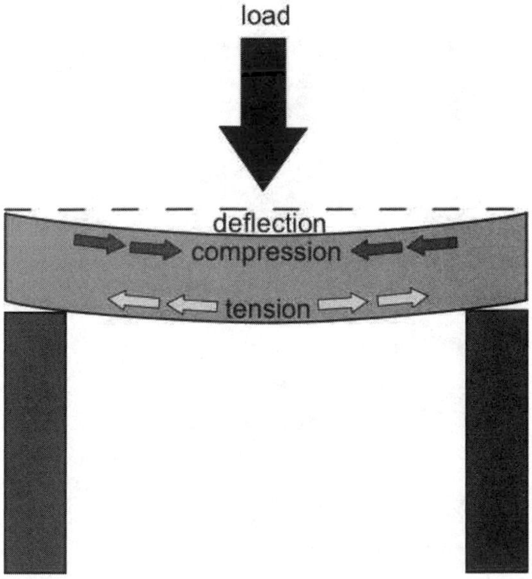

Spanning Openings

There are quite a few ways to carry a building load across an opening: beams, trusses, lintels, arches, corbels, and even cantilevers.

Wood beams have a long history. Beams cut from large trees are used in heavy-timber construction. Light wood-frame construction uses dimensional lumber beams that are uniformly cut and designed to carry loads across specific spans. Spaced beams are made with blocking and open spaces to keep weight light. Laminated beams, which are made from pieces of wood glued together, can be very strong. There are also a number of types of built-up beams.

Stone beams are good in compression but relatively poor in tension. They are also very heavy and limited to shorter spans than steel beams.

Steel beams are strong and good in both tension and compression. They are also relatively easy to assemble into grid patterns with steel columns, making it possible to create interiors with large open spaces.

Another way to span an opening is a **truss**. A truss could be thought of as a type of built-up beam that utilizes the inherent stability of a triangle to spread and support a load. Unlike a beam with its combination of tension and compression, in a truss, all of the structural members are in tension.

Steel trusses are composed of structural steel angles and tees bolted or welded together into a triangle-based framework. Steel trusses can take on many angled, curved, flat, and triangular forms.

Laminated wood trusses are composed of smaller pieces of wood glued together into large trusses. Laminated wood trusses can be designed to be stronger than solid wood trusses; they are also easier to shape into curves.

Figure 3-2 Compression, deflection, tension. When a load is applied to a beam supported by two columns, the beam bends downward (deflection). The top of the beam is then in compression, while the bottom is in tension.

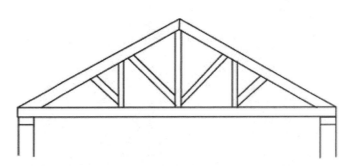

Figure 3-3 Truss. Some trusses look like large triangles with smaller triangles inside. Others are rectilinear— or even curved on top—but are still composed of smaller triangles.

LINTELS AND ARCHES

Openings weaken the structure of a rigid wall. Building a **lintel** or **arch** above a door or window opening supports the load and carries compressive forces around the opening to either side of the wall.

A lintel is a linear horizontal structural member placed over a door or window to transfer the load from the area above the window opening. Concrete lintels usually contain steel reinforcing to improve their tensile strength. Such lintels are often used in stone, brick, or other masonry construction. Wood lintels are called

Figure 3-6 Roman arch. A Roman arch is semicircular. Each of the stones in the arch (*voissoirs*) presses against the adjacent stones. The keystone at the top holds all of the stones in place.

Figure 3-4 Lintels. This building has precast concrete lintels over its door and window.

Figure 3-5 Masonry arch. This stone arch is in the Shaker Church Family Dwelling House near Enfield, New Hampshire.

Figure 3-7 Gothic arch. This gate at Moret-sur-Loing, France, was built of stone in the twelfth century. The pointed arches identify it as an example of Gothic architecture.

Figure 3-8 Corbels. This Syrian cut-stone hood is supported over a doorway on corbels; it was built in either the fifth or the sixth century. Corbels work best in such applications and are generally inferior to arches for spanning openings.

headers and are often made by doubling up standard wood **dimension lumber** for greater strength.

Arches, like columns, are structural members that are frequently used decoratively and expressively. Many historic architectural styles have their own type of arch. Some arches are able to stand alone because they transfer the load in both directions from each part of the arch. Other arches use buttresses to carry the load to the ground while keeping the arch from spreading.

An arch uses a curved structure to span an opening. Arches are designed to support a vertical load primarily by compression along its **axis** and to transfer the load to load-bearing surfaces adjacent to the two sides of the arch. Masonry arches are constructed of individual wedge-shaped stones or bricks. Rigid arches of curved, rigid timber, steel, or reinforced concrete are used where it is necessary to carry some bending stress.

Corbels consist of masonry units stacked with each row extending past the row below. They are held in place by the weight of the construction on top of them. A corbelled arch is made from such masonry units as bricks or stone blocks, with each row extending from the side of the opening farther into the opening; the opening gets smaller as it becomes higher. Corbels are not able to stand alone; they depend on the weight of masonry above the extending units to keep them from falling into the arch.

VAULTS, DOMES, AND OTHER CURVED FORMS

The ceiling over a hall or room can be spanned by a **vault**, which is an arched structure of stone, brick, or reinforced concrete. A vault functions like a three-dimensional arch. The supporting walls along the length of a vault are buttressed against outward stresses, similar to the sides of an arch.

A **barrel vault** is essentially a series of Roman arches lined up along an axis. It is semicircular in cross section.

Groin or **cross vaults** are formed by the perpendicular intersection of two vaults, creating the appearance of two arches that intersect diagonally. When the arches are elaborately curved, the vault takes on an ornate three-dimensional form.

Figure 3-9 Barrel vault. This barrel vault is built of bricks; others are made of stone, wood, or steel.

Figure 3-10 Groin vault. This straightforward groin vault is formed by the intersection of two barrel vaults.

Figure 3-11 Domes, pillars, and arches. Rigestan Square in Samarkand, Uzbekistan, features Islamic domes, pillars, and arches.

Domes span circular openings with a spherical surface structure consisting of stacked blocks, reinforced concrete, or short linear elements (as in a **geodesic dome**). One way to visualize a dome is to imagine it as an arch spun on its vertical axis. Domes can cover large, open interior spaces. They are supported by bearing walls, columns and arches, or piers.

Shell, membrane, and cable structures are other ways to cover an area with three-dimensional forms. We will look at them in Chapter 4: Structural Forms.

Cantilevers

It is possible to support a horizontal structure from one end only, with the structure extending past the support; this is called a **cantilever**. The weight of the cantilevered structure and any load on it is transferred back to the supporting wall. A simple example of a cantilever is a diving board. Balconies and overhangs are also often cantilevers.

Vertical Supports

Some of the vertical structural members available for use in buildings include columns, pilasters, piers, posts, and piles.

COLUMNS

Compression and tension occur in a **column**, which is a vertical structural member that is longer than it is wide or deep. When a load is placed on top of a column, the material in the column is compressed. Sometimes the load is great enough to compress the column until its material crumbles; this can happen to stone columns. With other materials, the column bends (deflects) along its length, much like a beam does. As a result, one side of the deflected area is in tension and the other is in compression. Thin wood columns tend to fail in this manner.

The goal in designing with columns and beams is to carry the load safely to the ground. A load on a beam is transferred

Figure 3-12 Cantilever: Fallingwater terrace. Located in Mill Run, Pennsylvania, Frank Lloyd Wright's Fallingwater features this cantilevered terrace above the waterfall. Cantilevers dramatically reach across an opening from a single side.

to the support (column) at each end, so that each column carries only half the load. The columns then carry the load to the ground. Well-designed and properly loaded columns and beams will deflect only within very well-defined parameters; they are designed to withstand loads greater than those anticipated in normal use.

Wood columns may be built of either solid wood or of wood pieces that are either laminated with glue or fastened together mechanically. Spaced wood columns are made of multiple structural members with blocking and spaces inside. A wood column fails under a compression load when wood fibers are crushed. Slender wood columns also fail by buckling.

Masonry columns and pilasters are made up of small, usually uniform units that are strong in compression. The bricks or blocks are stacked a minimum of 12 inches (305 mm) in both width and length, and a maximum of thirty times as long as they are wide. A row of columns connected by arches is called a **colonnade**.

A **pilaster** looks like a column protruding from a wall; it may stick out on one side or on both sides. The pilaster buttresses the wall, making it stronger and less likely to fall over when lateral forces are applied.

Stone columns can be carved from a single giant block of stone or built of large blocks that are stacked one on top of another. The columns rely almost entirely on compression to carry a load to the ground. Stone columns with stone beams are laid

Figure 3-14 Masonry pilasters. When the interior of the historic Town Hall building in Belmont, Massachusetts, was renovated, new wall finishes abutted the existing brick columns, creating pilasters.

Figure 3-13 Wood columns. These tall wood columns line the street face of a building in Saratoga Springs, New York.

out close together; the classic Egyptian column was often assembled in a densely packed **hypostyle** hall.

The reinforcing used in concrete columns helps resist applied forces. Concrete columns are laid out on a regular grid in order to facilitate the economical formation of beams and slabs. The columns are designed as continuous units from the foundation to their tops. When used with a grid of steel or timber beams, concrete columns are connected to the other components with steel connectors.

Precast concrete columns are used with precast beams to form structural assemblies. The joints between precast columns and beams are not usually rigid; typically, they are assembled with shear walls. Precast columns are commonly 10, 12, or 16 inches square.

Steel columns carry the building loads to the foundation. They may be placed in front of, within, or behind the exterior wall plane of the building. Steel columns are most commonly made in the wide-flange or W shape, but they are also available as round pipes and square or rectangular tubes. Some concrete columns have structural steel columns inside. Columns are conventionally designed to have an effective length of 12 feet (366 cm).

PILLARS AND POSTS

Pillars and **posts** are much like columns: linear vertical structural members. They may function like columns to carry a building load to the ground. Pillars can also be freestanding; monuments are basic examples. The term "post" is often used for wood columns made from a single tree trunk; it may also refer to shorter wood or metal vertical pieces used in fences and other construction.

Lateral Forces

If you support the ends of a simple beam on two columns, then push one of the columns from the side, they will tend to topple over. This structural arrangement does not resist **lateral forces** (perpendicular to the direction of the support) very well. Bracing the corners where the columns meet the beam can strengthen this arrangement.

Imagine a picture frame without a picture in it; the frame will easily shift out of alignment. However, when you put a stiff rectangular piece of cardboard in the frame, it will regain its right-angle corners. The flat surface of the cardboard will also help spread the stresses evenly and keep the frame straight. In the beam and columns example above, corner bracing will enable the columns and beam to effectively become a rigid frame.

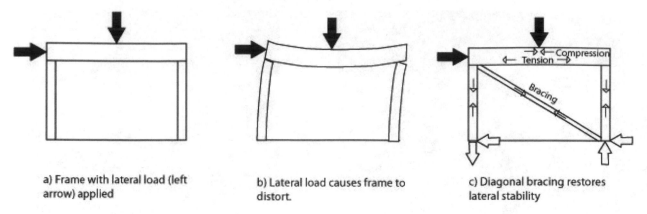

a) Frame with lateral load (left arrow) applied

b) Lateral load causes frame to distort.

c) Diagonal bracing restores lateral stability

Figure 3-15 Lateral stability. Lateral stability is the ability of a structure to resist lateral forces without sliding, overturning, buckling, or collapsing.

A load-bearing wall is designed to spread a load over its entire surface. In the case of a structural building frame, filling the opening with a load-bearing wall makes the area that carries the compressive forces to the ground much greater. The area that the wall stands on is greater than that provided by end columns alone; consequently, the load is spread over a greater area. Evenly applied loads are the easiest for structural elements to carry.

The wall will be strongest along the direction of its surface. If the load is perpendicular to the plane of the wall, the wall will need extra support for lateral stability. This support can be provided by buttressing the wall with pilasters, adding cross walls or transverse rigid frames, or inserting horizontal slabs between pairs of walls. A **buttress** is a thickening in a wall that provides additional structural support. It may be a relatively simple pilaster, a heavy exterior buttress, or a more complex flying buttress. All of these serve to increase the area that helps carry the load and resist lateral forces.

Another way to accommodate lateral loads is to locate other walls, called cross walls, perpendicular to the bearing wall. These walls become part of the building's structural system and are necessary for the building's stability. Even if the walls do not carry loads from above, they help the load-bearing walls do their work.

Lateral stability can also be increased by building pairs of walls connected by horizontal slabs. The slabs help even out the load between the walls as well as resist sideways forces.

Shearing Forces

A **shear wall** is a wood, concrete, or masonry wall that transfers a load to the foundation and resists changes in shape. In the picture-frame example above, the rigid cardboard in the frame acted as a shear wall, keeping the frame's corners at right angles. Shear walls are designed to deal with shearing forces.

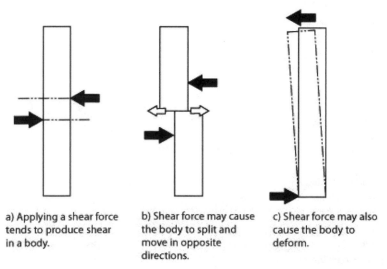

a) Applying a shear force tends to produce shear in a body.

b) Shear force may cause the body to split and move in opposite directions.

c) Shear force may also cause the body to deform.

Figure 3-16 Shear. Shearing forces occur when parallel surfaces move in opposite directions.

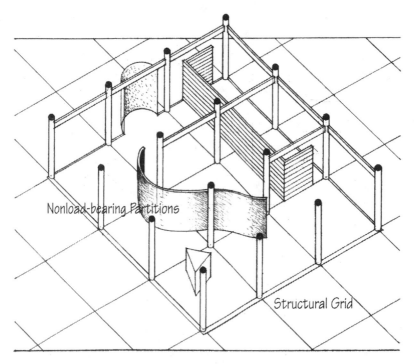

Figure 3-17 Structural grid. A structural grid creates regular open spaces between structural elements. Interior designers are then free to design nonload-bearing partitions of varying heights and configurations to shape the interior space.

A **shearing force** describes what happens when two parallel surfaces move in opposite directions. This is why scissors are called "shears": the parallel blades move past each other. A shearing force can occur during an earthquake, when one of the earth's tectonic plates rises up while the adjacent plate edge drops. Shear walls are found in buildings, filling structural frames and making it harder for building components to shift past each other.

A **braced frame** is composed of timber or steel with diagonal bracing members. The diagonal members pick up the loads that would otherwise twist the frame and prevent the corners from moving closer together or farther apart. Diagonal bracing members can save both materials and weight as compared to sheets that fill the entire frame.

As a building becomes taller and thinner, it is more likely to twist or sway. High-rise buildings require additional bracing with diagonal bracing and/or a rigid core. Many high-rise buildings employ tube structures, which consist of bracing systems at the perimeter of the building connected by rigid floor planes.

Grid Frameworks

Large and complex structural forms can be made of smaller structural units. Linear column and beam frameworks create a grid that can be added to with ease both horizontally and vertically. Within that framework, designers are free to add nonload-bearing walls that do not follow the grid.

☑ **Structural grids can be modified by using additional columns or by eliminating supporting elements. In the latter situation, the support for the load must be transferred away from the missing column. Sometimes this is a complex process, so the interior designer must consult an architect or structural engineer before removing existing structural elements.**

In this chapter, we have explored the basic structural forces that influence building design. In Chapter 4: Structural Forms, we will take a look at the components that make up a building's structure.

4

. . . .

Structural Forms

As we read in Chapter 2, the building envelope, consisting of the roof, exterior walls, and foundation, separates the inside from the outside, provides protection from weather, and controls access. The building envelope also helps to control ventilation and the gain or loss of heat. Within this envelope are a building core, floor and ceiling structures, walls, windows, doors, stairs, and ramps.

In some buildings, the exterior walls serve as both structure and enclosure. The exterior walls of a steel frame structure are often nonbearing **curtain walls**. Curtain walls are nonload-bearing surface treatments. The framing or panels of the curtain wall are supported by the columns alone, by columns and **spandrel beams**, or by the edges of the floor slab.

The windows, doors, floors, walls, and roofs that make up the building envelope may be simple surfaces or may include a wide variety of components. For example, windows can include operable and fixed glazing, skylights, clerestories, screens, shutters, blinds, shades, curtains, and drapes. They may be made of diffusing, insulating, or reflecting glass; glass blocks; or photoelectric panels.

To promote energy efficiency in a building envelope, architects and engineers seek to:

- reduce surface areas exposed to the exterior
- reduce the factors that permit energy loss through surface areas
- reduce the difference in temperature between the exterior and the interior
- reduce the amount of unconditioned air entering the building

These actions have important implications for both the form of the building's exterior and the conditions in its interior. They affect the orientation, angle, surface reflectance, and thermal capacity of the materials used in the building envelope.

Building code requirements for thermal envelope performance of nonresidential buildings in North America are usually those set forth in *ANSI/ASHRAE/IESNA Standard 90.1*. Typically, residential buildings are subject to the requirements of the *International Energy Conservation Code* or *ASHRAE Residential Energy Standard, Standard 90.2*.

The standards in these codes are intended as minimum requirements for building envelopes. The Green Building Council (USGBC) LEED rating system requires envelopes designed to exceed these requirements by 15 to 60 percent. Buildings that meet LEED standards usually employ elements that control daylight and solar heat. We will look at some of these, including window treatments and passive solar design, in Chapter 11: Heating and Cooling.

The more flexibility built into the building envelope, the more important it is to provide adequate controls. For example, thermal shades and other window treatments can block the passive solar collection of warming infrared radiation on a cold, sunny day.

Conventionally engineered buildings without readily adjustable user controls, such as adjustable window treatments and operable windows, use sophisticated air conditioning controls to control airflow and temperature. The resulting sealed spaces eliminate connection with the outdoors and limit flexibility in response to changing weather and occupant needs. Operable windows and user-controlled window treatments enable building occupants to modify their indoor environment.

WINDOWS AND DOORS

Windows in the building envelope introduce both fresh air and daylight. Windows that open can help cool a space in warm

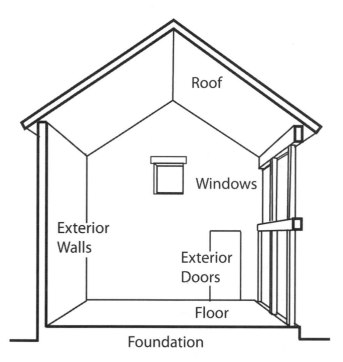

Figure 4-1 Building envelope. The building envelope includes windows and doors that are fabricated and tested off-site. Other envelope materials are assembled either on-site according to standard construction details or in innovative, unique designs.

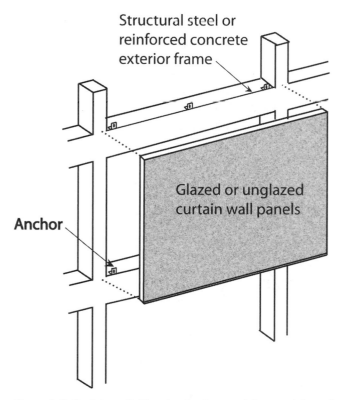

Figure 4-2 Curtain wall. The structural support for a curtain wall may be located in front of, within, or behind its surface plane.

weather by admitting cooling breezes and allowing excess heat from lighting and equipment to escape. However, large expanses of glass can permit building heat to escape in cold weather. Transparent and translucent envelope components, such as windows, routinely have the lowest resistance to heat loss of any building components. They also allow outdoor air to infiltrate, adding to the need for cooling or heating inside, and admit solar heat.

Fenestration is the technical name for windows in the building envelope. The **National Fenestration Rating Council (NFRC)** has developed a standardized rating for window performance. Each window or skylight manufactured in the United States bears an NFRC label certifying that the window has been independently rated. The label carries a brief description of the product and lists U-factor, solar heat gain coefficient (SHGC), and visible-light transmittance.

The thermal performance of exterior doors is also important. The thin film of air that forms on the inside surface of a closed door resists the passage of heat through the door. When this film is disturbed by forced-air-supply registers or return grilles, the door's thermal effectiveness is compromised.

Doors set into entry vestibules help prevent indoor air from mixing with outdoor air. This, in turn, helps control the interior environment and reduces the amount of unconditioned air that must be heated or cooled.

VAPOR PRESSURE

Air contains water vapor, which moves from an area of greater concentration to one of lesser concentration. This **vapor pressure** forces moisture to flow through the components of a building envelope. Additional water vapor is carried directly by airflow through gaps in the envelope. Water vapor condensing within the building envelope construction can render insulating materials ineffective, damage wood structural elements, and harbor mold and mildew.

Vapor retarders are materials that resist the flow of water vapor through the envelope assembly. They are very thin membranes that take up almost no space inside the building envelope. Nonetheless, their placement within a wall, roof, or floor is critical and varies with the type of construction and the local climate.

Water will readily permeate many building materials, including gypsum board, concrete, brick, wood, and glass fiber insulation as well as most interior finish materials. In cold climates, cold outside air contains little moisture, while inside air contains much more moisture comparatively. The difference in vapor pressure drives the flow of water vapor from the warm interior to the cold exterior.

In a cold climate, the vapor retarder is typically a plastic film installed within the building envelope, as close to the warm side as possible. This is usually located just behind the interior surface, such as gypsum board or wood flooring. Where the envelope has high insulation **R-values**, the vapor retarder can be located about one-third of the distance from the interior to the exterior, thereby allowing space for wiring or plumbing on the warm interior side.

Plastic films in the proper location within the envelope assembly provide better protection from migrating water vapor than vinyl wallpaper or vapor retarder paints on interior surfaces. Such films also help block airflow through the envelope.

Another problem in cold climates occurs when water vapor condenses on cold interior surfaces. This often occurs at windows and can cause damage to interior surfaces. Proper insulation of exterior walls helps keep interior surface materials warm and dry.

ROOFS

The roof system of a building shelters the interior space. The roof structure must be strong enough to span the space, carry its own weight, and support attached equipment as well as the weight of snow or rain. In addition, the roof must resist lateral and seismic forces and the uplifting of wind forces. Several types of pitched roof are used for light-frame buildings.

A flat roof can provide extra living space or space for a garden or green roof. Flat roofs may be built of reinforced concrete slabs, flat timber or steel trusses, timber or steel beams and decking, or wood or steel joists and sheathing.

The construction of a flat roof is similar to that of a floor, but even flat roofs must have some slope and a provision for water from rain and melting snow to drain. Flat roofs are usually drained by interior drains that run vertically through the building.

A reinforced concrete roof slab is covered with a vapor retarder, insulation, a roofing membrane, and a wear course of gravel or other material. Flat, structural steel–framed roofs are built much the way steel floors are. Sloping steel roofs rely on steel truss structures.

- A **pitched** roof has one or more slopes.
- A **shed** roof has a single pitched slope.
- A gable roof slopes down in two directions from a central ridge, forming a triangular **gable** at each end.
- **Gambrel** roofs are pitched roofs with a shallower upper slope and a steeper lower slope on each side.
- A hip, or **hipped**, roof has sloping sides like a gable roof, but the ends also slope in to meet the central ridge.
- A **mansard** roof resembles a shallow hipped roof set on top of a steeper lower part.

Concrete roofs can be designed as flat, folded, domed, or shell-shaped structures. Space frames are three-dimensional steel structures based on rigid triangles made of linear steel elements.

In cold climates, an uninsulated attic beneath a roof is sometimes separated from the living space of a house by an insulated ceiling. Although the attic is not insulated, it may still be warmer than the outside temperature. Venting the attic to the outdoors will enable it to disperse moisture that migrates through the insulated ceiling.

FOUNDATIONS

A building rests on a foundation made of concrete, concrete block, or stone that supports the floor structure and anchors the rest of the building. A foundation may be deep enough for a basement, only leave room for a crawl space, or consist of a slab-on-grade.

A **basement** is surrounded by a continuous foundation wall that resists the surrounding earth and provides support for the

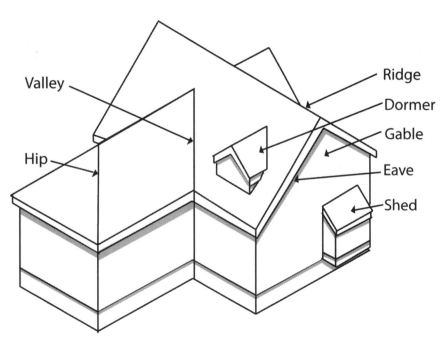

Figure 4-3 Roof terminology.

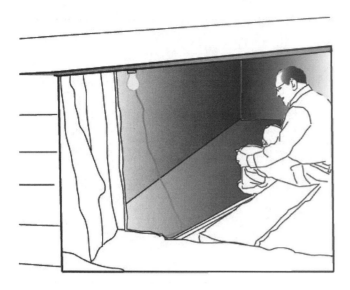

Figure 4-4 Crawl space. A crawl space may be literally that: a space that is too low for people to stand or even sit. A crawl space that allows reasonable movement provides space for utilities and even some storage.

exterior walls and the columns of the superstructure above. The depth of the basement affects how much heat will flow through basement walls and floors.

A **crawl space** is created under the superstructure by a continuous foundation wall or piers. Crawl spaces provide access to electrical, plumbing, and mechanical equipment.

It is becoming common practice to provide a continuous layer of insulation below floor framing above a crawl space. The crawl space remains vented to the outdoors, but generally it will not be affected by the extremes of outdoor air temperatures. This greatly reduces the amount of thermal transmission through the floor from the exterior.

A **concrete slab-on-grade** is supported directly on the earth and made thick enough to carry the wall and column loads for a one- or two-story building.

A foundation consisting of a grid of **piers** or poles can be used to elevate the building's superstructure well above ground level in order to prevent damage from flooding, accommodate a steeply sloping site, or allow cooling air to circulate below the building.

Foundations also serve to keep the rest of the building above wet earth and to keep water out of the building. Although the soil surrounding the foundation will help hold building heat in, foundations are often given an exterior layer of insulation as well. It is considered normal for the structure of a building to settle slightly, gradually subsiding as the soil below compacts under the building's loads, but architects and engineers take great pains to provide a stable base for the building's foundation.

At the base of the foundation, **footings** spread the load over a wider area. Some buildings on unsuitable or unstable soil require especially deep foundations. **Pile** and **caisson** foundations rest on layers of rock or on dense sands and gravels farther below the surface.

Foundation walls are usually made of concrete or of concrete masonry units, although older buildings may have stone foundations. **Concrete masonry units (CMUs)** are small units 8 inches (20 cm) high and wide and 16 inches (40 cm) in length. They can be handled easily and do not require formwork. Concrete foundation walls are cast in place within forms.

Figure 4-5 Cast-in-place concrete foundation wall forms. Concrete foundation walls have fewer joints that could admit groundwater than CMU walls.

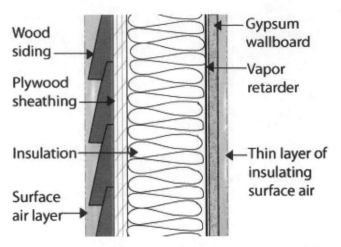

Figure 4-6 Exterior wall section. This section shows the insulating surface air layers and interior insulation in an exterior wall.

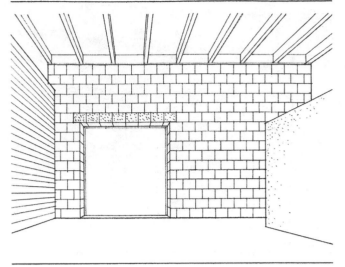

Figure 4-7 Load-bearing walls. Load-bearing walls provide support for both the building envelope and the interior structure.

EXTERIOR WALLS

The amount of heat that flows either into a building from outside or out of a building from inside, depends on:

- the difference in temperature between the inside and the outside
- the thermal resistance of the building-envelope materials
- the ability of the building envelope to store heat

The ability of a material to store heat is called its **thermal capacity**. A building envelope constructed with materials with high thermal capacity may be able to reduce the heat flow by storing heat during the daytime and emitting it at night. This slows down and may diminish the amount of excess heat that enters a building.

Building form also affects how heat moves into and out of a building. Tall, thick buildings shelter larger amounts of floor space from the outside climate. The heat generated by their electrical lighting can be more than enough to keep the building warm in winter. These buildings are called **internal load dominated** and require air conditioning throughout the year.

Almost all the interior spaces in thinner buildings have an exterior wall that needs to be heated in cold weather and cooled in hot weather. Electric lighting does not provide as much heat because daylight suffices for most daytime needs. These buildings are called **skin load dominated**.

LOAD-BEARING WALLS

Typically, vertical structural support for a building is provided either by load-bearing walls or by a framework of columns and beams. Load-bearing walls are commonly built parallel to each other.

Exterior walls are part of the building envelope and support vertical loads as well as horizontal wind loads. Exterior walls control the passage of heat, air, sound, moisture, and water vapor in and out of the building. These walls are constructed to endure the sun, wind, and rain and to be fire-resistant. Rigid exterior walls serve as shear walls to transfer lateral wind and earthquake loads to a building's foundation.

Load-bearing wall systems depend upon structural frames for stability.

- Concrete frames are rigid, noncombustible, and fire-resistant.
- Noncombustible steel frames require fireproofing for fire resistance.
- Timber frames gain lateral stability from diagonal bracing or shear planes. When a timber frame uses heavy timbers along with noncombustible, fire-resistant exterior walls, the assembly can meet the requirements for heavy timber construction, which is considered inherently fire-resistant.

Concrete and masonry bearing walls are classified by building codes as noncombustible construction. They support loads in compression by the mass of their material and are, therefore, heavy and solid. To accommodate tensile (pulling) stresses, concrete and masonry walls can be reinforced with steel. They are designed to carry relatively heavy loads across 20- to 40-foot (6 to 12 m) spans.

☑ **Interior surfaces of concrete and masonry walls are often left exposed, creating texture and pattern.**

Load-bearing walls can also be built with metal or wood **studs**. Stud wall frames can be assembled on-site or panelized off-site. The relatively small, lightweight components are easily worked into a variety of forms.

Wall stud rules of thumb:

- Wall studs are spaced 16 inches or 24 inches (405 or 610 mm) apart to carry vertical loads.

- Wall studs are usually either 2 × 4s or 2 × 6s.
- The maximum unsupported height for 2 × 4s spaced 16 inches on center is 14 feet (4265 mm), and 10 feet for studs 24 inches (610 mm) on center.
- Twenty-foot-long 2 × 6 studs can be spaced 24 inches apart, but they are spaced only 16 inches apart when supporting two stories and a roof.

The cavities between the studs are used for thermal insulation, vapor retarders, mechanical distribution, and mechanical and electrical service outlets. The fire-resistance rating of a stud wall assembly depends on its finish materials.

A building's superstructure and foundation enclose other building components, including walls, ceilings, floors, stairs, windows, and doors. These elements define interior spaces, connect to the outdoors, and facilitate movement through the building's interior. We will review these in Chapter 5: Horizontal Structures and Vertical Movement.

STRUCTURAL TYPES

The remainder of this chapter will introduce basic construction types and examine how they affect building interiors. Structural types include:

- light frame structures
- post-and-beam and heavy timber structures
- masonry structures
- concrete structures
- metal structures
- other structural types

Embodied Energy and Construction Materials

Many materials used to construct building structures are brought to the site from other places. Because such materials are not

TABLE 4-1. EMBODIED ENERGY IN BUILDING MATERIALS

Building Material	Material Type	BTU Per Unit
Masonry	Brick, clay fired	14,000/brick
	Brick, ceramic glazed	33,4000/brick
	Adobe, semistabilized	3700/block
	Concrete block	24,100–34,800/block
	Quarry tile	51,000/sf
	Ceramic tile	25,160/sf
Concrete	Ready-mix	1,500,000–2,000,000/cu yard
Metal Framing	Steel framing	19,200/lb
	Steel shapes	780,400–1,217,800/ft
	Aluminum shapes	469,900–811,800/ft
Wood Framing	2 x 4	3750/ft
	Lumber	7600–9800/bd ft
	Glue-laminated timbers	13,400/bd ft
	Plywood	5000–5800/sf
Metal Sheets	Steel 22 ga	29,400/sheet
	Galvanized 22 ga	49,800/sheet
	Aluminum plate ¼ in	420,700/sheet
	Stainless steel	138,300/lb
	Copper	265,140/lb
	Lead	105,620/lb
Plaster and Lath	Gypsum board	2600/sf
	Steel lath	12,000/lb
Glass	Flat glass, double strength	15,430/sf
	Plate or float glass ⅛–¼ in.	48,000/sf
	Laminated plate glass ¼ in.	212,500/sf
Flooring	Linoleum	7350/lb
	Wood flooring	10,300–14,300/bd ft
	Vinyl	22,560–27,730/lb
	Vinyl composition tile	5900/lb
	Modified resin vinyl tile	68,370/sf

locally produced, they require the use of energy in order to be transported to the job site. One energy-saving alternative is the use of locally produced materials.

Wood is a widely used and renewable construction material in North America. However, the largest trees—those of old-growth forests—are vanishing. Younger, smaller trees are fabricated into laminates, particle board, and engineered lumber, replacing the heavy timber used in earlier construction. Large wood members salvaged from old buildings continue to grow in value.

Stone is an extremely durable building material, but it is very heavy and expensive to ship. Using local stone helps relate a design to its region and efficiently uses a local resource.

Brick reflects the color and qualities of the clay from which it is produced. Fired and sun-dried brick are heavy to transport to distant sites, but they reflect the character of local settings beautifully. Used brick is highly valued as a sustainable building resource.

One of the most difficult green-design tasks is verifying that imported wood is sustainably produced and efficiently transported. Using locally produced wood makes certification much easier and, once again, reflects the climate of the project locale. Wood recycled from local buildings at the end of their useful life adds richness to a design's regional character.

Concrete is made from readily available materials and is usually produced near where it is to be used. Its durability and design flexibility make it a desirable material; however, its production and transportation are energy-intensive.

Each type of building material contains embodied energy. This energy can be measured in **British thermal units (BTUs)**.

The BTUs in the materials in Table 4-1 on page 45 are measured in varied units, making direct comparison difficult. Nonetheless, we can see that:

- the production of ceramic-glazed brick uses much more energy than that of plain, clay-fired brick
- quarry tile uses more energy than ceramic tile
- concrete uses significant amounts of energy
- glue-laminated timbers are more energy-intensive than lumber
- aluminum sheets use much more energy than steel sheets
- laminated plate glass is significantly more energy-intensive than plain plate glass

LIGHT FRAME STRUCTURES

Framing is the process of fitting and connecting relatively slender members to shape and support a structure. **Light frame construction** forms the structural elements from closely spaced and **sheathed** members made of dimension lumber or **light-gauge metal**. Light frame structures are common to many cultures and climates. Typically, they are built on-site from readily transported materials. Locally sourced materials are often used. Light frame structures may not be intended to last for the ages, but they are often preserved as representative of their time and place.

Light Frame Wood

Because of the availability of lumber from extensive forests, wood-frame construction traditionally has been used to build private

Figure 4-8 Platform framing model. A platform-framed wooden building is constructed of stacked floors, each made with studs only a single story high. Each story rests on the top plates of the story below or on the sill plates of the foundation wall.

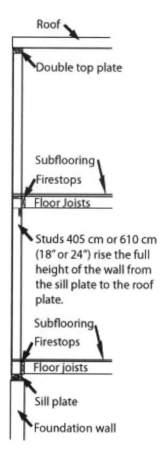

Figure 4-9 Balloon framing. The studs of a balloon-framed wooden building rise the entire height of the frame from the sill plate to the roof plate. Joists, which rest on supports that are set into the studs, are nailed to the studs.

residences and small public buildings in North America. A building's frame, which is a skeleton of relatively slender members, supports and shapes the superstructure, the part of the building that is aboveground.

A frame house is constructed with a timber skeleton that is usually sheathed with siding. **Sheathing** is a rough covering of boards, plywood, or other panels applied to the frame as a basis for siding, flooring, or roofing. **Siding**, such as shingles, boards, or sheets of metal, cover the exterior walls of frame buildings.

Strength is given to corners by assembling two or three studs at the intersection of two framed walls. Corners are further reinforced by diagonal **corner braces** attached to the studding.

Light Frame Steel

Light-gauge steel studs are cold-formed from sheets or strips of steel. Light-gauge studs are easy to cut and assemble in the field and are frequently used for lightweight, noncombustible, and damp-proof wall structures. These studs are used for bearing walls that support light-gauge-steel joists as well as for nonbearing partitions. Like wood studs, light-gauge-steel stud walls have cavities for insulation and utilities and can be finished with a wide array of materials.

Light-gauge-steel studs, which are manufactured as channels or C-shapes, are usually prepunched to allow piping, wiring, and bracing to be run through them.

Light-gauge-steel joists are lighter and more dimensionally stable and can span longer distances than wood joists. They can be cut and assembled in the field to create lightweight, noncombustible, and damp-proof floor structures. Metal joists are

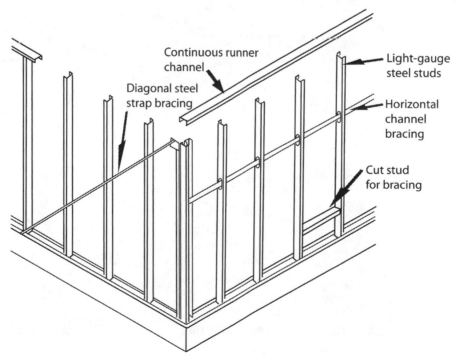

Figure 4-10 Light-gauge steel framing. Studs are given additional support by runner channels, horizontal channels, and diagonal corner braces.

assembled much the way wood joist framing is. Electric or pneumatic tools drive self-drilling, self-tapping screws or pins to connect them; they can also be welded.

POST-AND-BEAM AND HEAVY TIMBER

Post-and-beam construction (also called post-and-lintel construction) uses vertical posts and horizontal beams to carry floor and roof loads. The interior spaces formed by the grid of posts and beams can be left open to one another or divided into smaller spaces by nonbearing partitions. The skeleton frame of posts and beams is often left visible.

In wood post–and-beam construction, the posts or columns are supported by either individual piers or a wall foundation. Rigid shear walls or diagonal bracing provides resistance to lateral wind and seismic forces.

The foundation wall is topped by a **sill plate**, on which the stud wall is built. Wood beams for the first floor can be recessed into a concrete foundation wall. Where **open-web steel joists** are used, they are attached to steel base plates anchored into a concrete foundation wall or to a continual **bond beam** in a masonry wall.

Plank-and-beam construction uses a framework of wood timber beams to support wood planks or decking for floors or roofs.

The planks or sheets of decking span the framework of horizontal (or in the case of pitched roofs, sloping) beams.

Plank-and-beam floor and roof systems are used with post-and-beam wall systems to form three-dimensional structural grids. When these grid elements are left exposed on the interior of a building, the aesthetic appearance of the wood and the detailing of the joints must be high quality.

Plank-and-beam framing can sometimes qualify as **heavy timber construction**. Heavy timber construction with large wooden posts and beams is more fire-resistant than light wood-frame construction. Noncombustible, fire-resistant exterior walls combine with wood members and decking that meet minimum size requirements specified in the building code.

A type of heavy timber construction called **mill construction** was used in early mill buildings in North America. The combination of fire-resistant brick walls, large open-floor spaces, and daylight streaming through large windows provided an ideal setting for New England's textile industry. Many of these buildings still stand and have been converted into office spaces, housing and studios for artists, and museums.

Pole construction uses a vertical structure of pressure-treated wood poles firmly embedded in the ground. This **pier foundation** supports the building above the surface of land or water. Pole construction enables buildings to be constructed on steeply sloping land without removing all of the trees and grading the area to a flat surface.

Figure 4-11 Post-and-beam construction. This historic photograph of an interior in Winooski, Vermont, illustrates the large, open interior spaces that post-and-beam construction facilitates.

MASONRY STRUCTURES

Masonry construction dates back to the earliest civilizations. Building units of natural or manufactured products, such as stone, brick, or concrete block, are usually held together with mortar. Masonry walls are durable, fire-resistant, and structurally efficient for compression loads.

Masonry walls can be unreinforced or reinforced with metal wall ties. Reinforced masonry walls have steel reinforcing bars inside grout-filled cavities and joints.

Typically, masonry walls are constructed in parallel sets to support steel, wood, or concrete spanning systems. They are often spanned by open-web steel joists, timber or steel beams, or site-cast or concrete slabs.

Masonry Openings

Openings in masonry walls are spanned by arches or by stone or concrete lintels. Precast concrete lintels are available for brick and concrete masonry walls. Concrete masonry lintels rest on at least 8 inches of masonry on each side of the opening and are reinforced with steel in Portland cement grout. Paired steel angles can support the facing and backup wythes across an opening. Reinforced brick lintels are built four to seven courses high and 8, 10, or 12 inches (205, 255, or 305 mm) wide. Steel reinforcing bars are embedded in portland cement grout in the center of the brick construction.

Masonry Wall Construction

Solid masonry walls are constructed of solid or hollow masonry units, with joints filled with mortar. Masonry units can be assembled into solid walls, cavity walls, or veneered walls.

Figure 4-13 Glass block wall. Translucent, hollow blocks of glass have clear, textured, or patterned faces. Inserted into openings in exterior walls, they let in light while limiting views. As interior partitions, they contribute sparkle, translucency, and texture.

In grouted masonry walls, two wythes are bonded into a single mass with **grout** (fluid portland cement mortar). Where the facing and backing units of a masonry wall are completely separate (except where connected by metal ties), the result is called a **cavity wall**. The space between the two parts of the cavity wall

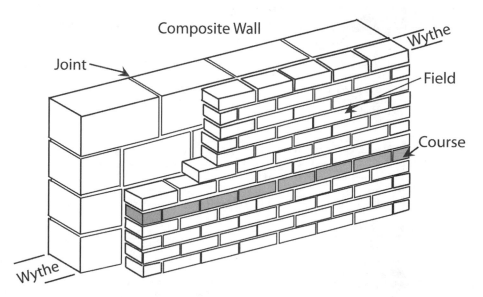

Figure 4-12 Masonry terms. A single horizontal row of masonry units is called a **course**. Multiple courses stacked together are referred to as a **field**. The continuous vertical section of a masonry wall one unit in thickness is called a **wythe** (or withe).

prevents water from penetrating through the entire wall into the interior. The air-filled cavity serves to insulate the wall and provides space for thermal insulating material. The outer wythe is provided with weep holes and flashing to allow water to leak back out to the outside. The cavity is usually 2 to 4½ inches (51 to 115 mm) wide. Each of the wythes is a nominal 4 inches thick.

A wall that has a nonstructural facing of stone, brick, concrete, or tile bonded to a supporting structure is known as a **veneered wall**. The surface veneer sometimes obscures the actual structural material, which may be concrete or masonry.

Masonry bearing or shear walls are required to have a minimum thickness of 8 inches (205 mm). With reinforcing, this can be reduced to 6 inches (150 mm). Solid 6-inch masonry walls in single-story buildings are limited to 9 feet in height.

☑ **Because masonry is composed of small units, it can be assembled into curving or irregular forms. Masonry walls provide texture and color to interior spaces.**

Masonry walls are assembled with mortar, which is usually composed of **portland cement**, sand, and water. Masonry cement is available with added ingredients for strength or setting properties, ready to be mixed with sand and water at the construction site.

Movement Joints

Masonry materials expand and contract with changes in temperature and moisture content. Clay masonry units absorb water and expand, and CMUs shrink as they dry after manufacture.

Movement joints are incorporated into masonry walls to control these changes: expansion joints are designed to close slightly when masonry materials expand, and control joints are constructed to open slightly as concrete masonry shrinks. Movement joints are located each 100 to 125 feet (30 to 38 m) along unbroken lengths of masonry walls; at changes in wall height or thickness; at columns, pilasters, and wall intersections; and near corners. They are also installed on both sides of openings greater than 6 feet (183 cm) wide, and on one side of openings less than 6 feet wide.

Stone

Masonry of natural stone is durable and weather resistant. Stones may be simply laid in mortar as double-faced walls or may be used as a facing veneer tied into a concrete or masonry backup wall.

☑ **Stone is finished to varying levels of smoothness and assembled into a variety of patterns.**

The types of stone most commonly used in building structures in the United States include:

- granite: very hard, strong, and durable, with good weathering- and abrasion-resistance
- marble: high compressive strength; most durable in dry climates or in areas protected from precipitation
- limestone: softer and more porous than granite; becomes harder when exposed to weather; durability greatest in dry climates

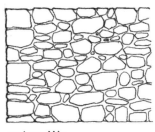

random rubble
A rubble wall having discontinuous but approximately level beds or courses.

coursed rubble
A rubble wall having approximately level beds and brought at intervals to continuous level courses.

squared rubble
A rubble wall built of squared stones of varying sizes and coursed at every third or fourth stone.

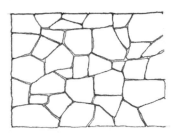

cyclopean
Formed with large, irregular blocks of stones fitted closely together without the use of mortar.

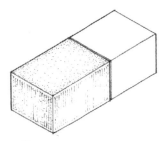

ashlar
A squared building stone finely dressed on all faces adjacent to those of other stones so as to permit very thin mortar joints.

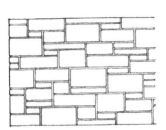

random ashlar
Ashlar masonry built in discontinuous courses.

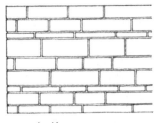

coursed ashlar
Ashlar masonry built of stones having the same height within each course, but each course varying in height.

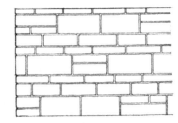

broken rangework
Ashlar masonry laid in horizontal courses of varying heights, any one of which may be broken at intervals into two or more courses.

Figure 4-14 Stone masonry patterns. Structural stone masonry patterns are sometimes visible on interior walls. Interior walls built with stone add scale, color, and texture. In other instances, stone is used to face walls constructed of other materials.

- sandstone: highly porous; easy to work with but relatively low durability
- slate: splits into slabs easily; extremely durable

Brick

Brick is a rectangular masonry unit made of clay and hardened by being exposed to the sun or by firing in a **kiln** (a furnace or oven). **Common brick** is used for general building purposes and is given no special color or texture. **Facing brick** (also called face brick) is used on surfaces, where its color and surface texture can be admired. Facing brick is made of special clays or is treated to create desired colors and textures.

Bricks absorb water and are graded for durability when exposed to weather. They are made by molding relatively wet or dry clay to produce a variety of surface textures and densities. Flashed bricks are fired alternately with too much and then too little air to produce a varied face color. Firebrick is made of high-temperature–resistant **refractory** clay; it is used for lining furnaces and fireplaces.

Bricks are made in a variety of standard sizes, which are given in **nominal dimensions**. These are larger than the actual brick dimension; the added size accounts for the thickness of a mortar joint. The dimensions and proportions of bricks affect the scale and appearance of brick walls. The types and thicknesses of mortar joints are chosen for both their appearance and their ability to shed water.

The orientation of each brick in a wall affects the wall's solidity and appearance. The arrangement of masonry units into regular patterns takes many forms.

- **Running bond** is perhaps the most common; it is composed of overlapping stretchers.
- **Common bond** inserts a course of headers between every five or six courses of stretchers.
- **Soldier course** consists of a continuous row of bricks in the soldier position. It is usually used as a single row.
- **Stack bond** (or stacked bond) vertically lines up the head joints of successive courses of stretchers.
- Other more complex bond patterns include **English bond** and **Flemish bond** and their variations as well as **garden-wall bond**.

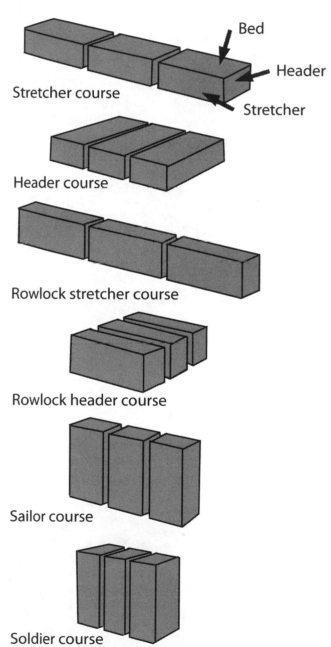

Figure 4-16 Brick positions.

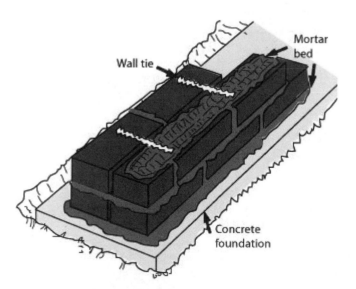

Figure 4-15 Brick construction. In this illustration, a brick wall is begun on a concrete foundation. The two wythes of the wall are linked by metal wall ties, and the bricks are held together by mortar.

Concrete Block

A CMU is a precast concrete masonry unit made of Portland cement, fine aggregate, and water. CMUs are available in many shapes and styles. **Concrete blocks** are solid or hollow CMUs; they are often incorrectly referred to as cement blocks. Several CMUs are shown in Figure 4-17; the following are some others:

- Bond-beam blocks have a depression in which reinforcing steel can be embedded in grout; they are used to construct structural bond beams.
- Lintel blocks are U-shaped and used in much the same way for bond beams or lintels.
- Sound-absorbing masonry units are CMUs with solid tops and slots in their faces. A fibrous filler material is sometimes added for increased sound absorption.
- Faced blocks have ceramic, glazed, or polished faces; they are often used in building interiors.
- Concrete bricks are solid, rectangular units that are similar to bricks in size and shape.

Concrete blocks are assembled into walls with a single wythe, with reinforcing embedded in the mortar of the horizontal joints. The vertical cells of CMUs may be filled with steel reinforcing embedded in grout. Steel reinforcing increases a wall's ability to carry vertical loads and its resistance to buckling and lateral forces. Multi-wythe, solid masonry walls are also bonded with grout, metal wall ties, or horizontal joint reinforcement.

Unfired Earth Constructions

Sun-dried bricks made of mud and water have been used for thousands of years. Bricks of sun-dried mud can be made resistant to erosion by water and wind through the addition of emulsified asphalt. The combination must be carefully tested to determine the amount of asphalt emulsion necessary to make the bricks waterproof.

Although unfired stabilized earth has low tensile strength and is unsuited for tall structures, its high compressive strength, ability to store heat, low cost, and ability to be locally sourced on a small scale have made it widely used in areas of little rainfall throughout the world.

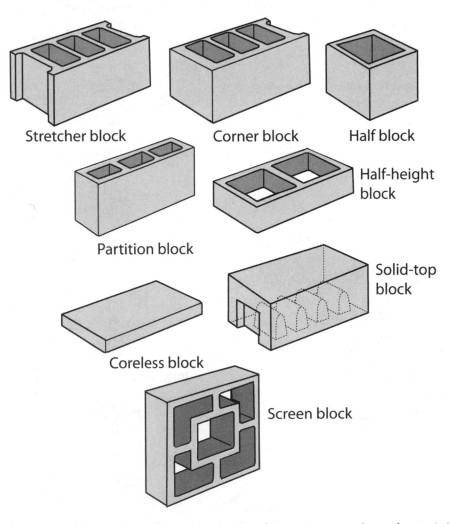

Stretcher block

Corner block

Half block

Partition block

Half-height block

Coreless block

Solid-top block

Screen block

Figure 4-17 Concrete block shapes. These are only a few of the most common forms of concrete blocks.

Adobe construction is made of sun-dried clay masonry mixed by hand or machine and cast in wood or metal forms. Straw is sometimes added to the mix. Adobe bricks are fragile until completely dry. They vary in size, although typically they are 10 by 14 inches and 2 to 4 inches thick (255 x 355 mm and 51–100 mm). Adobe bricks are very heavy: each weighs 25 to 30 pounds (11– 4 kg). They are mortared together with mortar of the same material into walls that are usually plastered on both the inside and the outside. Openings are traditionally spanned by rough-hewn wood beams called vigas.

Rammed-earth construction is another unfired, stabilized earth technology consisting of a stiff mixture of clay, silt, sand, and water that is compressed and dried within wall forms. The damp soil is compacted by hand or machine into lifts or layers 6 inches (150 mm) high before being set onto the previously placed layers.

Both adobe and rammed-earth structures use embedded wood anchors for attaching doors and windows. The thick walls vary from 8 inches (205 mm) for interior nonbearing walls to 18-inch-thick exterior walls capable of supporting two stories up to 22 feet high.

CONCRETE STRUCTURES

Concrete has been used as a structural material since the Roman Empire. It is made by mixing cement that has been **calcined** (heated to a high temperature without melting or fusing) and mineral aggregates with water. **Cement** is made from finely pulverized clay and limestone and is used as an ingredient in concrete and mortar; the term is often used incorrectly for the term "concrete."

The water used in concrete is free of organic material, clay, and salts; drinking-quality water is acceptable. **Aggregates** added to concrete are hard, inert mineral materials, such as sand and gravel. Aggregates make up 60 to 80 percent of the volume of concrete. They greatly affect its strength, weight, and fire resistance.

Other **additives** (also called admixtures) are combined with concrete to provide specific properties. These include:

- air-entraining agent: disperses tiny spherical air bubbles in a concrete or mortar mix for improved workability, either to increase resistance to damage by de-icing chemicals or to produce lightweight insulating concrete

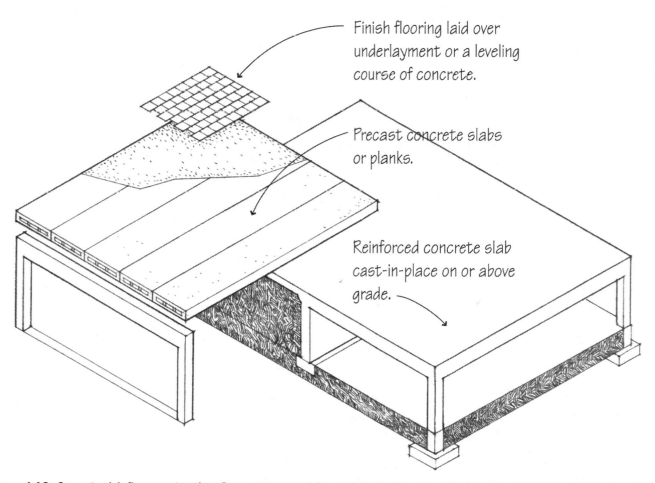

Finish flooring laid over underlayment or a leveling course of concrete.

Precast concrete slabs or planks.

Reinforced concrete slab cast-in-place on or above grade.

Figure 4-18 Concrete slab floor construction. Precast concrete slabs or planks (left), reinforced concrete slab (right). Cast-in-place reinforced concrete floor slabs are integrated into their supporting concrete beams. Precast concrete slabs or planks may be supported by beams or by load-bearing walls.

- accelerator: increases the rate of setting and strength development
- retarder: slows setting to allow more time for placing and working the mix
- surface-active agent (also called a surfactant): helps water wet and penetrate the mix or aids in distributing other additives
- water-reducing agent (also called a superplasticizer): reduces the amount of water required to keep concrete workable; this generally increases concrete strength
- coloring agent: a pigment or dye that alters concrete color

Freshly mixed concrete is tested for consistency and workability with a **slump test**. A sample is put in an open-ended, truncated, sheet-metal cone and tamped. When the cone is removed, the sample is measured and examined to determine if it is:

- a wet mix: sags from too much moisture, thereby decreasing strength, durability, and water tightness
- a dry mix: stiffly retains the cone shape with too little water or too much aggregate, thereby decreasing workability
- a plastic mix: flows sluggishly without segregating; is ready to mold

Compression tests determine the compressive strength of cured concrete using a hydraulic press. Pressure is applied either to a specially poured test cylinder or to an actual core sample taken from the job site and measures the maximum load that the cylinder can take.

Concrete is either **cast-in-place**, where it will be used by a concrete mixer or agitator truck, or **precast** off-site in factory-controlled conditions. Concrete used for construction is usually reinforced with **steel-reinforcing bars** or with **welded-wire fabric**.

The reinforcing in concrete beams is designed to tie into the reinforcing of other structural elements, such as columns, slabs, and walls. Cast-in-place concrete beams are usually formed and cast with the slabs they support. This structural integration strengthens the building.

Cast-in-place concrete slabs are classified by whether they have steel reinforcing running in one, two, or three directions. The reinforcing pattern affects how the slabs carry the stresses created by loads to other structural members or the ground. Slabs are usually cast with their supporting beams. Some slabs are made of closely spaced concrete joists supported by parallel beams, giving them the necessary strength for long spans and heavy loads.

Site-Cast Concrete

Site-cast concrete is cast into formwork that is usually made of prefabricated, reusable panels. The form surfaces that contact the wet concrete are coated with oil, wax, or plastic to aid in removal.

Form ties are used to hold formwork in place during pouring and setting, and the holes made by the ties are visible in the concrete's surface. These holes may be patched to match the surrounding finishes, filled with plastic caps, or left exposed as part of the concrete's finished surface. When an architect intends to leave tie holes exposed, their locations must be carefully planned as part of the surface design of the wall.

When concrete is site-cast, special forms can be added to create linear recesses and other patterns on the concrete's surface. The woodgrain pattern of plywood forms can be emphasized by sandblasting or wirebrushing the concrete. Sheathing lumber can be used for forms to create a board-and-batten pattern. Metal or plastic form liners create ribs and other textures.

☑ **Other aspects of the concrete's appearance can be controlled during or after it is cast. The use of colored cement and aggregates offers color variety. Exposed aggregate finishes can be designed with fine or coarse aggregates, and sandblasted, acid-etched, or scrubbed before they are completely cured. Finally, after it is set, the concrete's flat surface or ribs can be brush-hammered to produce a rough, irregular finish. The surface can also be sandblasted, rubbed, or ground smooth, then painted or dyed.**

Tilt-up construction consists of reinforced concrete wall panels cast in a horizontal position on-site, then tilted up with a crane into their final vertical position. They are usually cast on the concrete ground slab created for the building under construction, although molds of other materials are sometimes used. Tilt-up panels are designed to withstand the stresses of being lifted and moved, which may be greater than those of in-place loads, and to resist seismic forces that could pull the walls away from the roof, causing roof collapse.

Precast Concrete

Precast concrete structural elements are cast and steam-cured off-site, transported to the site, and set in place with cranes. Precast building components offer consistent strength, durability, and finish quality as well as eliminate on-site formwork. They may be reinforced or prestressed for extra strength or reduced thickness.

Prestressed concrete is reinforced by putting tension on high-strength steel tendons inside concrete. The tensile stresses in the tendons are transferred to the concrete, which deflects in a direction opposite to the deflection that will take place when the concrete is subjected to a load. The two forces, from the prestressed concrete and cables and from the load, cancel each other out, thereby allowing the prestressed concrete to span greater distances and heavier loads.

Precast, prestressed concrete structural elements include:

- solid flat slab: plank used for sort spans and uniformly distributed loads
- hollow-core slab: plank with hollow cores that reduce weight; used for uniformly distributed loads over medium to long spans
- single and double tees: T-shaped plank with single or double stem and broad, flat slab
- ledger beams: beam with projecting ledges to support the ends of joists or slabs; L or inverted-T shapes

Precast concrete wall panels are used for bearing walls that support site-cast concrete floors or steel–floor-and-roof systems. They are usually 8 feet wide but are available up to 12 feet wide. When used with precast concrete columns, beams, and slabs, the form precast structural systems that are modular and fire-resistant.

Precast concrete columns are commonly produced to support the following approximate areas:

- A 255 x 255 mm (10 × 10 in.) column supports 185 square meters (2000 ft²).
- A 305 x 305 mm (12 × 12 in.) column supports 255 square meters (2750 ft²).
- A 405 x 405 mm (16 × 16 in.) column supports 418 square meters (4500 ft²).

Shell Structures

A shell is a thin, curved plate structure designed to transmit applied forces by compression, tension, and shear. Shells can withstand relatively large uniformly applied forces, but they lack the bending resistance necessary to accommodate concentrated loads. Thin shell structures are constructed of reinforced concrete. A barrel shell is a rigid, cylindrical shell structure. A shell surface may be circular, elliptical, or parabolic; these are all geometric forms generated by straight lines.

A saddle surface curves upward in one direction and downward in the perpendicular direction.

METAL STRUCTURES

Iron has been used since at least 1200 BCE. During the Middle Ages, craftsmen handcrafted steel in Damascus, Syria. The introduction of the Bessemer process in the nineteenth century industrialized the process of removing impurities from molten iron, and cast iron, wrought iron, steel, and stainless steel became available for building construction.

Cast Iron and Wrought Iron

Cast iron is a brittle, iron-based alloy that contains carbon and small amounts of silicon. It is cast in a sand mold and machined to make building and ornamental products. Cast iron is strong in compression but weak in tension and bending; it becomes structurally unreliable in fires.

Cast-iron columns have been used since the nineteenth century to support glass-enclosed buildings, such as London's Crystal Palace. Their lightweight and elegant appearance has encouraged preservation of historic examples, although today, most architectural cast iron is purely decorative.

Wrought iron is durable, malleable, and relatively soft. Easy to work with, it is often forged into beautiful linear designs.

Figure 4-19 Shell structure. The Kresge Auditorium at the Massachusetts Institute of Technology is a striking shell form designed by Eero Saarinen.

Figure 4-20 Cast-iron columns. Cast-iron columns in Saratoga Springs, New York, are a valued part of the elegant resort area's historic downtown.

Wrought iron is used for gates, fences, and other architectural components with relatively light loads.

Steel Framing

Steel is an alloy of iron with carbon; sometimes, other materials are added to steel for specific properties. The strength, hardness, and elasticity of steel depend on its carbon content and heat treatment. Adding carbon to iron increases steel's strength and hardness but decreases its ductility and weldability.

Structural steel framing is made of hot-rolled steel beams and columns spanned by open-web joists and metal decking. Steel framing is most efficiently used in a regular grid pattern of girders,

Figure 4-21 Structural steel framing. This 1906 image shows New York ironworkers working on a skyscraper.

beams, and joists. Columns are spaced according to the spans of girders or beams. Lateral wind or seismic loads are resisted by shear planes, diagonal bracing, or rigid framing using special connectors.

Structural steel is manufactured in a variety of forms, including:

- W-shape (or wide flange): named for its wide, parallel flanges; has an H-shaped form; is often used for beams and columns
- S-shape (or American standard beam): has an I-shaped section with sloped, inner-flange surfaces
- American standard channel: has a rectangular, C-shaped section with sloped, inner-flange surfaces
- angle (or angle iron): has an L-shaped section with equal or unequal leg lengths; a pair of angles joined back to back forms a double angle
- bar: a long, solid piece with a square, rectangular, or other simple cross-sectional shape
- structural tubing: a hollow, structural shape with a square, rectangular, or circular cross section; round structural tubing is known as pipe
- plate: a thin, flat sheet of uniform thickness; may have a distinctive waffle surface pattern
- sheet metal: a thin sheet or plate of metal; corrugated metal used as decking has ridges and furrows that increase its strength
- open-web steel joist (or bar joist): a lightweight, fabricated steel joist commonly supported by its upper chord; the web often consists of a steel bar bent into a zigzag pattern; supported by bearing walls of masonry or reinforced concrete, steel beams, or joist girders

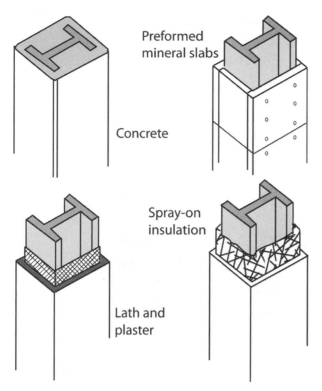

Figure 4-22 Fire-resistant structural steel column assemblies. Steel structural forms can be embedded in concrete or wrapped in plaster, mineral slabs, or spray-on insulation.

In general, rolled structural steel is as strong in tension as in compression, making it an excellent structural building material. However, steel rusts when exposed to water and air. Because steel can deform at high temperatures, steel structures must be coated with fire-resistant materials or combined into assemblies that are rated for fire resistance.

The outer walls of a steel structure may consist of exterior panels rigidly connected to the frame, which stiffen the structure and resist wind loads. As discussed earlier, curtain walls are exterior walls that are supported by the structural frame and carry a load other than their own weight and the wind load.

A rigid steel frame is frequently used for single-story light industrial buildings, warehouses, and recreational facilities. The frame consists of two columns and a beam or girder, fastened together with rigid connections.

☑ **Structural steel frames are well adapted to buildings with open interior spaces. A row of long-span beams or girders supported by pairs of exterior columns, called a one-way beam system, generates long, narrow, column-free spaces.**

Metal decking is corrugated to increase its stiffness, which, in turn, allows for increased spans. Metal decking can also be used as formwork for site-cast concrete slabs and left in place after the concrete cures. Decks are welded to steel joists or beams that they rest on and screwed, welded, or seamed to each other along their lengths.

OTHER STRUCTURAL TYPES

Cable structures use flexible wire rope or metal chains with high tensile strength as a means of support. **Suspension** structures support applied loads with cables suspended and prestressed between compression members. **Cable-stayed** structures employ cables extending from vertical or inclined masts to support parallel or radially arranged horizontal spanning members.

A **membrane structure** is a thin, flexible surface that transmits loads primarily along lines of tensile stress. Types of membrane structures include:

- **tent structure:** prestressed by external forces to be completely taut under all anticipated load conditions; usually have sharp curvatures in opposite directions
- **net structure:** a surface of closely spaced cables rather than fabric material
- **air-supported structure:** a single membrane supported by internal air pressure and securely anchored and sealed along the perimeter; air locks at entrances prevent air leaks
- **air-inflated structure:** a double-membrane structure supported by pressurized air within building elements

Many buildings are made of a mix of materials, and some even combine different structural types. By understanding the nature of structural materials, designers are often able to determine that a brick-covered building is actually a concrete structure. It is not uncommon for a building to have a structural frame of one material, with infill panels of another material forming the exterior walls.

Figure 4-23 Cable structure. This historic photograph of the roof of the TWA Maintenance Hangar at Philadelphia International Airport shows a cable-stayed structure.

Figure 4-24 Tent structure. Denver International Airport was opened to the public in 1993. Its main terminal is covered by a tent structure that is supported by steel poles.

Figure 4-25 Concrete and brick building. This small office building has a concrete structure filled in with glazed-brick panels.

There is a great deal more that could be said about building structural types; perhaps this short survey will whet your curiosity to learn more about historic and innovative buildings. In Chapter 5: Horizontal Structures and Vertical Movement, we will look at both the horizontal elements of building interiors and the building systems that allow movement from one layer of the building to another.

5

· · · · · · · · · · · · · · · ·

Horizontal Structures and Vertical Movement

HORIZONTAL STRUCTURAL UNITS

The basic horizontal structural units used in buildings are either reinforced concrete slabs or grids of **girders**, beams, and joists that support planks or **decking**. Rigid planar structures, such as reinforced concrete slabs, spread loads in many directions along the plane.

The stresses from the loads generally take the shortest and stiffest routes to the vertical supports. Rigid floor structures act like flat, deep beams, transferring lateral loads to rigid frames, shear walls, or braced frames. Rigid frames are usually constructed of steel or reinforced concrete with rigid joints. Rigid frames are used in low- and medium-rise buildings.

Floor and Ceiling Assemblies

As the base of an interior design, a floor supports the people and furnishings inside a building. A floor must be designed to withstand the use intended for that specific space. Floor systems fall into two general categories: a series of linear beams and joists topped with a plane of sheathing or decking, or a slab of reinforced concrete.

The depth of a floor system affects the interior ceiling to floor heights as well as total building height. In general, a floor system's depth is related to the size of the structural bays that it spans. The design of a floor system may also have to accommodate mechanical, plumbing, and electrical equipment.

The way that a floor structure's edges connect to the supporting foundation and structural wall systems affects a building's structural integrity and physical appearance. The details of these connections determine the building's ability to control airborne and structure-borne sound and affect the fire-resistance rating of the assembly.

Concrete Floor Systems

In concrete construction, concrete slab floors are reinforced with steel and either poured in place or delivered to the site as precast planks. The subflooring material must be smooth and level and suitable for installation of the floor's finish material. Sometimes, an existing floor receives a new subfloor or the application of a leveling material to smooth out irregularities.

Concrete floors are built with joints that allow materials to expand with changes in temperature or moisture.

- **Construction joints** are found between adjoining pours of concrete.
- **Expansion joints** between two parts of a structure allow for thermal expansion and contraction.
- **Control joints** are continuous grooves or separations inserted in concrete or masonry structures that create areas of weakness, thereby controlling where and how much cracking can occur.
- **Isolation joints** separate two sections of a structure to allow movement or settlement between the parts.

Concrete **slab-on-grade** floors are built in direct contact with the ground. The temperature of the ground is often different than that of outdoor air, and earth conducts heat more readily than air. A few inches of insulation can make a significant difference in the heat flow from a slab.

Precast concrete floor systems use precast concrete slabs, beams, and structural tees. These structural members are

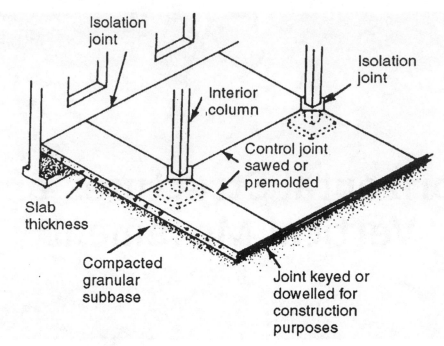

Figure 5-1 Concrete slab joints. Construction, expansion, control, and isolation joints accommodate joint movement in concrete floors

supported by concrete or masonry bearing walls or by steel or concrete frames.

Precast concrete floor units are cast and cured in an off-site plant, then transported to the site and set into place with cranes. Factory fabrication ensures consistent quality and eliminates the need for concrete formwork on-site.

Precast concrete slabs are usually installed with a reinforced concrete topping that is between 51 millimeters and 90 millimeters (2–3½ in.) thick. This topping may be eliminated with smooth-surfaced slabs when they are finished with carpet and pad. The undersides of precast slabs can be caulked and painted. A ceiling finish may be applied or suspended below the slab.

Wood Floor Systems

In wood light-frame construction, a floor usually consists of wood **joists** (small parallel beams) resting on larger beams or load-bearing walls. A structural subfloor, such as plywood or steel decking, is laid across and secured to the joists.

Wood joists are made of **dimension lumber**, which is easy to cut on-site with simple tools. Nominal sizes range from 2 × 6, which can span up to 305 centimeters (10 ft.), through 2 × 12, which can span 549 centimeters (18 ft.). The distance spanned depends more on the material's rigidity than on its compressive strength. Wood joists can also be prefabricated from such composite materials as **oriented strand board (OSB)**.

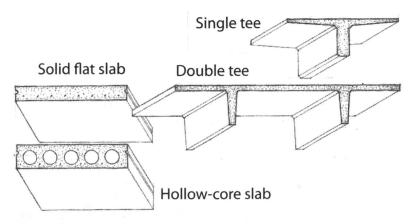

Figure 5-2 Precast concrete floor elements. Precast concrete slabs, beams, and structural tees are supported by cast-in-place or precast concrete, masonry bearing walls, or frames of steel or concrete.

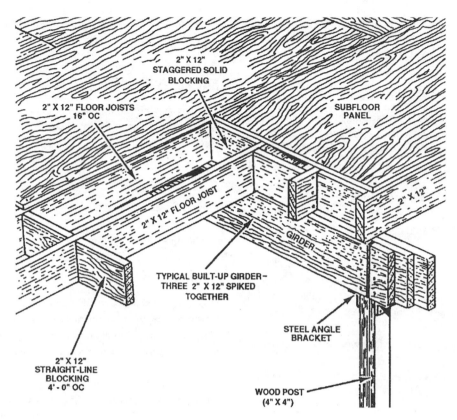

Figure 5-3 Wood floor framing. Wood posts support girders built up from 2 × 12 dimension lumber. The girders, in turn, carry the floor joists, which is covered with plywood subflooring.

The floor assembly is supported by girders, posts, or load-bearing walls. In areas where openings are cut into the floor or where concentrated loads are expected, the wood framing members are doubled up. Such is the case where nonbearing partitions run parallel to the length of the joists. The load from such partitions can be distributed across many joists when the partitions are perpendicular to them. Load-bearing walls must be supported from below.

Joist framing allows flexibility in the shape and form of a building. Wood plank-and-beam floor systems transmit impact sound. The optional installation of a ceiling below provides a concealed space for acoustic insulation, piping, wiring, and ductwork. Wood-frame construction is combustible, and requires fire-resistant ceiling and floor finishes for fire resistance.

Subflooring is a structural material that is used to span floor joists. Subflooring serves as a working platform during construction and provides a smooth base for the floor finish. Combined with joists, a subfloor can form a structural diaphragm that transfers lateral forces to shear walls. Plywood is usually used for subflooring, but OSB, waferboard, or particleboard is also sometimes used.

Underlayment is another layer, often made of plywood or hardboard, added on top of the subflooring. Underlayment helps spread out impact loads on the floor and prepares the surface for direct application of finish materials that require a smooth surface. The underlayment may be a separate layer over the boards or panels of the subfloor; alternately, it may be combined with the subfloor itself as a compound material.

Subflooring and underlayment panels are nailed into place over at least two open spans with their length perpendicular to the joists and their ends staggered. When glued and nailed to the floor joists, combined subfloor/underlayment panels work together with the joists like large beams, increasing the stiffness of the floor assembly and reducing floor creep and squeaking.

Wood joists and trusses can be factory assembled to an engineer's design, then shipped to the building site. They are assembled with similar methods to a conventional wood-joist-framed floor. Prefabricated, pre-engineered wood is lighter and more **dimensionally stable** than sawn lumber and can be manufactured in greater depths and lengths to span long distances. Prefabricated joists and trusses are best used for long spans across simple floor plans.

Wood beams are made of solid sawn lumber or glued-together smaller pieces of wood. These beams are supported and linked through the use of metal connections that are manufactured in many designs.

☑ **When left exposed, as is often the case with plank-and-beam or heavy timber construction, the quality of wood and details of construction are important to the appearance of a building's interior.**

Wood plank-and-beam framing is typically used to support moderate, evenly distributed loads. The beams support a structural floor plane of wood decking, plywood, or prefabricated stressed-skin panels. Most partitions in this type of framing are nonbearing and can be placed on a soleplate perpendicular to the planks. When aligned with the direction of the floor decking, nonbearing partitions may require extra support.

Steel Floor Systems

Steel-framed buildings usually employ steel decking, precast planks, or concrete slab floors. The steel beams that support the decking or precast planks are, in turn, supported by girders, columns, or load-bearing walls, which are usually parts of a steel-skeleton-frame system.

Light-gauge open-web joists are also used to support floors. They may be supported either by masonry or reinforced concrete bearing walls or by steel beams or joist girders (heavier versions of open-web joists).

Metal decking is corrugated for increased stiffness and spanning ability. The decking's perimeter is welded to steel supports when it is intended to transfer lateral loads to shear walls. The three types of metal decking include:

- form decking: provides permanent formwork for reinforced concrete slab
- composite decking: has embossed rib patterns that bond it to concrete slab and serve as tensile reinforcement
- cellular decking: made by welding corrugated decking to a flat steel sheet; the resulting spaces serve to protect electrical and communications wiring; when perforated cells are filled with glass fiber, cellular decking can serve as an acoustic ceiling

It is clear that many floor systems combine concrete and metal. Finish floor and ceiling treatments may help designers deal with the noise and equipment clutter problems of exposed ceilings.

Figure 5-4 Steel floor system. This floor-ceiling system shows steel beams that support metal decking, which, in turn, is topped with concrete. Structural-steel components are sprayed with fire-resistant material. Lighting, plumbing, HVAC ductwork, and electrical and acoustic equipment are all exposed.

However, suspended ceilings or raised floors reduce the floor-to-ceiling height of the finished space.

MOVING VERTICALLY

In buildings with multiple floors, it is necessary to provide ways for people and materials to move vertically inside the building. This is accomplished by:

- stairs
- ramps
- elevators and other lifts
- escalators
- materials-handling equipment

Stairs

The design of stairs is strictly regulated by building codes and by the Americans with Disabilities Act (ADA). Stairs that are part of building exits have additional fire-safety requirements. Codes also regulate the elements of stairs that make them safe to support weight and to move up and down.

Building codes may allow limited use of curved, winder, spiral, switchback, and alternating-tread stairs. This depends on the occupancy classification, number of occupants, use of the stairs, and the dimension of the treads.

- Most stairs must have a clear minimum width of 112 centimeters (44 in.).
- With an occupant load of less than 50 people, a 914-centimeter (36-in.) minimum width is permitted.
- Stringers and trim may project a maximum of 38 millimeters (1½ in.). They must be continuous without interruptions by a newel or other obstruction.

STAIR PARTS

A **railing** is a barrier made of horizontal rails supported by uprights or **balusters** (also called banisters). A railing with supporting balusters is called a **balustrade**. A **newel** (or newel post) is a post that supports one end of a handrail at the top or bottom of a flight of stairs. Stair handrails may be prohibited by code from being interrupted by a newel post.

The following are among established criteria for handrails:

- Handrails should be free of sharp or abrasive elements.
- Most stairs require handrails on both sides, except in individual dwelling units, when stairs are less than 1120 millimeters (44-in.) wide or when there are fewer than four risers.
- Extra-wide stairs require intermediate handrails.
- Handrails must be between 914 millimeters and 965 millimeters (36–38 in.) above the leading edge of treads or nosings.
- Handrails may project a maximum of 89 millimeters (3½ in.) into the required width.

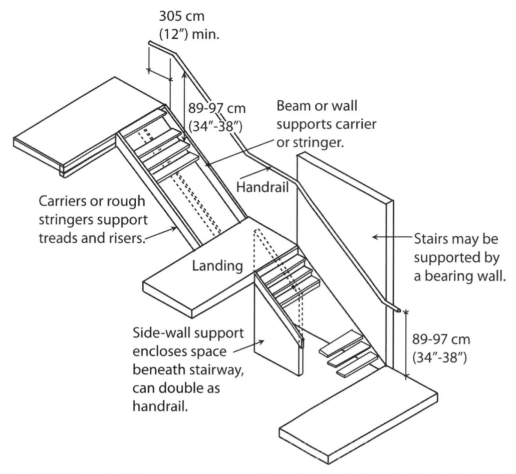

305 cm
(12") min.

89-97 cm
(34"-38")

Beam or wall
supports carrier
or stringer.

Handrail

Carriers or rough
stringers support
treads and risers.

Landing

Stairs may be
supported by
a bearing wall.

89-97 cm
(34"-38")

Side-wall support
encloses space
beneath stairway,
can double as
handrail.

Figure 5-5 Stair parts. Stairs require support from stringers, beams, or side walls. Handrails help steady users and prevent falls. Landings break up long runs of stairs and provide resting places.

- The handrail should extend a minimum of 305 millimeters (12 in.) beyond the top riser, and a minimum of 305 millimeters plus one tread width beyond the bottom riser.
- Handrail ends should return smoothly to the wall or the walking surface or continue to the handrail of an adjacent stair flight.
- The circular cross section of a handrail should be between 32 millimeters (1¼ in.) and 51 millimeters (2 in.) in diameter; other shapes with similar properties may be permitted.

A flight of stairs may not rise more than 36.5 meters (12 ft.) between floors or landings without intermediate landings. Each run of stairs requires a landing at the top and bottom as well as a flat floor or landing on each side of a door. The following are some criteria for stairways:

- Landings must be at least as wide as the stairway width, and a minimum of 1118 millimeters (44 in.) in length measured in the direction of travel.
- In dwelling units, a minimum of 914 millimeters (36 in.) is allowed.
- Doors must swing in the direction of egress and cannot reduce the landing to less than one-half of its required width.

- When fully open, doors must not intrude into the required stairway width by more than 178 millimeters (7 in.).

A **guardrail** is required when the side of a stair is exposed and not enclosed by a wall. Guardrails are usually 107 centimeters (42 in.) high and must not allow a ball with a 10 centimeter (4 in.) diameter to pass through.

Codes set requirements for stair treads, risers, and nosings:

- A minimum of three risers per flight is recommended to prevent tripping.
- The ADA sets a minimum tread depth at 28 centimeters (11 in.) and a riser height between 10 centimeters (4 in.) and 18 centimeters (7 in.).
- Risers and treads must maintain uniform dimensions, and open risers are not permitted on accessible egress paths.
- Where permitted, open risers must not allow a 102-millimeter (4-in.) diameter sphere to pass through.
- Nosings are limited to a maximum protrusion of 38 millimeters (1½ in.) and a maximum radius of 13 millimeters (½ in.).
- Nosings should be sloped; alternately, their undersides should have a 60-degree minimum angle from horizontal.

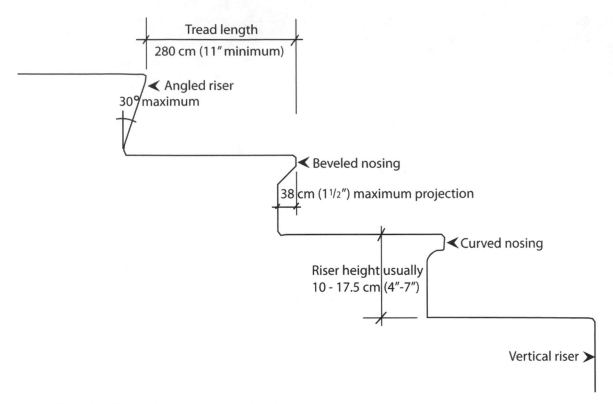

Figure 5-6 Treads, risers, and nosings. Treads and risers in a flight must be uniform within a small tolerance. Nosing dimensions, the slope of risers, and the projection of treads past risers are all covered by code.

The minimum ceiling height above a stair and its landing is usually required to be 229 centimeters (90 in.) measured vertically from the landing and the front edge of a stair tread to the ceiling directly above. Exceptions may be permitted for structural elements, light fixtures, exit signs, or other ceiling-mounted objects, with a minimum of 203 centimeters (80 in.) required.

People, especially those with disabilities, must be protected from low headroom in open spaces below stairs. This may present a design challenge involving changes in texture and material as well as guardrails or other obstructions. When the usable space under stairs is enclosed, it is required by code to be 1-hour fire-resistant-rated construction, with the exception of certain residential occupancies.

STAIR TYPES

Stairs create opportunities for dramatic three-dimensional openings and forms, inspiring vistas, and intriguing details. All stairs require careful planning for safety and support. Openings must be protected to prevent falls, unauthorized climbing of railings, and entanglements, particularly by children.

Common stair types include:

- straight-run stair: extends directly from one floor to another without turns
- quarter-turn stair: L-shaped stair with a landing between two flights of equal or unequal length
- half-turn stair: compact stair form that turns 180 degrees at an intervening landing

- winding stair: any stair constructed with winders, including circular and spiral stairs; may be restricted by building codes
- circular stair: usually designed with an inner circumference that is large enough to provide adequately sized winder treads
- spiral stair: wedge-shaped treads winding tightly around supporting central post that take up minimal amount of space; use severely limited by code

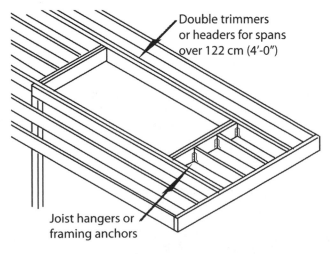

Figure 5-7 Framing for stair opening. Openings for stairways in wood-framed structures must be double-framed to be able to transfer loads around the open stairwell.

Figure 5-8 Single flight of stairs. This flight of stairs in the White House in Washington, DC, gracefully curves with the wall of the room.

Figure 5-10 Winding stair. This winding stair in a mill building in Manchester, New Hampshire, has fascinating lines but may be difficult—or even dangerous—to climb. The stairs continue around the corner as sharply triangular winders.

Figure 5-9 Stair. The finished underside of this stair creates an interesting form when viewed from below.

Figure 5-11 Circular stair. This graceful stair was built in 1846 in the Captain Charles L. Shrewsbury house in Madison, Indiana.

Figure 5-12 Spiral stair. A steel stair in the Stata Center at the Massachusetts Institute of Technology in Cambridge, Massachusetts, is tightly wound around a steel post and wrapped in a ribbon of wood. The railing at the bottom protects head clearance.

Figure 5-13 Steel stair. A stair can function like a sloped plane that connects one floor with another. This steel stair supports itself and its landing.

STAIR MATERIALS

Wood stairs are supported by **carriages** or rough **stringers** that serve as inclined beams. These sloping finish members that run along a staircase provide endpoints for treads and risers. Carriages running under the treads and risers may be attached to a supporting beam, header, or wall framing. The details of wood stringers are coordinated with the design of the balusters and railings.

Steel stairs are similar in design to wood stairs, with steel channels that serve as carriages and stringers. Steel stairs are available as pre-engineered and prefabricated components. Steel channels may be supported by beams, rest on masonry walls, or be hung on threaded rods from the floor structure above. Treads consisting of concrete-filled pans, bar grating, or textured-steel plates span the distance between the stringers; wood and precast concrete treads are also used. Metal-pipe handrails fabricated off-site are often used with utilitarian steel stairs. Such stairs must conform to building code and ADA accessibility requirements.

The ends and underside of steel stairs may be left exposed to view or finished with gypsum board or metal lath and plaster. Metals stairs may be noisy when in use and can be finished with resilient treads to dampen impact noise.

A concrete stair is designed as an inclined slab with steps formed as an integral part of its surface. Load, span, and support conditions for concrete stairs require careful structural design. The stair-slab thickness is related to the stair's span, which is the horizontal distance between slab supports. Concrete stairs are reinforced with steel that may extend into a side wall. Handrails are either inserted in cast-in-place sleeves or attached with brackets to the stairs or a low wall.

Concrete stairs are finished with slip-resistant nosings and treads. These may include:

- cast metal nosing with abrasive finish
- metal, rubber, or vinyl tread with grooved surface
- stone tread with abrasive strip

EXIT STAIRS

Stairs are an important part of the fire-safety provisions for a building. In a fire, elevators can become conduits for fire and smoke or they may stop and open at floors engulfed in flames. Firefighting ladders reach only to about the seventh floor of a building. Occupants of tall buildings must rely on stairs to get down from upper floors. This process can take hours in large and heavily occupied buildings.

Some stairs do not meet the strict requirements to be considered part of an exit and are not designated as exit stairs even though they may be very prominently located. In an emergency such as a fire, properly designed exit stairs provide safe ways to exit a building and allow firefighters to gain access.

Exit stairs, as defined by code, are the most common type of exit. An exit stair includes the stair enclosure, any doors opening into or exiting out of it, and the stairs and landings within the enclosure. The stair enclosure must meet fire-rating requirements. All doors in an exit stair must swing in the direction of discharge.

Figure 5-14 Exit stair. The enclosure for this exit stair was added onto an older existing building to provide safe egress. The high-contrast color scheme would help occupants in an emergency.

In the aftermath of the World Trade Center attack in September 2001, every aspect of egress safety in tall buildings has come under intense scrutiny. Some requirements for exit-stair widths in the *Life Safety Code, NFPA 101* were increased in 2005 to enable firefighters to move up while occupants move down. Code requirements continue to be strengthened.

Exit-stair requirements are similar to those of other stairs but are stricter. They include:

Minimum clear widths:
- Stairways shall not decrease in width along direction of exit travel.
- Stairways for occupancies of 50 or more should be 1.12 meters (44 in.).
- Stairways for occupancies of less than 50 should be 0.91 meter (36 in.).

Riser heights:
- minimum of 102 millimeters (4 in.)
- maximum for new stairs 178 millimeters (7 in.)
- maximum for Class A existing stairs 191 millimeters (7.5 in.)
- maximum for Class B existing stairs 203 millimeters (8 in.)

Tread depth minimum:
- new stairs: 279 millimeters (11 in.)
- existing Class A stairs: 244 millimeters (10 in.)
- existing Class B stairs: 229 millimeters (9 in.)

Headroom minimum: 2.03 meters (6 ft. 8 in.)

Height between landings maximum: 3.7 meters (12 ft.)

Dimension of landing in direction of travel minimum:
- Landing width must be equal to width of stair; it does not need to exceed 1.22 meters (4 ft.) when stair has a straight run.
- Intermediate landings shall not decrease in width along direction of exit travel.
- Doors may not open onto stairs without a landing at least the width of door.

Perhaps the greatest danger to building occupants in a fire is not flame but smoke. When an exit stairway is enclosed by walls of fire-rated construction and is accessible by a vestibule or open exterior balcony, the stairway is a smokeproof enclosure. This area is kept under positive air pressure so that smoke will not tend to enter even when a door is opened.

A smokeproof enclosure must be ventilated by natural or mechanical means to limit penetration of smoke and heat. Because stairs in smokeproof towers have direct access to outdoor air and to firefighting equipment on each floor, they are the safest stairs. Building codes usually require one or more of the exit stairways of a high-rise building to be protected by a smokeproof enclosure.

Smokeproof enclosures and exterior balconies also serve as places where people, including those who use wheelchairs, can wait for rescue. An **exterior balcony** is defined as a landing or porch that projects from the wall of a building and serves as a required means of egress. These areas of refuge will be discussed in more detail in Chapter 15: Basic Principles of Fire-Safety Design.

Ramps

Within a building, a **ramp** is a sloping floor or walk that connects two levels. A stepped ramp is a series of ramps connected by steps. A curved ramp is technically known as a **helicline**.

Ramps are designed to make travel from one level to another smooth and relatively unobstructed. If they are too steep or continue for too long without level resting areas, ramps become difficult or dangerous for people with mobility problems to use. Wheelchair ramps are limited to a rise of 1:12 but are more comfortable to use with a 1:20 rise. These translate to 12 feet and 20 feet in length for each inch in height.

Short, straight ramps have limited rise heights and are simply constructed as part of wood, steel, or concrete floors. Long ramps and heliclines are usually made of steel or reinforced concrete. Ramp surfaces should be stable, firm, and slip resistant.

Ramps are required to have a 915-millimeter (36-in.) minimum clearance between curbs or guardrails. A minimum 51-millimeter (2-in.) curb or barrier height is required.

Handrails are required along both sides of ramps with a rise of more than 15 centimeters (6 in.) or a run greater than 183 centimeters (72 in.). The top of the handrail should be between 865 millimeters and 965 millimeters (34–38 in.) above the ramp surface. Some ramps are provided with a second handrail at a lower level in order to accommodate wheelchair users.

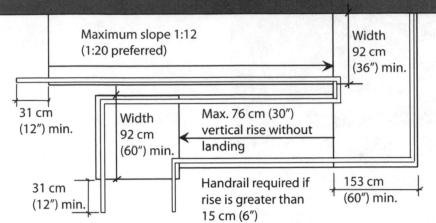

Ramps and landings not adjacent to a wall
must have curb, edge protection, and/or rail.

Maximum slope 1:12
(1:20 preferred)

Width
92 cm
(36") min.

31 cm
(12") min.

Width
92 cm
(60") min.

Max. 76 cm (30")
vertical rise without
landing

31 cm
(12") min.

Handrail required if
rise is greater than
15 cm (6")

153 cm
(60") min.

Figure 5-15 Ramp. Inserting landings into a long ramp enables it to bend back on itself. As a result, the ramp can be contained in a limited area rather than running throughout the space.

Elevators

Any multistory building needs ways to move people and objects from one floor to another. Stairs are the most basic means of vertical transportation, of course, and are included even in very tall buildings as secure exits in the event of fire. No one, however, wants to walk up 20 flights of stairs or carry furniture and supplies up them. This is why elevators and escalators are needed.

Elevator design has major implications for the architecture and structural engineering of a building. Historically, skyscrapers and elevators evolved together. Elevators and escalators are an important factor in determining a building's shape, core layout, and lobby design.

Although interior designers typically do not decide how many elevators a building will contain or where they will be located, these decisions will affect space planning because elevators take up a great deal of space at critical locations and are focal points for circulation paths.

☑ **Interior designers are often involved in selecting finishes for elevator cabs and lobbies as well as for the buttons and indicators in the cab and at each floor landing. Because people congregating at elevator lobbies are often forced to stand around waiting for an elevator, the design of these areas can have a great impact on the comfort of building occupants and visitors, and on the impression they have of the building and the businesses within it. This is especially important for people who have to use the elevators every day, when unpleasant, unsafe, or uncomfortable surroundings become a dreaded part of their daily routine. The design of elevators and their lobbies also has implications for security, fire safety, and maintenance of these semipublic areas.**

The ground-floor elevator lobby is also called the lower terminal and is usually located close to the main entrance, with a building directory, public telephones, elevator indicators, and possibly a control desk nearby. Lobbies are designed to be large enough for the peak load of passengers, with 0.5 square meters (5 square ft.) of floor space allowed per person waiting for one or more elevators. The same allowance should be made for hallways near the lobby. If the elevator's main lower terminal is on a mezzanine because of varied elevations of street entrances, escalators offer a valuable connection to a single, main lower elevator terminal.

The size of an elevator car and the frequency of trips determine the car's capacity. This is independent of the number of cars in the elevator bank. In practice, according to actual counts in many existing installations during peak periods, cars are not loaded to maximum capacity but are only 80 percent full.

Manufacturers and elevator consultants supply standard layouts for elevators, including dimensions, weights, and structural loads. The average trip time is determined by the time spent waiting in the lobby plus the time it takes to travel to a median floor stop. For a commercial elevator, a trip of less than one minute is highly desirable, with 75 seconds considered to be acceptable. A trip time of 90 seconds becomes annoying, and anything longer than 120 seconds exceeds the limits of toleration. For residential elevators, users often spend a minute or more of the trip time simply waiting for the elevator.

PARTS OF AN ELEVATOR

A landing is the part of the floor adjacent to the elevator where passengers and freight are received and discharged. The elevator's rise or travel is the vertical distance traversed by the elevator cab from the lowest to highest landings. Many of the elevator's parts are designed to increase safety:

- **cab (or car):** carries freight or passengers up and down in elevator shaft
- **shaft (or hoistway):** vertical space for travel of one or more elevators

- **guide rails:** vertical steel tracks on side walls of shaft that control travel of cab
- **guide shoes:** on sides of cab; fit onto guide rails; guide cab vertically in shaft
- **elevator pit:** extends from level of lowest landing to floor of shaft
- **cables:** connected to top beam of elevator; lift cab in shaft

- **counterweights:** rectangular, cast-iron blocks mounted in steel frame to counterbalance cab
- **elevator machinery:** in penthouse or elevator-machine room on roof
- **control panel:** with switches and buttons, regulates hoisting-machine velocity, acceleration, position determination, and car leveling
- **speed governor:** detects excessive speed or freefall; signals brakes to slow down and stop cab
- **limit switch:** automatically cuts off electric motor when elevator passes point near top or bottom of its travel
- **buffer:** piston or spring device that absorbs impact of descending car or counterweight at extreme lower limit of travel
- **hoistway door:** between elevator landing and hoistway; usually closed; open when car is stopped at landing
- **operating controls:** control car-door operation and function of car signals
- **car signals:** include floor call buttons and other indicators
- **supervisory controls:** allow group operation of multiple car installations

Elevators can be noisy. Noise-sensitive areas, such as sleeping rooms, should be located away from elevator shafts and machine rooms. Using vibration isolators between guide rails and the structure can reduce elevator noise. Properly designed controls also reduce system noise. Solid-state equipment eliminates the clatter and whirring sound of older machine rooms.

TYPES OF ELEVATOR MACHINES
Elevators are moved by geared traction, gearless traction, or hydraulic machines.

Geared-traction elevators:
- are found in medium-rise buildings
- are limited to a maximum rise of 107 meters (350 ft.)
- use a smaller, cheaper, high-speed motor that is geared down to provide car speed of up to 137 meters (450 ft.) per minute

Gearless-traction elevators:
- are used in high-rise buildings for passenger elevators
- operate at 6 meters (20 ft.) per second; have no gears; motor must run at same relatively low speed as drive sheave
- are used for medium- and high-speed elevators that run between 153 meters (500 ft.) per minute and 610 meters (2000 ft.) per minute
- are more efficient and quieter, need less maintenance, and last longer than geared traction elevators
- provide a very smooth, high-speed ride for rises above 76 meters (250 ft.)
- are more expensive than geared-traction elevators

Hydraulic elevators:
- have plunger attached to bottom of car that pushes against oil that is under pressure
- do not need penthouses but require machine room at or near bottom landing

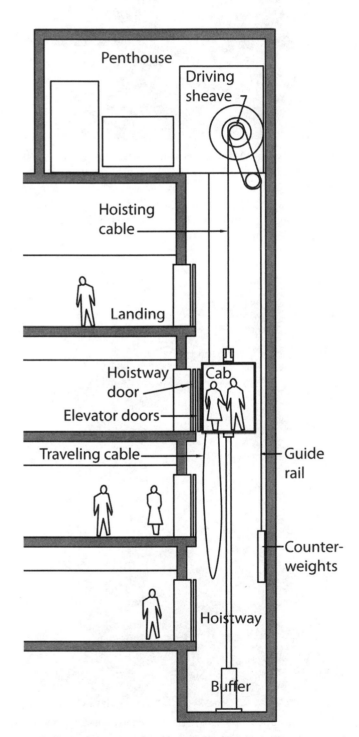

Figure 5-16 Parts of an elevator. The parts of an elevator are spread through a building from top to bottom.

- are used for low-speed, low-rise applications, such as office and residential buildings up to six stories high
- are relatively inexpensive to install but can be expensive to operate
- can be used with glass-enclosed observation cab
- can leak oil into the ground, leading to groundwater pollution

PASSENGER ELEVATORS

The architect makes the final decision on the type of elevator equipment for a building, based on the required passenger handling capacity, the trip time, and the cost. Usually, the architect consults with an elevator expert, who is either an independent consultant or a representative of a major elevator manufacturer. The interior designer and architect select finishes and details for the elevator cab and lobby. While cab interiors may be selected from the manufacturer's stock finishes, custom designs are also common.

Both the cab and the elevator lobby should be comfortably illuminated and have a pleasant atmosphere. The cars and shaftway doors pass from floor to floor, and their design reflects a building's architectural image. As an elevator rises from an impressive lobby through a building, it may open onto floors with well-designed tenant lobbies as well as on mundane spaces. The door designs of the cab and the shaftway should be compatible with the various conditions that may be found throughout the building.

Codes and Standards

Building codes heavily regulate elevator design, installation, and signals. These codes affect an interior designer's choices for lobbies and elevator cabs.

The American National Standards Institute and the American Society of Mechanical Engineers (ANSI/ASME Code A17.1, *Safety Code for Elevators, Dumbwaiters, Escalators and Moving Walks*) set strict installation requirements for vertical transportation equipment. Massachusetts, Wisconsin, Pennsylvania, and New York State as well as Seattle and Boston, among others, have their own, stricter codes. The NFPA 101 *Life Safety Code* establishes fire-safety requirements for elevators and escalators, and NFPA 70, the *National Electrical Code*, governs the electrical aspects of elevator construction. Other states and locales have additional requirements.

The ADA and ANSI A117.1 established barrier-free provisions for access by people with disabilities. Manufacturers follow the ADA access requirements as a minimum and may introduce additional conveniences as a particular project or local code requires. The main concerns of accessibility requirements are mobility, vision, and hearing.

Code requirements indicate that the clear opening for elevator doors should be at least 107 centimeters (42 in.); an opening of 122 centimeters (48 in.) is preferred. Smaller doors are appropriate only in residential or small, light-traffic commercial buildings. For elevators with small cars and a short rise, a swing-type, manual corridor door is permitted. Larger cars need power-operated sliding doors.

Figure 5-17 Single-passenger elevator doors. With a door that is only 91 centimeters (36 in.) wide, two people cannot pass each other at the same time, so loading is delayed until the unloading of passengers is complete. This adversely affects the speed and quality of the service. This example is from the Music Hall in New York City, initially constructed in 1891.

Figure 5-18 Double-passenger elevator doors. These elegant elevator doors are in the Library of Congress John Adams Building in Washington, DC.

TABLE 5-1. ADA ACCESSIBILITY GUIDELINES FOR ELEVATORS, 1991

Characteristic	Provision
Accessible elevators	Must be located on an accessible route
	Comply with ASME A17.1-1990 Safety Code for Elevators and Escalators
	Freight elevators are not used unless they are the only elevators available; in this situation, they must be used for both freight and passengers.
Automatic operation	Self-leveling feature that automatically brings cars to floor landings, correcting for under- or over-travel
Hall call buttons in lobbies and halls	Centered at 42 inches (1065 mm) above floor with button that registers up direction on top
	Visual signals that indicate when call is registered and answered
	Buttons, minimum of ¾ inch (19 mm) in smallest dimension, raised or flush
	Objects mounted beneath buttons shall not project into elevator lobby more than 4 inches (100 mm).
Hall lanterns	Visible and audible signal at each hoistway entrance that indicates which car is answering call
	Audible signals shall sound once for up direction and twice for down direction; otherwise, they have verbal annunciators saying "up" or "down."
	Hall lantern fixtures mounted with centerline at least 72 inches (1830 mm) above lobby floor
	Visual elements minimum of 2½ inches (64 mm) in smallest dimension
	Signals visible from vicinity of hall call button (may include in-car lanterns)
Raised and Braille characters on hoistway entrances	Raised and Braille floor designations on both jambs. Plates that are permanently affixed to both jambs are acceptable.
	Centerline of characters 60 inches (1525 mm) above finish floor
	Characters 2 inches (50 mm) high
Door protective and reopening device	Automatically opening and closing doors
	Device to stop and reopen car door and hoistway door automatically if door becomes obstructed by object or person without contacting object
	Reopening devices remain open for minimum of 20 seconds.
Door and signal timing for hall calls	Calculated for time and distance
	Minimum acceptable notification time shall be 5 seconds.
Door delay for car calls	Minimum time for elevator doors to remain fully open 3 seconds
Floor plan of elevator cars	Space for wheelchair users to enter car, maneuver within reach of controls, and exit from car
	See Fig. 5-19 Accessible Elevator Cab for further information.
	Clearance between car platform sill and edge of hoistway landing no greater than 1¼ inches (32 mm)
Illumination levels	Level at car controls, platform, and car threshold and landing sill at least 5 footcandles (53.8 lux)
Car controls for elevator control panels	All of the control buttons at least ¾ inch (19 mm) in smallest dimension. Raised or flush.
	All of the control buttons designated by Braille and by raised standard alphabet characters for letters, Arabic characters for numerals, or standard symbols.
	Call button for main entry floor designated by a raised star at left of floor designation
	Raised designations for control buttons shall be placed immediately to left of button to which they apply.
	Permanently applied plates are acceptable for raised control designations.
	Floor buttons shall have visual indicators to show when each call is registered and shall be extinguished when each call is answered.
	All floor buttons shall be no higher than 54 inches (1370 mm) above finish floor for side approach and 48 inches (1220 mm) for front approach.
	Emergency controls grouped at bottom of panel with centerlines no less than 35 inches (890 mm) above finish floor
Car-position indicators	Provided in elevator car above car control panel or over door, with numerals illuminating and audible signal sounding as car passes or stops at floor
	Numerals minimum of ½ inch (13 mm) high
	Audible signal no less than 20 decibels with frequency no higher than 1500 Hz. Automatic verbal announcement may be used instead.
Emergency communications	If provided, highest operable part of two-way communication system shall be maximum of 48 inches (1220 mm) from floor of car.
	Identified by raised symbol and lettering adjacent to device
	If system uses handset, cord length from panel to handset minimum of 29 inches (735 mm)
	Emergency intercommunication system shall not require voice communication.

Doors must have delayed door-closing capacity and detection beams that reopen a door without contact when they sense a passenger. Delayed door closings increase travel time, so in buildings with traffic peaks, one or more elevators can be designated for use by people with disabilities during busy periods.

Elevator cabs in public buildings must be able to accommodate people who use wheelchairs. According to the ADA, the inside car dimensions must permit a wheelchair to turn.

To assist people who use wheelchairs as well as those who walk, the ADA requires excellent car leveling, which means that the elevator car will come to rest at the same level as the floor onto which it is opening.

An elevator cab's interior is an almost inescapable and highly intimate place. It is important for a cab in a commercial or institutional building to make a positive impression. Cab interiors are subjected to and must be able to stand up to physical abuse, gravitational stress from rapid acceleration and deceleration, and shifting and vibration through constant movement. In addition, people in elevators are sometimes uneasy about traveling in a confined space and in close contact with strangers. Manufacturers' standard, original equipment choices often are not very compelling; in addition, a custom-designed elevator interior can be costly, time-consuming, and subject to cancellation. Elevator manufacturers offer standard cab interior dimensions that usually vary from those of their competitors, making standardization of design difficult.

An interior designer is likely to be involved in the decor of elevator cabs and the styling of hallway and cab signals. Typically,

Figure 5-20 Antique elevator cab. Elevators have evolved from elaborate cages with a full-time operator to sleek, minimal boxes. This wrought-iron elevator, made by Edward Darby & Sons, Philadelphia, in 1896, would look at home in a garden.

the elevator specification describes the intended operation of the equipment and includes an amount to cover the cabs' basic finishes. The type and function of signal equipment, along with finishes and styling, are options that the architect and interior designer specify.

Elevator-cab interiors may be finished in wood paneling, plastic laminate, stainless steel, and other materials. The choice of material depends on the building's architectural style, the available budget, and the practicality of the material for the elevator's intended use. One set of protective wall mats is usually provided for each bank of elevators, especially if there is no separate service car. Many elevators have small pegs, located high on the cab walls, on which to hang these mats.

Ceiling coves, ceiling fixtures, or completely illuminated ceilings provide lighting for an elevator cab. Lighting fixtures may be standard or special designs. Many designs cause glare and unflattering shadows. The goal in lighting cabs should be to provide pleasant, even illumination from sources that are resistant to vandalism and abuse.

Pre-engineered systems exist for designing and installing elevator cab interiors, offering architects and interior designers a well-designed product at a reasonable price. The systems offer a wide range of optional features in a fixed price range and come complete with panels, handrails, trim pieces, and a ceiling. The solution places a framework of mullions in the raw shell of the cab that have enough dimensional latitude to accept a variety of panel sizes, shapes, and materials. The emphasis is on the panels: these tend to be of more concern to architects and interior designers than the mullions, which appear as a grid. Designed to make a strong visual statement as well as to be economical and

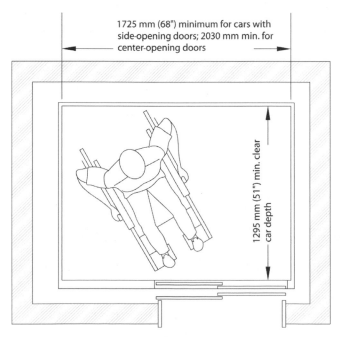

1725 mm (68") minimum for cars with side-opening doors; 2030 mm min. for center-opening doors

1295 mm (51") min. clear car depth

Figure 5-19 Accessible elevator cab. Accessible elevator cars with doors opening to one side must have a minimum width of 173 centimeters (68 in.). Cars with center-opening doors must be a minimum of 203 centimeters (80 in.) wide. The minimum clear depth is 130 centimeters (51 in.).

provide durability, these pre-engineered systems offer affordable prices, easy installation, reduced labor costs, rugged components, and fast delivery times.

Car finishes should be appropriate for use by people with disabilities. Many people with vision problems are able to see with sufficient, nonglare lighting. Sturdy handrails and nonslip finishes help people who have mobility problems. Well-designed signals and call buttons avoid confusion for everyone, including people with perceptual problems.

Elevator Signals

Elevator-cab and hallway signals and lanterns are designed to fit with the decor of cabs and corridors. The ADA specifies requirements for signals that are appropriate for people with disabilities:

- Codes mandate the location of visible and audible call signals or lanterns within sight of the floor area adjacent to the elevator.
- Signals must be centered a minimum of 183 centimeters (72 in.) above the floor at each hoistway entrance.
- Both jambs of the elevator hoistway entrances must have signage with raised characters and Braille floor designations, centered 152 centimeters (60 in.) above the floor.
- Call buttons must be centered 107 centimeters (42 in.) above the floor in each elevator lobby.
- Hall buttons indicate the direction of travel and confirm visually that a call has been placed.
- A hall lantern at each car entrance provides a visible indication of an arriving elevator's direction of travel and of its current location.
- An audible signal of an elevator car's imminent arrival enables people to move toward the arriving car and speeds service.
- Hall stations may have special switches for fire, priority, and limited-access service.

Cab Operating Panels and Signals

Within an elevator cab, signals that indicate its travel direction and current location are either part of the cab panel or are separate fixtures. A voice synthesizer may announce the floor, direction of travel, and safety or emergency messages inside the car. Voice synthesizers are very helpful for people with vision problems.

The ADA mandates the following:

- Buttons and emergency controls must be within easy reach from a wheelchair.
- Easily seen and understood visible signals in the car and at landings should be accompanied by audible signals.
- Signals should indicate that a call has been registered, when a car is approaching and landing, a car's direction of travel, the floor, and a car's position.
- Car floor buttons are required to have adjacent Braille plates.
- Large, easily recognized symbols should be adjacent to emergency controls for passenger use. The best designs are easily distinguishable from the call buttons themselves.

- People with hearing impairments also benefit from large visual signals that indicate when a call is placed and turn off when a call is answered.

A car's operating panel must have full-access buttons for call registry, door opening, alarm, emergency stop, and firefighters' control. An intercom connected to the building control office offers additional security. Sometimes, a door-closing button is provided if hand operation is anticipated.

Controls that are not intended to be used by passengers are grouped in a locked compartment. These include a hand-operation switch; light, fan, and power-control switches; and other security and emergency controls. Located in a cab compartment that is accessible only to elevator technicians are door-motion controls, car signals, door- and car-position transducers, load-weighing controls, door- and platform-detection-beam equipment, a speech synthesizer, and visual-display controls.

Elevator Fire Safety

In an elevator, a firefighter's return emergency service is required by ANSI and other local fire codes. Emergency personnel should have a means of two-way communication with cars and the control center. Other emergency controls allow switching of power between cars during emergency generator use.

Building codes generally require elevator shafts to have smoke vents at the top, thereby allowing the hoistway to become a smoke-evacuation shaft in an emergency. If there is a fire on a lower floor, an elevator shaft fills with smoke, which helps clear smoke from the area of the fire. However, this prevents firefighters and other people from using the elevator.

People have died while riding elevators down through smoke-filled shafts or being trapped in cars midshaft, so codes require that in the event of a fire, all elevator cars close their doors and return without stopping to the lobby or another designated floor, where they park with their doors open. They can then only be operated in manual mode with a firefighter's key in the car panel. All car and hall calls are cancelled, and car signals turned off. This way, firefighters can be sure that all of the elevator cars are secured and that no one is trapped in an elevator. In an emergency, a light or message panel in each car is activated to inform passengers of the nature of the alert and that the cars are returning to the designated terminal.

In emergencies, traveling cars stop at the next landing without opening their doors, then proceed to the designated terminal. Door sensors and in-car, emergency-stop switches are deactivated in order to prevent the cars from potentially stopping and opening at burning floors. Once they arrive at the terminal, cars may be used by trained personnel to transport fire personnel and equipment and to evacuate people from the building.

The lobby control station can override false alarms and return the system to normal use. This is especially important in large buildings with hundreds of fire, smoke, and water-flow detectors and automatic fire-alarm systems. The frequency of false alarms or alarms that respond to a very limited threat would immobilize a system without overrides.

Elevator Security

If a person is being attacked in an elevator, the attacker can render the enclosed space of the elevator cab inaccessible by pressing the emergency-stop button. An attacker can then restart the elevator and escape at any floor. In an effort to counter this danger, alarm buttons are provided that alert building occupants and security personnel.

Elevators must be equipped with communications equipment by code. A two-way communication system with hands-free operation is an effective method of providing security in an elevator cab. Security improves with a closed-circuit television monitor with a wide-angle camera in each car. Such systems require continuous monitoring at a building-security desk.

Sometimes, it is necessary to restrict access to or from a given floor or elevator car. Pushbutton combination locks and coded cards may work, but a second person can follow an authorized person into a car. The best systems combine automatic monitoring and access devices with continuous supervision by persons who know the appropriate action to take in an emergency.

Elevator System Controls

Large elevator systems use very sophisticated controls. The controls for small systems may be much simpler. Solid-state systems are universal on new elevators.

The simplest elevator control system is the single, automatic-pushbutton control. It answers one call at a time with one uninterrupted trip per call. Calls are registered at each floor only when a car is not in motion. Single, automatic-pushbutton controls are used only for private residences and light-use freight elevators.

Selective collective operation systems are used in apartment houses, small office buildings, and professional buildings with moderate service requirements. They may tend to bunch cars, resulting in long waits. The system collects all waiting "up" calls on the trip up and all "down" calls on the trip back down. The operation of more than two cars with this system is not recommended, and operating more than three cars is not feasible. Long lobby waiting times are seen as a major drawback when a company is considering renting space in a building.

Modern group supervisory systems treat any call that has been waiting more than 50 seconds as a priority call. Elevator computerized system control uses a central computer to collect and process enormous amounts of data. The system must continually monitor demand and control each car's motion. The system also analyzes all of the possibilities and answers each call in the most efficient manner.

Lobby elevator panels used to be wall-mounted adjacent to the related elevator bank, but today, they are more likely to be one or more computer screens at a lobby desk. Sometimes, an information-only screen is wall-mounted next to the elevators for passenger information. Such monitors provide information on car locations, movement direction, waiting corridor calls, and other status data.

In very tall buildings, an attractively decorated sky lobby on a high floor with an appealing view can break up the long trip.

This lobby is used when a building has office areas below and residences above, and most of the lower-section occupants never use the upper lobby. The upper-level occupants can use a shuttle that goes from the building's entry level to the sky lobby.

Elevator controls and mechanisms are complex, diverse, and subjected to heavy wear. They are designed with large safety factors and require thorough and frequent maintenance. Specialists associated with manufacturers must service elevators at close intervals. Local municipal representatives inspect them regularly for safety.

SERVICE ELEVATORS AND ELEVATORS FOR SPECIAL USES

In office buildings, one service car is provided for every 10 passenger cars. Service cars can function as passenger cars at peak times. A service car has a door that is between 122 centimeters and 137 centimeters (48–54 in.) wide for furniture, and should have access to a truck door or freight entry as well as to the lobby. Service elevators for bulky furniture should be designed for up to 1816 kilograms (4000 lb.) with a 122-centimeter (48-in.) wide door and a high ceiling.

Because hospital elevators must accommodate gurneys, wheelchairs, beds, linen carts, and laundry trucks, the cabs are much deeper than normal cabs. A hospital elevator can hold more than 20 people, and service is slow. Large hospitals generally have some passenger-only elevators. Through the use of dumbwaiters, food carts, laundry, and pharmaceuticals can be kept out of busy elevators.

Retail stores generally have one or two elevators for use by staff and by people who are unable to use escalators. These elevators are commonly located off the main circulation paths.

SPECIAL ELEVATOR DESIGNS

An observation car is a glass-enclosed car that is attached to a traction lift mechanism behind the car. The back is treated as a screen to hide the equipment. Observation cars can also be designed with hydraulic lift mechanisms and cantilevered cars. When an observation car is located on an outside wall, no shaft space is used within the building, thereby increasing usable interior space and reducing costs.

Inclined elevators are cars that ride up a diagonal path on inclined rails, pulled up by a traction cable. For example, the St. Louis Gateway Arch has a 10-passenger inclined elevator on each side.

Rack–and-pinion elevators ride up and down a rack. They are simple and safe for an unlimited rise with low maintenance and operating costs and use little space. A rack-and-pinion system was used for a 64-meter (210-ft.) rise in the 1986 renovation and rehabilitation of the Statue of Liberty in New York City. The elevator is used for medical emergencies, such as evacuating a person who is having a heart attack, as an alternative to carrying him or her down 171 spiral stairs from the observation platform in the crown to the main upper landing; such an emergency occurs about once a year. Rack-and-pinion elevators are used indoors and outdoors in industrial environments for passenger and materials vertical transport.

Figure 5-21 Glass-enclosed observation car. This hotel atrium is dominated by two glass-enclosed elevator cars that ride up and down between light-decorated tracks. The elevator machinery is painted black and streamlined as much as possible because it is constantly in view.

PLATFORM LIFTS AND RESIDENTIAL ELEVATORS

Vertical platform lifts are safe, economical, and space-conserving ways to overcome architectural barriers up to 12 feet high. These lifts are an alternative to elevators for limited rises. They are manufactured with a stationary enclosure, including gates and doors, as needed for each application, as compared with stair-mounted lifts, which are discussed below.

Vertical platform lifts do not require a hoistway or runway. Enclosures may be made of steel panels or clear or tinted acrylic panels, which enable a passenger to have a view from the lift during operation. They can be enclosed overhead when used outdoors. Designs can be customized to fit special decorative requirements. Most platform lifts are not allowed to be used as a means of egress, although the ADA does allow exceptions.

One way to enable a person who uses a wheelchair to move from one floor to another is to install a platform lift on a staircase. Winding-drum platform lift designs can traverse only straight runs of stairs. Inclined platform lifts with a rack-and-pinion drive are able to make turns on stairs, so they can accommodate landings and longer floor-to-floor distances.

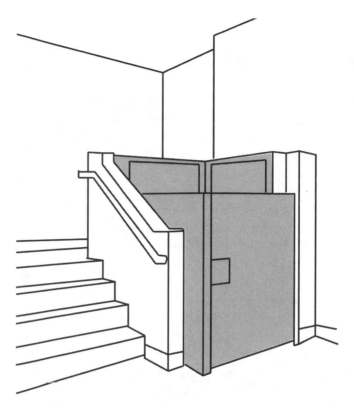

Figure 5-22 Vertical platform lift. Unless a vertical platform lift can be tucked in next to a stair landing, it takes up a significant amount of space.

Figure 5-23 Inclined platform lift on stair. This lift is folded up; in use, the facing surface would open toward the floor. The railings for the lift are in addition to handrails for stair users.

Figure 5-24 LU/LA elevator. LU/LA elevators provide high-quality access for people in wheelchairs as well as their companions.

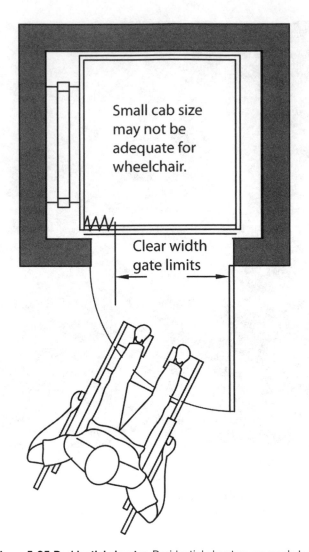

Figure 5-25 Residential elevator. Residential elevators are marketed for people with mobility problems. However, the small cab size may not accommodate a wheelchair or another person who provides assistance.

The rack-and-pinion–driven unit protrudes less than 32 centimeters (12½ in.) from the wall when folded. Pressing a button unfolds the platform lift. The safety-barrier arm moves to the vertical position, and the access ramp folds down to allow the person to enter the lift. When the unit reaches the destination level, the safety-barrier arm rises to a vertical position, and the access ramp lowers to allow the user to exit the lift. Pressure-sensitive features stop the unit if it encounters an obstruction. Platforms are available up to 81 × 122 centimeters (32 × 48 in.), which accommodates a wide variety of wheelchairs.

Since the enactment of the ADA, there has been a need for another type of vertical transportation: the limited-use/limited-application (LU/LA) elevator. LU/LA elevators were created to fill the void between the commercial elevator and the vertical platform lift or wheelchair lift. Typical applications include schools, libraries, small businesses, churches, and multifamily housing.

LU/LA elevators are available with cabs in the following sizes:

- 91 × 152 centimeters (36 × 60 in.)
- 107 × 137 centimeters (42 × 54 in.)
- 107 × 152 centimeters (42 × 60 in.)

ADA-compliant telephones and control panels are available accessories. The elevator uses a roped hydraulic-drive system, which requires additional space for a machine room. The pit depth varies from 33 centimeters to 97 centimeters (13–38 in.).

Residential elevators are available with laminate or wood cab interiors. The doors, which can be designed to look like residential wood doors, have concealed safety locks.

Cabs can have a single opening or two openings opposite each other or at right angles. Separate machine space is required. Small private-residence elevators are also used as wheelchair lifts. Because standard traction elevators require overhead equipment space, they are uncommon in private residences. Similarly, hydraulic elevators must have a plunger bore hole below.

A special section of the ASME elevator code A17.1b, part XXV, *Limited Use/Limited Application Elevators*, limits the size of private residence elevators to 1.67 square meters (18 square ft.) and the load to 635 kilograms (1400 lb.). They may not rise more than 7.6 meters (25 ft.) or exceed 9.15 meters (30 ft.) per minute. These and other safety, drive, and space limitations result in lower costs.

Escalators

An elevator is an efficient way to move people from one floor to another without taking up an excessive amount of floor space. However, no one likes to wait for an elevator. Escalators move more people faster. Passengers cannot be trapped on an escalator in a power failure, and escalators do not require emergency power; passengers simply walk up or down a stationary escalator as they would a staircase.

An escalator is a power-driven staircase that consists of steps attached to a continuous circular belt. Escalators move large numbers of people efficiently and comfortably up to six floors, although they are most efficient for connecting two or three floors. Elevators, on the other hand, are preferred for moving a distance of more than three floors. The decorative design of escalators enables passengers to observe panoramic views. In addition to the standard straight escalator, special escalator designs include curved escalators.

Escalators require space for floor openings and for circulation around the escalators. In many buildings, escalators and elevators are used together, with the elevators providing transportation for people with limited mobility.

Escalator drive machines are efficient up to a 7.6-meter (25-ft.) rise and can be modified up to an 18.3-meter (60-ft.) rise with a separate machine room. Machine controls are contained in a control cabinet.

The following are the parts of an escalator.

- truss (a welded steel frame): supports escalator and provides space for mechanical equipment
- support: located on both ends as well as in center if rise is more than 5.5 meters (18 ft.)
- tracks: steel angles that are attached to truss
- drive system: consists of sprocket assemblies, chains, and machine; works in a way similar to a bicycle chain drive
- emergency control button: located at both ends of escalator; when pressed, it stops drive machine and applies brake

- control switch: located at top and bottom newels; has key to start, stop, and reverse escalator's direction
- elongated newels: must have minimum of two horizontal treads before landing plate to enable passengers to adjust before stepping off escalator
- handrails: synchronized with tread motion
- balustrades (side panels of escalator): made of Fiberglas, wood, or plastic; crystal balustrades are made of tempered glass

Storeowners prefer escalators to elevators because they enable customers to see merchandise while changing levels. They are located on the main line of traffic so customers can see them readily and identify their destination. When laying out a retail space, avoid blocking the line of sight to escalators with large displays. Customers should be able to move toward escalators easily and comfortably.

In the United States, all escalators rise at an angle of 30 degrees from horizontal. There must be a 2.14-meter (7-ft.) clearance overhead for passengers. Escalators move at a standard speed of 30.5 meters (100 ft.) per minute.

The dimension between balustrades signifies the size of an escalator, while the width is the tread width. For example:

- An 81-centimeter (32-in.) dimension has a tread width of 61 centimeters (24 in.).
- A 122-centimeter (48-in.) dimension has a tread width of 102 centimeters (40 in.).

Theoretically, a tread width of 102 centimeters (40 in.) could accommodate two people. In reality, for psychological and physical reasons, one person per tread in an alternating diagonal pattern is the most common use. Half of the treads on an escalator that is 61 centimeters (24-in.) wide are unused.

An escalator requires an adequate queuing space at each loading and discharge point. Backups are dangerous when people are continually exiting the escalator, especially in theaters and stadiums with peak traffic flows. To avoid backups, well-marked escalators with adequate capacity must be provided.

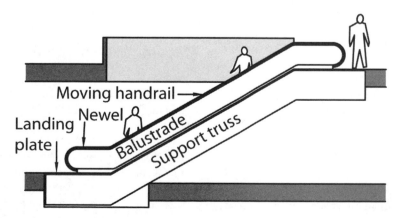

Figure 5-26 Parts of an escalator. Escalators take up a great deal of floor space, but they show off retail displays to passengers.

☑ **Collecting space at intermediate landings relieves pressure. Physical divisions at intermediate landing-turnaround points guide riders away from the discharge points. Dividers provide adequate space and time for riders to leave at that level or follow the guide around to continue the trip. A setback for the next escalator eases a 180-degree turn, so that people do not have to bunch up where they step onto the next escalator.**

Escalators should exit to an open area without the need for turns or changes of direction. However, if turns are required, large, clear signs should be posted to direct users. The landing space for an escalator that is 81 centimeters (32 in.) wide should be a minimum of 1220 centimeters (8 in.). For a an escalator that is 122 centimeters (48 in.) wide, the landing should be a minimum of 3 meters (10 ft.). For escalators that can reverse direction, landings must be provided at both ends.

ESCALATOR SAFETY FEATURES
- Handrails and steps should travel at exactly the same speed of 30.5 meters (100 ft.) per minute.
- Large, steady steps prevent slipping, as do proper step design and leveling with comb plates.
- Close clearances at comb plates and step treads lower the risk of items being caught in an escalator.
- Proper balustrade design also prevents clothes or packages from catching.
- Adequate illumination should be provided at landings and comb plates as well as along escalator stairways. Some escalators have built-in lighting.
- An automatic service brake will stop the escalator if the equipment breaks down or if an object becomes jammed in the handrail or steps.
- When pressed, an emergency stop button at each end of an escalator will stop its progress.
- Escalators will stop during power failures; when fire-safety devices operate; when a tread sags, rises, or breaks; or when the drive motor malfunctions.
- A governor shuts down an escalator that is traveling over or under the proper speed; it also prevents a reversal of direction and operates a service brake. In such situations, passengers must walk down the steps.

Typically, escalators are not allowed to act as a means of egress. Exceptions are made for escalators in existing buildings if they are fully enclosed within fire-rated walls and doors. Codes may also require specific sprinkler-system configurations.

As noted earlier, an escalator must provide adequate illumination for safety reasons, especially on the comb plate at the end of the escalator. In addition, as a featured part of the decor, lighting should enhance the visual design of the escalator.

ESCALATOR FIRE PROTECTION
When an escalator connects more than two floors, there are several methods to prevent a fire from spreading through the escalator opening:

- A fire shutter activated by temperature and smoke detectors shuts off the wellway of a given floor and prevents drafts and the spread of fire up through the building.
- Fireproof baffles surround the wellway and hang 51 centimeters (20 in.) from the ceiling, thereby creating a smoke and flame deflector. An automatic curtain of water from sprinkler heads on the ceiling further isolates the escalator.
- A close-spaced, high-velocity water nozzle produces a spray nozzle-like compact curtain of water, similar to a smoke guard, that prevents smoke and flames from rising through the wellways. Automatic thermal or smoke relays open all of the nozzles simultaneously.
- A sprinkler-vent fire-control system uses a fresh-air intake on the roof. A blower drives air down through the escalator floor openings, and an exhaust fan on the roof creates a strong draft upward through the exhaust duct, drawing air from just under the ceiling of each floor opening. The system includes spray nozzles on the ceiling.

ARRANGEMENT OF ESCALATORS
The most common arrangement for escalators arranges the entrances and exits to their upper and lower ends. This is called a crisscross arrangement. They can be built more cost-efficiently, take up a minimal amount of floor space, and have the lowest structural requirements.

Separated crisscross arrangements consist of only an up or a down escalator in one location. They allow space at the end of the run for merchandise. If the distance to the next run is more than 3 meters (10 ft.) or if the next escalator is not in sight, passengers may become confused and annoyed by the walk, potentially resulting in resentment. Such reactions to this inconvenience are made worse when the floor space for the trip between escalators is inadequate, leading to crowding, pushing, and delays. If passengers who need to travel more than three floors do not have access to an elevator, the problem is exacerbated even further.

Parallel escalators face in the same direction. They use more floor space than crisscross arrangements but have an impressive appearance. However, they are less efficient and more expensive than crisscross escalators. Parallel escalators can use spiral arrangements or stacked parallel arrangements.

Moving Walks and Ramps
Moving walks eliminate the need for people to walk long distances in a building; they are also used to speed up walkers. They eliminate congestion and force movement along a designated path. Like conveyor belts, they consist of power-driven, continuously moving surfaces. Moving walks can be used to transport large, bulky objects easily. They allow parking to be located away from airports and rail and ship transportation terminals. They are also useful for people with mobility problems. A moving walk must not incline more than 5 degrees from horizontal.

A moving ramp is a moving walk that inclines between 5 degrees and 15 degrees. Moving ramps offer a way for wheeled

Figure 5-27 Moving walk. Moving walks in airports are often accompanied by repeated announcements that ask stationary users to keep to the right so that fast-walking people can pass.

vehicles and large, heavy packages to move vertically and horizontally through a building. Moving ramps provide an option for people who would have difficulty using an escalator. Multilevel stores use moving ramps to transport shopping carts to rooftop parking lots. Transportation terminals use such ramps to carry luggage carts that are unable to easily negotiate escalators.

Like moving walks, moving ramps are limited in length to about 305 meters (1000 ft.). They are constructed much the way escalators are, but they have a flattened pallet instead of a step. The depth of the supporting truss is just 107 centimeters (3 to 6 in.) to prevent it from impinging on the ceiling of the floor below.

MATERIAL HANDLING

Until the late 1970s, materials were transported within commercial and institutional buildings primarily by hand, with some mechanical assistance. Office messengers carried mail. Hospitals used dumbwaiters, service elevators, conveyors, or chutes. Large stores used pneumatic tubes to carry money. Today, most of these tasks can be accomplished automatically and usually much more rapidly. The initial cost of automatic systems is high, but the reduction in labor and faster speed result in a short payback period and an increase in efficiency.

There are four major types of systems for material handling in commercial and institutional buildings: vertical lift car-type systems, horizontal and vertical conveyors, pneumatic systems, and automated and track-type container-delivery systems.

Vertical Lifts

Vertical lifts are related to elevators. They include freight elevators, dumbwaiters, and ejection lifts.

Design factors for freight elevators include the amount of weight that must be transported per hour, the size of each load, the method of loading, and the distance of travel. The type of load, the type of doors, and the speed and capacity of cars must also be considered.

For low rises less than 18 meters (60 ft.), hydraulic elevators provide accurately controlled, smooth operation and accurate automatic leveling. Cabs are made of heavy-gauge steel with a multilayer wood floor designed for hard service. Ceiling lighting fixtures must have guards against breakage. Freight-elevator gates slide up vertically and must be at least 1.8 meters (6 ft.) high. Hoistway doors lift vertically or have center openings, and are manually or power operated.

Hydraulic and mechanical vertical lifts are available for warehouse and industrial use. Such lifts are open frameworks that are custom-fit to the application; they range from simple, two-level applications to sophisticated, multilevel, multidirectional systems.

Manual load-unload dumbwaiters are used in department stores to transport merchandise from stock areas to selling and pickup centers. Hospitals use dumbwaiters to transport food, drugs, and linens. Restaurants with more than one floor carry food from the kitchen and return soiled dishes in dumbwaiters. Dumbwaiter designs include traction and drum styles as well as automated and programmable types.

Automated dumbwaiters can carry loads of up to 454 kilograms (1000 lb.) at speeds of up to 107 meters (350 ft.) per minute. The maximum cart size is approximately 81 cm (32 in.) wide × 173 cm (68 in.) long × 178 cm (70 in.) high.

Automated dumbwaiters are also called ejection lifts. Institutional and other facilities use them for rapid vertical movement of relatively large items. These dumbwaiters can deliver food carts, linens, dishes, and bulk-liquid containers, for example. Each load is carried in a cart or basket, which is manually or automatically loaded.

Some dumbwaiters have programmable controllers for automatic loading, dispatching, and ejection. Electronic sensors determine if space is available for a load, and the system automatically returns unloaded carts. Automated dumbwaiters are relatively expensive and require a large shaft area.

Conveyors

Industrial facilities and commercial buildings, such as mail-order houses, use horizontal conveyors. They are relatively inexpensive and can carry large quantities of merchandise. However, they demand an inflexible right-of-way, are noisy, and may be dangerous if used improperly.

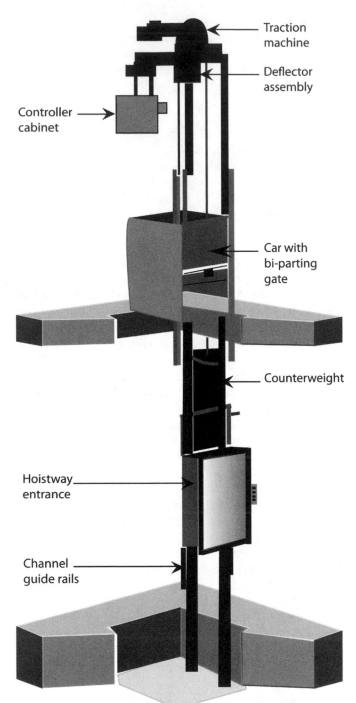

Traction machine

Deflector assembly

Controller cabinet

Car with bi-parting gate

Counterweight

Hoistway entrance

Channel guide rails

Figure 5-28 Dumbwaiter. Many dumbwaiters are limited to 50 feet in height and 300 to 500 pounds in load. This model exceeds these limitations.

A selective vertical conveyor picks up and delivers tote boxes (also called trays) by carrying them along a continuous chain. The operator puts up to 27 kilograms (60 lb.) in a tote box, electronically addresses the box, and places it at a pickup point. There, the chain picks up the box and delivers it. The process is monitored by a microprocessor. Vertical conveyors are available at a moderate cost. They require a large shaft and are noisy. It is difficult to switch from a horizontal conveyor to a vertical one.

Pneumatic Systems

Pneumatic tubes continue to be used for the physical transfer of materials, including cash, although electronic data transfer is replacing their use for carrying information that is printed on paper. Pneumatic tube systems are reliable, rapid, and efficient. They are relatively low cost if installed during initial building construction. Pneumatic tube systems consist of single or multiple loops of tubes whose diameters are between 57 millimeters and 152 millimeters (2¼–6 in.).

A single, large, noisy compressor was used to pressurize older systems. Newer systems are computer controlled with a small blower in each zone. They operate on a combination of vacuum and pressure and are relatively quiet. Newer systems can be of unlimited length. The carriers within the tubes travel at 7.6 meters (25 ft.) per second.

Pneumatic trash and linen systems provide for the rapid movement of bagged or packaged trash and linen from numerous outlying stations to a central collection point. Health codes require separate systems for trash and linen. Linen systems are commonly used in hospitals. Trash systems are found in many types of buildings, often along with trash compactors.

A pneumatic trash or linen system consists of large pipes under negative pressure, with loading stations throughout the building. The pipes are 41 centimeters, 46 centimeters, or 51 centimeters (16 in., 18 in, or 20 in.) in diameter. They carry one load at a time at speeds of between 6 meters and 9 meters (20–30 ft.) per second.

The compressors for trash and linen systems are large and quite noisy. The system requires a main vacuum system, a high-pressure line for the doors, and sprinkler heads every few floors. The cost of such systems is low to moderate.

Automated Container-Delivery Systems

In an automated container-delivery system, containers are locked onto a motorized carriage, which, in turn, is locked onto a track system. Containers can be moved at speeds of up to 37 meters (120 ft.) per minute horizontally and at a somewhat slower speed vertically. Containers come in various sizes and can carry up to 9 kilograms (20 lb.).

A container-delivery route may be either a simple point-to-point or loop system with simple controls or a complex system with loops and branches operated by a centralized computer. Automated container-delivery systems are easy to retrofit into a building because of their small size and flexible track layout.

In another variation, floor tapes below a carpet invisibly route robotic battery-powered vehicles. Such vehicles can connect to elevators for vertical transport. The sensing, instruction, power, and vehicle controls are all on the vehicles. These automated self-propelled vehicles can carry up to a 136-kilogram (300-lb.) load and can operate for an 8-hour day without recharging at speeds of between 6 meters and 37 meters (20–120 ft.) per minute. The vehicles are used for pickup and delivery of parts in industrial settings, for food and supplies distribution in hospitals, and for mail and document pickup and delivery in offices.

Interior designers with an understanding of how buildings stand up and how people move through them are trained to work with architects and structural engineers. It is critical that interior designers consult these other design professionals when interior design meets building structure. An understanding of building structures helps interior designers make welcome contributions to the design process.

Now that I have introduced the building and its environment, we will move on to Part III: Water-Supply, Distribution, and Waste Systems. These systems are essential to supporting building occupants and their work.

WATER SUPPLY, DISTRIBUTION, AND WASTE SYSTEMS

When the tap is turned on, out comes fresh, cool, clean water. This is the water we drink, cook with, bathe with, launder our clothes with, wash our cars with, and flush down the toilet. It is easy to think of water as a free, readily available resource.

However, this view is not the reality. Interior designer and educator Shashi Caan forecasts that "water will be one of our major concerns, and we will be exploring alternative water resources." Douglas Wittnebel of Gensler predicts that "in 10 years [there will] be a recognition that the true scarcity is potable water. And all design and construction projects will be based on comprehending the limits and systems of all the water resources and usage." (*Contract*, January 2008, p. 136)

In some parts of the world, including the southwestern United States, water resources have been a long-standing and constant concern. Yet water-efficiency standards are relatively limited compared with energy-use standards. Public awareness has centered on requirements for low-flow toilets and showerheads, and self-closing public toilet room faucets.

Building design professionals are beginning to respond to these concerns. "The overall public good could be well served by a mixture of public networks of pure water and electricity and individual cisterns and solar applications. The environmental benefits would be substantial—less water withdrawn from rivers, lakes, and underground aquifers; less energy and chemicals used to treat and deliver such water; less storm water discharged to pollute rivers; less fuel used to generate electricity; and less environmental damage from power plants. Yet we continue to economically discourage the individual who uses the rain and the sun." (Reynolds et al., *Mechanical and Electrical Equipment for Buildings*, p. 867)

Water-Supply Systems

Freshwater resources were a small percentage of total world resources at the turn of the twenty-first century. Salt water made up 97.5 percent of the water in the world. Of the freshwater that made up the remaining 2.5 percent, 68.9 percent was held in glaciers and permanent snow cover and another 0.9 percent was in swamps, permafrost, and other locations. This left only 29.9 percent in fresh groundwater and 0.3 percent in freshwater lakes and river storage, which are considered renewable. The largest freshwater resources were available in Asia and South America; the smallest, in Europe, Australia, and Oceania. The greatest renewable water resources were concentrated in Brazil, Russia, Canada, the United States, China, and India.

The world's population is expected to continue to grow dramatically, while water resources are fixed. The growing population is related to diminished natural resources and water pollution; the amount of water available per person in the future is destined to decrease.

According to the U.S. Geological Survey, withdrawal of water from U.S. supplies has varied less than 3 percent since 1985 and was estimated at 408 billion gallons per day (Bgal/d) in 2000. (Hutson, Barber, Kenny, Linsey, Lumia, and Maupin. *Estimated Use of Water in the United States in 2000. U.S. Geological Survey [USGS] Circular* 1268, March 2004, revised February 2005)

- Thermoelectric power uses 48 percent of all freshwater and saline water. About 52 percent of fresh surface-water and 96 percent of saline-water withdrawals were for thermoelectric-power cooling.
- Irrigation has accounted for about 34 percent of freshwater withdrawals since 1950. Irrigated acreage more than doubled between 1950 and 1980, remained constant between 1980 and 1995, then increased nearly 7 percent between 1995 and 2000.
- The public water supply used 43 Bgal/d in 2000, up from 14 Bgal/d in 1950.
- Self-supplied industrial uses accounted for 20 Bgal/d in 2000, or 12 percent less than in 1995 and 24 percent less than in 1985.

The dominance of thermoelectric-power production in water use is related to the use of electricity in buildings for power, heating and cooling, and lighting. Ways to use less electricity will be discussed in Part V: Electrical and Lighting Systems.

TABLE 6-1. WATER RESOURCES AVAILABLE PER CAPITA

Continent	billion cubic meters per year per person
World Average	7.60
Australia and Oceania	83.7
South America	38.2
North America	17.4
Africa	5.72
Europe	4.23
Asia	3.92

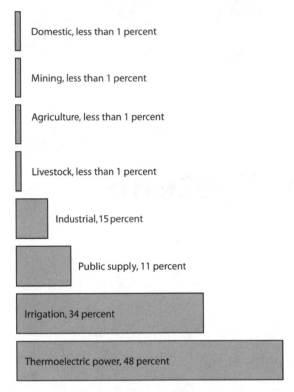

Domestic, less than 1 percent

Mining, less than 1 percent

Agriculture, less than 1 percent

Livestock, less than 1 percent

Industrial, 15 percent

Public supply, 11 percent

Irrigation, 34 percent

Thermoelectric power, 48 percent

Figure 6-1 U.S. water use. The majority of water used in the United States is for the generation of electric power and for irrigation. All of the remaining uses make up only 18 percent of the total. Water used in homes is less than 1 percent of the total amount.

A great deal of water is used to create materials for building construction. Plastic uses the most water per ton of material produced; steel also uses substantial amounts. Concrete is 16 percent water, but much more is used for processing and cleaning. Such water becomes acidic and difficult to reuse, although some can be recycled.

Although electrical production, irrigation, and industry all use substantial amounts of freshwater, residential water use remains a major factor—and one that interior designers can help control.

The use of freshwater supplies by toilets should be the primary focus in the home. Flushing toilets and washing clothes make up nearly half of all residential use. Another area of concern is the nearly 14 percent of water lost to leaks.

☑ **Interior designers work to help clients conserve water while maintaining a high-quality interior environment.**

TABLE 6-2. WATER USE IN CONSTRUCTION

Material	Quantity, ton (kilograms)	Water used, gallons (liters)
Bricks	1 (907)	580 (2200)
Steel	1 (907)	43,600 (165,000)
Plastic	1 (907)	348,750 (1.32 million)
Concrete	1 (907)	124 (470)

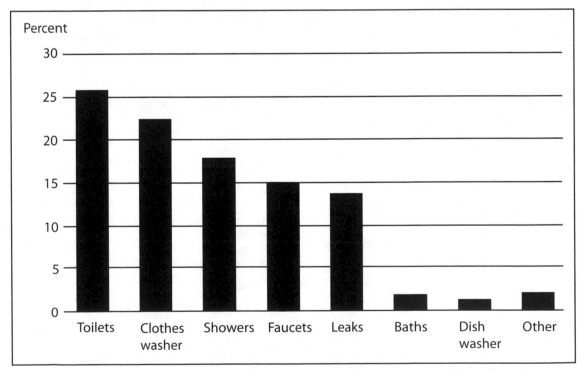

Figure 6-2 Household water use by percentage. In U.S. homes, toilets and clothes washing make up almost half of all of the water used. Showers and faucets are responsible for the second highest use, with leaks responsible for 13.7 percent of water use. Dishwashers and baths make up the remainder, which is less than 10 percent of the total amount.

THE HYDROLOGIC CYCLE

The total amount of water on the earth and in the atmosphere is finite (with the exception of comets, which may contribute a small additional amount). The water we use today is the same water that was in Noah's proverbial flood. Ninety-nine percent of the earth's water is either saltwater or glacial ice. A quarter of the solar energy reaching the earth is employed in constantly circulating water through evaporation and precipitation, a process known as the hydrologic cycle.

The most accessible sources of water are precipitation and runoff. Any daily precipitation that does not evaporate or run off is retained as soil moisture. After plants use this form of water to grow, it evaporates back into the atmosphere or runs down to fill voids in the ground with water. This zone is known as **groundwater**. The upper surface of groundwater is called the **water table**. Groundwater makes up the majority of the water supply. It can serve to store excess building heat in the summer for use in the building in winter. However, groundwater can harm building foundations when it leaks into spaces below ground.

RETAINING RAINWATER

Rain, snow, and other precipitation spread a supply of relatively pure water over a large area. Precipitation can be captured directly either in cisterns or as a more concentrated flow of runoff.

Historically, rain falling in the countryside ran into creeks, streams, and rivers, and rivers rarely ran dry. Rainfall was absorbed into the ground, which served as a huge reservoir. The water that accumulated underground either emerged as springs and artesian wells or created lakes, swamps, and marshes. Most of the water that leaked into the ground cleansed itself in the weeks, months, or years it took to get back to an **aquifer** (water-bearing rock formation).

Figure 6-3 Storm sewer. This storm-sewer plaque in Boston, Massachusetts, reminds people not to dump pollutants. The storm sewer drains directly into the Charles River and on into Massachusetts Bay.

Streets in towns that developed near rivers sloped to drain into the rivers, which ran to river basins and the sea. As marshy areas were filled in and buildings were constructed, paved streets and sidewalks channeled water to storm sewers and pumping stations. The rapid runoff increased the danger of flooding and concentrated pollutants in waterways. Water ran out of the ground into overflowing storm sewers, without replenishing groundwater levels.

When cities began to pave their streets in the nineteenth century, natural streams were enclosed in storm sewers. The sewer pipes then channeled water to local rivers. With the advent of flush toilets, the pipes became **combined sewers** that carried both storm runoff and building wastes to rivers. Eventually, the rivers and associated bodies of water became too polluted for use, and separate **sanitary sewers** and **sewage-treatment plants** were built.

Today, subdivisions slope from lawns at the top to street storm drains at the bottom. Once water enters a storm drain, it is dumped into rivers far away from its point of origin. Huge amounts of storm water also leak into sewer pipes in which it is mixed with sewage and taken even farther away to be processed at sewage-treatment plants. The result is a suburban desert, with lawns that need watering and restricted local water supplies.

In most of the United States, rainwater that falls on the roof of a home is of adequate quality and quantity to provide about 95 percent of indoor residential water requirements. However, members of a typical U.S. suburban household could not meet all of their needs with rain off the roof without modifying their water-use habits.

Rainwater can make a significant contribution to the irrigation of small lawns and gardens when a rain barrel below a downspout or cisterns located above the level of the garden collect and store water for later release. For centuries, traditional builders have designed for rainwater retention. In the world's drier regions, small cisterns within the home collect rainwater to supplement unreliable public supplies. With the advent of central water and energy supplies in industrial societies, rainwater collection and use became less common. It has become easier to raise the funds (with the associated costs spread among consumers in the form of monthly bills) to build a water-treatment plant with the related network of pipes than to convince individuals to collect, store, and recycle their own water. Individuals who choose to use rainwater to flush toilets must pay for their private system upfront and continue to pay for municipal water treatment through taxes. As a result, conservation can lead to additional expenses.

Acid rain, which is a result of air pollution in the northeastern United States, Canada, and some other parts of the world, makes some rainwater undesirable. Bird droppings and dust on collection surfaces along with fungicides used for moss control can pollute the water supply. Steep roofs tend to stay cleaner and collect less dirt in the rainwater than roofs with smaller inclines.

Snow—where it occurs—has a great impact on building and site design. Water stored as snow delays runoff after a storm. Snow is a great insulator, both thermally and acoustically. As one of the most reflective natural surfaces, snow bounces light into interior spaces; sometimes, glare can be a problem. Exterior building parts can be damaged or impeded by the weight and mass of snow.

PROTECTING THE WATER SUPPLY

Potable water is free of harmful bacteria and safe to drink as well as to use for food preparation. Water carried from the public water supply to individual buildings in water mains, which are large underground pipes, must be potable.

Current practices use large amounts of potable water for such low-grade tasks as flushing toilets. Better conservation practices reserve high-quality water for such high-quality tasks as drinking and preparing food, reduce overall use, and recycle water for lesser–quality uses.

Protecting and conserving clean water supplies is critical to people's health. Until recently, a reliable supply of clean water was not always available, and epidemic diseases continue to be spread through unsanitary water supplies. Water from ponds or streams in built-up areas is unsafe to drink because it may contain biological or chemical pollution.

Contaminated Water Supplies

For centuries, people knew the benefits of living near a source of freshwater. Unfortunately, it took a long time for people to realize that their own wastes and those of their animals could pollute water sources and cause disease and death. Bacteria were unknown to science until they were discovered in Germany in 1892.

Waterborne bacterial diseases are responsible for an estimated 2 million deaths annually worldwide, mostly children. These diseases include cholera, typhoid fever, dysentery, and Brainerd diarrhea, all of which produce abdominal symptoms and diarrhea. They are caused by such bacteria as *vibrio cholera, campylobacter, salmonella, shigella*, and *E. coli*.

These bacterial diseases are spread by contaminated surface-water sources and large, poorly functioning municipal water distribution. The diseases can be prevented by chlorination and safe water handling. However, water-treatment systems are expensive to build and to operate and have not been able to keep up with growth in population and human migration. Effective alternatives include point-of-use disinfection and safe water-storage vessels; low-cost, locally controlled technologies are becoming more prevalent.

Although the earth is largely a water planet, freshwater is not evenly distributed. Approximately one-sixth of people living today do not have enough water, and many more lack basic sanitation. In addition to geological and climatic issues, political and economic barriers prevent access to clean water. Some water supplies are contaminated by industry, while others contain naturally occurring pollutants.

The availability of clean water determines where homes and businesses are located, as well as how many people can live in or visit an area. Proper collection, treatment, and distribution of water protect the water supply.

Rainwater contains almost no bacteria and only small amounts of minerals and gases. Many communities collect clean water from rain running down mountainsides into valleys in reservoirs and limit human access to these areas to prevent contamination. Large aqueduct pipes carry water from reservoirs to communities, usually by gravity flow. Communities without access to relatively uninhabited mountain areas make do with water of less purity from rivers or tap underground water flows with wells.

Water from wells and mountain reservoirs requires relatively little treatment. River water is sent through sand filters and settling basins, where particles are removed. Additional chemical treatment precipitates iron and lead compounds. Special filters are used to remove hydrogen sulfide, radon, and other dissolved gases. Finally, chlorine dissolved in water kills harmful microorganisms. The result is an increased supply of clean water to support the development of residential and commercial construction.

WATER-SUPPLY SYSTEMS

Water mains are large pipes that transport water for a public water system from its source to service connections at buildings. A **service pipe** installed by the public water utility runs from the water main to the building, far enough underground to prevent freezing in winter. Inside the building or in a curb box, a **water meter** measures and records the quantity of water passing through the service pipe; typically, the meter also monitors sewage-disposal services. A **control valve** is located in the curb box to shut off the water supply to the building in an emergency or if the building owner fails to pay the water bill. A **shutoff valve** inside the building also controls the water supply.

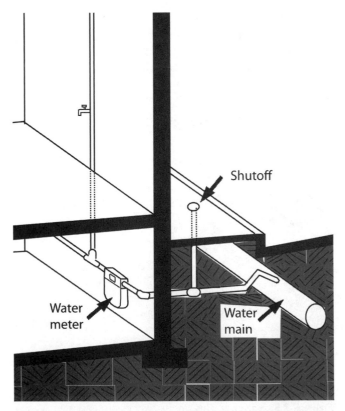

Figure 6-4 Water main. Water mains underneath sidewalks and streets carry water from reservoirs to buildings. The water main is connected to each building by a supply line.

Figure 6-5 Water control valve. The flow of water from a water main can be shut off outside a building, where a control valve is located under a cap.

Well Water

Wells supply water of more reliable quantity and quality than rainwater systems. Because water near the surface may have seeped into the ground from the immediate area, it may be contaminated by sewage, barnyard wastes, outhouse wastes, or garbage dumps nearby.

Deep wells are expensive to drill, but the water deep underground comes from hundreds of miles away, and the long trip filters out most bacteria. Well water sometimes contains dissolved minerals, most of which are harmless but may result in hard-water conditions.

Well water is usually potable when the source is adequately deep. It should be pure, cool, and free of discoloration and odor problems. The local health department will check samples for bacterial and chemical content before use. Wells are sunk below the water table so that they are not affected by seasonal fluctuations in the water level. Pumps bring the water from the well to the surface, where it is stored in tanks under constant pressure to compensate for variations in the flow from the well. The water can be filtered and chlorinated at this point. Pumps and pressure tanks are usually housed in outbuildings kept above freezing temperatures.

Municipal Water-Supply Systems

The water in a community's water mains is under pressure to offset friction and gravity as it flows through the pipes. The **water pressure** in public water supplies is usually at or above 345 kilopascals (kPa), which is equal to 50 pounds per square inch (psi). This is also approximately the maximum pressure that is achieved by private well systems and is adequate pressure for buildings up to six stories high. For taller buildings or locations in which the water pressure is lower, water is pumped to a rooftop storage tank and distributed by gravity—a system called **gravity downfeed**. The water storage tank can also double as a reserve for a fire-protection system.

Figure 6-6 Water pressure. This exhibit demonstrates how the weight of the water above an opening increases the pressure at that opening. The highest water pressure is produced by the lowest opening in the cylinder; the opening near the top is considerably weaker.

Once the water is inside the building, its pressure is controlled by the size of the pipes it travels through. Bigger pipes put less pressure on the water flow, while small pipes increase the pressure. If the water rises up high in the building, gravity and friction combine to decrease the pressure. The water pressure at individual fixtures within the building may vary between 35 kPa and 204 kPa (5–30 psi).

Too much pressure causes splashing; too little produces a slow dribble. Water-supply pipes are sized to regulate the difference between the service pressure and the pressure required for each fixture. If the pressure is still too high, pressure reducers or regulators are installed on fixtures.

WATER QUALITY

Pesticides, cleaning solvents, and seepage from landfills pollute groundwater in some rural areas of the United States. In urban areas, the level of chlorine added to prevent bacterial contamination sometimes results in bad-tasting water as well as deterioration of pipes and plumbing fixtures.

Electrical power plants discharge great amounts of waste heat into water, which can change biological and chemical conditions and threaten fish.

☑ **Steel, paper, and textiles are the most polluting industries. The textile industry employs large quantities of water in fiber production and processing and in fabric finishing, especially dyeing. Interior designers have the power to avoid products whose manufacturing includes highly toxic technologies and to seek out ones with low environmental impact.**

Water-Quality Characteristics

Communities routinely check on the quality of their municipal water supplies. If home or business owners are unsure if their building's supply meets safety standards, a government or private water-quality analyst will provide instructions and containers for taking samples and assess the water supply's purity. The analyst's report will reveal numerical values for the water supply's mineral content, acidity or alkalinity (pH level), contamination, turbidity, total solids, and biological purity as well as an opinion on the sample's suitability for its intended use.

Water Treatments

It is best to prevent the contamination of safe water supplies and to conserve them for high-quality uses. When all else fails, contaminated water is treated. Primary water treatment begins with filtration, followed by disinfection to kill microorganisms.

Secondary treatment keeps the level of disinfectant high enough to prevent microorganism regrowth.

WATER DISTRIBUTION

Throughout history, a primary concern of architects, builders, and homeowners has been how to keep water out of buildings. Not until the end of the nineteenth century did supplying water inside a building become common in industrial countries. Indoor plumbing is still unavailable in many parts of the world today. Interior designers work with architects, engineers, and contractors to ensure that water is supplied in a way that supports a client's health, safety, comfort, and intended use.

For indoor plumbing to work safely without spreading bacteria and polluting the freshwater supply, it is necessary to construct two separate systems. The first, the **water supply system**, delivers clean water to buildings. The second, a system of drains called the **sanitary** or **drain, waste, and vent (DWV) system**, channels all the waste downward through a building to the sewer beneath it.

In small wood-frame buildings, indoor plumbing usually is hidden in floor joist and wall construction spaces. Masonry buildings require spaces that are built out with wood furring strips or metal channels to hide horizontal and vertical plumbing.

In large buildings with many fixtures, piping is located in pipe chases, which are vertical and horizontal open spaces with walls (or ceiling and floor) on either side. Pipe chases often have access doors to the pipes so that they may be worked on without disrupting the building's occupants. The water-supply plumbing and the sanitary drainage plumbing must be coordinated with the building's structure and with other building systems.

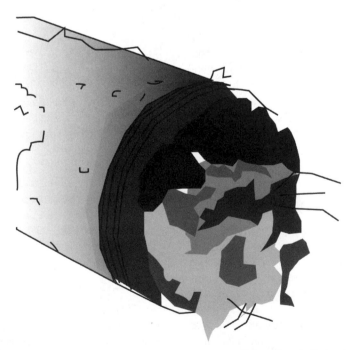

Figure 6-7 Scale clogging pipe. Corrosive materials in water create flakes of scale that, when combined with hair and other debris, clog water pipes.

TABLE 6-3. WATER QUALITY

	Description	Cause	Problem
Physical	Turbidity: Muddy or cloudy appearance	Suspended clay, silt particles; plankton or other small organic material	Aesthetically objectionable; usually does not affect health
	Visible color changes	Dissolved vegetation or microorganisms, rust	Usually not health threat; unpleasant
	Taste, odor	Organic compounds, inorganic salts, dissolved gases	Chemical analysis before treatment
	Temperature	Preference for cool drinking water	Cooling wastes water, energy
	Foaming	Concentrations of detergents	May indicate contact with domestic wastes
Chemical	Alkalinity	Bicarbonate, carbonate, hydroxide components	Testing required to determine treatment
	Hardness	Calcium and magnesium salts; carbonate hardness removed as scale when water is heated; permanent hardness not removed by heating	Inhibits cleaning action of soaps and detergents; deposits scale inside hot water pipes and cooking utensils
	pH	Measure of water's hydrogen ion concentration, relative acidity or alkalinity	pH of 7 is neutral; below 7 indicates acidity (corrosive); pH higher than 7 indicates alkalinity
	Toxic substances	Arsenic, barium, cadmium, chromium, cyanides, fluoride, lead, selenium, silver	Leaking waste dumps contaminate groundwater
	Chlorides	Noticeable taste in excess of 250 mg/l	Pollution from seawater, brine, industrial or domestic wastes
	Copper	Natural copper deposits, copper piping carrying corrosive water	Undesirable taste in excess of 1.0 mg/l
	Iron	Frequently present in groundwater; corrosive water in iron pipes	Brownish stains on washed clothes; can affect taste of water
	Manganese	Natural laxative	Color and taste effects similar to those of iron
	Nitrates	Can indicate seepage from deposits of livestock manure into shallow wells	High nitrate concentrations can cause methemoglobinemia ("blue baby" syndrome) in infants
	Pesticides	Wells near home treated for termite infestations	Avoid using pesticides near wells
	Sodium	Salts used on roads for ice control; some water softeners	Dangerous for people with heart, kidney, circulatory ailments
	Sulfates	Natural deposits of Epsom salts or Glauber's salt	Laxative effects
	Zinc	Can cause undesirable taste	Not usually a health threat
Biological	Disease-producing organisms	Bacteria, protozoa, viruses; presence of E. coli indicates contact with fecal wastes; destroyed at treatment facilities	Keep organic fertilizers and nutrient minerals out of surface water; store water in dark at low temperatures
Radiological	Radioactive chemicals	Mining; use in industry and power plants	Cumulative health effects

TABLE 6-4. WATER TREATMENTS

Treatment	Description	Purpose	Comments
Distillation	Heating water to produce water vapor	Eliminates pollution; purifies water for drinking, cooking, lab use	Simple method; distilled water is pure but tastes flat
Disinfection	Chlorination, nanofiltration, ultraviolet light, bromine, iodine, ozone or heat treatment	Destroys microorganisms	Required for surface water, or for groundwater in contact with surface water
Filtration	Water passes through permeable fabric or porous beds of filtering material	Removes suspended particles and some materials affecting color or taste	Removes some bacteria, including *Giardia* cysts
Aeration, also called oxidation	Water is sprayed or run down turbulent waterfalls to expose as much of its surface to air as possible	Improves taste and color; helps remove iron and manganese; may make water more corrosive	Improves flat taste of distilled or cistern water; removes hydrogen sulfide and algae odors
Fluoride	Added to public water supplies	Reduces childhood tooth decay	Not needed for adult teeth; too much can cause yellow mottling

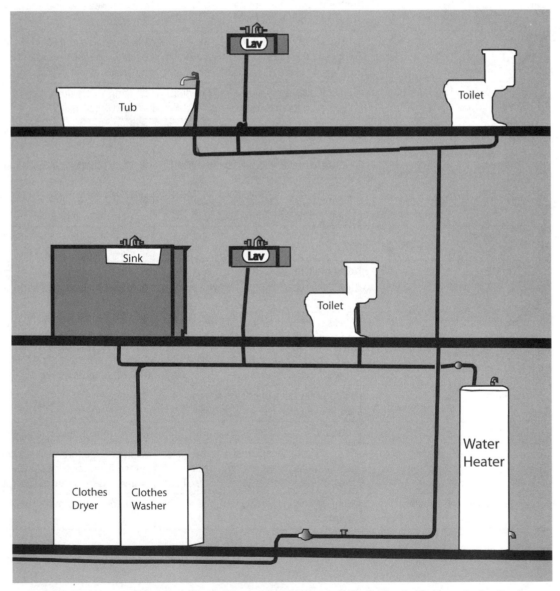

Figure 6-8 Water supply system. Some of the water entering a building is diverted to the water heater; from there, it travels in hot water supply piping to fixtures and appliances that need it. The rest of the water goes through cold water supply piping to appliances and fixtures.

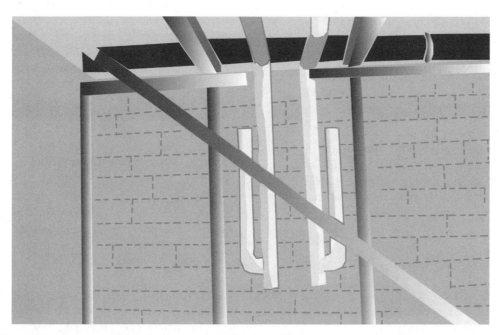

Figure 6-9 Masonry wall with furring for plumbing. It is difficult to run plumbing piping through masonry walls, and it is not recommended for walls that are subject to freezing. Light-gauge steel channels or wood studs are used for furring, in which the interior wall surface is built out to accommodate pipes.

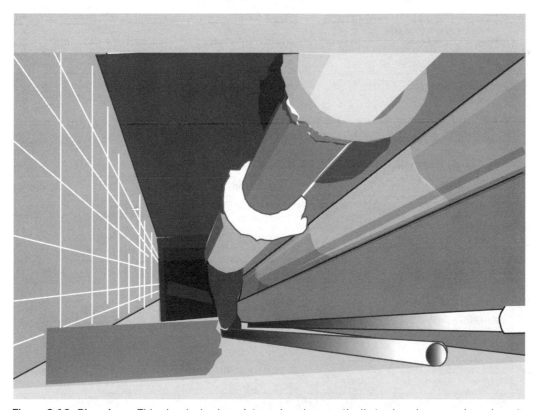

Figure 6-10 Pipe chase. This view looks down into a pipe chase vertically to show how supply and waste piping travels from floor to floor.

The weight of the vertical supply pipes and the water they contain is supported at each story and horizontally every 1.8 meters to 3 meters (6–10 ft.) apart. Adjustable hangars are used to pitch the horizontal waste pipes downward for drainage.

Distribution Systems

A water storage tank shares the uppermost zone in most high-rise buildings with two-story elevator penthouses, chimneys, plumbing vents, exhaust blowers, and air conditioning cooling towers. Solar collectors for hot water heating are sometimes also located on the roof. All of this equipment is usually surrounded by a band or screen two or more stories high.

Supply Pipes

The Romans used lead for plumbing pipes 2000 years ago, and the word "plumbing" is derived from the Latin word for lead, "plumbum." Roman baths combined hot and cold pools, exercise spaces, and even libraries and dining areas.

Lead pipes were used through the 1950s. As a result, the Environmental Protection Agency is concerned even today that lead may leach out of both lead pipes and copper pipes joined with lead solder and enter the water supply. Fortunately, lead on the inside surface of a pipe quickly reacts with sulfates, carbonates, and phosphates in the water to form a coating that prevents it from leaching out of the pipe. Experts believe, however, that the lead content in water is likely to exceed safe guidelines when the water is highly acidic or is allowed to sit in the lead pipes for a long time. Today, plumbing supply pipes are made of copper, red brass, galvanized steel, and plastic.

Solder, which was formerly made of lead, is now 85 percent tin and 5 percent antimony. Molten solder is drawn into the joint, which allows piping to be set up without having to turn the parts to be connected, thereby greatly facilitating installation. Solder also permits pipes to have thin walls because no threads need to be cut into their thickness. The smooth interiors contribute less friction to flowing water.

Plastic pipes require more access points for joint repair than are needed for metal pipes with soldered joints. Plastic pipe used for potable water is required to have a seal from the National Sanitation Foundation (NSF). Because plastic pipes are shockproof, they are used in mobile homes where vibration would be a problem for other types of plumbing.

TABLE 6-5. TYPES OF WATER DISTRIBUTION SYSTEMS

Type	Application	Description	Comments
Upfeed distribution	Small low buildings with moderate water use	Water main pressure	Too much pressure causes splashing; use flow restrictor
Pumped upfeed distribution	Medium-sized buildings with inadequate water pressure	Pumps provide extra pressure	Hydropneumatic systems force water into sealed pressurized tanks
Downfeed distribution	Water raised to rooftop storage tanks; water drops down to plumbing fixtures	Rooftop tanks may need to be heated to prevent freezing	Water available for fire hoses; requires extra structural support

TABLE 6-6. TYPES OF PLUMBING PIPES

Material	Description	Disadvantages	Comments
Galvanized steel	Strong, inexpensive	Corrosion, rust, leaks; mineral deposits reduce water pressure	Standard for supply until 1960s; pipes last 20 to 50 years
Red brass	Good corrosion resistance	More expensive than copper	Large brass pipes use threaded connections
Copper	Acid resistance; lighter weight than brass; lasts longer than steel	About twice as expensive as galvanized steel per foot	Can be soldered
Plastic pipe (general)	Lightweight, low cost, corrosion-resistant, easy to work	Made from synthetic petroleum and coal-based resins	Flexible for outdoor use; also rigid pipe
Rigid PVC plastic pipe	Cold-water applications	Heat sensitivity; not used for hot water	White or gray thermoplastic
ABS plastic pipe	Cold-water applications	Heat sensitivity; not used for hot water	Black thermoplastic
CPVC plastic pipe	Hot or cold water	Higher temperatures than PVC or ABS	Cream thermoplastic
PB plastic pipe	Flexible; can be snaked through walls	Cannot be solvent welded; uses compression fittings	Less susceptible to freezing damage than other plastics

Figure 6-11 Roman bath. Indoor plumbing reached a height in the Roman Empire. This Roman bath, located in Bath, England (its namesake), features grand, sunlit spaces.

Engineers determine pipe sizes by the rate at which the pipes transport water when demand is highest. Pipes in the supply network tend to be smaller as they get farther away from the water source and closer to the point of use since not all of the water has to make the entire trip. The pipe sizes are determined by the number and types of fixtures to be served and pressure losses caused by friction and vertical travel. Water flowing through a small pipe is under greater pressure than the same amount of water flowing through a larger pipe.

Each type of fixture is assigned a number of fixture units. Based on the total number of fixture units for the building, the number of gallons per minute (gpm) is estimated. The engineer assumes that not all of the fixtures are in use at the same time, so the total demand is not directly proportional to the number of fixture units.

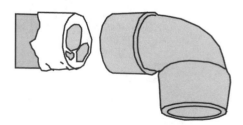

Figure 6-12 Plumber opening trap. Plumbing pipes must be accessible for cleaning and repairs. This plumber is opening a trap in a waste pipe.

Figure 6-13 Gluing plastic pipe fittings. Plastic pipes are glued together rather than soldered. While this makes them more difficult to take apart than metal pipes, they are easier to cut.

☑ An interior designer needs to give the engineer specific information about the number of plumbing fixtures and their requirements as early in the process as possible.

INSULATING WATER PIPES

Pipes sweat when moisture in the air condenses on the outside of cold pipes. This **condensation** drops off the pipes, wetting and damaging finished surfaces. Cold water pipes should be insulated to prevent condensation. Insulation also keeps heat from adjacent warm spaces from warming the water in cold pipes. When pipes are wrapped in glass fiber between 13 millimeters and 25 millimeters (½–1 in.) thick with a tight vapor barrier on the exterior surface, the moisture in the air cannot reach the cold surface.

Hot water pipes are insulated to prevent heat loss. When hot and cold water pipes run parallel to each other, they should be a minimum of 15 centimeters (6 in.) apart to prevent them from exchanging heat.

In very cold climates, water pipes in exterior walls and unheated buildings may freeze and rupture. For this reason, locating fixtures along exterior walls should be avoided. If water-supply pipes must be located in an exterior wall, they should be placed on the warm side (on the inside, in a cold climate) of the wall insulation. A drainage faucet located at a low point will allow the pipes to be drained before being exposed to freezing weather.

Supply Lines and Valves

From a **branch supply line**, a line runs out to each fixture. **Roughing in** is the process of getting all of the pipes installed, capped, and pressure-tested before actual fixtures are installed. The rough-in dimensions for each plumbing fixture should be verified with the fixture manufacturer so that fixture supports can be built in accurately during the corresponding phase of construction.

PLUMBING VALVES AND VACUUM BREAKERS

It is a good idea to have a **shutoff valve** to control the flow of water at each vertical pipe (known as a **riser**), with branches for kitchens and baths as well as at the runouts to individual fixtures. Additional valves may be installed to isolate one or more fixtures from the water-supply system for repair and maintenance.

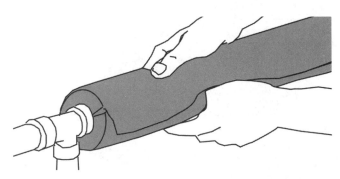

Figure 6-14 Pipe insulation. Pipe insulation is available preformed to wrap around water pipes, making home improvement easy.

Compression-type globe valves are used for faucets, drain valves, and hose connections.

Vacuum breakers prevent dirty water from flowing back into clean supply pipes. They also isolate water from dishwashers, clothes washers, and boilers from the water supply.

A dead-end upright branch of pipe located near a fixture is called an **air chamber**. When a faucet is shut off quickly, the water's movement in the supply pipe stops almost instantly. Without the air chamber, the pressure in the pipe momentarily becomes very high and produces a sound like banging the pipe with a hammer—appropriately called **water hammer**—that may damage the system. The air chamber absorbs the shock and prevents water hammer.

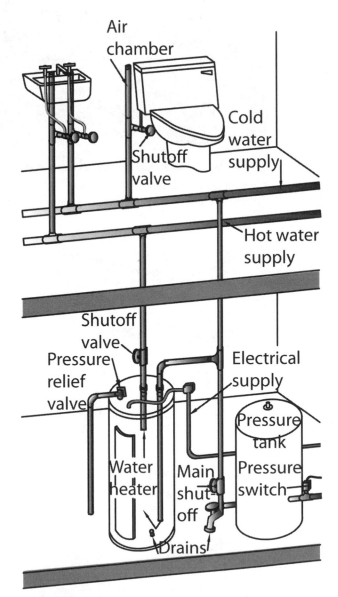

Figure 6-15 Branch lines to fixture. Hot and cold water supply lines often run close to each other. If the hot water supply lines are not insulated, heat from the hot water can be lost to the adjacent cold water lines.

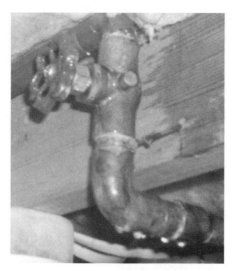

Figure 6-16 Shutoff valve with condensation. Drops of condensation are visible on the horizontal pipe below the shutoff valve.

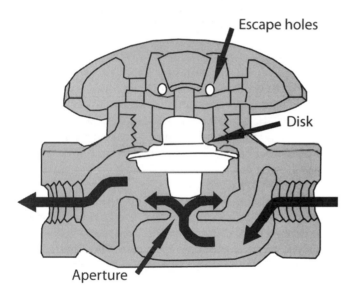

Figure 6-17 Vacuum breaker. Vacuum breakers are required when dirty water could come in contact with supply piping, such as in hair-washing sinks in beauty salons.

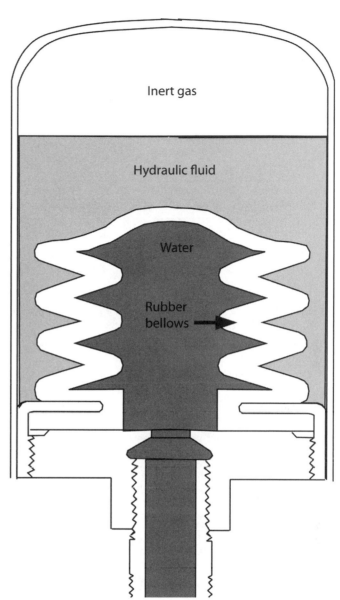

Figure 6-18 Water hammer shock absorber. When the water hammer–afflicted valve near a shock absorber closes, the initial shock expands the rubber bellows. This displaces the hydraulic fluid, and the shock is absorbed by the inert gas.

CHILLED WATER

Most public buildings provide chilled drinking water. Previously, a central chiller with its own piping system was used to distribute the cold water. Today, water is chilled in smaller water coolers at each point of use, providing better quality at less cost. Some systems involve a central water-purification system that distributes water throughout an office; water is then chilled at individual water coolers. These systems require more plumbing, but they eliminate the need to install heavy water bottles on coolers.

Standard hot and cold bottled-water coolers can use more energy than a large refrigerator; Energy Star–qualified coolers use only about half as much. Drinking fountains are usually specified with point-of-use water coolers but are also available without coolers.

HOT WATER

The hot water that is used for bathing, washing clothes, washing dishes, and many other tasks other than those involved in heating building spaces is called **domestic** or **service hot water**. Sometimes, when a well-insulated building uses very little water for space heating but uses a great deal of hot water for other purposes, a single, large hot water heater supplies water to both.

Hot Water Temperatures

In many buildings, water is heated and stored at high temperatures in large tanks to ensure that hot water will always be available in sufficient quantities. Inevitably, some heat is lost during

TABLE 6-7. RESIDENTIAL DOMESTIC HOT-WATER CONSUMPTION

Machine Type	Cycle	Small Machine, 14 lb. (6.4 kg), gallons (liters)	Large Machine, 18 lb. (8.2 kg), gallons (liters)
Clothes washing	Hot wash/hot rinse	38 (144)	48 (182)
	Hot wash/warm rinse	28 (106)	36 (136)
	Hot wash/cold rinse	19 (72)	24 (91)
	Warm wash/cold rinse	10 (38)	12 (45)
Dishwashing	Dishwashing machine	10 (38)	15 (57)
	Sink washing	4–8 (15–30)	
Personal hygiene	Tub bathing	12–30 (45–134)	
	Wet shaving, hair washing	2–4 (8–15)	
	Showering	2–6 /minute (13–38/minute)	A 5–6 minute shower is equivalent to a tub bath

storage and delivery. Occasionally, the water must be run for an extended period in order to access water at the desired temperature. To save both energy and water, wise consumers use water at lower temperatures whenever feasible.

People generally take showers in water that is between 41°C and 49°C (105°F–120°F), often by blending 60°C (140°F) hot water with cold water from the tap with a mixing valve in the shower. Most people find temperatures above 43°C (110°F) uncomfortably hot. Higher water temperatures allow smaller hot water tanks to be installed because the super-hot water is mixed with cold water before use.

Excessively hot water temperatures can result in scalding. Water temperatures above 60°C (140°F) can cause serious burns and lead to scalding if the water is hard. However, high temperatures limit the growth of the harmful bacterium *Legionella pneumophila*, which causes Legionnaires' disease. Codes may regulate or limit high water temperatures.

While lower temperatures are less likely to cause burns, they may be inadequate for sanitation. Lower-temperature water loses less heat when stored and in pipes, which, in turn, saves energy.

Smaller heating units are adequate, but larger storage tanks are needed. Solar and waste heat–recovery sources work better with low-temperature water heaters.

Water Heaters

According to the U.S. Department of Energy (DOE), water heating accounts for up to 17 percent of national residential energy consumption. Hot water is commonly heated using natural gas or electricity. It is also possible to use heat from other systems that would otherwise be wasted as well as heat from steam, cogeneration, or wood-burning systems.

Water heaters are selected based on their energy efficiency, tank storage capacity, and time required for the water temperature to rise a specified amount. Capacity affects how many fixtures can use hot water simultaneously. Rise time relates to how long a water heater takes to produce more hot water. If hot water is conserved, it is possible to specify a smaller tank; this directly affects energy efficiency and may make the use of such technologies as tankless water heaters desirable.

TABLE 6-8. REPRESENTATIVE HOT WATER TEMPERATURES

Use	Activity	Degrees Fahrenheit (degrees Celsius)
Lavatory	Hand washing	105 (40)
	Shaving	115 (45)
	Surgical scrubbing	110 (43)
Bathing	Showers, tubs	110 (43)
	Therapeutic baths	95 (35)
Laundry	Commercial, institutional	Up to 180 (82)
	Residential	140 (60)
Dishwashing	Commercial spray-type:	
	Wash	150 (65) minimum
	Final rinse	180–195 (82–90)

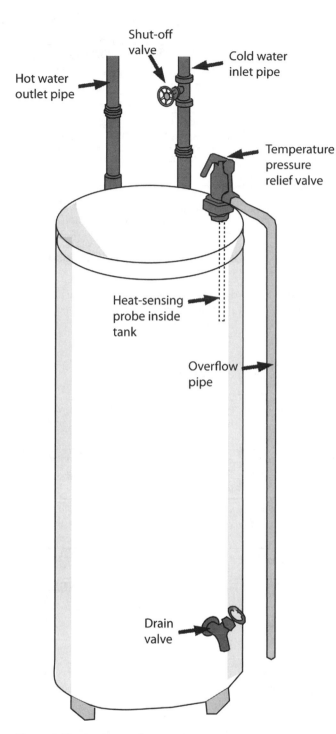

Shut-off valve

Hot water outlet pipe

Cold water inlet pipe

Temperature pressure relief valve

Heat-sensing probe inside tank

Overflow pipe

Drain valve

Figure 6-19 Storage tank water heater. The water enters at the bottom of a storage tank, where it is heated, and leaves at the top. The heat loss through the sides of the tank continues even when no hot water is being used, so storage water heaters continue to use energy to maintain water temperature. Typically, the tanks are insulated in order to retain heat, but some older models may need more insulation. Local utilities will sometimes insulate hot water tanks at no charge. Energy Star® water heaters are better insulated and use less energy.

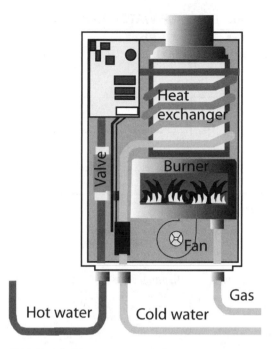

Heat exchanger

Valve

Burner

Fan

Hot water   Cold water   Gas

Figure 6-20 Tankless water heater. Small tankless water heaters (also called instantaneous or demand heaters) raise the water temperature very quickly within a heating coil, from which it is immediately sent to the point of use. A gas burner or electrical element heats the water as needed. Because these water heaters do not have storage tanks, they do not lose heat. With modulating temperature controls, demand water heaters will keep water temperatures constant at different rates of flow. Gas tankless water heaters may require expensive or complex venting.

SOLAR WATER HEATERS

Solar water heaters are designed as either active systems with circulating pumps and controls or as passive systems. Active solar water systems use energy to operate pumps that circulate water through the solar collector. Passive solar water heating systems are typically less expensive than active systems. Although passive solar systems are usually less efficient than active systems, they are often more reliable and last longer.

Solar water heaters use either direct or indirect systems. In a direct system, the water to be used in the building circulates through a solar collector in a simple and efficient manner. An indirect system circulates a fluid, usually a nonfreezing solution, through the collector and storage tank. The fluid does not mix directly with the water in the tank but transfers its heat through a heat exchanger.

The storage tanks of solar water-heating systems have an additional outlet to and inlet from the solar collectors. In solar water-heating systems with two storage tanks, the solar water heater heats water before it enters a conventional storage tank. In a one-tank system, the backup heater is combined with solar storage in the same tank.

TABLE 6-9. TYPES OF WATER HEATERS

Water Heater	Type	Use	Heat Source/Energy Use
Storage tank	Direct	Residential, small commercial; central 20–80-gallon tank, some with small tank at point of use	Electric, gas, oil; uses energy to maintain constant heat
Circulating storage	Direct	Coils containing steam or fluids submerged within tanks or set within boilers	Sun, steam, hot exhaust gases, very hot water; reuses heat from another source
	Indirect	Coils with water placed outside boiler within casing containing heat source	Electric or gas; reuses heat from another source
Tankless (instantaneous) water heaters	Large size	Central hot water systems	Electric or gas
	Smaller sizes	For wall mounting next to remote plumbing fixtures or isolated baths, laundries, etc.	Electric (less efficient) or gas (must be vented)
	Instant hot water taps	Kitchen or bar sinks	Electric; quick response; tend to be low efficiency
Heat pump water heaters	Built-in storage tank	Can run on heat given off by refrigeration machines, such as ice-making, grocery-display, walk-in units; move heat from one location to another; do not work well in cold spaces	Heat pump takes excess heat from air in hot place, such as restaurant kitchen or hot outdoor air; uses it to heat water; also dehumidifies; high efficiency
	Added on to existing tank	Takes up little extra space; fan, compressor add some noise	Improves efficiency
Active solar water heaters	Direct circulation system	Solar storage tank with circulating pump and controls; household water circulates through collectors and into home; subject to freezing	Heat from sun captured directly in water by solar collectors; not used in very cold climates
	Indirect circulation system	Pumps circulate nonfreezing heat-transfer fluid through collectors and heat exchanger to heat water	Heat from sun collected in heat-transfer fluid and transferred to water; used in low temperatures
Passive solar water heaters	Integral collector storage passive system	Black tanks or tubes in insulated glazed box collect solar heat for preheating water; used with backup water heater	Outdoor pipes can freeze in cold climates; best used for daytime, evening hot water needs
	Thermo siphon systems	Collector below storage tank; warmed water rises up into tank	Heavy storage tank affects roof design; usually more expensive
Water heating with space heating	Indirect water heaters may be separate component or part of system	Hot water from boiler is circulated through heat exchanger in separate insulated tank; less commonly, water in heat-exchanger coil circulates through furnace, then through water-storage tank	Gas, oil, or propane boiler or furnace as heat source; one of the least expensive ways to provide hot water when used with a new high-efficiency boiler
	Integrated water heating and space heating	Powerful water heater provides hot water for domestic use, supplements fan-coil unit that heats air for space heating; warmed air is then distributed through ducts	Integrated gas heaters are inexpensive to purchase and install; take up less space; more efficient at water heating

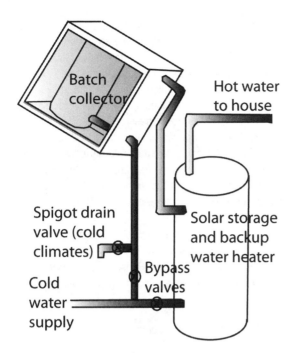

Figure 6-21 Solar water heater. Solar hot water is one of the most common solar applications. Even in climates that are relatively less sunny, solar hot water can provide most of the needs for a residence.

More complex systems are available for heating indoor pools, hot tubs, and spas in colder climates.

Water-Heater Energy Efficiency

The U.S. DOE uses **Energy Factor (EF)** as a measurement of relative energy efficiency for a water heater. The higher the EF is, the more energy efficient the water heater is.

Even though electric water heaters have a higher EF than gas types, electric resistance is a very expensive way to generate heat. In addition, generating plants are often sources of pollution.

Water heaters will lose less heat if they are located in a relatively warm area. Putting a water heater in an unheated basement should be avoided. By locating the water heater centrally, an interior designer can reduce heat loss in long piping runs to kitchens and bathrooms.

Existing water heaters can be upgraded for improved efficiency. Installing heat traps on both hot and cold water lines is inexpensive and will save money by preventing heat loss. The cold water pipe should be insulated between the tank and the heat trap. If heat traps are not installed, both hot and cold pipes should be insulated for several feet near the water heater.

Spas and hot tubs must be kept tightly covered and insulated around the bottom and sides. Most waterbeds are heated with electric coils underneath the bed and use a very high amount of energy. Keeping a comforter on top, insulating the sides, and putting the heater on a timer will help conserve energy.

Hot Water Distribution

Hot water is carried through a building by pipes arranged in distribution trees. When hot water flows through a single hot water distribution tree, it will cool off as it gets farther from the hot water heater. To get hot water at the end of the run, the cooled-off water already in the pipes must be wasted. With a looped hot water distribution tree, the water circulates constantly. There is still some heat loss in the pipes, but less water has to be run at the

After the decision to go solar is made, the next step is to make the existing water heater as efficient as possible. A careful analysis of the building site will determine if there is adequate sun for solar collectors, which will need to face within 40 degrees of true south. Trees, buildings, and other obstructions should not shade the collectors between 9 AM and 3 PM.

Solar energy can heat outdoor swimming pools during the months with most sun. Solar pool heating extends the swimming season by several weeks and pays for itself within two years. The pool's existing filtration system pumps water through solar collectors, where the water is heated and pumped back to the pool.

TABLE 6-10. DEPARTMENT OF ENERGY WATER-HEATER STANDARDS

Water-Heater Category	Minimum Energy Factor	Effective Date	Comment
High performance gas storage	0.62	January 1, 2009	Uses natural gas
	0.67	September 1, 2010	
Whole home gas tankless	0.82	January 1, 2009	Uses natural gas
Advanced drop-in or integrated heat pump	2.0	January 1, 2009	Used with storage tank, gas, electric
Solar	Depends on storage tank	January 1, 2009	Minimum solar function of 0.50, Og-300 certification by third party Solar Rating and Certification Corporation (SRCC)
Gas condensing	0.80	January 1, 2009	Uses natural gas

fixture before it gets hot. Hot water is always available at each tap in one to two seconds.

Hot water is circulated by use of the **thermosiphon** principle. Water expands and becomes lighter as it is heated. The warmed water rises to where it is used, then cools and drops back down to the water heater, leaving no cold water standing in pipes. Thermosiphon circulation works better the higher a system goes.

Forced circulation is used in long buildings that are too low for thermosiphon circulation and where friction from long pipe runs slows down the flow. The water heater and a pump are turned on as needed to keep water at the desired temperature. It takes five to ten seconds for water to reach full temperature at the fixture. Forced circulation is common in large one-story residential, school, and factory buildings.

Computer controls can save energy in hotels, motels, apartment buildings, and large commercial buildings. The computer provides the hottest water temperatures at the busiest hours. When usage decreases, the supply temperature is lowered and more hot water is mixed with less cold water at showers, lavatories, and sinks. Distributing cooler water to the fixture results in less heat loss along the pipes. The computer stores and adjusts a memory of the building's typical daily-use patterns.

Expansion bends are installed in long piping runs to accommodate expansion of the pipes caused by heat. Where the pipes branch out to a fixture, capped lengths of vertical pipe about 0.6 meters (2 ft.) long provide expansion chambers to lessen the shock of hot water expansion. Rechargeable air chambers on branch lines that are adjacent to groups of fixtures are designed to deal with the shock of water expansion. They require service access to be refilled with air.

Having looked at how water is supplied and distributed in buildings, we will turn our attention to what happens after the water is used. Chapter 7: Water, Waste, and Reuse Systems addresses waste plumbing, wastewater reuse, and solid-waste recycling.

7

....

Water Waste and Reuse Systems

Each building has a sanitary plumbing system that channels all of the waste downward through the building to the municipal sewer or a septic tank below. The sanitary system begins at the sink, bathtub, toilet, and shower drains.

The sanitary system has large pipes to prevent clogs. Since the system is drained by gravity, all of the pipes must run downhill. The large size of waste pipes, their need to run at a downward angle, and the expense and difficulty of tying new plumbing fixtures into existing waste systems means that the interior designer must be careful when locating toilets.

Until the advent of indoor plumbing, wastes were removed from a building daily for recycling or disposal. Historically, table scraps were fed to animals or composted. Human wastes were thrown from windows into street gutters or deposited in holes beneath outhouses. Urban inhabitants continued to dump sewage and garbage in gutters until the 1890s. People who lived in rural areas dumped wastes into lakes, rivers, or man-made holes in the ground called cesspools, which were fed by rainwater or spring water. These cesspools generated foul smells and created a health hazard.

In the 1700s, shallow wells, springs, or streams provided potable water for farms. Widely separated dry-pit privies (outhouses) produced only limited ground pollution. By the nineteenth century, natural streams were enclosed in pipes under paved city streets. Rain ran into storm sewers, then to waterways. When flush toilets were connected to storm sewers later in the nineteenth century, the combined storm water and sanitary drainage was channeled to fast-flowing rivers, which kept pollution levels down. Some sewers continued to carry storm water only, and separate sanitary sewers were eventually installed that fed into sewage treatment plants. Older cities still may have a complex network of storm sewers, sanitary sewers, and combined sewers that would be difficult and expensive to sort out and reroute.

WASTE-PIPING NETWORKS

With the advent of readily available supplies of water inside houses, water began to be used to flush wastes down the drain. Water pipes from sinks, **lavatories** (for washing hands), tubs, showers, **water closets** (toilets), urinals, and floor drains form a network drained by gravity. In order to preserve the gravity flow, large waste pipes must run downhill and normal atmospheric pressure must be maintained throughout the system at all times. Cleanouts are located to facilitate removal of solid wastes from clogged pipes.

Engineers size waste-plumbing lines according to their location in the system and the total number and types of fixtures they serve. Waste piping is laid out as directly and as straight as possible to prevent deposit of solids and clogging. Bends are minimized in number and angled gently, without right angles. Horizontal drains should have a 1:100 slope (⅛ in. per foot) for pipes up to 76 millimeters (3 in.) in diameter, and a 1:50 slope (¼ in. per foot) for pipes larger than 76 millimeters.

These large drainpipes can gradually slope from a floor through the ceiling below and become a problem for an interior designer.

Cleanouts are distributed throughout the sanitary system between fixtures and the outside sewer connection. Cleanouts are located a maximum of 15 meters (50 ft.) apart in branch lines and building drains up to 10 centimeters (4 in.) wide. On larger lines, cleanouts are located a maximum of 30.5 meters (100 ft.) apart. Cleanouts are also required at the base of each stack, at

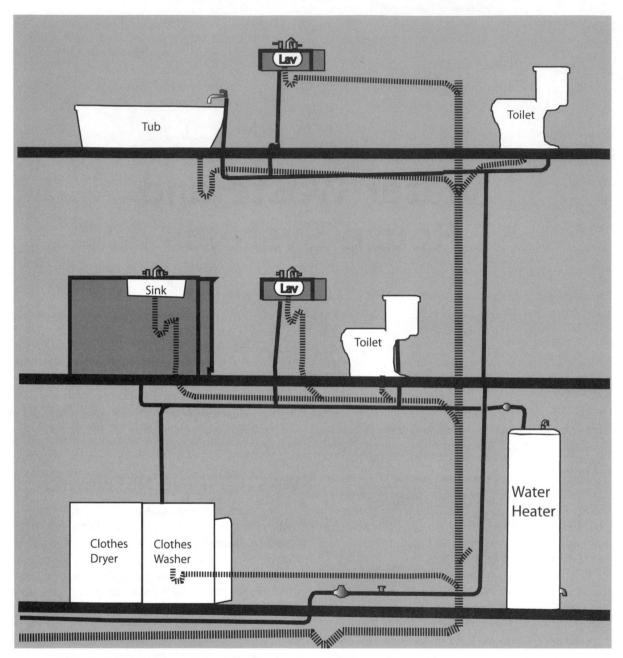

Figure 7-1 Waste and vent piping networks. A sanitary plumbing system carries wastewater downhill, joining pipes from other drains until it connects with the sewer buried beneath a building. Underground pipes for sewage disposal are made out of vitrified clay tile, cast iron, copper, concrete pipe, or polyvinyl chloride (PVC) or acrylonitrile-butadiene-styrene (ABS) plastic.

every change of direction greater than 45 degrees, and at the point where the building drain leaves the building.

Wherever a cleanout is located, there must be access for maintenance and room to work, which may create problems for an interior designer.

Fixture drains extend from the trap of a plumbing fixture to the junction with the waste or soil stack. **Branch drains** connect one or more fixtures to **soil stacks** or waste stacks. A soil stack is a waste pipe that runs from toilets and urinals to the building

drain or building sewer. A **waste stack** is a waste pipe that carries wastes from plumbing fixtures other than toilets and urinals.

It is important to admit fresh air into the waste plumbing system, to keep the atmospheric pressure normal, and to avoid vacuums that could suck wastes back up into fixtures. A fresh-air inlet connects to the building drain and allows fresh air into the building's drainage system. The building sewer connects the building drain to the public sewer or to a private treatment facility, such as a septic tank.

Figure 7-2 Cast-iron waste pipe. Cast iron is used for waste plumbing in both small and large buildings. Invented in Germany in 1562, cast iron was first used in the United States in 1813. It is durable, corrosion-resistant, and hard to cut; it was formerly joined at its hub joints using molten lead. Today, cast-iron pipes use hubless or bell-and-spigot joints and fittings or a neoprene (flexible plastic) sleeve.

Figure 7-3 Plastic waste pipe. Plastic pipes made of ABS or PVC plastic are lightweight and can be assembled in advance. This waste pipe is suspended by a pipe hanger.

Figure 7-4 Copper pipes. Copper pipes are used for water supply and may also be used for fixture vents on waste piping.

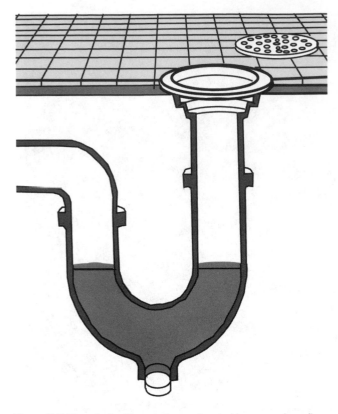

Figure 7-5 Floor drain. Floor drains are located in areas where floors need to be washed down after food preparation and cooking. These drains also allow floors to be washed or wiped up easily in shower areas, behind bars, and in other places where water may spill.

The function of **interceptors**, also known as traps, is to block undesirable materials before they get into the waste plumbing. Among the 25 types of interceptors are ones designed to catch hair, grease, plaster, lubricating oil, glass grindings, and industrial materials. Grease traps are the most common.

Sewage ejector pumps are used when fixtures are located below sewer level. Drainage from the below-grade fixture flows, via gravity, into a sump pit or other receptacle and is lifted into the sewer by the pump. Sometimes, backwater valves are used when plumbing fixtures are installed in basements as an alternative to a sewage sump and ejector.

☑ **It is best to avoid locating fixtures below sewer level when possible because if the power fails, the equipment will shut down and the sanitary drains will not work. Sewage ejector pumps should be used only as a last resort.**

Residential Waste Piping

Waste piping for a residence usually fits into a 15-centimeter (6-in.) partition. In smaller buildings, 10-centimeter (4-in.) soil stacks and building drains are common.

Fitting both the supply and the waste plumbing distribution trees into the space below the floor or between walls is difficult because larger wastes pipes must slope continually down from the fixture to the sewer. Some codes require that vertical vents that penetrate the roof must be a minimum of 10 centimeters (4 in.) to prevent blocking by ice in freezing weather. This adds another space requirement between walls.

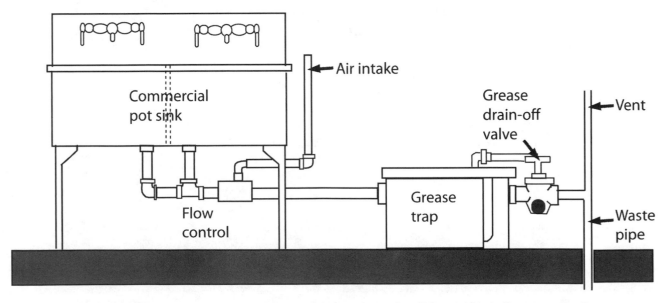

Figure 7-6 Grease trap. Grease rises to the top of a grease trap, where it is caught in baffles, preventing it from congealing in piping and slowing down the digestion of sewage. Grease traps are often required by code in restaurant kitchens.

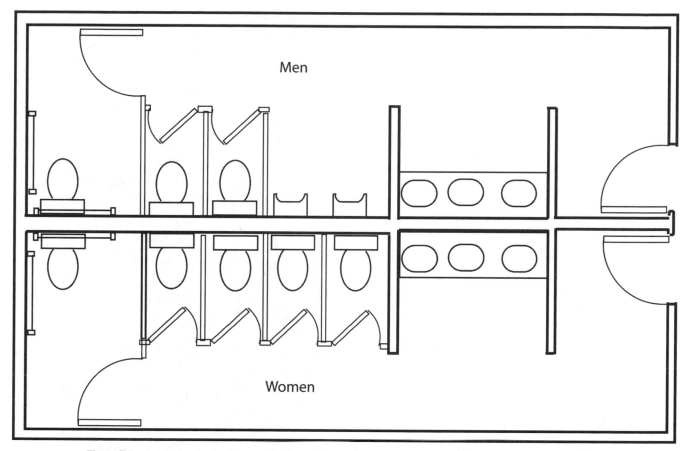

Figure 7-7 Back-to-back plumbing wall. It is common to locate bathrooms and kitchens back-to-back so that the piping assembly can pick up the drainage of fixtures on both sides of the wall. Sometimes, an extra-wide wall serves as a vertical plumbing chase, which is a place between walls for plumbing pipes.

Large Building Waste-Piping Systems

In large buildings, the need for flexibility in the use of space and the desire to avoid a random partition layout means that plumbing fixtures and pipes must be carefully planned early in the design process. The location of the building core with its elevators, stairs, and shafts for plumbing, mechanical, and electrical equipment affects the access of surrounding areas to daylight and views.

When offices call for a single lavatory or complete toilet room away from the central core (such as an executive toilet), pipes must be run horizontally from the core. In order to preserve the slope for waste piping, the farther the toilet room is located from the core, the greater the amount of vertical space taken up by the plumbing. **Wet columns** group plumbing pipes away from plumbing cores to serve sinks, private toilets, and other fixtures, and provide an alternative to long horizontal waste-piping runs.

When pipes are run vertically, a hole in the floor for each pipe is preferred over a slot or shaft, because the hole interferes less with the floor construction. In places where waste piping drops through the floor and crosses below the floor slab to join the branch soil and waste stack, it can be shielded from view by a hung ceiling. An alternative method involves laying the piping

above the structural slab and casting a lightweight concrete fill over it. This raises the floor between 127 millimeters and 152 millimeters (5–6 in.). Raising the floor in only the toilet room creates access problems, so the whole floor is usually raised. This creates space for electrical conduit and heating, ventilating, and air-conditioning (HVAC) as well.

Waste Components of Plumbing Fixtures

Originally, a pipe that carried wastewater from a plumbing fixture ran directly to the sewer. Foul-smelling gases from the **anaerobic** (without oxygen) digestion in the sewer, such as methane gas, could travel back up the pipe and create a health threat indoors.

The **trap** was invented to block the waste pipe near the fixture so that gas was not able to back up into the building. A trap is a U-shaped or S-shaped section of drainpipe that holds wastewater. The trap forms a seal to prevent the passage of sewer gas while allowing wastewater or sewage to flow through it. Traps are made of steel, cast iron, copper, plastic, or brass. On water closets and urinals, they are an integral part of the vitreous china fixture, with wall outlets for wall-hung units and floor outlets for other types.

Figure 7-8 Built-out plumbing chase. Plumbing that is adjacent to jogs in a wall can be enclosed and finished to hide its presence.

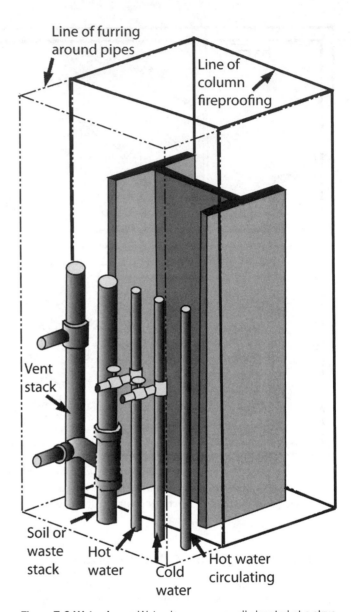

Figure 7-9 Wet column. Wet columns are usually located at a structural column, which requires coordination with the structural design early in the design process. Individual tenants can tap into these lines without having to connect to more remote plumbing at a building's core.

Drum traps are sometimes found on bathtubs in older homes. A drum trap is a cylindrical trap made from iron, brass, or lead, with a screw top or bottom. Water from the tub enters near the bottom and exits near the top, so the wastewater fills the trap and creates a water plug before flowing out. Sometimes the screw-off top, called a cleanout, is plated with chrome or brass and left exposed in the floor so that it can be opened for cleaning. Drum traps can cause drainage problems because debris settles and collects in the trap. If not cleaned out regularly, these traps eventually become completely clogged. Drum traps should be replaced during remodeling.

Each time a filled fixture trap is emptied, the wastewater scours the inside of the trap and washes away debris. Some fixtures have traps as an integral part of their design, including toilets and double kitchen sinks. There are a few exceptions to the rule that each fixture should have its own trap. Two laundry trays and a kitchen sink, or three laundry trays, may share a single trap. Three lavatories are permitted on one trap.

Traps should be within 0.61 meters (2 ft.) of a fixture and be accessible for cleaning. If a fixture is not used often, the water may evaporate and break the seal of the trap. Occasionally, this happens in unoccupied buildings and with rarely used floor drains.

VENT PIPING

The invention of the trap helped keep sewer gases out of buildings. However, traps are not foolproof. When water moving farther downstream in the system pushes along water in front of it at higher pressures, negative pressures are left behind. The higher pressures could force sewer water through the water in some traps, and lower pressures could siphon water from other traps, thereby allowing sewer gases to get through.

Every fixture must have a trap, and every trap must have a **vent**. Vent pipes are added to the waste piping a short distance downstream from each trap to prevent the pressures that would allow dirty water and sewer gases to get through the traps. Vent pipes run upward, join together, and eventually poke through the roof.

☑ **Because a roof may be several floors up and the pipes may have to pass through other tenants' spaces, adding vent pipes in new locations can be difficult.**

A vent pipe allows air to enter a waste pipe and break the siphoning action. Vent pipes also release the gases of decomposition, including methane and hydrogen sulfide, to the atmosphere. By introducing fresh air through the drain and sewer lines, air vents help reduce corrosion and slime growth.

The vent pipes connect an individual plumbing fixture to two treelike configurations of piping. The waste piping collects sewage and leads down to the sewer. The vent piping connects upward with the open air, allowing gases from the waste piping to escape and keeping the air pressure in the system even. This exerts con-

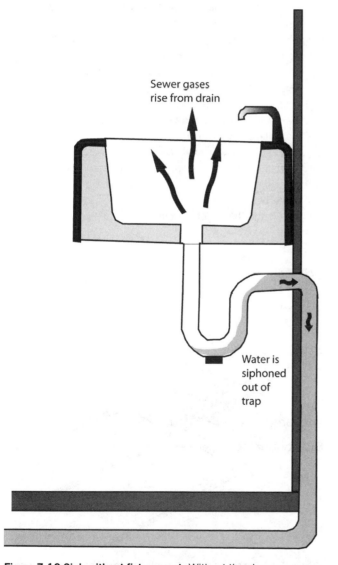

Figure 7-10 Sink without fixture vent. Without the air pressure provided by a fixture vent, water can be siphoned out of a trap. The resulting open piping can allow sewer gases to rise from the drain.

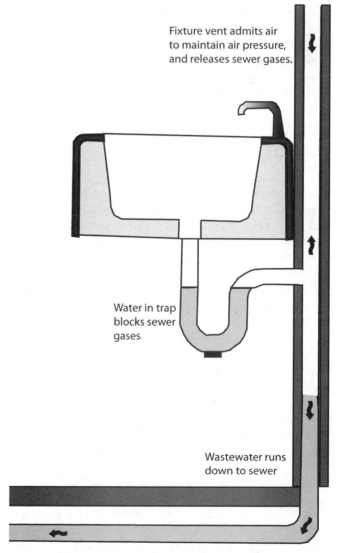

Figure 7-11 Sink with fixture vent. A fixture vent fulfills two purposes: providing air pressure to push wastewater down to the sewer and allowing sewer gases to rise up and out of the building.

tinuous pressure on foul gases so that they cannot bubble through the trap water, and gives them a local means of escape to the outdoors.

A vent must run vertically to a point above the spillover line on a sink before running horizontally so that debris will not collect in the vent if the drain clogs. Once the vent rises above the spillover line, it can run horizontally and then join with other vents to form the **vent stack**, eventually exiting through the roof.

When all of the fixtures are on nearly the same level, a separate vertical vent stack standing next to the soil stack is not required. In one-story buildings, the upper extension of the soil stack above the highest horizontal drain connected to the stack becomes a vent called the **stack vent**. It must extend 31 centimeters (12 in.) above the roof surface and should be kept away from vertical surfaces, operable skylights, and roof windows.

☑ **In some kitchen designs, a sink is located in an island, resulting in no place for the vent line to go up. An alternative is to run a waste line to a sump at another location, which is then provided with a trap and vent. A fresh-air vent, also called a fresh-air inlet, is a short air pipe connected to the main building drain just before it leaves the building, with a screen over the outside end in order to keep out debris and animals.**

TREATING AND RECYCLING WATER

In the United States, each person generates almost 75,700 liters (20,000 gallons) of sewage each year. Fruits, vegetables, grains, milk products, and meats derived from nutrients in the soil are brought into cities, to be later flushed out as sewage. Some communities discharge bacteria-laden sewage into nearby lakes, rivers, and/or the ocean. Most cities and towns send the sewage to treatment plants, where the solid matter (**sludge**) settles out. The remaining liquid is chlorinated to kill bacteria, then dumped into a local waterway.

The sludge is pumped into a treatment tank, where it ferments anaerobically for several weeks. This kills most of the disease-causing bacteria and precipitates out most minerals. The digested sludge is then chlorinated and pumped into the local waterway.

Because waterways cannot finish the natural cycle by returning the nutrients back to the soil, over time they accumulate increasing amounts of nutrients. This nutrient-rich water promotes the fast growth of waterweeds and algae. The water becomes choked with plant growth, and the sun is unable to penetrate more than a few inches below the surface. Masses of plants die and decay, consuming much of the oxygen in the water in the process. Without oxygen, fish suffocate and die. Eventually, the waterway itself begins to die. Over a few decades, it becomes a swamp, then a meadow. Meanwhile, the farmland is gradually drained of nutrients. Farm productivity falls, and produce quality declines. Artificial fertilizers are applied to replace the wasted natural fertilizers.

☑ **Designers can step into this process when they decide how wastes will be generated and handled by the buildings they design. Sewage treatment is expensive for the community and becomes a critical issue for building owners when private or on-site sewage treatment is required.**

Sewage disposal systems are designed by sanitary engineers and must be approved and inspected by the health department before use. The type and size of private sewage treatment systems depend on the number of fixtures served and the permeability of the soil as determined by a percolation test. Rural building sites are often rejected for lack of suitable sewage disposal.

Rural Sewage Treatment

In times past, rural wastes ended up in a cesspool, a porous underground container of stone or brick that allowed sewage to seep into the surrounding soil. Cesspools did not remove disease-causing organisms. Within a short time, the surrounding soil became clogged with solids, and the sewage overflowed onto the surface of the ground and backed up into fixtures inside the building.

Most cesspools have been replaced by septic systems. A typical **septic system** consists of a septic tank, a distribution box, and a leach field of perforated drainpipes buried in shallow, gravel-filled trenches. **Septic tanks** are nonporous tanks of precast concrete, steel, fiberglass, or polyethylene that hold sewage for a period of days while the sewage decomposes anaerobically.

During this time, the sewage separates into a clear, relatively harmless effluent and a small amount of mineral matter that settles to the bottom of the tank. Soaps and slow-to-degrade fats and oils float to the top of the tank to form a layer of scum. Inlet

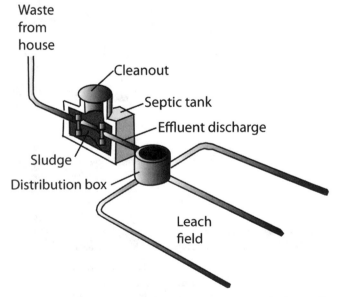

Figure 7-12 Septic system. A septic system has limited capacity and a limited lifetime. It requires regular maintenance as well as care when in use.

and outlet baffles in the tank prevent this surface scum from flowing out. The liquid moves through a submerged opening in the middle of the tank to a second chamber. Here, finer solids continue to sink, and less scum forms. This part of the process is known as **primary treatment**.

When the effluent leaves the septic tank, it is about 70 percent purified. The longer sewage stays in the tank, the less polluted the effluent is. If a building and its occupants practice water conservation, less water and waste flow through the septic tank, the effluent stays in the tank longer before being flushed out, and it emerges cleaner. Every few years, sludge is pumped out of the septic tank, hauled away, and processed until it assumes a harmless state at a remote plant. The methane gas and sewage odor remain in the tank.

Each time that sewage flows into a septic tank, an equal volume of nitrate-rich water flows out and is distributed to the leach field, which provides **secondary treatment**. There, the water is absorbed and evaporates. Nitrate-hungry microbes in the soil consume the potentially poisonous nitrates. In the process, plant food is manufactured in the form of nitrogen.

Nothing that can kill bacteria should be flushed down the drain into a septic system. Paints, varnishes, thinners, waste oil, pesticides, and photographic solutions can disrupt anaerobic digestion. Coffee grounds, dental floss, disposable diapers, cat litter, sanitary napkins, tampons, cigarette butts, condoms, gauze bandages, paper towels, fat, and grease add to the sludge layer in the bottom of the tank. Some septic systems include a grease trap in the line between the house and the septic tank, which should be cleaned out twice a year.

Trained professionals must clean septic tanks at regular intervals. As sludge and scum accumulate, there is less room for the bacteria that digest the waste, and the system becomes less effective. If scum escapes through the outlet baffle into the leach field, it clogs the earthen walls of the trenches and decreases the necessary absorption. Most tanks are cleaned every two to four years.

Most septic systems eventually fail, usually in the secondary treatment phase. If the septic tank or the soil in the leach field is not porous enough, or if the system is installed too close to a well or body of water or beside a steep slope, the system can malfunction and contaminate water or soil. Most communities have strict regulations requiring soil testing and construction and design techniques for installing septic tanks. If the site cannot support the septic tank, the building cannot be built.

Aerobic (with oxygen) **treatment units (ATUs)** can replace septic tanks in troubled systems. By rejuvenating existing drainfields, ATUs can extend a system's life. They accomplish this by bubbling air through the sewage or stirring the sewage, thereby facilitating aerobic digestion. After about one day, the effluent moves to the settling chamber where the remaining solids settle and are filtered out. Because aerobic digestion is faster than anaerobic digestion, the tank can be smaller. However, the aerobic process is energy intensive and requires more maintenance than anaerobic digestion. The effluent then moves on to the secondary treatment phase.

Secondary treatment can use a number of different techniques, with varying impact on a building site. Disposal fields are relatively inexpensive and do not require the soil to be very porous or the water table to be very deep below the surface. Drain lines of perforated pipe or agricultural tile separated by small openings are located in shallow trenches on a bed of gravel and covered with more gravel. The effluent runs out of these lines and through the gravel, until it seeps into the earth. The gravel's spaces hold the liquid until it is absorbed.

Buried sand filters that use sand, crushed glass, mineral tailings, or bottom ash are also used for secondary treatment. They are applied where the groundwater level is high, or in areas of exposed bedrock or poor soil. A large site area is required, but the ground surface can become a lawn or other non-paved surface. Buried sand filters can be a remedy for failed disposal fields.

Seepage pits are a form of secondary treatment appropriate for only very porous soil and a low water table. Seepage pits can also be used as dry wells to distribute runoff from pavement gradually.

Municipal Sewage Treatment Plants

Large-scale sewage treatment plants continue to improve the efficiency of their processes, and municipalities are actively reducing the amount of sewage they process. Large plants use aerobic digestion along with chemical treatment and filtration and can produce effluent that is suitable for drinking. Clean effluent is pumped into the ground to replenish depleted groundwater. Digested sludge is dried, bagged, and sold for fertilizer. Some plants spray processed sewage directly on forests or cropland for irrigation or fertilizer.

On-Site Large-Scale Treatment Systems

For many years, sending sewage to distant treatment plants was common practice. Today, it is becoming more common for groups of buildings to treat their wastes on-site. Advantages of this system include savings for the community, reusable treated water for landscaping and other purposes, and pleasant and attractive outdoor or indoor environments. In some campus-type industrial, educational, or military facilities, septic tanks are installed at each building, and the outflow is combined for the secondary treatment process. Use of sand filters for secondary treatment offers simple maintenance, very low energy use, and greater available usable land area.

CONSTRUCTED WETLANDS

Through the construction of an environment that filters and purifies used water and recycles it for additional use, municipal sewage-treatment costs can be reduced and local plant and animal life can be supported. Free-surface (open) wetlands use effluents to nourish vegetation growing in soil. Human contact with these secondary treatment areas must be controlled.

Subsurface-flow wetlands consist of a lined basin with large gravel or crushed rock and a layer of soil with plants above. Plants

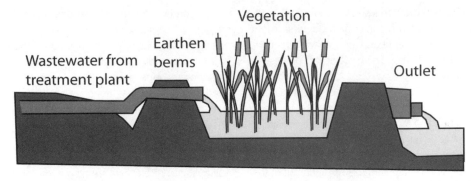

Figure 7-13 Greenhouse ecosystem. A greenhouse ecosystem is quite complex, but the resulting facility is a pleasant interior space that processes wastes in an ecologically friendly way.

encourage the growth of both anaerobic and aerobic microorganisms and bring air underwater through their roots. Then the effluent is filtered through sand and disinfected. At this point, the effluent is safe to use for many purposes, including landscape watering. This secondary-treatment option is also safer for human contact and attracts birds.

GREENHOUSE ECOSYSTEMS

Greenhouse ecosystems are secondary sewage-treatment systems that are constructed wetlands moved indoors. Marine biologist John Todd developed *Living Machines* at Ocean Arks International. They consist of a series of tanks, each with its own particular ecosystem. The first is a stream, and the second is an indoor marsh that provides a high degree of **tertiary wastewater treatment**. The system costs less to construct and about the same to maintain as a conventional sewage treatment system. A greenhouse ecosystem may use less energy, depending on solar energy for photosynthesis and on gravity flow. There is no need for a final, environmentally harmful chlorine treatment. The system produces one-fourth of the sludge of other systems.

Greenhouse environments are pleasant to look at and smell like commercial greenhouses. They are welcome in the neighborhoods they serve and can eliminate huge expenses for sewer lines that would otherwise run to distant plants. Greenhouse ecosystems offer an opportunity to enrich the experience of an interior environment while solving a serious ecological problem.

Within the greenhouse ecosystems, aerobic bacteria eat suspended organic matter and convert ammonia to nitrates, producing nitrites. Algae and duckweed eat the products of the bacteria. Snails and zooplankton then eat the algae. The floating duckweed creates shade that discourages algae growth in the later stages of production. Finally, fish eat the zooplankton and snails. The systems support water hyacinth, papyrus, canna lilies, bald cypress, willows, and eucalyptus, which remove phosphorus and heavy metals during the lives of the plants, returning them to the earth when the plants die. Small fish (shiners) are sold as bait, and dead plants and fish are composted.

☑ **On-site wastewater treatment has a significant impact on the design of a building's site. Interiors are also affected because the system may use special types of plumbing fixtures and may include indoor greenhouse filtration systems.**

Recycled Water

Water is categorized by its purity. Graywater may contain soap, hair, or human waste from dirty diapers and other laundry. It can be treated and recycled for such uses as toilet flushing and filtered drip irrigation. Dark graywater comes from washing machines with dirty-diaper loads, kitchen sinks, and dishwashers and is

TABLE 7-1. WATER GRADES IN BUILDINGS

Grade	Description	Uses
Potable Water	Water suitable for drinking; usually has been treated	Most household uses, including flushing toilets
Rainwater	Pure water distilled by hydrologic process; runoff from roofs may contain contaminants	Bathing, clothes washing, toilet flushing, irrigation, evaporative cooling
Graywater	Wastewater from sinks, baths, showers, not from toilets or urinals	Treatment required for reuse to flush toilets; filtering required for drip irrigation; usually limited to underground irrigation for single-family houses
Dark Graywater	Wastewater from kitchen sinks, dishwashers, washing diapers	Usually prohibited from reuse
Blackwater	Water containing toilet or urinal waste	Requires high level of treatment

usually prohibited by codes from being reused. Recycling gray-water that contains kitchen wastes, grease, and food solids can be a problem.

Future water conservation measures may include the use of water from bathing for flushing toilets, saving 21 gallons per person each day. The 14 gallons per person used daily for laundry can help with irrigation. Conversion kits are available that save water from lavatories and send it to the toilet tank for use in flushing.

SOLID WASTE SYSTEMS

The design of a building distribution system to bring supplies in and solid waste out requires careful planning. Mechanical equipment for solid waste systems can take up more space than is required for water and waste systems. In addition, handling of solid wastes may present fire-safety dangers and could create environmental problems.

☑ **As part of the building design team, interior designers are responsible for ensuring that the solid wastes generated during construction and building operation are handled, stored, and removed in a safe, efficient, and environmentally sound way. Whether designing an office cubicle to include a recycling basket or making sure that an old fireplace mantle is reused rather than discarded, interior designers can have a significant impact on how the building affects the larger environment.**

Nature operates in closed cycles. One organism's waste is another's food; nothing is wasted. Insects and microorganisms feed on the excrement and corpses of other animals, releasing soil nutrients for plants. Dead vegetable matter is attacked, broken down, and used again.

In agrarian societies, people, along with water, air, earthworms, and bacteria, convert animal and vegetable wastes into rich soil. Sun and rain on the soil encourage plants to grow, feeding people and animals and providing fuel for heating and cooking. Animals also provide food and clothing for people. Ashes from spent fuel and animal excrement return to replenish nutrients in soil.

Today, people discard many more materials: paper, plastics, glass, and metals; cinders, dust, dirt, and broken or worn-out machinery; kitchen garbage; old clothes; industrial by-products; and radioactive and chemical wastes from laboratories and industries. All of this averages out to about 45 kilograms (100 lb.) of waste per person annually in the United States. Some of these materials, such as food scraps and paper, are links in the biological recycling chain. Others, such as metals and plastics, represent nonrenewable resources. Many waste substances contain useful energy, but the separation and recycling of the mingled refuse is a Herculean task.

After the agricultural use of pesticides and fertilizers, solid waste is the next most serious source of land and soil pollution. Most cities either burn waste and bury the ashes or bury the refuse itself in landfills. The organic components decompose but glass, metals, and plastic remain.

Construction Waste

To conserve resources and prevent waste, it is best to reduce, then to reuse, and to recycle last of all. This general principle applies to the construction and operation of a building.

☑ **Interior designers can work with contractors to ensure that the materials removed during renovation and the waste generated by construction has a second life, possibly by including recycling requirements in demolition specifications. Interior designers can prolong the life of interior spaces by designing flexible spaces that accommodate change.**

Design for building recycling can include:

- An easily separated structure that facilitates remodeling and reuse of structural elements
- A building designed with extra space to accommodate expansion without rebuilding
- Less complex mechanical and electrical equipment that maximizes the use of sun and wind
- Distinct use of materials and building components to make recycling easy

In 1996, construction and demolition (C&D) debris added up to 136 million tons of waste in the United States. Current waste-reduction and recycling incentives are attempting to reduce this. Techniques for reducing C&D waste include the following:

- Use less material; for example, space wood-framing studs 24 inches rather than 16 inches apart.
- Know what is thrown out. Usable material can end up in a dumpster. A fenced debris pile is easier to monitor.
- Require subcontractors to purchase their own materials rather than to use those purchased by the general contractor; the subcontractors will waste less of materials they have purchased themselves.
- Reuse scrap materials in other ways; for example, large pieces of foam insulation can be laid below concrete floors.
- Donate doors and cabinets with dents or scratches to nonprofit organizations that build affordable homes.
- Neatly store extra sheet flooring, paint, and other materials for the building owner's later use.
- Use brick and concrete waste under paved walks and driveways.

Manufacturers currently sponsor programs that take back used carpet, which is ground up for attic insulation or recycled into new carpet. Plate glass becomes fiberglass insulation. Acoustic tiles can be recycled into new acoustic tiles.

Demolition by hand salvage produces useful building components and even some architectural gems. Architectural salvage warehouses are a goldmine for interior designers. When checking out a building for a renovation project, consider which elements can be reused in your design or salvaged for another project.

TABLE 7-2. CONSTRUCTION AND DEMOLITION (C&D) WASTE

Material	C&D Debris, %	Recycling or Reuse
Concrete and mixed rubble	40–50	About half is recycled as aggregate or subbase; some is used in new concrete
Wood	20–30	Ground up for mulch, composting, animal bedding, landfill cover, industrial fuel
Asphalt roofing	1–10	Asphalt paving and patching, new roofing, fuel
Drywall (gypsum wallboard)	5–15	Drywall is 85%–90% gypsum and 7%–15% paper; some manufacturing plants use recycled gypsum for up to 85% of new product; some is used in agriculture; scraps can be reused but process is labor-intensive
Metals	1–5	Recycled into new metal products
Bricks	1–5	Reused in renovation and new construction
Plastics	1–5	Crushed or melted into new product
Salvaged building components	1–5	Doors, windows, plumbing fixtures can be reused on other projects
Cardboard	1–4	Reduce packaging; recycle into new packaging
Carpet and carpet pad	1–2	Recycled into new carpet and pad

TABLE 7-3. DEMOLITION BY HAND SALVAGE

Material	Examples
Stone	Granite, marble, brownstone, bluestone, fieldstone, cast stone. Steps, capitals, lintels, sculptures, mantels, pavers
Metal: Cast iron, brass, bronze, copper	Radiators, clawfoot tubs, sinks, fireplace andirons and fenders, hardware, lighting fixtures, mailboxes, floor registers, window grilles
Bricks	Antique brick, used brick, pavers, flooring, veneer made from old bricks
Wood	Posts, columns, doors, windows, flooring, mantels, stair parts, millwork, cabinetry, cupboards
Ceramics, glass	Mirrors, stained glass, wall and floor tile, terracotta architectural details, art mosaics

Planning for Recycling

The design of a building includes tracking the flow of supplies in and of refuse out. Solid wastes can take up more space than waterborne waste systems. The accumulation of solid wastes in a building can pose fire-safety issues, and their removal may present severe local environmental problems. The separation of solid waste to permit resource recovery has significant energy and environmental consequences. Today, it is common to install mechanical equipment for handling solid waste in buildings.

Paper and some plastics can be collected and stored within a building. Glass bottles can be returned for reuse or recycling. If recyclable materials are kept separate at the site of their use, resource recovery is much easier. Glass bottles should preferably be washed for reuse, not broken and recycled.

Recycled paperboard (cardboard or pasteboard) saves 50 percent of the energy required to process pulp from wood. Recycled aluminum saves an astounding 96 percent of the electrical energy required for its original production. A 52 percent energy savings is achieved by recycling steel.

Recycling plastic uses significant amounts of energy. Thermoplastics can be melted and reformed into new products. Thermoset plastics, on the other hand, do not melt and must be ground up and combined with other materials. Recycled plastic pellets are used in building materials, toys, and sports products. Recycled plastic bottles are used in fabrics and some carpets. Because of consumer regulations and preferences, recycled plastic is not often used in food-related items.

Wood scrap chopped into wood fiber is worth more than when it is burned as a fuel. **Oriented strand board (OSB)**, made of wood chips and scraps, is used in the manufacture of **structural insulated panels (SIPs)**, window frames, and other building products.

Some materials that are impractical to recycle can be burned for fuel. These are referred to as low-grade resources and include gaseous wastes, liquid and semiliquid wastes, and solid wastes. Some industrial wastes give off a lot of heat when burned but some are very toxic. Some cities use the heat generated by burning rubbish to fuel electric power plants and/or central-heating installations. Trash burning is limited by environmental regulations. Burning vinyl wallcoverings poses serious environmental problems.

When composted in landfills, some of these materials produce methane gas, which can be collected for use as a high-grade fuel. Cities extract methane gas from old garbage dumps by drilling wells that tap underground pockets of decomposition gas. The quantities of gas produced by livestock farming or sewage treatment plants are sufficient to justify building gas-generating equipment. Many municipal water treatment plants are heated, illuminated, and powered by methane gas from the plants' digesters.

Incineration reduces the volume of materials that are sent to landfills. Incinerator plants are fed by dumping wastes down a chute, where they are then consumed by a gas- or oil-fueled fire at the bottom. The resulting toxic ashes are carried out of the building. Incinerators can create air pollution and are rarely installed in buildings because of the strict regulations.

☑ **Sorting and storing recyclable materials within a building requires more time and effort by its occupants. In an urban apartment, space and odor issues can make recycling difficult. Containers for different recyclables take up floor or cabinet space. A good community recycling program with curbside pickup helps minimize accumulation and organizes the process. Some recycling programs are set up to automatically recycle valuables in trash via mechanized sorting.**

Solid Waste Collection in Small Buildings

Trash compactors take up space in kitchens and may pose odor and noise problems. Some trash compactors have a forced-air-activated charcoal filter to help control odors as well as sound insulation to control noise. Solar-powered trash compactors are used outdoors to reduce trash pickup traffic.

In-sink garbage disposals use about 2 gallons of water per minute and create organic sludge that places an additional burden on the septic tank or sewage system. Most of the materials that are put down garbage disposals could be composted instead, providing a source of nutritious soil for other growing things.

Composting is a controlled process of decomposition of organic material. Naturally occurring soil organisms recycle nitrogen, potash, phosphorus, and other plant nutrients as they break down the material into humus. This is a dark brown, powdery material that is produced when decomposition is complete. The rich earthy aroma of humus indicates that the finished compost is full of nutrients essential for the healthy growth of plants and crops. Composting occurs as long as there is air and water to support it.

Large Building Solid Waste Collection

Large apartment complexes fence in their garbage can areas to keep out dogs and other pests. This contained area is a good place for recycling bins and even a compost pile for landscaping. The solid waste storage area requires sanitation truck access and noise control and should be located with concern for wind direction in order to control odors.

In a large building, both the building's occupants and its custodial staff must cooperate for successful recycling. Office building operations generate large quantities of recyclable white paper, newspaper, and box cardboard, along with nonrecyclable but

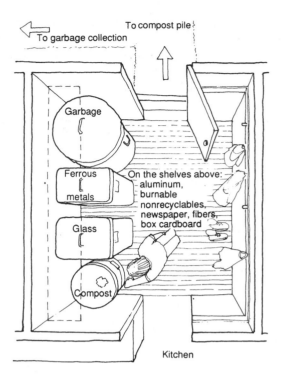

Figure 7-14 Residential solid waste storage. Most of the waste in a home comes from the kitchen. Finding recycling space in a pantry, air-lock entry, or cabinet or closet that opens to the outside makes daily contributions easier, facilitates weekly removal, and simplifies cleaning.

burnable trash that may include floor sweepings. Offices also produce food scraps including coffee grounds, and metals and glass from food containers. Dumping all of this into one collection bin saves space, but because of the related high landfill use costs, separation and recycling spaces are becoming more common.

The collection process for recycling in larger buildings has three stages. First, white paper, recyclables, compostables, and garbage are deposited in separate compartments near employees' desks. To make an office building's recycling system work, an interior designer must often design a whole series of multiple bins and the trails that connect them. Office-systems manufacturers are beginning to address some of these issues. The process often needs to be coordinated with the sources of the materials, such as paper suppliers, and with the recycling contractors who pick them up.

Next, custodians dump the separate bins in a collection cart. There are also bins for white paper in the computer and copy rooms and for compostables and garbage in the employee lunchroom. Floor sweepings are added to the garbage. Custodians take the full cart to a service closet at the building's core and deposit each type of separated waste in a larger bin. The storage closet also has a service sink to wash the garbage bins and may have a paper shredder.

Finally, white paper is shredded and stored for collection by recycling and sanitation trucks at the ground-floor service entrance, near the freight elevator. Compostables are either stored or sent to a roof-garden compost pile. Garbage is compacted and bagged. Compactors reduce wastes to as little as one-tenth of their original volume. The storage area should be supplied with cool, dry, fresh air. Compactors and shredders are noisy and generate heat and must be vibration-isolated from the floor. A sprinkler fire-protection system may be required, and a disinfecting spray may be necessary. Access to a floor drain and water for washing is recommended.

In some buildings, wastes are ground up and transported by a system of very large vacuum pipes, which suck the wastes to a central location for incineration or compression into bales. Garbage grinders flush scraps into sewers, adding to sewage-system loads.

Interior designers who understand water supply and conservation, wastewater treatment options, and solid waste recycling are well prepared to design environmentally friendly interiors. In Chapter 8: Toilet and Bath Design, we will put this knowledge to work in the design of public toilet rooms and residential bathrooms.

8

....

Toilet and Bath Design

Interior designers are often involved in the selection and specification of plumbing fixtures. The discussion of this topic will start with a brief look at the history of plumbing fixtures.

PLUMBING HISTORY

Indoor bathrooms were not common in homes until around 1875, but they date back thousands of years. Archeologists in Scotland's Orkney Islands discovered a latrine-like plumbing system dating to 8000 BCE that carried wastes from stone huts to streams in a series of crude drains.

Hygiene has been a religious imperative for Hindus since 3000 BCE, when many homes in India had private bathroom facilities. In the Indus Valley of Pakistan, archeologists found ancient private and public baths fitted with terracotta pipes encased in brickwork, with taps controlling water flow.

The most sophisticated early baths belonged to Minoan royal families. In the palace at Knossos on Crete, bathtubs were filled and emptied by vertical stone pipes cemented at their joints. Eventually, these pipes were replaced by pottery pipes slotted together much like modern pipes. The pottery pipes provided both hot and cold water and removed drainage waste from the royal palace. The Minoans also had the first flush toilet, a latrine with an overhead reservoir fed by trapping rainwater or by filling buckets from a cistern.

From medieval times on, wastes from chamber pots legally were supposed to be collected early in the morning by night soil men, who carted them to large public cesspools. However, many people avoided the expense of this service by throwing waste into the streets. Many cartoons of the period show the dangers of walking under second-story windows late at night.

Gentlemen let women keep to the inside of sidewalks to avoid the foul gutters.

By the 1600s, plumbing technology reappeared in parts of Europe, but indoor bathrooms did not. The initial seventeenth-century construction of Versailles included a system of cascading and gushing outdoor water fountains, but it did not include plumbing for toilets and bathrooms for the French royal family, 1000 nobles, and 4000 attendants who lived at the palace.

In the 1700s, urbanization and industrialization in Britain resulted in overcrowding and squalor in cities. There was no home or public sanitation, and picturesque villages turned into disease-plagued slums. Cholera decimated London in the 1830s, and officials began a campaign for sanitation in homes, workplaces, public streets, and parks. Throughout the rest of the nineteenth century, British engineers led the western world in public and private plumbing innovations.

In 1596, Queen Elizabeth I had a toilet installed by Sir John Harrington, who came from Bath, giving us two euphemisms still in use today. A high water tower was located on top of the main unit, with a hand-operated tap for water flow to the tank, and a valve that released sewage to a nearby cesspool. Harrington's toilet was connected directly to the cesspool, with only a loose trapdoor in between. The queen complained about cesspool fumes in this toilet without a trap. The new toilet fell into disuse because Harrington wrote an earthy, humorous book about it, which angered the queen.

British watchmaker and mathematician Alexander Cumming put a backward curve into the soil pipe directly underneath the toilet bowl, which retained water and cut off the smell from below. Cumming's patent application for a "stink trap" introduced the trap that has been used on all subsequent designs.

Figure 8-1 Victorian commodes. Before the installation of indoor toilets, the options included outhouses (cold in winter, odiferous in summer) and chamber pots (indiscreet). These Victorian commodes hide their function under lids.

What most people call a toilet is technically called a **water closet**. Toilets are not usually designed to facilitate proper washing during elimination. A toilet seat that provides a cleansing spray is available from several U.S. manufacturers for use on existing toilets. **Bidets**, which are popular in Europe but less often seen in the United States, are designed for personal cleansing. Toilets are available without a separate toilet seat, with a warmer for the seat, and with warm water within the toilet for washing. Combination toilet/bidet fixtures are available with water-conserving features.

Water closets, urinals, and bidets are made of vitreous china. Toilet bowls could never be leakproof and free of contamination until all of the metal and moving parts were eliminated. In 1885, Thomas Twyford, an English potter, succeeded in building the first one-piece earthenware toilet that stood on its own pedestal base. Porcelain toilets do not accumulate bacteria-harboring scratches when cleaned. His toilet design is essentially the same as the one used in the modern bathroom.

Water closets and urinals cannot be designed to have the type of air gaps found in lavatories. For example, water closets and urinals in public buildings have a supply pipe connected directly to the rim. Consequently, it is a legal requirement in most areas that at each fixture where a connection between the supply and waste plumbing is possible, a **vacuum breaker** must be installed on the supply line. When the pressure fails, air is allowed to enter the line, destroying the siphon action and preventing contaminated water from being sucked into the system. The chrome-plated flush valve on every public-toilet fixture contains a vacuum breaker. Vacuum breakers are also manufactured for outdoor faucets, where the end of a hose may be left in a swimming pool or garbage pail filled with water.

Most codes require that all water closets designated for public use have elongated bowls and seats with open fronts. Specific clearances are required on each side and in front of the bowl. Automatic flushing controls increase the accessibility of toilets and help keep them clean. The controls work by radiant heat from body pressure or by reflecting a light off the user and back to the control. Toilets designed for handicapped accessibility are usually wall-hung and have elongated fronts.

☑ **The ADA does not apply to private residences, but many designers incorporate the principles of universal design to accommodate clients' present or future needs. The Fair Housing Act (FHA) applies to multiple-unit housing built with government funds and may require partial or full accessibility or provisions for the easy conversion of some units. Structural reinforcement for future grab bars and wall-mounted water closets may be required—and is a good idea in any event.**

TOILETS

The modern toilet emerged in the 1940s with a tank that holds approximately 19 liters (5 gallons) of water and mounted on the back of the bowl. When the handle on the toilet is tripped, a flapper valve opens in the bottom of the tank to release the water to both flush waste away and rinse the bowl clean. A portion of the water flows out around the top rim, swirling to wash down the sides of the bowl. Most of the water flows rapidly through a hole near the bowl bottom and propels waste through the drain trap.

Because the volume of water needed to do a thorough job determines the size of the tank, some tanks are bigger than others, depending on the bowl design. Once a tank empties, the flapper valve falls closed, and the tank and bowl refill from the household water supply.

Water closets have large traps that are forced to siphon rapidly during the flushing process and are refilled with fresh water

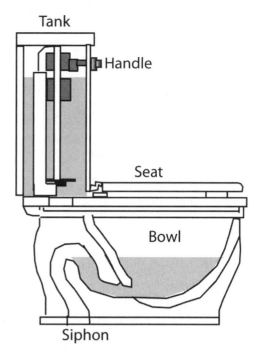

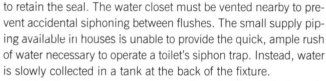

Figure 8-2 Toilet bowl. A toilet bowl is designed to clean itself with each flush. A portion of the water flows out around the top rim, swirling to wash the sides of the bowl.

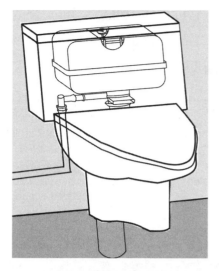

Figure 8-3 Pressure-assist flushing system. Pressure-assist toilets can be installed in the same amount of space as conventional toilets and require 138 kPa (20 pounds per square inch) of water pressure, which is typical in residential housing. Pressure-assist toilets are used in homes, hotels, dormitories, and light commercial applications and are available in handicapped-accessible models. More and more states are mandating the use of pressure technology in commercial structures, to prevent blockages and limit leaks.

to retain the seal. The water closet must be vented nearby to prevent accidental siphoning between flushes. The small supply piping available in houses is unable to provide the quick, ample rush of water necessary to operate a toilet's siphon trap. Instead, water is slowly collected in a tank at the back of the fixture.

A toilet may have a round or an elongated bowl; the latter is more comfortable for most people but takes up more space. Round bowls extend 28 inches from the wall, while elongated bowls may extend as much as 31 inches. Most toilets bolt to the floor 12 inches from the back wall, although some models have 10-inch or 14-inch dimensions; it is important that the plumber know the model of toilet selected.

The height of a conventional toilet seat is a compromise. A lower toilet seat is healthier for the average person as it approximates a squatting position and is easier for children to use, but it is more difficult for an average standing man to use. Higher toilets provide more support for tall and elderly people as well as for people with some disabilities.

Toilets are often used as chairs in the bathroom, and low ones are not at comfortable chair height. The standard 14-inch-high toilet seat falls somewhere between the lower and higher limits. Toilet manufacturers offer toilets with seats at the same height as a standard chair seat, which is marketed as comfortable for people of all ages and statures. The recommended height for a toilet that is accessible for people with disabilities is 457 millimeters (18 in.). Toilets are available at this height; alternately, an existing toilet can be retrofitted with special thick seats or a spacer

ring placed between the toilet rim and a standard seat. In addition, a grab bar next to the toilet will help users sit down and get up. Urinals for use by men in wheelchairs are either wall-mounted at lower heights or floor-mounted.

Most residential toilets are either one-piece, with a combined tank and bowl, or two-piece, with the tank bolted to the top of the toilet bowl. Two-piece toilets are generally less expensive than one-piece toilets, as well as easier to carry upstairs. Without a seam, one-piece toilets are easier to clean. Wall-mounted residential toilets are even easier to clean, but they are more expensive to install than their floor-mounted counterparts.

In the United States today, residential toilets are usually either gravity-flush toilets, which use the weight of water to create flushing pressure, or pressure-assisted toilets. The latter are somewhat more expensive and may make more noise, but do the job exceptionally well. Water is compressed in a vessel inside the tank and forced into the bowl quickly, for a clean flush with fewer clogs.

In public buildings with frequent flushing of toilets, slow-filling tanks could not keep up with the demand. Consequently, commercial toilet installations use larger supply pipes with special valves to regulate the strength and duration of each flush.

In addition to the flush toilet, many other types of toilets are used throughout the world (Table 8-1). An alternative type of toilet made by Incinolet consists of a toilet or urinal with no plumbing connections that reduces waste to a small volume of ash. This type of toilet requires connection to electrical power and a 10-centimeter (4-in.) diameter vent to the outside.

TABLE 8-1. TYPES OF TOILETS

Toilet Type	Description
Squat toilet	Various types; essentially hole in ground; pedestal squat toilet is same height as standard flush toilet
Chemical toilet	Uses chemicals to deodorize waste; used as portable toilets and on airplanes, trains, buses, and in motor homes; disinfects by mixing formaldehyde or less environmentally objectionable proprietary chemicals with toilet water
Double-vault dry toilet (Ecosan or urine-diverting, dry-composting toilet)	Toilet has two vaults, one in use and one inactive; urine is channeled by hose to storage and can be used for fertilizer later; excrement falls in other chamber and is covered by lime, ash, or soil; sanitary use depends on lack of humidity, alkaline environment, and lengthy storage period to produce organic soil conditioner
Composting toilet	Converts human waste into organic compost and usable soil by aerobic bacteria and fungi; solar-powered fan continually draws air into chamber and vents through roof

Figure 8-4 Composting toilet. Composting toilets use no water and keep wastes out of the wastewater system. Properly ventilated, a composting toilet is not unpleasant to use.

Figure 8-5 Wall-hung urinal. A standard wall-hung urinal may not meet accessibility mounting-height requirements.

URINALS

Urinals reduce contamination from water-closet seats and require only 46 centimeters (18 in.) of width along the wall. Urinals are not required by code in every type of occupancy. Typically, urinals are substituted for one or more of the required water closets. Many bars and restaurants install urinals along with the number of required toilets in order to accommodate large crowds. A wall-hung urinal stays cleaner than the stall type, but it tends to be too high for young boys and for men in wheelchairs. Where provided, the Americans with Disabilities Act Accessibility Guidelines (ADAAG) require that a minimum of one urinal comply with access requirements: a stall-type urinal or a wall-hung fixture with an elongated rim at a specified maximum height above the floor; grab bars are also now required. Clear space in front of the urinal must be provided to facilitate a front approach.

Although uncommon, urinals can be built into residential walls for pullout use, where they might be a solution to the eternal male/female toilet-seat dilemma.

High-efficiency urinals use a pint of water per flush compared to standard urinals that use a gallon per flush. As their name implies, waterless urinals eliminate the need for water. Some waterless urinals use a floating layer of a special biodegradable and long-lasting liquid or a layer of vegetable-based oil as a barrier to sewer vapors in the trap, which still allows urine to pass. Other waterless urinals employ an elastomeric (returns to original position after use) seal that permits urine to pass, then serves as a barrier to sewer gases. These urinals are not permitted in some jurisdictions because they are considered to be mechanical seals that could break and create a health hazard; making the elastomeric seal a replaceable component may solve this problem.

DESIGNING BATHROOMS

Bathrooms may be utilitarian, or unpleasant necessities or luxurious spaces for sensual relaxation. The design of bathrooms and public restrooms involves not only the plumbing system, but also the mechanical and electrical systems. There are also special space-planning considerations in bathroom design that have an impact on the plumbing layout.

Bathing facilities have a long and varied history. By 1500 BCE, aristocratic Egyptian homes used copper pipes for hot and cold water. Whole-body bathing was part of religious ceremonies, and priests were required to immerse themselves in cold water four times a day. The Mosaic Law of the Jews (1000–930 BCE) related bodily cleanliness to moral purity, and complex public waterworks were built throughout Palestine under the rule of David and Solomon.

Bathing became a social occasion in the second century BCE in Rome, when massive public-bath complexes included gardens, shops, libraries, exercise rooms, and lounge areas for poetry readings. The Baths of Caracalla offered body oiling and scraping salons; hot, warm, and cold tubs; sweating rooms; hair shampooing, setting, and curling areas; manicure shops; and a gymnasium. Shops sold cosmetics and perfumes. Up to 2500 members at a time visited the spas and the adjacent gallery of Greek and Roman art, library, and lecture hall. In another room, slaves served food and wine to spa visitors. All of these luxurious accommodations were open to men only; women had to use a smaller spa nearby. Eventually, men and women mixed at spas, but apparently without significant promiscuous behavior, a practice that lasted well into the Christian era until the Catholic Church began to dictate state policy.

All of this luxury ended around 500 AD, when invading barbarians destroyed most of the tiled baths and terracotta aqueducts, leading to a decline in bathing and personal cleanliness during the Middle Ages. The Christian view at the time emphasized the mortification of the flesh, and whole-body bathing was linked to temptation and sin. No one bathed, but the rich used perfume to cover body odors. Outhouses, outdoor latrines and trenches, and chamber pots replaced indoor toilets. Christian prudery and medical superstitions about the evils of bathing resulted in an end to sanitation and the rise of disease and epidemics.

In the 1500s, the Reformation's emphasis on avoiding sin and temptation led people to expose as little skin as possible to soap and water. There was almost no bathroom plumbing, even in grand European palaces. A 1589 English royal-court public warning that was posted in the palace, quoted in Charles Panati's *Extraordinary Origins of Everyday Things* (p. 202), read, "Let no one, whoever he may be, before, at, or after meals, early or late, foul the staircases, corridors, or closets with urine or other filth." Apparently, this was quite a common problem. Around 1700, a French journal cited by the same source noted, "Paris is dreadful. The streets smell so bad that you cannot go out.... The multitude of people in the street produces a stench so detestable that it cannot be endured."

Plumbing-Fixture Selection and Installation

☑ **On commercial projects, the architect and mechanical engineer usually select and specify plumbing fixtures. On residential projects, the interior designer or architect helps the client make the selection. An interior designer is often a client's primary contact for the selection of fixtures and presents the client's preferences and provides specification information to the engineer. Kitchen and bath designers, who may work for businesses that sell fixtures, often help owners select residential fixtures on renovation projects.**

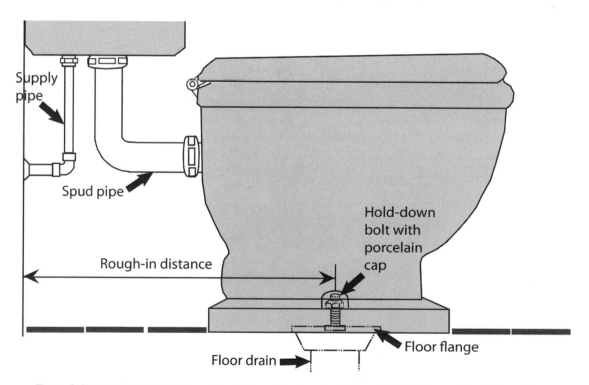

Figure 8-6 Installing a toilet. The critical dimension when installing a toilet is the rough-in distance from the wall to the center of the floor drain.

TABLE 8-2. MINIMUM NUMBER OF PLUMBING FACILITIES

Occupancy	Water Closets, Urinals: Minimum 1 per Number of People Indicated		Lavatories	Bathtubs, Showers	Drinking Fountains	Others
	Male	Female				
Assembly						
Theaters	125	65	200		1000	1 service sink
Nightclubs	40	40	75		500	
Restaurants	75	75	200			
Halls, museums	125	65	200		1000	
Coliseums, arenas	75	40	150			
Churches	150	75	200			
Stadiums, pools	100	50	150			
Business	25		40		100	
Educational	50		50			
Factory and industrial	100		100		400	
High hazard	100		100		1000	
Institutional						
Residential care	10		10	8	100	1 service sink
Hospitals, ambulatory nursing-home patients	50		1 per room	15	100	1 service sink per floor
Day nurseries, sanitariums, nonambulatory nursing-home patients	15		15	15	100	1 service sink
Employees, other than residential care	25		35		100	
Visitors, other than residential care	75		100		500	
Prisons	1 per cell		1 per cell	15		1 service sink
Asylums, reformatories, etc.	15		15	15	100	
Mercantile	500		750		1000	
Residential						
Hotels, motels	1 per guestroom		1 per guestroom	1 per guestroom		1 service sink
Lodges	10		10	8	100	
Multiple family: per dwelling units	1		1	1		1 kitchen sink. Clothes washer connection: 1 per 20
Dormitories	10		10	8		1 service sink
One- and two-family dwellings: per dwelling unit	1		1	1		1 kitchen sink, 1 clothes washer connection
Storage	100		100		1000	1 service sink

Several inspections by a local building inspector are required during the construction process to ensure that the plumbing is properly installed. Roughing-in is the process of getting all of the pipes installed, capped, and pressure-tested for leaks before the actual fixtures are installed.

☑ **At this point, an interior designer should check to ensure that the plumbing for the fixtures is in the correct location and at the correct height. The first inspection usually takes place after roughing-in the plumbing.**

A contractor must schedule an inspection promptly because plumbing work cannot continue until it passes inspection. The building inspector returns for a final inspection after the pipes are enclosed in the walls and the plumbing fixtures are installed.

☑ **The design of the building and the choice of fixtures affect the water and energy consumption over the life of a building. The designer can encourage conservation both by selecting appropriate fixtures and by increasing the user's awareness of the amount of water being used. Visible consumption measures allow a user to see how much water is being used, and to modify use patterns for better conservation. Rainwater storage tanks with visible water-level indicators outside the bathroom window show how much water is used in each flush. Slightly undersized pipes enable users to hear the water flowing. This is especially useful for outdoor taps, where water may be left on.**

LAVATORIES AND SINKS

Despite the hundreds of lavatory designs available in the interior design market, few take into account the way our bodies work and the way we wash. Lavatories are designed as collection bowls for water, but we use them for washing our hands, faces, and teeth quickly with running water. Because of spout design, we typically have to bend at the waist and splash water upward to wash our faces. Most lavatory fittings dump running water directly down the drain. They are hard to drink from and almost impossible to use for hair washing. Most handles are hand operated, as their name implies, and we have to move our hands out of the water stream to turn them on and off. The sink and adjacent counter area are often difficult to keep clean and dry.

☑ **For cleanliness and durability, lavatories must be made of hard, smooth materials that can be scrubbed, such as porcelain, stainless steel, and resin-based solid surfacing materials. Faucet designs should be washerless, drip-free, and splash-free, and made of noncorrosive materials. Models are available that have permanent lubrication, easy-to-change flow-control cartridges, and controlled compression to eliminate overtightening and wear on seals. Check for fixed faucet-handle travel as well as features that make servicing easy.**

☑ **ADA-compliant faucets come in variety of spout heights and feature single-lever, easy-to-grab models, wing handles, and 4-inch and 5-inch blade handle designs.**

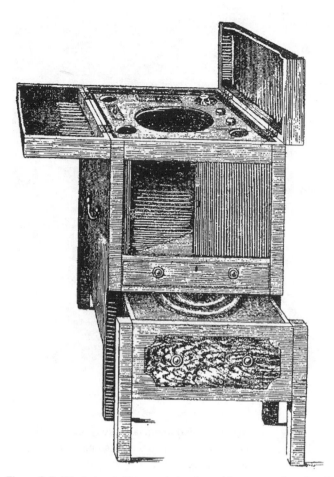

Figure 8-7 Washstand. This washstand combines space for a bowl of water for washing, covers that double as trays for accessories, and a slide-out commode.

Public restroom lavatories should have self-closing faucets that save water and water-heating energy. Faucet flow should be limited to a maximum of 1.9 liters (0.5 gal.) per minute.

Low-flow faucets that use between 1.89 liters and 9.46 liters (0.5–2.5 gal.) per minute employ aerators, flow restrictors, and mixing valves which control temperatures. These faucets function as well as or better than standard faucets that use between 15 liters and 19 liters (4–5 gal.) per minute. Low-flow aerators save up to half the amount of water used.

The term **sink** is reserved for service sinks, utility sinks, kitchen sinks, and laundry basins. Utility sinks are made of vitreous china, enameled cast iron, or enameled steel. Kitchen sinks are made of enameled cast iron, enameled steel, or stainless steel. The building code requires sinks in some locations, and local health departments may set additional requirements. Kitchen or bar sinks in break rooms and utility sinks for building maintenance are often installed even when the local code does not require them. Kitchen sinks are limited to a maximum flow of 11.4 liters (3 gal.) per minute. Foot-operated and automatic shutoff faucets free the hands, saving water at kitchen sinks.

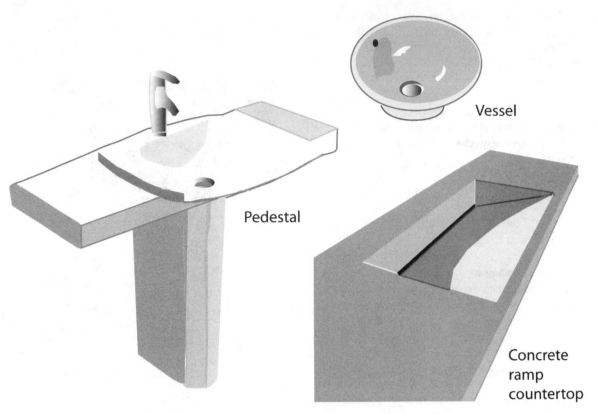

Vessel

Pedestal

Concrete
ramp
countertop

Figure 8-8 Bathroom lavatory types. Pedestal sinks are freestanding, without a cabinet below. Vessel sinks sit on top of a countertop. The image on the lower right shows a concrete countertop sink that drains along its back edge.

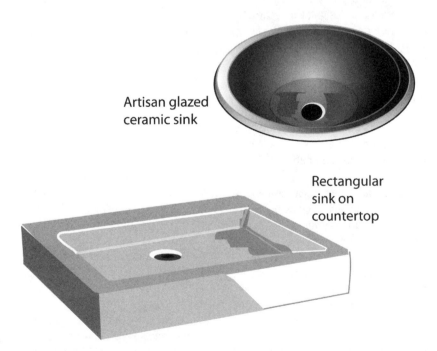

Artisan glazed
ceramic sink

Rectangular
sink on
countertop

Figure 8-9 Bathroom lavatory styles. Artisan-produced ceramic sinks can be set into a countertop and come in many beautiful and practical designs. The lower image shows a sleek, shallow rectangular sink that sits on top of a counter.

Figure 8-10 Drainboard kitchen sink. This double sink is made with its own drainboard, which contains both clutter and water efficiently.

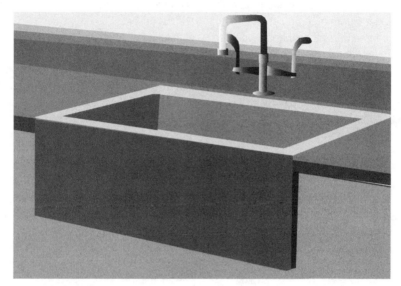

Figure 8-11 Farm-style kitchen sink. Farm-style sinks are wide and deep and have a large face set into the countertop and cabinet below. Both antique and newly manufactured farm-style sinks are available in enameled porcelain, soapstone, and copper.

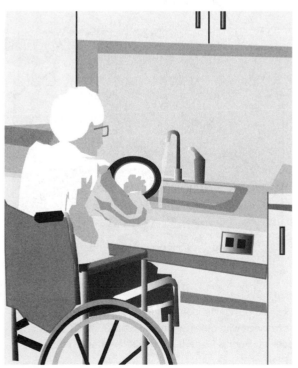

Figure 8-12 Adjustable-height kitchen sink. The idea of an adjustable-height sink that raises and lowers at the touch of a button is appealing. However, the expense is significant, and its practicality may be questionable.

The ADA sets standards for accessible kitchen sinks, including a maximum depth of 15 centimeters (6 in.). Service sinks, also called slop sinks, are located in janitors' rooms for filling buckets, cleaning mops, and other maintenance tasks. Wash fountains are communal hand-washing facilities sometimes found in industrial facilities.

Lavatories and other plumbing fixtures should have an air gap, which is a clear, vertical distance between the spout of the faucet or other outlet of the supply pipe and the flood level of the receptacle. The flood level is the level at which water would overflow the rim of the plumbing fixture. Bathroom sinks have overflow ports that drain excess water before it can reach the end of the faucet. Air gaps are required to prevent the siphoning of used or contaminated water from the plumbing fixture into a pipe supplying potable water as a result of negative pressure in a pipe. As a result, even if the water pressure fails, there is no chance of contaminated water being drawn into pipes as freshwater is drained back away from the fixture.

BATHTUBS

Modern bathing is done on a very personal scale, in private, although tubs for two are sometimes in style. Social bathing is limited to recreation, not cleansing, in swimming pools, bathhouses, and hot tubs with spouts, jets, and cascades.

While standing water is good for wetting, soaping, and scrubbing, running water is better for rinsing. We use tubs primarily for whole-body cleansing, but also for relaxing and soaking muscles. We follow a sequence of wetting our bodies, soaping ourselves, and scrubbing—all of which can be done well with standing water. Then we rinse, preferably in running water. Tubs work well in the wetting through scrubbing phases, but they leave us trying to rinse soap off while sitting in soapy, dirty water. This is particularly difficult and troublesome when washing hair.

Bathtubs come in four basic styles and are available either left- or right-handed, depending on the location of the drainhole (see Table 8.3). Air tubs have a champagne bubble-type effect, while river jets simulate the undulating motion of white-water–river flow. Underwater lights, vanity mirrors, and wall-mounted compact disc/stereo systems with remote controls are other luxurious options. Some tubs have built-in handrails and seats, while others have integrated shower and/or steam towers.

☑ **Clients may request big, two-person tubs with whirlpools, but often they do not use them as much as they think they will. Whirlpool baths are available in a great variety of shapes, including corner tubs that are 150 × 150 cm (60 × 60 in.) with built-in television monitors. A practical maximum size is 183 × 107 cm (72 × 42 in.). As people become more conscious of water use, they do not necessarily want to fill up a 1136-liter (300-gal.) tub.**

☑ **For safety's sake, all tubs should have integral braced grab bars horizontally and vertically at appropriate heights, and no unsafe towel or soap dishes that look like grab bars. Manufacturers offer very stylish grab bars that do not look institutional. Tubs should be well illuminated and have nonslip floors that can be cleaned easily.**

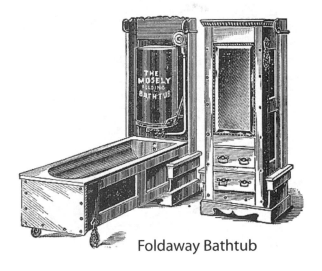

Foldaway Bathtub

Clawfoot bathtub with shower ring

Figure 8-13 **Antique bathtubs.** The Saturday-night bath was a U.S. institution well into the twentieth century. Bathing vessels were portable and sometimes were combined with other furniture. A sofa might sit over a tub or a metal tub might fold up inside a tall wooden cabinet. Homes had a bath area rather than a bathroom, and the bath and the water closet were not necessarily near each other.

TABLE 8-3. BATHTUB STYLES

Style	Description	Sizes, inches	Material	Comments
Recessed tub (three-wall alcove tub)	Unfinished on 3 wall sides; only front has decorative finish	Varied; lengths 60, 66, 72; widths 32, 42; depths 16–24	Porcelain on steel (POS); enameled cast-iron; expensive	Heavy cast-iron tubs may require floor reinforcing
Corner	Varied shape; usually triangle with 2 unfinished wall sides; finished front	Triangle 60 × 60 × 21; other sizes available	Usually acrylic or gel-coated fiberglass (FRP)	Also standard rectangle with front and end finished, two unfinished wall sides
Drop-in	Mounted on platform or sunk below floor level	Similar to recessed or corner tubs	Lightweight acrylic or FRP; cast iron needs floor support	Installed overlapping deck or undermounted
Freestanding	Most have 4 legs; some fit into frame; all surfaces finished	Varied; lengths 60–75; widths 29–44; depths 18–27	Lightweight materials; reconditioned antique cast iron; needs floor support	Reconditioned antique claw-foot tubs available
Whirlpool	Motorized circulation jets; available in all styles; usually platform-installed	Lengths 48", 60", 65". up to 75" round. Corner styles.	Lightweight materials	Some models have pump located separately for noise control, service ease

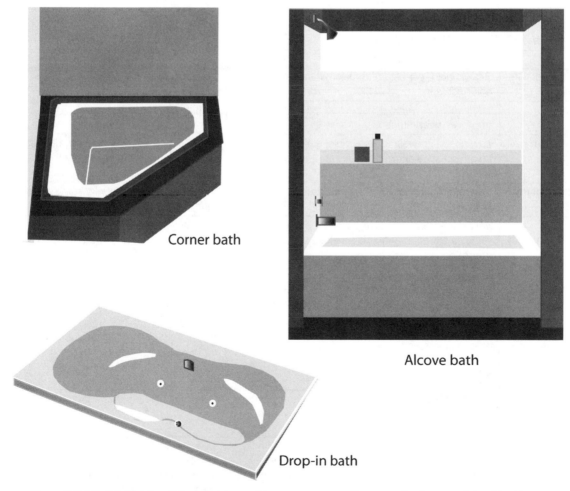

Corner bath

Alcove bath

Drop-in bath

Figure 8-14 Bathtub styles. Tub materials must be nonporous, sanitary, easy to clean, and durable. Heavy materials, such as cast iron, may require extra floor support. Surrounding surfaces should be easy to clean and waterproof.

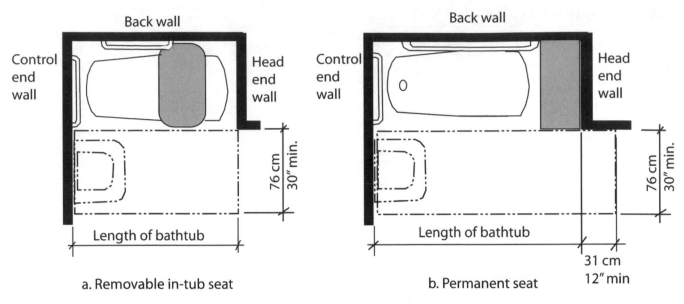

Figure 8-15 ADA bathtub clearances. People in wheelchairs have to transfer onto a tub seat by sliding across from the wheelchair. This can be an awkward maneuver, and allowing enough access is important. A roll-in shower is easier to use.

TABLE 8-4. BATHTUB MATERIALS

Material	Description	Problems
Porcelain on steel (POS)	Resists acid, corrosion, abrasion; flameproof; colorfast; sanitary; durable	If chipped, can rust; can be noisy
POS composite	Lightweight, layered construction reduces sound, improves heat retention	If chipped, can rust
Acrylic reinforced with fiberglass	Low cost; lightweight; repairable; easy to clean; color and style choices; feels warm; keeps water warm longer	Finish may scratch or discolor; damaged by strong chemicals; no abrasive cleansers
Gel-coated fiberglass (FRP)	Layers of fiberglass and foam insulation; low cost; lightweight; easy to install	Less durable than acrylic; some are better quality than others; no abrasive cleansers
Cast iron with extra-thick enamel	Very chip-, dent-, scratch-, and impact-resistant; reduces vibration and noise; helps keep water warm longer	Extremely heavy; difficult to repair; sandblasted, nonskid bottom very hard to clean if scuffed; expensive
Cultured marble (man-made)	Crushed limestone and polyester resin with gel-coated finish; tough, durable, transparent surface; stronger than quarried marble; can repair slight chips; less expensive than cast iron	More expensive than acrylic; surface can be scratched; very brittle; can crack from thermal shock; maximum water temperature 150°F; no abrasive cleansers
Natural marble stone	Not recommended	Very porous; hard water will etch and roughen surface; acidic cleaners will crumble it; oils will stain; extremely brittle; will crack if too hot or in rapid temperature change
Solid surfacing	Warm to touch; retains water temperature; hard to damage; repairable; outperforms cast iron and acrylic; white exterior can be painted	Relatively new product
Wood	Traditional Japanese bath for soaking uses hinoki (Japanese cypress); antimicrobial properties; will not rot; soaping, washing done outside tub	Most woods will warp, crack, or rot; teak is better; will dry out and split if not used regularly; room should have waterproof floor, floor drain; may not meet codes
Mosaic ceramic tile	Durable; great variety of patterns, shapes, sizes; use water-resistant grout	Requires skilled installation; tile cleans well; grout may not

Moderately priced all-in-one shower/bath enclosures in acrylic or fiberglass are very common, along with tubs and enclosures made of solid surfacing materials. Fiberglass is the most cost-effective choice, but acrylic is more durable and has more luster. Showers and tubs are often installed as separate entities and are sometimes divided by a half wall or a door.

☑ **Tubs are often uncomfortable and dangerous for people to get into and out of. The design of a tub should ideally support the back, with a contoured surface and braces for the feet. A seat allows most of a person's body to be out of the water and makes it easier for him or her to enter and exit the tub safely. A handheld shower is very helpful for rinsing the body and hair. Bathtubs are made of vitreous china, enameled cast iron, or enameled steel.**

Old-fashioned cast-iron claw-foot tubs are still available. Thermaformed acrylic tub liners that can be installed over existing fixtures are a fast and economical way to upgrade a bathroom. Tubs are available with integral skirts for easy installation and removable panels for access.

A single-lever faucet offers two advantages. First, for those who do not have full use of their hands, the lever is easier to manipulate than two round handles. Second, both temperature and flow rate can be adjusted with a single motion. To protect children and people with disabilities who have limited skin sensation, scald-proof, thermostatically controlled or pressure-balanced valves should be used to control hot water flow.

When a bathtub is required to be accessible, the ADA specifies the clear floor space in front of the tub, a secure seat within the tub, the location of controls and grab bars, the type of tub enclosure, and fixed/handheld convertible shower sprays. One of the best tub seats extends from outside the tub into the head of the tub, thereby allowing an individual to maneuver outside the tub before sliding in.

SHOWERS
Showers are considered to be a quick, no-nonsense way to clean your whole body. However, they waste a great deal of running water while you soap and scrub, even if they do an excellent job of rinsing skin and hair. With luck, your back gets an invigorating massage, but a real soak is impossible. If you drop the soap, you may slip and fall when retrieving it. It is safer to sit when scrubbing, especially the legs and feet, so an integral seat is a good idea.

Showerheads are available in two basic types. Regular stationary showerheads are hands-free but permit only limited aim adjustments. Handheld showerheads are attached to a flexible hose, which can be clipped onto a wall-mounted hanger, swivel, or bar for hands-free use. Although a bit more expensive than regular models, handheld showerheads are more versatile. They may help save water by directing it only where it is needed and by reducing the distance between the showerhead and the body, which encourages the use of cooler water temperatures. Both standard and handheld showerheads are available with adjustable sprays; those with rings outside the head are easier to adjust than those with controls in the head's center. A shutoff at the head reduces water to a trickle, thereby saving water. Low-water-pressure heads are designed to produce a satisfying stream at pressures below 80 pounds per square inch (**psi**).

Showerheads installed before 1992 may use up to 5.5 gallons per minute (**gpm**); some of these are still in use. Most codes now regulate showerhead flow; a low-flow showerhead uses a maximum of 2.5 gpm (9.5 liters per minute). There are two types of low-flow showerheads. Aerating heads mix air and water into a misty spray. Laminar-flow showerheads form individual streams of water; because they produce less steam and moisture, they are good for use in humid climates.

☑ **When helping children bathe, you should be able to reach the controls from the outside without wetting your arm. Even with soap in your eyes, you should be able to manipulate controls from inside the shower without seeing them. Shower controls and showerheads are available grouped together into a cleanly designed panel. Some showers feature multiple shower sprays and a steam generator. Systems that allow the sprays to be moved accommodate people of different sizes, and some systems come with programmable showerheads.**

When there is more than one shower in a public facility, the ADA requires that at least one must be accessible. There are two types of accessible showers: transfer showers and roll-in showers. Accessible showers have specified sizes, seats, grab bars, controls, curb heights, shower enclosures, and shower-spray units. How an individual with disabilities will enter the shower is an important design issue, particularly if the person is in a wheelchair. For a person who can physically transfer from a wheelchair to a shower seat, the seat and grab bars must be positioned to facilitate his or her entry. For a person who must shower while seated in a wheelchair, the threshold cannot be more than 25 millimeters (¼ in.) high to permit roll in, and the shower floor must be sloped to contain the water.

Moderately priced shower stalls are made of fiberglass or acrylic. More upscale options include marble and other stones, large-sized ceramic tile with borders, glass block, and solid surfacing materials. Preplumbed, all-in-one shower enclosures that include a steam generator are also available. Shower pans are typically made of terrazzo or enameled steel and are available in solid surfacing materials as well. Some shower pans are barrier-free. Grab bars, seats, antiscald valves, nonslip bases, and adjustable shower arms all add to safety.

Typically, shower enclosures are made of enameled steel, stainless steel, ceramic tile, or fiberglass. Frames for shower doors come in a variety of standard metal finishes. The handle that comes with a shower door can be upgraded to match the bathroom decor. Etched glass doors add a design element to the bathroom. Glass-panel antiderailing mechanisms improve safety, too. Open, walk-in styles of showers with no doors are also an option.

Heavy-glass frameless enclosures that can be joined with clear silicone are available up to 13 millimeters (½ in.) thick, although a thinner 10-millimeter (⅜-in.) enclosure is usually adequate. Body sprays with many jets pounding directly at a frameless door will inevitably leak, so pointing them against a solid wall is a better option. A vinyl gasket may prevent leaks, but it may defeat the visual effect of the frameless glass. In addition, it is unlikely to be effective for very long. Completely frameless enclosures always lose a certain degree of water, and glass doors generally do not keep steam in and retain the heat as well as framed doors. Complete water tightness may encourage mildew growth, so a vented transom above the door may be necessary.

Prefabricated, modular-acrylic steam rooms are available in a variety of sizes that can comfortably fit between two and eleven people. Steam rooms include seating and low-voltage lighting. An average steam bath consumes less than one gallon of water. Steam generators are usually located in a cabinet adjacent to the shower enclosure, but they may be located up to 6 meters (20 ft.) away. Equipment with minimal temperature variations, an even flow of steam, quiet operation, and steam heads that are cool enough to touch are good choices. Plumbing and electrical connections are similar to those of a common residential water heater. Controls can be mounted inside or outside the steam room.

Modular saunas combine wood and glass in sizes that range from 122 × 122 cm (4 × 4 ft.) to 366 x 366 cm (12 × 12 ft.). There are even portable and personal saunas that can be assembled in minutes. Heating units are made of rust-resistant materials and hold rocks in direct contact with the heating elements. Models are available in cedar, redwood, hemlock, and aspen.

Showers may be required by code in such communal locations as gyms, health clubs, manufacturing plants, warehouses, foundries, and other buildings where employees are exposed to excessive heat or skin contamination. Codes specify the type of shower pan and drain required.

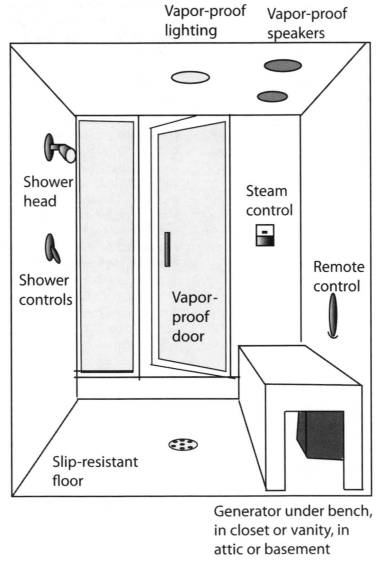

Figure 8-16 Steam room. Steam rooms can be custom-designed or installed as a prefabricated package. In either case, a steam generator must find a home nearby but out of the way.

There are alternatives to typical showers and tubs. Traditional Japanese baths have two phases. You wet, soap, and scrub yourself on a little stool over a drain; rinse with warm water from a small bucket; then, freshly cleansed, you soak in a warm tub. An updated version uses a whirlpool hot tub for the soak. If the hot tub is located in a small bathhouse with a secluded view, a person using it may approach bliss.

A shower pan that converts a standard 152-centimeter (60 in.) tub into a shower without moving the plumbing can improve safety. In this process, the old tub is removed and replaced with a slip-resistant shower pan. An acrylic wall surround can cover old tile and any unsightly construction work.

Different kinds of shower seats are available: adjustable, fold-up, and stationary. Regardless of type, the seat must be installed where it will allow a seated individual to reach the showerhead, valves, and soap holder. An adjustable showerhead can be hand-held by a seated person or bracketheld by a standing individual.

Grab bars, positioned to help an individual enter and exit the shower, cannot extend more than 38 millimeters (1.5 in.) from the wall in order to prevent a hand or arm from getting caught between the bar and the wall. Walls behind the seat and grab bars must be reinforced to support up to 114 kilograms (250 lb.) by installing 2 × 4 or 2 × 8 blocks horizontally between framing joists. Controls should be installed above the grab bar.

Designing Private Bathrooms

The minimum code requirements for a residence include:

- one kitchen sink
- one water closet
- one lavatory
- one bathtub or shower unit
- one washing-machine hookup

In a duplex, both units may share a single washing-machine hookup. Each water closet and bathtub or shower must be installed in a room that offers privacy. Some jurisdictions require additional plumbing fixtures based on the number of bedrooms. Many homes have more than one bathroom. Related bathroom-design terminology and bathroom-area requirements are shown below (Table 8-5).

Designing bathroom storage that is practical and efficient can be a challenge. Pullout step stools help children reach lavatories. Counters and mirrors at varying heights for seated and shorter people help accommodate everyone. Families often buy toilet paper and other supplies in bulk and need storage for at least some of these supplies in the bathroom itself (the rest can be stored nearby). Towels should also be stored in the bathroom. Multiple users can leave a plethora of toiletries and grooming supplies on counters and shelves, and designing appropriate, easy-to-maintain built-in storage areas can reduce clutter. Cleaning supplies need to be convenient but kept away from small children, and preferably out of sight. Specially designed accessories are available to accommodate a scale, toilet brush, and plunger.

Designing Public Toilet Rooms

On many projects, the interior designer allocates the space for public restrooms and places the fixtures. Toilet rooms in public facilities are often allotted minimal space and have to be designed with ingenuity to accommodate the required number of fixtures. The location of public restrooms should be central without being a focal point of the interior design.

Typically, a licensed engineer designs a building's plumbing system. On small projects like adding a break room or a small toilet facility, an engineer may not be involved; in this situation, a licensed contractor will work directly off the interior designer's drawings or supply his or her own plumbing drawings. The design of public restrooms also involves coordination with the building's mechanical system. The type of air-distribution system; ceiling height; location of supply diffusers and return grilles on ceilings, walls, or floor; and the number and locations of thermostats and **heating, ventilating, and air conditioning (HVAC)** zones influence the interior design.

Interior designers must be aware of the specific numbers and types of plumbing fixtures required by codes for public buildings. The *International Plumbing Code (IPC)*, although geared toward plumbing engineers and professional plumbing contractors, helps interior designers determine the minimum number and types of fixtures required for particular occupancy classifications. Plumbing-code requirements also include privacy and finish requirements and minimum clearances.

TABLE 8-5. TYPES OF BATHROOMS

Type	Description	Size/Comments
Basic three-fixture bathroom	Lavatory, toilet, combination tub/shower designed for one user at a time	Minimum of 3.25 square meters (35 square ft.); master baths may be much larger
Compartmented bathroom	Lavatory in hallway, bedroom, or small alcove, with toilet and bath in a separate space close by; toilet can also be separate, with its own lavatory	Convenient for couples or multiple children using components simultaneously; often found in hotels
Guest bath	Lavatory, toilet, shower stall rather than full bathtub	Minimum of 3 square meters (30 square ft.)
Half bath	Lavatory, toilet	2.3 square meters (25 square ft.); powder room under stairs is half-bath; often located near mudroom entrance

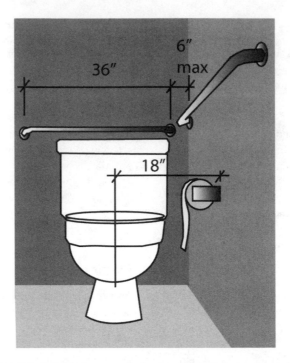

Figure 8-17 Accessible toilet stall: front approach. In general, washroom accessories must be mounted so that the part that the user operates is between 97 centimeters and 122 centimeters (38–48 in.) from the floor. The bottom of the reflective surface of a mirror must not be more than 102 centimeters (40 in.) above the floor. Grab bars must be between 84 centimeters and 91 centimeters (33–36 in.) above the floor.

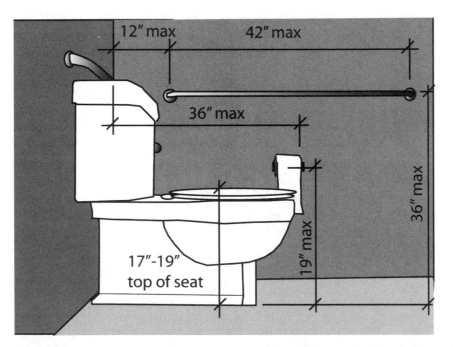

Figure 8-18 Accessible toilet stall: side approach. In general, wheelchair access requires a 152-centimeter (5-ft.) diameter turn circle. The turn circle should be drawn on a floor plan to show compliance. When this is not possible, a T-shaped space is usually permitted. Special requirements pertain to toilet rooms serving children aged 3 to 12 years. States may have different or additional requirements, so interior designers must check the latest applicable accessibility codes.

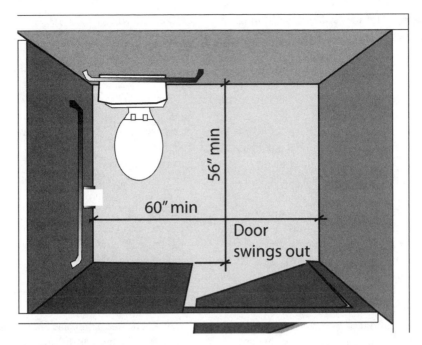

Figure 8-19 Accessible toilet stall: shorter, wider stall. An alternative layout is wider but may be shorter than standard accessible toilet stalls

The entrances to public restrooms must strike a balance between accessibility and privacy, so that they are easy to find and enter but also preserve the privacy of users. Frequently, men's and women's toilet rooms are located next to each other, with both entries visible but visually separate. This eliminates having to split up families across a public space, is convenient for those waiting, makes finding the restrooms easier, and saves plumbing costs. The area just outside the restroom should be designed to allow people to wait for their companions and should avoid closed-off or dark areas for safety reasons.

Restrooms with multiple water closets must have toilet stalls made of impervious materials, with minimum clearance dimensions and privacy locks. Urinals have partial screens but do not require doors. In general, lavatories are located closer to the door than toilets, in part to keep the most private functions out of the line of sight and to encourage hand washing after toilet use.

☑ **Both men's and women's rooms should have baby-changing areas where appropriate. Some facilities, such as health clubs, have family changing and toilet rooms, which are small rooms designed for use by one or both parents and their children. This eliminates the dilemma of a father with a four-year-old daughter or a mother with a young son, especially when changing clothes.**

Toilet rooms can preserve acoustic privacy several ways:

- isolation from acoustically sensitive spaces by closets or hallways
- construction of doors, walls, ceilings, and floors of bathrooms to block sound

- avoiding cracks around bathroom door
- avoiding back-to-back electrical outlets between adjacent spaces
- avoiding air grilles into ducts where there are adjacent grilles
- avoiding other open windows near bathroom window
- using masking sounds, such as music, fan noises, or recirculating fountains
- muffling sound of water moving inside pipes by placing them on less acoustically critical wall, and wrapping and resiliently mounting them

The *International Building Code (IBC)* references 1998 *ICC/ANSI A117.1 (Accessible and Usable Buildings and Facilities)* from the International Code Council. The ADAAG and American National Standards Institute (ANSI) accessibility standards list access requirements. These include minimal clearances, location requirements, and easy-to-use controls.

☑ **The conventional height of a toilet seat is 38 centimeters (15 in.). The recommended height for toilet seats for people with disabilities is between 43 centimeters and 48 centimeters (17–19 in.). In general, doors on accessible stalls should swing out, not in, with specific amounts of room on the push and pull sides of the doors.**

The ADA requires that all restrooms—even if only partially accessible—be fully accessible to the public, with adequate door width and turning space for a wheelchair. A single-toilet facility is usually required to be accessible or at least adaptable for use by a person with disabilities. A door is not allowed to impinge on the fixture clearance space, but it can swing into a turn circle. The ADA also regulates such accessories as mirrors, medicine cabinets, controls, dispensers, receptacles, disposal units, air hand dryers, and vending machines. The heights of light switches and electrical receptacles are also specified. When nonaccessible toilets already exist, it may be possible to add a single, accessible unisex toilet rather than one toilet per sex.

The ADA requires a minimum of one lavatory per floor to be accessible, but it is not usually difficult to make them all usable by everyone. An accessible lavatory has specific amounts of clear floor space leading to it, space underneath for knees and toes, covered hot water and drain pipes, and lever or automatic faucets. The ADA lists detailed requirements for clearance and height.

The number of required plumbing fixtures must be calculated for new construction, building additions, and occupancy classification changes. The number of required fixtures is based on the total number of occupants within a building or space. Typically, each floor requires a minimum of one toilet or restroom. Some tenant facilities may require their own toilet facilities, which can then be deducted from the total building requirements. The fixtures that may be required include water closets, lavatories, urinals, drinking fountains, bathtubs, showers, and washing machines. Code requirements are minimum numbers, and buildings in which many people may need to use the restrooms at the same time may want to install additional facilities.

Urinals may be required in some restrooms for men depending on the occupancy. Schools, restaurants, lounges, transportation terminals, auditoriums, theaters, and churches may have specific requirements. Facilities that tend to have heavy restroom use by men, such as bars, often install more than the number of urinals required by code.

Some occupancies with limited square footage and minimal numbers of occupants, such as small offices, retail stores, restaurants, laundries, and beauty shops, are permitted to have one facility with a single water closet and lavatory for both men and women. These facilities must be unisex and fully accessible. Adjustments may be made for facilities used predominantly by one sex if the owner can provide satisfactory data to the code officials.

In larger buildings, fixtures may be grouped together on a floor if maximum travel distances are within the limits established by code. Employee facilities can be either separate or included in the public customer facilities. It is common to share employee and public facilities in nightclubs, places of public assembly, and mercantile buildings.

Wherever there are water closets, there must be lavatories. However, lavatories are not required at the same ratio as toilets. Large restrooms usually have more water closets than lavatories.

☑ **As with other plumbing, fixtures should never be installed in exterior walls where there is any chance of below-freezing weather. Small-scale fixture plumbing will fit into a 15-centimeter (6-in.) interior partition, but wall-hung fixtures require chases between 46 centimeters and 61 centimeters (18–24-in.) thick. Plumbing chases are required when there are more than two or three fixtures. Plastic pipes are not allowed in residences in many jurisdictions.**

Fixtures should be located back-to-back and one above the other wherever possible for economical installation. This conserves piping space and permits greater flexibility in the relocation of other partitions during remodeling. Wherever possible, all fixtures should be located in a room along the same wall.

Bathroom fixtures should be located with space around them for easy cleaning as well as for easy access for repair and part replacement. Faucets and toilet valves are subject to constant repairs, and drains must be kept free of obstructions. Waste piping can be clogged with hair, paper, cooking fats, and tree roots. When water-supply piping fills with mineral scale, it must be replaced, which is something to be checked when a bathroom is undergoing a major renovation.

Access panels may be required in the walls of rooms behind tubs, showers, and lavatories. Trenches with access plates may be required for access to pipes in concrete floors. Water heaters are especially prone to scale from mineral-rich water, and their electrical or fuel-burning components need periodic attention.

☑ **Prefabricated bathrooms are available, with manufactured assemblies of piping and fixtures. One-piece bathrooms have no seams between the fixtures and the floors. Fixture replacement is difficult and expensive, and access for plumbing repairs must be provided through adjacent rooms.**

Some types of occupancies present special plumbing-design challenges. Plumbing fixtures for schools should be chosen for durability and ease of maintenance. Abuse-resistant materials like stainless steel, chrome-plated cast brass, precast stone or terrazzo, or high-impact fiberglass are appropriate choices. Controls must be designed to withstand abuse, and fixtures must be securely tied into the building's structure with concealed mounting hardware designed to resist exceptional forces.

Prisons employ extreme measures to prevent plumbing fixtures from becoming weapons. Heavy-gauge stainless-steel fixtures with nonremovable fittings are very expensive and require tamper-proof installation.

DRINKING FOUNTAINS

Access to fresh drinking water is necessary for good health; for some people, frequent drinks of water are an essential health need. The following are some guidelines for the location of drinking fountains:

- Drinking fountains are not permitted in toilet rooms or in the vestibules to toilet rooms, but they may be located in the corridor outside.
- One drinking fountain (water cooler) is typically required for each 75 occupants.
- In multistory buildings, each floor must have its own fountain.
- The ADA requires that one drinking fountain per floor be accessible. If there is only one fountain on a floor, it must have water spigots at wheelchair and standard heights.
- When there are multiple drinking fountains on a floor, typically half must be accessible.

TABLE 8-6. WATER USE BY APPLIANCES

Appliance	Type	Water Use		Hot Water	
		Gallons	Liters	Degrees Fahrenheit	Degrees Celsius
Dishwasher	Standard cycle	12 to 18	45 to 68	Above 120	Above 48
	Shorter cycle	7	26.5	Above 120	Above 48
Clothes washer	Top-loading	40 to 55	151 to 208	Above 120	Above 48
	Horizontal-axis			Above 120	Above 48

- Accessible drinking fountains have controls on the front or side for easy operation, and they require clear floor space for maneuvering a wheelchair.
- Cantilevered drinking fountains require space for a front approach and minimum knee space. Freestanding fountains require floor space for a parallel approach.

Drinking fountains are available with filter systems that remove lead, chlorine, and sediment from the water, as well as cysts, such as *cryptosporidium* and *Giardia*. Such systems use a quick-disconnect cartridge and may have an optional audible filter monitor to indicate when the filter needs to be changed. Safety bubblers flex on impact to prevent mouth injury.

PLUMBING FOR APPLIANCES AND EQUIPMENT

Although such appliances as dishwashers and clothes washers are not usually considered to be plumbing fixtures, they are included here as an aid to interior designers, who frequently assist clients in selecting them and who locate them on their plans. (Appliances are also discussed in Chapter 14: Electrical Appliances and Communications Equipment.)

Dishwashers and clothes washers have relatively simple plumbing requirements. Both use vacuum breakers to prevent clean and dirty water from mixing. Kitchens need regular water-supply lines for the sink and dishwasher, and waste lines for the sink, garbage disposal, and dishwasher. Adequate space must be provided for access, especially in front of front-loading machines.

In some urban locations, vacuum lines, compressed-air lines, or high-pressure water mains for driving tools were once run below streets as utility systems. Today, gas, electric, and steam are the only energy utilities in common use.

An electric-powered compressor in a building furnishes compressed air, which is supplied through pipelines for use in workshops and factories. Compressed air is used to power portable tools, clamping devices, and paint sprayers. Air-powered tools tend to be less expensive, lighter, and more rugged than electrical tools. Vacuum lines are installed in scientific-laboratory buildings.

This concludes the discussion on water and waste. In Part IV: Thermal Comfort: Heating and Cooling Systems, we will consider how buildings keep us warm (or cool) enough, and how that affects their design and energy use.

PART

IV

· · · · · · · · · · · · · · · ·

THERMAL COMFORT: HEATING AND COOLING SYSTEMS

When we are able to give off heat and moisture at a rate that maintains a stable, normal body temperature, we achieve a state of **thermal comfort**. This state is the result of a balance between the body and its environment.

Thermal comfort is affected by factors under your control, such as your body's metabolism and the clothing you wear; you can choose to move to a more comfortable place or consume warm or cold foods.

Engineers are directly concerned with measurable environmental factors that affect thermal comfort, including air temperature, surface temperature, air motion, and humidity. We will be looking at these factors in this part of the book.

In *Regenerative Design for Sustainable Development* (John Wiley & Sons, Inc., 1994, p. 106), John Tillman Lyle writes:

To control the flow of energy within a building, the materials and the details of their assembly must augment the form. Five elements of a building are particularly important for their roles in the thermal regime:

- insulation to contain or exclude heat as needed
- transparent surfaces to admit solar radiation as needed
- thermal mass to store heat and release it as needed
- shading materials to block solar radiation from transparent surfaces where desired
- openings to control air movement

Interior designers are skilled at manipulating the psychological factors affecting thermal comfort. By working with color, texture, sound, light, movement, and scent, interior designers create spaces that support the thermal (as well as spatial) comfort of users.

Principles of Thermal Comfort

Over time, our tolerance for a range of indoor temperatures that changes with the seasons has become more limited. Until the 1920s, most people in the United States preferred indoor temperatures around 20°C (68°F) in the winter and tolerated higher temperatures during the summer. They saved the cost of expensive energy in the winter months by wearing warm clothes. Low energy costs between 1920 and 1970 led to a preference for year-round indoor temperatures in the range of 22°C to 25.5°C (72°F–78°F). Today, we look at our energy needs in light of energy savings.

Our body's internal heating system slows down when we are less active, and we expect a building's heating system to make up the difference. Air movement and drafts, the thermal properties of the surfaces we touch, and relative humidity also affect our physical comfort.

The complex physical and chemical processes involved in the maintenance of human life are called our **metabolism**. The rate at which our bodies generate heat is called our **metabolic rate**. Excess heat is carried away by perspiration evaporating off our skin. Thinner people, who have less insulation (fat), stay cooler than heavier people.

Our fingertips, nose, and elbows are more sensitive to heat and cold than other parts of the body. Our upper lip, nose, chin, chest, and fingers are the body parts most sensitive to cold. Our fingertip temperature is usually in the high 20 degrees Celsius (high 80 degrees Fahrenheit); fingertips readily detect the rate at which heat is being conducted away from our bodies.

Materials that conduct heat rapidly may feel cooler to the touch than they actually are when in fact they are warmer than the air temperature. The high **thermal conductivity** of these materials gives interior designers a tool for creating spaces that feel cooler than their surface temperatures suggest they are.

Both the heating and cooling systems of a building help control how much heat our bodies give off. Typically, heating systems do not actually raise body temperature directly; they adjust the thermal characteristics of the indoor space to reduce the rate at which our bodies lose heat. Engineers refer to heating, ventilating, and air conditioning systems and equipment with the acronym HVAC.

In general, a man may feel warmer than a woman upon entering a room of a certain temperature, but later on will feel cooler than a woman will. It takes a man one to two hours to feel as warm or cold as a woman does in the same space.

Each individual has his or her own temperature sensitivities as well as consistent preferences from day to day. Each person's thermal requirements will vary depending upon whether he or she is exercising vigorously, digesting a heavy meal, or sleeping. No matter what the temperature of a space is, some occupants will probably be dissatisfied.

The **American Society of Heating, Refrigeration, and Air-Conditioning Engineers (ASHRAE)** has published research that building occupants in typical winter clothing prefer indoor temperatures between 20°C and 24°C (68° F–74°F). When dressed in summer clothes, occupants prefer temperatures between 23°C and 26°C (73°F–79°F). Their preferred temperature for more than one hour of a sedentary occupation is 17°C (65°F) or higher.

Where people remain in one location for long periods of time, as in an airplane, theater, office, or workshop, personal control over at least one environmental element helps them feel comfortable.

☑ When building interiors are designed with a variety of conditions within one space, people can move to the area in which they are most comfortable. Sunny windows and cozy fires offer many degrees of adjustment as a person moves closer or farther away.

Our bodies become used to seasonal temperature changes. In the summer, our bodies adjust to higher outdoor temperatures. When we go into an air-conditioned interior, it takes some time for us to readjust to the lower temperatures and lower humidity. After we are in a space for a long time, our bodies adjust to the conditioned interior environment. Stores and lobbies where people stay for short times try to maintain a relatively warm, dry climate in the summer, so that our perspiration rate does not change dramatically. In many commercial facilities, the HVAC-system designer must compromise between the long-term needs of the employees and the short-term preferences of the more transient customers.

The temperatures inside a building are affected by the outdoor air conditions on its exterior envelope. The sun's heat warms buildings both directly and by reradiating from the warmed earth. Warm air enters buildings through windows, doors, and the buildings' **ventilation system**. Building temperatures tend to be lower in the winter than in the summer at the perimeter and on the top floors, where most heat is lost. In the summer, sun and high air temperatures have their greatest influence at the perimeter.

The heat given off by buildings' occupants—their **metabolic heat**—affects temperatures in buildings. The heat of the people in, for example, crowded auditoriums, full classrooms, and busy stores warms these spaces. Cooking, laundry, bathing, lighting, computers, and other equipment also generate heat within a building. Small residential buildings usually gain less heat internally than larger office buildings housing many people and a great deal of equipment; their heating systems may be turned on sooner than larger buildings as outdoor temperatures fall.

Heat leaves buildings when heated air is exhausted or leaked to the outdoors. A building's materials also conduct heat to the outdoor air. Additional heat is radiated to cooler surfaces outdoors and carried out with heated water into the sewers.

PRINCIPLES OF HEAT TRANSFER

One way to visualize how heat moves from one place to another is to think of it as the energy of molecules bouncing around. The bouncing causes nearby, less active molecules to start moving around, too. The motion that is transferred from one group of molecules to another also transfers heat from the more active group to the less active group. A cold area is simply an area with quieter molecules; therefore, it has less thermal energy. A warm area is one with more active molecules.

As long as there is a temperature difference between two areas, heat always flows from a region of higher temperature to a region of lower temperature; this means that heat flows from an area of active movement to one of less movement. This tendency lowers the temperature and the amount of activity in the area with the higher temperature and increases the temperature and the level of activity in the area with the lower temperature. When

Figure 9-1 Heat transfer: Maxwell's teacup. "For instance, if we put a silver spoon into a cup of hot tea, the part of the spoon in the tea soon becomes heated, while the part just out of the tea is comparatively cool. On account of this inequality of temperature, heat immediately begins to flow along the metal from A to B. The heat first warms B a little, and so makes B warmer than C, and then the heat flows on from B to C, and in this way the very end of the spoon will in course of time become warm to the touch. The essential requisite to the conduction of heat is, that in every part of its course the heat must pass from hotter to colder parts of the body." (James Clerk Maxwell, *The Theory of Heat*, Dover Publications 2001, p. 12. Unabridged republication of ninth edition, published by Longmans, Green and Co., London and New York, in 1888)

there is no longer a temperature difference, both areas reach a state of **thermal equilibrium** and the molecules bounce around at similar rates.

The greater the difference between the temperatures of the two places or objects, the faster the heat is transferred from one to another. In other words, the rate at which the amount of molecular activity is decreased in the more active area and increased in the quieter area is related to the temperature difference between the two areas. Other factors involved include conditions surrounding the path of heat flow and the resistance to heat flow of anything between the two areas.

Heat energy is transferred in three ways: radiation, conduction, and convection. The movement of energy from more active (warmer) areas to less active (cooler) areas occurs through radiation, conduction, convection, and evaporation. **Radiation** occurs when heat flows in electromagnetic waves from hot surfaces through any medium, even the emptiness of outer space, to detached, colder surfaces. With **conduction**, heat is transferred by contact directly from the molecules of warm surfaces to the molecules of cooler surfaces. In **convection**, molecules of cool air absorb the heat from warmer surfaces and then expand in volume, rise, and carry away the heat energy. **Evaporation** carries heat away from wet surfaces. We will investigate each of these methods in upcoming sections.

HEAT TRANSFER AND THE BUILDING ENVELOPE

The amount of heat that the building envelope—the construction that separates the interior spaces from the outside environment—gains or loses is influenced by the construction of the outside of the building envelope as well as the wind velocity. Each layer of material that makes up the building's exterior shell helps resist the flow of heat into or out of the building. The amount of resistance depends on the properties and thickness of the materials making up the envelope. Heavy, compact materials usually have less resistance to heat flow than light materials.

The surface inside the building also resists heat flow by holding a film of air along its surface; the rougher the surface, the thicker the film and the higher the insulation value. Think of how an animal's very thick fur coat creates a rough insulating surface that traps a lot of air around the animal. Warm room air that mixes with cooler air gently flows against the inside surface of the building envelope, disturbing the insulating air film.

A layer of air slows down the transfer of heat through a building envelope. An **air space** is a sheet of air contained on two sides by drywall, brick, insulation, or other building materials. The amount of resistance to heat gain or heat loss that it provides is determined by its width, position (horizontal, vertical, tilted), and surrounding materials.

Some parts of walls and roofs, including framing members and structural ties in metal and masonry construction, transmit heat more rapidly than others; these **thermal bridges** can increase heat loss significantly in an otherwise well-insulated assembly. Metal studs also can create thermal bridges. When a thermal bridge exists in a ceiling or wall, the cooler area can attract condensation and the water can stain the interior finish.

Architects increase thermal resistance either by adding insulation or reflective sheets or by creating more air spaces. Air enclosed between two surfaces in the building envelope effectively resists air flow only when it lacks substantial air circulation. Typically, the thickness of the air space is not critical, but the number of air spaces makes a difference. Highly efficient insulation materials, such as fiberglass batt insulation, which hold multiple air spaces within their structure, are better than empty air spaces alone. High levels of insulation maintain comfortable interior temperatures, control condensation and moisture problems, and reduce heat transmission through the building envelope.

Superinsulated buildings are designed to eliminate the need for a central heating system. Although they vary with climate and building style, all superinsulated buildings are constructed to be air-tight, have a high level of insulation, and use a ventilation system to control air quality. The heat generated by people and equipment is adequate to maintain a comfortable temperature overnight without additional heating, although more heat may be needed after a cold winter night.

Radiation

The internal energy that sets molecules vibrating produces **electromagnetic waves**. Electromagnetic energy comes in many forms, including cosmic-ray photons, ultraviolet radiation, visible light, radio waves, heat, and electric currents. Infrared (IR) radiation is made up of a range of longer, lower-frequency wavelengths between shorter visible light and even longer microwaves. The sun's heat takes the form of mostly wavelengths from the shorter, and hotter, end of IR.

IR is an invisible part of the light spectrum and behaves exactly like light. IR travels in a straight line, does not turn corners, and can be instantly blocked by objects in its path. You can visualize whether radiated energy will be spread or blocked by determining if the source object can "see" the other object through a medium that is transparent to light (e.g., air, a vacuum). Breaking the line of sight breaks the transmission path.

Buildings get heat in the shorter IR wavelengths directly from the sun. Buildings also receive thermal radiation from sun-warmed earth and floors, warm building surfaces, and contact with human skin, which is emitted at much lower temperatures and at longer IR wavelengths. Radiation warms our skin when

TABLE 9-1. HEAT FLOW

Heat-Transfer Process	Heat-Flow Mechanism	Extent of Heat Transfer	Factors Affecting Heat Transfer
Conduction	Heat transferred directly from molecule to molecule, within or between materials	Proximity of molecules (material density)	Surface temperature
Convection	Exchange between a fluid (typically air) and a solid	Motion of the fluid caused by heating or cooling	Air temperature, air motion, humidity
Radiation	Heat flow via electromagnetic waves from hotter surfaces to detached, colder surfaces	Across empty space and potentially great distances	Surface temperature, orientation to the body
Evaporation	Moisture flow carries heat away from wet surfaces	Flow through envelope assemblies and via air leakage is principal means of latent heat gain or heat loss	Humidity, air motion, air temperature

Figure 9-2 Radiation. You will feel the radiated heat from a fireplace if you are sitting in a big chair facing the fire, but if you are behind the chair, the heat will be blocked.

the sun strikes it as well as when we stand near a fire. Conversely, when we stand near a cold wall or under a cool night sky, radiation cools our skin.

☑ **Typically, a cold window in a room has the greatest effect of draining radiated heat away from our bodies, making us feel colder. Closing the drapes slows down the heat transfer and helps keep us warm.**

Infrared electromagnetic waves emanating from an object carry energy to all bodies within a direct line of sight of that object. They excite the molecules in the objects they hit, thereby increasing both the internal energy and the temperature. All objects give off heat in the form of infrared electromagnetic radiation, and all receive radiation from surrounding objects. When objects are close in temperature, the transfer of heat from the warm object to the cooler object is comparatively slower than if there were a great

difference in temperature. If two objects are at the same temperature, they will continue to radiate to each other, but no net exchange of heat will take place.

When electromagnetic waves contact an object or a medium, they are reflected from the surface, absorbed by the material, or transmitted through the material. Materials that reflect visible radiation (light), such as shiny, silvered, or mirrored surfaces, also reflect radiant heat. Glass is transparent to visible light and to radiant energy from the hot sun but is opaque to wavelengths of thermal radiation released by objects at normal earth temperatures. That is why the sun warms plants inside a glass greenhouse, but the heat absorbed and reradiated by the plants and soil cannot escape through the glass. This is known as the greenhouse effect. Radiation is not affected by air motion.

HOW BUILDING MATERIALS RADIATE HEAT

Three properties describe the ways that building materials interact with heat from thermal radiation: reflectance, absorptance, and emittance. Each of these can be influenced by the interior design of a space.

Reflectance refers to the amount of incoming radiation that bounces off a material, leaving the temperature of the material unchanged. If you think of radiant heat acting like visible light, a heat-reflective material is similar to a mirror. The electromagnetic waves bounce off the reflective material without entering it, so its temperature remains the same. New white paint will reflect 75 percent of the IR radiation striking it; so will fresh snow.

Absorptance allows thermal energy to enter a material, thereby raising its temperature. For example, when the sun shines on a stone, the stone becomes warmer. Dark green grass will absorb about 94 percent of the IR shining on it.

All the radiant energy that reaches a material is either absorbed or reflected. A building painted white reflects about three-quarters of the sun's direct thermal radiation but absorbs about 98 percent of the longer wavelength IR that bounces back onto it from its surroundings.

Having absorbed the sun's heat during the day, a stone will radiate the stored heat out to cooler surrounding objects through the night air. This ability of a material to radiate heat outward to

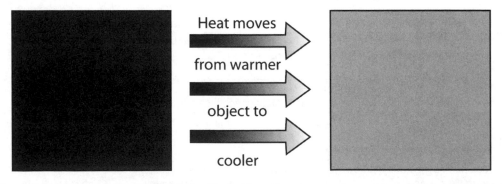

Figure 9-3 Heat transfer between objects. Heat will continue to move from a warm area to a cooler area until both objects reach the same temperature. The greater the difference in temperature between the two objects, the faster the heat transfer will take place.

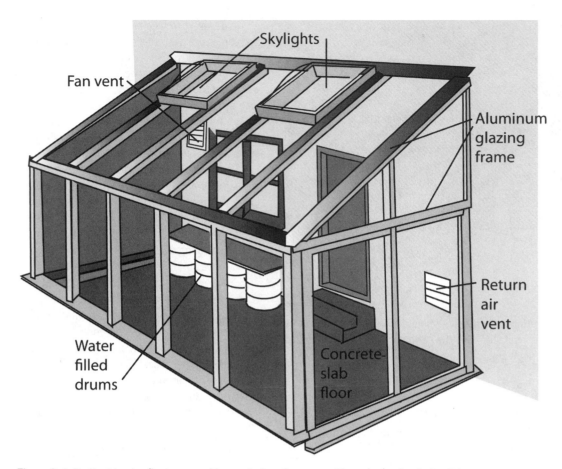

Figure 9-4 Radiant heat reflectance and transmission: Sunspace. The solar heat entering this space warms the concrete slab floor and the row of water-filled drums, both of which are capable of storing large amounts of heat and slowly releasing it at a later time.

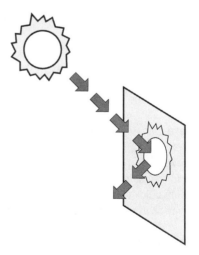

Figure 9-5 Reflectance. Sunlight is reflected at the same angle at which it strikes a surface.

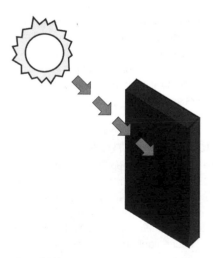

Figure 9-6 Absorptance. A white surface reflects heat back into space, while a black surface absorbs most of the heat striking it.

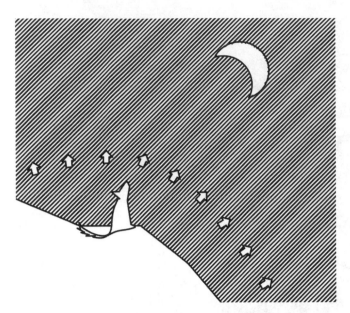

Figure 9-7 Emittance. In desert climates, hot days are followed by cool nights. The heat stored by the earth during the day is emitted into the cooler night sky.

other objects is called **emittance**. The amount of energy available for emittance depends upon the amount absorbed, so a highly reflective material has less absorbed energy to emit.

Black surfaces absorb then emit the sun's heat. Sun-heated lawns and pavements emit almost as much heat to the building as they would if they were painted black. A building with a bright metallic exterior reflects most of the radiation emitted from the earth back out into its surroundings.

Materials can emit radiation only through a gas that is transparent to IR wavelengths or through a vacuum. They do not radiate heat when they are sandwiched tightly between other layers of construction materials. Metal foils are often used inside walls; although they are good heat conductors, they work as a mirror-like insulation to prevent radiation from being emitted when there is a space with air on one or both sides. In cold climates, metal foils are installed facing the warmer interior to keep heating energy indoors. In hot climates, they face the sunny outside to keep the building from heating up.

MEASURING TEMPERATURE

Air temperature alone does not adequately measure comfort in a space: radiant temperature or air motion may be more important in creating comfort, especially in spaces that use passive solar heating or passive-cooling techniques. If you lose a great deal of body heat to a cold surface nearby, you will feel chilly, even if the air temperature is acceptably high. In the winter, when the surfaces surrounding you are warm, the air temperature can be somewhat lower without your feeling chilled. In the summer, buildings that have thick, massive walls, such as adobe houses, are likely to have cool interior surfaces, helping you remain comfortable, even at higher air temperatures.

In an effort to take such conditions into account, engineers sometimes use a calculation called the **mean radiant temperature (MRT)**, which measures the temperature of each surface in a space and defines the specific spot in the space where the MRT will be measured. It takes into account how much heat each surface emits and how the surface's location relates to the point where the MRT is being measured. Because an MRT is derived by a detailed analysis and complex calculations, it is quite abstract and cannot be directly measured.

The **operative temperature** is the average of the dry-bulb temperature and the MRT. The **dry-bulb temperature** is straightforward: it is the ambient air temperature as measured by a standard thermometer or similar device. Engineers use the MRT or operative temperature to help determine the amount of supplementary heating or cooling needed in a space.

Averages of the surface temperatures and air temperature in a room may not tell the whole story. People may be in a room with a comfortable average air temperature, but those who face a fireplace on one side of the room may be very hot while those who face an open window on another side of the room may be very cool. Most of the room's heat may be up by the ceiling, leaving the people's feet cold. Similarly, the distribution of heated surfaces may be uneven, and large cold windows and uninsulated walls may radiate heat outside so rapidly that people feel chilly even in a room with a warm air temperature.

Heating Floors and Ceilings

A building's heating system can warm very large surfaces, such as floors and ceilings, by heating them to a few degrees above body skin temperature. However, both ceilings and floors have disadvantages as radiant heat sources.

Heated floors warm feet; however, they have some drawbacks:

- The amount of heat needed to warm the rest of the body results in hot feet.
- Furniture blocks radiant heat to the upper body.
- Carpets reduce the floors' effectiveness as heat sources.
- Floors react slowly to changes in the demand for heat.
- Repairs can be messy and expensive.

Heated ceilings have both advantages and disadvantages:

- Less contact allows system to run at high temperatures.
- They are easier to maintain and repair than heated floors.
- Ceilings react fairly quickly to changing demands.
- Air movement may be inadequate to bring warm air down from ceiling.
- Legs and feet blocked from radiant heat by furniture may be cold.

Typically, actively cooling a surface does not make a space feel cooler because even a moderately cold surface is moist and unpleasant in humid summer weather. Alternatives that work better are:

- shading and insulating roofs, walls, and windows from the summer sun
- using highly reflective surface coatings on external surfaces
- using materials in the interior that heat up and cool down slowly to maintain cool temperatures throughout the day
- opening the building to allow heat to radiate back to the cool night sky

Conduction

Conduction is the flow of heat through a solid material, unlike radiation, which takes place through a transparent gas or a vacuum. Molecules that vibrate at a fast rate (at a high temperature) bump into molecules that vibrate at a slower rate (at a lower temperature) and transfer energy directly to them. The molecules themselves do not travel to the other object; only their energy does. For example, when a hot pan comes in contact with our skin, the heat from the pan flows into the skin. Conduction is responsible for only a small amount of the heat loss from our bodies. When an object we touch is cold, such as an iced drink in a cold glass, the heat flows from our skin into the glass. Conduction can also take place within a single material when the temperature is hotter in one part of the material than in another.

Convection

Convection is similar to conduction in that heat leaves an object as it comes in contact with something else, in this case, a moving stream of a **fluid** (liquid or gas) rather than another object. Our

Figure 9-8 Conduction. The heat in a warm cup of tea is conducted directly from the teacup to the cooler hands holding it.

Figure 9-9 Convection. Convection always involves a medium that picks up and transfers heat from one location to the other. In this case, the medium is the water in the pot.

skin may be warmed or cooled by convection when it is exposed to warm air or cool air, respectively, passing it. When the air molecules pass by the molecules on the surface of our skin and absorb heat, we feel cooler. This also occurs when we run cold water over our skin. The amount of convection depends upon how rough the surface is, its orientation to the stream of fluid, the direction of the stream's flow, the type of fluid in the stream, and whether the flow is free or is forced. When there is a large difference between the air temperature and the skin temperature, along with more air or water movement, more heat will be transmitted by convection.

Convection can also heat objects. A hot bath warms us thoroughly as the heat from the water is transferred by convection to our skin. Hot air from a room's heating system flowing past us will also warm our skin.

Evaporation

Evaporation is a process that results from the three types of heat transfer (radiation, conduction, and convection). When a liquid evaporates, it removes a large quantity of heat from the surface it is leaving. For example, when we sweat, the moisture evaporates and we feel cooler as some of the heat leaves our body. In order to understand evaporation, we need to look at the difference between latent heat and sensible heat. This will also be helpful later on in understanding how air conditioning works.

The kind of heat we have been talking about up to now that comes from the motion of molecules is known as **sensible heat**. Sensible heat is a form of energy that flows whenever there is a temperature difference; it is apparent as the internal energy of atomic vibration within all materials. The extent of this vibration is what temperature measures. Every material has a property called **specific heat**, which is how much the temperature changes due to a given input of sensible heat. **Latent heat** is sensible heat used to change the state of a material, for example to change water vapor to liquid water to ice (evaporate or condense). Latent heat results in a change in moisture content, such as the

Figure 9-10 Evaporation. The energy used to evaporate water comes from body heat.

humidity of air. Sensible heat flows combined with latent heat flows equal the total heat flow.

Sensible heat is all about the motion of molecules; latent heat describes the structure of the molecules themselves. The **latent heat of fusion** is the heat needed to melt a solid object into a liquid. The **latent heat of vaporization** is the heat required to change a liquid into a gas. When a gas liquefies (**condenses**) or a liquid solidifies, it releases its latent heat. For example, when water vapor condenses, it gives off latent heat. The same process takes place when liquid water freezes into ice. The ice is colder than the water because the water gave off its latent heat to its surroundings.

Our bodies contain both sensible heat (most of the body's heat) and latent heat (heat given off when perspiration evaporates). **Evaporative cooling** takes place when moisture evaporates and the sensible heat of the liquid is converted into the latent heat in the vapor. We lose the water and its heat from our bodies, so we feel cooler. Adding humidity to a room reduces evaporative cooling and is a useful technique for healthcare facilities and housing for seniors, where people may feel cold even in a warm room.

Air motion increases heat loss caused by evaporation, which is why a fan can make us feel more comfortable, even if it does not actually lower the room temperature. This sensation is called **effective temperature**, producing apparently higher or lower temperatures by controlling air moisture without actually changing the temperature of the space.

AIR TEMPERATURE AND AIR MOTION

Air motion may be caused by natural convection, be mechanically forced, or be a result of the body movements of a space's occupants. The natural convection of air over our bodies dissipates body heat without additional air movement. When temperatures rise, we must increase air movement in order to maintain thermal comfort.

Insufficient air movement is perceived as stuffiness as air stratifies, with cool air near the floor and warmer air near the ceiling.

A noticeable amount of air movement across the body when there is perspiration on the skin is experienced as a pleasant, cooling breeze. When surrounding surfaces and room air temperatures are 1.7°C (3°F) or more below the normal room temperature, we experience that same air movement as a chilly draft. When the moving air stream is relatively cooler than the room air temperature, its velocity should be less than the speed of the other air in the room to avoid the sensation of a draft. Air motion is especially helpful for cooling by evaporation in hot, humid weather.

AIR TEMPERATURE AND RELATIVE HUMIDITY

Relative humidity (RH) is the ratio of the amount of water vapor present in air to the maximum amount that air could hold at the same time; RH is expressed as a percentage. Hot air temperature and high RH are very uncomfortable; the higher the RH of a space, the lower the air temperature should be. RH is less critical within normal room-temperature ranges.

☑ **High humidity can cause condensation problems. Humidity below 20 percent can create a buildup of static electricity as well as dry out wood in furniture and interior trims.**

THERMAL CAPACITY AND RESISTANCE

Thermal capacity is the ability of a material to store heat and is roughly proportional to a material's mass or weight. A large quantity of dense material, such as a large rock, holds a large quantity of heat while light, fluffy materials and small pieces of material hold small quantities of heat. Thermal capacity is measured as

Figure 9-11 Bricklayer. Brick, a material with high thermal capacity, slows the transfer of heat from one side of a wall to the other. The bricklayer is building an interior brick wall.

the amount of heat required to raise the temperature of a unit (by volume or weight) of the material one degree.

Water has a higher thermal capacity than any other common material at ordinary air temperatures. Consequently, the heat from the sun retained by a large body of water during the day will only gradually be lost to the air during the cooler night. This is why once a lake or ocean warms up, it stays warm even after the air cools off.

Thermal Mass

Thermal mass refers to a quantity of material that exhibits good retention of heat; an example would be a thick concrete wall. Thermal capacity is the amount of heat that a material can hold; for example, air has high thermal capacity but is not massive. Materials with both high thermal mass and high thermal capacity heat up slowly and release heat gradually. For example, a cast-iron frying pan takes a while to heat up but releases an even heat to the cooking food and stays warm even when off the burner.

Materials with high thermal capacity have low **thermal resistance**. When heat is applied on one side of the material, it moves fairly quickly to the cooler side until a stable condition is reached. At this point, the process slows down.

Brick, earth, stone, plaster, metals, and concrete all have high thermal capacity. Fabrics have low thermal capacity. Thin partitions of low-thermal-capacity materials heat and cool rapidly, so the temperature fluctuates dramatically; for example, a tin shack can get very hot in the sun and very cold at night. Insulating materials have low thermal capacity since they are not designed to hold heat; they prevent heat from passing through them by incorporating many air spaces between their thin fibers. It is the air that has high thermal capacity.

Massive constructions of materials with high thermal capacity heat up slowly, store heat, and release it slowly. Consider how a brick or stone fireplace works. The effect is to even out the otherwise rapid rise and fall of temperatures as the fire flares and dies. Masses of masonry or water can store heat from solar-heat collectors to be released at night or on cloudy days.

The operative temperature of a room can be radiant energy stored in thermal mass, thereby allowing the room's air temperature to even out over time. This thermal lag can help moderate changes and is useful in passive solar design, but it may also mean that the room will not heat back up to the desired level quickly enough. Heating or cooling the room's air temperature more than the usual amount can compensate for this slow change in temperature during warm-up or cool-down periods.

High-thermal-mass materials can be an integral part of the building envelope and may be incorporated into the furnishings of the space. For maximum benefit, the materials must be within the insulated part of the building. A building's envelope with a large amount of mass may delay the transmission of heat to the interior for several hours or even for days; the greater the mass, the longer the delay. When thermal mass is used inappropriately, excessively high temperatures or cooling loads may result on sunny days and insufficient storage may occur overnight.

Figure 9-13 Taos Pueblo, New Mexico. Heavy mud or stone buildings with high thermal mass, such as these adobe structures at the Taos Pueblo in New Mexico, work well in hot desert climates with extreme changes in temperature from day to night. The hot daytime outdoor air heats the exterior face of the wall and migrates slowly through the wall or roof toward the structure's interior. Before much of the heat reaches the interior, the sun sets and the air cools off outside. The radiation of heat from the ground outside to the sky cools the outdoor air below the warmer temperature of the building exterior; then the warm building surfaces are cooled by convection and radiation. The result is a building interior that is cooler than its surroundings by day and warmer by night.

Figure 9-12 Concrete expansion joint. Concrete is a material with high thermal mass that is used for both the interiors and exteriors of buildings. This joint is designed to accommodate expansion and contraction caused by changes in temperature and humidity.

Figure 9-14 Treehouse in Buyay, Mount Clarence, New Guinea. In a hot, humid climate with high night temperatures, a building with low thermal capacity work best. The building envelope reflects away solar heat and reacts quickly to cooling breezes and brief reductions in air temperatures. This treehouse in Buyay, Mount Clarence, New Guinea, was elevated on wooden poles, light thatch was used for the roof, and the walls were made from open screens of wood or reeds. The cooling breeze passing through these open constructions prevents heat from being retained in the building.

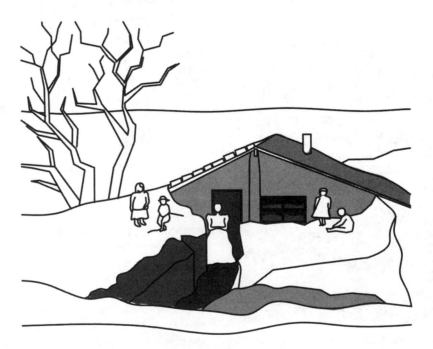

Figure 9-15 Dugout home near McCook, Nebraska, 1890s. The temperatures inside this 1890s dugout house belonging to a pioneer family are moderated by the surrounding earth, which also keeps out cold winds.

The choice of whether or not to use high quantities of thermal storage mass depends on a building's climate, site, interior design conditions, and operating pattern. High thermal mass is appropriate when outdoor temperatures swing widely above and below the desired interior temperature. Low thermal mass is a better choice when the outside temperature remains consistently above or below the desired temperature.

In a cold climate, a building that is occupied only occasionally, such as a ski lodge, should have low thermal capacity and high thermal resistance. This will help the building warm up quickly and cool quickly after occupancy, with no stored heat wasted on an empty interior. A well-insulated frame coupled with a wood-paneled interior is a good combination. In locations where the weather is very cold with high winds, the earth can shelter the building and moderate temperature changes. The high thermal capacity of soil ensures that basement walls and walls banked with earth stay fairly constant in temperature, usually around 13°C to 15°C (mid-fifties Fahrenheit) year-round. Earthbound walls should not be exposed to extreme air temperatures in cold weather. Instead, they should be insulated to thermal resistance values similar to the aboveground portions of the building. Burying horizontal sheets of foamed plastic insulation just below the soil's surface can minimize frost penetration into the ground adjacent to the building.

Thermal Conductivity

We have discussed how our bodies perceive the movement of heat from warm to cooler objects and how our senses are influenced by the rapidity with which objects conduct heat to and from our body rather than by the objects' actual temperatures. Steel, for example, feels colder than wood at the same temperature because heat is conducted away from our fingers more quickly by steel than by wood.

Figure 9-16 Thermal conductivity. Although the muffins and metal pan are hot right out of the oven, heat will travel more rapidly through the highly conductive pan than through the less conductive muffins.

☑ **This sensation is very useful to interior designers, who can specify materials that suggest warmth or coolness regardless of their actual temperatures.**

If you touch a material that conducts heat rapidly—for example, a metal shelf that is out of the sun—it will probably feel cool to your touch. This is because the metal will conduct the heat from your fingertips quickly away from your body and off into the surrounding air. **Conductivity** is a measurement of the rate at which heat flows through a material. High conductance encourages heat transfer between a solid material and the air.

Good conductors tend to be dense and durable and to diffuse heat readily. Smooth surfaces make better contact than highly textured ones, resulting in better conduction of heat and a cooler feeling.

Thermal Resistance

Resistance indicates how effectively any material serves as an insulator; measurements of resistance are very helpful when comparing insulating materials. A good insulating material resists the conduction of heat. The higher the thermal resistance of a part of the building envelope is, the slower the heat loss. The larger the difference between the temperature inside and outside the building, the faster the building gains or loses heat. Designing a building's walls, roofs, and floors for the maximum amount of thermal resistance results in optimal body comfort and energy conservation.

If you keep air from moving by trapping it in a loose tangle of glass or mineral fibers, you will create materials with very high thermal resistance. The fibers themselves have poor resistance to heat flow, but they create resistance to air movement, thereby trapping the air for use as insulation. When the air is disturbed, this insulating property drops to about one-fourth of its value. If air circulates within a wall, a convective flow will be created, which transfers heat from warm to cooler surfaces quickly.

Glass has a low resistance to heat flow, so double glazing or triple glazing with air trapped in thin layers between sheets of glass is used for a significant increase in thermal resistance. Increasing the thickness of the air space up to one inch increases the resistance slightly because the friction between the glass surface and the air prevents convective heat flow. Spaces wider than one inch offer no additional advantage; the wider space allows convective currents, and the moving air is less effective.

TABLE 9-2. ARCHITECTURAL MATERIALS AND THERMAL RESISTANCE

Material	Thermal Resistance
Metals	Very low
Masonry	Moderately low
Wood	Moderately high
Glass	Low
Air	Best resistor commonly found in buildings

TABLE 9-3. LOW-E COATINGS AND FILMS

Product Type	Use	Application	Use	Light Transmission
High-transmission low-e coating	Passive solar heating	Coating on inner glazing	Traps outgoing infrared radiation	Exterior summer shading to avoid overheating
Selective-transmission low-e coating	Winter heating, summer cooling	Coating on outer glazing	Blocks incoming infrared radiation	Relatively high for daylighting
Low-transmission low-e coating	Lower heat gain	Coating on outer glazing	Rejects more of solar-heat gain	May use tinted exterior glazing for lower light transmission
Selective-transmission low-e film	Retain heat emitted by warmed objects	Applied as separate sheets to new or existing windows	Reflects far-infrared radiation back into room	High visibility

TABLE 9-4. R-VALUES FOR INTERIOR MATERIALS

Category	Material	R-value
Interior finishes	Drywall ½ in.	0.45
	Drywall ⅝ in.	0.56
	Paneling ⅜ in.	0.47
Flooring	Plywood ¾ in.	0.93
	Particle board underlayment ⅝ in.	0.82
	Hardwood flooring ¾ in.	0.68
	Tile, linoleum	0.05
	Carpet, fibrous pad	2.08
	Carpet, rubber pad	1.23
Windows	Single glass	0.91
	With storm	2.00
	Double insulating glass ³⁄₁₆-in. air space	1.61
	¼-in. air space	1.69
	½-in. air space	2.04
	¾-in. air space	2.38
	Insulating glass ½-in. with low-e	3.13
	With suspended film	2.77
	With 2 suspended films	3.85
	With suspended film and low-e	4.05
	Triple insulating glass ¼-in. air space	2.56
	½-in. air space	3.23
	Addition for tight-fitting drapes or shades, or closed blinds	0.29
Doors	Wood hollow core flush 1¾ in.	2.17
	Solid core flush 1¾ in.	3.03
	Solid core flush 2¼ in.	3.70
	Panel door 1¾ in. with ⁷⁄₁₆-in. panels	1.85
	Storm door wood with 50 percent glass	1.25
	Metal	1.00
	Metal insulating door 2 in. with urethane	15.00
Air films	Interior ceiling	0.61
	Interior wall	0.68
Air spaces	Approximately ¹⁄₂₄ in.	1.00

Using a gas of lower thermal capacity than air can increase the thermal resistance of insulated glass. A thin metallic coating (a **low emissivity coating**, or a **low-e coating**) on the surface of the glass facing the airspace can reduce both the emittance of the glass and the conductivity of the entire glazing assembly. Low-e films are classified as hard-coat or soft-coat. Hard-coat films are durable and less expensive than soft-coat films but are less effective.

R-Values

R-values measure the thermal resistance of a given material. As discussed above, the greater the temperature difference from one side of a material to the other, the faster the heat will flow from the warm side to the cooler side. To determine the R-value, testers set up an experimental situation in which heat flows through a unit of material at the rate of one heat unit per hour. When this condition is established, the temperature on each side of the material is measured; the R-value is an expression of that difference in temperature. R-values are used for comparing the effectiveness of solid materials as insulators and refer to the material's resistance to heat flow.

The materials and construction assemblies used in a building's envelope affect its R-value. Different building shells vary in their ability to block heat transmission depending upon the way they are constructed and the materials they are made from. The structure's orientation to the sun and exposure to strong winds also influence the amount of heat that will pass through the barrier. By knowing the R-value along with the desired indoor temperature and outdoor climate conditions, an engineer can estimate the building envelope's ability to resist thermal transfer and to regulate indoor conditions for thermal comfort.

The insulating effectiveness of any airspace or air-containing building material is determined by its position and the direction of the heat flow. In the winter, heat flows up to the roof and the warm air within the roof assembly rises to the cold upper surface, where it gives up its heat. In hot weather, the heat flow through the roof is reversed. Air warmed by the hot upper roof surface remains stratified against that surface, and heat transfer through the roof is slowed. The hot air below the roof does not drop to circulate with the cooler air below. A reflective foil surface will eliminate about half of the heat flowing out through roofs and walls and about two-thirds of the heat flowing downward through floors. Foil surfaces can also reduce the transmission of heat from the sun on the roof into the building in the summer.

Types of Insulation

Insulation is the primary defense against heat loss transfer from the building envelope. The walls are the most important area to insulate because they have the largest area.

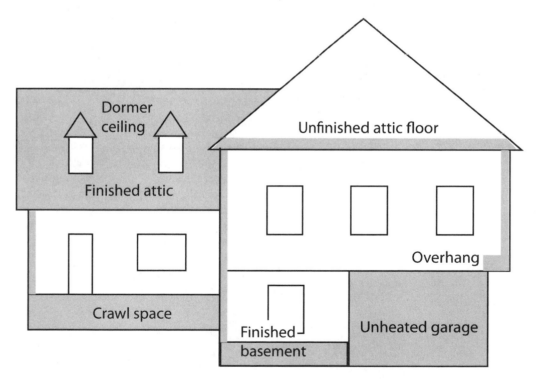

Figure 9-17 Where to insulate a house. In a cold climate, a house should be insulated wherever a heated area comes in contact with an unheated area. You can check if an existing building's walls are insulated by removing an electrical outlet cover and looking inside, or by drilling two 6-millimeter (¼-in.) holes above one another about 100 millimeters (4 in.) apart in a closet or cabinet along an exterior wall, and shining a flashlight in one while looking in the other. An insulation contractor can blow cellulose or fiberglass insulation into an existing wall.

Figure 9-18 Insulating an attic. To add insulation to an unheated attic without flooring, a layer of unfaced batts about 305 millimeters (1 ft.) deep is placed across the joists. To insulate a space with a finished cathedral ceiling, either the interior drywall is removed to install insulation or a new insulated exterior roof is built over the existing roof.

TABLE 9-5. MATERIALS USED FOR INSULATION

Insulation Material	R-value per Inch
Fiberglass batt	3.14–4.30
Blown (attic)	2.20–4.30
Blown (wall)	3.70–4.30
Rock wool batt	3.14–4.00
Blown (attic or wall)	3.10–4.00
Cellulose blown (attic)	3.13
Blown (wall)	3.70
Vermiculite	2.13
Autoclaved aerated concrete	1.05
Urea terpolymer foam	4.48
Rigid fiberglass (greater than 4 lbs. per cubic foot)	4.0
Expanded polystyrene (beadboard)	4.0
Extruded polystyrene	5.0
Polyisocyanurate (foil-faced)	6.25
Polyurethane (foamed-in-place)	7.20
Gas-filled panels (gfp): thin polymer-film bags with baffle inside, argon gas	7.0
Gfp, krypton gas	12.5
Gfp, xenon gas	20.0

Figure 9-19 Insulating basement walls. To insulate an unheated, unfinished basement, unfaced fiberglass batts are installed between floor joists, supported from below with wire or metal rods as necessary. The underside of the batts can be covered with a moisture-permeable air barrier. Heated basement walls can be insulated by adding frames made of 2 × 4 wood studs filled with fiberglass insulation against the concrete foundation walls and covering them with drywall. It is important to correct any drainage problems before insulating a basement.

Figure 9-20 Loose-fill insulation. Loose-fill insulation can be poured or blown into irregular open spaces within walls and above ceilings.

Uninsulated foundation walls are responsible for as much as 20 percent of a building's heat loss. Insulating the foundation or basement floor can save several hundreds of gallons of oil or therms of gas (one therm equals 100,000 British thermal units [BTUs]).

Insulation comes in many forms. Loose-fill insulation is poured by hand or blown through a nozzle into a cavity or over a supporting membrane above ceilings on attic floors.

Foamed-in-place materials include expanded pellets and liquid-fiber mixtures that are poured, frothed, sprayed, or blown into cavities, where they adhere to surfaces. By filling all corners, cracks, and crevices for an airtight seal, foamed insulation eliminates random air leakage, which can account for up to 40 percent of heating energy. Environmentally sound foamed insulation made without formaldehyde, chlorofluorocarbons (CFCs), hydrochlorofluorocarbons (HCFCs), or volatile organic compounds (VOCs) is available that is safe for use by persons who are chemically sensitive or who have allergies or asthma.

Flexible and semirigid insulation is available in batts and blankets. Batt insulation may be faced with a vapor retarder of Kraft paper, metal foil, or plastic sheeting and is also used for acoustic insulation.

Rigid insulation comes in blocks, boards, and sheets or preformed for use on pipes.

Rigid insulation with closed-cell structures, made of extruded polystyrene or cellular glass, is moisture resistant and may be used in contact with the earth. This type of insulation is often applied to the outside of the building and covered with fabric-reinforced acrylic. Sheets and rolls of insulation with reflective surfaces offer a barrier to radiant heat. Reflective insulation uses material of

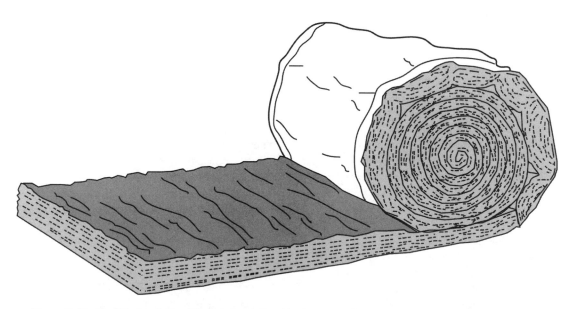

Figure 9-21 Flexible insulating blanket. Insulating blankets come in various thicknesses and lengths, and in widths of 41 centimeters and 61 centimeters (16 in. and 24 in.) to fit between studs, joists, and rafters in light frame construction.

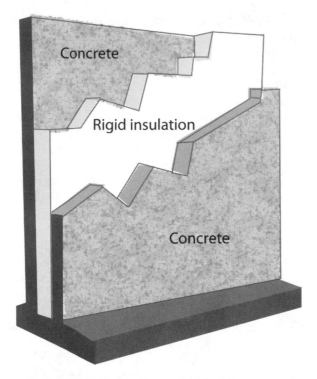

Figure 9-22 Rigid insulation. Sheets of rigid polyisocyanurate insulation are installed as part of the construction of foundation walls.

high reflectivity and low emissivity, such as paper-backed aluminum foil or foil-backed gypsum board, in conjunction with a dead-air space to reduce the transfer of radiant heat.

Thermal Feel

Interior designers can use an awareness of how people perceive the temperature of different materials to select appropriate materials for projects. A wood edge on a bar is usually perceived to be warmer than a brass edge. Some of the materials we like close to our skin—wood, carpeting, upholstery, bedding, some plastics—feel warm to the touch regardless of their actual temperature. We perceive materials to be warm that are low in thermal capacity and high in thermal resistance as well as those that are quickly warmed at a thin layer near their surfaces by our bodies. Materials that feel cold against the body, such as metal, stone, plaster, concrete, and brick, are high in thermal capacity and low in thermal resistance. They draw heat quickly and for extended periods of time from our body because of the relatively larger bulk of cooler material.

For example, a room with a temperature of 22°C (72°F) will likely be perceived as warm, while a 22°C (72°F) bath will likely feel cool to us. The air is a poor conductor of heat; water is an excellent conductor of heat. Our body gives off heat to the 22°C (72°F) air at a comfortable rate but loses heat rapidly to the 22°C (72°F) water. Similarly, a carpeted floor is comfortable to bare feet at 22°C (72°F), while a concrete floor at that temperature is perceived as cold.

U-Factors

U-factors are expressions of the steady-state rate at which heat flows through architectural envelope assemblies. U-factors are used in codes and standards and by engineers to specify envelope thermal design criteria. The U-factor includes all elements in a building envelope assembly and all sensible modes of heat transfer (convection, conduction, radiation). This includes heat flow through windows and skylights, where the situation becomes more complicated by differences in heat-flow rates between various parts of the window or skylight unit. The National Fenestration Rating Council (NFRC) devised the U-factor to combine these variations into a single value for an entire unit. The lower the U-factor, the lower the heat flow for a given temperature difference.

Solar Heat Gain Coefficient

The **solar heat gain coefficient (SHGC)** is a measure of a window's ability to resist heat gain from solar radiation. The SHGC value looks at the performance of the entire glazing unit rather than just at the glass itself. It represents the percentage of solar radiation striking a window or skylight that becomes building heat as a number from 0 to 1.

A high SHGC, such as 0.9, indicates poor resistance, which is desirable for solar heating applications. A lower SHGC (e.g., 0.2) indicates good resistance and would be a good choice when cooling is the issue. The SHGC depends on the type of glass, the number of panes, tinting, reflective coatings, and shading by the window or skylight frame.

HUMIDITY

Water vapor is a colorless, odorless gas that is always present in air in widely varying quantities. The warmer the air, the more water vapor it can hold. The amount of water vapor in the air is usually less than the maximum possible, and when the maximum is exceeded, it condenses onto cool surfaces or becomes fog or rain.

As indicated earlier, relative humidity (RH) is the amount of vapor actually in the air at a given time divided by the maximum amount of vapor that the air can contain at that temperature. For example, an RH of 50 percent means that the air contains half as much water vapor as it can hold at a given temperature. Cold air can hold less water vapor than warmer air. If the temperature drops low enough, it reaches the **dew point**, which is the point at which the air contains 100 percent RH. When the RH is raised to 100 percent, as in a gym shower room or a pool area, fog is produced. Cooling below the dew point causes the water vapor—a gas—to turn into liquid droplets of fog. The vapor condenses only enough to maintain 100 percent RH, and the remaining vapor stays in the air as a gas.

People are comfortable within the 20 percent to 50 percent RH range. In the summer, RH can be as high as 60 percent when temperatures rise to 24°C (75°F); above that RH, we are uncomfortable because the water vapor (sweat) does not evaporate off our bodies well to help us cool off.

Humidity levels affect interior design materials:

- Too much moisture causes dimensional changes in wood, most plant and animal fibers, and even masonry.
- Steel rusts, and wood rots and warps.
- Frost action causes spalling (chips or fragments breaking off) in masonry.
- Surface condensation damages decorative finishes and wood and metal window sashes as well as structural members.

With the advent of smaller, tighter homes, moisture problems in residences have increased. A typical family of four produces about 11 kilograms (25 lb.) of water vapor per day from cooking, laundering, bathing, and breathing. Humidifiers and clothing dryers release even more moisture. The drying of concrete slabs, masonry, or plaster in new construction and the bare earth in crawl spaces and basements adds to moisture in buildings.

Condensation

When hot, humid air comes in contact with a cold surface, condensation forms. For example, when you take a glass of iced tea outside on a hot humid day, little drops of water will appear on the outside of the glass and run down the sides. The water vapor in the air condenses to form visible droplets of water on the cooler surface. In cold climates, water vapor can condense on the cold interior surfaces of windows. Condensation can result in water stains and mold growth.

Cooled air in summer may reach the dew point, where it condenses on pipes and windows. Air in buildings can be cooled below the dew point by coming into contact with cold surfaces. In humid summer weather, condensation forms as "sweat" on cold drinks, cold water pipes, the cold-water tanks of toilets, and cool basement walls. In the summer, concrete basement walls, floors, and slabs on grade that are cooled by the earth will collect condensation. Carpets on the floor or interior insulation on basement walls inhibit the rise in the concrete-slab temperature and exacerbate the problem. Both carpets and insulation may be damaged if the RH is very high or if condensation occurs. Insulating the exterior or below the slab with well-drained gravel can help.

In the winter, air cooled below the dew point fogs and frosts windows, and condensation can cause rust or decay when it collects under window frames. Wintertime condensation collects on cold closet walls, attic roofs, and single-pane windows.

Visible condensation can be controlled with methods that do not require additional energy (as do fans, heaters, and dehumidifiers). In addition, they do not increase heat loss in the winter and heat gain in the summer. The methods are:

- Blowing warm air across perimeter windows artificially warms cold surfaces and prevents condensation.
- Designing room arrangements that avoid creating pockets of still air and surfaces shielded from the radiant heat of the rest of the room.

- Interior surfaces should be insulated from the cold outdoors in the winter.
- Enough air motion should be provided to keep condensation from settling on cold surfaces in the winter.
- Cold water pipes and ductwork should be insulated in the summer.
- Reducing the amount of water vapor in the air prevents condensation in all seasons.
- Ventilating moist air out of the space reduces water vapor in the air. When the dew point is higher outdoors than inside, ventilation rates should be reduced.

☑ **Insulated curtains that can be moved over windows can contribute to condensation problems because the interior surface of the window is shielded from the heating source in the room and becomes cold. If warm room air can pass around or through the insulating window treatment, moisture will condense on the window. Thermal window treatments designed to seal out cold air need to be properly gasketed or sealed at the top, bottom, and sides to prevent moist room air from entering the space between the insulation and the glass, where it will condense against the cold window. The insulating material must also be impervious to moisture that might accumulate.**

High Humidity

In the summer, high humidity reduces the evaporation of moisture from our skin surfaces as well as encourages mold and fungus growth in buildings. **Refrigerant dehumidifiers** are an option for spaces that do not require mechanical cooling but do need a reduction in humidity.

A dehumidifier chills air, which lowers the amount of moisture the air can hold, leading to water vapor condensing on its cooling coils. Then the condensed water falls into the dehumidifier's collection container. Water accumulating in the dehumidifier may harbor disease-causing bacteria. Refrigerant dehumidifiers do not work well below 18°C (65°F) because frost forms on their cooling coils, so they might not be an appropriate choice in a cool basement.

Low Humidity

Heated winter air can be very dry, causing wood in buildings and furniture to shrink and crack. Wood shrinks in the dimension perpendicular to the grain, leaving unsightly cracks and loose furniture joints. Very low humidity also causes plants to wither. Furthermore, our skin becomes uncomfortable and dry, and the mucous membranes in our nose, throat, and lungs become dehydrated and susceptible to infection. Added moisture helps, as do lower air temperatures that reduce evaporation from the skin (and lower heating costs).

Dry air creates static electric shocks. Carpeting is commercially available with a conductive material (copper or stainless steel) woven into its pile and backing that reduces voltage buildup and helps alleviate static electric shocks.

In warm-air heating systems, moisture can be added to the air as it passes through the furnace with water sprays or absorbent pads or plates supplied with water. Pans of water on radiators are an old-fashioned but effective method of raising humidity in the winter. Boiling water, washing, and bathing all release steam. Plants release water vapor into the air, and water evaporates from the soil in their pots. Spraying plants with a mist increases the air humidity, and the plants benefit, too. We also release water vapor when we breathe.

Electric humidifiers help relieve respiratory symptoms but may harbor bacteria or mold in their reservoirs if not properly maintained. Some humidifiers include an ultraviolet (UV) light bulb to inhibit bacterial growth.

Controlling Hidden Moisture

When the moisture content of the air inside a building rises, it creates **vapor pressure**, which, in turn, drives water vapor to expand into areas of lower vapor pressure, such as exterior walls, seeking equilibrium. When there is moist air on one side of a wall and drier air on the other, water vapor migrates through the wall from the moist side to the drier side. Water vapor will also travel along any air leaks in the wall.

Most building materials have relatively low resistance to water vapor. When the temperature at a given point within a wall drops below the dew point at that location, water vapor condenses and wets the interior construction of the wall. This condensation causes an additional drop in vapor pressure, which then draws more water vapor into the area. The result can be very wet wall interiors, with insulation materials saturated and sagging with water or frozen into ice within the wall. The insulation becomes ineffective, and the heating-energy use of the building increases. The wall-framing materials may decay or corrode, and hidden problems may affect the building's structure. The amount of vapor pressure within a building depends on the amount of vapor produced, its inability to escape, and the air temperature.

Indoor air in cold climates may be more humid than outdoor air; in this situation, vapors will flow from the warmer interior to the colder exterior surfaces of the walls, ceilings, and floors. This can leave the building envelope permeated with moisture. Wet insulation becomes less effective, and dry rot, a fungal disease of timber that can cause it to become brittle and crumble into powder, can afflict wood structural members.

In hot, humid climates, you need to prevent the moisture from getting into the building's interior. A drainage plane inside the exterior surfacing material, such as tar paper, will let moisture that gets through wick away to the inside. This is safer than using a vapor barrier that may trap the moisture in the wall.

A solid coat of exterior paint that prevents the water vapor from traveling out through the building's wall will trap vapor inside. Vapor pressure can raise blisters on a wall surface that will bubble the paint right off the wall. This is sometimes seen outside kitchens and bathrooms, where vapor pressure is likely to be highest.

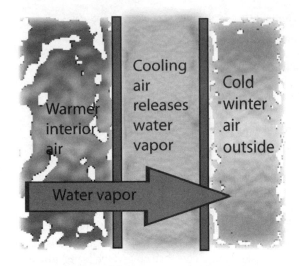

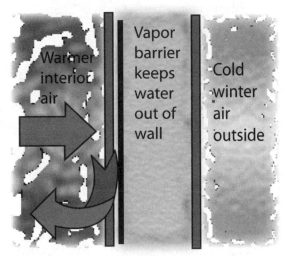

Figure 9-23 Wall vapor barrier. When the interior side of a wall is warmer than the exterior side, the warm inside air will release water vapor as it moves to the drier air outside.

Through the use of a **vapor barrier** as close to the warm side of the building envelope as possible, the creeping water vapor can be prevented from traveling through the wall. The vapor barrier must be positioned between the main insulating layer and the warm side of the wall. In a cold climate, the vapor barrier should be just under the plaster or paneling inside the building. In an artificially cooled building in a warm climate, the warm side is the outside.

Vinyl wall coverings and vapor-barrier paints on interior surfaces offer some protection, but they do not eliminate the need for a vapor barrier. Aluminum foil-faced insulation is effective for thermal insulation, but it does not make an adequate vapor barrier. Plastic films are tight against both moisture and infiltration. When adding a vapor barrier to an older building is not practical, plugging air leaks in walls, applying paint to warm-side surfaces, and providing ventilation openings on cool-side surfaces clear moisture from the construction interior. Special vapor-retardant interior paints are available for this purpose.

MECHANICAL ENGINEERING DESIGN PROCESS

The decisions made by the designers of a building's HVAC system are crucial in determining thermal comfort, indoor-air quality, and the efficiency of the building's energy use. Air-exchange rates affect the amount of energy used to heat or cool fresh air, and the energy lost when used air is exhausted. ASHRAE requirements for ventilation include minimum rates for replacing previously circulated air in the building with fresh air.

Energy costs can be reduced or eliminated by improving building insulation, lighting design, and the efficiency of HVAC and other building equipment. Buildings that allow natural ventilation as well as those that employ such techniques as heat reclamation, thermal-storage systems, and flexible air handling and chiller units lower energy use and reduce costs.

Typically, the architect and engineers decide which systems to employ, but the responsibility for finding appropriate solutions depends on the creativity and integrated efforts of the entire design team, in which the interior designer should play a significant role.

☑ **As an interior designer, you will rarely need to refer to the mechanical codes, but you should be familiar with some of the general requirements and terms, especially those that affect energy-conservation requirements. In buildings where there is a minimum of mechanical work, the mechanical engineer or contractor will work directly off the interior designer's drawings. For example, the interior design drawings may be the source for information in a renovation project where a few supply diffusers or return grilles are being added to an existing system. In any event, you may need to coordinate your preliminary design with the mechanical engineer or contractor to make sure you leave enough room for clearances around HVAC equipment.**

The goals of the mechanical engineer, like those of the interior designer, are to achieve an environment in which people are comfortable and to meet the requirements of applicable codes. By calculating how much heating or cooling is required to achieve comfort, the engineer develops design strategies that affect both the architecture and the mechanical systems of the building, such as the optimal size of windows, or the relative amounts of insulation or thermal mass. The engineer will:

- figure out how big the HVAC system components should be in order to provide enough heating and/or cooling for the most extreme conditions the building is likely to experience
- calculate the amount of energy used for normal conditions in a typical season and adjust the design to reduce long-term energy use
- consider the number of people using the building both seasonally and hourly
- consider the amount of heat gained or lost from the outside environment
- evaluate the materials, areas, and rates of heat flow through the building's envelope to determine how they affect this calculation

- look at the volumes of the spaces in the building and the rates of fresh-air exchange to determine the amount of fresh air needed
- suggest window locations and other design elements that minimize the heat gain within the building

Phases of the Design Process

The phases of the engineering design process are similar to those of architects and interior designers: preliminary design, design development, design finalization and specification, and construction.

During the preliminary design phase, the engineer:

- considers the most general combinations of comfort requirements and climate characteristics
- lists the schedule of activities that will take place in the space along with the conditions required for comfort during performance
- analyzes the site's energy resources
- lists design strategies to accommodate the climate
- considers building-form alternatives with the architect
- reviews available systems, including both passive (nonmechanical) and active alternatives
- figures out the size of one or more alternative systems using general design guidelines

In small buildings, the architect may do the system design. For larger, more complex buildings, the mechanical engineer will work as a team with architects, landscape architects, and the interior designer. The team approach helps assess the value of a variety of design alternatives arising from different perspectives. When mutual goals are agreed upon early in the design process, this team approach can lead to creative innovations. The more that the site position, layout, and orientation of the building reduces heat loss, the less energy the heating and cooling equipment consume. Opportunities may arise for the design of the HVAC system to be expressed in the form of the building. Creative teamwork can also lead to new designs that offer better environments with less energy use; this strategy can be applied to many other buildings later on.

During the design-development phase, one alternative is usually chosen as the best combination of aesthetic, social, and technical solutions for the building's program. The engineer:

- is given the latest set of drawings and programming information for the building
- lists, with the architect, the range of acceptable air and surface temperatures, air motions, relative humidities, lighting levels, and background-noise levels for each activity to take place in the building
- develops a schedule of operations for each activity
- determines the **thermal comfort zones** by considering these activities and their schedule, the amount of heat that will be generated by the activities, and the building's orientation

- establishes the **thermal load** (the amount of heat gained or lost) for the worst winter and summer conditions, and for average conditions during the majority of the building's operating hours for each zone
- may estimate the building's annual energy consumption
- selects the HVAC systems (More than one system may be used to meet different conditions in a large building. For example, one system may serve zones that are completely within the interior of the building, with a separate system for perimeter zones.)
- identifies the components of the HVAC system and locates them within the building (Mechanical rooms, **distribution trees** [vertical chases and horizontal runs of ductwork], and components like **fan-coil units** under windows and air grilles within specific spaces all have to be selected and located.)
- specifies sizes for the components of the HVAC system

Once the engineer lays out the system, it is time to coordinate conflicts with other building systems, such as the structure, plumbing, fire safety, and circulation. By drawing sections through the building, architects and engineers can identify clearance problems and see opportunities to coordinate the HVAC system with other building systems.

The process of design finalization involves the designer of the HVAC system verifying the load on each component, and the component's ability to meet this load. Then the final drawings and specifications are completed. During construction, the engineer may visit the site to ensure that work is proceeding according to design as well as to deal with unanticipated site conditions.

Thermal Comfort Zones

Each thermal comfort zone has its own set of functional, scheduling, and orientation concerns that determine when and how much heating, cooling, or ventilation is needed:

- Functional factors depend on activity levels or users' heat tolerances and include the need for daylight and the effect of one function on the air quality of others.
- Scheduling factors affect the need for electric lighting and the heating and cooling needs of unoccupied spaces.
- Orientation factors consider the degree of exposure to daylight, direct sun, and wind, which is especially relevant for perimeter spaces. Cooling for interior spaces overheated by electric lighting is also considered.

In multistory buildings, interior spaces on intermediate floors—those spaces not at the building's perimeter or on the top or ground floors—may be able to use ventilation air as their only heating load source. These areas are so well shielded from the building's exterior that they may not need additional heat and can be served only by cooling. The amount of electrically generated heat along with that produced by human activity and other heat-generating sources usually outweighs the cooling effect of the

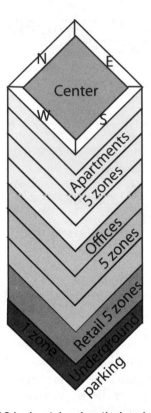

Figure 9-24 HVAC horizontal and vertical zoning. The way that a mechanical engineer sets up zones for heating and cooling has implications for the architectural and interior design of a space. Zones may occupy horizontal areas of a single floor or may be vertically connected between floors. The function of a space affects both its vertical and its horizontal zoning. Some functions may tolerate higher temperatures than others. Some functions require daylight, which may add heat to the space, while others are better located away from the building's perimeter. In some areas, such as laboratories, air quality and isolation are major concerns. The input of the interior designer can be an important component in ensuring that the client's needs are met.

amount of outdoor air supplied by minimal ventilation, even in winter weather. In the summer, most interior cooling loads are generated inside the building. The perimeter areas of the building are much more weather sensitive.

Heating and Cooling Loads

Heating and cooling loads are the amounts of energy required to compensate for heat loss and heat gain in the building. The rate of flow of hot or cold air coming into the building from ventilation and infiltration influences the size of the heating or cooling load. It also depends on the difference in temperature and humidity between the inside air and the outside air. The amount of outside air coming in is expressed in liters per second (cubic feet per minute [cfm]).

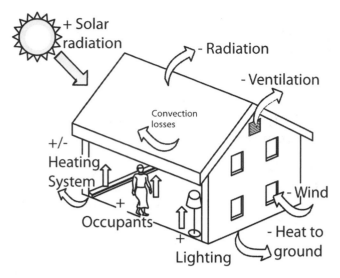

Figure 9-25 Heat losses and heat gains in buildings. Buildings may switch from losing heat to gaining heat in a short time. Different parts of a building may be gaining or losing heat simultaneously.

HEAT LOSS AND HEATING LOADS

A heating load is created when a building loses heat through the building envelope. Cold outside air that enters a building through ventilation, such as an open window, or is the result of infiltration, such as when air leaks through cracks in the building envelope, also add to the heating load.

Convection, radiation, or conduction of heat through the building's exterior walls, windows, and roof assemblies and the floors of unheated spaces are the main sources of heat loss in cold weather. Wind passing the building both draws warm air out and forces cold air in. Infiltration of cold air through cracks in the exterior construction, particularly around doors and windows, contributes significant heat loss. This heat loss places a heating load on the building's mechanical system, which must make up heat in spaces that lose it through cracks and poorly insulated areas. Energy auditors use equipment to locate air leaks and areas with inadequate insulation. They know what to look for in new and older buildings, and the cost of an energy audit is a good investment for a building owner. Some utilities will supply basic energy audits for free. Trained experts, sometimes called house doctors or home-performance contractors, look at the building as a system and evaluate safety, comfort, energy efficiency, and indoor air quality. You can get a listing of qualified, trained energy auditors from your state energy office or cooperative extension service.

The most common sources of air leaks are places where plumbing, wiring, or a chimney penetrates through an insulated floor or ceiling or along the sill plate or band joist on top of the building's foundation wall. Fireplace dampers and attic access hatches are other likely sources.

Anywhere that walls and ceilings or floors meet or where openings pierce the building's exterior provide opportunities for air

to infiltrate. Air can leak where the tops of interior partition walls intersect with the attic space as well as through recessed lights and fans in insulated ceilings. Missing plaster allows air to pass through a wall, as do electrical outlets and switches on exterior walls. Window, door, and baseboard moldings can leak air, as can dropped ceiling soffits above bathtubs and cabinets. Air can also leak at low walls along the exterior in finished attics, especially at access doors, and at built-in cabinets and bureaus.

Gaps less than 4 millimeters (¼ in.) wide can be sealed with caulk, which is available in a variety of types for different materials. Caulks with 20-year flexibility lifetimes should be specified. Either colored or paintable caulk should be selected for visible use. The least expensive caulks do not hold up well. Larger cracks and holes that are protected from the sun and moisture can be filled with expanding one-part polyurethane-foam sealant. A safe-for-ozone label identifies foam sealants without CFCs.

For even larger cracks and for backing in deep cracks, backer rod or crack filler, usually in the form of a round coil that is between 4 millimeters and 25 millimeters (¼–1 in.) in diameter and is made of a flexible foam material is specified. Then the crack is sealed with caulk. Rigid foam insulation or fiberglass insulation wrapped in plastic can be used for very large openings, such as plumbing chases and attic hatch covers. Plastic in places with high temperatures may melt. Metal flashing with high-temperature silicone sealants may be permitted around chimneys by some building codes.

HEAT GAINS AND COOLING LOADS

Buildings gain heat from occupants and their activities. **Cooling loads** are defined as the hourly rate of heat gain in an enclosed space and are expressed as BTUs per hour. Cooling loads are used as the basis for selecting an air-conditioning unit or a cooling system.

Cooling loads represent the energy needed to offset the heat gained through the building envelope in hot weather or from hot air entering the building via infiltration or ventilation. Body heat, showering, cooking, lighting, and using appliances and equipment also create cooling loads.

The heat generated by lighting is often the greatest part of a building's total cooling load. All types of electric lighting convert electrical power into light and heat. Eventually, the light is also converted to heat within the space (consider a lamp shining on a desk and the desk becoming warmer). All of the electrical power that enters a lighting fixture ends up as heat in the space.

Some of the heat from lighting is convected from the lighting fixture to the surrounding air and becomes part of the cooling load. The rest is radiated to surrounding surfaces, with the exception of a small amount that is conducted to adjacent material. This radiated and conducted heat is then convected to the air, becoming part of the cooling load. Recessed fixtures tend to heat the surrounding structure, while hanging fixtures convey heat more directly to the air. Some fixtures are designed so that air returns through them, absorbing heat that would otherwise go into the space.

Electric, gas, and steam appliances and equipment in restaurants, hospitals, laboratories, and such commercial spaces as beauty salons release heat to interiors. Hoods over kitchen appliances that exhaust air may reduce heat gain, but the exhausted air must be replaced with outdoor air, which may need to be cooled. Steam or hot water pipes that run through air-conditioned spaces and hot water tanks within spaces contribute to the cooling load.

In both warm and hot weather, buildings gain heat by convection, radiation, and conduction through the exterior walls and window and roof assemblies. The amount of heat gain varies with the time of day, the orientation of the affected building parts to the sun, the exposure to the wind, and the amount of time it takes for the heat to reach the interior of the building (thermal lag). The heat gain from sun shining on windows varies with the orientation to the sun and the ways the windows are shaded.

In hot weather, warm **make-up air** enters when spaces are ventilated to remove odors or pollutants. The use of a dehumidifier to lower relative humidity in a space adds to heat gain because of the latent heat released into the space when moist air is condensed and the heat produced by running the dehumidifier's compressor.

MEASURING HEATING AND COOLING LOADS

A **degree-day** is a unit used in computing heating and cooling loads, sizing HVAC systems, and calculating yearly fuel consumption. It represents one degree of difference in mean daily outdoor temperature from a standard temperature. A heating degree day is one degree-day below the standard temperature of 18°C (65°F) and is used in estimating fuel or power consumption by a heating system. A cooling degree-day is one degree-day above the standard temperature of 24°C (75°F) and helps calculate energy requirements for air conditioning and refrigeration systems. Degree-day information is usually published in daily newspapers.

Systems are rated in tons of refrigeration, which is the cooling effect obtained when a ton of ice at 0°C (32°F) melts to water while at the same temperature over a period of 24 hours. It is equal to 3.5 kilowatts (12,000 BTU/hour).

The **energy efficiency rating** is an index of the efficiency of a refrigerating unit. It expresses the number of BTUs removed per watt of electrical energy input.

Energy Use Calculations

Mechanical engineers perform load calculations to determine the correct size for heating and cooling equipment, airflow rates, and duct and pipe sizes. Architects calculate loads to ensure that the building envelope is adequately insulated, compare alternative envelope designs, estimate preliminary mechanical-system costs, and evaluate the potential benefits of solar-energy design. Load calculations provide the basis for estimates of annual building energy use. They can become very complicated when used for detailed cost comparisons of alternative systems.

When one design costs less to install but another is more energy efficient, engineers may perform energy design value

analyses. For example, an analysis may help with decisions about optimizing the quantity of insulation, choosing between double and triple glazing, selecting types of lighting, deciding on solar energy use, and balancing aesthetic considerations with their cost to the client.

Heating and Cooling System Components

☑ **Although an interior designer does not design the HVAC system, you will have to consider the space that components take up, their noise, their terminal outlets in occupied rooms, and the access space needed for repair and maintenance.**

HVAC systems consist of three main parts: the equipment that generates the heating or cooling, the medium by which the heat or cooling is transported, and the devices by which it is delivered. For example, a building might use an oil-fired boiler to generate hot water. The water is the medium that carries the heat throughout the building, and the pipes and radiators are the delivery devices.

The front end (or head end) of the system is where the energy or fuel consumption or heat collection occurs. The equipment here is selected for its capacity to offset the peak load of the zones that it serves and to bring them back from their lower temperature setting when not in use to their normal operating condition.

The front end may consist of a central heat source, such as a furnace, steam or hot water boiler, solar-heat collector, geothermal well, or heating water converter. It may also include a central cooling source like a chiller, DX (which stands for direct expansion) air conditioner, or evaporative cooler.

The conveying medium transports the heated or cooled steam, water, or air through a system of pipes or ducts throughout the building. Steam travels under its own pressure, air is moved by fans, and water is moved by pumps.

Terminal delivery devices are located within the spaces to be heated or cooled. The heated or cooled medium is delivered to the space by air registers and diffusers, hydronic radiators or convectors, or fan coil units.

It is becoming more common for buildings to be designed for localized, rather than centralized, HVAC production and control. Multipurpose buildings with fragmented occupancy schedules call for many diverse HVAC zones. Digital-control systems allow both overall building coordination and localized thermal response. Employees are more satisfied when they can control their interior environment. Self-contained package units can provide heating and/or cooling directly to the space, combining all three components in one piece of equipment.

Architectural Considerations

The design of the HVAC system affects a building's architecture and interior design. The architect must coordinate with all consultants from the beginning of the project to allow realistic space allotments for HVAC equipment. The design of the mechanical system must merge with the architectural and structural planning and should be developed concurrently. Spaces requiring quiet, such as bedrooms and conference rooms, should be located as far away as possible, both horizontally and vertically, from noisy HVAC equipment.

☑ **Interior design issues, such as whether to use an open office plan with modular furniture systems or private enclosed offices, have a significant impact on the mechanical system and should be shared with the engineer early in the design process.**

In addition to deciding which HVAC system will be used in a large building, the mechanical engineer selects the system based on initial and **life-cycle costs**, suitability for the intended occupancy, availability of floor space for the required equipment, maintenance requirements and reliability of the equipment, and simplicity of the system's controls. The architect must communicate and coordinate with the engineer and ask questions about the engineering system's impact on the architectural and interior designs.

Together, the architect and engineer evaluate issues that affect the thermal qualities of the building, such as the amount and type of insulation and the shading of the building from the sun's heat, and influence the mechanical-equipment size and fuel consumption. The architect may develop design elements that reduce the system's operating expenses and lower the size and initial cost of HVAC equipment, but that increase the initial cost of the building's construction. The use of cost-effectiveness analyses helps determine the optimal economic balance between passive (built into the building's architectural design) and active (mechanical-system) approaches.

Early in the project, the architect must consider the number, position, and size of central HVAC stations and ensure that they are located near the areas they serve and have access to outdoor air. Clearances must be allowed around the equipment for access during normal operation, inspection, routine maintenance, and repair. Plans should be made for eventual replacement of major components without substantial damage to existing building

materials. Space for flue stacks, access for fuel delivery, and room for fuel storage may be needed. HVAC requirements can have a substantial impact on the space plan, ceiling heights, and other interior design issues, so getting involved early in the process is a good idea.

Mechanical rooms often take up approximately 5 to 10 percent of the gross building area. Furnace and boiler rooms, fan rooms, and refrigeration rooms may be separate spaces or may be combined. They may require doors of adequate width for equipment replacement, and the doors may need to be louvered to allow air to enter the space. Their size, location, and noise can be important interior design considerations.

The locations and dimensions of piping and ductwork will determine where chases must be located for clusters of piping and ductwork running vertically between floors. Ductwork, and especially areas where ducts connect, requires regular access for maintenance. Suspended ceiling grids allow easy duct access. Gypsum wallboard ceilings may require access doors at specific locations, including at all fire dampers within ducts. With proper early planning, only minor changes in the floor plan will need to be incorporated into the final mechanical design.

☑ **Within occupied areas, space must be allocated along exterior walls for exposed terminal-delivery devices, such as registers and diffusers. Their form and position must be coordinated with the interior design to prevent conflicts between furniture arrangements and the location of grilles or wall-mounted units. Thermostat locations are determined by the engineer and depend on the surrounding heat sources, but they have a significant effect on the visual quality of the interior space. The architect is also concerned with the appearance of grilles and openings in outside walls on the building's exterior.**

Buildings are continuously gaining and losing heat. Much of this heat gain and heat loss occurs when buildings take in fresh air; limiting ventilation reduces such gain and loss. As we will see in Chapter 10: Indoor Air Quality, ventilation is essential to ensure acceptable air quality indoors.

10

·················

Indoor Air Quality

The American Society of Heating, Refrigeratiing, and Air-Conditioning Engineers (ASHRAE, 2004) has defined acceptable **indoor air quality (IAQ)** as "air in which there are no known contaminants at harmful concentrations as determined by cognizant authorities and with which a substantial majority (80 percent or more) of the people exposed do not express dissatisfaction." This definition depends more on consensus than on quantifiable data. It reflects the complexity of identifying contaminants and their sources in indoor air; it also speaks to the difficulty of diagnosing illnesses caused by contaminants in indoor air. Engineers consider four approaches when confronting IAQ problems:

- choosing materials and equipment that limit pollution
- isolating sources of pollution
- providing adequate fresh and filtered recirculated air
- maintaining a clean building and clean equipment

As buildings become more tightly controlled environments, IAQ and its effects on our health become an increasingly critical issue. Today, there are more than 80,000 synthetic chemicals in use, most of which have not been tested individually or in combination for their effects on human health. Materials used in building, furnishing, and maintaining a building potentially contain many toxic chemicals.

Three major reasons for poor IAQ in office buildings are:

- the presence of indoor air pollution sources
- poorly designed, maintained, or operated ventilation systems
- unanticipated or poorly planned uses of the buildings

☑ **Interior designers play a significant role in specifying materials that may contribute to indoor air pollution. They also are key players in the renovation of buildings for new uses and to accommodate new ways of working.**

Air pollution problems can start with a building's materials and finishes and with the construction methods used to build or renovate the building. IAQ is compromised when inadequate ventilation does not provide enough outside air. Chemicals used in cleaning and office products that become trapped inside a building, as well as outdoor pollutants caught inside, add to the problem. Mold or other microorganisms that grow, multiply, and disperse particles through heating, ventilating, and air conditioning (HVAC) systems are other significant sources of IAQ problems as well. Poor design and maintenance of the HVAC system supports the growth of microorganisms.

People contribute skin scales, exhaled carbon dioxide (CO_2), airborne particles, vapors, and gases. Cleaning, cooking, broiling, gas and oil burning, personal hygiene, and smoking all add pollutants to indoor air. Pesticides from pest-management practices can also pollute a building's air. Indoor air pollutants can be circulated from portions of the building used for specialized purposes, such as restaurants, print shops, and dry-cleaning stores, into offices in the same building.

Contaminants in buildings are so widespread that almost every building contains one or more recognized contaminants. Asbestos and lead have been used in building products for many years in the past. Heating systems can give off carbon monoxide (CO). Interior finishes and building materials often contain formaldehyde. Both benzene and chlordane are petroleum products found in detergents, insecticides, and motor fuels. Mercury, ozone, and radon can contaminate buildings as well. Paper copying and inks produce irritating fumes, and dust and tobacco smoke contain particles that adversely affect the respiratory system. Plastics can give off offensive gases. Fabrics treated with fire-retardant chemicals can cause respiratory problems for some people.

Sick Building Syndrome

The overall result of these pollutants can be **sick building syndrome (SBS)**, which is diagnosed when more than 20 percent of a building's occupants complain of such symptoms as headaches, upper respiratory irritation, or eye irritation and when these symptoms disappear after leaving the building on weekends. Symptoms may also include irritation of mucous membranes, dizziness, nausea, throat irritation, and fatigue. Although the specific causes are not identified, the symptoms coincide with time spent in a particular building and disappear once the affected person leaves the premises.

Building related illness (BRI) describes the same range of ailments, from mild allergic reactions to more serious infections, including pneumonia; however, BRI is the term used in cases for which the specific cause is known. Both SBS and BRI are largely the result of poor IAQ.

Symptoms that appear suddenly after a change in a building, such as painting or pesticide application, are another indication of IAQ problems. Some people may be affected by IAQ problems, while others who share the space may not be.

Complaints about BRIs may result from other causes, such as illness contracted in another location; acute sensitivity, including allergies; job-related stress or dissatisfaction; and other psychosocial factors. "Nevertheless studies show that symptoms may be caused or exacerbated by sick building syndrome," according to the U.S. Environmental Protection Agency (EPA).

Inadequate ventilation has been identified as a major factor in BRI. Opening a building up to outside air can result in the need for greatly increased energy use to properly heat, cool, humidify, and distribute that air. In addition, already conditioned air in the building is lost to the outside. ASHRAE has attempted to address both IAQ and energy conservation concerns by revising its ventilation standard to provide a minimum of 15 **cubic feet per minute (cfm)** of outdoor air per person, increasing this minimum to 20 cfm per person in office spaces.

☑ **In order to improve IAQ and prevent contamination by pollutants, the building's architect, engineers, and interior designer must work together. The interior designer can**

- **specify appropriate materials, products, and equipment**
- **evaluate the amount and toxicity of emissions given off during installation or use, especially where surfaces of possible pollutants are exposed to the air and to people**
- **review maintenance requirements for cleaning processes, stain-resistant treatments, and waxing that emit pollutants**
- **provide the building's management, users, and owners with appropriate information about maintenance requirements**

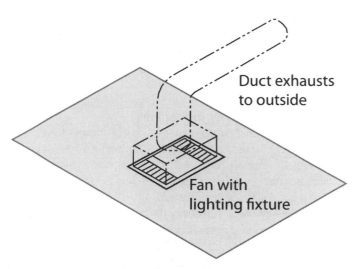

Figure 10-1 Bathroom ventilation. Bathroom exhaust fans should exhaust directly to the outside.

Many of the problems people have with adverse reactions to building contaminants develop after new construction or renovation. Renovations in occupied buildings are especially likely to introduce pollutants into the buildings' interiors. SBS problems can be prevented by

- maintaining the HVAC system, including periodic filter replacement
- replacing water-stained ceiling tile and carpet
- prohibiting smoking
- venting restrooms, copy rooms, printing facilities to the outside
- storing and using paints, adhesives, solvents, and pesticides in well-ventilated areas
- using paints, adhesives, solvents, and pesticides when a building is unoccupied
- allowing time for building materials in new or remodeled areas to off-gas pollutants before occupancy

During construction, interior contamination can be prevented by

- compartmentalizing construction with partitions and doors with closers
- blocking connecting plenums and air-conditioning returns
- isolating work areas from occupied spaces
- supplying extra ventilation via window- or door-mounted fans
- keeping the construction area under negative pressure to prevent contaminants from spreading throughout the building
- complying with IAQ requirements
- protecting construction workers

Allergies and Multiple-Chemical Sensitivity

Interior designers are more and more often being called on to help people with allergies or other physical sensitivities in the design of healthy, nonpolluting homes. Businesses, too, are becoming more aware of the costs of ill employees as well as more concerned about the health of the indoor environment. Some interior designers have made environmentally sensitive and healthy design a specialty. As homes and workspaces are exposed to increasing levels of more exotic chemicals, it becomes more important that designers have the knowledge and skills necessary to create safe indoor environments.

The causes, symptoms, and treatment of allergies have been recognized by health professionals as an immune-system problem. Allergies to mold, household dust, and dust mites are quite common. Interior designers are often asked to consider allergies when designing residential interiors.

Multiple-chemical sensitivity (MCS) is a controversial illness. There is no standard medical definition, diagnosis, or cure. The Centers for Disease Control and Prevention (CDC) does not recognize MCS, and scientists and physicians argue about whether the disorder is real or imagined. Skeptics claim that persons who complain of chemical sensitivities often have a history of other problems, including depression, which has led many to label MCS a behavioral health condition.

The Social Security Administration and the U.S. Department of Housing and Urban Development (HUD), however, recognize MCS as a disability and as a chronic condition in which people develop increased sensitivities to synthetic chemicals or irritants. Although the medical origins of MCS have not been identified (leading to the aforementioned skepticism), it has been associated with acute and high-level or chronic and low-level exposure to chemicals in building materials (including formaldehyde), furnishings, office equipment, carpets, personal care and laundry products, and biological contaminants. MCS is credited with injuries to the nervous, endocrine, immune, and respiratory systems that make individuals sensitive to even minute amounts of common synthetic chemicals. Symptoms may vary widely from person to person and may appear unrelated. Continued exposure to the irritants causes a person to react to many other synthetic chemicals. Symptoms may become disabling or life threatening. As the level of sensitivity increases, extreme sensitivity to a wide range of chemicals may occur.

MCS is usually triggered by an acute and sometimes continuous exposure to toxic chemicals, after which a person develops an intolerance to lower levels of a range of substances. In other words, a person can develop MCS after one massive exposure to, for example, a pesticide spraying or a chemical spill, or after years of working at a factory that uses toxic substances. Less commonly, it can result from built-up exposure to the chemicals we all come into contact with each day.

Persons with heightened sensitivity to materials in the built environment are often forced to make changes in the way they live and work. Interior designers who are aware of these issues can help create safe, healthy interior spaces.

Odors

Foul-smelling air is not necessarily unhealthy, but it can cause nausea, headache, and loss of appetite. Our noses are more sensitive than most detection equipment available today; they can detect harmful substances by their odors so that they can be eliminated before they reach dangerous levels. Sources include

- building intakes, which pick up auto exhaust, furnace and industrial effluents, or smog, and bring the contaminants into a building's air supply
- industrial odors from such chemical products as printing inks, dyes, and synthetic materials and from manufactured products
- body odors in offices, assembly rooms, and other enclosed and densely occupied spaces that accumulate on furnishings and are released after the people who produced them have left the space
- smoking
- materials such as cotton, wool, rayon, and fir wood that absorb odors readily and give them off later at varying rates, depending on temperature and relative humidity (RH)
- moisture or certain kinds of metals and coatings used on air-conditioning coils, which emit odors
- linoleum, paint, upholstery, carpets, drapes, and other room furnishings that may add odors and that usually are reduced with lower RH
- offensive odors from food, cooking, and the decomposition of animal and vegetable matter

As our environment is freed of multiple odors, we become more sensitive to those that remain. The obvious presence of human body odor in a space is usually an indication of inadequate ventilation.

Control odors by

- removing gases or vapors or reducing their concentration below perceptible levels
- ventilating with clean outdoor air
- using air washers or air scrubbers
- adsorbing (assimilating) odors by using activated charcoal filters
- removing odors by chemical reactions, odor modification, oxidation, or combustion

VOLATILE ORGANIC COMPOUNDS

Volatile organic compounds (VOCs) are chemical compounds that tend to evaporate at room temperature and normal atmospheric pressure (and, thus, are volatile), and that contain one or more carbon atoms (and, thus, are called organic compounds). They are invisible fumes or vapors. Some VOCs have sharp odors, while others can be detected only through the use of sensitive equipment. Almost any manufactured or natural product may give off VOCs in a confined space; VOCs commonly evaporate from building and furnishing products. Plywood, plastic, fibers, varnishes, coatings, and cleaning chemicals are common sources. Solvents used in paints, waxes, consumer products, and petroleum fuels all emit VOCs, many of which are toxic and can affect the central nervous system, the eyes, and the respiratory system.

Building occupants may experience intoxication, loss of judgment, and panic, in addition to the many symptoms typical of exposure to formaldehyde.

VOCs enter the air when the surfaces of solid materials evaporate or **off-gas** at room temperatures. Some products will off-gas VOCs for a period, during which time the space must be ventilated, then revert to a safe state.

Most of the more serious effects of VOCs are the result of exposures at levels higher than those normally expected indoors. However, some common situations are likely to cause mild to serious health effects from VOC exposure. These include

- installation of large volumes of new furniture or wall partitions
- dry cleaning of large volumes of draperies or upholstered furniture
- large-scale cleaning, painting, or installation of wall or floor coverings
- high air temperatures

Both building-maintenance workers and other building occupants are exposed to higher levels of VOCs when the HVAC system is shut down at night or during weekends. VOCs are not adequately cleared from the building, and the accumulation is circulated through the building when the system is turned on again.

Some building materials may act as sponges for VOCs, absorbing them for later release. Carpeting, ceiling tiles, and freestanding partitions with high surface areas absorb VOCs. Rough surfaces and low ventilation rates increase absorption. VOC emissions can be managed by limiting sources, providing proper ventilation, and controlling RH.

☑ **The stability of materials has an impact on IAQ over an extended period. Interior design finishes that do not produce or retain dust as well as designs that limit open shelving or dust-collecting areas help control VOC retention in a space. Durable materials, such as hardwoods, ceramics, masonry, metals, glass, baked enamels, and hard plastics, generally have low VOC emissions. Low-VOC paints are available as well. Fibers, including cotton, wool, acetate, and rayon, have low VOCs, but their dyes and treatments may release toxic chemicals.**

The rerelease of VOCs that have been absorbed by furnishings can be controlled by increasing outside air ventilation during and after the installation of finishes and furnishings. Fresh air should be introduced constantly and exhausted directly to the outside rather than through the HVAC system. Fiber-lined HVAC ducts and return-air plenums should be protected, especially the exposed upper surfaces of ceiling panels and exposed spray-on insulation. Newly occupied buildings should be operated at the lowest acceptable temperatures to slow VOC emissions.

The period immediately following the completion of the building's interior is critical in terms of VOC exposure. The process of aging materials before installation may help release some of the VOCs outside of the space. If possible, occupancy should be delayed to allow for **off-gassing** from adhesives, paints, and other materials and finishes. Installed materials can be protected from collecting VOC emissions from other products by sealing them in plastic vapor barriers.

During a **bake-out period**, the unoccupied building is sealed and the temperature is raised to approximately 27°C (80°F). The space is periodically completely ventilated, over a period of 72 hours to a week (168 hours). This process increases the aging rate for shorter-lived VOC sources. Baking-out must be thoughtfully planned and professionally monitored. The effectiveness of bake-out procedures is mixed and depends on the materials and procedures involved.

VOC emissions from ceiling and wall materials are highest immediately after installation. Most wall finishes have a slow decay rate, emitting VOCs gradually for a prolonged period. Finishes that are applied wet give up their VOCs more quickly and become inert after a shorter ventilation period. When looking for products that emit low amounts of VOCs, consider

- how much of a product's surface area is exposed
- how much of the product is used in the building
- what is known of the toxicity or irritation potential of the product's primary chemical constituents
- how stable the product is in the intended use

☑ **The process of painting or plating furniture can create air and water pollution and toxic waste. Coating processes are less polluting and safer. Metals can be coated with powder coating. Polymer coating has replaced cadmium plating, which produced air and water pollution. Check specifications on metal tables and chairs to see how they are coated.**

Chemicals Affecting Indoor Air Quality

Of the ever-expanding number of chemicals in the environment, a number stand out as particularly damaging to IAQ:

Formaldehyde
- is a colorless, strong-smelling gas used in the manufacture of synthetic resins and dyes, and as a preservative and disinfectant
- is the most widespread VOC and a major contributor to SBS
- is present in urea-formaldehyde foam insulation (UFFI), pressed-wood products, and furnishings
- irritates mucous membranes of eyes, upper respiratory tract, and skin, causing difficulty breathing, coughing, wheezing, chest tightness, nausea, vomiting, histamine allergic reactions, and/or asthmatic attacks
- may produce pulmonary edema, lung inflammation, pneumonia, and death at high concentrations
- may increase risk of cancer in humans at high concentrations

Phenol-formaldehyde (PF) resins
- resist moisture degradation
- are added to products for exterior applications, interior plywood, and as bonding for laminates on wood and steel surfaces
- emit formaldehyde at lower rates than UF resins

Figure 10-2 Copier isolation and exhaust. Copiers and printers that produce ozone should be located away from areas in which people work and should exhaust directly to the outside.

Urea-formaldehyde (UF) resins
- are less expensive
- are used only for interior applications
- off-gas 10 to 20 times as much as PF resins

Carbon monoxide (CO)
- is an odorless gas produced by incomplete combustion in furnaces, stoves, and fireplaces
- is found near garages, combustion equipment, or indoor air tobacco smoke
- interferes with oxygen intake
- causes headaches, dizziness, sleepiness, and muscular weakness
- may cause unconsciousness and death at high concentrations

Carbon dioxide (CO$_2$)
- is an odorless gas that we exhale every time we breathe
- is generated by fossil-fuel combustion and contributes to the greenhouse effect
- causes stuffiness and discomfort and dulls the ability to think at high concentrations
- is an indicator of an inadequate ventilation rate in enclosed or high-occupancy spaces

Sulfur dioxide (SO$_2$)
- is produced by heating with coal and oil and power plants that use coal, oil, gas
- is found in acid rain and smog
- causes irritation of respiratory mucous membranes as well as cardiovascular problems

Nitrogen dioxide (NO$_2$)
- is a yellowish-brown gas
- is produced by high-temperature combustion, heating buildings with oil and gas, biomass burning, and tobacco smoke
- causes respiratory irritation that interferes with breathing, may cause lung damage, and may suppress the immune system

Hydrocarbons
- are compounds of hydrogen and carbon
- are found in aerosol sprays, refrigerants, and foams
- contribute to the greenhouse effect and stratospheric ozone depletion

Chlorofluorocarbons (CFCs)
- are produced by heating buildings, cooking appliances, and dry-process photocopiers
- are imperceptible in the air at first, then cause increased distress over time
- cause itching or burning eyes, sneezing, coughing, dry nose and throat, sore throat, and/or tightness in chest
- can be replaced by HCFCs for upholstery foams and insulating foams, but this contributes to the greenhouse effect

Ozone
- is an irritating, pale blue gas composed of three oxygen atoms
- is produced by copy machines, high-voltage electronic equipment, and electrostatic air cleaners
- is explosive and toxic at low concentrations
- causes wheezing, shortness of breath, dizziness, and/or asthma

☑ **Interior designers have a responsibility to ensure that building owners, managers, and maintenance staff understand the original IAQ design elements and principles in order to guarantee benefits in the future. Maintaining and monitoring the HVAC system reduce SBS risk and enable problems to be identified and corrected at minimum expense. Interior designers will benefit by visiting the space a few months after the construction is finished and again a few years later to learn how to improve the process on future projects. Feedback from an environmental consultant can be very helpful as well.**

Manufacturers are becoming much more aware of the dangers of VOCs in their products. The following are other VOCs to watch out for:

- **Methylene chloride (methol chloride)** in paint strippers, adhesive removers, and aerosol-spray paints causes cancer in animals and is converted to CO in the body.
- **Xylene**, which is found in varnishes, solvents for resins, and enamels, is a narcotic irritant that affects the heart, liver, kidneys, and nervous system.
- **Toluene**, which is a petrochemical found in various adhesives and solvents and in chipboard, is a narcotic that may cause anemia.
- **Styrene** is found in many paints, plastic foams, plastics, and resins and is a possible carcinogen.
- **Benzene**, which is found in cigarette smoke as well as in paints, stains, and varnishes used on furnishings, is a respiratory-tract irritant and carcinogen.
- **Ethyl benzene** is found in some solvents and causes severe irritation to the eyes and the respiratory tract.
- **Trichloroethylene**, which is found in furniture varnishes, may affect control of the nervous system and is most likely a carcinogen.
- **Methylene chloride**, which is found in acoustical office partitions, is a narcotic that can affect the central nervous system and probably causes cancer.
- **Methylethylketone**, also called **2-butanone**, is found in fiberboard and particleboard and depresses the central nervous system.
- **Phenylcyclohexene (4-PC)** is an odorous VOC from styrene-butadiene (SB) latex, which is used to bind carpet fibers to jute backings. Using heat-fusion bonding for carpet backing eliminates the high-VOC latex bond.

Perchloroethylene (perc), the chemical most widely used to dry-clean fabrics and draperies, is also called tetrachloroethylene. It can irritate the skin and eyes, can depress the central nervous system, and has been shown to be a carcinogen in animals. Dry cleaners recapture perc during the dry-cleaning process for reuse and remove more during the pressing and finishing processes. Some dry cleaners do not remove as much perc as possible all of the time; their goods repeatedly have a chemical odor.

Fumes can be produced by polymers or by additives used as colorants or plasticizers in plastics that are used to make wall coverings, carpets, padding, plumbing pipes, and electric wires; their insulation emits toxic chemicals, including NO, cyanide, and acid gases. Plasticizers soften plastics, making them less stable. **Polyvinyl chloride (PVC)** plastics are safe to use, but their manufacturing process produces health risks, and they emit toxic fumes in fires. Most plastic laminates have very low toxicity levels.

Other Indoor-Air-Quality Contaminants

Indoor air also includes other impurities, including biological and radiological substances.

Particulates are liquid or solid particles smaller than 500 micrometers from building-construction materials and equipment and building occupants. In locations where smoking is permitted, it contributes 50 to 90 percent of such particles. Pollen grains responsible for seasonal allergies are larger than dust particles and can be mechanically filtered out.

Respirable small particles (RSPs) are particles less than 10 microns in diameter (100 microns is about the diameter of a human hair) and are linked to SBS. Many people become increasingly sensitive through repeated contact, which results in allergic reactions.

Pesticide residues may remain in basements, foundations, ceilings, wall cavities, cabinets, closets, and soil outside foundations treated before 1980 for termites, roaches, and mice with pesticides containing toxic substances. Pesticide residues may be neurotoxins and may present a long-term risk of liver or kidney disease or cancer. If the history of the contamination is known, the materials can be identified and removed by experts. The pesticides may also be able to be sealed permanently.

Fibrous mineral and glass particles in wall insulation, duct insulation, fire-resistant acoustic ceiling tiles, and fabrics can break down, burn the eyes, cause the skin to itch, and may increase a person's long-term risk of lung damage and cancer. These particles should be handled only by persons wearing a respirator and gloves, should be sealed and enclosed, and should be left in place. Man-made mineral fibers are generally larger and less dangerous than asbestos fibers. An initial blowout period for duct insulation removes broken fibers.

Asbestos is white, light gray, or light brown and looks like coarse fabric or paper or a dense pulpy mass of light gray stucco-like material applied to ceilings, beams, and columns. Before the 1980s, asbestos was used in steam-pipe and duct insulation, furnaces and furnace parts, drywall joint-finishing material and textured paint, acoustic tiles, fiber cement shingles and siding, floor tiles and adhesive, and some sprayed and troweled ceiling finishing plaster.

Most asbestos can be left undisturbed as long as it does not emit fibers into the air. If disturbed, asbestos must be encapsulated or removed by asbestos-removal professionals. Inhalation of asbestos fibers presents a long-term risk of cancer, asbestosis (fibrous scarring of the lungs), and fluid in the lungs. Asbestos can be sealed and covered with sheet metal if it is not crumbling. Encapsulation may cost more than removal. Avoid drilling holes, hanging materials onto walls or ceilings, causing abrasion, or removing ceiling tiles below materials that contain asbestos. Removal may release fibers if not done correctly, so it is imperative to hire a properly certified and licensed expert to identify and remove the asbestos.

Areas in which asbestos is being removed must be isolated by airtight plastic containment barriers and kept under negative pressure with high-efficiency particulate air (HEPA) filtration (see Table 10-1, page 176) within the barrier. The asbestos-containing material must be wetted before removal and disposed of in leak-tight containers. After the removal is completed, all surfaces should be wet-mopped or HEPA-vacuumed for two consecutive

Figure 10-3 Vinyl asbestos tile. Through the 1970s, vinyl asbestos tile (VAT) was installed widely in residential and commercial projects, and remains in some buildings today. There is little risk as long as the asbestos is not disturbed. However, expert removal is required during demolition.

days, the work site should be inspected, and the air quality should be tested.

Lead is a neurotoxin that accumulates in the body. It is particularly harmful to fetuses, infants, and young children, causing learning disabilities, nausea, trembling, numbness in the arms and legs, seizures, convulsions, coma, and death. Particles are suspended in the air or settle on surfaces. Children inhale and ingest lead from paint chips by playing on floors and near other dusty surfaces, and then putting their hands in their mouths.

Lead-based paint was used in 75 percent (nearly 60 million private homes) of U.S. homes built before 1975. Lead is also used for leaded-glass artwork. Until 1985, solder used to connect pipes contained lead, and although this did not ordinarily leach into the water within the pipes, older pipes and solder should be checked.

A professional licensed contractor should remove lead. Occupants must be out of the building during the process, and workers must be properly protected. Lead paint should not be sanded or burned off. Moldings and other woodwork should be replaced or chemically treated. Wood floors must be sealed or covered, belongings should be removed or covered, and dust should be contained during the process. The final cleanup should be done using a HEPA vacuum.

If the condition of the lead-based-painted surfaces is clean and intact and there is no cracking, peeling, blistering, or flaking of existing paint, the surfaces are sometimes permitted to be encapsulated with a coating applied in liquid form that provides flexible, impact-resistant barriers. This coating product can be used on almost any surface, including wood, concrete, brick, cement, drywall, plaster, and gypsum. Some coatings contain a bitter-tasting ingestion deterrent, approved by the U.S. Food and Drug Administration (FDA), to discourage oral contact or ingestion by children. Encapsulation is the simplest and most economical procedure and does not require hazardous-waste removal or the relocation of building occupants. Some products are formulated for professional use only, while others are designed for homeowners and do-it-yourselfers. The effectiveness of encapsulation compared with that of removal remains a controversial issue.

Radon is a colorless, odorless radioactive gas produced by the decay of radioactive uranium that occurs naturally in soil, groundwater, and air. As radon rapidly decays, it releases radiation that can move through soil and into buildings through cracks and openings in their foundations around plumbing, especially those below grade. If concentrated in a building, radon gas may result in an increased risk of lung cancer over a long period.

Radon can be easily measured in a building. It is controlled by minimizing and thoroughly sealing penetrations of below-grade walls and floors. In areas of high risk, under-slab ventilation may be used.

Tobacco smoke is a complicated mixture of more than 4700 chemical compounds, irritating gases, and carcinogenic tar particles. Tobacco smoke causes cancer, emphysema, cardiovascular diseases, and other significant diseases.

Methane and other soil gases are released by decomposing garbage in landfills, leaking sewage lines, and toxic waste. Methane can be explosive or toxic and can have obnoxious odors. To dissipate methane, soil is removed, foundation and floor drains are sealed, and subsoil is ventilated if necessary.

Biological Contaminants

Most of us do not want to think about bacteria, fungi, viruses, algae, insect parts, dead mice, and dust in the air we breathe. These microorganisms release **bioaerosols**, which include tiny spores from molds and other fungi that float through the air and irritate skin and mucous membranes. However, all of these contaminants are less common than human-skin scales. We shed skin cells continually from our skin and in our breath, and our environment is littered with our dead cells. It is estimated that a person sheds 40,000 biological particles containing bacteria per minute when sitting at a desk, and as many as 45 million such particles per minute when exercising.

Office buildings provide an exceptionally favorable environment of high humidity and standing water in circulation and air conditioning ducts, ceiling tiles, insulation, and even ice machines. The number of bacteria able to reproduce in an office environment is often in the range of 1000 colony-forming units per cubic meter.

Mold in carpets eats skin scales, as do dust mites, and produce excrement that can cause allergies. Other biological particulates include pollens, spores, cat-dander allergens, and finely ground food products, such as grains, coffee, and cornstarch. A protein in rat and mice urine is a potent allergen that can become airborne when it dries.

It is often difficult to test for biological contaminants because many of the specific test substances are not widely available; in addition, the symptoms vary and are similar to those from other causes. Estimates of the impact of RSPs on building problems vary from 5 to 50 percent of SBS cases.

Biological contaminants need four items in order to grow in a building:

- a source that enters buildings with outdoor air or on occupants, pets, and houseplants and that lives in air-handling and humidification systems, building materials, and furnishings
- water that is produced by roof and plumbing leaks, vapor migration and condensation, houseplants, humidifiers, aquariums, and building occupants
- nutrients that include skin cells, dust, dirt, food, water, houseplants, dead plant tissue, building materials, and furnishings
- favorable temperatures between 4.4°C and 37.8°C (40°F–100°F

Biological contamination is often the result of inadequate preventive maintenance. The internal components of air-handling units, fan-coil units, and induction units are seldom cleaned.

Drain pans hold stagnant contaminated water that should be drained. Wet cooling coils and porous insulation collect dirt and debris, especially in air-conditioning systems. Access doors to heat exchangers, air-handling units, and heat pumps may be in inaccessible locations over ceiling tiles. Fan-coil and induction units are often difficult to disassemble for cleaning. Outdoor intakes within 7.6 meters (25 ft.) of a cooling tower or other unsanitary location allow microorganisms to enter the building. Whenever an area is flooded, cleanup must be thorough and prompt.

☑ **According to *Contract* associate editor Sofia Galadza (*Contract*, May 2007, p. 118), mold develops when the combination of right temperature, mold spores, moisture, and a food source is present. That food source is often cellulose; paper is cellulose-based, and mold occurs in paper-faced drywall. In 2003, the average commercial financial impact from a mold cleanup was close to $450,000, with an average liability settlement of approximately $1.7 million. Mold damage is no longer covered by insurance companies, although some efforts are being made to change this so that coverage is available if insured parties take steps to control mold.**

Dust mites are relatively large, so they settle out of the air and usually live at floor level; they become airborne only when the dust is disturbed. Dust-mite allergens include enzymes in mite feces, mite saliva, and the soluble proteins from mite body parts.

Filters are rarely effective for bacteria, and evaporative humidifier filters may harbor bacteria that eat cellulose and thrive in the warm, wet environment. Air-conditioning coils can hold skin cells, lint, paper fibers, and water and are a perfect environment for mold and bacteria. Building air-quality specialists tell horror stories of mold-covered mechanical systems that supply air to an entire building.

Contamination of the central-air system and lack of proper ventilation create breeding conditions for microorganisms. Incorrectly specified building and interior materials or finishes provide homes for bacteria and fungi. For example, carpet that is not moisture-resistant can become wet in the wrong location and harbor microorganisms.

Fungus particles and dust mites grow in basements, damp carpets, bedding, fabrics, walls, ceilings, and closets. Covering beds and upholstery with barrier cloth and increasing ventilation can contain them. Borax treatments can retard fungi proliferation. Many types of bacteria and fungi produce toxic substances called endotoxins as by-products of their metabolic processes.

Synthetic carpets containing large amounts of dust make excellent mold environments, especially after water damage. Thoroughly clean and dry water-damaged carpets and building materials within twenty-four hours if possible, or consider removal and replacement.

Installing and using exhaust fans that are vented to the outdoors in kitchens and bathrooms and venting clothes dryers outdoors can reduce moisture and reduce the growth of biological contaminants. Ventilate the attic and crawl spaces to prevent moisture buildup. If using cool mist or ultrasonic humidifiers, clean appliances according to the manufacturer's instructions and refill with fresh water daily.

☑ **Keeping a building clean limits exposure to house dust mites, pollens, animal dander, and other allergy-causing agents. Interior designers should avoid specifying room furnishings that accumulate dust, especially if they cannot be washed in hot water. Using central vacuum systems that are vented to the outdoors or vacuums with high-efficiency filters may also help. A basement below ground level should not be completed unless all water leaks are patched and outdoor ventilation and adequate heat to prevent condensation are provided. A dehumidifier should be run in the basement if necessary in order to maintain RH levels between 30 and 50 percent.**

BIOLOGICAL CONTAMINANTS IN INDOOR AIR

Biological contaminants are almost universally present in building interiors. In conditions that favor their growth, they can cause major health problems. For example, humidifier fever is associated with exposure to amoebas, bacteria, and fungi in humidifier reservoirs, air conditioning, and aquariums. Humidifier fever produces flu-like symptoms, including fever, chills, difficulty breathing, muscle aches, and malaise. Biological contaminants also damage interior construction and finish materials and furnishings. Keep the following biological contaminants in mind as you work:

Fungi
- are plant-like organisms (e.g., molds, mildew, yeast) that lack the chlorophyll needed for photosynthesis
- live on decomposed organic matter or living hosts and reproduce by spores (dry spores can become airborne)
- can result in allergic reactions as well as other immune-system disorders and toxic reactions
- have a distinctive odor that often first indicates their presence and include such VOCs as ethanol
- are controlled by scheduled maintenance (e.g., changing filters often, keeping RH low, eliminating standing water)

Molds
- are a type of fungi that grow where there is moisture or RH exceeds 70 percent
- are often produced by water damage from leaks in pipes or floods or from condensation on walls and ceilings.
- are slimy spores that grow on glass, paint, rubber, textiles, electrical equipment, mineral wool or fiberglass duct-lining materials, paper, and adhesives

Mildew
- is a fungus that appears as a thin layer of black spots on a surface
- grows on drywall; use drywall with fiberglass nonwoven mat facing
- grows on cellulose; use noncellulose adhesives for wall coverings and hardwood flooring

Mycotoxins
- are toxins produced by fungi
- are usually found in contaminated food
- are spores that can enter the respiratory tract

Dust mites
- are allergens that cause allergic reactions in many people
- cause allergic reactions that include nasal inflammation, asthma, itching, inflammation, and rash
- require at least 60 percent RH to survive; maintain RH of 30 to 50 percent

Legionella pneumophila
- causes Legionnaire's disease, a progressive form of pneumonia that infects only about 5 percent of those who inhale droplets of water with the bacteria (however, 5 percent of those infected die of the disease)
- causes Pontiac fever, a flu-like illness that infects 95 percent of exposed persons and lasts between 2 and 3 days

Free-living amoebas
- are microscopic protozoa that can form dormant cysts when food is not available and hide away until food is plentiful
- can be dispersed through the humidification and HVAC systems from areas of standing water
- keep alive some bacteria that they have eaten and protect them from disinfectants, such as chlorine

Viruses
- are submicroscopic organisms that reproduce in living hosts and can cause disease

Blue-green algae
- are single-celled microscopic organisms that grow in fresh or salt water and sunlight
- are implicated in some BRIs

Interior Materials and Volatile Organic Compounds

VOCs are used in the manufacture and installation of many interior design products. Interior designers must check the current availability of alternative or reformulated materials in order to protect IAQ. Newly constructed and furnished buildings present a greater threat than older buildings, where VOCs have had time to dissipate.

PRESSED-WOOD PRODUCTS

Pressed-wood products are made with VOC-emitting chemicals to provide strength and moisture resistance, including formaldehyde, α-pinene, xylenes, butanol, butyl acetate, hexanal, and acetone. Such products are used extensively in residential and commercial interiors projects for work surfaces, drawer fronts, cabinet doors, furniture tops, and shelving. Common pressed-wood products include particleboard, medium-density fiberboard (MDF), hardwood plywood, chipboard, and hardboard such as pegboard.

In mobile homes, where pressed-wood products cover almost every surface within a confined space, formaldehyde is concentrated and poses an increased threat to the health of the occupants. Since 1985, HUD has permitted the use of only plywood and particleboard that conform to specified formaldehyde-emission limits in the construction of prefabricated and mobile homes.

Some sealants are applied by the manufacturer before shipping; others are applied on-site after installation. Sealants can prevent formaldehyde release and block moisture from seeping into the material. Some products react with the formaldehyde to create nonemitting or inert compounds. Thin liquid coatings that form a hard surface after curing and drying, including acid-curing lacquers, polyacrilamide, polyurethane lacquer or varnish, and latex paints, may also emit VOCs while drying, but the end effect is to seal in the long-term formaldehyde emissions. If pressed-wood products are sealed with veneers or laminate, check that all surfaces are completely sealed, including edges, backs, under-desktop surfaces, and tabletops as well as inside cabinets and drawers. If they are not, request an application of a liquid sealer that is formulated especially for formaldehyde reduction. Pressed-wood products include the following:

Particleboard, which is also called **chipboard**, is made of wood particles and fibers and is used as an underlay for carpet, furniture, and cabinetry. Particleboard is a major source of formaldehyde in homes and may give off small quantities for years; the average half-life of decay from newly manufactured, unfinished products is about seven months. Substitute formaldehyde-free particleboard or exterior plywood or low-density panels made from recycled paper; alternatively, seal particleboard with a secure coating to encapsulate the VOCs.

Interior laminated panels can be used to seal base materials, such as particleboard, MDF, and plywood. Any unsealed areas will continue to emit VOCs. Laminate is available that emits formaldehyde levels low enough to meet third-party certification standards.

Thick high-pressure laminates (HPLs), **phenolic** impregnated backer sheets more than 20 mils thick, and vinyls more than 6 mils thick are more effective than thin low-pressure laminates (LPLs), such as resin-saturated papers, thin vinyls, low-basis-weight papers, or foils. Melamine LPL (thermally fused melamine) is also effective.

MDF is made of wood pieces and chips pressed together in a hot hydraulic press. It is used to back thin sheets and veneers of such hardwoods as oak and maple, in cabinets and furniture, and as the innermost layer of many modular office partitions. MDF emits formaldehyde, acetone, benzene, and other VOCs at high temperatures and humidity. MDF should be sealed with a secure coating to encapsulate.

Hardwood plywood, which is also called interior-grade plywood, emits formaldehyde, acetone, benzene, and other VOCs at high temperatures and humidity. It should be encapsulated with a secure coating.

Softwood plywood produced for exterior construction use contains PF resin, which emits less formaldehyde than interior plywood.

Hardboard is made of wood fibers that are pressed into a dense sheet while applying heat. Natural resins hold the sheet together without glue. Hardboard is used for pegboard and other inexpensive functions. Relatively small amounts of formaldehyde resins are added along with other chemicals to improve its strength and moisture resistance.

Flake or **oriented strand board (OSB)** produced for exterior construction use contains PF resin.

Adhesives for pressed-wood products may be solvent-based with toluene, xylenes, acetone, and other hazardous solvents. Water-based adhesives are safer, but they may still contain some solvents, including benzene, toluene, acetone, and xylenes. The lowest toxicity is found in water-soluble casein or polyvinyl acetate (PVA)–based plain white glue. UF resins and glues constitute 6 to 14 percent of the weight of various pressed-wood products and are used for interior products. They are a major interior source of VOCs. PF resins and glues make up 2 to 3 percent of product weight. The dark or red/black adhesives are used in products intended for exterior use or for those that may be exposed to water.

PAINTS, COATINGS, AND SEALANTS

In addition to the laminating materials discussed above, paints and coatings can be used to seal VOCs in pressed-wood products. However, some of these coatings are detrimental to IAQ. Many manufacturers offer VOC-free paint products. Information about VOCs is available on paint can labels. A rating of less than 100 grams per liter (about 13 oz. per gallon) is recommended.

Paints:

- Formaldehyde is added to alkyds and acrylics in order to improve curing.
- Water-, oil-, or solvent-based paints all emit aromatic hydrocarbons, alcohols, and aliphatic hydrocarbons.
- Latex and solvent-based paints may give off benzene, toluene, xylenes, ethanol, methanol, and other VOCs.
- Some paints may emit VOCs as long as six months after drying.
- Solvent-based paints contain hydrocarbons and other VOCs. They react with sunlight and pollutants to produce ozone and require hazardous solvents for thinning and cleanup.
- Latex water-based paints release much lower VOCs and may emit butanone, ethyl benzene, and toluene. Latex paints with mercury-based preservatives and antimildew agents can increase the risk of liver and kidney damage and if inhaled, can affect the lungs and brain. Despite this, they are less hazardous than solvent-based paints
- Solvents for the mixing, removal, and application of paints also emit VOCs.

Varnishes:

- Most varnishes are solvent-based urethanes. They are highly noxious to handle but are stable when cured.

- Polyurethane varnish emits a variety of VOCs.
- Water-based emulsion urethanes are low-emission and perform well.

Acid-cured or acid-catalyzed coatings:
- These coatings are applied to pressed-wood surfaces to seal in the emissions from UF resin.
- Acid-cured coatings contain formaldehyde, acetone, toluene, and butanol, but they emit short-lived VOCs. Emissions from sprayed-on coatings decline 90 to 96 percent within sixteen weeks of application, while brushed-on coatings decline 82 to 96 percent during this period.

Wood stains:
- These stains emit a variety of VOCs.

Polymer oils:
- These oils are used for floor and cabinet finishes.
- They contain formaldehyde gas and remain toxic for several weeks after application.

Furniture polishes and waxes:
- These emit a range of VOCs.
- Low-toxicity sealers and wax finishes are recommended.

Paint stripper:
- This emits methylene chloride.

TEXTILE PRODUCTS
Fabric treatments:
- Natural and synthetic fabrics, including draperies, treated with chemicals for strength, permanent-press features, fire resistance, water-repellant properties, and soil-repellant properties may release VOCs.
- Formaldehyde-free treatments are available and should be substituted.

Upholstered furniture:
- Coverings may emit formaldehyde, chloroform, methyl chloroform, and other VOCs.
- Polyurethane foam used in cushions and upholstered furniture emits toluene di-isocyanate (TDI) and phenol; emissions decrease over time.
- Other furniture components, such as pressed-wood products, adhesives, and formaldehyde resins, emit VOCs.

FLOORING MATERIALS
Carpeting:
- Carpets may emit VOCs, including formaldehyde, toluene, benzene, and styrene.
- 4-PC is used to bind carpet fibers to jute backings; emissions may be initially high but tend to diminish quickly.
- Low-emission carpets have fusion-bonded backing and use alternative fastening systems to eliminate latex and adhesives.
- Carpets, especially shag or plush carpets, can collect particles, including lead.

- Low-emission carpets, adhesives, and cushions are recommended.
- Ask the installer to unroll and air out carpet in a clean, well-ventilated area before installation.
- Avoid occupying space during and immediately after carpet installation.
- Open doors and windows, increase ventilation, and exhaust air with fans and air conditioning during installation and for 48 to 72 hours afterward.
- Specify that the installer follow the Carpet and Rug Institute's installation guidelines.
- Carpets should not have an objectionable odor; contact the supplier if they do.
- Carpet-cleaning solutions may include highly toxic chemicals.

Carpet pads:
- Pads made of foamed plastic or sheet rubber are high in VOCs.
- Felt pads with recycled synthetic fibers or wool or jute backings have low VOC emissions.
- Cork, which is a quick-growing natural resource, can also be used.

Carpet adhesives:
- Tacking with nail strips rather than gluing down carpet lowers emissions.
- Use water-based or low-toxicity glue. Some carpet adhesives emit xylenes, toluene, and a variety of other VOCs for up to one week.

Vinyl flooring and linoleum:
- Vinyl floor tiles emit formaldehyde, toluene, ketones, xylenes, and many other VOCs for a long time.
- Alternative is natural linoleum made of linseed oil, cork, tree resin, wood flour, clay pigments, and jute backing. However, linoleum may emit VOCs, including toluene, hexanal, propanal, and butyl formiate, when initially installed.
- Floor-tile adhesives may emit toluene, benzene, ethyl acetate, ethyl benzene, and styrene. Adhesives with low VOCs are available.

Hardwood flooring:
- UF or polyurethane coatings on hardwood flooring briefly emit butyl acetate, ethyl acetate, ethyl benzene, xylenes, and formaldehyde VOCs.
- Some of the adhesives used with wood flooring also emit VOCs.

WALL COVERINGS
VOC emissions for all types of wall coverings drop significantly a few days after installation. The adhesives used for heavy wall coverings can be a problem; wallpaper paste may emit a wide variety of VOCs. Low-toxic adhesives are available. Lightweight papers can be applied with light, water-based glue. Metal foils are made by a highly polluting manufacturing process, produce very low emissions, and pose disposal problems.

Vinyl and vinyl-coated wall coverings are made of soft plastics in a polluting manufacturing process and emit vinyl-chloride monomers and other VOCs for long periods. Paper, plant fiber, silk, cotton, and other natural-fiber wall coverings often use organic dyes and water-based inks with few VOCs. Some may emit methanol, ethanol, toluene, xylenes, and more formaldehyde than vinyl wall coverings. Acoustic panels, tiles, and wall coverings with mineral fibers or fiberglass backings and fabric coverings can be long-term sources of formaldehyde. They also tend to retain dust. Wood fibers, tapestry, and cork panels are preferred, if permitted by fire codes. PVC paneling emits phenol, aliphatic and aromatic hydrocarbons, and glycol ethers and esters.

Plastic tiles can emit formaldehyde, phenol, aliphatic and aromatic hydrocarbons, ketones, and other VOCs. Some solid hardwood wall coverings may emit VOCs.

OTHER INTERIOR MATERIALS AND PRODUCTS

Caulking compounds used in interiors include silicone, latex, and uncured rubber. Silicone caulking used to seal cracks and seams is very safe and stable. Latex caulking is safe once it has cured, but some types contain benzene and toluene and produce VOCs and odors for weeks after installation. Uncured rubber caulkings (e.g., butyl caulk, acoustical sealant, polysulfide caulk) may emit formaldehyde, acetic acid, toluene, and xylenes.

UFFI was used for home insulation in the 1970s, but is no longer used. Most existing sources have out-gassed the majority of VOCs.

Bonding agents for overlays to furniture and case goods panels may emit VOCs; they should be sealed with a secure coating to encapsulate.

Interior flush doors are available with flaxboard or wheatboard cores instead of particleboard.

Laminated countertops with particleboard core surfaces should be completely sealed with laminate and nonformaldehyde adhesives. Using a formaldehyde-free core material for countertops is recommended.

Modular office partitions absorb pollutants, then release them back into the air. Long-term use (and reuse) of old panels can increase their impact on IAQ. The chipboard, hardboard, and treated fabrics they contain may emit VOCs.

Panels are in close proximity to office workers and often nearly surround them, cutting off air circulation and keeping the VOCs near the workers. Manufacturers may treat panels with chemicals for soil and wrinkle resistance that may contain formaldehyde and other VOCs just before wrapping and shipping. Methylene-chloride solvents used to clean panels during manufacture and storage can be released when panels are unwrapped and installed.

Textured fabric surfaces can absorb VOCs emitted by carpets, paints, copying fluids, and tobacco smoke; absorption increases with higher temperatures and decreased ventilation on weekends. These surfaces later emit surges of VOCs when the air conditioning is turned back on and ventilation is increased.

Some manufacturers will precondition office partitions during storage, shipping, and installation. Most off-gassing occurs immediately after removal of the packaging; avoid VOCs by unpacking and exposing materials before installation.

☑ **When choosing a finish, interior designers should consider where and how it will be used, the client's level of concern about avoiding VOCs, whether proper ventilation will be provided before occupancy, and what alternatives might have less impact on IAQ. It is not always possible to completely avoid VOC emissions on a project, but with care and resourcefulness, designers can maintain high standards for appearance and maintenance, while cutting pollutants and observing budget constraints.**

Material Safety Data Sheets

Manufacturers of products that have health and safety implications are required to provide a summary of the chemical composition of the material(s) used, including health risks, flammability, handling, and storage precautions. Material Safety Data Sheets (MSDSs) list all of the chemical constituents that make up a minimum of 1 percent of a material and are not proprietary. The sheets do not predict VOC emission rates, and you have to make assumptions about whether higher percentages of a chemical imply higher out-gassing rates. It is best to require MSDSs for all products and materials used indoors. If questionable components are present, you may have to obtain additional information on chemical formulations, storage, drying times, and airing procedures.

Some definitions are useful to decipher the information in an MSDS:

- **Threshold limit value (TLV):** the accepted toxicity for a hazardous material. The lower the TLV, the more toxic the material.
- **Time weighted average (TWA):** The allowable exposure limit over a working day. The lower the TWA, the more toxic the material.
- **Lethal dose, 50 percent (LD50):** The dose at which, when ingested, half of tested lab animals will die. The U.S. government permits other tests that do not result in high mortality for lab animals. The lower the LD50, the more toxic the material.
- **Total volatile organic content (TVOC):** The volume of the product that will evaporate over time. High TVOC increases the indoor air pollution.

Indoor-Air-Quality Equipment

Once the sources of IAQ problems have been removed or isolated wherever possible, increased ventilation and improved air filtration are usually the next most practical measures. The following building system components address IAQ issues. These factors will be discussed in more detail later, so consider this an introduction to some of the terminology and design considerations.

Building codes specify the amount of ventilation required for specific purposes and occupancies in terms of air changes per hour, or in cfm per person. ANSI/ASHRAE Standard 62.1-2004 *Ventilation for Acceptable Indoor Air Quality* has tables covering

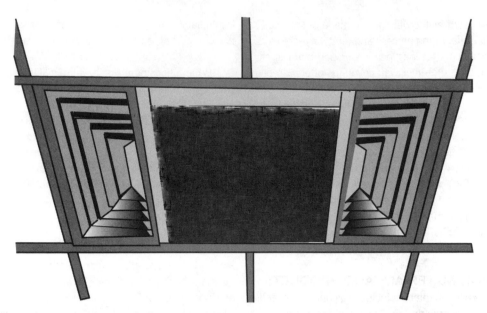

Figure 10-4 Stand-alone electrostatic air filter. Each unit has a fan that operates with or without the central HVAC fan and circulates air 6 to 10 times per hour. The air is ducted to diffusers, from which it circulates across a space to return air intakes on the opposite side of the space.

most buildings; its companion is Standard 62.2 *Ventilation and Acceptable Indoor Air Quality in Low-Rise Residential Buildings.* As of this writing, three proposed addenda to Standard 62.1 are being considered that would include coverage of high-rise buildings and could possibly increase ventilation rates significantly. The mechanical engineer will use the appropriate figure to determine what equipment is needed for a specific project.

Increasing ventilation for improved air quality must strike a balance with energy conservation. Energy-conservation efforts have resulted in reduced air-circulation rates in many central air-handling systems. Fewer fans use less power, but distribution is poorer and the air mix within individual spaces suffers. Individual-space air-filtering equipment provides a higher circulation rate and a proper air mix.

There are a number of ways that good ventilation can be ensured while controlling heat loss. Heat exchangers recover heat from air that is being exhausted and transfer it to make up outside air coming into the building, thereby saving heating energy.

Figure 10-5 Heat exchanger. Heat exchangers recover heat from air that is being exhausted and transfer it to make up outside air coming into the building, thereby saving heating energy.

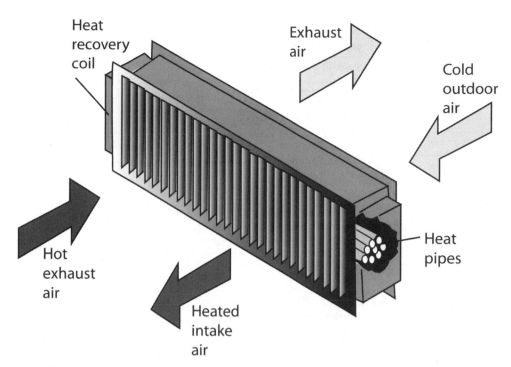

Figure 10-6 Heat pipes. Heat pipes can help dehumidify and cool incoming air. Refrigerant inside a heat pipe alternately evaporates and condenses as it travels through a porous wick. Only the self-contained refrigerant moves, promoting very low maintenance and long life.

Through the tracking of occupancy patterns in the building, ventilation can be tailored to the number of people in the building at any one time. Opening outside-air dampers for one hour after people leave an area for the day when possible can dilute large volumes of room air and dissipate collected contaminants.

Engineers find that it is easiest to get good IAQ with a heating and cooling system that uses forced air motion (fans and blowers), with some filtering equipment built into the air-handling equipment. Separate air-cleaning systems are commonly used with radiant-heating systems. Cooling systems can use economizer cycles at night, when they vent warm indoor air to the outside and bring in cooler outdoor air for overnight cooling. Evaporative cooling systems use a continuous flow of outdoor air to add humidity to the indoor air.

AIR CLEANERS

The general types of technologies used by air cleaners include mechanical filters, electronic air cleaners, and hybrid filters for the capture of particles, along with gas-phase filters to control odors. Air cleaners that operate by a chemical process, such as ozonation, also exist. The selection of the type of air filter should depend on the intended use of the filter, as explained below.

Air filters protect the HVAC equipment and its components and the furnishings and décor of occupied spaces. They also protect the general well-being of residents as well as reduce housekeeping, building maintenance, and furnace and heating-equipment fire hazards. The lower-efficiency filters generally used in central HVAC systems will usually cover all of these functions except protecting the health of the occupants, when much higher performance filtration is required. It may not always be possible to install this equipment in older existing environmental systems, so self-contained, portable room air cleaners must sometimes be used to obtain sufficiently high levels of filtration effectiveness.

Both outside air and recycled air must be filtered. Inadequate filtration is a result of low-efficiency filters; improper installation;

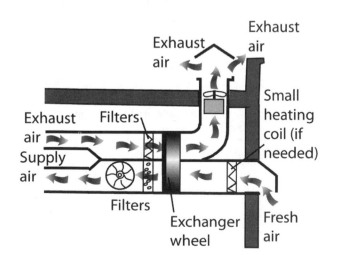

Figure 10-7 Energy transfer wheels. In cold weather, energy-transfer wheels recover heat from exhaust air. In hot weather, they both cool and dehumidify incoming fresh air.

TABLE 10-1. TYPES OF AIR CLEANERS

Type	Use/Description	Comments
Portable, room-sized air cleaners	Residential use when continuous, localized air cleaning is necessary	Sized for particular room; can be moved from room to room; can be more efficient than in-duct units
In-duct air-cleaning units	Installed in residential, unducted return air grilles or ducted air plenums of central heating, air-conditioning, or HVAC system	Building-wide air cleaning; recirculate building air through unit; HVAC must have fan always on for air cleaning; residential fans usually can be turned on or off as needed for cooling
Panel (flat) filters	Used in portable units with fans; protect central HVAC equipment from large particles	Little resistance to air moving through filter; allow small particles through; must be replaced regularly; remove 75 to 85 percent of particles from air
Pleated media filters	Catch large and small particles; pleats add efficiency and useful life	Increased density increases resistance to air flow
HEPA filters	Provide best protection; used in hospital, lab, and some portable residential air cleaners	Dense weave requires larger fans; require more energy and cost to run; are noisy; replacement filters are expensive; last up to five years with prefilter
Negative-ion generators	Electronically charges particles to remove them from indoor air; personal air purifiers can reduce airborne particles	Require frequent maintenance and cleaning; have low energy costs
Electrostatic precipitators	Charge and collect airborne particles; have high initial cost when installed in HVAC systems	Have low energy costs; precipitating cell is reusable but requires frequent cleaning; become less efficient with use; produce ozone
Hybrid filters	Incorporate two or more technologies	May combine mechanical filters plus electrostatic precipitator or ion generator in integrated system; may be single device
Chemisorption filters	Active material attracts, bonds polluting gas molecules onto its surface	Absorbing material requires regular replacement
Adsorption filters	Remove specific gaseous contaminants from air; use activated-charcoal or chemically impregnated porous pellets	Filters must be regularly regenerated or replaced; may re-emit pollutants if saturated; effective but capture only small percent of specific gases
Air washers	Used to control humidity and bacterial growth in large ventilation system	If not well maintained, moisture in air washer can add to pollution
Ozone generators	Ozone released in air attaches to and destroys wide range of contaminants: chemical gases, bacteria, mold; and mildew; primarily act to reduce sense of smell	According to the U.S. Environmental Protection Agency (EPA), available scientific evidence shows that at concentrations that do not exceed public health standards, ozone has little potential to remove indoor-air contaminants
UV light	Destroys viruses, bacteria, fungi; installed within HVAC systems or directly in kitchens, sickrooms, overcrowded dwellings, hospitals, lab fume hoods, and some personal air purifiers	May be expensive; must be mounted high in room, shielded from sight (can damage eyes, skin); National Renewable Energy Laboratory developing UV to control VOCs by breaking down cigarette smoke, formaldehyde, and toluene into water and CO_2

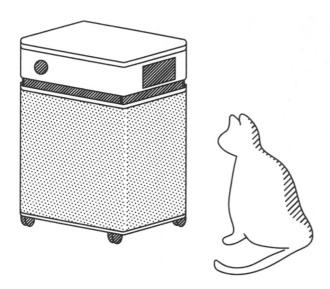

Figure 10-8 Room air cleaner. These air cleaners can be easily moved from one room to another in order to efficiently handle localized air-cleaning needs.

or torn, clogged, or otherwise ineffective filters. Ductwork is often installed without any provision for access or cleaning, leading to a massive buildup of contamination that can spread to building occupants. Poor maintenance in the ducts puts even more demands on the filters. It is best to remove pollutants at the source. ASHRAE recommends dust collectors at the source rather than filters for dusty areas. For example, the maintenance workshop in a hotel may have a vacuum that removes sawdust immediately from a worktable rather than a filter in the air-conditioning system that would allow the dust to spread throughout the area.

When the sources of allergy problems are present in a residence, air cleaning alone has not been proven effective at reducing airborne allergen-containing particles to levels at which no adverse effects are anticipated. Cats, for example, generally shed allergens at a much higher rate than air cleaners can effect removal. Dust mites excrete allergens in fecal particles within carpet and/or bedding, where air cleaners are ineffective. For individuals who are sensitive to dust-mite allergens, the use of impermeable mattress coverings appears to be as effective as the use of an air-cleaning unit above the bed. Source control should always be the first choice for allergen control in residences.

☑ **If the choice is made to use an air cleaner, select one that ensures high efficiency over an extended period and does not produce ozone levels higher than 0.05 ppm.**

Mechanical filters are used in central filtration systems as well as in portable units that use a fan to force air through the filter. Mechanical filters capture particles by straining first larger and then smaller particles out of the air stream through increasingly smaller openings in the filter pack. Very small sub-micron–sized particles are captured by being drawn toward the surfaces of the filtration medium, where they are held by static-electricity charges. This is the factor responsible for the effectiveness of the highest-efficiency mechanical filters' removal of sub-micron–sized particles.

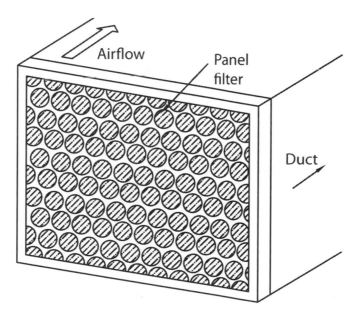

Figure 10-9 Flat or panel filter. Typically, flat or panel filters contain a low-packing-density fibrous medium that is dry or can be coated with a sticky substance, such as oil, so that particles adhere to it. Less-expensive, lower-efficiency filters that employ woven fiberglass strands to catch particles restrict airflow less, so smaller fans and less energy are needed. The typical low-efficiency furnace filter in many residential HVAC systems is a flat filter, 13 to 25 millimeters (½–1-in.) thick, which collects large particles efficiently but removes only between 10 and 60 percent of total particles and allows most smaller RSPs through.

Figure 10-10 HEPA filter. Typically, HEPA filters are made from a single paper-like sheet of water-repellent glass fiber that is pleated to provide more surface area on which to catch particles. To qualify as a HEPA filter, a filter must allow no more than 3 particles out of 10,000 to penetrate the filtration media. This is a minimum particle-removal efficiency of 99.97 percent and includes smaller RSPs. Similar HEPA-type filters with less-efficient filter paper may have 55-percent efficiencies. These filters, which are still very good when compared with conventional panel type and even pleated filters, have higher airflow, lower efficiency, and lower cost than their original version.

Media filters are approximately 90 percent efficient. Typically, they are a minimum of 15 centimeters (6 in.) deep and have a minimum life cycle of six months. Filters, particularly media filters, require regular maintenance. When blocked, they can damage HVAC equipment, so they must be replaced frequently. Filters for large units can cover an entire wall in a room-size air-handler plenum.

Electronic filters, which are generally marketed as electronic air cleaners, employ an electrical field to trap particles. Like mechanical filters, they may be installed in central filtration systems as well as in portable units with fans. Electronic air cleaners require less maintenance than systems with filters, but they produce ozone. Air rushing through a mechanical filter produces static electricity, which causes large particles to cling to the filter. Electronic filters lose efficiency in response to more humidity and high air velocity. Negative-ion generators and electrostatic precipitators are two types of electronic air cleaners.

Compared with particulate control, gas-phase pollution control is a relatively new and complex field that seeks to remove gases and associated odors. Two types of gas-phase capture and control filters are physical adsorption and chemisorption.

Activated carbon adsorbs some gaseous indoor air pollutants, especially VOCs, sulfur dioxide, and ozone, but it does not efficiently adsorb volatile, low–molecular-weight gases, such as formaldehyde and ammonia. Although relatively small quantities of activated charcoal reduce odors in residences, many pollutants affect health at levels below odor thresholds.

Engineers use a combination of panel filters, high-efficiency particle filters, and adsorption filters to achieve high IAQ. Panel filters are placed ahead of the HVAC unit's fan (upstream), and the high-efficiency systems are located downstream from the HVAC's cooling units and drain pans. This enables microbiological contaminants in wet components of the system to be removed before they are distributed with the air through the entire building.

CENTRAL CLEANING SYSTEMS

Central cleaning systems have been used in homes and commercial buildings for years. Essentially, they are built-in vacuum cleaners with powerful motors. As such, they can be used to trap dirt and dust inside the power-unit equipment and away from rooms where people live and work; alternately, they can be vented outdoors, decreasing exposure for people with dust allergies. The power unit is usually installed in a utility room, basement, or garage. Tubing that runs under the floor or in the attic connects through the walls to unobtrusive inlets placed conveniently throughout the building. When it is time to vacuum, a long, flexible hose is inserted into an inlet and the system turns on automatically. The noise is kept at the remote location of the power unit.

Most power units operate on a dedicated 15-amp normal residential electrical circuit, but some larger units may require heavier wiring. Systems come with a variety of hoses and brushes. Installation is simplest in new construction. Building owners with some knowledge of electricity, a builder, a plumber, or a system dealer can install systems in a day or two. Central cleaning systems are commonly found in commercial office buildings and restaurants.

Plants and Indoor Air Quality

Indoor plants can help reduce stress and improve the aesthetics of a space as well as increase humidity in overly dry indoor air. Over the past few years, it has been suggested that houseplants have been shown to reduce levels of some chemicals in laboratory experiments. However, there is currently no scientific evidence that a reasonable number of houseplants remove significant quantities of pollutants in homes and offices. Instead, overly damp planter-soil conditions may promote the growth of biological contaminants. In restaurants and other places with water and food, planters can provide a home for cockroaches and other unwanted pests.

Controls for Indoor Air Quality

Older, simple HVAC systems controlled IAQ by measuring the concentration of CO_2 in parts per million (ppm) in the air and adjusting ventilation rates to compensate for it. This indicates whether the ventilation rate is adequate for the number of people using the space, but it ignores other contaminants. Newer systems monitor for CO_2 along with possible leakage of such fuels as propane, butane, and natural gas and inadequate levels of oxygen. Alarms activate equipment automatically when levels are too high. The system can regulate ventilation heat exchangers, especially in unoccupied spaces, to prevent the buildup of VOCs from finishes and furnishings, thereby avoiding the need for Monday-morning flushing of a room's air. The unit's size is about that of a programmable thermostat, and the mounting height depends on the gas being monitored.

VENTILATION

Before the invention of mechanical ventilation, the common high ceilings in buildings created a large volume of indoor air that diluted odors and CO_2. Fresh air was provided by **infiltration**, the accidental leakage of air through cracks in the building, which along with operable windows created a steady exchange of air with the outdoors. The high ceilings of old auditoriums harbor a reserve where fresh air can build up when the building is unoccupied between performances.

Natural Ventilation

There are two discrete reasons for introducing outdoor air to buildings. **Ventilation** involves bringing in fresh air to provide oxygen and to help carry away CO_2 and body odors. Ventilation is always needed whatever the climate.

Natural ventilation moves a source of fresh air at an appropriate temperature and humidity through a building without fans. Wind or convection moves air from high- to lower-pressure areas. Mechanical controls adjust the volume, speed, and direction of the airflow. Contaminated air is either cleaned and reused or exhausted from the building.

Passive cooling replaces heated indoor air with cooler outdoor air. Cooling breezes are available only at specific times and in specific places. Much greater amounts of airflow are required for passive cooling than for IAQ control.

WIND VENTILATION

The simplest system for getting fresh air into a building uses outdoor air for its source and wind for its power. Wind creates local areas of high pressure on the windward side of the building, and areas of low pressure on the leeward side. Fresh air infiltrates the building on the windward side through cracks and seams. On the opposite side of the building, where pressure is lower, stale indoor air leaks back outside. Wind-powered ventilation is most efficient when there are windows on at least two sides of a room, preferably opposite each other. The process of infiltration can be slow in a tightly constructed building. Loose-fitting doors and windows result in buildings with drafty rooms and wasted energy. Manual controls for openings are a necessary part of a natural-ventilation design.

Depending on the leakage openings in a building exterior, the wind can affect pressure relationships within and between rooms. The building should be designed to take advantage of the prevailing winds in the warmest seasons when it is sited and when the interior is laid out.

☑ **Very leaky spaces have two or more air changes per hour. Even when doors and windows are weatherstripped and construction seams are airtight, about one-half to one air change per hour will occur; however, this rate may be useful for the minimum air replacement needed in a small building. In general, weatherstripping materials have a lifespan of less than ten years and must be replaced before they wear out.**

CONVECTIVE VENTILATION

In **convective ventilation**, differences in the density of warm and cool air create the differences in pressure that move the air. Convective ventilation is based on the principle that hot air rises, which is known as the **stack effect**. The warm air inside a building rises and exits near the building's top. Cool air infiltrates at lower levels. The stack effect works best when the intakes are as low as possible and the height of the stack is as great as possible. The stack effect is not noticeable in buildings less than five stories or about 30.5 meters (100 ft.) tall. In cold weather, fans can be run in reverse to push warm air back down into the building. Fire-safety codes restrict air interaction between floors of high-rise buildings, thereby reducing or eliminating the stack effect. To depend on convective forces alone for natural ventilation, you need relatively large openings. Insect screens keep out bugs, birds, and small animals as well as admit light and air, but they reduce the amount of airflow. Systems that use only convective forces are not usually as strong as those that depend on the wind.

AIR-SUPPLY RATES

Defining minimum outdoor air-supply rates has proven to be controversial. The current ASHRAE ventilation standard (Standard 62.1-2004—*Ventilation for Acceptable Indoor Air Quality*–for other than low-rise residential buildings) establishes minimum rates on the basis of an occupancy component and a building component in recognition of these distinct contaminant sources. Some building professionals feel that the outdoor-air requirements are too high; others, that they are too low. Recommended rates, including those for naturally ventilated buildings, are currently being reassessed.

The ventilation rate is measured in **liters per second (L/s)** or in cfm. It takes only very small amounts of air to provide enough oxygen for us to breathe. Low ceilings create greater densities of people per volume and as such require higher rates of ventilation.

Especially high rates of air replacement are needed in buildings that house heat- and odor-producing activities. Restaurant kitchens, gym locker rooms, bars, and auditoriums require extra ventilation. Lower rates are permissible for residences, sparsely occupied offices, warehouses, and light-manufacturing plants.

Using natural ventilation helps keep a building cool in hot weather and supplies fresh air without resorting to energy-dependent machines. However, in cold climates, energy loss through buildings that leak warm air can offset the benefits of natural cooling. Careful building design can maximize the benefits of natural ventilation while preventing energy waste.

☑ Opportunities for natural ventilation may be limited by outside noise. Unfortunately, almost all methods of blocking noise will also slow breezes.

ATTIC VENTILATION

Thermal buoyancy—the rising of warm air—is a primary cause of air leakage from a building's living space to the attic. Ventilating an attic reduces temperature swings, makes the building more comfortable during hot weather, and reduces the cost of mechanical air conditioning.

Warm air rising up through plumbing, electrical, and other penetrations into the attic will also heat the roof sheathing. Adding ventilation without sealing air leaks into the attic can actually increase the amount of air leaking from the house, wasting valuable heat. Air leaking out of air handlers and ducts and heat leaving the system by conduction can be major sources of heat loss in cold weather.

Ventilation alone cannot prevent moisture in the attic. Keeping dampness out of the building, especially in the basement and crawl space, helps protect against condensation and mildew in the attic. An airtight ceiling is also important.

Installing rigid insulation in the **eaves** (the projecting overhangs at the lower edge of a roof) reduces heat loss in the eave area. Another option is to change the framing detail to one that leaves more room between the top plate and the rafter. Cardboard or foam baffles precut to fit 16- or 24-inch-on-center framing can eliminate wind blowing across insulation.

Eliminate air leaks that allow heated air to escape into the attic at top plates, wiring penetrations, plumbing vents, and chimney and duct chases. Recessed lights are responsible for significant heat loss; be sure to use fixtures rated for insulation contact (IC rated) and air tightness.

Placing HVAC equipment and ductwork in attics wastes leaking air and should be avoided. If there is no alternative, all ducts should be sealed tightly and run close to the ceiling, buried in loose-fill insulation to the equivalent R-value of the attic insulation.

Roof windows, also called **operable** or **venting skylights**, can create the same updraft throughout the house as an old-fashioned cupola. When shaded to keep direct sunlight out, they are one of the best natural-ventilation devices available. However, their value for cooling alone does not compensate for their initial cost.

Roof ventilators also increase natural ventilation. Some roof ventilators are spun by the wind, drawing air from the room below. Others rely on convective flow, while still others create low-pressure areas that are then filled with interior air. Wind-gravity or wind-turbine ventilators create suction when wind blows across the top of a stack, pulling air up and out of the building. Roof ventilators require control dampers to change the size of the openings as necessary.

☑ **In residences, ventilation is tied to the number of exterior windows and the amount of natural ventilation they supply. If a bathroom does not have a window, it is required to have a fan with a duct leading directly to the exterior. The window also provides daylight and possibly a room-expanding view. A percentage of the windows must be operable in order to provide ventilation and emergency egress. Doors should not be relied on for essential building ventilation unless they are equipped with a holder set at the desired angle. An ordinary door cannot control the amount of air that flows past it.**

Figure 10-11 Roof window. Roof windows allow moisture to escape from kitchens, bathrooms, laundry rooms, and pool enclosures. They are available with remote controls and rain sensors.

Mechanical Ventilation

Mechanical-ventilation options include unit ventilator fans on the outside wall of each room to circulate room air and replace a fraction of it with outdoor air. Window or through-wall air-conditioning units can also be run as fans. A central-heating and -cooling system with coils of hot or chilled water tempers the air in room-ventilation units. Fixed-location fans can provide a reliable, positive airflow to an interior space.

Any time that air is exhausted from a building, makeup air must be supplied. This can be done in a limited manner by infiltration through the building envelope. Opening windows and doors can also provide a supply of fresh air. When mechanical equipment exhausts a large volume of air, makeup air is introduced through vents in the building envelope and directed to the equipment through ducts.

In addition to ceiling mounts, exhaust fans come in models for mounting through the wall without ducting, with a concealed intake behind a central panel that can be decorated to match the room. Other models move air from one room to another through the intervening wall via grilles on both sides.

☑ **ANSI/ASHRAE Standard 62.2-2004,** *Ventilation and Acceptable Indoor Air Quality in Low-Rise Residential Buildings*, **requires intermittent (user-controlled) exhaust fans of at least 50-cfm (25-L/s) capacity for bathrooms and 100-cfm (50-L/s) capacity for kitchens.**

Codes prohibit discharging exhaust fans into attics, basements, or crawl spaces. ANSI/ASHRAE 90.2-2004, *Energy-Efficient Design of New Low-Rise Residential Buildings*, requires user-controlled exhaust fans for bathrooms and kitchens. The intake should be as close as possible to the source of the polluted air, and the air path should avoid crossing other spaces. Kitchen fans

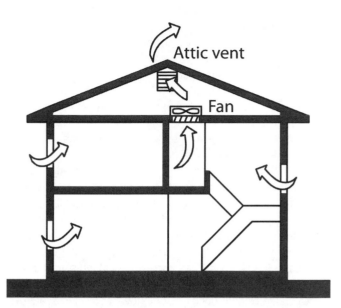

Figure 10-12 Whole-house fan. This whole-house, motor-driven fan pulls stale air from living areas of the house and exhausts it through attic vents. Without an adequate exhaust fan, the building may not have enough air for combustion equipment, such as furnaces and stovetop barbeques, and fumes may not be exhausted properly. Equipment that demands a large amount of exhaust should have another fan that supplies makeup air running at the same time.

can exhaust grease, odors, and water vapor directly above the range, with a duct that exhausts vertically through the roof, directly through an exterior wall, or horizontally to the outside through a soffit above wall cabinets. Self-ventilating cooktops may exhaust directly to the outside or, when located in an interior location, through a duct in the floor.

TABLE 10-2. MECHANICAL VENTILATION

Type	Function	Comments
Exhaust fans	Remove odorous or overly humid air from bathrooms, kitchens, and process areas; create negatively pressurized space that helps control spread	May be very noisy; discharge into attics, basements, or crawl spaces is prohibited by code; Energy Star® fans available
Whole-house fans	Quiet, continuous-use fan in central location; outdoor air must be temperature-controlled	Heated or cooled air is dumped outside, resulting in energy loss; Energy Star® fans are available
Bathroom fans	Over tubs and showers	Should be UL listed and connected to GFCI-protected branch circuits
Large, multiport exhaust fans for master bedroom suites	Vent toilet area, shower, and walk-in closet with single unit	Acoustically insulated motor is mounted in remote location; flexible ducts run to three separate unobtrusive grilles
Computerized fans for small offices	Ensure regular exchanges of air	Quiet operation; high energy efficiency available
Blower fans	Use activated-charcoal filter to remove odors; available unducted to filter and recirculate air in room	Do not exhaust air
In-line fan systems	Residential and light commercial applications	Fans in flexible round or rigid square and rectangular ducts exhaust air from several rooms

In bathrooms, the exhaust fan should be in the ceiling above the toilet and shower or high on the exterior wall opposite the door. It should discharge directly to the outside, at a point a minimum of 91 centimeters (3 ft.) away from any opening that allows outside air to enter the building. Residential exhaust fans are often combined with a lighting fixture, a fan-forced heater, or a radiant-heat lamp.

Models are available with a high-efficiency centrifugal blower that provides virtually silent performance, and an illuminated switch that indicates when the fan is on. Highly energy-efficient motors are available that use about one-third of the electricity of standard versions and that may qualify for local utility rebates. Some designs allow easy installation in new construction as well as retrofit applications. Models are available that activate automatically to remove excess humidity. Fluorescent- or incandescent-lighting fixtures and even nightlights are included in some designs.

Operable exterior openings (windows or skylights) are permitted instead of mechanical fans, but they must have an area of not less than one-twentieth of the floor area, and a minimal size of 0.14 square meters (1.5 square ft.). If natural ventilation is used for kitchen ventilation, openings must be a minimum of 0.46 square meters (5 square ft.).

Public toilet-room plumbing facilities must be coordinated with the ventilation system to keep odors away from other building spaces while providing fresh air. The toilet room should be downstream in the airflow from other spaces. The air from toilet rooms should be exhausted outdoors, not vented into other spaces. By keeping slightly lower air pressure in the toilet rooms than in adjacent spaces, air flows into the toilet room from the other spaces, thereby containing toilet-room odors. This is accomplished by supplying more air to surrounding spaces than is returned. The surplus is drawn into the toilet rooms, then exhausted. Exhaust vents should be located close to and above toilets.

Overall room-exhaust fans are also used in storage rooms, janitor closets, and darkrooms. The amount of outdoor air supplied is slightly less than the amount exhausted, resulting in negative air pressure inside the room. This draws air in from surrounding areas, preventing odors and contaminants from migrating to other areas.

LOCALIZED EXHAUST SYSTEMS

Industrial-process areas, laboratories, and critical medical-care areas may require one or more fans and ductwork to the outside. Kitchens, toilet rooms, smoking rooms, and chemical-storage rooms also should be directly exhausted to the outside. Photocopiers, and other equipment may need localized exhaust ventilation. Healthcare and laboratory buildings often have "clean" and "dirty" zones. High air pressure in clean areas and lower air pressure in dirty areas help contain contaminants. Buildings with many exhausts have greater heating and cooling loads.

In open offices with few walls and copying machines, a designer can erect a barrier around a contamination-producing machine and provide mechanical ventilation to **task-ventilate** the area immediately.

Hoods can be built over points where contamination originates. Commercial kitchen hoods collect grease, moisture, and heat at ranges and steam tables. Sometimes, outside air is introduced at or near the exhaust hood with minimal conditioning, then quickly exhausted, which saves heating and cooling energy.

Residential kitchen hoods work best when located directly over a range, catching the hot air as it rises. Fans that pull from several inches above the burner surface at the back of the stove and downdraft fans, including those on indoor grills, require significantly more airflow to be effective. It is best to install a fan that is no larger than needed. In general, wall-mounted hoods are more effective than freestanding island hoods because there are fewer air currents to blow fumes away from the hood.

The Home Ventilating Institute, a fan manufacturers' trade association, recommends:

- a range-hood capacity of 40 to 50 cfm per linear foot of range, or about 120 to 150 cfm for the standard 76-centimeter (30-in.) range
- a range hood at least as wide as the stove with an extra 76 to 152 millimeters (3–6-in.) for good measure
- a range hood that is located no more than 51 to 61 centimeters (20–24 in.) above the stovetop
- a 51-centimeter-deep (20-in.-deep) range hood, which captures fumes better than the typical 43-centimeter-deep (17-in.) models.

Slide-out ventilation hoods are mounted below wall cabinets and can be vented or unvented. Some manufacturers offer hoods with dishwasher-safe grease filters. Retractable downdraft vents behind cooktop burners also have washable grease filters.

Commercial-style residential ranges require increased airflow capacity for range fans. More airflow is required to remove the heat from high-output ranges and to make up for the reduced effectiveness of more stylish, slimmer hoods.

Keep in mind that high-powered kitchen range hoods may create health hazards. Typical range hoods are rated at 175 to 250 cfm. Some fans remove air at a rate of more than 600 cfm, and some exceed 1000 cfm. These high-capacity fans are powerful enough to pull exhaust gases out of a fireplace, woodstove, water heater, or furnace—a problem called **backdrafting**. Backdrafting exposes building occupants to fumes that containing CO, oxides of nitrogen, and other pollutants. A reliable source of makeup air must be supplied to replace the air that is being exhausted. Codes may require minimum window openings for this purpose.

Range-hood manufacturers may not provide an integrated makeup air solution, so a range-hood installer must find a way to activate the supply fan when the exhaust fan starts. After installation, it is essential to verify that the exhaust fan is not depressurizing chimneys or flues. It is possible to get an idea whether backdrafting is occurring by using a stick of incense or a smoking match, closing all interior doors except those between the kitchen and combustion appliances. While the fan is running, watch to see if the smoke rises up the flue. The test should also be performed while the furnace blower is operating because unbalanced air flows in ductwork can also contribute to depressurization problems. A contractor can use a pressure device called a manometer for a more exact reading.

Most buildings are designed to have a positive air pressure as compared to the outdoors, so unconditioned air does not enter through openings in the building envelope. Corridors should be supplied with fresh air, and residential units, including apartments, condominiums, hotels, motels, hospitals, and nursing homes, should have exhausts.

Multistory buildings have chases for exhaust ducts through successive floors, which can double up with plumbing in apartments, hotels, and hospitals. Kitchen exhausts, however, must remain separate because of the risk of fires. In large laboratory buildings, many exhaust stacks can be seen rising high above the roof.

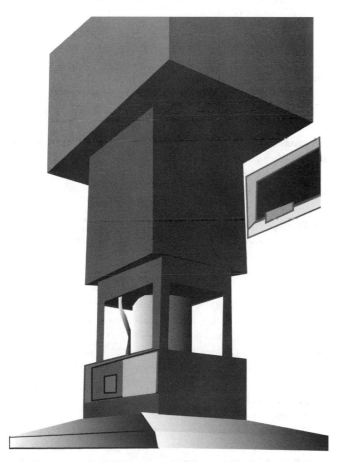

Figure 10-13 Residential range hood. Residential range hoods are available in a wide variety of styles and materials, including stainless steel and glass. Some models extract air almost noiselessly. Innovative self-cleaning features and lighting fixtures are included with some styles. When hoods are installed without ducts, heavy-duty charcoal filters are used to ensure the removal of smoke and odors.

FENESTRATION

A building's **fenestration**—its windows, skylights, and **clerestories** (high windows)—greatly influences the amount of heat gain and loss as well as the infiltration and ventilation. The proportion of glass on the exterior affects energy conservation and thermal comfort.

Windows can be used to improve energy conservation by admitting solar thermal energy, which provides natural ventilation for cooling and reduces the need for artificial illumination. The proper amount of fenestration is determined by architectural considerations, the ability to control thermal conditions, the first cost of construction versus the long-term energy and life-cycle costs, and the human psychological and physical needs for windows.

Most windows do not provide for air filtering. Their use can have a significant impact on the functioning of mechanical heating and cooling systems.

Window Orientations

In temperate northern-hemisphere locations:

* North-facing windows lose radiated heat in all seasons, especially in the winter.
* East-facing windows gain heat very rapidly in the summer when the sun enters at a very direct angle in the mornings.
* South-facing windows receive solar heat most of the day in the summer, but at a low intensity because the higher position of the sun strikes at an acute angle. In the winter, the low sun angle provides sun to south-facing windows all day.
* West-facing windows heat up rapidly on summer afternoons when the building is already warm; this causes overheating, leading to hot bedrooms at night.

Planting shade trees to the west and installing deep awnings over windows can help. East and west windows must be shaded in tropical latitudes. Horizontal skylights gain the most solar heat in the summer, when the sun is overhead, and the least solar heat in the winter, when the sun angle is lower.

Windows and Natural Ventilation

The open position of a window determines how well it provides natural ventilation. The wind will be deflected if it strikes the glass surface. The direction of wind is unpredictable, so in order to provide ventilation without cold drafts, you have to keep the wind away from people. When you want the wind to provide cooling, it needs to flow across the body. Windows with multiple positions can offer control.

Skylights can be prewired for sun-screening accessories, including sun-blocking shades, pleated shades, venetian blinds, and roller shades. Energy Star® skylights use low-emissivity (low-E) glass coatings, warm-edge technology that ensures that the areas around the frames do not reduce the insulating properties of the glazing, and energy-efficient blinds that improve overall energy efficiency.

Sashes that pivot 90 or 180 degrees around a vertical or horizontal axis at or near their centers are used in multistory or high-rise buildings. They are operated only for cleaning, maintenance, or emergency ventilation.

Figure 10-14 Casement windows. Casement windows open fully, and the swing of the sash can divert a breeze into a room.

Windows ventilate best in the presence of wind. In calm conditions, taller buildings may still admit—or exhaust—air because of the stack effect.

Thermal Transmission

Windows and doors account for about one-third of a home's heat loss, with windows contributing more than doors. Windows should be replaced or at least undergo extensive repairs if they contain rotted or damaged wood, cracked glass, missing putty, poorly fitting sashes, or locks that do not work.

Glass conducts heat very efficiently. Windows and skylights frequently have the lowest R-value of a building envelope, allowing infiltration of outdoor air and admitting solar heat. Without some kind of adjustable insulation, they are much less thermal-resistant.

In the winter, glazed areas at the perimeter of a building cool adjacent interior air, and the cool, dense vertical layer of air along the glass drops to the floor, creating a carpet of cold air. The inside and outside surfaces of a pane of glass are close to the same temperature, which, in turn, is about halfway between the indoor and the outdoor temperatures. Consequently, where there are windows, the temperature inside the building is strongly affected by the exterior temperature. In walls with a great deal of glazing, the interior surface and air temperatures approach the exterior temperature.

☑ **Windows can give off surprisingly large amounts of heat. Each square foot of unshaded window facing east, south, or west in midsummer admits about as much heat as one-half square foot of cast-iron radiator at full output. This may be an impossible amount to cool in the summer. A comparatively large energy loss occurs in the winter.**

In order to conserve energy, building codes and standards prescribe relatively small windows in relationship to residential floor areas and commercial wall areas unless a designer can prove a significant benefit. Large glass areas for daylighting increase heating requirements but use less electricity for lighting. Less exposed glazing is needed for daylighting in the summer than in the winter. Increasing insulation in walls or roofs may also justify more glass areas.

When sunlight and heat transmission through glass is controlled properly, light and warmth enter the space without glare and radiant-heat buildup. Solar heat gain can be collected within the space with control devices that admit heat but control glare. When added heat is not wanted in a building's interior, it is best to use exterior controls.

Sunlight that passes through glazing warms objects, but the radiant heat then emitted by the objects cannot escape quickly back through the glazing, so the space warms up. A window's **solar heat gain coefficient (SHGC)** is a measurement of the amount of solar energy that passes through a window (see page 188). The SHGC measures how well a product blocks heat caused by sunlight and is expressed as a number between 0 and 1; the lower the SHGC, the less heat gain. Typical SHGC values range

Figure 10-15 Double-hung windows. Double-hung windows can open only half of their area, either at the top, the bottom, or part of each. The window on the right has been fitted with a storm window.

Figure 10-16 Awning windows. Awning windows that swing open from the top outward allow air through while keeping rain out. These windows vent the upper story of a residence.

Figure 10-17 Hopper window. Hopper windows open from the bottom inward to direct breezes in and up. This example is fitted into a metal frame below fixed glazing.

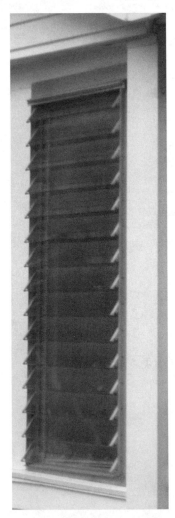

Figure 10-18 Jalousie window. Jalousie windows are horizontal glass or wood louvers that pivot simultaneously in a common frame. They are used primarily in mild climates to control ventilation while cutting off visibility from the outside. This example is one of several on an enclosed porch in New England.

from 0.4 to 0.9. The SHGC is particularly important in warm climates, where keeping most of the solar heat outside is preferable.

Solar heat gains through windows and skylights range from none at night to 1058 watts per square meter (335 BTU per square foot) per hour. The amount of heat gain depends on the time of day, the time of the year, cloudiness, the orientation and tilt angle of the glass, the latitude of the site, and the type and number of layers of glazing. Internal and external shading devices also affect solar heat gain. Solar heat gain is a desirable quality for passive solar heating but is undesirable when you want to prevent overheating in the summer.

☑ **An interior designer's choice of window frames and glazing materials can influence the interior climate of a building. Windows and skylights are responsible for up to one-fourth of a building's energy loss. Today, all windows produced for use in a building's exterior have two layers of glass. Using low-E coatings, which affect the windows' ability to absorb or reflect radiant energy, may cost 10 to 15 percent more, but they can reduce energy loss up to 18 percent. Adding low-E coatings to all of the windows in the United States would save half a million barrels of oil per day.**

Energy-efficient windows can reduce the cost of a building's HVAC by minimizing the influence of outside temperatures and sunlight. This also reduces maintenance, noise, and condensation problems. Over time, the windows' extra initial expense usually pays for itself.

Ordinary window glass passes about 80 percent of the infrared (IR) solar radiation and absorbs most longer-wave IR radiation from sun-warmed interior surfaces, keeping the heat inside. In cold weather, this type of glass loses most of the absorbed heat by convection to the outside air; a single-glazed window has an insulating value of about R-1. Because ordinary glazing prevents the passage of heat from sun-warmed interior surfaces back to the outdoors, greenhouses and parked cars get hot on sunny days. This principle is also used in the design of flat-plate solar collectors.

Insulating glass consists of multiple layers of glass with air spaces between them. Double-glazing is almost twice as efficient as single-glazing, but it has no effect on air leaking through the edges of the window sash. Double-glazed windows have an insulation value of approximately R-2.

The type of glass used greatly affects the insulating value of a window. **Low-E glass** uses a nearly invisible metallic coating to block radiant-heat transfer; it also reduces ultraviolet (UV) rays in order to protect carpets and furnishings from fading. So-called "super" windows have two low-E coatings for an insulating value of up to R-8.

An alternative approach with return at the perimeter is variously called an air-extract window, an air curtain window, or a climate window. Developed in Scandinavia in the 1950s, this triple-glazed window passes room air between a typical outer double-glazed window and an inner single pane. The inner pane is consequently kept at very nearly the same temperature as the room air, which greatly increases comfort near windows on very cold or very hot days. Venetian blinds can be inserted in this cavity, where they can intercept direct sun and redirect its light toward

the ceiling. The solar heat intercepted by these blinds is carried off by the room air to a plenum above the ceiling, where such air can be either exhausted or recirculated and its heat content either reclaimed or rejected.

Weatherstripping all window edges and cracks with rope caulk is a quick, inexpensive way to improve window thermal transmission. The rope caulk can be removed, stored in foil, and reused until it hardens. Compression-type or V-strip type weatherstripping is a little more expensive but is more permanent, is not visible, and allows windows to be opened. The upper sash of a double-hung window can be permanently caulked if it is not routinely opened for ventilation.

Weatherstripping is also available in metal, felt, vinyl, and foam-rubber strips that are placed between a door or a window sash and frame. These strips can be fastened to the edge or face of a door, or to a doorframe and threshold. Weatherstripping provides a seal against windblown rain and reduces the infiltration of air and dust. The material chosen should be durable under extended use, noncorrosive, and replaceable. Spring-tensioned strips of aluminum, bronze, or stainless or galvanized steel; vinyl or neoprene gaskets; foam-plastic or foam-rubber strips; or woven pile strips all are options. Weatherstripping is often supplied and installed by manufacturers of sliding glass doors, glass entrance doors, revolving doors, and overhead doors. An automatic door bottom is a horizontal bar located at the bottom of a door that drops automatically when the door is closed to seal the threshold to air and sound.

A **storm window** is a separate sash added to a single-glazed window that cuts thermal conductivity and infiltration in half. A single sash with insulated glazing in combination with a storm window results in one-third as much heat transmission and half as much infiltration. Storm windows will save about 3.8 liters (1 gal.) of home heating oil per .09 square meters (1 square ft.) of window per year in a cold climate. They also reduce heating loss by 25 to 50 percent.

The simplest storm window is a plastic film taped to the inside of a window frame, which is very inexpensive and will last from one to three years. The plastic is heated with a blow dryer to shrink tight. A slightly more complex interior storm window consists of a sturdy aluminum frame and two sheets of clear glazing film, creating a layer of air between them. A secondary air layer is established between the existing window and the interior storm window. The windows are held in place by fasteners screwed into the sash or molding; they are sold as do-it-yourself kits or manufactured panels for interior use.

Exterior removable or operable glass or rigid-acrylic storm windows are more common than internal styles. The tightest aluminum-framed combination storm/screen windows have air-leakage ratings as low as 0.01 cfm per foot, although some leak more than 1 cfm per foot. Storm/screen windows rated lower than 0.3 cfm per foot should be specified. Storm/screen units are available with low-E coatings on the glass at somewhat higher prices. Aluminum frames should be tightly sealed when they are mounted to the window casings. All cracks should be caulked, but the small weep holes at the bottom edges must not be sealed in order to prevent moisture buildup.

Old, wood-framed storm windows can be repainted and used and may be more energy-efficient than newer styles. Wood-framed storm windows have separate screens that must be put up and taken down every year.

Double- or triple-sealed panes filled with a **low-conductivity gas**, such as argon, krypton, CO_2, or sulfur hexafluoride, can reduce heat loss even more than windows with air between the glazing layers. The inert gas reduces convective currents, and the inner surface stays close to the indoor temperature, which produces less condensation. These windows require very reliable edge seals.

Low-E coatings are applied to one glass surface facing the air gap. They consist of thin, transparent coatings of silver or tin oxide that allow the passage of visible light while reflecting IR heat radiation back into the room, thereby reducing the flow of heat through the window.

Hard-coat low-E coatings are durable and less expensive than soft-coat ones, but they are less effective. Soft-coat low-E coatings have better thermal performance but can be degraded by oxidation during the manufacturing process. Low-E coatings reduce UV transmission, thereby reducing fading.

High-transmission low-E coatings are used in cold climates for passive solar heating. The coating on the inner-glass surface traps outgoing IR. Variations in design are available for different climate zones and applications. Selective-transmission low-E coatings are used for winter heating and summer cooling. They transmit a relatively high level of visible light for daylighting. The coating on the outer glazing traps incoming IR, which is convected away by outdoor air. Low-transmission low-E coatings on the outer glazing reject more of the solar gain than their high-transmission counterparts.

A building may need multiple types of low-E coatings on different sides of the building. The south side may need low-E and high solar heat gain coatings for passive solar heating, while the less sunny north side may require the lowest U-value windows available (see below). Some window manufacturers offer different types only at a premium cost.

☑ Selecting windows for energy efficiency
- Select windows with air-leakage ratings of 0.3 cfm or less (Energy Star® windows are recommended).
- Look for the National Fenestration Rating Council (NFRC) label that indicates certification of window performance.
- Install new windows correctly to avoid air leaks around the window frame.
- Select windows with both low U-values and low SHGC ratings in climates with both heating and cooling seasons.
- Specify a window with at least double glazing and a low-E coating, with a U-value of 0.35 or lower in cold climates.
- Apply sun-control or other reflective films on south-facing windows to reduce solar gain in warm climates.
- Create seasonal shading on south-facing windows by using plants and trees to reduce summer solar heat gain in cold climates.
- Keep windows clean to maximize the winter sunlight.

- Install awnings on south- and west-facing windows.
- Install white window shades, drapes, and/or blinds to reflect heat away from the house (close shades, drapes, and blinds during the day).
- Install exterior or interior storm windows (low-E storm windows are recommended because they save energy).
- Repair and weatherize existing storm windows, using weatherstripping at all movable joints; strong, durable materials; and interlocking or overlapping joints.
- Install tight-fitting insulating shades to drafty windows after weatherizing.
- Conduct an energy audit to find air leaks and check insulation levels. Look for cracks around windows, doors, baseboard gaps, and mail chutes; in brick, siding, stucco, and the foundation; and in places where phone, cable, electric, and gas lines enter the building.
- Close fireplace dampers when not in use to keep warm air from escaping.

U-VALUES

The NFRC was established in 1992 to develop procedures that accurately determine the U-value, also known as the U-factor, of fenestration products. The NFRC is a nonprofit collaboration of window manufacturers, government agencies, and building trade associations that seek to establish a fair, accurate, and credible energy-rating system for windows, doors, and skylights. The U-value measures how well a product prevents heat from escaping from a building. Most U-value ratings range between 0.20 and 1.20. The lower the U-value, the less heat that is transmitted. The U-value is particularly important in cold climates.

The "U" in U-value is a unit that expresses the heat flow through a constructed building section including air spaces of 19 millimeters (3/4 in.) or more and of air films. After an independent laboratory completes the testing and evaluation of a window, the window manufacturer is authorized to assign the product its U-value. Most windows are given two U-values, one for the glass only and one for the whole assembly with the frame.

Designers, engineers, and architects can evaluate the energy properties of windows using U-values. Because the ratings are based on standard window sizes, windows of the same size should be compared. The use of U-values makes heat-gain and heat-loss calculations more reliable. A U-value is the inverse of an R-value, which indicates the level of insulation, so a low U-value correlates to a high R-value.

SOLAR HEAT GAIN COEFFICIENT

In addition to the U-value, the NFRC also provides solar heat gain ratings for windows that indicate how much of the sun's heat will pass through into a building's interior. Solar heat gain is helpful in the winter when it reduces the load for the building's heating equipment. In the summer, however, additional solar heat increases the cooling load. As mentioned earlier, the SHGC is a number from 0 to 1.0. The higher the SHGC, the more solar energy passes through the window glazing and frame.

Windows used in colder climates should have SHGCs greater than 7.0, while those used in warmer climates should have lower SHGCs. Energy Star® products for northern climates must have a U-factor of 0.35 or less for windows and 0.45 or less for skylights. Central climate Energy Star® windows should have 0.40 U-factors and SHGCs of 0.55 or less. Windows for warm, southern climates should have 0.75 U-factors and SHGCs below 0.40 to earn the Energy Star® label.

Overall, Australia's climate is the same as that of the southern United States, except for Tasmania and the southeast edge of the mainland, both of which have a cold climate. The Australian Window Energy Rating Scheme (WERS) gives windows ratings from 0 to 5 stars for their ability to respond to both summer cooling and winter heating. Canada uses a rating similar to that used in the United States, with four climate zones rated A, B, C, and D from south to north.

Selecting Glazing Materials

The material selected for windows and skylights should be appropriate for the amount of light that needs to pass through for their intended use. Thermal performance and life-cycle costs are important economic considerations. The strength and safety of glazing materials must also be considered, as should sound reduction. The aesthetic quality of the glazing's appearance, size, location, and framing has a major impact on both the interior and the exterior of the building.

☑ **The color of glazing can be critical for certain functions. Artists' studios, showroom windows, and community-building lobbies all require high-quality visibility between the interior and the exterior. Warm-toned bronze or gray glazing can affect interior and exterior color schemes. Tinted glazing controls glare and excess solar heat gain year round, so solar warmth is decreased in the winter as well as in the summer. Tinted glazing can modify distracting or undesirable views as well as provide some privacy for occupants, while allowing some view out when the illumination outside is substantially higher than that inside during the day. Unfortunately, this effect may be reversed at night, putting occupants on display. Reflective glazing may bounce glare onto nearby buildings or into traffic.**

Keep in mind that tinted or reflective glass is especially vulnerable to thermal stress. Warm air from a floor register can cause the glass to break from tension stresses on the glass edges.

Window Films

Plastic films glued to the inside face of window glass act like reflective and absorptive glass to intercept the sun's energy before it enters a building. Plastic window films can be reflective or darkening.

During the winter, tinted windows reflect radiated heat back inside a room and increase its operative temperature. They also reduce drafts resulting from cold glass surfaces and make the window glass more shatter-resistant. Tinted-glass coatings

TABLE 10-3. GLAZING MATERIALS

Glazing Type	Use/Description	Comments
Ordinary window glass	Single- and double-glazed windows, doors, skylights	Passes about 80 percent of IR solar radiation; absorbs majority of longer-wave IR radiation from sun-warmed interior surfaces, keeping heat inside
Heat-absorbing glass	Usually solar bronze or solar gray; absorbs selected wavelengths of light	Absorbs about 60 percent of solar heat, half of which is reradiated and convected into building's interior
Heat-reflecting glass	Bounces off most of sun's heat	Large glass wall can reflect enough sun to overheat adjacent buildings and cause severe glare
Shatter-resistant glass	Tempered, laminated, or wired glass; some plastics	Required by code in some circumstances; plastic may scratch or degrade in sunlight

TABLE 10-4. WINDOW FILMS

Film Type	Use/Description	Comments
Silver-, gold-, bronze-, and smoke-tinted films	Block out almost as much visible light as radiated heat	Silver reflects up to 80 percent of solar radiation; bronze and smoke intercept even more solar radiation
Selective-transmission films	Admit most of solar radiation but reflect long IR radiation from warm objects back into room better than ordinary glass	Available as separate sheets to apply to existing windows

TABLE 10-5. TYPES OF WINDOW FRAMES

Frame Type	Description	Performance
Wood	Most common material; remains warm to the touch in winter; stays at room temperature in summer	Moderate insulator; requires staining or painting
Vinyl	Vinyl (PVC) frames with fiberglass can insulate better than wood	Usually not paintable; maintenance-free; radical climate change may eventually cause joint failure and water penetration
Aluminum	Common in western United States; lightweight; must have thermal break or will conduct heat rapidly and feel cold to the touch in winter and hot in summer	Usually not paintable; maintenance-free; slowly oxidizes to dull, pitted appearance

continue to be improved, and lightly tinted coatings that reduce visibility less are available for climates with high cooling loads.

Plastic window films can cause cracking of thermal panes and other windows through thermal expansion and contraction of the self-contained insulated window units. Plastic films should not be used on tinted glass or on very large areas of glass. The films themselves are relatively fragile and have a limited service life.

Window Frames

A window's dimensions affect its energy performance. The glass, low-E coating, and gas fill, such as argon or xenon, work better at conserving energy than the edge spacer, sash, and frame, so the center of the window is actually more efficient than the edges. True **divided lights** (many small panes, each in its own frame) have a great deal more edge area per window and are much less efficient.

Window Treatments

The type of window coverings that an interior designer specifies can affect the heating and air-conditioning load in a space. The location of drapery may interfere with supply-air diffusers or other heating units near a window. It is important to check the proposed type, size, and mounting of window treatments to verify that they will not interfere with the HVAC system.

Insulating draperies fitted with foam or other insulating backing can be used as thermal barriers for windows. Insulating curtains and drapes are available that fit into tracks.

Insulating shades are available in a great variety of styles and stop up to 80 percent of winter heat loss and 86 percent of summer heat gain. They insulate and seal a window on all four sides, providing an added R-value of 4.99. Five layers of air- and moisture-tight fabric are ultrasonically welded without perforating the internal solar barrier. Systems are available for sunrooms with straight or curved eaves and wood or aluminum framework.

Skylight shades use a high-temperature track and can be surface-mounted or recessed into the opening of the frame. Some shade styles use hook-and-loop attachments instead of tracks, which are appropriate for window shades that do not have to be opened and closed frequently.

Roman-shade styles can be covered in the manufacturer's fabrics or custom fabrics. They can be made of insulated materials.

Figure 10-19 Thermal shade. Thermal shades can be made in many different ways. Sealing the curtain tightly against the wall prevents cold air from flowing into the interior space. Insulating fabric is available that is made up of a layer of cotton, then insulation, then a mylar (plastic and aluminum material) layer that acts as a vapor barrier and reflects the IR component of heat back to the room, followed by a second layer of insulation. One side comes unfinished so that fabric can be added to match the room's décor. The fabric can simply be wrapped around a 1×2-inch wood strip and stapled, and the strip is either screwed in above the window or hung from a wooden pole or other type of bar. A heavy wooden dowel is inserted at the bottom so that the curtain hangs straight. The curtain can be attached to the wall with magnets, snaps, hook-and-loop fasteners, or channels. The curtain can be rigged like a Roman shade or rolled up by hand and tied.

Figure 10-20 Japanese shoji screen. Traditional Japanese window treatments are designed to either slide out of the way or to lift out and stack in a custom-fit alcove. This drawing of a shoji screen is by Edward S. Morse and appeared in *Japanese Homes and Their Surroundings* (Dover Publications, 1961, originally published by Ticknor and Company in 1886).

Honeycomb window shades over double-glazing offer improved winter R-values. Translucent 10-millimeter (⅜-in.) shades produce a rating of R-3.23, while 19-millimeter (¾-in.) translucent shades are rated R-3.57 and opaque shades are rated R-4.2. Cellular honeycomb shades can be mounted in tracks and can move horizontally or vertically on flat or curved surfaces. Motor or manual operation is available.

Operating insulating shutters can act as rigid window insulation. Shutters may be hinged, sliding, folding, or bifold. Interior shutters are usually manually operated, and exterior shutters are mechanical.

Both draperies and shutters require storage space when they are not in place across the window. An airtight seal around the edges keeps thermal performance high and prevents condensation from forming.

Loosely woven fiberglass mesh fabric shades are designed to intercept specific percentages of sunshine. These shades are mounted in frames over windows and have fairly long life spans. Mesh shades with different dot densities are specified by transmittance. They control brightness while permitting a view of the outside.

Motorized window-treatment controls are available for both residential and commercial installations as well as for vertical blinds, drapery, metal or wood blinds, roller or Roman shades, and cellular-shade systems. Systems for blinds offer either a single motor or separate motors for tilting and traversing along with the ability to control multiple windows with one remote. The headrail may serve as its own valance. Factory-preset limit switches make installation easier. Controls are either low-voltage modular switches or wireless remote controls.

DOORS

Doors also contribute to heat loss. The entire perimeter of a door should be weatherstripped, with a door sweep at the bottom of the door. In general, storm doors are not cost-effective when added to old, uninsulated metal or fiberglass doors, and trapped heat may damage their plastic trim.

The NFRC has established a rating procedure for determining the thermal performance of doors and sidelights, as it has for windows. A permanent label attached to the edge of a door slab lists the certified U-factor. A temporary label also appears on the face of the door. The energy rating is listed as a U-factor (the rate of heat loss). Higher numbers indicate more heat loss. The values presented include the door and its frame.

In Chapters 9 and 10, we have reviewed the principles of thermal comfort and ventilation. Chapter 11: Heating and Cooling examines the equipment used for heating, cooling, and ventilating buildings.

11
· · · · · · · · · · · · · · · ·

Heating and Cooling

The building envelope's design influences comfort in the way it transmits heat to surfaces and slowly changes air temperature. Air and surface temperatures can often be controlled by passive design techniques. Air motion and air humidity contribute to comfortable cooling. Access to outdoor air improves air quality as well as provides daylight, a view, and solar heat on cold days.

In the preface to the ninth edition of *Mechanical and Electrical Equipment for Buildings*, the authors explain how the perspective of engineers has changed:

"Buildings today contribute to negative global consequences of the future, and our approach to mechanical and electrical systems must consider how best to avoid environmental impacts....

"We have moved from systems that centralize all sources of heating, cooling, water, and electricity toward those that encourage more localized production and control." (Benjamin Stein et al., John Wiley & Sons, Inc., Hoboken, NJ, 2006, p. xvii)

SOLAR HEATING

Estimates suggest that if the sunlight that reaches the earth's surface in one day were converted into useful energy forms, it would satisfy the energy needs of the world for more than 50 years. The amount of sunlight falling on a building typically has enough energy to keep it comfortable throughout the year. Solar energy offers insurance against the possibility that conventional-energy technologies could suddenly become too expensive, unavailable, or undesirable for social, political, or physical reasons. The ability to produce energy on-site leads to decentralization and social stability. Most solar-heating systems can handle 40 to 70 percent of a building's heating load.

The limited supply of fossil fuels encourages their conservation. Electric energy is an inefficient source of heat and may be generated by fossil fuels or by nuclear power plants. Solar energy offers an alternative with fewer air-polluting emissions and no danger of harmful radioactivity.

Despite the availability of free energy from the sun, the cost of solar-energy systems has not been competitive with cheaper conventional-fuel systems. With the recent increased awareness of the importance of energy conservation, solar energy is rising in popularity and, one hopes, falling in price.

The part of the radiation from the sun that is not scattered or absorbed and reaches the earth's surface is called **direct radiation**. When the sunlight has been scattered or re-emitted, it is called **diffuse radiation**.

Solar energy is available in four useful forms:

- **Photosynthesis** is the process by which the sun maintains life by producing food and converting carbon dioxide (CO_2) into oxygen; photosynthesis is also necessary for the growth of wood and indirectly for fossil fuels derived from plants and animals.
- **Natural daylight** provides illumination outside and inside buildings.
- **Photovoltaic (PV)** cells convert sunlight directly into electrical energy.
- **Thermal energy** is used for space heating, domestic hot water, power generation, distillation processes, and the heating of industrial processes.

Wind power could be considered a fifth form since the sun's heat drives the wind. Solar heating is primarily concerned with the

193

sun's thermal energy, but solar-heating designs have implications for PVs, lighting, and even photosynthesis.

A **passive solar-heating system** is actually the building itself, which has no moving parts and depends on local site and climate conditions. Passive systems incorporate solar collection, storage, and distribution into the architectural design of a building's structure, without pumps or fans. This is accomplished by selecting the optimal location, type, and size of windows as well as by employing overhangs and shading. Thermal-storage mass is integrated into the building's construction.

Passive solar-heating systems can present conflicts between access to the sun and space use, view, and ventilation because collecting the sun's radiation for heating may dictate a massive wall where a window would offer a great view instead. Avoiding glare and overheating are major concerns.

Compared with passive solar-heating systems, **active solar-heating systems** offer better control of the environment within a building and can be added on to most existing buildings. Active systems use pumps, fans, heat pumps, and other mechanical equipment to transmit and distribute thermal energy via air or a liquid. Most systems use electricity continually to operate the system. Many buildings use hybrid systems with passive solar-design features and electrically driven fans or pumps.

When a building is designed to take advantage of solar heating, provisions must be made to prevent overheating in warm weather. Roofs provide a barrier to excess summer solar radiation, especially in the tropics where the sun is directly overhead. The transmission of solar heat from the roof to the interior of a building can result in high ceiling temperatures. Surfaces that reflect most infrared (IR) rays heat up very little in the sun. High ceiling temperatures can be reduced with thermally resistant materials, materials with a high thermal capacity, or ventilated spaces in the roof structure.

Orienting building entrances so that they are at a distance from or are protected from prevailing cold winter winds as well as buffering entries with airlocks, vestibules, or double entry doors dramatically reduces the amount of interior and exterior air change when people enter. Locating an unheated garage, mudroom, or sunspace between the doors to a conditioned interior space is a very effective way to control air loss in any building.

The interior layout of a passive solar-heated building should be designed at the same time as the building's siting, rough building shape, shading, and orientation for maximum compatibility. Spaces with maximum heating and lighting needs should be located on a building's south face. Buffer areas, such as toilet rooms, kitchens, corridors, stairwells, storage, garages, and mechanical and utility spaces, need less light and air conditioning, so they can be located on a north or west wall. The areas with the greatest illumination level needs, such as those for accounting,

Figure 11-2 Active solar equipment. This solar thermal collector is designed to be built directly underneath an exterior roof or wall, where it absorbs heat from the sun without interfering with the building's appearance. This solar hot water system can be installed with PV exterior materials to provide combined electrical power and heat.

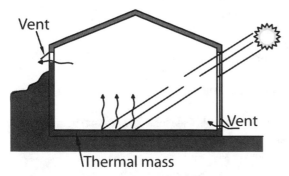

Figure 11-1 Passive solar design. This illustration shows a direct-gain passive solar design, through which the sun's heat directly supplies the energy to heat the space.

typing, reading, and/or drafting, should be next to windows and have access to natural lighting. Conference rooms, which require few if any windows for light and views, can be located farther away from windows. Spaces that need a great deal of cooling because of high internal heat gains from activities or equipment should be located on the north or east side of a building.

PASSIVE SOLAR DESIGNS

All passive solar systems utilize south-facing glass or transparent plastic for solar collection. The low winter sun emits 90 percent of its energy between 9 AM and 3 PM. When other buildings or tall trees block access to the sun during this critical period, solar-energy systems are not practical. The area of the glazing amounts to 30 to 50 percent of the floor area in cold climates and 15 to 25 percent in temperate climates, depending on the average outdoor winter temperature and projected heat loss. Glazing materials must be resistant to degradation by the sun's ultraviolet (UV) rays. Double-glazing and insulation are used to minimize heat loss at night.

A second essential component of a passive solar design is the presence of thermal mass for heat collection, storage, and distribution, oriented to receive the maximum amount of solar exposure. Concrete, brick, stone, tile, rammed earth, sand, water, or other liquids can be used.

Some systems use materials that hold and release energy through **phase changes** (changing from liquid to gas, for example), such as eutectic salts and paraffins. Dark-colored surfaces absorb more solar radiation than lighter ones. Vents, dampers, movable insulating panels, and shading devices can assist in balancing heat distribution.

Passive solar heating types are classified as

- **Direct gain:** Sunlight enters space to warm exposed thermally massive surfaces.
- **Indirect gain:** The sun strikes thermal mass, then is gradually passed as heat to the space behind.
- **Isolated gain:** The sun gently heats a sunspace or greenhouse, which then passes some of its heat to the space behind.

Daily temperatures in **direct-gain passive solar spaces** typically fluctuate between 6°C and 17°C (10°F–30°F). A well-designed system can be 30 to 70 percent efficient in capturing and using the solar energy that strikes a building. Direct-gain design demands skillful and total integration of all architectural elements within the space, including walls, floor, ceiling, and interior surface

TABLE 11-1 THERMAL STORAGE THICKNESSES

Material	Thickness for Effective Thermal Storage
Concrete	30 to 46 centimeters (12–18 in.)
Brick	25 to 36 centimeters (10–14 in.)
Adobe	20 to 31 centimeters (8–12 in.)
Water	15 centimeters (6 in.) or more

finishes. The patterns of sun and shade create texture and rhythm, and the shadows cast on the exterior have a strong impact on the appearance of the building façade. Direct-gain-system characteristics include the following:

- The sun entering south-facing windows or skylights reaches an open-plan top floor, providing good outdoor views and access to the south.
- A large thermal-mass surface is required, with dark colors but no rugs or wall hangings that would absorb heat. Light-colored surfaces near glass reduce glare.
- The space warms up quickly and may overheat at midday. Large temperature swings occur. Heat is lost to bare windows at night when they are not insulated. Warmth spreads throughout the space.
- There is high daylighting glare potential near lower windows. Summer shading helps prevent this. Both side- and top-lighting are used.
- Large south-facing windows provide cooling cross ventilation. Clerestories help stack ventilation. Thermal mass ventilation is used at night.

Indirect-gain systems include **thermal-storage walls** (masonry Trombe walls or water walls) or roof ponds. The overall efficiency of indirect-gain systems runs between about 30 and 45 percent, with water walls being slightly more efficient than masonry.

Characteristics of **Trombe walls** include the following:
- The location on the south wall of the building restricts the outdoor view to the south.
- The inner wall is kept clear of hangings and furniture; the rest of the space is unrestricted.
- The wall is slow to warm up or cool off; small temperature swings occur because of thermal mass.
- Radiant heat is greatest in evening (after sunset) and near the wall surface.
- No daylighting passes through the Trombe wall.
- Cross ventilation is discouraged.

Water-wall characteristics include the following:
- It is made of corrugated galvanized steel culverts, steel drums, or fiberglass-reinforced plastic tubes.
- Water filling wall allows convection to move heat more rapidly through the wall.
- Opaque wall blocks sunlight from entering interior.
- Custom-made walls can be fitted below windows or in another exterior wall location.
- Translucent water wall may provide diffuse lighting.

Direct-gain systems collect heat directly within an interior space. The surface area of the storage mass, which is built into the space, accounts for 50 to 60 percent of the total surface area of the space, including interior partitions. Surfaces are constructed of concrete, concrete block, brick, stone, adobe, or other thick, massive materials. Brick veneer or clay tile over a bed of grout is an effective finish. Floors are typically slab-on-grade without carpets or rugs. The sun should strike directly or be reflected onto the massive surfaces as soon as possible after entering the space. During the winter, the warm surfaces raise the mean radiant temperature (MRT) in the room higher than the air temperature, allowing comfortable conditions between 3°C and 6°C (5°F–10°F) below normal. The mass also keeps room temperatures from becoming too hot in the summer. When additional cooling is needed, ventilation is provided with operable windows and walls.

Direct-gain systems are simple and offer daylight and views to the south. Site conditions and window treatments must prevent bright winter sun from creating glare. Too much heat may enter the space on sunny days. Operable window insulation at night keeps the heat inside the space. Glass filters out much of the sun's UV light, but enough gets through to the interior to bleach paints, interior furnishings, and other building materials. Fade-resistant colors and materials should be selected if they will be exposed directly to the sun for a long time.

Greenhouses and sunspaces combine direct- and indirect-gain systems. When used as part of a solar-heating system, a greenhouse has a masonry or thermal water wall between it and the occupied space. Solar-greenhouse efficiency can be as high as 60 to 75 percent. Only 10 to 30 percent of the energy entering the greenhouse is supplied to the occupied space unless an active heat-storage system is used. The remainder of the heat is used to heat the greenhouse itself.

Isolated-gain systems combine qualities of both direct- and indirect-gain systems. A sunspace or greenhouse is an example of an isolated-gain solar-heating system. Roof ponds are another example.

Sunspaces and greenhouses are available as manufactured systems with wood or metal frames, complete with glazing or flashing. The system can be insulated from the rest of a building, becoming a collector for heat that is stored in a subterranean rock bed. The floor above the rock bed must be kept free of rugs for maximum solar absorption. The system is designed to provide filtered views from a building's interior to the south. The sunspace or greenhouse also shades the interior from summer sun. Night ventilation cools the system as well as the building interior.

Sunspaces and greenhouses are subject to extreme temperature swings, with radiant heat losses at night. Installation of movable insulation can facilitate limited nighttime use. Little or no daylight makes its way through the common wall.

A **roof pond** is another isolated-gain solar-heating system, one that exposes water to the sun during the day and to the cool sky at night. In a typical roof pond installation, water in large plastic bags is supported by a metal deck and roof structure, which serves as the finished ceiling of the room below. The metal deck radiates heat collected and stored in the water bags to the interior space below. An insulating panel is moved mechanically over the roof pond at night, ensuring that stored heat radiates downward into the space.

Roof ponds facilitate an unrestricted interior plan with side-lighting, views, and access to the outdoors. Using very light color on the underside of the roof aids top-lighting. Temperatures remain mostly steady year-round, despite occasional and limited temperature swings. The potential for interior cross ventilation is excellent, especially along the underside of the roof as the pond cools during the night.

Roof ponds are limited to one-story buildings. The roof structure must be able to support the dead load of the water. Spraying or flooding the outside of the roof-mounted water bags adds to evaporative cooling in the summer, increasing the cooling effect fourfold.

Shading for Solar-Heat Control and Cooling

In many climates, the right combination of properly implemented natural methods can provide cooling that is equivalent to mechanical air conditioning. At the very least, natural cooling allows the installation of smaller cooling equipment that will run fewer hours and consume less energy.

Providing shade from the sun is essential for passively cooled buildings as well as for passively heated buildings that might become overheated in hot weather. The best shading occurs before the sun's heat reaches the building.

Even though in the northern hemisphere, the sun moves in a southern arc, northern windows may also need to be shaded in the summer against early-morning rays or near sunset.

Movable shading devices are preferable to fixed shades because they can be adjusted seasonally. Shading options in order of effectiveness are trees and shrubs, trellises, overhangs, awnings, shade screens, window coatings, and interior shades.

Trees throw shade over a building and its surrounding area and cool themselves by pumping water from the ground into their leaves. As this water evaporates from the surface of the leaves, it cools the tree and surrounding area. A tree or vine that foliates early in the spring, defoliates late in the fall, and has low transmissivity in the summer provides shade that varies with the availability of solar heat.

Deciduous shade trees are best for south yards because their canopies are broad and dense. Deciduous trees and vines can provide shade for low buildings while allowing more sunlight through when their leaves fall in the winter. Evergreens can work well for north and northwest yards.

Trellises are permanent structures that partially shade the outside of a building. Clinging vines that grow over the trellis add more shade and evaporative cooling. A special trellis designed to shade air conditioners, heat pumps, and evaporative coolers improves the equipment's performance and appearance without restricting airflow to the equipment.

Fast-growing vines create shade quickly, while trees can take years to provide useful shade. Deciduous vines, such as grape, clematis, and wisteria, lose their leaves in the winter, enabling the sun's heat to strike a building. Trellises and climbing plants are an attractive, flexible design solution.

Roof overhangs block high-angle summer sun but allow the lower winter sun to strike the building. They are effective only for the upper story of a multistory building and do not provide relief for east and west windows. Roof overhangs or horizontal shading

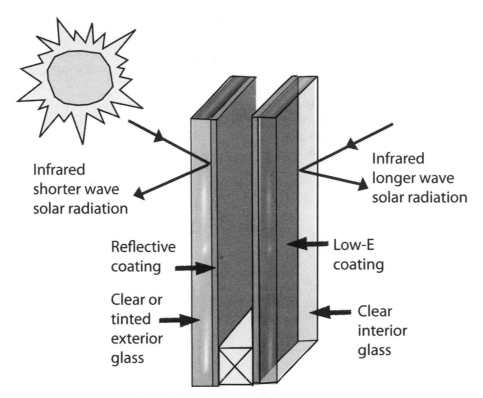

Infrared shorter wave solar radiation

Infrared longer wave solar radiation

Reflective coating

Low-E coating

Clear or tinted exterior glass

Clear interior glass

Figure 11-3 Solar-heat-control window. When the sun's rays are intercepted before passing through window glass, the air-conditioning cooling load can be cut in half, saving between 10 and 50 percent of energy costs. The highest priority should be placed on the surfaces that receive the most summer heat, usually the east and west surfaces.

devices at each floor of taller buildings can block high summertime sun angles on south-facing walls while admitting lower winter sun.

Horizontal louvers parallel to a wall permit air circulation near the wall and reduce conductive heat gain. Manual or timer-controlled photoelectric controls allow the louvers to adapt to the sun's angle.

Slanted louvers offer more protection than parallel ones, with angles varying to coordinate with solar angles. Louvers hung from a solid overhang protect against low sun angles but may interfere with the view. Vertical louvers are most effective on the east or west side. Egg-crate louvers, which are known as a **brise soleil**, combine horizontal and vertical elements to produce a great deal of shade and are very efficient in hot climates.

Outside shade screens (sun screens, shade cloths, or solar shields) on windows exposed to direct sunlight prevent the sunlight from entering a window. These lightweight, durable, and easy-to-install devices are made from aluminum or plastic and are designed to block a certain amount of the sun's energy, typically between 50 and 90 percent.

The **shading coefficient** is the amount of heat that penetrates the screen; low numbers indicate that less energy gets through. Although you can see through a shade screen, the view is obscured. Fixed sunshades can block the sun in the early spring, when it is desirable to have the sun penetrate the interior.

Adjustable sunshades, such as awnings, avoid this problem. Manual controls for adjustable sunshades are inexpensive and relatively trouble-free; occupants make adjustments when necessary. Motorized devices are effective for large or heavy devices in remote places, such as clerestory windows. Automatic systems with computerized controls can be set to consider the thermal needs of an entire building.

Awnings can cover individual windows or sections of outside walls and are most effective on the south side of the building. Awnings come in a variety of shapes, sizes, and colors to match many building designs. Fixed awnings block light at a given angle; adjustable awnings can be rolled up in the winter to allow low-angle sun to reach into a building. Awnings have the disadvantage of blocking the view from the top half of the window.

Exterior shading rejects about 80 percent of the solar energy that strikes a window. Interior shading devices absorb and reradiate 80 percent into the interior, increasing interior temperatures dramatically. Outside louvers can cool off in a breeze; conversely, draperies become part of a heat trap, giving off radiant heat in hot weather.

Interior-shading devices, including roller shades, blinds, and curtains, absorb solar radiation and convert it to convected heat in the interior air. They prevent direct solar radiation from striking occupants and furnishings but do not block sunlight as well as exterior shades do. Interior shades can reduce solar radiation by as much as half, depending on their reflectivity, and reduce visual glare from direct sunlight. Compared with exterior shades, they are exposed to less dirt and weathering and are usually easy to adjust manually.

☑ **To provide the most benefit, interior shades should have a light-colored surface on the side facing the window and be made of an insulating material. They should fit tightly to prevent air movement into the room and cover the whole window.**

Solar Collectors

Types of solar collectors include flat-plate, solar-concentrating, and solar-storage collectors. Two or three 0.9 × 2.1 m (3 × 7 ft.) panels provide domestic hot water for a typical family of four. The array size will depend on the energy load required, the amount of backup storage needed, the proposed application, and the cost of competing local energy sources. As a rule of thumb, 5 square meters (54 sq ft.) of collectors per residential user should be allotted for heating domestic hot water. Collectors should equal one-quarter to one-half of the internal floor area served for space heating, with even larger amounts for cooling.

South-wall installations of collectors work best for space heating in northern climates, where the winter sun is very low in the sky and strikes vertical walls directly. Collectors must be kept free of snow cover.

Flat-plate collectors:
- These are a more common and less expensive type of collector panel.
- They can use both direct and diffuse solar radiation.
- The sun's rays pass through the cover plate and strike an absorbent, blackened metal surface that collects the solar radiation.
- The fluid circulating through tubes or channels in the plate picks up the heat and carries it to an isolated storage unit.
- Plates made of glass, clear plastic, or fiberglass block some of the solar radiation but slow down heat loss to the environment. An insulating box contains the heat loss at the back and sides of the collector.
- As the sun warms the air or water in the solar collector, it rises either to the space where it is used or to a thermally massive storage area until it is needed.
- Simultaneously, cooler air or water is pulled from the bottom of the thermal-storage area, using a natural convection loop.

Solar-concentrating collectors:
- use only direct solar radiation
- can be used for cooling or to produce steam for electrical-generation turbines
- use optical lenses or reflectors to focus solar radiation onto a point much smaller than the area that receives the sun's rays, thereby concentrating energy and producing higher temperatures
- use tracking mechanisms to follow the sun throughout the day

Solar storage attached to collectors:
- This system typically holds one to three days' output.
- Most systems need to be drained when not collecting to prevent freezing. Antifreeze and heat exchangers are also used.
- Some systems store heat in air spaces in a large bed of river rocks.

The reflections from solar collectors on walls and sloped roofs can produce glare into neighboring buildings. Although the heat reflected into neighboring buildings may be welcome in the winter, it adds to their cooling load in the summer. Strategically placed external projections on the building and foliage can eliminate the problem.

ACTIVE SOLAR DESIGNS

Active solar systems use solar-collector panels, circulation and distribution systems, a heat exchanger, and a storage facility to absorb, transfer, and store energy from solar radiation for building heating and cooling. Systems use air, water, or another liquid for the heat-transfer medium, which carries collected heat energy from solar panels to the heat-exchange equipment or storage utility for later use.

Liquid active solar systems:
- These systems use pipes for circulation and distribution.
- They are protected from freezing with antifreeze solutions.
- Aluminum pipes require the use of a corrosion-retarding additive.

Air active solar systems:
- These systems use ductwork, which requires additional installation space.
- Larger collector surfaces are required because air transfers heat less efficiently than liquids.
- They are easier to use since leaking, corrosion, and freezing are not problems.

The storage facility for active systems holds heat for use at night and on overcast days in an insulated tank filled with water or another liquid or in a bin of rocks or phase-change salts for air systems.

Heat distribution in an active solar system is similar to that in a conventional heating system, using all-air or air-water delivery. A heat pump or absorptive cooling unit accomplishes cooling.

For efficiency, a building should be thermally efficient and well insulated. The siting, orientation, and window openings should take advantage of seasonal solar radiation. A backup heating system is recommended.

Solar Water Heating, Cooling, and Other Applications

Using solar energy to heat water is one of the most cost-effective solar applications. Solar water heaters manufactured as packages including collectors, storage tank, and controls are available in many countries.

Solar energy is also used for the heating loads of industrial processes, including drying lumber or food, chemical- or metallurgical-process extraction operations, food processing and cooking, curing masonry products, and drying paint. Solar cooling is used for the refrigeration of food or chemical preservation.

The need for cooling with a solar design coincides with the time when the greatest amount of solar energy is available. Most glass and plastics do not pass long-wave thermal radiation, so closed windows and glass or plastic-covered solar collectors do not radiate much heat to the night sky. Open windows work better, but if warm trees, buildings, or earth are within the radiation's path rather than colder open sky, less heat will be removed.

Solar energy can be stored as hot water as it comes out of collectors or as chilled water. Solar air-conditioning systems operate by absorption; by the **Rankine cycle**, in which solar steam turns a turbine to power an air conditioner; or by **desiccant cooling**, which uses dehumidification to cool. The equipment for solar cooling is expensive, so it is used only where cooling loads cannot be avoided by good building design.

HEATING SYSTEMS

Heating and cooling systems have evolved over time as equipment has become more complex. Interior designers should be aware of how heating and cooling equipment works as well as how the equipment will affect the design, energy efficiency, and the client's comfort.

Mechanical and electrical systems are made primarily of non-renewable plastics and metals that offer strength, durability, fire-resistance, and varying amounts of conductivity or resistance to heat or electricity. These materials use significant amounts of energy to manufacture and deliver.

History of Heating Systems

As we look for innovative and energy-efficient ways to heat buildings, we can benefit from reviewing how the systems in use today developed. The Romans developed the first centralized heating systems in the first century CE. Charles Panati, in his *Extraordinary Origins of Everyday Things* (Harper & Row, New York, 1989, p. 131), says that according to the Stoic philosopher and statesman Seneca, several patrician homes had "tubes embedded in the walls for directing and spreading, equally throughout the house, a soft and regular heat." The hot exhaust from wood or coal fires in the basement was collected under the floor in an area called a hypocaust and distributed through terracotta tubes. The remains of these systems have been discovered in parts of Europe where Roman culture flourished. Unfortunately, central heating disappeared with the fall of the Roman Empire.

About 80 percent of the heat went up the chimneys of the huge central fireplaces in vast, drafty eleventh-century castles, while people huddled close to the fire to keep warm. Sometimes, a large wall of clay and brick that extended several feet behind the fire was used to absorb and reradiate the heat later on, but this type of construction was relatively rare until the eighteenth century.

In 1642, French engineers installed single-room heating systems in the Louvre in Paris that drew room-temperature air through passages around the fire and discharged heated air back into the room. This continual reuse resulted in stale air and stuffy rooms.

The Industrial Revolution brought steam heat to Europe in the eighteenth century. Steam conveyed in pipes heated schools, churches, law courts, assembly halls, greenhouses, and wealthy people's homes. The extremely hot surfaces of the steam pipes dried out the air uncomfortably and generated the odor of charred dust.

Eighteenth-century America used a system similar to the Roman hypocaust. A large coal furnace in the basement sent heated air through a network of pipes with vents in major rooms. Around 1880, many U.S. buildings were converted to steam systems. A coal furnace heated a water tank, and hot air pipes carried both steam and hot water to vents connected to radiators. These steam radiators are still seen in many older homes.

Building Heating Fuels

We have already discussed the most powerful heating source at our disposal: the sun. Any building heating system must start with an assessment of the available free heat from the sun, then look to other fuel sources as supplements. Currently, solar energy supplies only about 2 percent of U.S. energy needs, although this is likely to change. Our primary source of building energy is fossil fuels.

Fossil fuels include gas, oil, and coal. Heating systems in the United States generate more than one billion tons of CO_2 per year, and about 12 percent of the sulfur dioxide and nitrogen oxides that pollute the air. The heating system is the largest energy expense in most homes, accounting for two-thirds of the annual energy bill in colder climates. Buildings consume more than 30 percent of all energy used in the United States.

Oil:
- derived from refined crude petroleum
- delivered by truck; size of storage tank depends on proximity of supplier and space available in building
- supplies subject to international political and economic maneuverings

Natural gas:
- second most common heating fuel
- piped thousands of miles directly from wellhead to consumer
- burns cleanly
- does not require storage space in building
- a distinctive odor added so that leaks can be readily detected.

The American Gas Association (AGA) conducts research and provides information on safe and efficient installation and operation of gas-fired equipment; it also issues standards and proposes installation requirements that in many cases are incorporated in major building codes.

Local gas utilities that work with governmental agencies offer rebates to encourage customers to purchase and install high-efficiency gas-heating systems. Equipment covered includes Energy Star® hot water boilers, hot air furnaces, and steam boilers.

Liquefied gas:
- Propane and butane are petroleum gases that become liquids under moderate pressure.
- Liquefied gas is transported in pressurized cylinders and is connected to a building's gas piping.
- It is most often used for small installations in remote locations.
- It burns cleanly.
- It is slightly more expensive than natural gas.

Coal:
- Coal is much more plentiful than oil or gas.
- It is rarely used for heating new residential construction.
- It requires a complex heating system with high maintenance requirements.
- It is bulky, heavy, and dirty to distribute, store, and handle.
- It is difficult to burn efficiently and cleanly.
- It requires expensive emissions control.

Figure 11-4 Propane gas cylinder. Propane is a petroleum gas in a pressurized cylinder that is delivered to a site and connected to the gas piping of a building. In this situation, propane supplements this building's primary heat source, firewood.

- Heavy, dusty ash generated by burning coal must be removed.
- Mining coal underground is dangerous; in addition, open pits destroy the countryside.

Wood (cordwood):
- When properly harvested, wood is a sustainable resource.
- Destroying trees in desert areas can expand the desert, cause famine, result in habitat destruction, and endanger the survival of forest animals.
- Wood requires extensive covered, ventilated, and easy-to-access storage space.
- Wood brought directly into the house from a woodpile may contain insects.
- The incomplete combustion of wood can give off dangerous gases.
- Fires leave deposits of highly combustible **creosote**, which is an oily product of burning wood tar, inside chimneys; creosote can spontaneously erupt into a chimney fire at high temperatures. To prevent this, chimneys must be cleaned often.

Wood pellets
- are dense pellets of quality sawdust
- are highly efficient and produce less pollution
- are cleaner and need less storage space than cordwood
- are more expensive than solid wood
- are automatically fed into special stoves by an electric auger

Electrical energy
- has lowest installation cost of common fuels but is very expensive in most parts of the world
- is clean and easy to distribute within a building
- is much less efficient to generate remotely than is direct combustion of another fuel in the building itself
- can be an efficient fuel when used in an electric heat-pump system

Electricity generated from fossil fuels or nuclear energy discards two or three units for every unit of heat released through electric resistance into a room because of losses in electrical generation and transmission.

BUILDING ENERGY CONSERVATION

Today, architects and engineers design buildings with systems that will eventually wean us from our dependence on nonrenewable fuels. With an eye to protecting natural resources and preserving the environment, building engineers are seeking ways to share heating and cooling tasks between mechanical systems and natural ventilation and daylighting.

Energy Star® certifications have been developed by the U.S. Environmental Protection Agency (EPA) and the U.S. Department of Energy (DOE) for energy-efficient furnaces, central and room air conditioners, and heat pumps. Energy Star® homes are identified as at least 30 percent more energy-efficient than the current International Energy Conservation Code requirements.

Utility companies have realized that it costs less to offer rebates for the purchase of energy-efficient appliances than to build new power plants. Some local electric utilities and gas companies offer rebates for high-efficiency (HE) heat pumps and central air conditioners. Gas companies may offer rebates for HE furnaces and boilers.

Many existing home-heating systems dating back to the 1950s and 1960s are much too large for their buildings. Consequently, they keep cycling on and off first to heat the building, then to allow it to cool off, a process that wastes energy. A heat-loss analysis of the building can determine the proper size for the equipment.

Modifying an existing heating system can produce significant energy savings. A new, more efficient oil burner is another option. Possible modifications include

- **Modulating aquastat:** a device for hot water (hydronic) systems that senses the outdoor temperature and keeps the boiler only as hot as necessary
- **Hot water time-delay relay:** circulates already-warmed water through radiators without turning on the boiler to heat more water
- **Pilotless ignition:** a feature of gas heaters that eliminates the amount of gas needed to run the pilot light
- **Flue economizer:** recovers heat from hot gases that go up the flue

Fireplaces and Woodstoves

Wood is popular for heating homes in regions where energy costs are high and local regulations permit burning wood. Not all fireplaces are good heaters, and any fireplace or woodstove requires regular maintenance if it is to remain reliable and safe.

To burn properly, a fire requires a steady flow of air. Traditional fireplaces draw the air for combustion from inside the house.

Wood-burning fireplaces and woodstoves burn seasoned wood or manufactured wood logs; both can add to indoor and outdoor air pollution by emitting CO, irritating particles, and sometimes nitrogen dioxide (NO_2). Wood smoke causes nose and throat irritation and can trigger asthma attacks. To keep chimneys clean and minimize pollution risks, burn small hot fires, not large smoky ones; use seasoned wood; and provide adequate ventilation. Coal and peat are also used as fireplace fuel sources.

A fireplace is actually a framed opening in a chimney that is designed to hold an open fire and sustain fuel combustion. Modern fireplaces combine masonry and steel construction; some are made almost entirely of steel. Fireplaces should be designed to carry smoke and other combustion by-products safely outside and to radiate the maximum amount of heat comfortably into the room. The designer must keep the fireplace adequate distances from combustible materials. Multifaced fireplaces are sensitive to drafts in a room; avoid placing their openings opposite an exterior door.

- **Firebox:** a chamber where combustion takes place; traditionally steel-lined with noncombustible firebrick
- **Throat:** a narrow opening that connects firebox and smoke chamber.

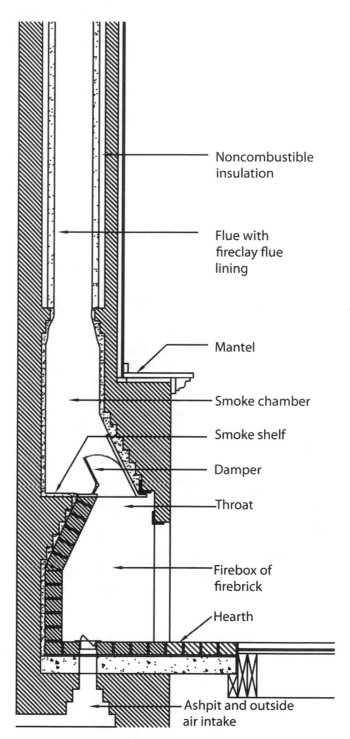

Figure 11-5 Fireplace and chimney section. A building's chimney may serve more than one fireplace and may even vent other heat sources. The chimney breast and mantel are often treated as a focal point in a room.

- **Damper:** regulates draft in fireplace
- **Smoke chamber:** connects throat to chimney flue
- **Smoke shelf:** deflects downdrafts from chimney, preventing cold air and smoke from entering room
- **Flue:** creates draft and carries smoke and gases safely outside; usually metal or tile liner inside masonry chimney
- **Grate:** sits on fireplace floor; holds logs so air can stoke fire from underneath
- **Air intake:** located underneath fireplace floor; pulls in outside air
- **Flue damper:** regulates draft; can be closed to keep air from escaping up flue when fireplace is not in use
- **Hearth:** made of noncombustible material (brick, tile, stone); extends floor of fireplace out into room to prevent flying sparks
- **Ash drop:** in hearth; can be opened to dump ashes into pit underneath
- **Gas starter:** sets logs ablaze without kindling
- **Chimneybreast:** located on wall of room; often projects a few inches
- **Mantel:** may trim top of fireplace

Strict environmental laws may prohibit burning of wood on certain days to all but certified, clean-burning appliances, which usually means factory-built fireplaces or woodstoves. The EPA certifies prefabricated fireplaces and woodstoves for burning efficiency and allowable particulate emissions. New models that meet EPA requirements are quite clean-burning.

Traditional brick or stone masonry fireplaces:
- radiate most of heat in immediate area and lose much up chimney
- are susceptible to creosote fire damage; require regular cleaning

HE or hybrid wood-burning fireplaces:
- Basically, these are wood-burning furnaces.
- Fire burns in a combustion chamber behind glass doors.
- Air enters the firebox at the top of the glass; air wash keeps the glass cleaner.
- Controlling the combustion air produces more heat and long burn times.
- Smoke is burned when passing through a catalyst or secondary combustion chamber.
- Heat is held in the firebox longer, which heats the air plenum that carries air to the rest of a home.

Masonry heating stoves (Russian or Finnish stoves):
- burn combustible wood solids plus gases totaling 99 percent of wood
- radiate energy stored in thermal mass back into space slowly and evenly over many hours; heat solid objects that reradiate into air
- produce very gentle heat and almost imperceptible warmth
- are slightly cooler in morning than when fueled in evening
- can be used with passive solar heating
- have much lower particle emissions than woodstoves

Manufactured prefabricated fireplaces:
- Most of their heat warms air circulating inside one or two shells that surround the firebox.
- The room air intake underneath the firebox lets cool air in; a damper controls the intake.
- Heated air rises to the warm air outlet at the top of the fireplace.
- HE heat-circulating fireplaces have an outside air intake and do not require room air for combustion.
- A fan may increase the airflow and speed up heat transfer.
- Convection currents circulate warm air in the room and direct cool air to the fireplace.

Some clean-burning fireplaces are variations of the Rumford design that was developed in England in the late 1700s. The Rumford is a tall, shallow fireplace that is about as high as it is wide; it burns hot and easily radiates heat into the room. To prevent smoking, the fireplace is built with a rounded throat that draws air up into the smoke chamber. Some current models can be used in new construction or retrofitted into an existing fireplace.

Heat-circulating fireplaces:
- An enclosed sheet-metal firebox has a double- or triple-walled metal pipe that runs up inside a wood-framed chase.
- The chase cover and cap keep sparks in and animals out.
- The firebox holds some of the flue gas heat and radiates more heat to a room, thereby replacing masonry fireplaces.
- They may rust within 100 meters of salt water.

Zero-clearance fireplaces:
- do not need space between their enclosures and nearby combustible materials
- are relatively low-cost

Fireplace inserts:
- These are airtight boxes inserted into fireplaces.
- Most draw air from a room, circulate it around themselves, then return warmed air to the room.
- They mimic some effects of wood-burning stoves.
- Some have blowers to help distribute heat.

Glass fireplace enclosures:
- These enclosures control air intake so wood burns more slowly and retains more heat in the firebox.
- They mount securely against the face of the fireplace, overlapping the opening.
- They may be left unattended.
- They provide a clear view of the fire and keep smoke and sparks out of the room.

Gas fireplaces require only a small vent. Direct-vent models expel CO out the rear, which means that the fireplace can be vented directly through an exterior wall and that a chimney to the roofline does not need to be built. Some gas fireplaces also draw combustion air from the outside.

Figure 11-6 Masonry heater. A masonry heater can be purchased as a prefabricated unit or can be built in place. Plans and instructions for masonry heaters are commercially available.

Gas logs and gas fireplaces burn natural or propane gas to provide flames that are largely decorative, although some units also provide quite a bit of heat. Ceramic gas logs can be hooked up to an existing gas starter in a fireplace or to a new line brought to the firebox. Gas logs should be installed only in a fireplace that is designed to burn wood. They should always be operated with the damper open, so CO will vent up the chimney.

Vented gas fireplaces:
• These fireplaces use natural or low pressure (LP) gas.
• Conventional models require a venting system, while new models vent through a wall power vent.
• Built-in units do not require a special floor or hearth in front.
• These fireplaces can be converted to wood-burning fireplaces.

Vent-free gas fireplaces:
• Most of these fireplaces are not approved for use in bedrooms, bathrooms, or confined spaces.
• Their flame height and heat output are adjustable.
• They may produce an objectionable odor.

Vented gas logs:
• These logs require venting via a smoke dome or chimney.
• The chimney damper must remain open, resulting in heat loss.
• They are made of high-temperature ceramic or concrete.
• They are used behind protective glass and are placed directly on a fire grate or a flame pan that is covered with a bed of volcanic granules to simulate wood fire.
• They fit fireplaces that have a gas hookup and can be used in any Underwriters Laboratories (UL)–listed solid-fuel-burning fireplace.

Vent-free gas logs:
• These logs operate with the chimney damper closed to prevent heat loss.
• An oxygen-depletion sensor (ODS) shuts off the heater and gas flow when the oxygen level in the room is inadequate.
• An auto-shut-off valve stops the gas flow when the pilot light is extinguished or the gas flow is interrupted.
• These logs are placed directly on a fire grate or a flame pan that is covered with a bed of volcanic granules to simulate wood fire.
• They fit fireplaces that have a gas hookup and can be used in any UL-listed solid-fuel-burning fireplace or AGA-listed, design-certified vent-free fireplace.

Electric fireplaces:
• These fireplaces feature plug-in installation and a realistic flame appearance.
• They operate with the heater on or off.
• Electric radiant heat is not energy efficient.
• They can be installed in any room.

Woodstoves:
• Woodstoves may be more energy efficient than heat-circulating fireplaces.

• Some woodstoves only radiate heat, while others also heat air passing around the firebox in convection currents.
• These stoves must be located at safe distances from combustible surfaces.
• Their catalytic combustors reduce air pollution by igniting wood smoke at a lower temperature, thereby burning up gases and producing more heat and less creosote.
• Woodstoves with catalytic combustors cannot burn plastic, colored newsprint, metals, or sulfur.
• Their precision dampers and other controls adjust heat output.

☑ **A stove's location affects furniture arrangements and circulation paths. Areas that "see" the stove get most of the radiant heat, resulting in hot spots near the stove and cold spots where visual access is blocked. Circulation paths must be left around hot stove surfaces. In addition, space must be made available for wood storage; this space should be covered, well ventilated, accessible, and large enough for an ample supply. Wood-burning stoves require a minimum of 46 centimeters (18 in.) between uninsulated metal chimneys and combustible wall or ceiling surfaces. The stove must be at least 91 centimeters (36 in.) from the nearest wall. This distance may be reduced to 46 centimeters if the wall is protected by a noncombustible heat shield or 25 millimeters (1 in.) of clear air space.**

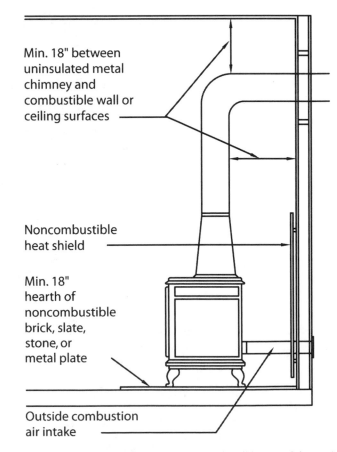

Min. 18" between uninsulated metal chimney and combustible wall or ceiling surfaces

Noncombustible heat shield

Min. 18" hearth of noncombustible brick, slate, stone, or metal plate

Outside combustion air intake

Figure 11-7 Woodburning stove. Noncombustible materials must be used below and around a woodstove, with a minimum clearance provided for combustible materials.

Chimneys and Flues

Chimneys are usually associated with fireplaces, but boilers and furnaces have chimneys, too. Burning produces carbon monoxide (CO) and CO_2. Chimneys carry these gases and other products of combustion up and out of buildings. Older, less efficient fuel-burning equipment uses chimneys to carry high-temperature flue gases. These must be isolated from combustible construction. Traditional flues are built 10 to 12 meters (35–40 ft.) high to provide an adequate draft. In new flues, fans provide this draft.

Chimneys in homes are usually constructed of a terracotta flue lining surrounded by 8 inches of brick, with a 2-inch space between the brick and any wood. This space is filled with incombustible mineral wool. Prefabricated chimneys are replacing heavier, bulkier field-built masonry. HE boilers and furnaces remove so much heat from exhaust gases that the flues used can be smaller and can be vented through a wall to the exterior, eliminating a chimney.

Masonry chimneys must have a minimum clearance of 5 centimeters (2 in.) from combustible construction. Typically, fire-stopping is provided between the chimney and wood framing.

Thermal expansion caused reinforced concrete chimneys that had been built during the 1970s and 1980s to crack when heated. Vertical exterior cracks became worse as steel reinforcing bars rusted. This technique is now obsolete.

Chimneys work by convection, with warmer air and gases rising up and out of the chimney. The removal of air through the chimney leaves a room with a fireplace at a lower air pressure than the outdoors. This lower pressure often draws air from the surrounding room. Oxygen is only about one fifth of the air, so it takes a great deal of air to provide enough oxygen for combustion.

This makeup air should be drawn from the outdoors via either an intake that is located close to the fuel burner or a duct that is connected to a more remote intake. A duct or grille draws air directly from the outdoors to the fire without passing through the room. When an intake is not supplied, outdoor air enters a building interior through cracks, creating a draft through the room that can negate the heat from the fireplace. If all of the air leaks are plugged, the fire will becomes smoky and sluggish, and

the chimney will not work properly. Smoke buildup in the room depletes oxygen.

Most of the heat from a fireplace goes up the chimney, which can result in a net heat loss. The colder it is outside, the more heat is lost. Masonry masses around the fireplace can store and release some heat, especially when the fireplace is surrounded by the building and is not on an exterior wall. The ANSI/ASHRAE Standard 90.2-2004, *Energy Efficient Design of New Low-Rise Residential Buildings*, requires a tight-fitting damper, firebox doors, and a source of outside combustion air within the firebox for a safe, efficient fireplace.

Gas-Fired Heaters

Vent-free gas heating appliances include unvented, wall-mounted, and freestanding gas heaters and gas fireplaces (discussed earlier). These appliances require that a nearby window be kept open a couple of inches for an adequate supply of fresh air to prevent oxygen depletion, which results in heat loss.

Hot Water and Steam-Heating Systems

Originally, mechanical systems in buildings were designed to provide additional heat in cold weather. Cooling was provided by the way buildings were sited, shaded, and ventilated. This initial discussion of mechanical systems will consider these heating-only systems. Today, in practice most heating equipment is used in conjunction with cooling and ventilating equipment, which will be considered later in this chapter (see page 219).

Hot water systems were the residential standard until about 1935. These hydronic systems heat a building by means of water heated in a boiler and circulated by a pump through pipes to a fin-tube radiator, a convector, or a unit heater for heating only. Fan-coil units (FCUs) and radiant panels are used for both heating and cooling. Hydronic systems are used in residences as well as in perimeter areas of commercial buildings with separate cooling-only ducted systems in the interior spaces. Steam boilers generate steam that is circulated through piping to radiators.

TABLE 11-2. TYPES OF GAS HEATERS

Type	Description	Comments
Unvented gas heaters	Produce nitrous oxides that cause nose, eye, and throat irritation, along with CO; produce a great deal of water vapor that can cause condensation, mildew, and rot in wall and ceiling cavities	Unvented gas heaters are prohibited in homes by many state and city codes throughout the United States and Canada
Gas-fired IR heating units	Used in semi-outdoor locations, such as loading docks and repair shops; use natural gas or propane	If vented, can be installed in warehouse-type retail stores; heat surfaces first, not the air, providing thermal comfort without high air temperatures; are large and usually noisy
Gas-fired baseboard heaters	Use natural gas or propane to heat by convection and radiation; built-in fan vents directly to outside, so heaters are located at or near exterior wall	Gas-fired baseboard heaters come in lengths of 1.2 meters (4 ft.) and 1.9 meters (6 ft.)

Figure 11-8 Electric recessed wall heater. This electric recessed wall heater is shown without its protective grille and gasketed frame.

BOILERS

Boilers heat recirculating hot water systems for building heating. A boiler is a closed arrangement of vessels and tubes in which water is heated or steam is generated. A horizontal pipe carries exhaust gas from the boiler and is connected to a vertical flue section called the stack. Boilers also need ventilation air, with an inlet and an outlet on opposite sides of the room.

Boiler systems require a fuel, a heat source, and a pump or fan to move the water. A distribution system, heat exchanger, or terminal within the space to be heated along with a control system complete the equipment. Any heat that escapes through the boiler's walls also helps heat the building. If a boiler is too small for the building, the building temperatures will be too low. Boilers that are too large waste money and space.

The type of boiler used depends on the size of the heating load, the heating fuels available, the efficiency needed, and whether the boilers are single or modular. To receive Energy Star® certification, a boiler must have an annual fuel-usage efficiency of 85 percent or higher.

Boilers are often fueled with oil and gas. Coal boilers require antipollution equipment to control fly ash, which consists of various sizes of particles, and flue gas, which contains sulfur and nitrogen. Flue gases contribute to acid rain. Boilers sometimes use recovered industrial waste heat to generate steam, often in combination with oil or gas. Hot water converters use a steam or hot water heat source, such as a geothermal source, district heating, or a central steam boiler to heat hot water for building use.

Boilers heat water that is then distributed through the building. Steam boilers are used for space heating and domestic hot water as well as for generating electrical power for hospitals, kitchens, and industrial processes.

STEAM AND HOT WATER SYSTEM DISTRIBUTION

In **steam-heating systems**, steam that is produced in a boiler is circulated under pressure through insulated pipes, then condensed in cast-iron radiators. In the radiator, the latent heat given

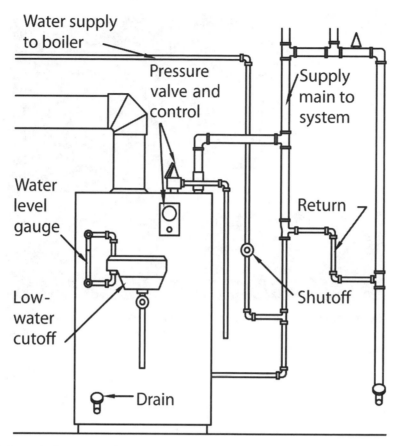

Figure 11-9 Steam boiler. A steam boiler heats water to generate steam, which is distributed through pipes to steam radiators or convectors.

TABLE 11-3. TYPES OF BOILERS

Boiler Type	Description	Comments
Electric boilers	Do not need combustion air or flues; no air pollution in building	Use high-grade electrical energy for low-grade task of heating
Cast-iron boilers	Used for low-pressure steam and low-temperature hot water systems	Generally less efficient than other types
Portable boilers	Small steel boilers assembled from welded-steel units	Prefabricated on a steel foundation; transported as single package from factory
Large boilers	Installed in refractory-brick settings built on-site	Most efficient when in constant operation
Modular boilers	Sections can be used as needed	Provide better efficiency, ease of maintenance, smaller size
Hot water converters	Similar to heat exchangers that transmit heat from steam or hot water	Heat hot water for building use

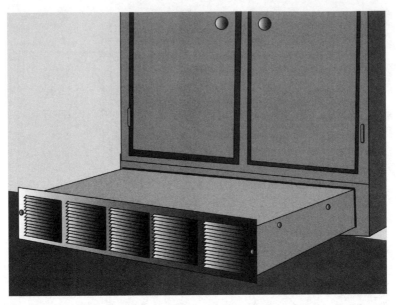

Figure 11-10 Electric heater in kickspace. Locating an electric heater in a kickspace below base cabinets takes advantage of unused space and puts the heat at the user's foot level for cozy warmth, with less direct heat at the cooking level.

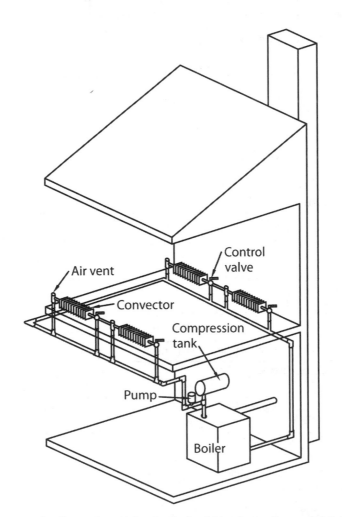

Figure 11-11 Hot water heating system. Hot water (hydronic) heating systems consist of a boiler that heats water, which is then distributed to radiators or convectors.

TABLE 11-4. TYPES OF HOT WATER CIRCUITS

Circuit Type	Description	Comments
Series-loop system	Water flows to and through each baseboard or fin tube in turn	Water cooler at end of circuit; no individual heating-element shutoff
One-pipe system	Fittings divert part of flow into each baseboard	Water cooler at end of circuit; more piping and higher cost than loop
Two-pipe reverse-return system	Return flow is reversed and does not mix with supply	Uniform water flow and temperature; more piping and higher cost than above
Two-pipe direct-return system	Return flow is longer; doubles back on return to boiler	Water at end of line may be considerably cooler; not recommended

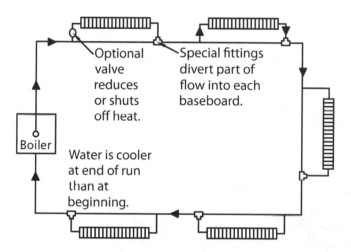

Figure 11-12 One-pipe hydronic system. Water circulates through a single pipe, becoming cooler toward the end of the circuit.

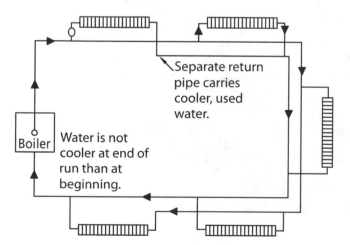

Figure 11-13 Two-pipe hydronic system. A separate return pipe keeps cooled water from mixing with warmer supply water.

off when the steam cools and becomes water is released into the air in a room. The condensed water then returns to the boiler through a network of return pipes. The system is reasonably efficient but difficult to control with precision because the steam gives off its heat rapidly.

Heat sources are often located just below windows even though some of this warmth will be driven through the exterior wall in cold weather. Well-insulated windows and walls stay warmer, and the need for heat at the building's edge is lower. The best-insulated spaces require little additional heat.

Steam pipes are larger than those for water but are smaller than air ducts. The steam moves by its own power, and unlike the rate and temperature of water, those of steam cannot be controlled. The condensation of steam in pipes is noisy, and hot water systems are now more common than steam systems. In order for the condensed water to collect and drain in the steam pipes, the drainpipes must be sloped, taking up more space in construction.

Hot water heating circuits that serve baseboards or radiators come in four principal arrangements (see Table 11-4).

Natural Convection Heating Units

Radiators and convectors are used to supply heat only in residential and small light-commercial buildings. What we usually call radiators, including both fin-tube radiation devices and old-fashioned cast-iron radiators, actually use convection as their primary heating principle. Various styles of baseboard and cabinet convection heating units are used in smaller buildings. Their appearance and the space they occupy are of concern to an interior designer. When located below a window, they can affect the design of window treatments.

Radiators consist of a series or coil of pipes through which hot water or steam passes. The heated pipes warm the space by convection and to a lesser extent by radiation. Leaks in radiators are easily repaired.

Cast-iron radiators:
• Old-style cast-iron radiators are located near outside walls and under windows in every room.

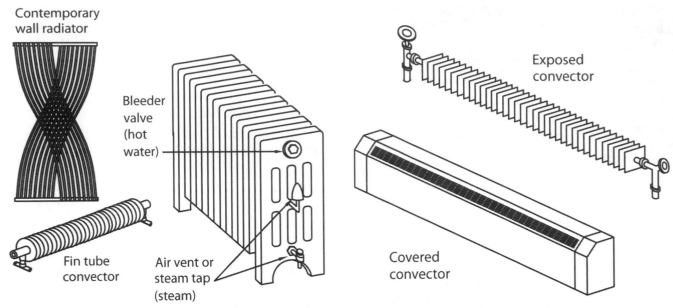

Contemporary wall radiator

Fin tube convector

Bleeder valve (hot water)

Air vent or steam tap (steam)

Exposed convector

Covered convector

Figure 11-14 Radiators. Radiators are easier to control in hot water systems than in steam systems. A very even release of heat to the air is achieved by regulating the water's temperature and rate of circulation. Hydronic systems are silent when properly installed and adjusted and produce comfortable heat.

Figure 11-15 Baseboard fin-tube radiator/convector. Fin-tube radiators are longer and smaller than old-fashioned cast-iron radiators. Although covered convectors are easier to clean and have a more finished appearance than fin-tube convectors, some buildings still have these exposed convectors.

Figure 11-16 Radiator cover. This custom-made radiator cover rests over an old cast-iron steam radiator. The back of the cover is open, so that the cover can be removed easily. The top surface provides usable horizontal space under a windowsill.

- Such radiators are not installed anymore.
- Cast-iron radiators are made of between 2 and 50 cast-iron sections, each with four or six tubes.
- Some models stand on the floor, while others hang on wall brackets.
- Radiator covers are available that obscure their appearance, but some designs may block convection of warm air currents.

Contemporary radiators
- are designed in a variety of colors and styles
- are based on simple components that can be combined in many heights and widths

Fin-tube radiators (fin-tube convectors):
- These radiators are typically used along outside walls and below windows.
- They raise the temperatures of glass and wall surfaces.
- A fin-tube radiator located along an interior wall would reinforce the cold air circulation pattern in the room; occupants would be too cold on one side and too hot on the other.
- Electric-resistance fin-tube units contain an electrical element instead of copper tubing.

Baseboard fin-tube unit:
- These enclosures usually run the length of a wall, but the element inside may be shorter.
- They tend to be less conspicuous than cabinet-style units.

Convectors:
- Convectors are a form of fin-tube radiator, with an output larger than a baseboard fin-tube convector for a given length of wall.
- They are housed in freestanding wall-hung or recessed cabinets that are 61 cm high × 91 cm wide (2 ft. high × 3 ft. wide). Air must flow freely around these units in order to be heated.

☑ Radiators lose a great deal of heat to adjacent exterior walls. Foil-covered-cardboard radiator reflectors are available at building-supply stores and can be placed between the wall and the radiator. Keeping a radiator clean will maximize heat reflection out into the room.

Radiant Heating

As discussed earlier, thermal comfort depends on more than air temperature. The temperature of surrounding surfaces also comes into play. Warm surfaces can maintain comfort even when the air temperature is low. Radiant heating is a more comfortable way to warm people than introducing heated air into a space.

Radiant heat can be more energy-efficient than hot air systems because it transfers heat directly to objects and occupants without heating large volumes of air first. The warmer surfaces that result mean that more body heat can be lost by convection without altering the room and becoming uncomfortably cold. As a result, the air temperature in the space can be kept cooler, and less heat will be lost through the building envelope.

Radiant-heating systems use ceilings, floors, and sometimes walls as radiant surfaces. The heat source may be pipes or tubing that carry hot water or electrical-resistance heating cables that are embedded within the ceiling, floor, or wall construction. Radiant heat is absorbed by surfaces and objects in the room and reradiates from the warmed surfaces. Radiant panel systems cannot respond quickly to changing temperature demands and are often supplemented with perimeter convection units. Separate ventilation, humidity-control, and cooling systems are required for completely conditioned air.

RADIANT-HEATED FLOORS
Floors can be heated by electrical-resistance wires, warm air circulating through multiple ducts, and warm water circulating

TABLE 11-5. TYPES OF RADIANT-HEATING SYSTEMS

System type	Description	Comments
Hydronic radiant panels	Circulate warm water through metal or plastic pipes, either encased in a concrete slab or secured under subfloor with conductive heat plates; better for floors than ceilings	Rug or carpet over the floor will interfere with heat exchange; special under-carpet pads can help with heat transfer; alternately, higher water temperatures can be used
Electric radiant floors	Can be used to heat whole house or to provide spot comfort in kitchens and baths	Easier and less expensive to install than hydronic panels; less expensive to design for different zones
Electric radiant ceilings	Wiring can be installed in ceiling; snap-together metal components available for easy maintenance	Wires hidden in ceiling can be punctured during renovations
Manufactured gypsum-board heating panels	Electrical heating element in 16-millimeter (⅝-in.) fire-rated gypsum wallboard; installed same way as gypsum wallboard; simple wiring connections	Panels are 122 centimeters (4 ft.) wide and 183 centimeters (6 ft.), 244 centimeters (8 ft.), 305 centimeters (10 ft.), or 366 centimeters (12 ft.) long
Electric towel warmers	Easy to install and fairly flexible as to location; attach to door hinge pins or wall or leave freestanding	Should not be located where they can be reached while person is in bath water
Hydronic towel warmers	Are connected to either home's heating system or to loop of hot water that circulates from home's hot water tank	More complicated to install than electric warmers; can be installed near tub or whirlpool

through coils of pipe to warm concrete or plaster surfaces. Heated floors warm feet by conduction and the convective currents they produce heat the room air evenly. Tables and chairs can block IR waves coming up from a floor, thereby blocking heat to the upper body.

Without adequate insulation, heated floors cannot provide all of the heat in a cold climate unless the floor temperature is increased to one that is too hot for feet. Rugs and carpets reduce the efficiency of heated floors. Heated floors cannot react quickly to small or sudden changes in demand because of the high thermal mass of concrete floors. Repairs are messy and expensive.

Electric radiant floor elements can consist of cables coated with electrical insulation or of fabric mats with the cables woven into them, which are more expensive. Like hydronic tubes, electric elements are embedded in the floor system. Cables are usually embedded in a 38-millimeter (1.5-in.) thick slab of gypsum underlayment or lightweight concrete. As with hydronic tubing, the ability of the framing to support the slab's weight and make adjustments to window and door heights for the slab's extra thickness must be considered.

In general, mats require less floor thickness than cables and can often be placed in a mortar bed beneath floor tiles. This adds as little as 3 millimeters (⅛ in.) to the floor height. Some mats can be rolled out on the subfloor beneath a carpet and pad. Mats are available in a range of standard and custom sizes and shapes. While mats heat up a tile floor faster than buried cables, the thermal mass of the cable system will keep the floor warm for a longer period.

RADIANT-HEATED CEILINGS

Ceiling installations are preferred over floor systems. Ceiling constructions have less thermal capacity than floors and, therefore, respond faster. They can also be heated to higher temperatures.

The system is completely concealed, with the exception of thermostats and balancing valves.

It is acceptable for ceilings to get hotter than walls or floors since they are not usually touched. However, downward convection is poor, and the hot air stays just below the ceiling. When the ceiling is at its warmest, the room may feel uncomfortable. Overall efficiency suffers, and cooler air may stratify at floor level. Tables and desks block heat from above, resulting in cold feet and legs.

Radiant-heating panels can be installed at the edges of a space to provide additional heat with variable air–volume systems. Applications include office building entryways and enclosed walkways. They are useful in hospital nurseries as well as in hydrotherapy, burn, and trauma areas. Residential uses include bathrooms, above full-height windows, and in other cold spots. Factory silicone-sealed panels are available for use in high-moisture areas. Some panels can be silk-screened to provide an architectural blend with acoustical tiles. Custom colors are also available. Radiant-heating panels operate at 66°C to 77°C (150°F–170°F).

Most of the heat from radiant-heating panels flows directly beneath the panels and falls off gradually with greater distance, dropping by about 5°F over the first six feet. This may seem like a disadvantage, but some occupants like to find a spot that is relatively cooler or warmer within the room. Proper placement of panels must be coordinated with ceiling fans, sprinkler heads, and other obstructions, which can pose a problem when installing panels in an existing building.

Radiant-heating panels avoid some of the problems inherent with forced-air systems, such as heat loss from ducts, air leakage, energy use by furnace blowers, and the inability to respond to local zone conditions. Installation costs for energy efficient radiant-heating panels are considerably less than those of a forced-air system, but unlike a forced-air system, radiant-heating panels cannot provide cooling.

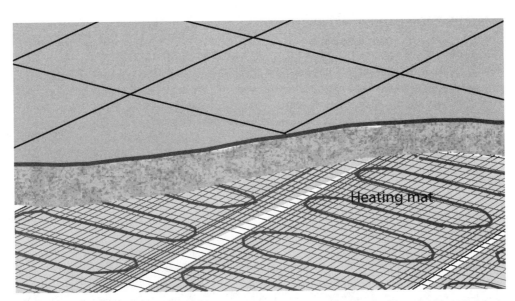

Figure 11-17 Radiant floor heating. In this illustration, a radiant-heating mat with embedded electrical cables is covered by ceramic tiles set in mortar.

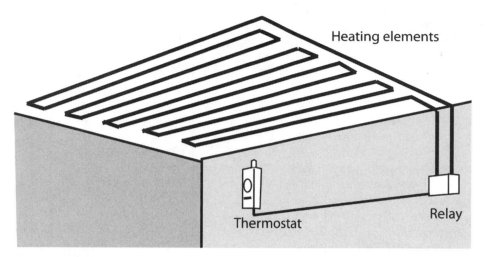

Figure 11-18 Radiant ceiling heat. Radiant-heating electrical cable is installed before the completion of a plaster ceiling.

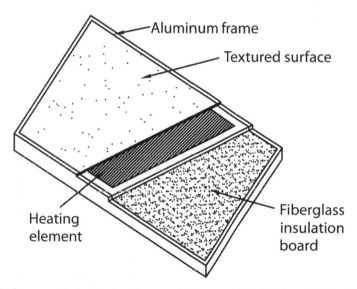

Figure 11-19 Surface-mounted radiant ceiling panel. Preassembled electric radiant-heating panels can be installed in a modular suspended ceiling system or surface-mounted to heat a specific area.

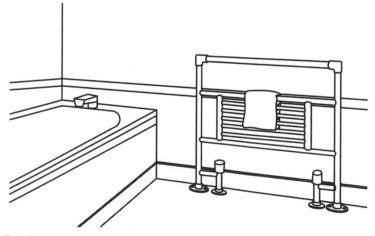

Figure 11-20 Towel warmer. As their name implies, towel warmers are designed to dry and warm towels. They also serve as a heat source in a bathroom or spa. They are available in electronic and hydronic models, in a variety of styles and finishes.

ELECTRICAL-RESISTANCE HEAT

When your feet get cold but you do not want to turn up the heat throughout the building, you might want to use an electrical-resistance space heater. These common, low-cost, and easy-to-install small heaters offer individual thermostatic control and do not waste heat in unoccupied rooms. However, they use expensive electricity as their fuel, so their use should be limited to spot-heating a small area for a limited time in an otherwise cool building.

An electrical-resistance system works like a toaster: wires heat up when it is turned on. Electrical-resistance heating takes advantage of the way electrical energy is converted to heat when it has difficulty passing along a conductor. Most of the time, such a system consists of baseboard units or small, wall-mounted heaters, both of which contain the hot wires. The heaters are inexpensive and clean and do not have to be vented. No space is required for chimneys or fuel storage.

Electrical-heating units designed for residential use combine a radiant-heating element with a fan and a light in a ceiling-mounted unit. Some units include a nightlight as well. Bulb heaters provide silent, instant warmth using 250 watt R-40 IR heat lamps. Bulb heaters are available vented and unvented, and recessed or surface-mounted. Auxiliary heaters are available for mounting in or on walls and in kickspaces below cabinets.

The elements of an electrical-resistance heating system can be housed in baseboard convection units around the perimeter of a room. Resistance coils heat room air as it circulates through the units by convection. Electrical unit heaters use a fan to draw in room air and pass it over resistance-heating coils, then blow it back into the room.

Units are available that can be wall- or ceiling-mounted for bathrooms and other spaces where the floor might be wet but where quick heat for a limited time in an enclosed space is needed. IR heat lamps are also installed in bathroom ceilings for this purpose.

Unit heaters take advantage of natural convection as well as a fan to blow forced air across their heating element and into the room. For direct combustion, fuel is piped directly to the unit; a flue vents the unit to the outdoors for the removal of combustion products. Through-wall models vent flue gases and introduce fresh outdoor air. Unit heaters are made of factory-assembled components, including a fan and a heating mechanism in a casing. The casing has an air inlet and vanes for directing the air out. Units are usually suspended from the roof structure or floor-mounted and are located at the building's perimeter. Mounting the unit overhead saves floor space.

Warm Air Heating

Around 1900, warm air heating systems began to take the place of fireplaces. The original warm air systems used an iron furnace in the basement, which was hand-fired with coal. A short duct from the top of the sheet metal enclosing the furnace delivered warm air to a large grille in the middle of the parlor floor, with little heat going to other rooms.

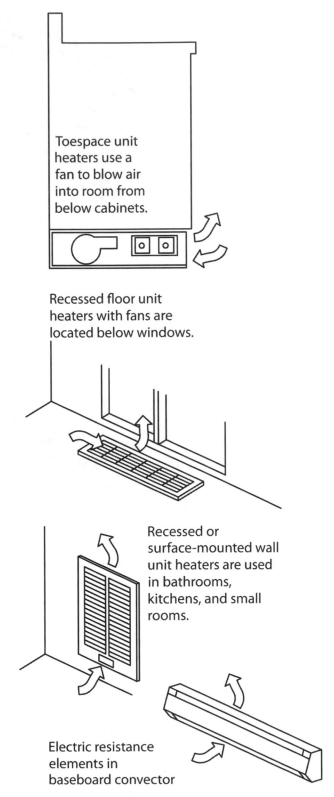

Toespace unit heaters use a fan to blow air into room from below cabinets.

Recessed floor unit heaters with fans are located below windows.

Recessed or surface-mounted wall unit heaters are used in bathrooms, kitchens, and small rooms.

Electric resistance elements in baseboard convector

Figure 11-21 Electrical resistance heating units. Electrical resistance heating units are compact and versatile, but they lack humidity and air-quality controls. Electrical resistance heaters use high-grade electrical energy for the low-grade task of heating. These heaters have hot surfaces, and their location must be carefully chosen in relation to furniture, drapery, and traffic patterns.

TABLE 11-6. TYPES OF SPACE HEATERS

General Type	Use
Toe space unit heater	Installed in low space under kitchen and bathroom cabinets
Wall unit heaters	Surface-mounted or recessed for use in bathrooms, kitchens
Fully recessed floor unit heaters	Typically used where glazing reaches floor, as at glass sliding door or large window
Small IR unit heaters	Radiate heat instantly from small area; beam where needed
High-temperature heaters (electrical, gas-fired, oil-fired)	May require venting. Temperatures greater than 260°C (500°F); radiant heat produced feels pleasant on bare skin in swimming pools, shower rooms, bathrooms
Industrial unit heaters	Metal cabinets with directional outlets suspended from ceiling or roof structure; used in large industrial buildings; outdoors, loading docks, grandstands, public waiting areas, garages, hangars; will melt snow over limited areas
Quartz heaters	Resistance-heating elements sealed in quartz-glass tubes that produce IR radiation in front of reflective background; heat within 15 feet; quiet
Electrical forced-air heaters	Blow warm air and circulate it throughout room; best used in room that can be closed off
Ceramic forced-air heaters	Ceramic heating element is safer than other electric space heaters
Oil-filled heaters	Electricity heats oil inside to heat room or temporarily replace main heat source
Portable electrical-resistance heaters	Heat small nearby area; may lead to fires from bedding, drapery, furniture when used for space heating

Over time, oil or gas furnaces that fired automatically replaced coal furnaces, and operational and safety controls were added. Air was ducted to and from each room, which evened out temperatures and airflow. Fans were added to move the air, making it possible to reduce the size of ducts. Adjustable registers permitted control within each room. Filters at the furnace cleaned air as it was circulated. Eventually, by adding both fans and cooling coils to the furnace, both hot and cold air could be circulated.

During the 1960s, fewer homes were built with basements, and sub-slab perimeter systems replaced basement furnaces. The heat source was located in the center of a home's interior, where any escaping heat would help heat the house. Air was delivered from below, above, and across windows and back to a central, high return grille in each room. The air frequently failed to return to the lower levels of the room, leaving occupants with cold feet. In addition, water below the house could penetrate the heating system, causing serious problems with condensation and mold.

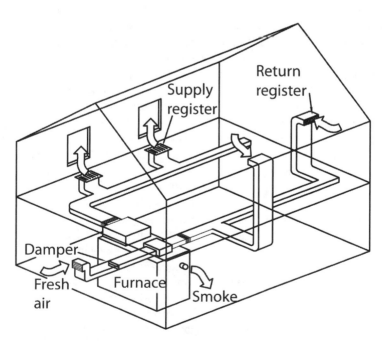

Figure 11-22 Warm air furnace and ducts. Technological improvements, such as forced-draft chimneys and heat exchangers, have greatly improved the efficiency of warm air furnaces.

Electrical heating systems became popular because they eliminated combustion, chimneys, and fuel storage. Horizontal electric furnaces were located in shallow attics or above ceilings that were furred out to provide access space. Air was delivered down from the ceiling across windows, then taken back through door grilles and open plenum spaces. For the most part, heat pumps have replaced less efficient electrical-resistance systems.

Today, air is heated in a gas, oil, or electric furnace and distributed by fans through ductwork to registers or diffusers in inhabited spaces. Forced-air heating is the most versatile and widely used system for heating houses and small buildings. The system can include filtering, humidifying, and dehumidifying devices. Cooling can be added with an outdoor compressor and condensing unit that supplies refrigerant to evaporator coils in the main supply ductwork. In most cases, fresh air is supplied by natural ventilation. Warm air distribution systems offer good control of comfort through air-temperature and air-volume control. The moving stream of air stirs and redistributes the air in the room. Warm air systems work especially well in tall spaces where air stratifies with warm air at the top and cold air at the bottom.

In general, well-designed warm air heating systems are considered to be comfortable. The air motion in a warm air heating system can create uniform conditions and reasonably equal temperatures in all parts of a building. A forced-air system usually burns gas or oil inside a closed heat exchanger located inside a furnace. A large blower also located inside the furnace compartment forces cool air across the hot outer surface of the heat exchanger to heat the air. Fans move the heated air through a system of supply ducts located inside the walls and between floors and ceilings. **Supply registers** are equipped with dampers within the ducts that balance and adjust the system by controlling airflow. The dampers' vanes disperse the air to control its direction and reduce its velocity.

A separate system of **exhaust ducts** draws cool air back through **return-air grilles** to be reheated and recirculated. Return-air grilles are located near the floor, on walls, or on the ceiling. Sometimes, they can be relocated during design or renovation projects to avoid conflict with another piece of equipment. In some cases, there is no separate ductwork for the return air. Return grilles are then placed in the suspended ceiling to collect return air. The mechanical system draws return air back to a central collection point, where it is then returned through ducts to the building's heating plant. This use of the space between the suspended ceiling and structural floor above as one huge return duct is referred to as a **plenum return**.

Filters and special air-cleaning equipment can clean both recirculated and outdoor air. The system circulates fresh air to reduce odors and to make up for air exhausted by kitchen, laundry, and bathroom fans; it can add humidity as needed. A wide variety of residential systems is available, depending on the size of the house. The heating system must be large enough to maintain the desired temperature in all habitable rooms.

Energy-saving designs for warm air systems start with insulated windows, roof, walls, and floors, reducing the amount of heat needed. Warming the windows directly is less essential when they are well insulated, so a central furnace or heat pump connects to short ducts to the inner side of each room. Air is returned to the central unit through open grilles in doors and the furnace or to a heat-pump enclosure.

Warm air systems can be noisy. A quiet motor with cushioned mountings should be selected for the blower (fan), and it should not be located too close to the return grille in order to avoid noise. The blower housing should also be isolated from conduits or water piping, with flexible connections attaching equipment to ductwork. Ducts can be lined with sound-absorbing materials, but care must be taken to avoid creating an environment for mold and mildew growth. Warm air distribution systems can circulate dust and contaminants as well as air through a building.

All mechanical systems require regular maintenance for efficient operation and proper indoor air quality (IAQ). The air filters of heating, ventilating, and air-conditioning (HVAC) equipment must be cleaned and replaced at regular intervals. Burners should be occasionally cleaned and adjusted for maximum efficiency of combustion. Motors, fans, pumps, and compressors should have their rubber belts checked and replaced as necessary. Ductwork may need to be vacuum cleaned.

FURNACES

Systems using air as the primary distribution fluid have a furnace as a heat-generating source, rather than the boiler used for water or steam. Warm air furnaces are often located near the center of a building.

The furnace is selected after the engineer determines the type of system and fuel source. Cool air returns from occupied spaces at around 16°C to 21°C (60°F–70°F) and passes through a filter, a fan or blower, and a heating chamber. When the air goes to the supply-air ductwork, it is between 49°C and 60°C (120°F–140°F). The bonnet or plenum is a chamber at the top of the furnace from which the ducts emerge to conduct heated or conditioned air to inhabited spaces. The furnace may include a humidification system that evaporates moisture into the air as it passes through.

Airborne dust is a common source of problems in a forced-air heating system. As air is pulled through the furnace, dust readily adheres to oily or greasy components. Because household dust usually contains atomized cooking grease, even nonoily parts acquire a coat of fuzz. This inhibits the cooling of the components, and when motors and bearings run hot, their lives are shortened. Dust can also clog furnace filters, restricting the flow of air. This places stress on the blower motor, which, in turn, reduces its efficiency and makes it run hotter. To avoid these problems, clients should be reminded to vacuum the registers in each room at least once a month. Air-return grilles should be removed and the return duct cleaned as far as the vacuum cleaner will reach. The furnace filter and blower also should be serviced regularly.

In residential design, the furnace burner is started and stopped by a thermostat, usually in or near the living room, in a location where the temperature is unlikely to change rapidly that is protected from drafts, direct sun, and the warmth of nearby warm-air registers. When the thermostat indicates that heat is

TABLE 11-7. TYPES OF FURNACES

Furnace Type	Description	Comments
Forced-air gas furnace	Thermostat controls valve that feeds gas to burner tubes, where it is lighted by electric spark or pilot light flame; air warmed in heat exchanger above burners is circulated by furnace blower	Exchanger should be checked for CO safety every few years; room must be left around access panels for maintenance
Oil-fired forced-air furnace	Very efficient and durable; more complicated than gas-fired furnace; oil pumped from storage tank into combustion chamber is atomized and ignited by spark; flame heating heat exchanger warms air circulated by blower	Safety switch opens if burner fails to ignite; photoelectric cell detects when chamber goes dark and shuts down system; reset switches should never be pushed more than twice because excess fuel pumped into combustion chamber could explode
Electric forced-air furnace	No combustion occurs, so there is no flue through which heat can escape; very high efficiency	Clean, simple; poses fewer problems than combustion furnaces; can be expensive to operate

needed, the burner and blower start up. The blower continues to run after the burner stops, until the temperature in the furnace drops below a set point. A high-limit switch shuts off the burner if the temperature is too high.

Conventional combustion techniques in furnaces are typically only around 80 percent efficient. Newer pulse-combustion and condensing combustion processes designed to be up to 95 percent efficient recover much of the heat that goes up the flue stack with other equipment. Pulse-combustion furnaces have simple connections, requiring only a small vent and outside air pipes, and a condensation drain pipe. To receive Energy Star® certification, a furnace must have an annual fuel usage efficiency of 90 percent. Furnaces can be expected to function for 15 to 20 years.

Gas and oil furnaces require combustion air and ventilation for exhausting combustion products to the outside. Gases rise up the flue from the furnace as a result of the chimney's heat and the temperature difference between the flue gases and the outside air. When either is increased, the force of the draft is increased. Flues extend past the top of the highest point of the building, so combustion products are not drawn back into the building. Where the chimney is not high enough, a fan can help create the needed draft.

Energy can be recovered from exhausted air with a **regenerative wheel**, which is a rotating device of metal mesh that uses its large thermal capacity to transfer heat from one duct to another. Air-to-air heat exchangers with very large surfaces also save energy.

FORCED-AIR HEATING DISTRIBUTION

Perimeter heating is the term for the distribution pattern of warm air to registers placed in or near the floor along exterior walls. A perimeter loop system consists of a loop of ductwork, usually embedded in a concrete ground slab, for distribution of warm air to each floor register. A perimeter radial system uses a leader from a centrally located furnace to carry warm air directly to each floor register.

Ducts are either round or rectangular and are made of metal or glass fiber. Flexible ducting is used to connect supply-air registers to the main ductwork to allow adjustments in the location of ceiling fixtures, but it is not permitted in exposed ceilings. Duct

TABLE 11-8. MINIMUM EFFICIENCY RATING SYSTEMS FOR HEATING AND COOLING EQUIPMENT

Rating	Definition	Use
Annual fuel utilization efficiency (AFUE)	Ratio of annual fuel-output energy to annual fuel-input energy	Heating and cooling equipment
Coefficient of performance (COP)	For cooling: ratio of rate of heat removal to rate of energy inputs in consistent units	For a complete cooling system or factory-assembled equipment
	For heating: ratio of rate of heat delivered to rate of energy inputs in consistent units	For a complete heat-pump system
Energy efficiency ratio (EER)	Ratio of net equipment cooling capacity in BTU/h to total rate of electrical input in watts	When consistent units are used, this ratio is same as COP
Integrated part load value (IPLV)	Single-number figure of merit	Part-load efficiency for air-conditioning and heat-pump equipment
Seasonal energy efficiency ratio (SEER)	BTU/h, divided by total electrical energy input during same period in watt-hours	Total cooling output for an air conditioner during normal annual usage period for cooling

sizes are selected to control air velocity. The dimensions for ducts on construction drawings are typically the inside dimensions; an extra 51 millimeters (2 in.) can be added to each dimension from the duct wall and insulation. Ductwork can be bulky and difficult to house compared with piping. With early coordination, ducts can be located within joist spaces and roof trusses as well as between bulky recessed lighting fixtures.

Vertical duct shafts take up about 1 to 2 square meters for every 1000 square meters of floor area served. In addition, fan rooms use up 2 to 4 percent of the total floor area served. This figure increases to between 6 and 8 percent for hospitals. Fan rooms are located to serve specific zones or levels. A single air-handling unit can serve between 8 and 20 floors. The smaller the number of floors, the smaller the vertical ducts can be.

Ductwork can be concealed or exposed. Concealed ductwork permits more effective isolation from the noise and vibration of equipment and from the flow of air. Surfaces are less complicated to clean and less visible. Construction can be less meticulous, and construction costs are lower. It costs more to install visually acceptable exposed ductwork than to construct a ceiling to hide standard ducts. Concealed ductwork also provides better architectural control over the appearance of the ceiling and wall surfaces. Access panels and doors or suspended ceilings must provide access for maintenance.

Rectangular medium- and high-velocity ducts can transmit excessive noise if not properly supported, stiffened, and lined with sound-absorbing material. Rigid, round ducts are stronger and have better aerodynamic characteristics than their rectangular counterparts, so they have fewer noise problems. High-velocity ducts can route air through a terminal box called a sound trap or sound attenuator, which is lined with an acoustic absorber, to diminish noise. Air can also be slowed down as it enters a room, reducing the noise of friction through the ducts.

Ducts should be insulated, and all joints and seams should be sealed for energy efficiency. All of the hot air ducts that pass through unheated spaces should be wrapped with insulation. Foil-faced, vinyl-faced, and rigid foam insulation can be used. Duct insulation should have a minimum rating of R-5 for cold climates; an R-8 rating is optimal. All joints and seams in the insulation should be sealed with duct tape.

Because ducts conduct noise from one space to another, they are sometimes lined with sound-absorbing material. During the 1970s, cheaply made materials prone to deterioration were used to reduce noise in high-velocity locations. Damaged or improperly stored material has also been installed in ducts. In such situations, delamination of fiberglass in the duct linings resulted in glass particles in the air. Duct linings are still in use, but better-quality materials are installed with more care. Even good-quality duct linings should not be used downstream from moisture, which can encourage the growth of mold and bacteria. In difficult acoustic situations, double-walled ducts with lining enclosed between the walls should be used.

Large commercial structures have fire-rated partitions, floors, and ceilings that confine fires for specified periods of time. Fire-safety codes require that air ducts through a fire barrier have **fire dampers** made of fire-resistant materials. A fire damper is normally held open by a catch, but a fusible link that melts releases the catch and automatically closes the fire damper in a fire. This prevents the spread of fire and smoke through the system. Access doors are usually installed at fire dampers for inspection and servicing.

Air for heating, cooling, and ventilation is supplied through registers and diffusers. The selection and placement of supply and return openings require architectural and engineering coordination and have a distinct effect on the interior design of a space. They are selected for airflow capacity and velocity, pressure drop, noise factor, and appearance.

Supply registers, diffusers, and **return grilles** include the following:

- **Grilles:** rectangular openings with fixed vertical or horizontal vanes or louvers through which air passes
- **Register:** grille with fire damper directly behind louvered face to regulate volume of airflow
- **Diffusers:** have slats set at angles for deflecting warm or conditioned air from outlet in various directions
- **Perforated metal faceplates:** placed over standard ceiling diffusers to create uniform perforated ceiling
- **Air-supply units:** designed to distribute air perpendicular to the surface.
- **Return grilles:** louvered, egg-crate, or perforated designs connected to duct; lead to undivided plenum above ceiling or transfer air directly from one area to another; may be called either grilles or registers

TABLE 11-9. BUILDING SYSTEMS EQUIPMENT CONCEALMENT AND ENCLOSURE

Criteria	Concealed	Exposed
Acoustic	Less noise from moving water and air	Possible acoustic interest
Maintenance	Fewer surfaces requiring cleaning	Maintenance access more difficult; access panels available
Construction quality	Less care needed for unseen work	Quality of visible elements more important
Appearance	More control	Honest and direct visual interest
Flexibility	Care needed in cutting holes in surfaces	Changes easily made
Partition height	Suspended ceilings create uniform height	Construction of partitions of varying heights

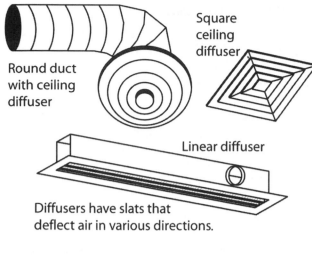

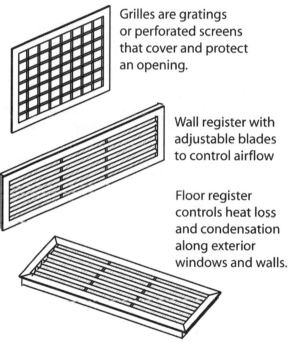

Figure 11-23 Registers, diffusers, and grilles.

Square ceiling diffuser

Round duct with ceiling diffuser

Linear diffuser

Diffusers have slats that deflect air in various directions.

Grilles are gratings or perforated screens that cover and protect an opening.

Wall register with adjustable blades to control airflow

Floor register controls heat loss and condensation along exterior windows and walls.

- **Return-air inlets:** usually located near floor and across space from supply outlets for heating systems; usually located in ceilings or high on walls to avoid removing cooled air that has just been supplied to room for cooling systems
- **Exhaust-air inlets:** usually located in ceilings or high on walls; are almost always ducted; supply outlets can also be used as return grilles

COOLING SYSTEMS

The invention of air conditioning has made sweltering summers more bearable. Sunbelt cities, such as Atlanta, Miami, and Houston, have grown larger thanks in part to air conditioning, which has made it easier for people to live and work there year-round by reducing the heat and humidity indoors. Mechanical cooling systems were originally developed as separate equipment to be used in conjunction with mechanical heating equipment. Today, cooling equipment is often integrated into HVAC systems, which will be discussed later.

The earliest known home air-cooling systems were in Egypt around 3000 BCE. Egyptian women put water in shallow clay trays on a bed of straw at sundown. The rapid evaporation from the water's surface and the damp sides of the tray combined with the drop in temperature at night to produce a thin film of ice on top, even though the air temperature was not below freezing. The low humidity aided evaporation, and the resulting cooling brought the temperature down enough to make ice.

Around 2000 BCE, a wealthy Babylonian merchant developed a home air-conditioning system. At sundown, servants sprayed water on the walls and floor of a room. Evaporation and nocturnal cooling brought relief from the heat.

Evaporative cooling was also used in ancient India. At night, wet grass mats were hung over openings on the westward side of a home. Water sprayed by hand or trickling from a perforated trough above the windows kept the mats wet through the night. When a gentle, warm wind struck the cooler wet grass, evaporation cooled temperatures inside the home as much as 30 degrees.

By the end of the nineteenth century, large restaurants and other public places embedded air pipes in a mixture of ice and salt and circulated the cooled air with fans. The Madison Square Garden Theater in New York City used four tons of ice per night. However, none of these systems addressed how to remove humidity from warm air.

The term "air conditioning" is credited to physicist Stuart W. Cramer, who presented a paper on humidity control in textile mills before the American Cotton Manufacturers Association in 1907. Willis Carrier, an upstate New York farm boy who won an engineering scholarship to Cornell University, produced the first commercial air conditioner in 1914. Carrier was fascinated with heating and ventilating systems. One year after his graduation from Cornell in 1902, he got his first air-cooling job for a Brooklyn lithographer and printer. Temperature and humidity fluctuations made paper expand and shrink. Ink flowed too freely or dried up, and colors varied. Carrier modified a conventional steam heater to accept cold water and fan-circulated cooled air. He calculated and balanced the air temperature and airflow and succeeded in cooling the air and removing the humidity. Today, Carrier is known as the father of modern air conditioning.

By 1919, Chicago had its first air-conditioned movie house. The same year, the Abraham & Strauss department store in New York City was air conditioned. In 1925, a 133-ton air-conditioning unit was installed in New York City's Rivoli Theater. By the summer of 1930, more than 300 theaters were air-conditioned, drawing in hordes of people for the cool air as well as the movie. By the end of the 1930s, stores and office buildings claimed that air conditioning increased workers' productivity enough to offset the cost. Workers were even coming early and staying late to stay cool.

Today, cooling accounts for 20 percent of the energy use in the United States, and 40 percent in the southern states alone. One-third of the U.S. population spends substantial amounts of time in air-conditioned environments. Two-thirds of U.S. homes have air conditioners. Residential air conditioning uses almost 5 percent of all energy in the United States—more than 10 billion dollars worth—and adds about 100 million tons of CO_2 to the atmosphere from the electrical-power generation stations that use fossil fuels.

Air Conditioning Energy Use

The combination of air conditioning with electric lights has had a profound effect on the design of buildings. With fewer windows needed for ventilation and daylighting, interior spaces became windowless. Less need for daylight penetration also lowered ceilings, encouraged less exterior wall area, and permitted less exterior land space for the building itself.

Although the term "air conditioning" is often associated only with cooling, it actually has a broader meaning. Air conditioning is the treatment of air so that its temperature, humidity, cleanliness, quality, and motion are maintained as appropriate for a building's occupants, a particular process, or some object in the space.

Engineers use some common terms when discussing air conditioning:

- **Cooling load:** rate at which heat needs to be removed from air
- **Capacity:** ability of equipment to remove heat
- **Heat gain:** total load on cooling system; almost identical to its cooling load, although from the engineer's viewpoint there is a technical difference

Design Strategies for Cooling

To make an air conditioner effective, people must close themselves up tightly in their building to keep the cooled air from escaping. When the summertime heat is shut out, people shut themselves in. Most people miss the fresh air, the smells and sounds of the yard, and the pleasure of relaxing on a shaded deck or porch. The natural cooling features of the building can decrease reliance on air conditioning during hot weather. When ventilation and air movement inside are improved and shade outside is provided, energy can be conserved, utility costs can be lowered, and people can enjoy summer more without being held hostage by the heat.

NATURAL-VENTILATION COOLING
Several design techniques that can reduce cooling loads and increase comfort have been discussed. Shading with horizontal overhangs on southern exposures is another such technique: it keeps out the sun's heat. Shaded areas on the building's face can also serve as balconies, porches, verandas, and cantilevered upper floors. Covered awnings, screens, landscaping plants, and other shading devices keep the sun's heat outside.

☑ **Cooling issues often have a relationship to building form and daylighting decisions. The number and location of openings that allow a breeze to enter the building and the need to close them sometimes to retain cool air affect its appearance and the amount of daylight admitted. East and west windows may be minimized to keep direct sun out of the building. The amount of exposure to daylight needed in the winter may be enough to cause overheating in the summer.**

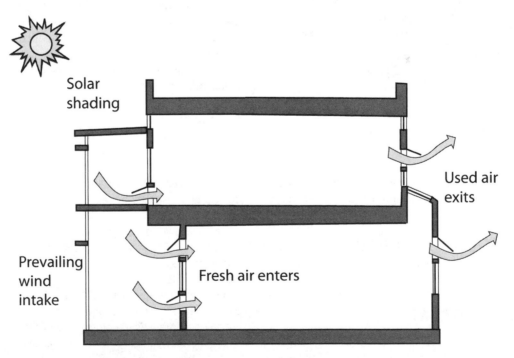

Figure 11-24 Natural ventilation. Natural ventilation relies on convection to move warm air up and cooler air down. Breezes also move air through a space, cooling it by evaporation. Varied ceiling heights and operable windows help with air movement.

Natural ventilation offsets higher air temperatures by increased air motion. This is especially effective in humid, hot climates with little change between day and night temperatures. Building designs for natural ventilation are very open to breezes but closed to direct sun. Such buildings are often thermally lightweight because night air is not cool enough in some locations to remove stored daytime heat. A good design for cooling brings in outdoor air when the exterior temperature is 25°C (77°F) or lower and closes the building up tight on hot days while opening it up at night. When designing for cooling, interior designers must balance the need to keep hot air out and the need for fresh air and comfortable breezes.

Cross ventilation is driven by wind through windows. Buildings with narrow floor plans with large ventilation openings on both sides favor cross ventilation. This type of layout also works well for daylighting. **Stack ventilation** uses very low openings to admit outside air, and very high openings to exhaust rising hot air. In general, stack ventilation is weaker than cross ventilation.

HIGH THERMAL MASS COOLING

The structure of a building may be able to absorb heat by day and be flushed by cool air at night. High thermal mass cooling works well in places with warm, dry summers. The thermal mass of the building stays cool during the hot daytime, and the heat drains away slowly during the cool night. Such buildings use thermal mass on the floors, walls, or roofs. Fans are often used with high thermal-mass systems. Large, high buildings with concrete structures are good candidates for high thermal mass cooling.

In a high thermal mass design, the building needs a heat sink, a place from which heat is ejected at night. The roof can radiate heat to a cold night sky, but it needs protection from exposure to the sun by day.

OTHER COOLING TECHNIQUES

When mechanical cooling is required, sometimes it can run at night when electrical power is least expensive. Incoming air can be precooled to reduce the equipment's cooling load. For buildings with relatively short but intense peak load periods, the space, its contents, and the surrounding mass can be precooled to a desired temperature before occupancy. This increases the amount of heat that the building can absorb when the daily heat gain is at its peak. Precooling minimizes the amount of heat released to the room air during the peak period. Precooling works where the building has high thermal storage capacity or where the cooling system is more efficient during cooler night periods. The occupancy patterns of churches and theaters offer opportunities to use precooling.

Fans

Fans can effectively cool small buildings. A person perceives a decrease of 1°C for every 2.5 meters per minute (1°F per 15 feet per minute [fpm]) increase in the speed of air past the body. The air motion produced varies with the fan's height above the floor, the number of fans in the space, and the fan's power, speed, and blade size.

According to the American Society of Heating, Refrigerating, and Air-Conditioning Engineers (ASHRAE), the acceptable temperature range for people wearing light summer clothes is 22°C to 26°C (72°F–78°F) at between 35 percent and 60 percent relative humidity (RH). A slow-turning, ceiling-mounted paddle fan can extend this comfort range to about 28°C (82°F).

Ceiling fans:
- Ceiling fans are part of the Energy Star® program for energy efficiency.
- Ceiling fans with aerodynamically curved fan blades are more efficient and can be run at lower speeds than other ceiling fans, thereby saving energy.
- Ceiling fans with fluorescent lamps with electronic ballasts are more energy efficient and produce less heat than incandescent lamps.
- Remote controls and temperature sensors encourage using a ceiling fan only when it will improve conditions in a room.
- When run at a low speed in the winter, ceiling fans bring warm air that has stratified at the ceiling back down to body level.

Two out of three U.S. homes have ceiling fans, most of which have inefficient blade shapes and motors. Residential ceiling fans often include incandescent lights, which increase the heat in a room. In addition, the heat from the motor adds to the room's heat, and the fan cools people only when it moves air past them.

Attic fans:
- Attic fans decrease air-conditioning costs by reducing the temperature in the attic.
- These fans protect attic spaces from condensation damage in the winter.
- They are activated by heat and moisture.
- Roof-mounted fans are available with energy-efficient, quiet motors.
- Gable fans with louvers can be automatically controlled to vent the attic.

Window fans:
- Window fans should be located on the downwind side of a house, facing outward.
- These fans are most effective when a window is opened in each room in a building and interior doors are left open.
- They do not work well in long, narrow hallways or in buildings with many small rooms and interior partitions.

TABLE 11-10. CEILING-FAN SIZES

Room Size	Fan Size
100 square feet (9 sq m)	36 inches (91 cm)
150 square feet (3.9 sq m)	42 inches (107 cm)
225 square feet (21 sq m)	48 inches (122 cm)
375 square feet (35 sq m)	52 inches (132 cm)
More than 400 square feet (37 sq m)	Two fans

Whole-house fan:

- Whole-house fans exhaust heat from a central area through a ventilated attic.
- They are mounted in the hallway ceiling on the top floor of the building.
- They blow air into the attic.
- They are covered on the bottom with a louvered vent.
- They draw air in through open windows and doors and blow it out through the attic.
- They maintain a steady, cooling breeze throughout the house.
- They cost about the same amount as three or four window fans to buy and less than air conditioning to run.

Mechanical Air Conditioning

When all else fails and the outdoor temperature climbs, people must choose to endure the heat or turn on the air conditioning. In order to understand the discussions that take place between the client, the architect, the engineers, and the contractors, an interior designer should have a basic understanding of air conditioning.

AIR-CONDITIONER OPERATION

An air conditioner works in the following way: A fan sucks warm indoor air across a series of coils that contain refrigerants and blows it back into the room. The refrigerant absorbs heat in the evaporator, then exhausts it outside through another system of fans and coils in the condenser. When the indoor air cools, it also dehumidifies. The moisture taken out of the air condenses on the cool coils just like water collects on a glass of iced lemonade on a hot day. The water runs down a drain or drips off the air conditioner outside. Dehumidified air contributes to the cooling effect people feel.

Air conditioning cools by removing sensible heat—the heat transferred by the motion of molecules—from the air. As discussed earlier, the transfer of sensible heat requires a temperature difference between a warm area and a cooler one. A surface, such as a coil or a cooling panel, is placed in contact with the air and kept at a temperature below that of the air by continuous extraction of heat. If the temperature of this surface is below the dew-point temperature of the air, condensation will form on it. The air, in losing moisture because of the condensation, also loses latent heat—the heat transfer that takes place because of a change in the structure of the molecules. Consequently, it is both cooled and dehumidified. The condensation must be drained away from the air conditioning equipment, so the equipment needs a drain.

A well-designed air conditioning system must eliminate both the heat and the humidity unintentionally leaking into a building or generated within it as well as the heat and humidity introduced with air for ventilation. Engineers try to design air conditioning systems that are large enough to ensure adequate comfort but not so large that they cycle on and off too frequently, which would wear out the equipment faster. With some equipment, excessive cycling on and off results in decreased efficiency and more energy use. There are two basic types of air conditioning cycles: compression refrigeration and absorption refrigeration.

The **compression refrigeration cycles** in small buildings transfer heat from one circulating water system (chilled water) to another (condenser water). This system is referred to as a water-to-water system. Cooling takes place by changing a refrigerant from a liquid to a vapor. Heat can be extracted from water or from air.

A **refrigerant** is a gas at normal temperatures and pressures, so it can vaporize at low temperatures. Until the mid-1990s, the most common refrigerants in the United States could allow chlo-

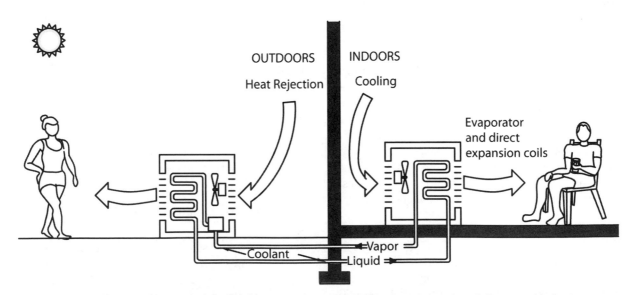

Figure 11-25 Cooling compression cycle. The compression refrigeration process essentially pumps heat out of a chilled water system and into a condenser water system, continually repeating the cycle. Water or air cooled by the expansion (evaporator) coils is distributed throughout the building, absorbing heat from occupants, machinery, lighting, and building surfaces, and then is returned for another chilling cycle.

rofluorocarbon (CFC) gases to escape from the equipment, contributing to ozone depletion and global warming. In addition, the large amount of electrical energy used to power cooling equipment adds CO_2 to the atmosphere. Today's more efficient equipment and new refrigerants are producing energy savings, and progress is being made in the reduction of escaped refrigerant and development of non-CFC refrigerants.

The **absorption refrigeration cycle** uses a salt solution to cool spaces. Absorption cycles are about half as efficient as compression cycles. Energy for the absorption system can come from the sun or from high-temperature waste heat from steam or hot water. Even though an absorption cycle is less efficient than a compression cycle, it may use less energy since it can use lower-grade heat to run a generator (as opposed to the electricity that a compression cycle uses for its compressor).

Air-Conditioning Equipment

As mentioned earlier, an air conditioner employs a condenser, which is a heat exchanger used in a refrigeration cycle to discharge heat to the outside environment. Air-cooled condensers, which are less expensive and do not require as much maintenance as water-cooled units, are common on small refrigeration systems. Medium-sized systems may use water or air. Large condensers are water cooled for higher efficiency, but they have higher installation and maintenance costs. Condenser water is usually recirculated through a cooling tower, where the heat is given off to the atmosphere. Evaporative condensers are a cross between a cooling tower and an air-cooled condenser. They use less energy than a water-cooled condenser with a cooling tower and are more efficient.

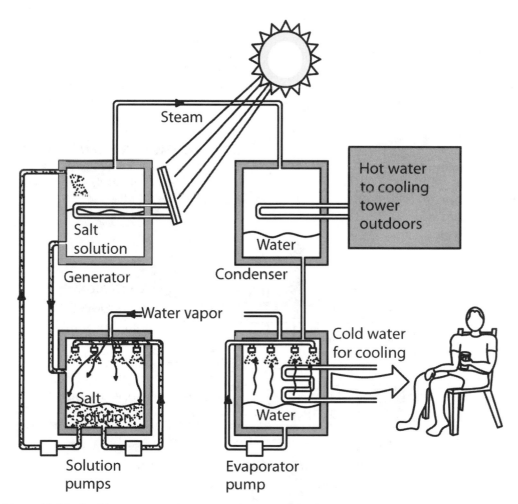

Figure 11-26 Cooling absorption cycle. In the cooling absorption cycle, water vapor is attracted to a concentrated salt solution, which absorbs water from the evaporator vessel. The water cools rapidly as it is evaporated. Then the water dilutes the salt solution in the evaporator. The diluted salt solution is drawn off from the vessel continually, sprayed into a piece of equipment called a generator that boils off excess water, and returned to repeat the absorption cycle. The steam that boils off condenses at a condenser with cool water or air, then returns to the evaporator vessel. The cooled water left in the evaporator can be tapped through a heat exchanger as a source of chilled water.

Packaged terminal air conditioners (PTACs):
- PTACs are factory-assembled units with a compressor, condenser, expansion valve, and evaporator.
- They include window air conditioners, through-wall room units, and heat pumps.
- Most through-wall units are located near the floor and look like a wall-mounted FCU below the window.
- They are simple to install and permit occupants to control cooling within a space.
- They provide individual metering for separate tenants.
- Their removal for repair or replacement is easy, and the failure of a unit affects only one room.
- No ductwork, central chiller, cooling tower, pumps, or piping is needed, which saves space and money.
- PTACs can be added to a building as needed and located in the space to be served.

Unit air conditioners:
- These are small, electrically powered PTACs mounted in windows or exterior walls.
- They are the most common piece of mechanical equipment in the United States.
- They are easy to select, install, and service or replace.
- They offer the option of separate zones for individual apartments or motel rooms.
- When turned on only as needed, they may offer energy savings.

Central residential air conditioners:
- These cool an entire house.
- They require a large compressor unit outside.

In many homes, a room air conditioning unit is installed in a window or wall, with the compressor located outside. The efficiency of air conditioning equipment is listed on an EnergyGuide label. Room air conditioners measure energy efficiency via the energy-efficiency ratio (EER), which divides the cooling output in British thermal units (BTUs) by the power consumption. As of October 2006 in the United States, new room air conditioners have to have an average EER rating of around 10, and even stricter regulations are under consideration by the federal government.

☑ **Window air-conditioning units are also best kept out of direct sun, so east or west windows should be avoided. The north and south walls of the house are possibilities.**

Some home air conditioners save energy with a fan-only switch that allows owners to use cool, nonconditioned outside air at night. A filter checklight reminder for maintenance and an automatic-delay fan switch that turns off the fan a few minutes after the compressor shuts off also improve energy efficiency. Quiet operation, which is not usually rated, is a valuable feature, but the air conditioner must be on to experience this. Highly energy-efficient units may not dehumidify as well as less efficient units. Air conditioners must be kept clean, and refrigerant must be recharged as needed to maintain efficiency.

AIR CONDITIONER ENERGY RATINGS
Central air conditioners are rated via the seasonal energy efficiency ratio (SEER), which takes the seasonal cooling output in BTUs and divides it by the seasonal energy input in watt-hours

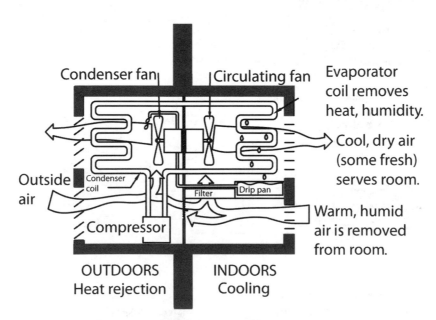

Figure 11-27 Unit air conditioner. Unit air conditioners are not as efficient as larger central units. Unit air conditioners are noisy and because of high air velocity can cause drafts. Sometimes the noise is welcome since it can mask street noise. In moderate climates, air can be circulated either through cold-side or hot-side coils, using the unit as a heat pump to cool in hot weather and to heat in cool weather. This use does not work economically in very cold weather when there is not enough heat outdoors.

for an average U.S. climate. Many older-home central air conditioners have SEERs between 6 and 7. In 1988, the average SEER for central air conditioners was around 9, but the minimum requirement has been raised to 10. To earn an Energy Star® certification, an air conditioner must achieve a SEER of 12 or higher.

☑ **Building codes regulate the permissible amount of energy use for residential heating and cooling systems. ASHRAE Standard 90.2-2007,** *Energy Efficient Design of New Low-Rise Residential Buildings* **and ANSI/ASHRAE/IESNA 90.1-2007** *Energy Standard for Buildings except Low-Rise Residential Buildings* **set minimum efficiency ratings for heating and cooling equipment.**

In addition to the EER and SEER, several other ratings apply, depending on the size and type of equipment. The annual fuel utilization efficiency (AFUE) rating is a ratio of the annual fuel output energy to annual input energy. The coefficient of performance (COP) assesses the rate of heat removal for cooling equipment and the efficiency of heat pump systems for heating. The integrated part load value (IPLV) expresses the efficiency of air conditioning and heat pump equipment.

Frequently, the location of air-conditioning equipment for a residence or small commercial building influences both the interior design and the landscaping close to the building. A cool, shaded outdoor location is best for the compressor. The north side of a house under trees or tall shrubs is a good choice as long as the plantings do not block the unit's ability to dump heat. Because of exposure to direct sun, a rooftop or the east or west side of a building is usually a poor choice of location. Compressors are noisy and should be kept away from patios or bedroom windows.

Other Heating and Cooling Equipment

When moisture is added to air, the RH increases and the temperature seems to have fallen. This works when the air is very dry and not too hot and requires a large quantity of water and outdoor air. For centuries, fountains have cooled courtyards in hot, arid climates. Passive evaporative cooling systems can be as simple as a sprinkler on the roof of a conventional building or as complex as a roof pond with adjustable louvers.

EVAPORATIVE COOLERS

Outdoor conditions in about half of the United States are suitable for mechanical evaporative cooling. Known as swamp coolers or desert coolers, evaporative coolers are also used in high-heat applications, such as restaurant kitchens. Dry fresh air from outdoors is circulated through a wet pad, where it absorbs moisture as water vapor. After use, the air exits the building through grilles or open windows. Evaporative coolers are often located on the roof. Through-wall coolers are also common.

Indirect evaporative cooling actually uses both direct and indirect evaporative techniques and may be combined with direct

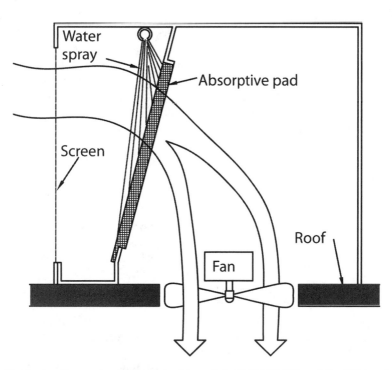

Figure 11-28 Evaporative cooler. When the outdoor air is 41°C (105°F) and the RH is a low 10 percent, evaporative cooling can produce indoor air with a temperature of 26°C (78°F) and 50 percent RH with only the power necessary to operate a fan. However, the fans that drive evaporative coolers are noisy, and the aroma of the wetted cooler may be unpleasant.

refrigerant cooling systems. Warm, dry outdoor air that has been cooled by evaporation is passed through a rock bed under a building at night. The next day, very hot dry air is cooled by passing through the rock bed, then through an evaporative cooler.

MISTING AND FOGGING SYSTEMS

Misting and fogging systems make people feel cooler with no total change in the heat content of the treated air. Roof sprays have been used in the past to keep poorly insulated roofs cool.

Misting can be used for small outdoor areas, such as team benches at football stadiums and refreshment pavilions. It has also been used in very large spaces in hot dry climates, including a railroad station in Atocha, Spain, and a conservatory in Michigan. Night roof spray thermal-storage systems cool water on the roof at night via radiation and evaporation. The water is stored on or below the roof for use the next day in building cooling or in a tank to precool entering air.

RADIANT COOLING SYSTEMS

Radiant cooling systems rely on water circulated through tubes to carry away excess heat.

Concrete core system:
- water circulated through plastic tubes in concrete floor slab
- carpet, pad, and insulation on concrete floor

Suspended ceiling panel system:
- usually aluminum facing connected to metal tubes
- suspended below concrete slab finished with flooring and carpet

Capillary tube system:
- cooling grids of capillary tubes embedded in ceiling plaster or gypsum board
- grids also mounted on ceiling panels
- grids mounted below concrete slab covered with insulation, flooring, and carpet

DEHUMIDIFICATION AND HUMIDIFICATION EQUIPMENT

Although lower humidity does not lower air temperature, it does increase comfort. Excessively low humidity can cause discomfort from dry skin.

Desiccant dehumidifiers:
- **Desiccants** are porous materials, such as silica gel, activated alumina, and synthetic polymers with a high affinity for water vapor, that lower humidity without overcooling the air.
- In active desiccant systems, desiccants are heated with natural gas or solar energy to drive out the moisture that they have removed from the air.
- Passive systems use the heat from a building's exhaust air to release and vent moisture removed from the incoming air.
- Desiccants raise the temperature of the dried air.

Refrigerant dehumidifiers:
- These humidifiers are appropriate for spaces that need only dehumidification rather than mechanical cooling; they are often freestanding units in small buildings.
- The air temperature remains essentially unchanged during dehumidification.
- Energy to run the refrigeration cycle is added to the space as heat.
- Accumulated water must periodically be removed to prevent disease.
- These dehumidifiers may encounter operating difficulties at air temperatures below 65°F (18°C), at which point frost forms on their cooling coils.

Task humidifiers:
- These humidifiers are used to relieve symptoms of respiratory illnesses.
- Bacterial and mold growth in water reservoirs is a problem; adding a UV lamp may counteract this threat

HEAT PUMPS

Heat pumps derive their name from their ability to transfer heat against its natural direction. As discussed earlier, heat usually flows from warm to cooler areas. But any air above absolute zero always contains some thermal energy. The higher the temperature, the more energy is available. A heat pump can deliver 1.5 to 3.5 units of heat for each unit of electricity it uses. This can save 30 to 60 percent over the cost of electric heating, depending on geographic location and the equipment used. Heat pumps do this without combustion or flues.

Heat pumps are used for indoor pools, athletic facilities, small-scale industrial operations, motels, hotels, and apartment buildings. In the heating mode, a heat pump extracts heat from outside the building and delivers it to the building, usually in conjunction with a forced warm air delivery system. When the heat pump uses air as the source of heat, the heat output and efficiency decline with colder weather. In general, air-to-air heat pumps that operate below freezing temperatures rely on electrical-resistance heating elements for backup heating. They work best in areas with mild winters, where there is a balance between heating and cooling loads, or where electrical heating is the only option.

In climates without extreme temperature changes, residents may employ heat pumps that can be reversed for heating their homes in the winter. For cooling, heat pumps use a normal compression refrigeration cycle to absorb and transfer excess heat to the outdoors. For heating, heat energy is drawn from outdoor air by switching the air heating and cooling ducts (the heat-exchange functions of the condenser and evaporator remain the same).

Earth tubes cool air before it enters a building. A fan forces air through long underground tubes. Sometimes, these tubes are located in trenches designed for underground water lines or other purposes.

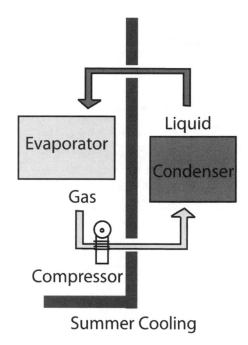

Summer Cooling

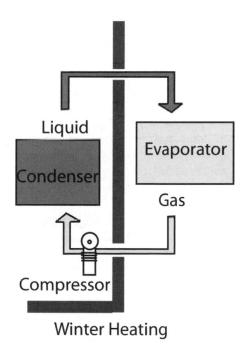

Winter Heating

7Figure 11-29 **Heat pump operation.** In a heat pump, a relatively small amount of energy is used to pump a larger amount of heat from a cold substance (e.g., the water, the ground, or outdoor air) to a warmer substance, such as the air inside the building. Heat pumps work especially well with relatively lower temperature heat sources, such as the water inside the jacket of an internal combustion engine or warm water from a flat-plate solar collector. The heat pump increases the heat from these sources to the higher temperatures needed for space heating. Heat pumps can be part of a total energy system, concentrating waste heat from an electrical generating system to heat the same buildings served by the electrical generators. Heat pumps that pump heat from water or ground sources are more dependable than air sources in cold weather.

TABLE 11-11. TYPES OF HEAT PUMPS

Type	Description	Uses
Air-to-air heat pump	Uses refrigeration cycle to both heat and cool; heat is pumped outdoors in summer and to inside in winter	Most common type used in small buildings
Air-to-water heat pump	Cool and dehumidify interior spaces; heat goes into useful water	Restaurants using heat pumps to cool hot cooking areas produce hot water for food preparation and dishwashing
Water-to-air heat pump	Water is heat source; delivers warmed air to space; closed piping loop uses heat rejected by one pump in cooling mode for another in heating mode	One zone of building can be heated while another is cooled; used for motels where rooms get varying sun, may be occupied or not, and hot water needs are high
Water-to-water heat pump	Replaces boiler and chiller	Dairies use them to simultaneously cool milk and heat water for cleaning
Ground-source heat pump (ground-to-air or geothermal heat pumps or geo-exchange systems)	Utilizes fact that underground temperatures are more constant year-round than air temperatures; supplies energy for heating, cooling, and domestic hot water	Used in schools with large land areas and historic structures with limited indoor mechanical equipment spaces; more costly and difficult to install than air-source pumps; life-cycle savings; low energy bills; requires less maintenance

HVAC SYSTEMS

Having discussed both mechanical heating and cooling systems, we will look at how they are used together. An HVAC system integrates mechanical equipment into one complex system that is designed to provide thermal comfort and air quality throughout a building. The difficulty of doing this is apparent when we consider that a building may be hot from the sun on one side, colder on the other, and warm in its interior, all at the same time on a winter day. Keeping all of the building occupants comfortable while conserving energy is a formidable task.

In the 1960s, when energy costs were low, architects, engineers, and building owners did not worry about how easily heat was transmitted through the building envelope. Dramatic architectural effects, such as all-glass buildings, took precedence over energy conservation. Omitting roof and wall insulation minimized initial building costs. HVAC system designers made building occupants comfortable by using as much mechanical equipment as necessary.

With increased fuel costs, energy has become one of the largest expenses in a building's operating budget. Some energy-conservation strategies came at the expense of comfort. The better the building interior is isolated from severe outside conditions, the more comfortable the occupants remain.

HVAC System Design

There are limits to what can be accomplished without mechanical systems. It is difficult to get a building itself to provide adequate air motion for comfort when temperatures exceed 31°C (88°F). Without some way to remove humidity from the air, most North American buildings are clammy in the summer and mold becomes a serious problem. It is difficult to filter air without the use of fans. All of these issues leave the mechanical designer with the job of deciding whether mechanical equipment will supplement and modify conditions occasionally, always modify and control the interior environment, or permanently exclude the outdoor environment.

HVAC systems simultaneously control temperature, humidity, air purity, distribution, and motion of air in interior building spaces. HVAC systems use air, water, or both to distribute heating and cooling energy. Systems include furnaces that supply hot air and boilers that heat water or produce steam. Some systems include electric heaters that use electrical resistance to convert electricity to heat.

The mechanical engineer selects the HVAC system based on performance, efficiency, and initial and life costs of the system. The engineer considers the availability of fuel, power, air, and water as well as the means for their delivery and storage; he or she also takes into account the need for access to outdoor air. The engineer also evaluates the system for its flexibility to serve different zones with different demands. He also reviews the type and layout of the distribution system in terms of heating and cooling, with an eye to laying out efficient, short direct runs and a minimum number of turns and offsets, to minimize friction losses.

HVAC equipment can take up between 10 and 15 percent of the building area. The size requirements for a building depend on the heating and cooling loads. Some pieces require additional access space for service and maintenance. Codes may require mechanical areas to have noise and vibration control and fire-resistant enclosures. Heavy equipment may need additional structural support.

CENTRALIZED VERSUS LOCAL EQUIPMENT

The designer of a building's mechanical system looks at whether the building's needs are dominated by heating or by cooling concerns. Because climate is such a strong factor in small buildings

TABLE 11-12. TYPICAL HVAC DESIGN PROCESS

Design Stage	Action	Team Members
Preliminary design	List activity comfort needs Develop activity schedule Analyze on-site energy resources List climate design strategies Consider building form alternatives Consider combinations of active and passive systems Alternatives sized by general design guidelines	Small buildings: architect Large projects: architects, engineers, landscape architects
Design development	Establishes design conditions by activity, schedule Determines HVAC zones using activities, schedule, orientation, internal heat gains Estimates thermal loads on each zone Selects HVAC systems Identifies and sizes HVAC components and locations: mechanical rooms, distribution trees, in-space components Lays out system	Architectural or mechanical engineer
Design finalizing	Compares HVAC system layout drawings with other building systems	Architects, other consultants
	Verifies match between loads and components Completes final layout drawings	HVAC-system designer

TABLE 11-13. CENTRAL AND LOCAL HVAC EQUIPMENT

System Type	Benefit	Disadvantages
Local HVAC system: differing but simultaneous needs; often skin-load-dominated buildings	Responds quickly to individual rooms' needs	Machine noise in room
	Does not need large central equipment spaces	Maintenance workers in occupied rooms
	Has shorter distribution trees	
	Localizes breakdowns	Many local filters to maintain
	Has simple control systems	
	Heating and cooling use limited for energy conservation	Few opportunities to use waste energy
Central HVAC system	Equipment located outside of occupied space	Mechanical rooms need to be centrally located near area served
	Offers better maintenance access	Breakdown of single piece of equipment may affect entire building
	Features energy recovery from boilers and chillers	Energy is wasted when entire system is activated to serve one zone
	Centralized mechanical spaces concentrate noise and heat for easy control	Direct access to outside for fresh air and for installation and removal of equipment
	Air intakes can be high above street pollution	Rooms for heating, cooling and AHU equipment need ceilings around 3.7 meters (12 ft.) high
	Regular maintenance of centralized air-filtering equipment results in long equipment life	Distribution trees are large and controls are complex

and heating and cooling needs may vary from room to room, localized equipment rather than a centralized system may be the better choice.

INTERIOR DESIGN IMPLICATIONS

Uniformity in the design of a building has implications for the HVAC system and for its interior design. Uniform ceiling heights, lighting placement, and HVAC grille locations increase flexibility in office arrangements and extend the building's useful lifespan. Four basic types of office space can be interchanged within a flexible overall plan: enclosed offices; bullpen offices with repeated, identical workstations with desk-height dividers; uniform, open-plan offices with higher partitions; and freeform, open-plan offices with partitions of varying heights. However, uniformity in ceiling lighting, air handling, and size can make design of connecting corridors, lounges, and other support services difficult.

TABLE 11-14. UNIFORMITY AND DIVERSITY IN INTERIOR DESIGN

Building Environment	Characteristic	Effect	Result
Uniformity	Mass production and speed	Rapidity of design and construction	Low initial costs
	Uniformity of ceiling heights, light fixture placement, grille locations	Flexibility in office arrangements	Can extend building's useful life
	Open offices	Loss of privacy; lack of stimulation	User discontent
Diversity	Corridors and service spaces at different heights	Complete and detailed design; complex construction	More interesting for designers and contractors; may help orient users
	Retail shops	Light, sound, heat, aroma	Distinguish shops from neighbors
	Thermal conditions	Warm offices and cool circulation spaces in winter	Enhanced user comfort; save energy; promote passive design strategies
	Varied light levels	Low, dark transition spaces	Make main spaces seem bright and high

On the other hand, diverse design elements require complete and detailed design of a space, but the resulting design may be a more complex and interesting building for designer, builder, and user. Variety aids user orientation and distinguishes spaces from one another.

Some spaces require diverse thermal conditions. In the winter, people expect offices to be relatively warmer than circulation spaces, which are transitional from the exterior to the interior. Just like a space can seem lighter and higher if preceded by a lower, darker space, transitional spaces that are closer to outside temperatures can make key spaces seem more comfortable without extreme heating or cooling, thereby saving energy over the life of the building.

The design of the air circulation and ventilation system interacts with the layout of furniture. Even furniture like filing cabinets and acoustic screens less than 1.5 meters (5 ft.) high can impede air circulation, especially if they extend to the floor. Some sources recommend an open space of at least 25 to 51 millimeters (1–2 in.) at the base, with 152 millimeters (6 in.) allowing even better airflow. If walls or full-height partitions enclose spaces, each enclosed space should have one supply vent and one return or exhaust vent.

HVAC Zones

The numbers and types of HVAC zones required for thermal comfort influence the selection of centralized versus local HVAC-equipment systems. A zone placed away from the building envelope may not have the access to outdoor air required for a localized system. Space must be available for equipment within a local zone.

Typically, large, multipurpose buildings conventionally use a system of 16 zones (see Fig. 9-24, page 158). Each function—apartments, offices, and stores—has five zones: north, east, south, and west sides and a central core. Underground parking is the sixteenth zone. Each of these zones may encompass more than one floor. Adding scheduling considerations may increase the number of zones. If apartments need individual controls, each apartment may become one zone.

HVAC-System Types

The design of HVAC systems for large buildings is continuing to undergo several changes:

- Increasing use of mechanical equipment combined with natural ventilation and daylighting, fostered by automated building controls
- More frequent use of underfloor plenum air supply rather than using ducts to diffusers and return grilles, both on the ceiling, along with full-access floors for power and data cabling
- Increased natural ventilation to avoid refrigerants that contain chemicals dangerous to the environment
- Use of fuel cells and PVs to supply on-site energy to larger buildings, rather than relying on fossil-fueled, grid-supplied energy

There are hundreds of types of HVAC systems in use in large buildings, but most can be classified as one of four main categories. One type, direct refrigerant systems, is heating and cooling systems that respond directly to the needs of individual zones. The other three—all-air, air-and-water, and all-water systems—produce heating and cooling in a central location, far from some zones. Air-handling equipment for these last three systems is either centrally located or located on each floor.

Direct refrigerant systems locate the heating and cooling device in or near the space served. Typically, they are used in smaller, skin-dominated buildings with extensive perimeter zones.

All-air systems provide the best overall comfort and well-controlled conditions. Air is heated, cooled, humidity controlled, and filtered, and fresh outdoor air is added. Thick distribution trees take up a great deal of space, and reducing duct sizes requires higher-velocity air, which generates more noise, friction, and energy use. A central mechanical room eases maintenance.

All-air systems are common in existing buildings and come in many varieties. The following are some of the most prominent systems:

- **Single zone systems:** Typically, these forced-air systems are used in small buildings and have a single thermostat. They are the least complicated all-air system and have a very low initial cost.
- **Single duct variable-air-volume (VAV) systems:** These systems are most popular for interior zones of internal-load–dominated buildings. Such systems require less duct space, and their variable air volume flow rate, rather than temperature, saves energy. Fans run at full volume only during peak hours.
- **Fan powered VAV systems:** Individual units can heat a space while the main supply cools it. These systems are used when simultaneous heating and cooling are needed (e.g., in perimeter zones). They provide additional air motion and mixing within a room.
- **Multizone systems:** Because these systems have huge distribution trees, they are used in medium-sized buildings or on single floors of larger buildings. A group of single zones is served by a single supply fan. Warm and cool airstreams are mixed at a central location to suit each zone. Leakage between zones is common.
- **Single duct with reheat systems:** This is the smallest distribution tree of the class. Formerly common, today it is restricted by codes and standards. A small reheat coil is added on for each zone. Central cold air must be as cold as the air in the coolest zone, which wastes a great deal of energy.
- **Double duct constant-volume systems:** These are two complete distribution trees. Frequently used in hospitals, they provide better comfort under reduced loads than VAV systems. However, they are very expensive to install, use a great deal of space, and usually consume a high amount of energy.

Air-and-water systems use a water distribution tree for most heating and cooling, with a small central airstream for fresh air. They have thinner distribution trees and require less total space; filters are maintained in that space. Humidity is less well controlled, and sometimes, the equipment has trouble knowing when to switch from air to water or vice versa. These systems include

- **Induction systems:** An air terminal below windows mixes fresh air with room air. These systems are used in perimeter zones of large buildings that require extensive heating and cooling, such as office buildings, hospitals, schools, apartment buildings, and laboratories.
- **FCU with supplementary air:** This unit is located below windows and distributes both fresh air and room air.
- **Radiant panels with supplementary air:** These are ceiling or wall panels with heated or cooled water. With this system, a large surface area must be kept clear of obstructions.
- **Water-loop heat pumps:** These systems make efficient use of discharge heat in large buildings in cold weather.

All-water systems control only air temperature, not air quality. They are located above ceilings, below windows, or in corners of rooms. They are very slim distribution trees that only heat and cool; there is little mixing of air between zones. All-water FCUs require a drain line, and water standing in pans can encourage bacterial or mold growth.

As the size of buildings' structural elements has decreased because of improved material strength, the size of building mechanical systems has increased. In buildings in which smaller structural elements leave more floor area open, more flexibility in space planning is possible. Mechanical components are often located at or within structural columns. It is common to have a structural column with an air duct crossing it at the top. Because the moving parts of a mechanical system need maintenance and change with user needs while the structure rarely changes, it is impractical to wrap the mechanical system completely inside the structural envelope.

Exposing the mechanical system within the space permits easy access for maintenance, repair, and alteration. Exposed systems may add visual interest. Sometimes, office buildings expose the HVAC system in corridors and service areas but conceal it in offices. Exposed systems both increase flexibility and reveal elements that users can manipulate, reminding them of the opportunity and encouraging user interaction.

The location of centralized HVAC equipment in a large building has implications for the building's space use and function. The heat, noise, moisture, air motion, and vibration from equipment may annoy occupants of adjacent floors or neighboring buildings. Mechanical floors can be used to separate floors of apartments from office floors, isolating daytime-use spaces from housing used more heavily at night. Very large buildings often require several intermediate mechanical floors. Basement locations offer noise isolation, utility access, and support for heavy machinery. Rooftops provide access to air for rejecting excess heat along with unlimited headroom. However, top-floor spaces often bring top rental fees, which are lost when these spaces are devoted to mechanical equipment.

HVAC Equipment

HVAC systems are made up of a number of separate pieces of equipment, which may be combined under the comprehensive term **air-handling unit (AHU)**. Types of AHUs include unitary AHUs, computer-room units, and central AHUs.

- **Preheaters** warm air that is below 0°C (32°F) to a temperature slightly above freezing before it is sent on for other processing.
- **Blowers** (fans) supply air at a moderate pressure to create the forced-air drafts that operate the HVAC system.
- **Humidifiers** maintain or increase the amount of water vapor in the air.
- **Chillers** that are powered by electricity, steam, or gas remove heat from a recirculating chilled-water system used to cool buildings.
- **Boilers** heat recirculating hot water for building heating.

TABLE 11-15. BASIC HVAC SYSTEM TASKS

System	Intake and Exhaust	Movers, Converters, and Processors	Distribution	Results
Heating	Intake fuel and combustion air	Boilers, furnaces, pumps	Pipes, ducts, electrical conduits	Warm air or surfaces; air motion often controlled; may need humidity control
	Exhaust heat and CO_2	Fans, filters, heat pumps	Diffusers, grilles, radiators, thermostats, valves, dampers	
Cooling	Intake air, water, fuel	Evaporative coolers, heat pumps, chillers and cooling towers, coils, pumps, fans, filters	Pipes, ducts, diffusers, grilles, radiators, thermostats, valves, dampers	Cool air or surfaces; air motion usually controlled; humidity control usually provided
	Exhaust air, vapor, water, heat, CO_2			
Ventilation	Air	Fans, filters	Ducts, diffusers, grilles, switches, dampers	Fresh air; air motion usually controlled; air-quality control often needed

- **Condensing water equipment** rejects heat removed from recirculating chilled-water systems by using a cooling tower or closed-circuit evaporative cooler.
- **Energy conservation equipment** includes boiler-flue economizers to preheat incoming boiler water, runaround coils, and economizer cycles.
- **Energy storage systems** include water and ice storage tanks.
- **Air-handling equipment** includes fans, filters, and coils for air heating and cooling.
- **Controls** include such individual controls as controllers, actuators, and limit and safety switches. A building management system (BMS) is found in most large buildings, laboratories, hotel rooms, and office buildings with more passive strategies.
- **Unitary AHUs:** These self-contained, weatherproof units have a fan, filters, a compressor, a condenser, and evaporator coils for cooling. They are installed on the roof directly above the space to be air conditioned, or mounted on a concrete pad along the exterior building wall.

Computer room units use a highly reliable AHU with extremely precise temperature, humidity, and dust controls for sensitive electronic equipment, all located in the space served. High-quality components, reserve capacity, and redundant components to take over in case of equipment failure add to the expense of computer room units.

Central air-handling unit systems are found in large buildings with multiple zones of at least 450 square meters (5000 sq ft.) and in tall multistory buildings. Hospitals with stringent air-quality controls use central AHU systems exclusively. Large central AHU systems require routine daily checking and regularly scheduled maintenance. They are built on-site and take longer to install than prefabricated units, but they may be more energy efficient. Central AHU systems have a 20- to 30-year life expectancy.

HVAC DISTRIBUTION TREES

The first multistory buildings, such as mill buildings in New England and the earliest skyscrapers, depended on daylight and cross ventilation, which worked well with high ceiling spaces and extensive perimeter exposure. Most of the heat gain and loss occurred at the perimeter, which was where the earliest HVAC distribution equipment was located.

As buildings began to use electrical lighting and air conditioning, they developed large central areas that had to be supplied with forced cooled air. Large centralized equipment rooms and bulky air distribution trees were standard.

The concurrent development of the glass curtain wall pushed unsightly air distribution trees to the building cores. The glass perimeter's extreme heating and cooling needs made it necessary for large air distribution areas to carry air horizontally from the core, above suspended ceilings, to the edges. The result was reduced interior floor-to-ceiling heights and spaces with low ceilings and without direct access to daylight.

Today, HVAC equipment is becoming decentralized, with small fan rooms on each floor with horizontal distribution trees spreading out from them. Office ceilings are being raised to provide more daylight. Exposed concrete structure and raised-floor air-supply and ventilation systems work well with thermal-mass night cooling. Building façades are becoming more three-dimensionally complex to take advantage of passive sun control, making it easier to accommodate perimeter distribution systems.

The effects of the increasing use of electrical lighting and air conditioning floor plans can be seen. The RCA Building in New York City's Rockefeller Center (1931–1932), which retained a slab-like floor plan to allow daylight to reach the working areas arranged around a core that contained elevators and other service spaces. Central boilers, chillers, and fan rooms supplied a great deal of forced cooled air through bulky air distribution trees.

☑ **In the mid-twentieth century, the advent of glass curtain walls and the slick, two-dimensional modern look made air distribution trees visually intrusive, and they were pushed to the building's core.**

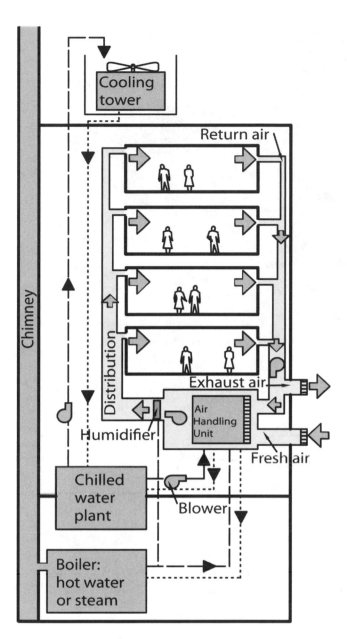

Figure 11-30 Centralized HVAC system. Centralized HVAC systems distribute heating and cooling through distribution trees that take up a great deal of space, both horizontally and vertically. They need to be coordinated with the lighting, ceiling design, and other interior design elements. Like trees in nature, distribution trees have roots: the machines that heat or cool the air or water. The trunk of the tree is the main duct or pipe from the mechanical equipment to the zone served. The tree's branches are the many smaller ducts or pipes that lead to individual spaces. The leaves are the point of interchange between the piped or ducted heating or cooling and the space served. This point may be a large, bulky FCU on an exterior wall below the window. The leaves could also be perforated ceiling tiles with thousands of small holes, similar to an almost invisible, widely spreading grille.

When a building's architect and engineers lay out the HVAC distribution pattern, the interior designer's work is directly affected. Ceiling heights are determined, and the transition from higher to lower spaces has a direct impact on interior volumes and relationships. Horizontal distribution takes up room at the ceiling and lowers ceiling heights, which may be an issue in daylighting design. Code-mandated building height limits may, in turn, limit floor-to-ceiling heights. Horizontal layouts are located at circulation paths, at structural elements, at the building perimeter, or in separate layers above or below other floors.

Horizontal distribution above corridors is very common, and the reduced headroom is not usually a problem. Typically, circulation spaces are away from windows, so daylight is not affected. Corridors provide logical connections from one space to another and are good paths for distribution trees. The change from lower service spaces to higher ceilings in office spaces enhances the openness of the higher spaces.

UNDERFLOOR DISTRIBUTION

Underfloor air supply with displacement ventilation provides fresh air, cooled to just below the design room temperature, at a low velocity. Using the underfloor area as a plenum, high volumes of low-velocity air are distributed without ductwork.

Fresh air enters the underfloor distribution space and rises as it picks up heat from occupants, office equipment, and lighting. Eventually, it stratifies at the ceiling, where it is collected. The provision of cool, fresh air near the floor and warmer, staler air at the ceiling provides better IAQ and thermal comfort than ceiling supply and return systems. Individual control of floor-mounted registers increases comfort.

Codes may restrict the height of the raised floor, and wiring is often required for a special wear-resistant coating. A ceiling must be least 2.7 meters (9 ft.) high for proper air stratification. Without a suspended ceiling, lighting, fire-safety, and other building systems are exposed; an option is to move some of these under the floor above.

If all of the components of an underfloor system are designed, installed, and maintained properly, the system will offer as great a degree of fire protection as any other cabling system. Wiring must conform to code no matter where it is placed, and there is no reason why an underfloor system cannot incorporate code-mandated smoke barriers. Noise transmission also is not a problem because the depth of the underfloor space and the carpet covering the floor provide acoustical insulation that is more than sufficient. Fears that an underfloor system might feel bouncy may have been true in the past, but today's dense, high-quality flooring products have eliminated this drawback.

☑ **Ceiling heights are important for the distribution of air from the ceiling. High ceilings above cubicles allow colder air to be used, which translates into small ducts. High ceilings also allow deep daylight penetration and a large pool of air, which stays fresher for a long period.**

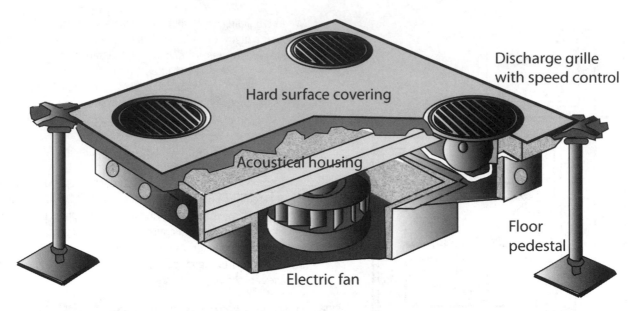

Figure 11-31 Underfloor distribution. Typically, a raised floor is supported on a 600 x 600-mm (2 x 2-ft.) module. The diffuser is also the location of power and data cabling outlets. The units allow multiple orientations and ease of reorganization.

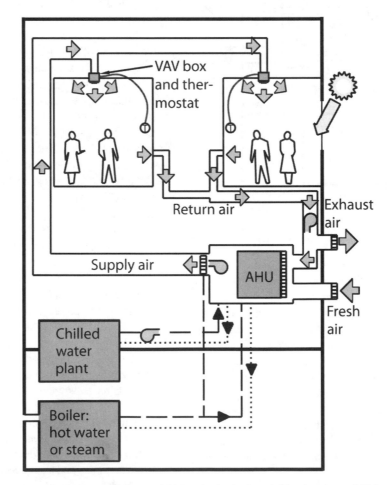

Figure 11-32 Single-duct VAV system. In the 1990s, single duct, variable air volume (VAV) systems became the most popular system. Each zone has its own thermostat that operates a damper. The dampers at terminal outlets control the flow of conditioned air to the local ductwork in that zone according to temperature requirements for each zone or space.

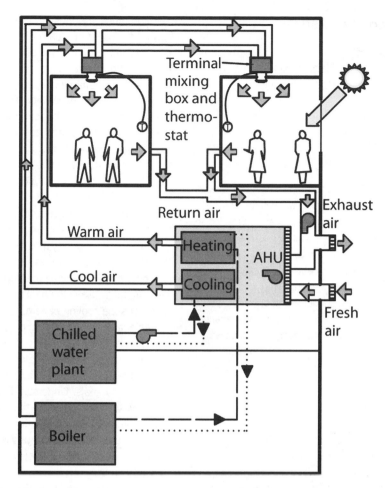

Figure 11-33 Double-duct system. When temperatures must be closely controlled in a large number of rooms or zones, double-duct systems circulate both heated and cooled air to a control box in each zone. These systems offer superior comfort control and flexibility for simultaneous heating and cooling zones.

INTERIOR AIR PRESSURES

In some spaces, such as shopping malls, corridors of apartment houses, and stair towers, more air is introduced into the space than is mechanically removed. These spaces are kept under positive pressure, so air does not tend to flow into them. This pressurization helps prevent unheated or uncooled outdoor air or smoke from a fire from entering these spaces. Higher air pressures also reduce discomfort from drafts and uneven temperatures from infiltration of air through the building envelope.

ENERGY-SAVING CONTROLS

A **thermostat** is a temperature-activated switch that turns heating and cooling equipment on and off in order to maintain a preset temperature.

A one-degree reduction in the thermostat setting can save 2 percent of the heating bill for a home. Clock thermostats lower the temperature automatically at night and turn it back up one-half hour before the home's occupants get up in the morning. Clock thermostats pay for themselves in about one year.

☑ A mechanical engineer determines the location of a thermostat based on the location of surrounding heat sources. Most thermostat malfunctions result from improper location, poor maintenance, or inappropriate use. To work properly, a thermostat must be mounted on an inside wall away from doors and windows, so that it will not be affected by the outdoor temperature or by drafts. Lamps, appliances, television sets, and heaters should not be placed under a thermostat because their heat will affect furnace operation. If the occupants of a space usually adjust the thermostat, it should be in an accessible location, although there is no specific Americans with Disabilities (ADA) requirement. The interior designer should make it a point to know where the thermostat is to be located to prevent it from ending up in the middle of a featured wall, right where he or she had planned to hang a piece of art. Thermostats are available with a flush-mounted wall plate, and with remote-sensing wires that could be wrapped around a picture, sculpture, molding, or other decorative element. When thermostats must be concealed for aesthetic reasons or to avoid damage to them, they can be located in a return air duct.

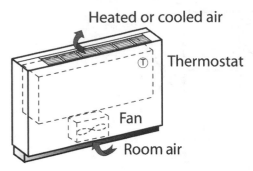

Figure 11-34 Fan coil unit. An FCU is a factory-assembled unit with a heating and/or cooling coil, fan, and filter. Wall, ceiling, and vertical stacking models are available. Some designs are concealed in custom enclosures, semirecessed into the wall, or installed as floor consoles with various cabinets. Recessed units are often found along corridors. Ceiling models are available in cabinets for exposed locations or without cabinets for concealed mounting. They should not be mounted above solid ceilings because condensation drains are prone to clogging and the drain pans can overflow, requiring maintenance. One ceiling unit can be ducted to supply several adjacent small spaces. Vertical stacking units are used in multiple-floor apartment buildings, condominiums, office buildings, and hotels. They eliminate the need for separate piping risers and runouts.

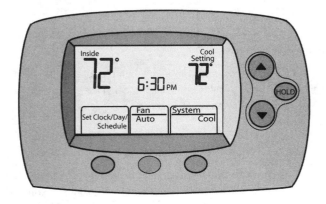

Figure 11-35 Thermostat. Thermostats control the flow of water to radiators and convectors. Fans that circulate warm air also use thermostats. A thermostat triggers a low-limit switch, which turns fans and pumps on for the heat distribution system when a preset low temperature is reached. An upper-limit switch shuts off the furnace when the specified temperature is reached. A safety switch prevents fuel from flowing to the heating plant when the pilot light or fuel-ignition system is not working.

Self-contained thermostats provide inexpensive room-by-room control for water or steam distribution systems. Self-contained thermostatic control valves can be mounted directly on cast-iron radiators, fin-tube radiators, FCUs, and unit heaters. They can be retrofitted in dormitories, apartments, and offices that have only one thermostat for each floor. They provide highly cost-effective energy conservation by controlling the temperature locally, thereby eliminating the need to open windows in overheated rooms. Self-contained microprocessor-based thermostats can be fine-tuned for flexible, simple control.

The HVAC controls for small buildings are usually thermostats. ANSI/ASHRAE Standard 90.2-2007, *Energy Efficient Design of New Low-Rise Residential Buildings*, sets standards for thermostats. Thermostats must be able to be set from 13°C to 29°C (55°F–85°F). They must also have an adjustable deadband, the range of which includes settings at 5.6°C (10°F) increments. The **deadband** is a range of temperatures separating a low temperature that triggers the heat to go on from a higher temperature that starts the cooling system.

As engineers and architects move away from designing buildings that are equipment-driven, interior spaces will reflect new energy-efficient priorities. Older buildings may gradually be refitted with new systems, and user demands may moderate to meet sustainability goals. Understanding how existing buildings work and how they can be made more resource-efficient is important to interior designers who work as part of a building design team. In Part V: Electrical and Lighting Systems, we will examine alternatives to heavily wired, energy-intensive, and artificially illuminated buildings.

PART

V

· · · · · · · · · · · · · · · · ·

ELECTRICAL AND LIGHTING SYSTEMS

Our reliance on electricity has serious implications for environmental quality and resource conservation. Much of the energy produced from coal, petroleum, and nuclear sources ends up as electricity distributed for building use.

Existing buildings were rarely designed for daylighting and rely strongly on electrical lighting. Lighting consumes 25 to 30 percent of the energy used in commercial buildings. This, in turn, adds heat to a building's interior and increases energy use for air conditioning.

According to the author of *Mechanical and Electrical Equipment for Buildings*, "Electricity generated by thermal processes (except for cogeneration) delivers to the end user less than one-third of the total energy that goes into its production; more than two-thirds is usually lost as waste heat at the generating plant." (Benjamin Stein et al., John Wiley & Sons, Inc., Hoboken, NJ, 2006, p. 29)

As we consume our planet's resources, including fossil fuels, many look to a return to renewable and sustainable energy. This vision will be partially implemented by solar energy converted directly to electricity (through photovoltaics [PV]) on or near the building requiring the electricity.

Existing buildings contain miles of wiring, much of which is no longer in use. Wireless technologies and underfloor distribution offer new ways to power equipment and send data. Workspaces are changing form and location rapidly to keep up with new ways of working. An interior designer's knowledge base for designing commercial offices is undergoing radical change.

12

....

Electrical Systems Basics

Electricity is the most prevalent form of energy in a modern building. Electricity supplies power to electrical outlets and lighting fixtures. Ventilating, heating, and cooling equipment depends on electrical energy. Electricity provides energy for elevators, material transporters, and signal and communication equipment.

Lighting is the primary user of electrical energy in most buildings. In commercial buildings, motors are the second largest user of electrical energy, for heating, ventilating, and air-conditioning (HVAC) systems; plumbing pumps; elevators; and most industrial processes.

☑ **Working with a building's architect and engineers, the interior designer is responsible for seeing that power is available where needed for the client's equipment and for ensuring that the lighting and appliances are appropriate and energy efficient.**

Until around 1870, only fire and muscle power were commonly used in buildings to perform useful work. Historically, coal and oil were burned for heat and light or converted into energy for machines that generated heat. Since the end of the nineteenth century, heat has been converted into electricity. Even nuclear energy produces heat for conversion to electricity. Converting heat to electricity is inherently inefficient, with about 60 percent of the energy in the heat wasted.

In the twentieth century, electricity offered a clean, reliable, and very convenient source of energy for illumination, heating, power equipment, and electronic communication. Electricity was not usually generated on a building site. Small generating units powered by internal-combustion engines, water, sun, or wind generally have been considered to be expensive to buy and maintain, to have limited capacity, and to be less reliable and efficient than central generating plants. However, this is beginning to change. Techniques for generating and storing energy are advancing, and we can look forward to a significant increase in locally produced electrical energy.

Currently, large, centralized electrical generating plants are usually powered by water or steam turbines. The steam is generated by coal, oil, gas, or nuclear fuel. In electrical generating plants, about $1\frac{1}{2}$ times as much heat goes up the chimney and into waterways as to transmission lines for energy. Additional losses occur in the transmission lines to users, so that the electrical energy people receive is only one-third of the initial energy available from the fuel. Compare this with modern heat-producing equipment that burns fuel in the building itself, which is generally 70 to 90 percent efficient.

PRINCIPLES OF ELECTRICITY

Electricity is a form of energy that occurs naturally only in uncontrolled forms, such as lightning and other static electrical discharges, or in natural galvanic reactions that cause corrosion. As Vaughn Bradshaw explains in *Active and Passive Control Systems, 3e* (John Wiley & Sons, Inc., Hoboken, NJ, 2006, p. 295):

No one knows exactly what electricity is or how it works. It does, however, behave in predictable ways, that is, when a light switch is thrown, the light consistently goes on, or if it doesn't go on, prescribed steps (such as replacing the lamp) can be taken to correct the problem. Because the experience is repeatable, observers have made up theories about what constitutes the electrical phenomenon. These theories have changed and evolved over time, and undoubtedly will continue to be improved upon.

The currently accepted theory is that electrical current consists of a flow of electrons along a conductor. The flow is induced by an imbalance of positive and negative charges. Like charges repel, and opposite charges attract. Electrons, with their negative charges, are repelled by a negatively charged area and attracted to a positively charged one. When a positive area is connected to a negative area by a material that conducts electricity, electrons flow from the negative side to the positive side.

Lightning

A lightning bolt is an instantaneous release of very high electrical potential between a rain cloud and the earth. Tall buildings and buildings in exposed locations are most susceptible to lightning strikes. Buildings are protected from lightning by pointed metal rods that connect directly with the earth through heavy electrical conductors. By leaking a charge off their points, they neutralize electrical charges of clouds before lightning bolts even form. If lightning still strikes the building, the lightning rods and conductors offer a path to the ground of much less resistance than the building itself, thereby protecting the building.

Protecting a building against lightning strikes should be done completely and properly, with Underwriters Laboratories (UL) label equipment and a UL-approved installer. Partial protection is improper protection and may be worse than none at all.

A typical residential lightning system consists of three parts: air terminals (lightning rods), conductors, and ground terminals. In many areas, the system should be supplemented with a surge arrester installed at the electrical service panel. Manufacturers of lightning protection equipment sell only to UL-listed installers.

Circuits

A **circuit** is any closed path followed by an electrical current. Electrons flow along a closed path (e.g., a wire) from a point with a negative charge to one with a positive charge. An electrical circuit is a complete conduction path that carries **electrical current** from a source of electricity to and through some electrical device (or **load**) and back to the source. Current will not flow unless there is a closed circuit back to the source.

Electrical circuits can be arranged in a couple of ways. In a **series circuit**, the parts of the circuit are connected one after another, and the resistances and voltages add up. The current is the same in all points of a series circuit.

When two or more branches or loads in a circuit are connected between the same two points, they are said to be con-

Figure 12-1 Lightning protection. A lightning strike has practically unlimited voltage and a very high current. A lightning conductor requires a wide clearance—more than one meter (3¼ ft.) from any other conductive material. The lightning arrester in this image will lure the lightning strike, which will then flash over into the water tube or antenna cable. *Photo credit: Stefan Fassbinder.*

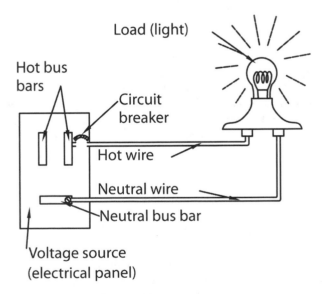

Figure 12-2 Circuit. Electrical power for this circuit originates at an electrical panel. It flows from the hot bus bars through the circuit breaker and along the hot wire to the load, in this case a light bulb. In order for the circuit to function, it must be completed, as shown here with a neutral wire, so that it can return to the electrical panel voltage source.

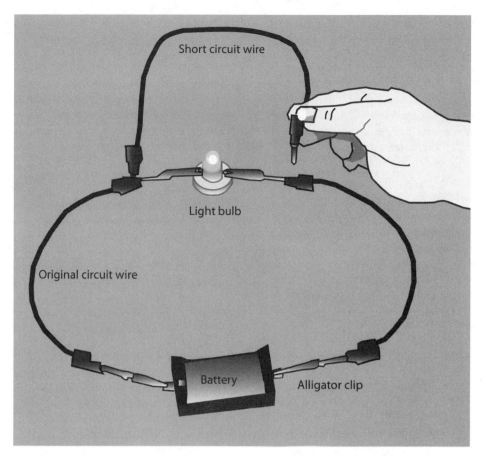

Figure 12-3 Short circuit. Electricity seeks the easiest route around its circuit to return to its source. This circuit starts at the battery and runs through wires to its load, here, a light bulb. The circuit has a return route back to the battery. When a wire is added that allows the electricity to head back home without doing its work—lighting the bulb—it will take this short circuit around the load.

nected in parallel. **Parallel circuits** are the standard arrangement in all building wiring. Each parallel group acts as a separate circuit. If one of these smaller circuits is broken, only the devices on that section are affected, and the rest of the circuit continues to circulate electricity.

Sometimes, because of worn insulation on a wire or another problem, an accidental connection is made between points on a circuit. This connection shortens the circuit and lets the electricity take a shortcut back to the source. The electricity does not encounter the resistance that would be in the normal wiring, and the current rises instantly to a very high level. This is called a **short circuit**. If the flow of electricity is not stopped by a fuse or circuit breaker, the heat generated by the excessive current probably will start a fire.

Amps, Volts, Watts, and Ohms

Electricity flows at a constant speed and moves almost instantaneously. The process of electricity flowing along a circuit is called **electrical current**, or **amperage**. It is measured in **amperes** (abbreviated **amps** or simply "**A**"), named after André Ampère, a

French mathematician and physicist who lived from 1775 to 1836. An ampere is defined as one coulomb per second that flows past a given point. A coulomb is, in turn, defined as 6.28×1018 electrons—a very, very large number of very, very tiny particles.

Electron movement and its energy—in other words, electricity—occurs when there is a higher positive electrical charge at one point on a **conductor** than at another point on that same conductor. For example, in an ordinary battery, chemical action causes positive (+) charges to collect on the positive terminal and negatively charged (−) electrons to collect at the negative terminal. Even when the battery is not connected to any load, the electrified particles at the positive and negative terminals tend to flow; this tendency or force is called **potential difference** or **voltage**. When a conductor runs between the positive and negative terminals, the voltage between the terminals causes current to flow in the conductor. The more voltage in a system, the more current flows, the more electrons move along the conductor each second, and the more amps are measured in the circuit.

A unit of voltage is called a **volt (V)**, after Count Alessandro Volta (1745–1827), an Italian physicist and a pioneer in the study of electricity. A volt is defined as a unit of electrical potential; it measures the difference in electrical potential between two points of a conductor that carry a constant current of one ampere, when the power dissipated between the two points is equal to one watt. To understand how much power is in a volt, build up a static charge by scuffing your feet on a wool carpet. You can actually generate about 400 volts by doing this, enough to make a visible spark jump between your finger and a metal object—or another person. A static shock has an extremely tiny current flow (amperage), so only a limited number of electrons are available to make the jump. Its effect is startling rather than harmful, despite the high voltage. However, the current flow available from the utility grid is almost unlimited, making 120-volt household systems powerful and dangerous. The electrical current could easily melt all of the wiring in a home.

Predictably, watts are named after James Watt (1736–1819), a Scottish engineer who invented the modern steam engine. A **watt (W)** is defined as one ampere flowing under the electromotive force of one volt. This is, if you think about it, a circular definition, but we already know that electricity is a mysterious subject. It helps to remember that a watt is used to measure how many electrons are passing a point and how much force is available to move them.

Utility meters measure electrical power use in **kilowatt-hours (kWh)**. In physics, energy is technically defined as the work that a physical system is capable of doing in changing from its actual state to a specified reference state. In building construction and design, power is defined as the ability to do work, or the rate at which energy is used in doing work. Power is energy used over time. A watt represents the rate at which energy is being used at any given moment, and 1000 watts equal one **kilowatt (kW)**. Electrical power is expressed in watts or kilowatts, and time is expressed in hours, so units of energy are watt-hours or kilowatt-hours (kWh). One kWh equals one watt of power in use for 1000 hours. The amount of energy used is directly proportional to the power of a system (the number of watts) and the length of time it is in operation (the number of hours).

Watts are familiarly known as indications of the amount of electricity a light bulb (technically referred to as a **lamp**) will use. A 60-watt incandescent lamp uses 60 watts of power to operate. When the lamp is placed in an electrical circuit, with voltage on one side 120 volts higher than voltage on the other side, then 1/2 ampere of current (60 divided by 120) will flow through the circuit. The current is said to be drawn through the circuit by the light bulb, which is called the load on the circuit. When the voltage is lower, more current is needed to get the same power at a lower voltage. If the voltage difference in this example were only 12 volts instead of 120 volts, the current draw would be 5 amperes (60 divided by 12). The amount of current (number of amperes) determines the size of the wire needed for a particular use.

Electrical resistance is believed to be a form of friction on the atomic level. It can be thought of as similar to friction or a constriction in the flow of water or another substance. Electrical current always flows through the path of least resistance. Good conductors are simply materials in which there many electrons that are free to move around, so that there is not a great deal of resistance to the electrons moving. All metals conduct electricity, although some do it better than others. Effective electrical conductors include silver, gold, and platinum, with copper and aluminum almost as good and much less expensive.

What makes a metal imperfect as a conductor is the presence of internal obstacles to the free motion of electrons that cannot be avoided because metals are made of atoms. These impede the flow of electrons and give rise to electrical resistance. Repeated collisions of electrons with these bumps lead to loss of energy in the form of heat. Materials with low electrical resistance are, obviously, very useful because they conduct electricity more efficiently and lose less energy to heat than those with high electrical resistance.

Insulators are materials that offer so much resistance that they almost prevent the flow of any electricity at all, so they are used to contain electricity in its path. Glass, mica, rubber, distilled water, porcelain, and certain synthetic materials are very good insulators. Rubber and plastic are used for wire coverings, porcelain is used for lamp sockets, and some switches are immersed in oil.

Electrical resistance is measured in units called **ohms**, named after George Simon Ohm, a German physicist who lived from 1787 to 1854. An ohm is equal to the resistance of a conductor in which a potential difference of one volt produces a current of one ampere.

Direct and Alternating Current

There are two types of electrical current. **Direct current (DC)** has a constant flow rate from a constant voltage source, such as a battery in which one terminal (or **pole**) is always positive and the other is always negative. The flow is always in the same direction; this is called **polarity**. Any current in which each wire is always of the same polarity, with one wire always positive and one always negative, is a direct current. Direct current is produced in batteries and PV equipment.

With **alternating current (AC)**, the voltage difference between the two points reverses in a regular manner. This means that the electrical current changes direction back and forth at a fixed **frequency** (rate). The change from positive to negative, to positive again is called one **cycle**, and the speed with which the cycle occurs is the frequency of the current. Commercial power from utility companies in the United States and Canada is AC and is typically supplied at 60 cycles per second, or 60 Hertz (Hz)—named after Gustav Hertz, a German atomic physicist (1887–1975). Many other countries supply commercial power at 50 Hz.

AC is more complex than DC and involves an electrical generator with a metal loop that rotates, changing the magnitude and direction of the induced voltage (and current). One complete rotation of the loop produces one complete cycle in voltage (and in the current).

Equipment made for one frequency is not compatible with any other frequency. Motors will not perform as desired at the

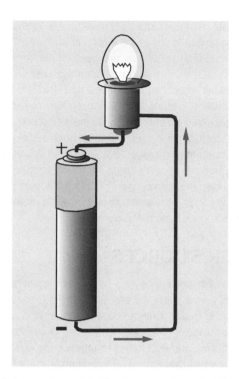

Figure 12-4 Direct current. Direct current does what its name implies: it flows in one direction around a circuit, here, from a battery through a light bulb and back to the battery.

wrong frequency and may overheat, burn out, or have a shortened life. In AC circuits, resistance (measured in ohms) is called **impedance**.

The advantages of AC over DC are the ease and efficiency with which the level of voltage can be changed by transformers. **Generators** put out currents at many thousands of volts. **Transformers** at the generating plant further increase the voltage before the electricity is passed to the main transmission lines, to keep amperage at a minimum. When the amperage is kept low, large amounts of energy can be transmitted through small wires with minimum transmission energy losses.

The electricity passes through substations on its way to local transmission lines. Once the electrical energy has reached the local area, it is reduced in voltage at another transformer for distribution to buildings. The local lines have higher transmission losses per mile than the main lines but are much shorter.

The voltage that reaches the building is still too high for consumer use, so each building or group of buildings has a small transformer to reduce the voltage even further before it enters the building. Electrical service for small buildings is provided at 230 or 240 volts. Large, cylindrical transformers on utility poles that reduce the voltage for small buildings are common sights. The voltage is again reduced to approximately 120 volts for household use. Some older homes have only 120-volt service. Near

Figure 12-5 Electrical transmission. The power that goes through these transformers to the transmission lines in the background is generated by a hydroelectric plant on the adjacent Merrimack River in Manchester, New Hampshire.

large cities, the supply may be 120/208 volts. Large buildings and building complexes often buy electricity at the local line voltage and reduce it themselves with indoor transformers before use.

Transformers for large buildings are usually mounted on poles or pads outside the building or inside a room or vault. The transformer for a large building steps down 4160-volt service to 480 volts for distribution within the building. A second transformer in an electrical closet steps down 480 volts to 120 volts for receptacle outlets.

The electricity within a home may not be exactly 120 and 240 volts. Typically, a city dweller may have 126 volts at an outlet, while a suburbanite may receive only 118 volts. Outlets at the far end of a branch circuit have lower voltages than those near the service entrance panel, but the wiring in a home should not vary by more than four volts. The minimum safe supply is 108 volts in order to avoid damage to electrical equipment.

Power Generation

Through the early twentieth century nearly all large buildings and groups of buildings supplied their own on-site or local power. On-site generators supplied electricity for elevators, ventilators, call bells, fire alarms, and lighting. All of this technology used DC electricity, which cannot be transformed to different voltages and must be generated and distributed at the voltage to be used in the building. The low voltages produced by these local DC power plants lost too much voltage to be distributed over long distances.

In 1882, Thomas Edison opened Pearl Street Station in New York City, the first centralized electrical utility, which provided DC electricity to homes and shops within one square mile. The success of the Pearl Street Station encouraged the building of other power stations all over the United States. Purchasing power from a central source was less expensive, less noisy, and took up less space than generating it on-site.

With the development and use of AC machines, electricity could be transmitted at high voltages over long distances. As a result, an extensive distribution system came into existence. High-voltage transmission reduced power losses through the wires. The high voltage was transformed down to usable voltages at the point of use. By the 1920s, larger, central power stations led to lower construction and operating costs per kilowatt. Electrical power companies bought fuel under large, long-term contracts, further reducing power costs. Some on-site generation was still used where utility power was unreliable or expensive.

In the 1960s, total energy systems that produced electricity and heat simultaneously from the same fuel source came into use for shopping centers, industrial plants, community buildings, motels, hospitals, schools, and multifamily residential projects. Because independent total energy systems had no connection to the local electrical utility, they had to run at a rate to meet the electrical demand even if this meant also producing more heat than needed. Excess heat was wasted through a cooling tower, in local ponds or rivers, or as steam.

In 1978, the Public Utilities Regulatory Policies Act (PURPA) decreed that utilities must buy on-site generated electricity sold by small, private power producers. Local total energy systems were now able to be connected to the electrical utility.

Today, fuel-fired generators are used on-site for emergency and standby power in hospitals and other critical processes. Larger, modular integrated utility systems (MIUS) link electrical energy production, heating and cooling, solid waste and sewage, and potable water, so that waste generated by one part of the system can be used as input by another. Such systems are often used with cogeneration plants that use one fuel source to produce more than one type of energy. Moderate-sized communities or large building complexes use MIUS to provide utility services at lower installation and operating costs, save natural resources, and minimize environmental impact.

POWER SOURCES

One source of electrical energy is **hydroelectric energy**. Producing electricity from moving water is clean and renewable. The huge dams required to generate huge quantities of electricity from water can displace people from their homes, devastate vast areas through flooding, and decimate fish populations that need open rivers to spawn. However, smaller waterfalls that produce energy for use near the site may be a viable alternative.

For thousands of years, **wind power** has been used to propel sailing ships, grind grain, and pump water. There is evidence that wind energy was used to propel boats along the Nile River as early as 5000 BCE and simple windmills were used in China to pump water in ancient times. Windmills that were erected as the American West was developed during the late nineteenth century pumped water for farms and ranches. Small electric wind systems were developed to generate DC by 1900, but most of these fell out of favor when rural areas became attached to the national electricity grid during the 1930s. By 1920, wind turbine generators were producing electricity in many European countries. In the 1950s in the United States, rural electrification offered electricity at rates below what could be produced locally, and the small-scale windmill became a thing of the past.

Recently, wind power has become an appealing alternative to fossil fuels, especially in countries with scarce petroleum and ample wind. Large wind farms are supplying power on a grand scale. Small residential windmill turbines are also becoming more common.

Today, wind power is growing in popularity as a sustainable resource. Its greatest problem, uneven availability, is mitigated by tying electrical energy produced by wind into the electrical-distribution grid. Large-scale wind farms use wind turbines to generate electricity profitably. Large offshore wind farms are popular in northern Europe and could be located off coastal regions in the United States, although they may be visible from very valuable seaside properties. Relatively small wind farms are becoming more feasible, and even solitary windmills are once again starting to be seen in the United States.

The term **windmill** is applied to devices that turn wind power into mechanical energy—to pump water or grind grain, for example.

Technically, the term **wind turbine** is used for equipment that produces electrical energy from wind power. Once the relatively high initial expense is incurred, the electricity is produced for free, offering a hedge against anticipated high future electrical costs. Windmills have a minimal impact on the environment and offer energy independence. The space around the wind turbines can still be used for agriculture, grazing, ranching, or most other uses. At remote sites without electrical service, it is more cost effective to install a windmill than to install and buy oil or natural gas for an engine generator set or to extend power from a distant utility.

The danger that birds will be killed by industrial wind farms seems to be limited to sites along avian flyways. Noise may be a concern, especially with large turbine blades that are close to the ground. Wind turbines are usually sited at high elevations to catch high-speed winds.

Photovoltaic Technology

Photovoltaic (PV) technology converts sunlight directly into electricity. It works any time the sun is shining, but more electricity is produced the more intense the light and the more direct the angle of the light. Unlike solar systems for heating water, PV technology does not use the sun's heat to make electricity. Instead, it produces electricity directly from electrons freed by the interaction of sunlight with certain semiconductor materials in the **PV array**.

PV electrical power systems are becoming increasingly important sources of energy. Advances in PV module materials, construction techniques, and product types have increased efficiency and lowered costs.

Site-generated PV uses DC, which is already being used in televisions, lighting, motors, and appliances for recreational vehicles. DC power is then converted to AC power and tied to the central electrical energy grid. During periods of low supply, the energy grid provides backup energy. When extra production is available on-site, the meter runs backwards, effectively selling the extra energy to the grid.

Individual PV cells are wired together to produce a PV module, the smallest PV component sold commercially. These modules range in power output from about 10 to 300 watts. Usually, individual modules are mounted onto an existing roof. Some modules can be designed directly into the roof and act as both a roofing material and an electricity generator. To connect a PV system to a utility grid, one or more PV modules are connected to an inverter that converts the modules' DC electricity to AC electricity. The AC power is compatible with the electric grid and can be used by lights, appliances, computers, televisions, and many other devices. Some systems include batteries to provide backup power in case the utility suffers a power outage.

Small commercial and industrial PV applications include lighting, traffic counters, signaling, and fence charging. Large systems provide electricity for residential, office, educational, and mobile electrical needs. Systems are not limited to sunny tropical areas. A solar electrical system in Boston, Massachusetts, will produce more than 90 percent of the energy generated by the same system in Miami, Florida. In areas with low-sun winter seasons, such as New England, these systems are frequently paired with a generator or other backup systems for extra power.

When the PV system generates more electricity than is needed at the site, excess energy can be fed directly onto electric lines for use by other electric customers. Through a **net-metering** agreement with the electric utility, PV system owners are compensated for the excess power they produce. The PV-system contractor installs an inverter that ensures that the electricity coming from the PV system is compatible with electricity coming from the power lines.

Figure 12-6 Photovoltaic cells. PV cells are made from a very pure form of silicon, an abundant element in the earth's crust that is not very difficult to mine. PV cells provide direct electrical current. When enough heat or light strikes a cell connected to a circuit, the difference in voltage causes current to flow. No voltage difference is produced in the dark, so the cell provides energy only when the sun shines. A cell connected to a battery can provide continuous power.

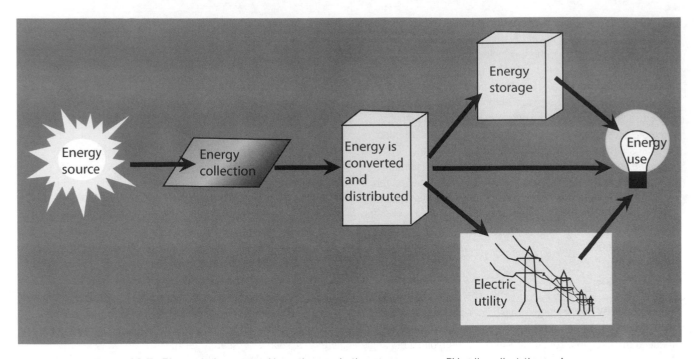

Figure 12-7 Photovoltaic system. Here, the sun is the energy source. PV cells collect the sun's energy, which is then converted from DC to AC. From there, energy is sent to storage (a battery), put immediately to work, or transferred to an electric utility and sent out over the electrical grid.

Stand-alone PV arrays:

- These are the oldest type of PV system.
- They are isolated from the utility electrical grid and designed for a specific job.
- They are used for sign lighting, motor homes, and isolated small residences.
- When a fuel-powered generator is added for a more reliable supply, the system becomes a hybrid stand-alone.
- Storage batteries store the excess from peak hours to use during cloudy days and at night.
- Some uses require a DC/AC inverter to change to AC power.
- Fluorescent lighting fixtures are available with inverter ballasts.
- Some kitchen appliances and power tools are DC-compatible appliances.

PV system arrays:

- These arrays complete connected sets of modules that are mounted and ready to deliver electricity.
- Building mounted arrays are stationary and usually consist of flat plates mounted at an angle.
- Tracking arrays follow the motion of the sun, providing more contact with the solar cells.

PV panels:

- These panels can substitute for other construction materials, providing cost savings.
- **Building integrated PV (BIPV)** elements combine PV modules into roof panels, roofing tiles, wall panels, skylights, and other materials.

- Solar roof shingles, structural metal roofing, architectural metal roofing, and window glass are now available.
- Structural metal panels are used for PV-covered parking, charging stations for electric vehicles, park shelters, and other covered outdoor spaces as well as for commercial buildings.

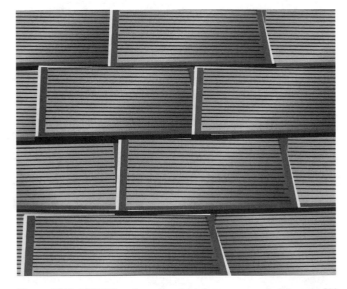

Figure 12-8 BIPV tiles. Inventors look for new ways to integrate PV cells into building construction materials. BIPV tiles are already available for use on roofs. They imitate traditional roof shingles in size and layout; some have an iridescent glow, while others try to blend in with ordinary roofing materials.

- Custom-color crystalline solar cells, including gold, violet, and green, are becoming available.
- Other architectural module designs have space between the cells and opaque backings to provide diffuse daylighting along with electric production.

As mentioned earlier, PURPA requires that electric utilities buy electrical power from small suppliers. Most states have adopted net-metering laws that require a utility to pay PV providers at the same rate at which it sells the electricity during PV-generating hours. The energy that a customer generates and uses is credited at the rate the utility would otherwise charge that customer. Only when a customer produces more energy than it uses does the utility pay at a lower rate. This means that small producers get fair credit for the energy they supply themselves and are able to sell any excess to the utility, even if at a low rate. When PV users buy from the utility, they pay at the conventional utility rate.

Net metering benefits both the customer and the utility. Some utilities have instituted PV installation programs, primarily for res-idences. The utility installs and maintains the PV system on the customer's property (usually the roof), and the customer pays a small surcharge to the utility. The result is an environmentally beneficial power supply.

National Electrical Code (NEC) *NFPA 70, Article 690 – Solar Photovoltaic Systems* sets standards for PV systems. If a PV system is connected to the electrical grid, the local utility will have additional interconnection requirements. The electric utility will also know about the option of offering net metering. Some home-owners associations require residents to gain approval for a solar installation from an architectural committee, which, in turn, may require a system plan and agreement from neighbors. In most lo-cations, building and/or electrical permits are required from city or county building departments. After the PV system is installed, it must be inspected and approved by the local permitting agency (usually the building or electrical inspector) and often by the elec-tric utility as well.

Fuel cells use electricity to extract hydrogen from water to make DC electrical energy without combustion. Almost no nitrous

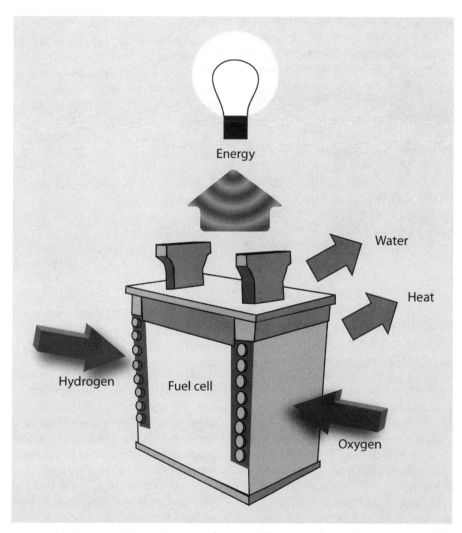

Figure 12-9 Fuel cell. Fuel cells take in hydrogen and oxygen and produce electrical energy, water, and heat. Their efficiency depends on how well the heat given off is utilized.

oxides or carbon monoxide are produced. An inverter converts the DC energy that the fuel cell produces to AC for building use. Fuel cells can provide a compact, safe, and highly efficient source of energy for electricity, heat, and water purification. A building's fuel-cell power plant adds a fuel processor to the fuel-cell stack and a power conditioner (or inverter) to convert the fuel cell's DC to AC.

Fuel cells are about 40 percent efficient for power production; when combined with a way to use that 60 percent waste heat, they climb toward a total of 90 percent efficiency. Other hydrocarbon fuels also can feed fuel cells: natural gas, propane, methane, methanol, and (with additional pretreatment) methane from landfills and anaerobic digester gas from sewage treatment plants.

Solid-waste incineration takes a large quantity of solid waste and uses it as refuse-derived fuel. Modern heat-recovery incinerators use a high-temperature process called **pyrolysis** to convert solid waste to carbon dioxide, water vapor, flue gases, and ash. Pyrolysis allows the system to meet U.S. Environmental Protection Agency (EPA) emission standards, even when using pathological wastes and plastics as refuse.

Hospitals generate up to 9.1 kilograms (20 lb.) of solid waste per patient per bed day. At this volume, incineration becomes a feasible fuel source for space heating, hot water, sterilization, kitchens, and laundries. On a smaller scale, preassembled domestic incinerators can be added to boilers as supplemental sources of heat.

Biopower is the process of using plant and other organic matter (**biomass**) to generate electricity, which can then be used for lighting, cooking, and heating. The biomass fuel comes from agricultural waste, forest products residue, and urban wood waste. Energy crops, such as willow, poplar, switchgrass, and eucalyptus, are grown specifically for this purpose; recently, a suggestion has been made to use kudzu, a ubiquitous and aggressive non-native plant that will crowd out almost any other crop. Corn is a controversial biomass fuel—a valuable food plant grown with petroleum-based fertilizers using gasoline-driven machinery on large, corporate farms.

Proper production of electricity from biomass can reduce both sulfur emissions that are linked to acid rain and the amount of waste sent to landfills.

Geothermal energy, which uses the earth itself for heat that can be tapped for use in buildings, is not directly used to produce electricity, but it is included here as a reminder that its use for space heating, domestic hot water, industrial processing, and occasionally cooling offsets substantial amounts of electrical energy. Geothermal energy is used in large building complexes or through direct wells into individual buildings.

High-pressure city steam is another energy source that is not used directly for producing electricity. In fact, this source is usually reheated exhaust steam from a local electrical generating plant distributed through underground mains and meters to urban users. By using the heat produced as a by-product of electrical generation, high-pressure city steam increases the efficiency of the generating plant's use of fuel. In itself, city steam generates no pollutants and presents almost no fire hazard, and it does not require installation of individual boilers and chimneys in buildings. In the past, city steam has been used for power for elevators, fans, and pumps. Currently, it is used for heating and absorption cooling.

ELECTRICAL SYSTEM DESIGN PROCESS

Electrical engineers start the process of designing electrical systems by estimating the total building electrical power load. Then they plan the spaces required for electrical equipment, such as transformer rooms, conduit chases, and electrical closets. The amount of energy that a building is permitted to consume is governed by building codes. A building energy-consumption analysis determines whether the building design will meet the target electrical energy budget. If not, the engineer must modify the electrical loads and reconsider the projected system criteria. The engineer will incorporate energy-conservation devices and techniques and draw up energy-use guidelines to be applied when the building is occupied. These techniques depend on the day-to-day voluntary actions of the building's occupants, which are hard to determine during the planning phase.

Once the electrical load is estimated, the engineer and the utility determine the point at which the electrical service will enter the building and the meter location. They also will decide on the type of service run, service voltage, and the building utility voltage. With the client, the engineer looks at how all areas of the building will be used and the type and rating of the client's equipment, including specific electrical ratings and service-connection requirements.

The electrical engineer gets the electrical rating of all of the equipment from the HVAC, plumbing, elevator, interior design, and kitchen consultants. This communication often takes place at conferences during which the electrical consultant makes recommendations to the other specialists regarding the comparative costs and characteristics of equipment options.

The electrical engineer is responsible for determining the location and estimated size of all required electrical equipment spaces, including switchboard rooms, emergency-equipment spaces, and electrical closets. Panel boards usually are located in closets but may be in corridor walls or other locations. The architect must reserve spaces for electrical equipment.

☑ **The electrical engineer, the architect, the interior designer, and the lighting designer design the lighting for a building. Drawings may have to separate the lighting plan from the layouts for receptacles, data, and signal and control systems. Underfloor, under-carpet, over-ceiling wiring, and overhead raceways are usually shown on their own plan. Then the engineer prepares a lighting-fixture layout. All electrical apparatus is located on a plan, including receptacles, switches, and motors. Data processing and signal apparatus are located. Telecommunications outlets, network connections, telephone outlets, speakers and microphones, television outlets, and fire and smoke detectors are shown. Control wiring and building management system panels are also indicated.**

Next, all lighting, electrical devices, and power equipment is circuited to appropriate panels. The engineer will detail the number of circuits needed to carry the electrical load; the types and sizes of electrical cables and materials and electrical equipment; and their placement throughout the building. Panel schedules are prepared that list all of the circuits for each panel, including those for emergency equipment. Panel loads are computed that show how much power is circuited through that panel. The engineer prepares riser diagrams that show how wiring is run vertically and designs the panels, switchboards, and service equipment. After computing the wiring sizes and protective equipment ratings, the engineer checks the work. Then the engineer coordinates the electrical design with the other consultants and the architectural plans and continues to make changes as needed.

Interior designers are also responsible for showing electrical-system information on their drawings. The electrical engineer uses the interior design drawings to help design the electrical system. In new buildings, the location and size of equipment rooms, including switching rooms and electrical closets, should be coordinated with the electrical engineer.

The interior designer:

- should be familiar with the location and size of the electrical panels, and with building systems that affect the type of wiring used, such as plenum mechanical systems
- must know the locations of existing or planned outlets, switches, dedicated outlets, and ground fault circuit interrupters (GFCIs) (see Fig. 12-18, page 257)

- must coordinate lighting fixtures, appliances, equipment, and emergency electrical systems with the interior design
- may need to coordinate the location of equipment rooms
- should be aware of the presence of an uninterrupted power supply or standby power supply

The interior designer does not usually need to be completely familiar with electrical code requirements, but there are several areas that may affect interior design work. Building codes set limits on the total amount of energy used by the building, including equipment and lighting. The NEC is also known as NFPA 70; it is revised every three years. The NEC sets the minimum standards for all electrical design for construction. Interior designers rarely use the NEC because it is the responsibility of the electrical engineer to design the electrical system. On smaller projects, a licensed electrical contractor will know the codes. However, since interior designers typically will specify the location of electrical outlets and fixtures, they need to know basic code requirements. For example, the NEC includes restrictions on the proximity of electrical components and plumbing.

Standards for electrical and communications systems are set by the following:

- American National Standards Institute (ANSI)
- National Electrical Manufacturers Association (NEMA)
- Underwriters Laboratories (UL)

The Americans with Disabilities Act (ADA) specifies mounting heights for outlets and fixtures in handicapped-accessible spaces.

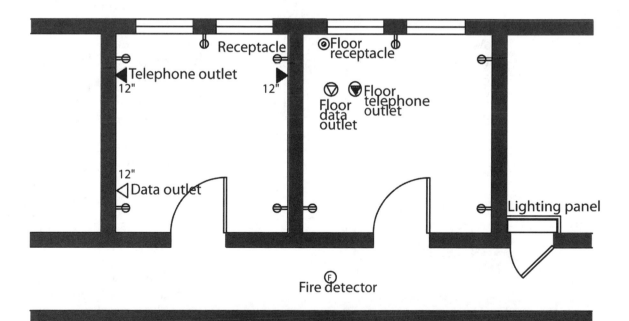

Figure 12-10 Interior design power plan. Interior design drawings often indicate all electrical outlets, switches, and lighting fixtures and their type. Large equipment and appliances along with their electrical requirements should be indicated. Communication system equipment, such as public telephones, telephone outlets and related equipment, and computer outlets are shown.

ELECTRICAL SERVICE EQUIPMENT

There are two separate electrical systems in most buildings. The **electrical power system** distributes electrical energy through the building. The **electrical signal** or **communication system**, which will be discussed later (see page 320), transmits information via telephone, cable television wires, and other separate data lines.

The electrical power service from a utility line may come into the building either overhead or underground. The length of the service run and type of terrain as well as the installation costs affect the decision of which to use. Service voltage requirements and the size and nature of the electrical load also influence the choice. Other considerations include the importance of appearance, local practices and ordinances, maintenance and reliability criteria, weather conditions, and whether some type of interbuilding distribution is required.

Installing overhead service costs from 50 to 90 percent less than underground service, but the cost of underground service is decreasing. Overhead service is preferred for carrying high voltages over long runs and in areas where the terrain is rocky. Access for maintenance is easier with overhead service. Wires on poles are more prone to problems in bad weather than underground cables.

Underground service is barely noticeable, very reliable, and has a long life. All of this comes at a higher cost. Underground service is used in dense urban areas. The service cables run in pipe conduit or raceways that allow for future replacement. Direct-burial cable may be used for residential service connections.

Main service panel
- is origin of network of wires carrying electrical current through building
- is usually located where power line enters building
- in a residence, is usually located in basement or utility room
- in larger buildings, is usually located in switchgear room near entrance of service conductors and is mounted on main switchboard
- is located as close as possible to service connection to minimize voltage drop and to save wiring

Main disconnect (or service) switch
- is on main service panel to protect firefighters
- must be in readily accessible spot near where service enters building
- must allow access

Transformer
- This is used when building voltage is different from service voltage.
- A transformer may be pole- or pad-mounted outside building or in room or vault within building.
- Step-down transformers lower voltage, while step-up transformers increase it.

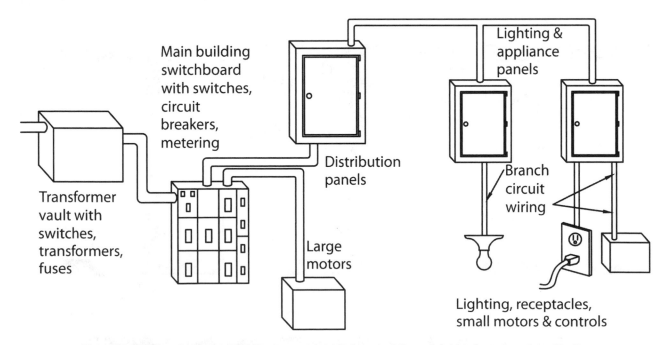

Figure 12-11 Electrical power distribution system. In a large building, electrical power from the utility line is stepped down to building use levels by transformers. Controls and protection devices are installed at the main building switchboard. From there, power goes directly to large equipment as well as to distribution panels and individual lighting and appliance panels. At this point, branch-circuit wiring carries electrical power to end uses.

- Typically, a transformer will step down incoming 1460-volt service to 480-volt service for distribution within the building; another transformer then steps down 480 volts to 120 volts for receptacle circuits. Low or secondary voltages used in buildings include 120, 208, 240, 277, and 480 volts.

Watt-hour electric meter
- measures and records quantity of electric power consumed over time
- is supplied by utility and placed ahead of main disconnect switch so that they cannot be disconnected
- is located either outside at service point or inside building
- must be available for inspection and service, even where remote readers are used

Unit substation or transformer load center
- This is an area where a step-down transformer, meters, controls, buswork, and other equipment are located.
- It may be located outdoors or indoors in ventilated basement, with access by authorized personnel only.
- Transformers produce heat that must be either ventilated or used.
- **Transformer vaults** are fire-rated enclosures that are provided in case an oil-filled transformer case ruptures. These vaults often have to be vented to the outside with flues or ducts.

In small office, retail, and other buildings, lighting panels may be mounted in a convenient area to facilitate the use of circuit breakers for **load switching**. Buildings six stories and higher use **electrical closets** for the panels and risers to connect floors. Larger buildings use strategically located electrical closets to house all electrical-supply equipment.

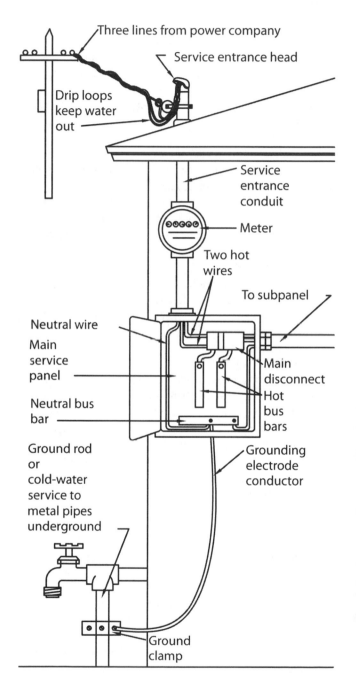

Figure 12-12 Electrical service equipment. Service conductors are the wires extending from the main power line or transformer to the building's service equipment. A grounding rod or electrode is firmly embedded in the earth to establish a ground connection outside the building. Other equipment includes service panels, switches, and meters.

Figure 12-13 Watt/hour meter. In single-occupancy buildings or in buildings where the landlord pays for electrical service, there is one meter. For multiple-tenant buildings, banks of meters are installed so that each unit is metered separately. A single meter is not allowed in new multiple-dwelling constructions by federal law because tenants tend to waste energy when they do not have to pay for it directly.

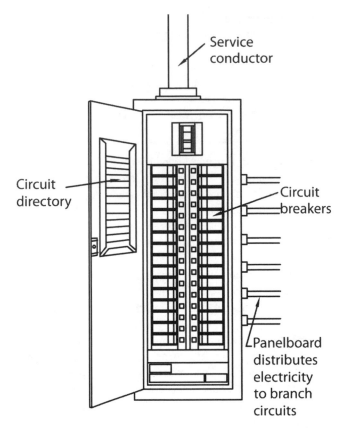

Figure 12-14 Electrical panel. In residences, the service equipment and the building's panel board are combined in one unit. The panelboard is often located in the garage, a utility room, or the basement, as close to major electrical loads as feasible. Sometimes, an additional subpanel is added near the kitchen and laundry. In apartments, the electrical panel may be located in the kitchen or in an immediately adjacent corridor, where they are used as the code-required means for disconnecting most fixed appliances. In small commercial buildings, they may be recessed into corridor walls.

A **switchboard** is the main electrical panel that distributes the electricity from the utility service connection to the rest of a building. It also distributes bulk power into smaller packages and provides protection for that process. Low-voltage switchboards with large circuit breakers and all high-voltage (more than 600 volts) equipment are referred to as switchgear. In commercial, industrial, and public buildings, switchgear is usually located in basements in a separate, well-ventilated electrical switchgear room.

Electrical closets are vertically stacked together to prevent blocking horizontal conduits. They should not have other utilities, such as piping or ducts, running through them either horizontally or vertically. Inside is space for current and expansion panels, switches, transformers, telephone cabinets, and communications equipment. Floor slots or sleeves allow conduit and bus risers to pass through from other floors. Electrical closets must have space, lighting, and ventilation for an electrician to work comfortably and safely on installations and repairs. Electrical closets and cabinets must be fire-rated because they are common places for fires to

start. In addition, they should not be located next to stairwells or other primary means of egress. The electrical engineer is responsible for locating electrical closets, and their location will have implications for the interior designer's space plan.

Energy Conservation and Demand Control

Energy conservation affects the work of the electrical engineer, the architect, the interior designer, and the building's owner and occupants. Legislation mandates energy-use limitations, including lighting controls in certain nonresidential buildings. The trend toward stricter regulations continues.

Conservation can start with the selection of high-efficiency motors, transformers, and other equipment. Electrical load control equipment is often necessary to meet code requirements for energy budgets. The electrical design should accommodate potential expansion by including additional equipment rather than by oversizing the original equipment.

A number of ways to conserve electrical energy have already been discussed. In residential buildings with multiple tenants, **individual user metering** makes the tenant financially responsible for energy use. The exceptions are hotels, dormitories, and transient residences. Electrical heating elements should be avoided because they use a high-grade resource for a low-grade task. When lighting design is discussed later (see page 295), we will examine how remote-control switching for blocks of lighting conserves energy.

Energy may leak from home electronics and small household appliances that require DC, such as televisions, videocassette recorders (VCRs), cordless telephones, telephone answering machines, portable tools, and rechargeable vacuum cleaners. These implements draw energy when in use as well as when the power is apparently off. The average U.S. household leaks 50 watts of electricity continuously, or around 440 kilowatt-hours per year. This adds up to more than three billion dollars in electricity in the United States per year. Televisions, VCRs, and cable boxes account for half of this amount, for instant-on, remote control, channel memory, and light-emitting diode (LED) clocks. Digital satellite systems also leak an average of 13 watts when not in use. DC transformers, such as those on electric toothbrushes, draw 2 to 6 watts of electrical power even when not in use or when the appliance is fully charged. To encourage clients to save energy, advise them to unplug equipment that is not in use and to look for Energy Star® appliances, which leak less energy.

Electrical-load control, also referred to as **demand control**, switches or modulates the electric load in response to a central signal. By limiting the maximum amount of energy used at peak times and the overall total amount of electricity needed, utilities avoid having to construct new power plants.

The oldest and simplest type of utility sponsored demand control is a utility-rate schedule that varies with the time of day, offering lower rates for off-peak hours. The utility installs a free, time-controlled circuit switch for use with water heaters, well pumps, battery chargers, and so forth, where time delay is possible. The equipment is energized only during hours of low demand, which are usually midafternoon and after midnight.

Industrial and commercial installations may adopt user-supplied demand control for a reduction of 15 to 20 percent in electric bills. These systems disconnect and reconnect electrical loads to level off demand peaks. These interruptions can be very short and almost unnoticeable. The systems control HVAC loads, lighting loads, and process loads in small commercial, institutional, and industrial buildings. Without a person to determine the safety of shutting off other loads, essential lighting, elevators, communication equipment, computers, and process-control and emergency equipment are not included in automatic systems. Manual systems also exist that trigger alarms indicating that it is time to connect or disconnect a load.

Intelligent panelboards are compact, centralized, programmable microprocessors that provide electrical load control and switching functions directly within the panelboard, thereby eliminating external devices and the associated wiring. The intelligent panelboard can also accept signal data from individual remote or network sources and provide status reports, alarm signals, operational logs, and local bypass and override functions. The system simplifies and improves facility operations and reduces maintenance costs and electric bills.

Other options for energy conservation include systems that conform to an ideal energy use curve automatically. Forecasting systems are the most sophisticated, most expensive, and most effective energy-control systems for large structures with complex needs. They are part of a computerized central control facility.

ELECTRICAL CIRCUIT DESIGN

Once a building is connected to a community's electrical grid, the next steps are to locate the places the electricity should be available and to provide a way to turn it on and off safely. During the design of a building, the electrical engineer or electrical contractor designs the type of circuiting, wire sizes, and so forth.

☑ **Interior designers should be familiar with the basic principles of power supply and distribution in order to be able to coordinate interior design issues with the rest of the design team.**

Because the location of outlets and switches is dependent on the layout of furniture and a room's intended use, they are often shown on interior design drawings. Power requirements and locations for special built-in equipment are also usually indicated on such drawings. The interior designer will want to approve the appearance of cover plates and other visible electrical devices.

The information that the interior designer supplies is integrated into the electrical engineer's drawings. The electrical engineer will take cost and safety into consideration in the design of the electrical system. In addition to the construction cost of the system, the electrical engineer must consider the cost of both materials over the life of the building and energy to run the system.

As discussed earlier, electricity must have a complete path or circuit from its source, through a device, and back to the source. An electrical circuit is a loop. Interrupting the circuit, as with a switch, stops the flow around the loop. When a lamp or appliance is turned on, AC electricity flows both ways in the loop, changing direction 60 times a second (60 cycles, or 60 Hz).

Lines from the power company run either overhead or underground to carry electricity from a transformer through the meter and into the service entrance panel. In small buildings, service is usually provided at 230 or 240 volts. Most homes have three-wire service, with two hot conductors each supplying 115 or 120 volts, and one neutral conductor. The actual pressure (voltage) supplied can vary between 115 and 125 volts within a given day.

The wires that carry the electrical service must be protected from damage within the structure of the building. In wood residential construction, a tough, protective plastic sheath houses all three wires. In heavier construction, the wires are run in steel or plastic pipes called **conduits**. Conduits provide better protection, and new wires can be installed by pulling them through existing conduits, which cannot be done with plastic-sheathed cable.

Electrical power distribution systems are designed to provide the amount of energy required at the location desired and to do so safely. Even the smallest part of the system is connected to a powerful utility network, so the potential for physical damage, injury, and fire are always present. The solution is to isolate electrical conductors from the structure of the building, with the exception of specific points, such as wall receptacles, where contact is wanted. Insulating conductors and putting them in protective raceways accomplish this.

The NEC sets minimum standards for electrical design for construction. Local inspection authorities visit a site at least two times during construction to determine whether the design, material, and installation techniques meet national and local code requirements. The first visit is after the raceways have been installed (called **roughing-in**) and before the wiring and closing-in of the walls. A second visit is made after the entire job is complete.

☑ **The quality of the installation is the contractor's responsibility. The interior designer must be wary of equipment substitutions by the contractor, whose bid was submitted on the basis of the plans and specifications. The contractor should be required to supply the equipment that is specified.**

Grounding

In order to receive a shock, a person simultaneously must touch a **hot wire** (or a metal object in contact with a hot wire) and must be grounded. An electrical circuit has three wires. The hot wire, which is covered by black insulation (or any other color but white, green, or gray), runs side by side with the neutral and ground wires. The **neutral wire** is covered with white or gray insulation. The **ground wire** is either bare copper or is covered with green insulation. Homes built before 1960 often do not have a ground wire.

The hot wire carries the electrical power generated by the local utility. It is always poised and waiting to deliver its charge from inside an outlet or behind a switch, but current will not flow and release its power until it has a way to get back to its source,

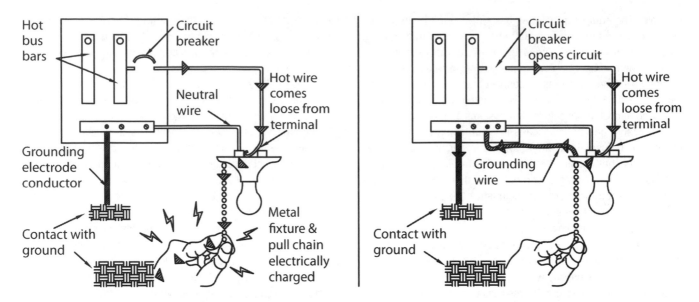

Figure 12-15 Grounding. Electrical circuits are grounded in the event that a faulty circuit allows electricity to travel an unintended route rather than returning to its source. The grounding literally carries electricity into the ground rather than letting it travel other undesirable routes.

thereby closing the circuit loop. The neutral wire closes the loop. When a person throws a switch to turn on an electric lightbulb, he or she is essentially connecting the hot and neutral wires and creating a circuit for electricity to follow.

The hot wire immediately senses this path and releases its energy. If nothing impeded the current flow, most of that energy would go unused. A lightbulb or other electrical device standing in the path between the hot and the neutral wire uses up almost all of the energy available in the hot wire, leaving little for the neutral wire to carry back to the source. This is why a person gets a shock from touching the hot wire but not the neutral one, even when current is flowing.

When a person gets a shock from a hot wire, the body acts like a neutral wire and completes the circuit to the damp ground below. This is because the earth itself is also an excellent path that leads back to the power source and closes the loop. In fact, the electrical system uses the earth as an alternate path for safety purposes. The neutral wire is connected to the ground at the main service panel. From there, a wire goes either to a copper-coated steel rod driven deep into the earth next to the building or to a metal water pipe that enters underground in old buildings. The power source is also grounded through a wire from the transformer on the utility pole to the earth. All building wiring is grounded. If a person is not in contact with the damp ground either by touching it directly or through wires, metal pipes, or damp concrete in contact with the soil, there will be no shock.

The human body is not as good an electrical path as a wire even though it is about 90 percent water, which can be a good conductor. Skin thickness, muscle, and other body characteristics make a person a poor path for electrical current. Even so, the body is very vulnerable to electrical shocks. Shocks kill by stopping the heart. A steadily beating heart relies on tiny electrochemical nerve pulses that carry a current in the range of .001 amps. Even a charge as small as .006 amps can shatter the heart's microcircuitry and disrupt its beating rhythm. Often, the nerves cannot stabilize quickly enough to restore the circuitry and save a person's life.

An electric drill draws about three amps, and an electric mixer draws about one amp, much more than the amount it takes for a fatal disruption of the heartbeat. Fortunately, it takes a fairly high voltage to push a significant amount of current through people. In general, a person will not receive a shock from circuits under 24 volts. Electric toys fall into this range, as do doorbells, thermostats, telephones, security systems, cable television, and low-voltage lighting. Even within this range, however, a shock can disrupt the heartbeat of a person with a pacemaker.

The best defense against a shock when handling electrical devices or appliances is to make sure that your body is not grounded. Remember, current will go through you only when you are a path to the ground. People should not work with electricity while standing on damp ground or damp concrete or on a metal ladder that is resting on damp materials. Using electric tools and other electrical devices around the plumbing system can be dangerous, too. All of these connect a person with the ground.

The NEC has introduced three features that make electrical systems safer: the equipment ground, the GFCI, and polarized plugs.

An **equipment-grounding conductor** is a third wire that does not ordinarily carry current. It is energized only momentarily when there is a fault between an ungrounded conductor and metal electrical equipment that could cause a shock. The equipment-grounding conductor is either a bare wire or has green insulation. Grounded equipment has a plug with a third prong that goes into the half-round hole in an outlet.

Faulty equipment grounds are most likely to occur when vibration and other types of movement wear out a wire's insulation or break the wire itself. Old refrigerators and washing machines, which vibrate a great deal, are typical culprits, as are lamps whose insulated cords harden as they age but still receive heavy use. When such leaks occur, a hot wire can be exposed or an entire metal appliance can be electrically charged, and a person risks a shock every time it is touched. Such a fault could connect the metal case of the appliance with the electrical power circuit. To touch the now-electrified metal case and a ground, such as a water pipe, will result in a very nasty 120-volt shock. If the person's hands are wet when making contact, the resulting shock could be fatal. Consequently, appliance manufacturers recommend that appliance cases be grounded to a cold-water pipe and supplied with three-wire plugs. Two of the three wires connect to the appliance, and the third connects to the metal case.

The ground wire runs alongside the hot and neutral wires and is attached to the metal parts of electrical boxes, outlets, tools, and appliances that could carry an electrical charge should a leak occur. The ground wire siphons off those leaks by providing a good path back to the main service panel, exactly like the neutral wire. In effect, any leak that is picked up by the ground wire will most likely blow a fuse or trip a breaker and shut down the circuit, signaling that there is a serious problem somewhere in the system.

To accept the three-prong plugs that accommodate the ground wire as well as to provide a safe ground path, the NEC requires that all receptacles be the grounding type and that all wiring systems provide a ground path separate and distinct from the neutral conductor. Electrical codes require that each 120-volt circuit have a system of grounding. This prevents shocks from contacts where electricity and conductive materials come together, including such parts of the electrical system as metal switches, junction and outlet boxes, and metal faceplates.

Where wiring travels through the building inside armored cable, metal conduit, or flexible metal conduit, the conductive metal enclosure forms the grounding system. When a metal enclosure is not used, a separate grounding wire must run with the circuit wires. Nonmetallic or flexible metallic wiring (e.g., Romex or BX) is required to have a separate grounding conductor. Nonmetallic cable already has a bare grounding wire within it. Insulated grounding conductors must have a green covering. These types of wiring will be discussed later (see page 264).

Replacing old two-slot outlets with the new standard three-slot, grounded outlets that accept all types of household plugs and conveniently allow a three-prong cord to be plugged in anywhere seems like a good solution. However, since old two-wire systems do not have an equipment ground, the ground prong on the plug does not actually go to ground. Installing a proper ground wire for these outlets is time-consuming and costly, but if is not done, the illusion of a ground wire will have been created—but it will not be safe.

Another way around the problem is the three-prong/two-prong adapter, more popularly known as a cheater plug. The NEC accepts this device provided that the screw that attaches the cover plate is inserted through the equipment ground tab. This screw connects to the metal yoke, which, in turn, connects to the metal electrical box. However, unless the metal electrical box has been grounded to the earth, this creates only the impression of a safe, grounded system. This false sense of security puts people one step closer to receiving a dangerous or even fatal shock.

Electrical Fire Risks

The NEC of the National Fire Protection Association (NFPA) defines fundamental safety measures that must be followed in the selection, construction, and installation of all electrical equipment. All inspectors, electrical designers, engineers, contractors, and operating personnel use the NEC. The NEC is incorporated into the Occupational Safety and Health Act (OSH Act) and has the force of law.

UL establishes standards and tests and inspects electrical equipment and publishes lists of inspected and approved electrical equipment. Many local codes state that only electrical materials bearing the UL label of approval are acceptable.

An electrical permit is required when doing electrical work. It ensures that the work is reviewed with a local building inspector in light of local codes. The inspector will check the work to make sure it is done right.

Circuit Protection

Because the amperage available from the utility grid is almost unlimited, a 120-volt household system is powerful and dangerous. The electrical current could easily melt all of the wiring in a home. Special devices that limit current are located in the main service panel. When a home owner opens the door of the electrical panel, he will find either fuses or circuit breakers (and sometimes both), each rated to withstand a certain amount of current, usually 15 amps. If the current exceeds the listed amount, the fuse will burn out (blow) or the breaker will trip, shutting off the current and protecting the wiring system from an overload. This is a signal that too much power is attempting to be drawn through the wires.

Overloaded and short-circuited currents can result in overheating and fires. Circuit protection devices protect insulation, wiring, switches, and other equipment from these dangers by providing an automatic way to open the circuit and break the flow of electricity.

FUSES AND CIRCUIT BREAKERS

If too much current flows in a wire, it can get hot enough to set fire to surrounding material. **Fuses** and **circuit breakers** protect against this possibility by cutting off power to any circuit that is drawing excessive power. They provide an automatic means for opening a circuit and stopping the flow of electricity.

During maintenance work, the circuit should be manually shut off. This will shut off the current to the circuit if more current starts flowing than the wire can carry without overheating and causing a fire. This may occur when too many appliances are plugged in at once or when a short circuit occurs. Circuit breakers are easily installed as needed for various circuits in the building.

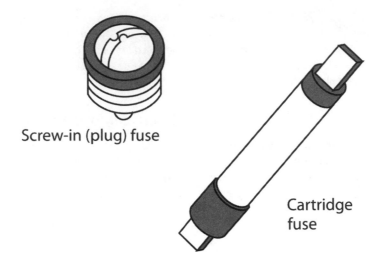

Figure 12-16 Fuses. The key element in a fuse is a strip of metal with a low melting point. When too much current flows, the strip melts, or blows, thereby interrupting power in the circuit. When the fusible strip of metal is installed in an insulated fiber tube, it is called a cartridge fuse. When encased in a porcelain cup, it is called a plug fuse.

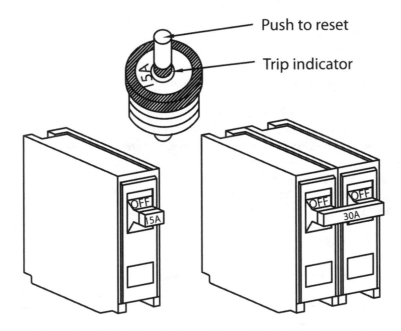

Figure 12-17 Circuit breaker. A circuit breaker is an electromechanical device that performs the same protective function as a fuse. It acts like a switch to protect and disconnect a circuit. A strip made of two different metals in the circuit breaker becomes a link in the circuit. Heat from an excessive current bends the metal strip because the two metals expand at different rates. This trips a release that breaks the circuit. Commercial and industrial applications use solid-state electronic tripping control units that provide adjustable overload, short-circuit, and ground-fault protection. Circuit breakers can be reset after each use.

A demand for too much power, called an **overcurrent**, occurs when too many devices are connected to a circuit or when a failed device or loose wire causes a short circuit. Overloading the circuit with too many appliances or lighting fixtures is the most common cause of fuses blowing repeatedly or circuit breakers tripping again and again. An overcurrent also may occur when high-wattage fixtures and appliance motors are turned on because they momentarily need much more electricity to start than they draw during operation. If a circuit is near capacity, a startup overcurrent can blow a fuse even though there is no real danger to the system.

Circuit breakers are built to withstand such momentary surges, but standard fuses are not. When a circuit often blows a fuse when an appliance such as a refrigerator or room air conditioner is turned on, a time-delay or slow-blow fuse can help cope with brief surge demands. Both plug and cartridge fuses are available in slow-blow designs that safely allow temporary overloads. Whether a fuse or a circuit breaker is the better choice depends on the application and on other technical considerations.

GROUND FAULT CIRCUIT INTERRUPTERS

The NEC recognizes a **ground fault circuit interrupter** (**GFCI** or sometimes **GFI**) as a way to protect against shocks when a building's wiring is not grounded. GFCIs are actually designed for another primary use. Water and electricity do not mix. Dampness in the soil or in concrete that rests in the soil makes both surfaces good electrical conductors and good grounds. Metal faucets and drains are also excellent grounds because the water-supply lines and sewers with which they connect are usually underground. Such plug-in devices as hair dryers, power tools, and coffee makers are commonly use around sinks, in the basement, or out in the garage and are part of the problem. Shutting off a faucet with one hand while holding a faulty hair dryer with the other could be fatal.

Unfortunately, the fuses or circuit breakers in the main service panel will not protect a person from a lethal shock in such circumstances. Fuses and circuit breakers protect the wires in a house

from overheating, melting the insulation, and causing a fire. They do not protect occupants against faults in the electrical ground.

The role of the GFCI is to protect people from a potentially dangerous shock. GFCI devices can be part of a circuit breaker or installed as a separate outlet.

When a person leaves a hair dryer with a frayed cord in a little spilled water that is in contact with the sink's metal faucet, he or she may receive a shock. A person could accidentally touch an exposed hot wire in the frayed cord while at the same time turning off the water faucet with the other hand. Even though the dryer is turned off, an electric current immediately flows from the cord, through the person's body, through the plumbing system, and eventually to ground. This is called a **ground fault** (current leak). It will not cause the circuit breakers or fuses in the main service panel to break the circuit, and the current will continue to flow through the body.

A GFCI instantaneously senses misdirected electrical current and reacts within one-fortieth of a second to shut off the circuit before a lethal dose of electricity escapes. When it senses a ground fault, the GCFI interrupts the circuit and switches it off.

Another function of GFCIs is to detect small ground faults and to disconnect the power to the circuit or appliance. The current required to trip a circuit breaker is high, so small leaks of current can continue unnoticed until the danger of shock or fire is imminent.

GFCIs permit the easy identification of ground faults. They are required along with circuit breakers in circuits where there is an increased hazard of accidental electrical shock, such as near bathroom sinks. If the GFCI senses any leakage of current from the circuit, it will disconnect the circuit instantly and completely. The GFCI does this by precisely comparing the current flowing in the hot and neutral legs of the circuit. When the amount of current is different, some current is leaking out of the circuit.

NEC requirements for GFCI protection for readily accessible outlets are regularly updated. Requirements in 2005 included

- bathrooms, kitchens, unfinished basements, wet bars, laundry rooms, utility rooms
- swimming pools, spas, hot tubs, hydromassage tubs, boathouses
- exterior outlets

To ensure that GFCIs are working, manufacturers added the "test" and "reset" buttons that are seen on them. Pushing the test button creates a small electrical fault, which the GFCI should sense and immediately react to by shutting off the circuit. The reset button restores the circuit. Repeated action by the GFCI to protect a leaking circuit will eventually wear out the GFCI. GFCIs should be tested every week and replaced immediately if they are not working properly.

Branch Circuits

Branch circuits carry the electrical power throughout the building to the places where it will be used. After passing through the main service disconnect, each hot conductor (wire) connects to

Figure 12-18 Ground fault circuit interrupter. GFCIs detect current leaks in faulty circuits and shut them off. GFCIs wear out from use and need to be tested regularly and replaced as necessary.

one of two hot bus bars in the distribution center. **Bus bars** are metal bars that accept the amount of current permitted by the main fuses or circuit breakers and allow the circuit to be divided into smaller units for branch circuits. Each branch circuit attaches to one or both hot bus bars by means of fuses or circuit breakers.

Each 120-volt branch circuit has one hot and one neutral conductor. The hot conductor originates at the branch circuit overcurrent protective device (fuse or circuit breaker) connected to one of the hot bus bars. A 240-volt circuit originates at the branch circuit overcurrent protective device connected to both hot bus bars.

All of the neutral conductors start at the neutral bus bar in the distribution center. All the neutral conductors are in direct electrical contact with the earth through a grounding conductor at the neutral bus bar of the service entrance panel. An overcurrent protective device never interrupts the neutral conductors, so the ground is maintained at all times. In effect, each branch circuit takes off from an overcurrent protective device and returns to the neutral bus bar.

In order to decide how many branch circuits to specify and where they should run, the electrical system designer takes into account a variety of loads:

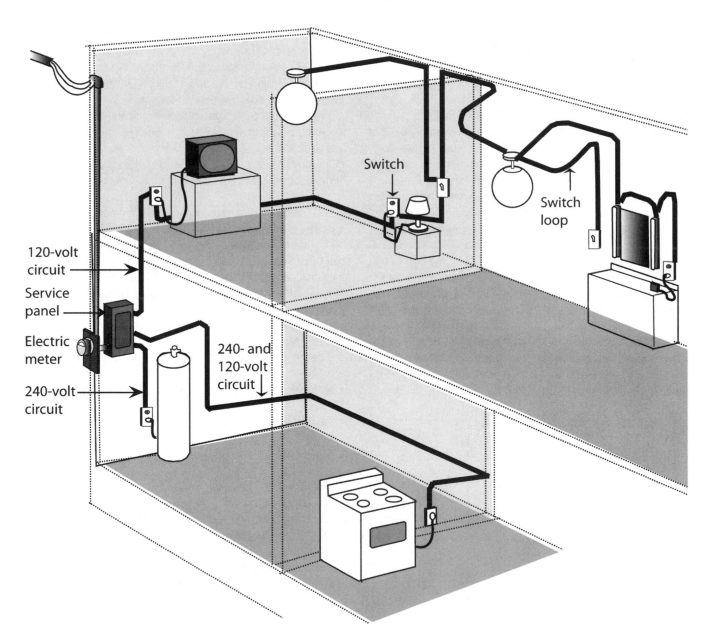

Figure 12-19 Branch circuits. Electrical engineers lay out branch circuits, but they may need specific information about lighting fixtures, appliances, and other equipment from the interior designer to do so. The client may have preferences about which equipment shares a given branch circuit.

- lighting: often the greatest load
- data-processing equipment, convenience outlets, desktop computers and their peripherals, plug-in heaters, water fountains, and other miscellaneous electrical power users
- HVAC and plumbing equipment, which use electrical energy for motors and switches
- elevators, escalators, materials-handling equipment, dumbwaiters, trash and linen transportation systems
- kitchen equipment in restaurants, most hospitals, and some office, education-related, and religion-affiliated buildings
- special loads, such as laboratory equipment, shop loads, display areas, display windows, floodlighting, canopy heaters, and industrial processes

Once the electrical-power requirements of various areas of the building are determined, the electrical engineer lays out wiring circuits to distribute power to points of use. Each circuit is sized according to the amount of load it must carry, with about 20 percent of its capacity reserved for flexibility, expansion, and safety. To avoid excessive drops in voltage, branch circuits should be less than 30 meters (100 ft.) long.

The electrical engineer will specify general-purpose circuits to supply current to a number of outlets for lighting and appliances. Manufacturers specify load requirements for lighting fixtures and electrically powered appliances and equipment, and the interior designer is often responsible for giving these specifications to the engineer. The design load for a general-purpose circuit depends on the number of receptacles that will be served by the circuit and on how the receptacles will be used.

Branch circuits with multiple general purpose 20-amp outlets or multiple appliance outlets have a maximum 50-amp capacity. Single-type outlets for specific pieces of equipment may be 200 to 300 amps depending on the equipment needs. Lighting, convenience receptacles, and appliances should each be grouped on separate circuits. Audio equipment may need to be on the same ground as the room it is serving to prevent interference problems. Similarly, dimmers may need to be shielded to protect sensitive electronic equipment.

Circuits are arranged so that each space has parts of different circuits in it. If receptacles within a space are located on more than one circuit, the loss of one receptacle will not eliminate all power to the space.

The layout of the branch circuits, feeders, and panels is designed for flexibility in accommodating all probable patterns, arrangements, and locations of electrical loads. Laboratories, research facilities, and small, education-related buildings require much more flexibility than residential, office, and fixed-purpose industrial installations. With the rapid changes in computers and other electronic equipment in home offices and small businesses, flexibility and access should be built into most electrical designs. It can be difficult to anticipate future uses and requirements, but overly specific design wastes money and resources, both during initial installation and in operation.

In addition to being flexible, the building's electrical service must be reliable. The electrical service works together with the building's distribution system. The quality of the electrical utility's service is a key element in determining reliability, and the quality of the building's wiring system is the other. Very reliable and expensive electrical service has no real value when the power cannot be reliably distributed to where it will be used. Because a system is only as reliable as its weakest element, redundant equipment is sometimes provided at anticipated weak points in the system. For especially critical loads within the system, as in health-care facilities, the electrical system designer designates reliable power paths or provides individual standby power packages.

In addition to ensuring that the electrical design is compliant with applicable codes, the system designer must prevent electrical safety hazards in the event of misuse, abuse, or failure of equipment. Large equipment may obstruct access spaces, passages, closets, and walls. Doors to rooms with electrical equipment should open out so that a worker cannot fall against a door and prevent rescue in an emergency. In some buildings, lightning protection is also a safety issue.

Economic factors influence the selection of equipment and materials for electrical systems. Equipment must function adequately and have a satisfactory appearance while minimizing costs. When there are many competing brands and types of equipment with similar qualities, cost is the deciding factor. The initial purchase and installation cost is only one consideration. Initial low-cost equipment may result in higher energy costs, higher maintenance costs, and a shorter useful life. The life-cycle equipment costs over the life of the structure may make a more expensive purchase a better choice in the long run.

Typically, buildings have energy budgets, such as a limited number of BTUs per square foot per year. Some codes also require energy-use calculations for heating and cooling as well as lighting equipment.

In general, wiring and conduits are small and take up relatively little space in a building. Panels, motor-control centers, busducts, distribution centers, switchboards, transformers, and other equipment are large, bulky, noisy, and highly sensitive to tampering and vandalism. Spaces for electrical equipment must be easy to maintain and well ventilated. They should be centrally located to limit the length of runs and should allow room for expansion. Spaces should limit access to authorized personnel only and should be designed to contain noise.

Electrical Design for Residences

Residential electrical requirements are established by NFPA 70A: *National Electrical Code® Requirements for One- and Two-Family Dwellings* (2005), which sets the distances for electrical outlets and mandates the use of GFCIs in wet locations. Electrical outlets are not permitted directly above baseboard heating units in new buildings. Ranges, ovens, open-top gas-broiler units, clothes dryers, and water heaters have their own specific code requirements or standards.

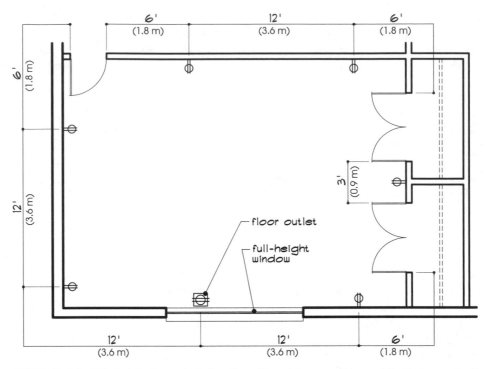

Figure 12-20 Residential electrical receptacle locations. No point on a wall is permitted to be greater than 1.8 meters (6 ft.) from a 20-amp grounding-type convenience receptacle. Any wall that is 61 centimeters (2 ft.) or more long, including walls broken by fireplaces, must have a receptacle. A receptacle must be installed within 1.8 meters (6 ft.) of any door or opening, including arches but not including windows. Receptacles should not be combined with switches into a single outlet unless convenience of use dictates that the receptacle should be mounted as high as a switch. In rooms without overhead lights, a switch control should be provided for one-half of a receptacle intended for a lamp in an appropriate place.

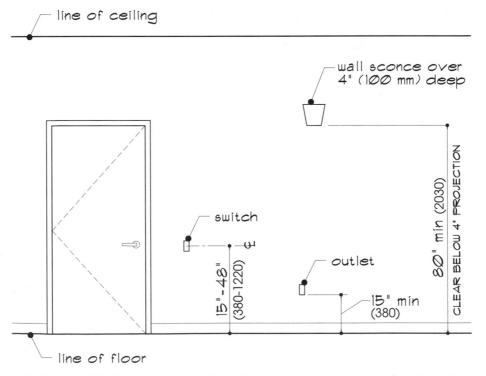

Figure 12-21 Accessible electrical device locations. Accessible design requirements include maximum and minimum heights for electrical switches and outlets. Projecting objects, such as wall sconces, have clearance requirements.

Electrical codes require the following:

- Every room, hallway, stairway, attached garage, and outdoor entrance must have a minimum of one lighting outlet controlled by a wall switch.
- A single wall switch in rooms other than the kitchen and bathroom can control one or more receptacles for plugging in lamps.
- Actual lighting outlets for ceiling- or wall-mounted lights are required for kitchens and bathrooms.
- One lighting outlet of any type is required in each utility room, attic, basement, or underfloor space that is used for storage or contains equipment that may require service.

The number of branch circuits required for a residence, including an allowance for expansion, is estimated by allotting one 15-amp circuit per 37 to 45 square meters (400–480 sq ft.) or one 20-amp circuit per 49 to 60 square meters (530–640 sq ft.) plus an allowance for expansion, with more provided as needed.

Code requirements are geared to prevent people from running an excess of appliance cords off an extension cord plugged into a single outlet. Too much power coming through a single extension cord can overheat the cord and cause a fire.

NEC requirements for residences include the following:

Kitchens:
- There must be a minimum of two 20-amp appliance branch circuits exclusively for receptacle outlets for small appliances in the kitchen, pantry, breakfast and/or dining room, and similar areas; clock outlets are allowed on these circuits.

- All kitchen outlets intended to serve countertop areas must be fed from at least two of these circuits, so that all countertop outlets are not lost if one circuit fails.
- No point on the wall behind the countertop can be more than 61 centimeters (2 ft.) from an outlet, and all countertop convenience receptacles must be GFCI types.
- Every counter space greater than 30 centimeters (12 in.) long should have a receptacle.
- With a maximum of four receptacle outlets per 20-amp circuit and an ever-increasing variety of small electrical appliances, people usually need more than two appliance circuits in the kitchen.
- Dishwashers, microwaves, refrigerators, and garbage disposals require their own separate 20-amp circuits. An electric range or oven requires an individual 50-amp, 120/240-volt major-appliance circuit.
- Gas appliances require their own separate fuel lines.
- Receptacles behind such stationary appliances as refrigerators do not count toward the 3.66-meter (12-ft.) spacing requirement.
- A readily accessible means for disconnecting electric ranges, cooktops, and ovens within sight of these appliances, such as a small kitchen panel recessed into the kitchen wall, is a good idea.

Bathrooms:
- Electrical switches and convenience outlets should be located wherever needed but away from water and wet areas.
- Such switches and outlets must not be accessible from the tub or shower.
- All bathroom outlets should be GFCI types.

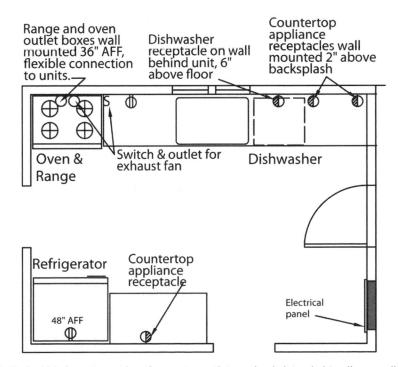

Figure 12-22 Typical kitchen power plan. Countertop outlet spacing is intended to allow small appliances to be plugged in with short cords and to discourage the use of extension cords.

- A minimum of one 20-amp wall-mounted GFCI receptacle should be supplied adjacent to the bathroom lavatory, fed from a 20-amp circuit that feeds only these receptacles.
- The receptacle near the lavatory should not be connected to the bathroom lighting, exhaust fan, heaters, or other outlets.

Bedrooms:

- A house without central air conditioning needs one additional circuit, similar to an appliance circuit, for use with a window air conditioner.
- Two duplex outlets should be located on each side of the bed, for clocks, radios, lamps, and electric blankets.
- For closets, switch controls are preferable to pull chains, which are a nuisance but considerably less expensive.

Home offices:

- Each study and workroom or large master bedroom should be equipped electrically to double as an office.
- At a minimum, six duplex 15-amp or 20-amp receptacles should be supplied, on a minimum of two different circuits, one of which serves no other outlets, and all of which have adequate surge protection.
- An additional separate, insulated, and isolated ground wire, connected only at the service entrance, should run to boxes containing two of these receptacles, where it should be terminated, clearly marked, and labeled. This will allow special grounding receptacles if the normal receptacles have too much electrical noise for computer use.
- Two telephone jacks should be installed in recessed boxes, with an empty 19-millimeter (¾-in.) conduit from the telephone entry service point to an empty 100-millimeter (4-in.) square box. The incoming telephone service lines need a surge suppressor.

Laundry rooms:

- A minimum of one 20-amp appliance circuit should be installed exclusively for laundry outlets.
- An individual 30-amp, 120/240-volt major-appliance circuit, separate from the laundry circuit and rated for an electric clothes dryer, must be supplied, along with a heavy-duty (HD) receptacle—unless it is certain that a gas dryer will be used.

Areas that are often used for workshop-type activities:

- These areas should have receptacles in appliance-type circuits, with a maximum of four receptacles per circuit.
- Basements are required to have a minimum of one receptacle.
- Receptacles in garages, sheds, crawl spaces, below-grade finished or unfinished basements, or outdoors must be GFCI types.
- GFCI-protected and weatherproofed receptacles must be located on the front and rear of the house, with a switch controlling them inside the house.

Electrical Design for Commercial Spaces

The electrical code establishes requirements for convenience receptacles in commercial spaces. The code seeks to ensure that there are enough outlets to prevent a spaghetti-like tangle of extension cords while respecting the total energy use in the space.

Requirements for other commercial spaces include the following:

Retail stores:

- There must be one convenience outlet per 28 square meters (300 sq ft.) for lamps, show windows, and demonstration appliances.
- The type of store and anticipated uses determine locations and quantities.

School classrooms:

- Classrooms require 20-amp outlets wired two per circuit at the front and back of each classroom for opaque, slide, and video projectors.
- Side walls also need similar outlets, wired six to eight per circuit.
- Computer areas in schools need to be laid out in detail, with two-section surface-mounted or recessed raceways on the wall behind a row of computers, and two duplex 20-amp receptacles at each computer station wired on alternate circuits.

TABLE 12-1. OFFICE CONVENIENCE OUTLET REQUIREMENTS

Office Size	Convenience receptacles per square meter (sq ft.) by wall length or meters (linear ft.)	Comments
Offices less than 37 square meters (400 sq ft.)	One per 3.7 square meters (40 sq ft.) or one per 3 square meters (10 linear ft.) of wall	Whichever is greater
Larger offices	10 outlets for the initial 37 square meters	Maximum of six per 20-amp branch circuit
	One outlet per 9.3 to 11.6 square meters (100–125 sq ft.) of additional space	
Each computer terminal	One 20-amp duplex receptacle	On adjacent wall, power pole, or floor near each desk
Office corridors	One 20-amp, 120-volt receptacle for each 15.3 square meters (50 linear ft.)	For vacuuming and waxing machines

- Another section of raceway for network cabling and wiring into peripherals helps contain all of these frequently changed wires.
- Special equipment in school laboratories, shops, and cooking rooms require adequate outlets.
- Public areas and corridors in schools require HD devices and key-operated switches, plastic rather than glass lighting fixtures, and vandal-proof equipment wherever possible.
- All electrical panels must be locked—and should be in locked closets.

Electronic Equipment Protection

Sudden power increases called surges, which momentarily disrupt a building's steady power flow, can destroy many electrical appliances and other devices. Electrical power can jump from its normal 120 volts to 400 volts or 500 volts. These electrical surges are invisible and give no warning, zipping right through the main electrical panel so quickly that the circuit breakers and fuses do not notice them. Fortunately, most such surges are small and do not cause much damage, with the exception of a massive surge caused by a direct lightning strike.

Microprocessors found in computers, stereos, television and VCR controls, garage-door openers, telephones, and an increasing number of other common devices are sensitive to power surges. Fax machines and printers are also sensitive to surges. Home appliances with microprocessor controllers include ranges, dishwashers, ovens, microwave ovens, and clothes washers. Intercoms and security systems, plug-in radios, answering machines, smoke alarms, programmable thermostats, dimmers, and motion detectors may all have microprocessors.

Microprocessors use much less voltage than electrical systems. Each microprocessor's built-in power supply converts 120-volt electricity to about 5 volts. Microprocessors like steady current. Small changes in power, even a split-second surge, can scramble electrical signals. A surge that slips past the power supply can destroy delicate chips and burn out circuits.

If an electrical system takes a direct hit, the electronic equipment will be destroyed, but the chances of this happening are small. It is more likely that lightning will induce a surge in the building's electrical system. A lightning strike generates a brief but very powerful magnetic field in the surrounding atmosphere. Electrical wiring from the utility pole and throughout the building acts like an antenna and picks up an electrical charge from the magnetic field as it briefly forms and collapses. The lightning does not even have to hit nearby power lines to cause damage. It could generate a charge from some distance away, and any power lines between the house and the lightning strike will conduct the surge.

Surprisingly, some of the most troublesome electrical surges come from inside the building itself. Large electric motors, like those in a refrigerator or air conditioner, generate a surge every time they switch on. Lightweight electric motors, like that in a vacuum cleaner, also cause surges. The surge can run through any wire in the system in any direction and out to any device on the branch circuits. Not all of these surges are harmful, but they occur regularly as motorized appliances cycle on and off.

All computer installations, even the smallest home-office installation, need to be protected from line transients with a surge suppressor. The multitap plug-in strips with built-in surge suppressors are inadequate unless they meet specifications for surge current, clamping voltage, and surge-energy suitable for the particular installation. Major data-processing installations require additional types of treatment, including voltage regulators; electrical-noise isolation, filtering, and suppression; and surge suppressors.

Sensitive equipment should be isolated on separate electrical feeders. It is helpful to separate sensitive equipment physically to avoid problems caused by switching, arcing, and rectifying equipment. Fluorescent, mercury, sodium, and metal-halide discharge-type lighting, especially with electronic ballasts, can cause interference. Separating the equipment grounding pole of the electrical receptacle from the wiring system ground is a good idea when electronic dimmers, ballasts, and switching devices are present. These specially grounded receptacles have orange faceplates or an orange triangle on their faceplates.

There is a wide range of plug-in devices called surge suppressors, surge protectors, or transient voltage surge suppressors (TVSS), of which high-quality surge suppressors cost more than their lesser-quality counterparts. They range from cord-connected multiple-outlet strips to large three-phase units located at a building's service entrance. All are designed to limit a surge in voltage to a level that the protected equipment can withstand without damage. This is done either by placing one or more devices in the path of the incoming voltage transient to obstruct the amount of current allowed through, or by placing devices that have lower impedance (resistance) across an incoming power line in parallel with the protected load, so that the higher transient voltage bypasses the current coming into the building. Hybrid units combine both methods.

Electrical Emergency Systems

Most buildings are required by code to have energy sources to operate lighting for means of egress, exit signs, automatic door locks, and other equipment in an emergency. Emergency systems supply power to equipment that is essential to human life safety during the interruption of the normal supply. The NFPA governs emergency systems under several codes. The NFPA 101®: *Life Safety Code®, 2009 Edition* covers emergency systems in chapters on the means of egress.

Emergency-lighting systems illuminate areas of assembly to permit safe exiting and prevent panic. The emergency power system provides power for the fire detection and alarm systems as well as for elevators, fire pumps, and public-address and communications systems. It also allows the orderly shutdown or maintenance of hazardous processes. Codes require that artificial lighting must be present in all exit discharges any time that a building is in use, with the exception of residential occupancies.

The intensity of emergency lighting must be at least 11 lux (one foot-candle) at floor level. This can be reduced during performances at some assembly occupancies. All exit lighting must be connected to an emergency power source that will ensure illumination for a minimum of 1 to 1½ hours in case of a power failure. The code official may need to designate which exit accessway must be illuminated by emergency lighting.

Standby power systems are sometimes required by code. NFPA 110: *Standard for Emergency and Standby Power Systems, 2005 Edition* and NFPA 111: *Standard on Stored Electrical Energy Emergency and Standby Power Systems, 2005 Edition* govern standby systems. Standby systems are required for power processes and systems whose stoppage might create a hazard or hamper firefighting operations as well as for safety measures. These could include HVAC systems, water-supply equipment, and industrial processes whose interruption could cause safety or health hazards. Optional standby systems are installed to carry any or all loads in a facility at the discretion of the owner. They protect property and prevent financial loss in the event of a normal service interruption and are used for critical industrial processes or for situations in which an ongoing research project cannot be shut down.

NFPA 99: *Standard for Health Care Facilities, 2005 Edition* governs emergency systems for healthcare facilities in most jurisdictions. Most codes require emergency systems. Some also require standby systems for essential water systems and water treatment systems. The emergency system must pick up loads within ten seconds of the power interruption. Legally required standby systems must pick up within one minute. Batteries and PV cells are major sources for emergency and standby power, which consequently is usually DC current. Emergency supply batteries must have a full-load capacity of 90 minutes. An emergency supply or legally required standby supply of batteries with an engine generator set must have a two-hour minimum. The wiring system for emergency power is separate from the normal power system, with the exception of where it is connected to the same equipment.

ELECTRICAL WIRING AND DISTRIBUTION

As discussed earlier, wires that carry electrical current are called conductors. They extend from the circuit breaker boxes to individual switches, lights, and outlets. Conductors are rated in amps for their capacity to carry current. Conductor ampacity (capacity in amperes) increases with increasing conductor size and the maximum permissible temperature of the insulation protecting the conductor. Conductors are surrounded by insulation that provides electrical isolation and physical protection. A jacket over the insulation offers added physical protection. Conductor materials include the following:

- **Silver and gold:** very good conductors; very expensive
- **Copper:** almost as good a conductor as silver and gold; commonly used for building wiring
- **Aluminum:** less expensive and lighter than other conductor materials; about 80 percent as conductive as copper; used for large conductors

Interior designers may find themselves involved in discussions about the type of electrical cables that can be run in a project. The type of electrical cable that is permitted has a very significant effect on the cost of the electrical work. Contractors will frequently use these terms when discussing conditions on a site with interior designers. There are actually many types of electrical cables, some of which are used only in specialized applications. The following are a few of the cables that interior designers are most likely to encounter:

- **NM and NMC (Romex) cable:** Its plastic outer jacket makes NM easier to handle but also easier to damage. This cable is used for small residential and other structures not exceeding three floors above grade.

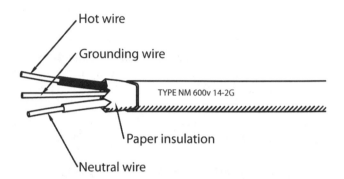

Figure 12-23 Nonmetallic sheathed cable. NEC cable types NM and NMC are commonly known by the trade name Romex. They are nonmetallic sheathed cables with a plastic outer jacket. The enclosing sheath is both moisture-resistant and flame-retardant. The NEC limits the use of Romex cable to residential one- and two-family dwellings not more than three floors in height. Typically, these are wood-frame buildings. Romex cables are easier to handle but more vulnerable to physical damage than BX cables.

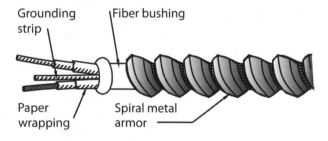

Figure 12-24 BX cable (metal-clad cable). AC or BX cable is the most common type of exposed wiring and is frequently used in residences and in rewiring existing buildings. BX cable is officially called NEC type AC cable, as well as flex cable or armored cable. Two or more conductors are wrapped in heavy paper or plastic and encased in a continuous, spiral-wound interlocking strip of steel tape. BX cable is common in commercial applications. It is installed with U-clamps or staples against beams and walls. In new construction, the NEC requires BX cable to be secured at specified intervals. In existing construction, it can be fished through walls, floors, and ceilings for renovations.

- **BX (AC) cable:** This cable is an assembly of insulated wires bound together and enclosed in protective, spiral-wound, interlocking steel tape armor. It is used for residences, rewiring existing buildings, and dry locations. It is also often used to connect rectangular fluorescent lights in suspended ceiling grids to allow for flexibility in relocation. This cable is restricted in some jurisdictions, even in some in which the NEC allows it.
- **Metal-clad (MC) cable:** This cable can be used either exposed or concealed in cable trays. With its moisture-proof jacket, it can be used in wet and outdoor locations. This cable looks similar to BX, but it has an additional green ground wire that provides extra grounding protection.

Raceways collect and protect cables:
- insulated cables in open raceways for industrial uses
- insulated conductors in closed raceways for offices
- buried in structure: conduit in floor slab, underground ducts
- attached to structure: surface raceways, including those suspended above hung ceilings
- part of structure: cellular concrete; cellular metal floors

Combined conductor and enclosure, factory-made assemblies are designed for the following specialized situations:

- **Busway:** Copper or aluminum bars are assembled in a rigid metallic housing. A plug-in busway allows easy connection. It is used to tap into a conductor at frequent intervals along its length.

- **Busduct:** Copper or aluminum bars are assembled in a rigid metallic housing. A feeder busduct has no plug-ins. It is used to carry large amounts of current.
- **Cablebus:** It is similar to a ventilated busduct but with cables instead of busbars. It is rigidly mounted in open space frame.
- **Light-duty plug-in busway:** This is a plug-in connection and simple installation. It is used for branch circuit wiring for direct connection of light machinery and industrial lighting.
- **Flat cable (FC) assemblies:** These are type FC cables with two to four conductors field-installed in a rigidly mounted, square structural channel. Pigtail wires extend from tap devices to devices or outlets with receptacles. Lights, small motors, and unit heaters, for example, are served without hard wiring.
- **Lighting track:** This consists of one to four circuits permanently installed in a factory-assembled channel. Special tap-off devices carry power to attached lighting fixtures along the track. It is used only for lighting.
- **Flat conductor cable (FCC):** This is for under-carpet use.

Conductors for general wiring (building wire) include manufactured wiring systems. These consist of a copper conductor covered with insulation and sometimes a jacket. There are a variety of special cable types, including

- high-voltage cables
- armored cables
- corrosion-resistant jacketed cables
- underground cables
- service entrance cables

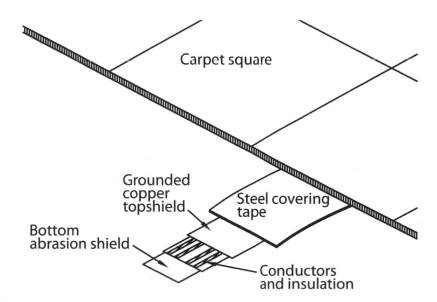

Figure 12-25 Flat conductor cable. NEC type flat conductor cable (FCC) is also called flat-wire cable. It is a small, factory-assembled cable in a flat housing and is used under carpet tiles without making a bump on the surface. Three or more flat copper conductors are placed edge-to-edge and enclosed in an insulating material. The assembly is covered with a grounded metal shield to provide physical protection and a continuous electrical ground path. The bottom shield is usually heavy polyvinyl chloride (PVC) or metal. The whole assembly is only about .76 millimeters (.03 in.) high, and is essentially undetectable under carpet.

Individual wires are run in protective coverings called **conduits**. Conduits are required for fire-resistant construction and include rigid metal conduit, electrical metallic tubing, and flexible metal conduit. This may affect an interior designer's decision to remove a suspended ceiling and expose the wiring and other equipment above because the cost of rewiring into conduits can be substantial.

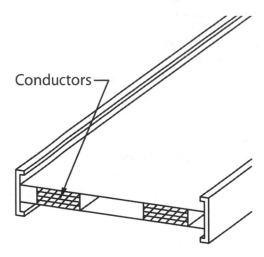

Figure 12-26 Busduct detail. Conductors are securely protected inside a busduct.

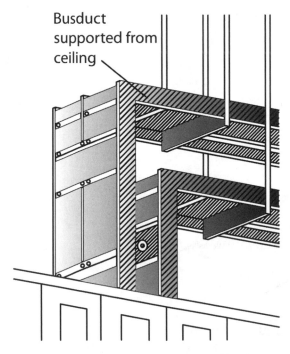

Figure 12-27 Busduct. The terms busway and busduct are often used interchangeably for assemblies of copper or aluminum bars in a rigid metallic housing. These assemblies are preferred when it is necessary to carry a large amount of current that can be tapped at frequent intervals along its length. Light-duty busduct or busway is used for feeder or branch circuits. Connections can be changed easily.

Steel conduit protects the enclosed wiring from mechanical injury and damage from the surrounding atmosphere. It provides a grounded metal enclosure for wiring to avoid shock hazards as well as a system ground path. Steel conduit protects its surroundings from fire hazard from overheating or arcing of the enclosed conductors. In most commercial construction and large multifamily residential construction, individual plastic-insulated conductors are placed in metal conduits. The NEC generally requires all wiring to be enclosed in a rigid metal corrosion-resistant conduit, which provides a corrosion-resistant support for the conductors. Wires are installed in the conduits after the conduit system has been inspected and approved.

Steel conduit
- protects enclosed wiring; provides grounding; supports conductors
- heavy-wall steel conduit (rigid-steel conduit)
- intermediate metal conduit (IMC)
- electrical metallic tubing (EMT, or thin-wall conduit)

Aluminum conduit
- lighter than steel; provides better corrosion resistance; nonmagnetic; nonsparking; painting not needed; used where steel conduit is used, with the exception of in concrete (usually) or buried in earth.
- **Armored or nonmetallic sheathed cable** may be used for frame construction.

Flexible metal conduit:
- **Greenfield:** Empty, spiral-wound interlocked steel or aluminum raceway used for motor connections; places where vibration, movement, or obstructions are present; wiring inside metal partitions; motor connections
- **Sealtite:** has liquid-tight plastic jacket; used in wet locations

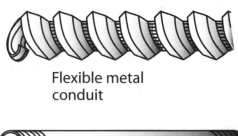

Flexible metal conduit

Steel conduit

Figure 12-28 Conduit. Flexible metal conduit is used to isolate the vibration from motors. Steel conduit is widely used to protect, ground, and support wiring.

Nonmetallic conduit:
- Raceways are formed from rigid PVC for indoor exposed use.
- Underground wiring is enclosed in plastic tubing or conduits.

Surface metal raceways:
- These are metallic and nonmetallic surface raceways and multiple-outlet assemblies.
- They are used in dry, nonhazardous, noncorrosive locations; in general, used only for wiring that operates below 300 volts.

All types of facilities use insulated conductors in closed raceways. Typically, the raceway is installed first, with wiring pulled in or laid in later. Raceways may be buried in a building's structure as conduit in the floor slab or as underfloor duct. They may be attached to the structure as surface raceways, including conduit and raceways suspended above hung ceilings. Wall and ceiling surface raceways are somewhat unsightly, but they allow for wiring where it is needed with excellent access and without opening up walls or ceilings. Cable protection and support equipment includes the following:

Cable trays:
- These trays provide continuous, open support for self-protected cables.
- For general wiring system use, cables in cable trays must be self-protected.

Figure 12-29 Cable tray. Cable trays give continuous, open support for cables. While used primarily in industrial applications, they are also found in offices with heavy data and communications requirements. *Photo credit: Herb Fremin*

- Wiring in cable trays is easy to install and maintain as well as relatively low cost.
- Cable trays are bulky and must either be exposed or accessible through a hung ceiling.

Floor raceways:
- **Individual floor raceways** are sometimes installed to get power for computers, telephone lines, and other equipment at locations in open-plan offices away from the structure, without installing a complete floor-raceway system. One labor intensive process involves channeling the concrete floor, installing conduit in the opening (or chase), connecting the wiring to the nearest wall outlet, and patching the chase.
- **Surface floor raceway:** This is usually unsightly and may cause tripping and problems with cleaning the floor. Surface floor raceways can be used only in dry, nonhazardous, noncorrosive locations. Surface raceways are used when the architecture does not permit recessed raceways, for economy of construction and anticipated expansion. They offer outlets at frequent intervals and access to the equipment in the raceways.
- **Underfloor raceways:** These are metal or plastic raceways added onto a structure and covered with concrete fill. Feeder ducts underfloor are used with flat cable undercarpet. In general, this type of raceway is installed first, with wiring pulled in or laid in later.
- **Cellular metal floor raceways:** These are integrated structural/electrical systems.
- **Precast cellular concrete-floor raceways:** These have single enclosed tubular spaces in precast cellular concrete slab floor. They are used in office buildings with random arrangements. They can also be used for air and water distribution. Their large capacity, versatility, and flexibility regarding outlet placement and movement are advantages.

Figure 12-30 Coring slab. This machine is drilling a hole in a concrete slab. This is how poke-through fittings are inserted to feed wiring from the floor below. *Photo credit: Herb Fremin*

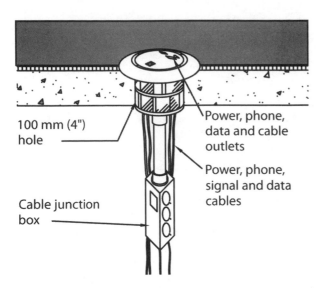

Figure 12-31 Poke-through fitting. Poke-through fittings are often used in existing commercial spaces to meet expanded desktop power and data wiring needs. The NEC requires that electrical penetrations in fire-rated floors, walls, ceilings, and partitions must be properly sealed.

Undercarpet wiring employs factory-assembled FC consisting of three or more flat copper conductors enclosed in insulation and grounded with a metal shield. This type of wiring is used under carpet squares for easily repositioned wiring and offers low cost and flexibility for open-plan offices. Undercarpet wiring is used in new construction and to rework obsolete wiring systems in existing buildings. The NEC prohibits its use in wet and hazardous areas and in residential, hospital, and school buildings. FC layouts are usually shown on a separate electrical plan.

Ceiling raceways provide wiring for lighting, power, telephones, and outlets for the floor above. They are used with vertical multisection raceways (service poles) fed from the top.

Over-the-ceiling FC assemblies are more flexible than underfloor systems. They are used for lighting, power, and telephone service, and can provide outlets for the floor above as well. Retail stores use ceiling systems to permit very rapid layout changes at low cost. They are easily altered for changes in functions of spaces as well as for furniture layout changes, making them very appropriate for educational facilities. FC assembly systems use a metallic or nonmetallic surface-type raceway hung from the concrete slab above in the ceiling plenum. They are used with lift-out suspended ceiling panels. Vertical poles carry the power from the top down to the desk or floor level. The poles may be prewired with several power outlets, telephone connections, and data cable outlets. Special conduits, raceways, troughs, and fittings are available for exposed installations. Many finishes are available, but the appearance of the poles usually belies their economical nature.

Lighting track is a factory-assembled FC assembly with conductors for one to four circuits permanently installed in the track. Tap-off devices carry power to attached lighting fixtures anywhere along the track. Lighting track is generally rated at 20 amps and may be used only to feed lighting fixtures. Taps to feed convenience receptacles are not permitted.

Full-Access Floors

The revolution in desktop electronics and the increasingly fast turnover rates for offices combine to make underfloor delivery of power, data, and telecommunications services a much more cost-effective option for many offices, because of both the greater ease with which wires and cables can be distributed and the flexibility that access floors permit. Full-access floors provide space for both air supply and cabling. The system allows rapid and complete access to an underfloor plenum.

Lightweight, die-cast-aluminum panels are supported on a network of adjustable steel or aluminum pedestals. The panels are 46 or 91 centimeters (18 or 36 in.) square, and the floor depth is usually between 31 and 76 centimeters (12–30 in.). Where air requirements are minimal, the pedestals can be as short as 15 centimeters (6 in.). The panels are made of steel, aluminum, a wood core encased in steel or aluminum, or lightweight reinforced concrete. They are finished with carpet tile, vinyl tile, or high-pressure laminates. Fire-rated and electrostatic-discharge-control coverings are also available. Access floor systems are designed for loads between 1220 and 3050 kilograms per square meter (250–625 lb. per sq ft.) and are available for heavier loads up to 5490 kilograms per square meter (1125 lb. per sq ft.). Seismic pedestals are available to meet building code requirements.

Electrical conduits, junction boxes, and cabling are run below full-access flooring panels for computer, security, and communications systems. The space under the flooring panels can also be used as a plenum to distribute the HVAC air supply, with a ceiling plenum for air return. Ducts for conditioned air can also run beneath the floor. By separating the cool supply air from the warm return air, the system helps reduce energy consumption. The construction is usually completely fire-resistant. The ceiling height must be adequate to accommodate the raised floor. Raised floors often require steps and ramps for level changes.

Access floor systems are used in offices, hospitals, laboratories, computer rooms, and television and communications centers. They provide accessibility and flexibility in the placement of desks, workstations, and equipment. Equipment can be moved and reconnected fairly easily with modular wiring systems, which also cut down on labor costs.

☑ **Conduits, busducts, panels, and communications wiring take up horizontal and vertical space as they travel throughout and between floors. Electricians must have access to wiring through doors, hatches, or removable panels. These access openings must be coordinated with the work of the interior designer.**

Low-Voltage Wiring

Low-voltage wiring is usually 12 to 14 volts, and is used for thermostat circuits and for switching complex lighting circuits or remote-control panels. This type of wiring cannot give shocks or cause fires, and it can run through a building without cable or conduit. Because the amperages required are also low, the wire can be small and inexpensive. A small transformer connected to a 115-volt circuit produces the low-voltage current. Most telephone and communications wiring is low voltage, with the current provided by the communications company.

Power Line Carrier Systems

Adding sophisticated building-management controls to an existing building would be very expensive if all new wiring had to be installed. **Power line carrier (PLC) systems** use existing or new electrical power wiring as conductors to carry control signals for energy management controls in existing large, complex facilities. Low-voltage, high-frequency, binary-coded control signals are injected into the power wiring. Only receivers tuned to a particular code react to the signals. In residential use, the control-signal generator can be a small, manually programmed controller. In commercial facilities, computers operate an energy-management or lighting controller.

☑ **The special design needs for data and communications may make it worthwhile to hire a design consultant who is familiar with the latest technology. The design will depend on the number, type, and location of data-processing terminals. The type of local area network determines the communications medium, such as coaxial cable, shielded and unshielded wire, or fiber optic cables. This, in turn, determines the types of connections and floor outlets.**

RECEPTACLES AND SWITCHES

In addition to understanding how electricity is distributed throughout a building, interior designers need to know how it is controlled and accessed at the end point. Whether a person turns on a wall switch, plugs an appliance into a receptacle, or uses a dimmer to lower the lights, he or she is using a **wiring device** installed in an **outlet box**. Even **attachment plugs (caps)** and **wall plates** are considered to be wiring devices. Outlet boxes are also used where light fixtures are connected to the electrical system. Low-voltage lighting control devices are considered wiring devices. **Junction boxes** are enclosures for housing and protecting electrical wires or cables that are joined in connecting or branching electrical circuits. Commercial attachments that are not usually considered wiring devices include premise wiring, such as data and communications wiring and raceways.

Electrical equipment is given ratings for voltage and current. Voltage ratings indicate the maximum voltage that can be safely applied to a unit continuously. An ordinary electric wall receptacle is rated at 250 volts, but is supplied with only 120 volts in normal use. The type and quality of insulation used and the physical spacing between electrically energized parts determine the voltage rating. Current ratings are determined by the maximum temperature at which the equipment's components can operate at full load. This depends on the type of insulation used. Wiring

devices are usually rated at 300 amps or less and frequently at 20 amps. They can be mounted in a small wall box.

Manufacturers classify wiring devices to indicate their quality and expected use. However, their grades are not standard among manufacturers, so if interior designers specify by grade without a manufacturer named, they will have little control over what they may actually get. The following are commonly used grades:

- **Hospital grade:** highest quality; built to withstand severe abuse while maintaining reliable operation; must meet UL requirements for the grade; has green dot on device face
- **Federal specification grade:** roughly equivalent to industrial (premium) and commercial specification grades; less stringent than hospital grade.
- **Industrial specification grade:** used for industrial and high-grade commercial construction
- **Commercial specification grade:** used for education-related and residential buildings and commercial work
- **UL general-purpose grade:** corresponds roughly to residential grade; is the least demanding quality
- **Standard or residential grade:** used in low-cost construction of all types; not necessarily used in all types of residential work

Each electrical receptacle, lighting fixture, or switch is housed in a metal or plastic box that is fastened securely to the structure, thereby supporting the device and protecting the box's contents. The cable or conduit serving the device is clamped tightly to the box where the wires enter. The bare neutral wire is connected to the box and to the frame of the device, ensuring that it will never cause shocks if the device becomes faulty. The black and white wires are stripped of insulation at their ends and connected to

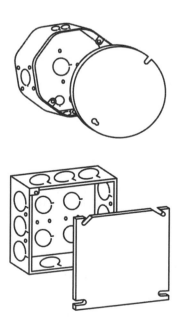

Figure 12-32 Junction boxes. Junction boxes are designed to fit within the dimensions of stud walls. They are also used with exposed steel conduit.

the device with screws or clamps. Then the circuit is tested for safe, satisfactory operation, and the device is screwed snugly to the box. A metal or plastic cover plate is attached to keep fingers out, keep electrical connections free of dust and dirt, and provide a neat appearance.

Outlet and device boxes are made of galvanized, stamped sheet metal. Nonmetallic boxes may be used in some wiring installations. Cast iron or cast aluminum boxes are used for outdoor work and in wet locations. Square and octagonal 10-centimeter (4-in.) boxes are used for fixtures, junctions, and electrical devices. Single switches and duplex outlets (one receptacle above another, as commonly found in homes) use a 102 × 57 mm (4 × 2¼ in.) box. Depths range from 38 to 76 millimeters (1½–3 in.).

Outlet boxes are wall- or floor-mounted for electrical receptacles. For lighting fixtures, they are wall- or ceiling-mounted. Floor boxes of cast metal are set directly into the concrete floor slab. Typically, switch boxes are mounted on the wall to control a lighting outlet box. They are usually mounted within the wall on a stud. Installation of an electrical box usually just penetrates the wall surface and does not require firestopping. The opening in the wall cannot allow a gap greater than 3 millimeters (⅛ in.) between the electrical box and the gypsum wallboard.

The NEC specifies the minimum number of electrical boxes allowed for some building types, especially dwelling units. Most electrical codes specify the maximum distance between receptacles in a room, so that a lamp or appliance with a standard-length cord can be placed anywhere around the room perimeter without using an extension cord. Codes also specify the number of receptacles per room and the maximum number of receptacles per circuit in order to prevent overloading wires with excessive flows of current. Typically, the NEC and model-building codes specify that no more than 645 square centimeters (100 sq in.) of electrical boxes can be installed per 9.3 square meters (100 sq ft.) of wall surface.

When an existing electrical box is not being used, it must either have a cover plate or be completely removed, including the box and all its wiring, with the wall opening properly patched. In fire-rated walls, boxes used on opposite sides of the same walls must be separated by 61 centimeters (24 in.) horizontally.

Electrical Receptacles

The electrical outlet that an electrical cord is plugged into is technically known as a **convenience receptacle**. The number of poles (prongs) and wires, along with whether they have a separate grounding wire or not, identify the different types of receptacles. Grounded receptacles are used on standard 15-amp or 20-amp branch circuits.

Technically, the term "wall plug" is the name for the cap on the wire that carries electricity to an appliance—the part on the end of a line cord that is plugged into a wall.

Receptacles installed on a standard 15-amp or 20-amp branch circuit must be of the grounding type. Receptacles connected to different voltages, frequencies, or current types (AC ver-

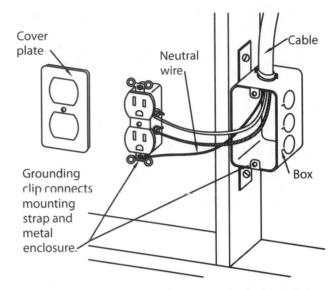

Figure 12-33 Duplex convenience receptacle. A receptacle is by definition a single-contact device. A normal wall convenience receptacle takes two attachment plugs and is called a duplex convenience receptacle or duplex convenience outlet. This is commonly shortened to duplex receptacle or duplex outlet.

sus DC) on the same premises must be polarized. Typically, receptacles are 20 amps and 125 volts, but they are available from 10 to 400 amps, and from 125 to 600 volts. Locking, explosion-proof, tamper-proof, and decorative-design receptacles are available. Some units, such as range receptacles, are designed for specific uses. Split-wired receptacles have one outlet that is always energized and a second outlet that is controlled by a wall switch. Sometimes, these are used for a lamp, with the switch near the room entrance.

Receptacles are usually mounted between 30 and 46 centimeters (12–18 in.) above the finished floor. In shops, laboratories, and other spaces with tables against walls, receptacles are mounted 107 centimeters (42 in.) above the floor. Receptacles above kitchen counters are mounted 122 centimeters (4 ft.) above the finished floor. In accessible spaces, the ADAAG requires a minimum height of 38 centimeters (15 in.) for outlets, with outlets above kitchen counters at a minimum of 107 centimeters (42 in.) above the floor. When work areas are required to be accessible, as in public library carrels and office workstations, receptacles should be located above the work surface whenever possible or, alternatively, under the front edge of the work surface. This requires careful planning.

Modern electronic equipment is very sensitive to random, spurious electrical voltages, which are called **electrical noise**. Two special receptacles help eliminate electrical noise:

- **Receptacles with built-in surge suppression** protect equipment from over-voltage spikes.
- **Receptacles with an insulated equipment-grounding terminal** that separate the device ground terminal from the system

(raceway) ground eliminate much of the unwanted electrical noise. This latter type is connected to the system ground at the service entrance only and is identified by an orange triangle on the faceplate.

Switches

A light can be turned on and off either by plugging a lighting fixture into an electrical outlet (receptacle) and turning the switch on the lighting fixture on and off, or by **hard-wiring** the lighting fixture directly into the building's power-supply system and using a wall switch to control the power. Switches up to 30 amps that can be outlet box mounted are considered wiring devices. Switches are installed in hot wires only. They disconnect an electrical device from the current, leaving the device with no voltage going through it and eliminating the possibility of shock when the switch is open.

Wireless systems are available in many homes, offices, and public places. They eliminate the need to connect lights, fans, and other equipment directly to a building's hard wiring. (Wireless data and communication will be discussed later; see page 323).

A common wall-light switch is a type of general-duty safety switch called a **contactor**. Contactors close an electrical circuit physically by moving two electrical conductors into contact with each other, allowing the power to flow to the lighting fixture. The contactor physically separates the two conductors in order to open the circuit, which stops the electrical flow and shuts off the light. Contactors are good for remote controls by manual or remote pushbutton or for such automatic devices as timers, float switches, thermostats, and pressure switches. Contactors are found in lighting, heating, and air conditioning equipment as well as in motors.

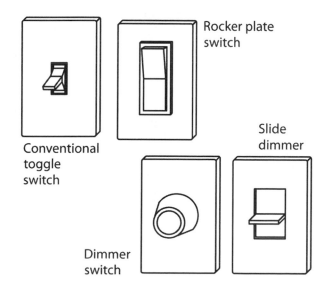

Figure 12-34 Wall-switch types. Wall-switch designs change style over time. Switchplates are available in a variety of colors and decorative designs.

Contactors can be operated by hand, electric coil, spring, or motor. A wall switch is an example of a small, mechanically operated contactor. A relay is a small, electrically operated contactor. The operating handles for contactors may be toggle, push, touch, rocker, rotary, or tap-plate types. Mercury and AC quiet types of handles are relatively noiseless, while toggle, tumbler, and AC/DC types are not. A toggle switch has a lever or knob that moves through a small arc and causes the contacts to open or close the electric circuit. Keyed switches are used where access needs to be limited to authorized individuals. Tumbler-lock controlled switches are used when a keyed switch does not provide adequate security, such as when keys may be stolen. Spring-wound timer switches are often used for bathroom heaters and ventilation fans.

Types of switches:
- **General-duty safety switches** are intended for normal use in lighting and power circuits.
- **HD switches** are used for frequent interrupting, high-fault currents and for ease of maintenance.
- **Three-way switches** are used in conjunction with another switch to control lights from two locations, such as from the bottom and top of a stairway. An ordinary single-pole switch has "on" and "off" written on it. A three-way switch has three terminals, so the on and off positions may change depending on the position of the other switch.
- **Four-way switches** are used in conjunction with two three-way switches to control lights from three locations.
- **Remote-control (RC) switches** are used for switching blocks of lighting as well as for exterior lights, whole floors, or whole buildings. They use electromagnets to operate fixtures from a distance without wiring. Ceiling fans and electrically operated window treatments often use remote controls.
- **Solid-state switches** are beginning to replace the common wall switch. Solid-state switches use an electronic device with a conducting state and a nonconducting state, similar to a conventional switch in closed position and open position. The change between the two states is accomplished by a control signal in the voltage. The change is made instantaneously, noiselessly, and without sending a flash of electricity across a gap. When an electronic-timing device is added, the result is a time-controlled electronic switch with no moving parts, acting independently of utility-line frequency.

☑ A switch with a solid-state rectifier makes it possible to switch incandescent lamps from high to off, to low. They cost little more than an ordinary switch and can save energy when a lower illumination level is often acceptable.

Programmable time switches add a small, programmable memory circuit. A programmable switch fits into a wall-outlet box just like an ordinary switch. It uses miniature electronics for lighting, energy management, automated building control, and clock and program systems. With a read-only memory (ROM) chip programmed with the sunrise and sunset information for the latitude involved, this becomes a "sun tracker," which can control circuits with dark-to-dawn control year-round.

Programmable controllers are even more sophisticated switches that add a microprocessor, enabling them to respond with a particular control plan to given input signals. They use programmable memory to store instructions that implement special functions. This amounts to a special type of computer that has a short program within its hardware for a specific type of function, such as logic, timing, or counting. These controllers are used in industrial controls, process controls, and elevators.

Interior designers often indicate switch locations on their drawings. Switches to control lighting or receptacles are usually on the handle side of the door of a room. An interior designer's drawings should show and identify plug-in strips on walls and special-purpose receptacles. These have special symbols and notes that indicate the locations of signal outlets for fire alarms, telephones, intercoms, data, communications radios, televisions, and other equipment. Typically, the circuits for this equipment are not indicated on the floor plan but on a separate power plan. Lighting-fixture outlets are usually included with wiring devices unless doing so leads to a cluttered drawing; in this situation, they are represented on their own drawing. Motors, heaters, and other fixed, permanently installed equipment are shown and identified on power plans rather than on lighting drawings. Equipment with a cord and plug is not usually represented, but receptacles for plug-in equipment are shown and identified.

☑ **Dimmers, switches, receptacles, fan controls, cable television, and telephone jacks are all available in a variety of colors. Cover plates specified in a bold color may have to be replaced if the wall color or other décor changes.**

Much of the wiring used in buildings is attached to lighting fixtures. In Chapter 13: Lighting Systems, we will see how daylighting can be combined with electrical lighting for round-the-clock use.

13

....

Lighting Systems

All interior design projects start with an investigation of existing conditions. The location of the space (e.g., its orientation and climate) as well as its neighbors and history will shape the interior. The location of an interior project within an existing or newly designed building, whether at the perimeter or at its center, affects light, view, and energy demands.

DAYLIGHTING

Sunlight is a highly efficient and comparatively cool source of illumination. Daylight varies with the season, the time of day, the latitude, and weather conditions. More sunlight is available in the summer than in the winter, and each day's sun peaks at noon. An overcast day is very different from a day with a clear sky, and conditions can change several times during a day.

On a bright day, sunlight provides illumination levels that are 50 times as high as the requirements for artificial illumination. Direct sun may be desirable for solar heating in the winter, but the glare from direct sun must be managed. Indirect sunlight produces illumination levels between 10 and 20 percent as bright as direct sun, but still higher than levels needed indoors. Daily changes in daylight controls and seasonal adjustments in the size of daylight openings may help accommodate the changing nature of daylight and the overabundance of sun. Mirrored or low-transmission glass does not solve glare problems as well as shading does.

It is almost impossible to carry out fine visual tasks, such as reading or sewing, in the glare of direct sun. The sky is brilliant with scattered sunlight, which is often bright enough to distract the eye. Direct sunshine bleaches colors, and the heat from direct sun in buildings is often intolerable, especially in the summer. Clouds often obscure the sun's glare partially or completely.

In addition to being an economical response to code-mandated energy budgets, daylighting can save businesses significant labor costs. The greatest costs for a business are related to the people who work in the building. Recent studies continue to link daylighting to increased productivity. A field study undertaken by the Lighting Research Center of Rensselaer Polytechnic Institute in 2001 and replicated in 2003 concluded that people in windowed offices spent 15 percent more time on work-related tasks than comparable people in interior offices. The promise of even a modest 1 percent increase in productivity is likely to appeal to a business owner more than a building that is 20 percent more energy efficient. The potential for a good daylighting design to improve productivity by even a small increment and increase corporate profits is a strong justification for a daylighting design.

Physiological Effects of Daylighting

In proper amounts, ultraviolet (UV) rays from the sun help human bodies produce vitamin D and keep the skin healthy. UV light dilates skin capillaries and causes blood pressure to fall slightly. UV creates a feeling of well-being, quickens the pulse rate and appetite, and stimulates energetic activity, perhaps even increasing work activity. Visible light affects biological rhythms, hormonal activity, and behavior. (The importance of infrared [IR] radiation in radiant heating was discussed earlier.)

On the other hand, overexposure to UV rays can damage skin and cause malignant tumors and cataracts. There is almost no UV in standard incandescent and fluorescent lighting, although some available lighting sources do include UV.

Daylight helps people relate the indoors to the outdoors. Colors appear brighter and more natural in daylight. The variations in light over the course of a day and in different weather conditions stimulate visual interest. Like most other living things, people need full spectrum light, which is a main characteristic of daylight. Without daylight, people tend to lose track of time, are unaware of weather conditions, and may feel disoriented. Even mail carriers who spend most of their day outdoors express a clear preference for daylight in their indoor workplaces, leading Maguire Group Inc. of Foxborough, Massachusetts, to add skylights to its design for the postal distribution center in Nashua, New Hampshire, in 1995.

Glare

Glare is a result of excessive contrast or of light coming from the wrong direction. The contrast between the bright outside environment viewed through a window and the darkness of the interior space creates glare. Glare results in discomfort and eye fatigue caused by repeated adjustment of the eye to one lighting condition after another. Direct sunlight or reflected sunlight from bright, shiny surfaces can be disturbing or even disabling, and it should never be permitted to enter the field of view of a building's occupants. Windows or skylights within the occupants' normal field of vision can appear distractingly bright next to other objects. A window next to a blackboard, for example, will produce glare.

There are two basic methods to avoid glare and reduce brightness contrasts: sensitive interior design and daylight light controls (see page 279 for a discussion of daylighting controls).

Interior design strategies to control glare include the following:

- Assign tasks where adequate natural light is available.
- Orient furniture so that daylight comes from the left side or rear of line of sight.
- Face workstations at an angle to windows unless they are on a northern exposure and no exterior glare sources are in the line of sight.
- Place windows away from internal focal points in a room.
- Use north-facing clerestories to reduce glare from very bright views and to avoid glare-related accidents.
- Employ diffuse light by varying the direction and intensity of light sources and creating soft, overlapping shadows.

Direct or **discomfort glare** occurs when a light source is within the field of vision. **Reflected glare** or **veiling reflection** is produced when a light source is reflected in a surface within view. Direct glare depends on:

- brightness, size, and position of each light source in vision field
- rapid adaptation of eye to average brightness of overall visual scene
- attraction of eye to highest **luminance** (brightness) in scene
- alternation of eye from overall scene to brightest point, causing visual fatigue

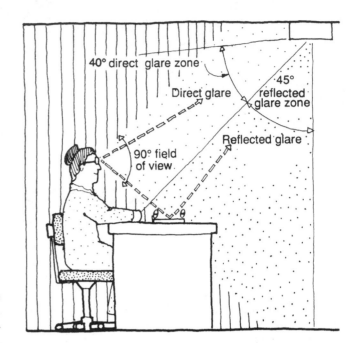

Figure 13-1 Glare zones. Direct glare is a problem when the glare source is within the viewer's normal, upright viewing position. Reflected glare is a problem when the viewer looks downward at a work surface.

Complete control of veiling reflections is difficult, but the following techniques help provide adequate illumination while minimizing their impact:

- Minimize reflected glare through the physical arrangement of sources, task, and observer.
- Minimize objectionable brightness to ease eye adaptation.
- Select light sources designed for minimum glare reflectance.
- Control the quality or nature of the task to accommodate reflections.

DESIGNING FOR DAYLIGHTING

Daylighting considerations affect the architecture of a building's exterior, determining the amount of fenestration and its appearance on the building façade. The building orientation and shape should be designed with daylighting in mind.

Daylight can be increased

- with a few carefully placed windows
- with appropriately selected interior finishes
- by keeping windows and interior surfaces clean for better reflectance

Lighting designer Bill Lam cites the modernist John Hancock Tower in Boston, Massachusetts, as an example of how architects get it wrong. The building was mirrored to keep light out, with the long sides of the building facing east and west. The glazing extended from the floor to about one foot above the ceiling. To reduce glare and control overheating, interior blinds were lowered and are left down—and the lights left on—all the time.

Basic daylighting can consist solely of making windows and skylights large enough for the darkest overcast days, as in many northern European buildings. True daylighting is more accurately defined as passive solar design. Daylighting involves the conscious design of building forms for optimum illumination and thermal performance. It is most challenging in workspaces with varied and demanding functions, such as schools, offices, laboratories, libraries, and museums, and least challenging in public spaces where comfort standards are less stringent and controlled lighting is less important.

Interior spaces need high ceilings and highly reflective room surfaces for optimal light distribution. The light source—the sun—is continuously changing in direction and intensity. Light reflected off the ground is ideal because it is both bright and diffuse, but adjacent buildings or trees often shade the ground. Light bouncing off the ground outside ends up on the ceiling.

In a daylighting design, heat and light are controlled through the form of the building. For example, in a Middle Eastern mosque in a sunny climate, limited sunlight enters the building through small windows located high on a decorated ceiling, then is diffused as it bounces off interior surfaces. Conversely, the large windows in a western European cathedral flood the interior with light that is colored by and filtered through stained glass. To take advantage of sunlight without an excess of heat or glare, buildings should be oriented so that windows are on the north and south sides. Architect Frank Lloyd Wright shaded the west and south sides from the most intense sun with deep overhangs. One way to study where light is coming from in an existing building is to look at the shadows in person or by using photographs.

Daylighting must be integrated with the view, natural air movement, acoustics, heat gain and loss, and electric lighting. Operable windows offer daylight and natural airflow, but they let in noise. Daylighting will not save energy unless lights are turned off, so lighting zones must be circuited separately, with lights turned off or dimmed when the natural light is adequate and left on where proper amounts of daylight are not available.

To be successful, the daylighting scheme must allow daylight to penetrate into the building and ensure that daylight will be available whether the sky is overcast or clear. An atrium can be used to bring large quantities of direct or reflected sunlight down into a building interior. In some buildings more than two stories high, **light wells** bring natural light into the interior building core. Light wells are smaller than atriums and can be created with skylights, clerestories, or window walls.

The bottom line of daylighting design involves achieving the minimal acceptable amount of natural illumination when the available daylight conditions are at their worst and screening out excess illumination at other times. For example, the daylight available at 9 AM in December is used as the basis for the worst-case conditions. The designer also seeks to provide adequate daylight under average sky conditions, with artificial lighting supplying added light for less-than-average daylight conditions. The goal is to provide adequate natural illumination during most of the daytime hours that the space is occupied. The design is balanced with supplemental artificial lighting in dark areas rather than with an overabundance of daylight in lighter areas.

Daylighting relies primarily on diffused sunlight or reflected, indirect sunlight to illuminate building interiors. The amount of natural light available in a room depends on how much sky is directly visible through windows and skylights from a given point in that room. The amount of indirect light from the sky also depends on how bright the visible areas of sky are. The sky at the horizon is about one-third as bright as the sky directly overhead, so the closer the window is to the ceiling, the more light it will gather—as long as it is not blocked by trees or buildings. Skylights are very effective at collecting the brightest light.

☑ **The shape and surface finishes of a space have an impact on daylighting. Tall, shallow spaces with high surface reflectances are brighter than low, deep rooms with windows at only the narrow end and with dark, cold surfaces. It takes fewer bounces off the walls for light to get deep into a room when the windows are high on the wall. High windows distribute light more evenly to all walls and allow light to penetrate into the interiors of large, low buildings. The ceiling and back wall of the space are more effective than the side walls or floor for reflecting and distributing daylight. Tall objects, such as office-cubicle partitions or tall bookcases, can obstruct both direct light and reflected light.**

The level of daylight illumination diminishes as it goes deeper into the interior space. In order to reduce glare, it is necessary to design a gradual transition from the brightest to the darkest parts of the space. The amount of light about 1.5 meters (5 ft.) from the window should not be more than 10 times as bright as the darkest part of the room. In a room with windows on only one wall, the average illumination of the darker half of the room should be at least one-third of the average illumination level of the other half with windows. By using windows on more than one side of the room, along with interior light wells, skylights, and clerestories, an interior designer can achieve more balanced daylighting. It is best to allow daylight from two directions for balance, preferably at the end of the room farthest from the main daylight source.

Sidelighting

Daylighting is broken into two conventional categories: sidelighting through windows in walls, and toplighting through skylights in roofs and clerestory windows very high up on walls.

The ground and nearby building surfaces may reflect sunlight into windows. Reflecting surfaces absorb most of the heat and scatter visual light at a much lower intensity than direct sunlight. Once inside the building, reflected light can reach indoor points directly or by reflecting farther off other interior surfaces. These successive reflections can bring daylight deeper into the space.

TABLE 13-1. SIDELIGHTING STRATEGIES

Strategy	Description	Effect	Comments
Design for bilateral lighting	Light from two walls	Evenly distributed light; reduced glare	Lighting from one side only produces more glare
Windows placed high on wall	Light from high on wall	Light penetrates more deeply into space; more uniform distribution	Raise ceiling heights; put window as close to ceiling as possible
Use adjacent walls as reflectors	Place windows close to adjacent walls	Reduces contrast at window edge; reflects light deeper into space	May reveal desirable patterns and colors from sunlight
Splay the walls of an aperture	Light washes across longer or rounder surface around window	Reduces contrast; increases visual comfort	Less potential for glare
Provide daylight filters	Block or diffuse daylighting	Use trees, vines, trellises on exterior; use blinds, drapes, translucent glazing on interior	Light-colored finishes reduce contrast with sky color beyond
Provide summer shading	Blocks direct sunlight from entering building at certain times of year	Use exterior louvers, overhangs, trellises, trees, light shelves	Block direct sunlight; reflect diffused sunlight; provide solar control

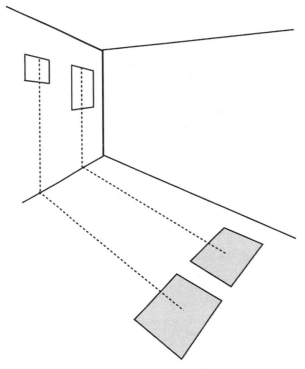

Figure 13-2 Window proportions for daylighting. The larger and higher the window, the more daylight enters the room. As a rule of thumb, daylighting can be used for task lighting up to a depth of two times the height of the window. By using the depth that light can penetrate into a given space as a guide, an interior designer can proportion rooms to take advantage of the maximum amount of daylighting. The ideal height from the top of the window to the floor should be about one-half the depth of the room in order to achieve maximum daylight penetration and distribution without glare. The standard for daylighting of offices, lobbies, and circulation areas is for glazing to equal 5 to 10 percent of the floor area served. For display, drafting, typing, and factory work, the glazing should be about one-fourth the floor area. Sill height is not critical because the lower part of the window does not contribute much light to the inner part of the room.

Openings for daylighting may also provide ventilation, views, and solar heat, but they should be considered to be potentially different from openings for those designed for these other functions. The size and orientation of window openings, the transmittance of the glazing, and the reflectance of the room and outdoor surfaces affect the quality of daylighting. As mentioned earlier, overhangs and nearby trees obstruct the sun. East and west windows must have shading devices to reduce bright early morning and late-afternoon sun. In the summer, the low angle of the morning and evening sun creates glare and generates excessive heat. South-facing windows are ideal for daylight when they have horizontal shading devices that can control excessive solar radiation and glare. Windows and skylights facing north in northern latitudes receive little or no direct sunlight and gather indirect light without significant heat gain.

Highly reflective surfaces absorb less light at each reflection and pass more light to the room's interior. Surface brightness should change gradually from the outside to the inside. White exterior surfaces and window frames gather more reflected light in through the windows. Light-colored window frames help reduce uncomfortable contrasts between the bright outdoor views and darker interiors, especially when splayed at an angle. Light-colored surfaces reflect and distribute light more efficiently, and dark colors absorb light. Large areas of shiny surfaces can cause glare. To reduce contrast, light colors and high reflectances for window frames, walls, ceilings, and floors should be used.

☑ **Interior surface colors and reflectances should be selected according to the primary source of incoming light. Direct and reflected skylight hits the floor first, while reflected sunlight hits the ceiling first. Light colors and reflectances on surfaces far from openings help increase the light in dim areas. When windows are placed adjacent to light-colored interior walls, reflected light goes through a series of transitional intensities rather than having an extremely bright opening surrounded by unlit walls.**

TABLE 13-2. TOPLIGHTING

Strategy	Description	Effect	Comments
Splay sides of skylight	Sides of skylight open wider toward interior	Skylight area appears larger	Reflects diffused light into space
Place toplights high in space	High ceilings with skylights	More surface area on which light can diffuse, thereby enlarging source	Works well in spaces with skylight well above field of view
Use interior devices to block, baffle, or diffuse light	Redirect sunlight with reflector	Diffuses light onto another surface	Reflector is positioned below skylight, clerestory, or roof monitor

Toplighting

Toplighting, or lighting from above, offers the best distribution of diffuse skylight, with deeper penetration and better uniformity of daylight. This type of illumination is best where light is desired but a view is not necessary. It offers better security and frees up wall space. In addition, toplighting may eliminate the need for electric lighting on the top floors of a building during daylight hours. Unlike sidelighting, it is easy to distribute uniformly. Toplighting controls glare from low-angle sunlight better than does sidelighting.

However, when direct sun enters a skylight, it may strike surfaces and produce glare and fading. Unshaded skylights exposed to the summer sun by day and the cold winter sky by night lead to heat loss. High windows or top lights work best for such horizontal tasks as reading at a desk, while lower sidelights (windows in walls) are best for such vertical tasks as filing.

SKYLIGHTS

Skylights allow daylight to enter an interior space from above. Skylights are metal-framed units preassembled with glass or plastic glazing and flashing. They come in stock sizes and shapes or can be custom-made. They are efficient and cost-effective sources of daylighting.

Angled skylights on a north-facing or shaded roof
- reduce the heat and glare associated with direct sun
- bounce sunbeams off angled interior ceilings to further diffuse the brightness
- may offer a view of sky and trees from the interior

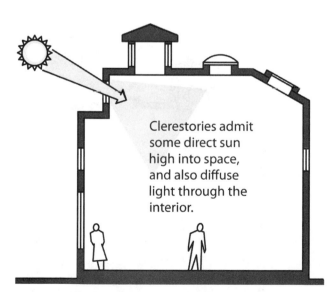

Figure 13-3 Clerestory window. Clerestories provide balanced daylight throughout the changing seasons better than skylights do. South east, or west facing clerestory windows that are designed so that the light bounces against a vertical surface and is diffused on its way to the interior capture the maximum amount of sun in December and the minimum amount of sun in June. Clerestories use standard weathertight window construction. In the northern hemisphere, south facing clerestories provide the most heat gain in the winter.

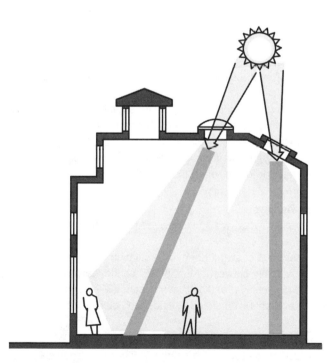

Figure 13-4 Skylights. Skylights can be mounted flat or angled with the slope of a roof. It is important for them to be installed correctly in order to prevent leaks. Controlling brightness and glare may also require louvers, shades, or reflector panels. A well-designed and installed horizontal skylight with a domed surface can bring daylight into an interior space and provide a view of the sky.

Horizontal skylights

- get less low-angle winter sun than skylights on sloped surfaces
- admit most heat in summer, adding to cooling load
- require shades when artificial cooling is used
- do not collect much solar heat in winter, are covered by snow, and may leak in rain
- work best in overcast conditions

Skylights are glazed with acrylic or polycarbonate plastic, or with wired, laminated, heat-strengthened, or fully tempered glass. Building codes limit the maximum area of each glazed skylight panel. Building codes also require wire screening below glazing to prevent broken-glass injuries when wired glazing, heat-strengthened glass, or fully-tempered glass is used in multilayer glazing systems. There are exemptions to these regulations for individual dwelling units.

Double-glazing a skylight promotes energy conservation and reduces condensation. Skylights with translucent glazing provide daylight from above without excessive heat gain. The process by which translucent materials diffuse light reduces contrast for a restful, long-term environment, but the light appears as dull as that from an overcast sky. Clear glass should be used when the sparkle of sunlight is desired.

OTHER TOPLIGHTING OPTIONS

Tubular skylights (also called light pipes or sun pipes):

- are metal or plastic tubes that deliver light from roof into otherwise dark room
- do not provide a view
- transmit and deliver varied amounts of light depending on diameter of shaft
- are convenient and economical for supplemental illumination in hallways, closets, and areas that do not require a great deal of control
- produce light quality comparable to that of ceiling-mounted fluorescent fixture (often indistinguishable)

Roof windows:

- are stock wood windows designed for installation in sloping roof
- either pivot or swing open for ventilation and cleaning
- are typically between 61 and 122 centimeters (2–4 ft.) wide and between 92 and 183 centimeters (3–6 ft.) high
- are available with shades, blinds, and electric operators

Sloped glazing systems:

- glazed curtain walls engineered to serve as pitched glass roofs

Heliostats and tracking devices:

- are dish-shaped mirrors that focus sunlight onto a stationary second mirror
- must be maintained to prevent dirt and dust accumulation from affecting their performance
- require source of energy (perhaps solar)

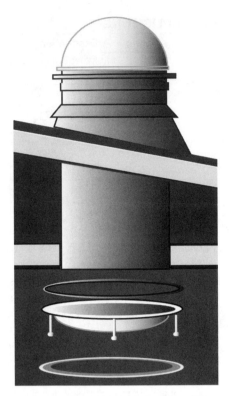

Figure 13-5 Tubular skylight. A typical light pipe includes a roof-mounted plastic dome to capture sunlight, a reflective tube that stretches from the dome to the interior ceiling, and a ceiling-mounted diffuser that spreads the light around the room. Installation is relatively simple.

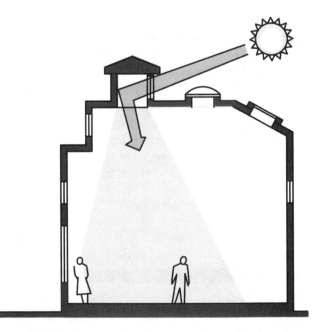

Figure 13-6 Roof monitor. Roof monitors reflect daylight into a space. The light enters a scoop-like construction on the roof, then bounces off the surfaces of the monitor opening and down into the space. Mirror systems that use a periscope-like device can bring daylight and views underground by reflecting them down through a space.

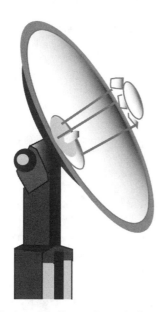

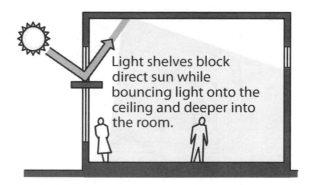

Light shelves block direct sun while bouncing light onto the ceiling and deeper into the room.

Figure 13-8 Light shelf. Light shelves are part of the exterior architecture of a building and must be planned as such. They work best in spaces with high ceiling reflectances.

Figure 13-7 Heliostat. A heliostat dynamically readjusts the primary mirror to track the sun and maximize the capture and use of sunlight at all times of the day. Collected light is distributed, often with a light pipe.

Daylight Control

Exterior shading strategies were discussed in Chapter 11: Heating and Cooling. Light shelves transition between exterior and interior.

Window treatments are more than interior decorations; they can play an important part in preventing glare. Interior devices to control daylight include the following:

Venetian blinds:
- adjust to changing exterior and interior conditions
- can block all daylight and view if desired
- permit light to enter room by reflection back and forth between slats, while still blocking glare
- can exclude direct sun and reflect light onto ceiling, where it will bounce into interior
- redirect daylight deeper into room when mirrored on one or two sides
- in upper 61 centimeters (2 ft.) of window, can beam daylight between 9 and 12 meters (30–40 ft.) into space to provide illumination at work surface
- can be rigged to cover only lower half of window
- are available as slender blinds between two window panels, thereby eliminating dirt and clumsy control cords

Figure 13-9 Venetian blinds. Styles of blinds range from thin-metal mini-blinds, such as those shown here, to blinds with wide wooden slats.

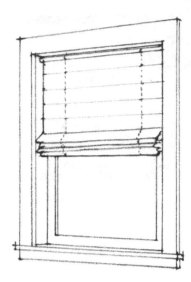

Figure 13-10 Roman shade. Roman shades are versatile window treatments. They can be made with insulating and custom materials.

Roller shades:

- diffuse direct sunlight, eliminate glare, and increase uniformity of illumination
- can be so bright that they become source of glare themselves
- come in off-white fabric colors or with additional opaque drapery in order to reduce brightness
- when opaque, can be pulled up from bottom of window to permit daylight into room while still eliminating glare

Automatic motorized shading systems:

- respond to sensors and continually adjust amount of daylight
- are expensive

Draperies:

- Their effectiveness depends on the weave and the reflectivity of the fabric.
- Any amount of light transmission from blackout through transparency can be achieved.
- More flexibility is possible with two separately tracked drapes over the same opening.
- Draperies allow user adjustment and soften the interior environment.
- Their exterior surfaces (like those of some shades, blinds, and insulating panels) are mirrored or highly reflective to reject most sunlight.

Tinted glass or **plastic** with metallic or metal-oxide coatings or films:

- reflects light to control amount of light that enters interior
- reduces the view into interior from outside during day
- changes way exterior looks from inside building
- puts interior on display while blocking occupant views at night
- transmits IR spectrum, which contains heat, at 10 to 15 percent below their visible light transmittance

Colored materials, such as bronze, distort the appearance of interior colors. Gray-tinted glazing is neutral in tone, so interior colors are rendered fairly accurately. Light-transmittance ranges from very dark with only 10 to 15 percent of light passing through to very light with 70 to 80 percent of the light passing through.

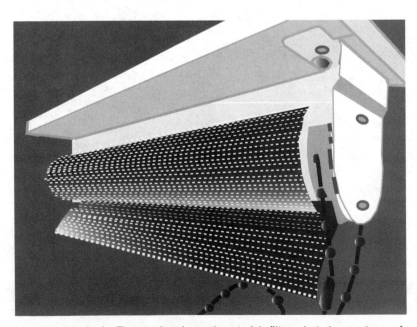

Figure 13-11 Mesh roller shade. The openings in mesh materials filter selected percentages of sunlight. The mechanisms range from simple roller shades to motorized commercial systems with remote controls.

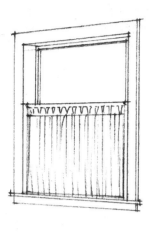

Figure 13-12 Curtains and drapery. Drapery designs tend to be more formal than those of curtains, which are often hung inside the window frame. Drapes are often used with sheer casements for maximum flexibility in light control.

Daylighting and Heat

Daylight brings with it solar heat, which may be welcome as a part of a building's sustainable energy plan or may raise energy use for air conditioning. Some solar-heating designs do not allow openings in the south wall for daylight. On the other hand, solar-heating designs that permit direct sun through south facing walls may admit too much daylight and glare for visual tasks. Large glazed openings that let in daylight can lose heat through those same cold glass surfaces. Designs that limit openings on north, east, and west facing walls to keep heat in the building may shut out daylight from these directions. One design option is to use overly warm sun-heated air from southern exposures to warm the cooler north, east, and west facing perimeters of the building.

In the summer, shaded windows produce less heat gain than the electric lights they replace, resulting in decreased energy use for both lighting and cooling. Electrical lighting introduces around twice as much heat per unit of light into a space as daylighting does. In the winter, there is some solar heat gain from south facing windows, but the use of daylighting eliminates some of the heat that would otherwise be generated by electric lighting, so supplemental heating may be needed.

LIGHTING DESIGN BASICS

Interior design schools routinely offer full-semester courses on lighting design. It is not the purpose of this book to try to cover all of the facets of lighting design to the degree that a lighting course would. Instead, we will look at how the current approach to lighting developed as well as how current lighting design practices affect relationships between architects, engineers, lighting designers, and interior designers. We will also look at some of the less glamorous aspects of selecting lighting sources and controls and will consider practical fixture requirements and lighting system maintenance.

History of Lighting

After the sun went down, fire was the first source of heat and light, and it is still a major source in many parts of the world. Indoor lighting most likely originated with the triangular stone oil lamp used by Cro-Magnon man around 50,000 years ago; a fibrous wick lying in a saucer-like depression was kept burning by rank-smelling animal fat. By around 1300 BCE, the Egyptians burned vegetable-oil lamps with bases of sculpted earthenware and papyrus wicks. Later, Greeks and Romans used wicks of oakum (hemp or jute fiber) or linen that had to be lifted and trimmed, and the lamps had forceps with scissors attached for this purpose.

In 1490, Leonardo da Vinci invented a high-intensity lamp by immersing a glass cylinder that contained olive oil and a hemp wick inside a large glass globe filled with water. The water magnified the flame and allowed him to work through the night.

The Romans invented candles made of nearly colorless and tasteless animal fat (tallow) before the first century AD. This edible substance led starving soldiers to eat their candle rations. In the nineteenth century, isolated British lighthouse keepers did the same.

By the eighteenth century, British chandlers (candle makers) used beef and mutton fat from small-town slaughterhouses to make candles for housewives; these candles had to be snuffed every half hour by snipping the charred end of the wick. Since matches had not yet been invented, the candles were hard to relight once the flame was out. Castles that used hundreds of candles each week kept a staff of snuff servants solely for this purpose. Tallow candles could rot or be eaten by rats if not stored properly.

The rushlight was made by holding a reed (rush) soaked in melted fat in the jaws of special holders, where they would burn for 15 to 20 minutes. Rushlights remained in use in rural England into the twentieth century.

By the late seventeenth century, the use of semi-evaporating beeswax candles was widespread. Although beeswax candles were three times the price of tallow, they burned with a brighter flame, less smoke, and a much more pleasant smell. In 1765, household records indicated that one of Britain's great homes used 100 pounds of wax candles per month. Glossy white English beeswax, hard yellow vegetable tallow from China, and green bayberry-scented candles from the northeast coast of America were prized for their quality.

In the early eighteenth century, an oil from the head of sperm whales called spermaceti was used for candles that burned with a bright, white flame. Vegetable-oil candles with plaited wicks that did not need snuffing were introduced in England in 1840 to celebrate Queen Victoria's wedding to Prince Albert. Inexpensive paraffin candles that burned as brightly as spermaceti were introduced in 1857.

Figure 13-13 Gas lamp poster. The poster's title reads, "French people economize natural gas."

By 1900, the availability of oil lamps and gaslights was cutting into the market for candles. The simplest oil lamp consisted of a shallow dish with a lip that supported a wick made from rush or twined cotton, which gave off about the same light as a candle. In 1784, French inventor Ami Argand enclosed a wick in a glass chimney below a large reservoir of oil. This produced the light of 10 candles and could burn unattended for several hours. By 1836, the glass oil lamp with a key to wind the wick was a common sight.

Oil lamps used whale oil, and the aggressive hunting of whales would have probably ended in their extinction if petroleum had not been discovered in Pennsylvania in 1859; distilled into kerosene, it burned with a clear, bright, and nearly smokeless light. Kerosene lamps appeared as elaborate chandeliers, functional kitchen lamps, and even tiny pressed-tin lamps for servants' quarters. Unfortunately, the lamp oil had a very unpleasant smell and was highly flammable, so lamps were stored out of the way in a separate lamp room when not in use and distributed by servants as daylight faded.

Three thousand years ago, people in China burned natural gas to remove the brine from salt. Early European tribes erected temples around natural gas jets to worship the eternal flames. In the seventeenth century, Belgian chemist Jan Baptista van Helmont manufactured coal gas. He believed in the use of the philosopher's stone to transform base metals to gold, and his invention was a bridge from alchemy to chemistry. His work inspired French chemist Antoine Lavoisier, who considered the possibility of lighting Paris streets with gas lamps and invented a prototype lamp in the 1780s. Unfortunately, Lavoisier was guillotined during the French Revolution.

Before the invention of the electric light bulb, gaslight supplied lighting for streets and buildings. The first gas company was established in London in 1813, leading to the advent of home gas lamps. By 1816, Westminster, England, boasted 26 miles of gas pipe. The heat and smell from gas fixtures relegated them to use outdoors until the middle of the nineteenth century.

German scientist Robert von Bunsen diminished the flicker of a pure-gas flame by premixing the gas with air. In 1885, one of Bunsen's students invented the gas mantle, which greatly increased illumination. The mantle was made of thread dipped in thorium and cerium nitrate. When lit, the thread was consumed, and the remaining skeleton of carbonized compounds glowed a brilliant greenish white.

British inventors had been experimenting with electric lights for more than 50 years before Thomas Edison invented the lightbulb. When a current is passed through a filament in a glass chamber without air, it glows white-hot. Joseph Swan had the idea of using carbon for the filament, and patented a lamp in England in 1878, a year before Edison had the same idea and registered a patent in the United States. Edison then proceeded to set up a system of electrical distribution and took the lightbulb out of the laboratory and into homes and streets. The two men sued each other but eventually cofounded an electric company.

Edison's Pearl Street Power Station in New York City was the first to supply electricity on consumer demand. By December 1882, more than 200 individual and business customers in Manhattan were using more than 3000 electric lamps, each with an average bulb life of only 15 hours (compared to around 2000 hours today). By early 1884, Edison had perfected a 400-hour light bulb and increased that to 1200 hours in 1886.

Despite initial curiosity, the growth of electricity in homes was slow at first. It took seven years for Edison's initial 203 residential customers to grow to 710 homes. Thanks to decreasing electric rates and word of mouth, by 1900, 10,000 people had electric lights. By 1910, the number was more than three million.

In 1859, Antoine-Henri Becquerel, the French physicist who had discovered the radioactivity in uranium, coated the inside of a glass tube with a chemical called a phosphor that fluoresced under electric current. His invention became the basis of the fluorescent tube. It took until 1934 for Arthur Compton of the General Electric Company to develop the first practical fluorescent lamp in the United States. Operating at lower voltages, the fluorescent lamp was more economical than the incandescent bulb, which wasted up to 80 percent of its energy as heat. General Electric had white and colored fluorescent tubes on display at the 1939 World's Fair. By 1954, energy-saving fluorescent tubes had edged out incandescent lamps for commercial use.

Today, two electrical light-source types dominate the lighting market. Incandescent and discharge lamps include tungsten-halogen types as well as the classic incandescent bulb. Fluorescent, mercury, metal-halide, sodium, and the more recent induction lamp are all gaseous-discharge types. Plasma-type lamps are a third type that uses a microwave-powered sulfur lamp.

Principles of Lighting Design

The goal of lighting design is to create an efficient and pleasing interior that is both functional and aesthetically pleasing. Lighting levels must be adequate for seeing the task at hand. By varying the levels of brightness within acceptable limits, the lighting design avoids monotony and creates perspective effects. **Ambient lighting** levels for general lighting should be at least one-third as high as task levels. **Accent lighting** levels that provide focus on a specific object should not be greater than five times the ambient level.

Another name for a lighting fixture is **luminaire**; its purpose is to house and provide electricity for the light source and to direct its output. The many variations available in luminaire design make choosing the correct fixture for a given use a difficult task. In addition to the light they contribute to a space, luminaires can serve as focal points, adding sparkle, style, and visual texture.

In an open office, the advantages of nonuniform lighting increase as the space between workstations increases. Nonuniform ceiling layouts may appear chaotic. Using uniform ambient lighting along with local **task lighting** near visually taxing activities eliminates this problem. By placing indirect lighting fixtures carefully and making sure that they are the correct distance from the ceiling, an interior designer can prevent bright spots on the ceiling that appear as direct and reflected glare.

By grouping tasks with similar lighting requirements and placing the most intensive visual tasks at locations that offer the best daylight, an interior designer can use fewer fixtures and less lighting energy. Movable fixtures work best for task lighting. Sometimes, it is more energy efficient to look at improving the way a difficult visual task is done than to provide higher levels of lighting.

☑ **Interior designers should specify effective, high-quality, efficient, low-maintenance, thermally controlled fixtures. High-quality, permanent finishes, such as Alzac, multicoated baked enamel, or aluminum finishes, will retain their performance for eight to ten years. For energy efficiency, look for a high luminaire efficiency rating (LER). Low-maintenance fixtures remain clean for extended periods and are designed so that all reflecting surfaces are easily and rapidly cleaned without demounting. Fixtures should permit simple and rapid relamping and should be located so as to provide adequate access.**

Lighting terminology and definitions:
- **Luminous transmittance** (which is also called transmittance, transmission factor, and coefficient of transmission) is a quality of a material, such as a luminaire lens or diffuser, and is a measure of its ability to transmit incident light; it is the ratio of the total transmitted light to the total incident light.
- **Reflectance** (which is also called reflectance factor and reflectance coefficient) is the ratio of reflected light to incident light.
- **Specular reflection** is the reflection that occurs on a smooth surface, such as polished glass or stone.
- **Efficacy** measures the relationship between the amount of light and the amount of heat produced by both daylight and electric light sources. It is measured in **lumens per watt (lm/W)** and is the ratio of lumens provided to watts of heat produced by a light source. Fixture efficiency is directly affected by temperature. Daylight introduces less heat per lumen than electric sources.

Light-colored finishes on ceilings, walls, floors, and furnishings in workspaces reflect more light and make better use of lighting energy than dark-colored finishes.

TABLE 13-3. SURFACE REFLECTANCES

Surface	Reflectance
Ceiling	80 to 92 percent
Walls	49 to 60 percent
Floors	20 to 40 percent
Furniture, office machines, equipment	25 to 45 percent

TABLE 13-4. KEY LIGHTING DESIGN PRINCIPLES

Design Principle	Strategy	Tactic	Effect
Design lighting for expected activity	Nonuniform lighting in multitask spaces where some tasks need additional light	Use readily movable fixtures	User puts light where needed
		Use fixed luminaries for general low-level lighting with supplemental task lighting	Saves energy; provides welcome contrast
		Use uniform layout for ambient lighting	Reduces distraction
		Group tasks with similar lighting requirements	Uses light efficiently
		Place difficult visual tasks at best daylight locations	Reduces use of electrical lighting
		Improve quality of difficult visual tasks rather than providing more light	Reduces need for higher lighting levels
Specify well-designed luminaires	Effective fixtures provide useful light and minimize direct glare	Specify luminaires with visual comfort probability (VCP) of 70 or more	Reduces likelihood of glare
	High-quality fixtures with permanent finishes	Specify Alzac, multicoat baked enamel, or high-quality permanent aluminum finishes	Maintains original performance for eight to ten years
	Energy-efficient fixtures	Specify luminaires with high luminaire efficiency ratings (LERs)	Rating combines photometric and energy efficiencies
	Low-maintenance fixtures	Specify luminaires designed so that all reflecting surfaces can be easily and rapidly cleaned without demounting	Reduces maintenance time, expense
		Specify luminaires that remain clean for extended periods	
	Thermally controlled fixtures	Use electronic ballasts, low-wattage lamps to reduce heat generated by fixtures	Reduces cooling expense, energy use
Select efficient light sources and accessories	Light sources and accessories that produce good-quality light efficiently	Use high-efficacy, high CRI, compact sources	Maximizes quality of lighting; minimizes energy use
	Spill light; borrowed light	Use glass in upper wall sections	Uses light efficiently
Select appropriate lighting system	Indirect: 90 to 100 percent of light is directed toward ceilings, upper walls	Correct spacing and hanging-stem lengths 12 to 18 inches from ceiling to avoid hot spots	Diffuse, shadowless illumination with low glare
	Semi-indirect: 60 to 90 percent of light is directed toward ceilings, upper walls	Downward light diffused by translucent element	Diffuse lighting with low glare
	Direct/indirect: 50 percent upward; 50 percent downward	Upward light reflected from room surfaces; downward light through diffuser	Good diffusion; satisfactory downward lighting levels
	General diffusion: light transmitted in all directions	Select luminaires with low luminance; lay out in patterns that reduce visual disturbance	Efficient for spaces with moderate lighting levels
	Semi-direct: 60 to 90 percent downward	Remaining upward lighting minimizes direct glare from fixtures	Shadows minimal with minimum of 25 percent upward lighting and 70 percent ceiling reflectance
	Direct: all light downward	Floor and horizontal surfaces reflect light; light sources may be spread or concentrated; luminaires may form ceiling surface	Low ceiling illumination; little vertical illumination; fixture adaptations to avoid glare
Use of daylight properly	Design to use when available	Plan to use daylighting when building-use schedule permits	Lower electrical-lighting energy costs
	Control of window luminance to avoid disabling glare	Provide easily adjustable, user-controlled window treatments	User can adjust to avoid glare
	Control of excessive heat gain	Select glazing and treatments to reduce IR radiation entering space	Reduces need for cooling
		Use thermally massive materials	Moderates and slows changes in temperature
	Reflect light back into space at night to avoid light loss via windows	Provide light-reflective window treatments for night use	Reduces light energy lost through windows; also reduces heat loss

TABLE 13-4. KEY LIGHTING DESIGN PRINCIPLES (continued)

Design Principle	Strategy	Tactic	Effect
Use energy-efficient lighting control strategies	Can reduce energy consumption by up to 60 percent without reducing lighting effectiveness	Appropriate controls are mandated in ANSI/ASHRAE/IESNA Standard 90.1	Reduces energy use; does not limit design
		Occupancy sensors; automatic daylight-compensation control	Reduces use of electrical-lighting energy when not needed
		Separate tasks or spaces with separate controls	Reduces amount of space lighted
Use light finishes on ceilings, walls, floors, furnishings	Produce higher illumination levels in room	Specify light-colored, highly reflective surfaces	Maximizes impact of lighting
	Minimize uncomfortable illuminance ratios	Avoid high contrasts between backgrounds and illuminated surfaces	Reduces eye fatigue, glare, distraction

The Process of Lighting Design

Until 1973, daylighting was considered to be part of architectural design, not part of lighting design. Since an artificial-lighting system had to be installed anyway, the practice was to ignore daylight, even to the extent of shutting it out completely. However, when the energy crisis occurred in the mid-1970s, the extensive use of electrical energy for lighting in nonresidential buildings drove designers to integrate the least expensive, most abundant, and in many ways most desirable form of lighting: daylighting. The lighting designer on a project considers the following:

- integration of daylight with electric light
- energy-use relationships among electric lighting, daylighting, heating, and cooling
- coordination of interior layout of space and lighting design
- source, characteristics, and equipment requirements for electric lighting
- visual requirements for specific tasks and occupants
- light and shadow patterns and ability to see visual detail
- color of both light and illuminated surfaces and their effects
- aesthetic qualities of daylight and electrical light
- effect of lighting on physiological and psychological well-being

The process of lighting design includes several phases similar to other design processes. The design process entails the following:

- **Task analysis** assesses difficulty, time factor, type of user, cost of errors, and any special requirements.
- **Preliminary design** evaluates the need for general, local, or supplementary lighting; choices of sources and systems; architectural-lighting elements; daylighting; and ambient lighting.
- **Detailed design** determines fixtures and ceiling systems, degrees of nonuniform lighting, and the use of fixed or movable lighting. It also involves making detailed calculations and considering maintenance requirements.
- **Evaluation** looks at the design's energy use, construction and operating costs, and **life-cycle costs**.

The lighting designer prepares specifications and drawings and may handle the ordering of fixtures and controls. Fixtures often have long delivery times, so advance planning is necessary. When fixtures arrive, their many parts must be inspected and accounted for. Although fixtures may be one of the last elements to be installed, they must be one of the first planned and ordered for interior projects.

After installation, light levels must be fine-tuned. The individuals responsible for day-to-day use must be trained in using controls, and those involved in maintenance must understand lamp types and replacement requirements. The lighting designer can expect to make additional visits after installation until everything works to the client's satisfaction.

The interior designer or lighting designer typically prepares a lighting plan and schedule that indicate fixture locations and selections. Then must coordinate the selections with the heating, ventilating, and air-conditioning (HVAC) engineers, who will monitor power loads. The result is a detailed, workable design that may involve relocating a space or changing lighting or HVAC-system details.

The best lighting designs blend seamlessly into an overall interior design. Differences inherent in the objectives of the interior designer and the electrical engineer often lead to difficulties in achieving this goal. These differences are rooted in the training and functions associated with each profession. The interior designer may focus on aesthetics to combine form with function and to strive for an interior space that supports the client's image and facilitates the client's work process. Often, the electrical engineer's perspective may conflict with a design concept. Focusing on technical issues, the electrical engineer creates designs that accentuate flexibility and efficiency. By standardizing lighting, fixture type, and fixture placement and by minimizing the number of different light sources, the engineer promotes energy conservation and maintenance simplicity while providing enough light for the tasks at hand.

The lighting design approach that engineers are most likely to use is analytical and data-oriented. An alternative approach called **brightness design** involves using a computer perspective of a space with the level of luminances desired; then the lighting is designed to meet these lighting levels. The model provides the designer with a picture of the space's brightness patterns and

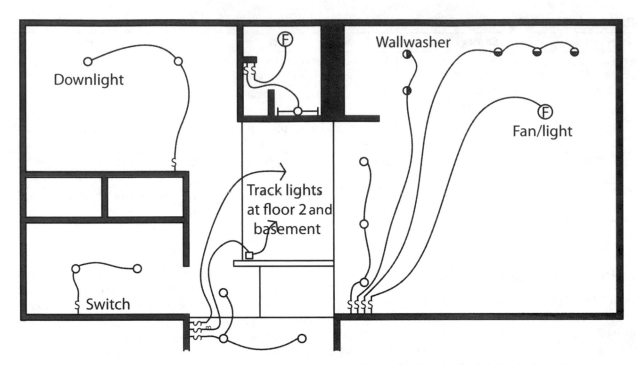

Figure 13-14 Interior designer's lighting plan. An interior designer's lighting plan is often the basis for the work of an electrical engineer.

encourages experimentation with window configurations and treatments, light sources, and shadows. Brightness design relies heavily on the experience of the designer and is more intuitive—and less quantifiable—than analytical lighting design.

The designer and the electrical engineer often have differing perspectives on the relationship with the client, and this can widen the gap between their approaches. The designer typically works with the client's executive management team to blend business objectives, work processes, and corporate image. The engineer might never meet this team and frequently works with the facility manager, who may also be one of the interior designer's contacts. Facility managers are looking for a lighting scheme that is flexible, efficient, and low-maintenance. A third client group comprises the users, including employees, whose needs focus on comfort and productivity. Unless the interior designer and the electrical engineer understand the needs of these three distinct client groups, they will not be able to work together effectively. When the interior designer and electrical engineer work well together, they help the client recognize and prioritize each client group's objectives and achieve a design that integrates each discipline's strengths and meets the client's overall needs.

Professional lighting designers can help bridge the gap. With expertise in the technical aspects of lighting and strong resources in the aesthetic and functional aspects of lighting design, the lighting designer is able to see both perspectives. Added to this are extensive knowledge of the fixtures on the market and the ability to speak the electrician's language.

Thoughtful architects, engineers, and lighting designers are conducting research into ways to satisfy real vision needs with minimal energy use. The Illuminating Engineering Society of North America (IESNA) is a research, standards, and publishing organization that develops stable scientific bases for lighting while remaining aware of its artistic aspects. The combination of science and art make lighting design a truly architectural discipline.

The amount of electrical energy used for lighting has been decreasing as consumers and business become more aware of energy conservation strategies. Good lighting design can save up to half of the electrical power used for lighting.

Lighting has been a major contributor to the building heat load. One watt of lighting adds 1 watt (3.4 BTUs per hour) of heat gain to the space. It takes about 0.28 watts of additional energy to cool 1 watt from lighting in the summer, but the added heat may be welcome in the winter. Reducing the lighting-power energy levels to below 2 watts per .09 square meter (1 sq ft.) in all but special areas results in less impact from light-generated heat on the HVAC system.

Lighting standards are set by a variety of authorities, depending on the type of building, whether it is government owned or built, and where it is located. The International Building Code (IBC) and other code authorities require energy conservation measures. Standards may also give credits for energy-saving lighting controls. Agencies that publish standards and code requirements for lighting include

- U.S. Department of Energy (DOE)
- U.S. General Services Administration (GSA)
- National Fire Protection Association (NFPA) codes, including the National Electrical Code (NEC)
- American Society of Heating, Refrigerating and Air-Conditioning Engineers (ASHRAE)
- Illuminating Engineering Society of North America (IESNA)
- National Institute of Science and Technology (NIST)

Energy budgets and lighting levels established by these standards affect the type of lighting source, the fixture selection, the lighting system, the furniture placement, and maintenance schedules. State codes may regulate the amount of energy permitted for lighting in various occupancies. With good design, lighting levels can be even lower than limits set by codes.

Selecting Light Sources

The most important decision made during the lighting design process is most likely the choice of light source. This choice of lamp affects color, heat generation, energy use, maintenance, and cost.

The human eye perceives the longest visible wavelengths as red and the progressively shorter wavelengths as orange, yellow, green, blue, and violet. White is a balanced mix of all of the wavelengths, and black is the absence of light. Human eyes evolved to see in sunlight, and we perceive sunlight as normal in color.

The color appearance of any object is strongly influenced by the illuminating lamp's spectrum and color temperature. The **spectrum** is the range of energies or wavelengths that, when reflected or transmitted by materials, are interpreted by our eyes and brain as colors. When materials absorb these energies, they become heat.

Chromaticity, the relative proportions of each of three primary colors (red, green, and blue) required to produce a given illuminant color, is the basis of the **Commission Internationale de l'Eclairage (CIE) color system**, the internationally accepted standard for designating illuminant color.

A lamp's **color temperature** indicates its own color appearance, for example, yellow, white, or blue-white. The color temperature is also usually a guide to the colors in which it has the most energy. Color temperature determines whether a light source is regarded as warm, mid-range, or cool; the higher the color temperature, the cooler the source.

Careful selection of lamps enables a lighting designer to modify the visual perception of illuminated spaces. These qualities change, of course, when electric lighting is turned off. Incandescent lamps, including halogen lamps, with color temperatures of between 2700 K and 3000 K and color rendering indexes (CRIs) well above 90 (see p. TK) are often used to enhance warm palettes:

- Standard incandescent lamps can distort cooler colors, especially at low light levels.
- Fluorescent lamps are available in a wide variety of color temperatures, ranging from 2700 K to 6500 K, and CRIs of 90 to the low 50s.

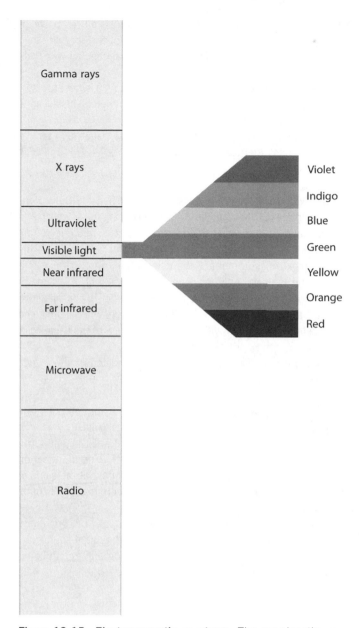

Figure 13-15 Electromagnetic spectrum. The wavelengths responsible for visible light make up only a small portion of the electromagnetic spectrum.

TABLE 13-5. EXAMPLES OF COLOR TEMPERATURES

Light Source	Color Quality	Color Temperature
Candle flame	Warm	1750 K
Standard incandescent lamp	Medium	2600 K to 3000 K
Cool-white fluorescent lamp	Cool	4250 K
Clear blue sky	Very cool	10,000 K

- Compact fluorescent lamps come in temperatures between 2700 K and 3000 K for warm palettes, 3500 K for mid-range or mixed palettes, and 4100 K for cool palettes, all with CRIs of 80 to 85.
- Linear fluorescent lamps, such as T8 and T5 types, are currently the leading choices in retail and commercial installations where color rendition is important.
- High-intensity discharge (HID) lamps (see page 291) have a range of color temperatures from 1800 K to 6400 K and CRIs from 60 to 85.

Along with other color-rendering considerations, the **Color Rendering Index (CRI)** should be considered during the selection and specification of lamps. The CRI is the only color-rendering rating published in lamp manufacturers' product literature. The CRI is a complex measurement of the color-rendering capability of a lamp and is useful only for comparing lamps with the same or very similar color temperatures. A CRI rating of 80 or higher indicates that there is very little shift in test colors when illuminated by the lamp compared with a reference source of the same color temperature.

The designer can alter light-source characteristics to reduce loss of contrast several ways:

- Dimming or switching lamps reduces the fixture output in the critical glare zone and can improve task contrast.
- Using large-area, low-output sources reduces source luminance in the ceiling glare zone and increases illumination from the outside glare zone for better contrast at the same or lower illuminance level; however, this increases the lighting fixture cost.
- A luminaire can be used to make a large, low-brightness source, such as a ceiling or wall a secondary light source.
- Reflected and direct glare only at offending angles can be reduced with diffusers and lenses.

INCANDESCENT LAMPS

The light from an open fire, a candle, or an oil lamp is incandescent, as is the glowing filament of a lightbulb. Incandescent light has fewer shorter wavelengths and, therefore, appears redder than sunlight. Up to 90 percent of the electrical energy used by an incandescent lamp is lost to heat, and only the remaining 10 percent is emitted as light. The additional heat increases the building's cooling load. Incandescent lamps have relatively short lives, with about 750 hours the standard. However, at least one incandescent lamp is available that has a 10,000-hour lifespan.

Where incandescent lamps are selected, using a single large lamp rather than several smaller ones limits energy use and increases the amount of overall light. One 100-watt incandescent lamp produces more light than three 40-watt lamps and uses 20 watts less electricity. Three-way lamps are a good choice because they can be switched to a lower wattage when bright light is not

TABLE 13-7. EFFICACY OF LIGHT SOURCES

Source	Efficacy (lumen/Watt)
Candle	0.1
Incandescent lamp (15 to 500 W)	8–22
Tungsten-halogen lamp (50 to 1500 W)	18–22
Fluorescent lamp (15 to 215 W)	35–80
Compact fluorescent lamp	55–75
Mercury vapor lamp (40 to 1000 W)	32–63
Metal-halide lamp (70 to 1500 W)	80–125
HPS (35 to 100 W)	55–115
Induction lamp	48–70
Sulfur lamp	90–100
Sunlight, varying conditions	90–115
White LEDs	20–60

TABLE 13-6. LIGHT SOURCE COLORS

Type	Lamp	Approximate CRI	Whiteness	Colors Enhanced	Colors Grayed
Fluorescent	Warm white	52	Yellowish	Orange, yellow	Red, blue, green
	Cool white	62	White	Yellow, orange, blue	Red
	Cool white deluxe	77	White	Green, orange, yellow	Red
	Triphosphor	75	Yellowish	Red, orange	Deep red, blue
		80	Pale yellowish	Red, orange, green	Deep red
Mercury	Clear	20	Blue-green	Blue, green	Red, orange
	Deluxe	45	Pale purplish	Deep blue, red	Blue-green
Metal-Halide	Clear	65	White	Blue, green, yellow	Red
	Phosphor-coated	80	White	Blue, green, yellow	None
HPS	Standard	21	Yellowish	Yellow, green	Red, blue
	Color-corrected	60	Yellowish-white	Red, green, yellow	Blue
	Incandescent	99 or higher	Yellowish	Red, orange, yellow	Blue, green

needed. Dimmers help add flexibility to the light load. Energy-saving incandescent lamps replace standard types without a visible difference; for example, 40-watt lamps are replaced by 34-watt lamps; 60-watt lamps by 52-watt lamps; and 75-watt lamps by 67-watt lamps.

Incandescent lamps were once ubiquitous, but they are now losing ground to sources that produce less heat and use less energy. Fluorescent lamps are leading the way.

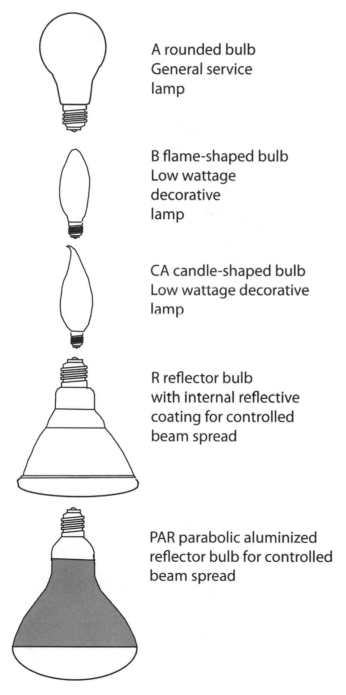

A rounded bulb
General service
lamp

B flame-shaped bulb
Low wattage
decorative
lamp

CA candle-shaped bulb
Low wattage decorative
lamp

R reflector bulb
with internal reflective
coating for controlled
beam spread

PAR parabolic aluminized
reflector bulb for controlled
beam spread

Figure 13-16 Common incandescent lamp bulb shapes. These are some of the most common incandescent lamp bulb shapes.

FLUORESCENT LAMPS

Fluorescent lamps are sealed glass tubes filled with mercury. An electrical discharge between the ends of the tubes vaporizes the mercury vapor and excites it into discharging UV light to a phosphor coating the tube's inner surface. The phosphor glows, with the color of the light it emits determined by the composition of the phosphor. Fluorescent light may lack the longer, warmer wavelengths and appear bluer than sunlight, but they are now available in 220 colors. Trichromic phosphor fluorescent lamps combine green, blue, and red for a highly efficient white light. They can be made cooler or warmer by changing the proportions of the primary colors. Compact fluorescent lamps have largely solved the problems of size and design of fixtures with a multitude of forms.

Technological improvements in dimmable fluorescent lamps are making this a feasible option. Dimming a fluorescent lamp system lowers energy consumption and allows flexibility in lighting levels. Currently, fluorescent dimming methods include analog, digital, and wireless IR.

Fluorescent lamps provide three to five times more light for the same amount of energy than conventional incandescent lamps. When a 75-watt incandescent lamp is replaced with an 18-watt compact fluorescent lamp, 570 kilowatt-hours (kWh) of electricity and eliminate 1300 pounds of carbon-dioxide emissions over the life of the fluorescent lamp. Fluorescent lamps give off less heat, reducing energy needed for air conditioning. Fluorescent lamp life ratings depend on how often the lamp is started. The more hours per start, the longer the lamp life. Ratings have increased to the point where lamps should be turned off when not needed for more than a few minutes. Fluorescent lamps operate best between 41°F and 77°F (5°C–25°C). High humidity makes them difficult to start, but precoating them with silicone breaks up moisture films and prevents leakage.

Fluorescent T8 lamps and T5 lamps with electronic ballasts can help meet energy-efficiency code requirements. T5 lamps are very highly efficient and use an ultraslim ballast case that can be hidden in slender fixtures. Because the T5 puts out the same amount of light as a T8 with 40-percent less lamp wall area, its surface brightness is about 60 percent higher than that of the T8. This allows for very efficient design, but it is too bright to look at. Today, new fixtures are being designed that take advantage of the T5's qualities while shielding glare.

Fluorescent lights require a ballast to operate. The ballast ignites the lamp with a high voltage, then controls the amount of electrical current for lamp operation. Recent advances in ballast technology have greatly changed the manufacturing and qualities of lighting ballasts.

Fluorescent ballasts regulate the electric current that flows through the fluorescent lamp. This activates the gas inside the fluorescent tube. Self-ballasted compact fluorescents have an electronic ballast as the part of the lamp that screws into the bulb socket. Modular compact fluorescent lamps have separate ballasts (adapters) that screw into standard light-bulb sockets. With a separate adapter, the ballast does not have to be replaced when the lamp fails. A fluorescent ballast will last 50,000 hours.

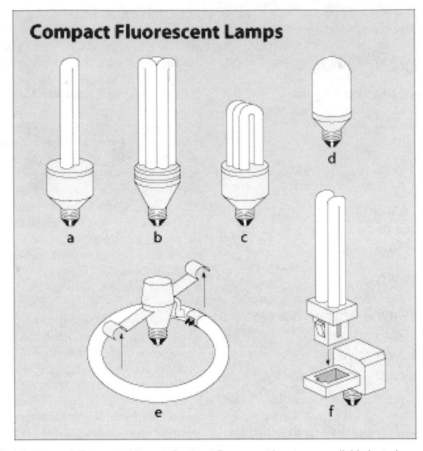

Figure 13-17 Compact fluorescent lamps. Compact fluorescent lamps are available in an increasing number of sizes and shapes that allow their use in lighting fixtures designed for incandescent lamps.

TABLE 13-8. LIGHTING BALLASTS

Ballast Type	Also Called	Description	Advantages	Disadvantages
Magnetic ballasts	Core-and-coil	Magnetic steel-plate core wrapped with copper windings	Formerly common; now obsolete; still in existing buildings	Operate at 60 Hz, causing humming sound; heavy; tend to flicker
Hybrid ballasts	Cathode-disconnect	Magnetic core-and-coil transformer with electronic switch	Better energy efficiency	Operate at 60 Hz, causing humming sound; heavy
Electronic ballasts	Solid-state electronic	Available as dimming ballasts	More energy efficient; generate less heat; virtually silent; lighter; start/stop without flicker	More expensive; may hum
Special ballasts	Low-current ballasts	Match specific low-current lamps: T8, slimline, others	Cost-effective; energy-efficient	Special ballasts must be specified to match specific lamps
	High-current ballasts	Used with high-output lamps	Increase output in existing installation; reduce number of fixtures in new installation	
	Energy-saving ballasts	Combine more efficient ballast design, lower current rating for lower wattage of lamp, special switching	Reduce total wattage of lamp/ballast combination	
	Multilevel ballasts	Used to change lighting levels evenly	Available with two or three levels	

Subcompact fluorescent lamps are smaller, brighter, and less expensive than earlier compact fluorescent lamps. With their subcompact size and screw-in bases, they fit in most lighting fixtures that are designed for incandescent lamps. Subcompact fluorescents offer the same energy-efficiency benefits as larger compact fluorescents and meet stricter technical specifications for color rendition and light output. They are available with the Energy Star® label.

Fluorescent and HID lamps contain mercury to generate UV energy that energizes the phosphor and produces light. Mercury, however, is a toxic material that accumulates in fish and other species. Mercury has been regulated as a hazardous material since 1980. The U.S. Environmental Protection Agency (EPA) initiated a new test, the Toxicity Characteristic Leaching Procedure (TCLP). Both fluorescent and HID lamps failed the TCLP.

In 2000, the EPA established the Universal Waste Rule, which requires that building owners and management dispose of their lamps in an environmentally sound manner. Conforming to this rule is easier when fixtures are relamped in a group rather than singly. Facilities may need to provide a storage area for storing spent lamps before disposal.

Today, fluorescent lamps contain greatly reduced amounts of mercury (under 5 mg). According to the EPA, production of the electricity used during the life of a 60-watt incandescent lamp releases about three times as much mercury from power plants as that used by a compact fluorescent lamp, even when the mercury in a landfilled (rather than recycled) lamp is added.

HALOGEN LAMPS

Tungsten-halogen lamps (commonly called halogen lamps) are an efficient, lightweight, compact, incandescent light source with a 2000-hour lifespan. Like a standard incandescent lamp, a halogen lamp produces light by heating a filament. The addition of a small amount of halogen gas to the bulb produces a brighter, whiter light than standard incandescent lamps and prolongs lamp life. Halogen lamps are available in standard or low-voltage designs, with the standard design around 20 percent more efficient

than a standard incandescent lamp. Low-voltage reflector lamps are about 40 percent more efficient.

Halogen lamps are available in a variety of designs and bases. They are smaller than standard incandescent lamps of the same wattage and are ideal for precision point sources. The light output of an aging halogen lamp is much better than that of an aging incandescent lamp. Halogen lamps with reflectors offer a variety of high-intensity beams for professional spotlighting, task lighting, and accent lighting.

It takes a great deal of heat for the halogen gas to heat the compact, high-temperature filament, and when the gas pressure inside the lamp becomes too great, the quartz-lamp envelope can break violently and scatter hot quartz fragments. Consequently, fixtures with halogen lamps should be screened or shielded. The high lamp temperature can also be a fire hazard. These hazards are avoided when the lamp is encapsulated inside a sealed envelope. Encapsulated halogen lamps are available in R, PAR, MR, and modified A lamp shapes and can replace standard incandescent lamps of the same shapes, with three times the lifespan.

HIGH-INTENSITY DISCHARGE LAMPS

High-intensity discharge (HID) lamps are even more efficient than fluorescent lamps and have a 24,000-hour lifespan. The overall efficiency of HID lamps is influenced by the design of the lighting fixture, the age of the lamp, and the regularity of cleaning. Their color properties formerly limited their use to outdoors

Tungsten-halogen lamp

MR multifaceted reflector bulb for controlled beam spread

Figure 13-18 Tungsten-halogen lamp types.

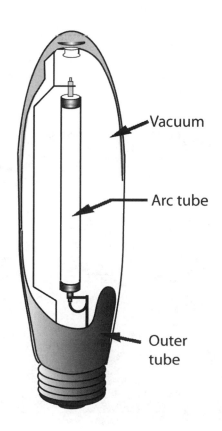

Vacuum

Arc tube

Outer tube

Figure 13-19 High-intensity discharge lamp.

or industrial spaces, but with more than 60 colors now available, they are more often used to replace incandescent and fluorescent lamps indoors.

HID lamps come in three main types, named for the materials in the lamp's arc tube that affect the light color.

- Mercury lamps tend to be somewhat blue-green.
- Metal-halide lamps provide the most natural-looking light and are used in stores and public spaces.
- High-pressure sodium (HPS) lamps tend toward the red-yellow wavelengths.

Newer HPS lamps have a whiter color than incandescent lamps and are suited for retail applications. HPS lamps are available with a CRI of 80—an outstanding rating—and a color temperature of 2700 K. They have a 10,000-hour lifespan and are highly energy efficient. HPS lamps can be used as accents as well as for display, wall-washing, and downlights. Their warm, crisp light has been described as like sunshine on a clear day. HPS lamps have some technical problems in terms of fixture design, but these are being worked out, so more-versatile, high-quality HPS lamps are expected to be on the market in the future.

LIGHT-EMITTING DIODES

Light-emitting diodes (LEDs) have been around for quite a while and are used in medical instruments, bar coders, telephones, digital cameras, laptop computers, consumer appliances, automobiles, and signals. They are also used in building signage, retail displays, and exit and emergency signs, and as pathway markers.

LEDs are available in a full range of colors, are small (1/8 inch [3 mm] across), have very low light output, use very little power, and have a fast response time. Today, LEDs are becoming mainstream lighting sources for luminaires.

FIBER OPTICS

Fiber optics are used architecturally for ambient, accent, and display lighting in many institutional and commercial buildings. A single, remote source can supply a large number of relatively small point-source lights, making star-sprinkled ceilings possible. Fiber optics eliminate heat, UV content, and electrical fields, along with much of the wiring present with other sources. Illuminators for fiber-optic systems utilize a variety of lamp types. The fiber bundle that carries the light can be buried in almost any substrate.

Fiber-optic lighting has its own terminology:

- **Attenuation:** degree of light reduction as it travels along fiber; amount of light and its color change with length of fiber
- **Axial mode** (also called end-light): optical fibers designed to carry light from its source to end of fiber with little leakage along the way
- **Core:** center of optical fiber that carries light
- **Glass optical fiber:** used for communications and data, but rarely for lighting because of its expense and large bending radius
- **Illuminator:** light source, usually metal box with metal-halide or halogen lamp and its accessories; may also contain optical controls, color filters, local and remote-control connections, and, almost always, fan or blower for forced-air cooling of source lamp
- **Lateral mode** (sidelighting): optical fibers designed to emit light along their entire length
- **Plastic optical fiber:** typically used in lighting work, usually clear-acrylic core sheathed with plastic compounds
- **Tail:** single optical fiber or bundle of fibers extending from illuminator to output point

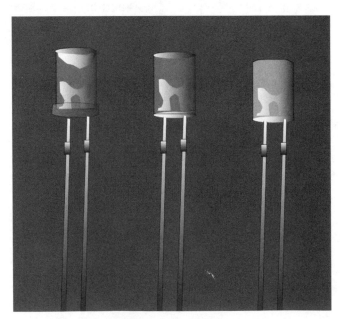

Figure 13-20 LEDs.

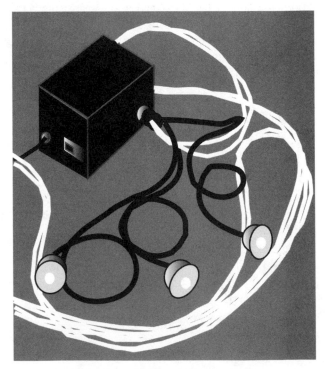

Figure 13-21 Fiber optic lighting system.

HOLLOW LIGHT GUIDES AND OPTICAL LIGHTING FILM

Hollow light guides channel light the way fiber optics do, with the exception that much of the distance is across air rather than through a fiber-optic core. Each guide has a specially designed channel that reflects light efficiently along its length for a particular application. Patterns made by special transmitting films on the channel surface allow light to pass out onto the task plane. A light ray that travels all the way down the pipe will strike a mirror at the end and return up the pipe.

Typically, hollow light guides use acrylic liner tubes six to eight inches wide and can be manufactured for almost any common length. Single-loaded, linear light guides send light down a single light tube. A double-loaded system feeds two linear guides; if mounted in a shared wall, the light can reach two rooms.

Hollow light guide tubes can be either integrated into recessed 2 × 4-foot ceiling systems or pendant-mounted. Distribution patterns can be similar to those of ordinary lens diffusers. Light can also be distributed asymmetrically in horizontal or vertical patterns.

A hollow light guide constructed with optical lighting film (OLF) can transport light long distances from a remote source with little attenuation. OLF is a plastic sheet material that both transmits and reflects light. It is transparent on one side and has very tiny prisms (microprisms) on the other. These microprisms reflect nearly 99 percent of the light striking them within a designated angle, yet transmit other light. On the smooth side of the OLF, a pattern of white dots scatters specular light.

SULFUR LAMPS

The very high light output of a sulfur lamp is diffused by a light pipe. A sulfur lamp is a golf ball-sized globe filled with an inert gas and a few milligrams of sulfur. Sulfur lamps emit full–spectrum light with very little UV or IR radiation, and with excellent color characteristics. Sulfur lamps maintain their efficiency and light output throughout their lifetimes, possibly up to 50,000 hours. They do not contain mercury.

Lighting-Fixture Selection

Lighting equipment should be unobtrusive but not necessarily invisible. Fixtures can be chosen to complement the architecture and to emphasize architectural features and patterns. Decorative fixtures can, of course, enhance the interior design.

Basic lighting-fixture types include:

- **Recessed and semirecessed fixtures:** Housings are all or partially hidden above the finished ceiling.
- **Surface-mounted fixtures:** These are mounted on walls or ceilings and usually are attached to a recessed junction box. They include cove, cornice, and valance fixtures as well as wall sconces.
- **Pendant-mounted fixtures:** These are attached to either a recessed or a surface-mounted junction box and hang below the ceiling on a stem, chain, or cord. They can throw light up, down, or at an adjustable angle.
- **Track and cable-mounted fixtures:** These are adjustable fixtures mounted on a recessed, surface-mounted, or pendant track or cable through which current is conducted. The fixtures are often low voltage, with a transformer either on the track or separately on each fixture.
- **Furniture-mounted fixtures:** These provide task lighting for work surfaces as well as uplighting from low partitions.
- **Portable lamps:** These are often decorative plug-in fixtures that provide task and accent lighting. They can stand on the floor or a table.

Luminaire diffusers vary in material, characteristics, and uses. Some are integral parts of the fixture, while others can be added as needed.

Translucent diffusers made of white opal glass, frosted glass, or white plastics effectively hide the lamp inside. Their circular distribution lowers lamp luminance over a larger area than more focused lighting does. Direct glare and veiling reflections can pose problems. They are useful for low-visual task areas, such as corridors, stairwells, spaces with high ceilings, and walls.

TABLE 13-9. LIGHTING FIXTURE DISTRIBUTION CHARACTERISTICS

Characteristic	Description	Example	Comment
Uniformity of illumination	Points distant from fixture centerline obtain same illumination as those below fixture	Flat-bottomed fixtures	Permits wider spacing of fixtures
High efficiency	Direct fixture output to work surface	Direct lighting fixtures	May create glare problems
Diffuseness	Light reaches work surface from multiple directions	Indirect and semi-direct lighting fixtures	Illuminance is reduced by multiple reflections off surfaces
Direct glare	Light output at high angles from vertical	Circular shields or cones on downlights	Horizontal or vertical baffles or small apertures
Reflected glare (veiling reflections)	Reflection of low output angles from task	Fixtures that limit output between 0 and 45 degrees	Shape of lamp reflector, baffles, shields
Ceiling illumination	Good ceiling coverage; no hot spots; good diffuseness	Indirect, uplight fixtures	Concentrated uplights may yield hot spots if too close to ceiling; uneven illumination

Figure 13-22 Recessed fixtures. Recessed downlights are often used when the focus of interest is the object or space being illuminated rather than the light source. When turned off, downlights often look like black holes in a light-colored ceiling.

Transparent to translucent diffusers:

- **Glass** is scratch-resistant, easily cleaned, and noncombustible. It has various grades of impact resistance, is nonyellowing, and blocks UV. Readily formed into a desired pattern, glass is heavy and expensive and is usable with all sources.
- **Acrylic (Plexiglas):** Clear to translucent acrylic is easily scratched and has low impact resistance. Acrylic is available in a UV-grade low-yellowing form. It resists brittleness, warping, and crazing. Acrylic molds well and is usable indoors and outdoors in temperatures above 90ºC.
- **Polycarbonate:** Initially very clear and highly impact-resistant, polycarbonate tends to lose strength and clarity with age. Its scratch resistance is good, and its thermal resistance is excellent. Readily molded into prismatic forms, polycarbonate is self-extinguishing. This is an expensive material that can be used indoors and outdoors with all sources.
- **Polystyrene:** This experiences rapid yellowing with UV exposure and discolors over time. It is slow-burning, but its smoke is problematic. Despite its good thermal resistance, ease of molding, and low cost, polystyrene is not scratch-resistant and is used indoors only.
- **Louvers and baffles:** These are usually rectangular metal or plastic. Louvers have average overall efficiency, but parabolic louver designs may have low efficiency. Specular aluminum or dark-colored louvers produce little direct glare, but they may cause serious veiling reflections.
- **Prismatic lens:** This is an efficient fixture, with good diffusion and wide permissible spacing. Veiling reflections may be a problem.
- **Fresnel lens:** This lens has a small housing without a reflector but still maintains beam control. It also has poor lamp-hiding power, high efficiency, and visual comfort. This type of lens is used in lighthouses.
- **Batwing diffusers:** These are high–efficiency and have low reflected glare and low to very low surface brightness.

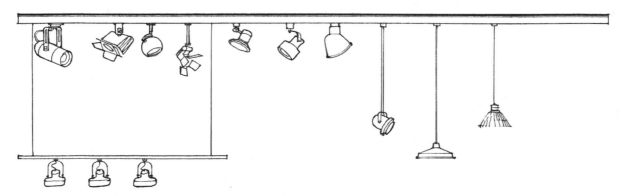

Figure 13-23 Track-mounted fixtures. Track-mounted fixtures come in a variety of styles. The track itself can become a linear design element, a shining curve, or a sleek cable winding through the space.

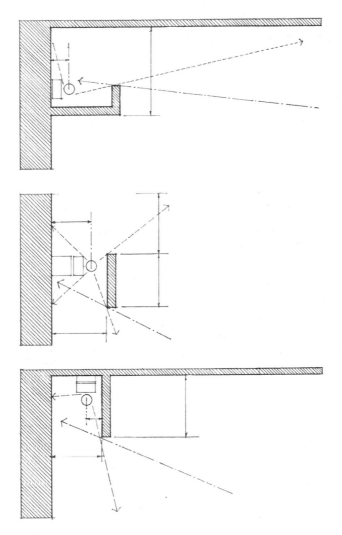

Figure 13-24 Cove, cornice, and valance lighting. Cove, cornice, and valance lighting techniques are usually designed as part of the interior architecture and become important parts of the form of the space.

Lighting Controls

A good lighting control design provides both flexibility and economy. It also allows a variety of lighting levels and lighting patterns while conserving energy and money. Energy efficient lighting-control strategies can reduce consumption over uncontrolled installations by up to 60 percent without reducing lighting effectiveness. Money is saved through reduced energy use, reduced air-conditioning costs due to less heat from lights, longer lamp and ballast life due to lower operating temperatures and lower energy output, and lower labor costs due to control automation. In order to meet building code energy budget requirements, employing energy-saving lighting controls that dim or shut off fixtures is frequently necessary.

Many building codes require that a lighting power budget be established by a mandated procedure for each project. The designer must create the lighting within these energy constraints. The nationally accepted standard that defines the establishment of a lighting power budget is ANSI/ASHRAE/IESNA

Standard 90.1: *Energy Efficient Design of New Buildings Except Low-Rise Residential Buildings*, published by ASHRAE and regularly updated.

☑ **Lighting controls include all of the ways that lighting systems can be operated, including both automatic and manual controls. Interior designers can help conserve energy by using occupancy sensors and automatic daylight-compensation controls where appropriate. Dimming, stepped switching, and programmable controls are sometimes recognized for credits from utility companies. Control systems decisions are made at the same time as the lighting is designed to ensure that controls are appropriate to the light source and that the system arrangement and accessories are coordinated with the control scheme.**

Light zones are defined to accommodate the scheduling and functions of various spaces. Ambient, task, and accent lighting are considered during the laying out of zones. Each zone should be separately circuited, and each task light should have its own switch. Traffic patterns are analyzed, and an on/off switch is located at every entrance. Convenient, easily accessible lighting controls encourage the use of all possible lighting combinations. The additional initial expense of extra switches and extra cable is made up in energy-cost savings. The result is good illumination where needed, and no wasted energy where a lower light level will serve just as well.

☑ **When designing a complex multiple-use space, such as a hotel banquet room, interior designers must talk to the people who use the space daily to discover how the space is used. Audiovisual technicians and banquet crews, for example, will be aware of common problems. Often, controls are located in places that are hard to reach during an event or where the presenter cannot see the result of an adjustment in lighting level while making it.**

The minimum number of lighting control points required by code is one per 40.5 square meters (450 sq ft.) plus one control point per task or group of tasks located in the space. Automatic controls are more effective than manual controls that depend on one person to select lighting levels for others, especially in open office spaces. Interior and exterior lighting systems in buildings larger than 465 square meters (5000 sq ft.) must have an automatic shut-off control, with the exception of emergency and exit lighting.

The designer of the lighting-control system selects the number of lighting elements to be switched together and establishes the number of control levels. Switching off entire fluorescent fixtures results in abrupt changes in light levels in a space. An option is to switch ballasts to allow four different light levels to be produced by a single, three-lamp fluorescent fixture with a two-lamp ballast and a one-lamp ballast. Maximum illumination is produced when all three lamps are on. When only the two-lamp ballast is on, lighting is at two-thirds strength. With only the one-lamp ballast, just one-third of the fixture's output is available, and with all lamps off, there is no light at all. Switching ballasts allows light reduction in small steps at low cost.

Fluorescent lamps can be dimmed to around 40 percent of their output without reduction in efficiency, even with conventional ballasts. A continuous fluorescent dimming between 10 and 100 percent is possible with special, individual magnetic silicon-controlled rectifier (SCR) dimming ballasts, with triac dimmers, or with electronic ballasts. New high-efficiency electronic ballasts enable linear fluorescent lamps to be dimmed from 100 percent down to 1 percent. Compact fluorescent lamps can now be dimmed from 100 percent down to 5 percent.

In general, manual lighting controls give employees a sense of control, leading to a feeling of satisfaction and increased productivity. However, manual systems can also waste energy because people tend to leave lights on at the maximum level even when daylight is sufficient or when they leave a room for an extended period. Manual dimmers in multiple-occupant spaces lead to personal dissatisfaction and friction. With remote-control dimming systems, occupants can adjust the lighting fixtures closest to their workstations without disturbing other employees, which can help them reduce glare on computer screens.

Static automatic lighting controls can be set for time schedules that contain regularly scheduled periods during which task lighting is not required, such as coffee and lunch breaks, cleaning periods, shift changes, and unoccupied periods. Programmed time controls save between 10 and 20 percent of energy use. The payback period for the installation of these controls ranges from one to five years. A relatively simple programmable controller can be substituted for a wall switch. More sophisticated units allow remote control of loads and circuits on a preprogrammed time basis. With tight programming, the system can save up to half the amount of energy use compared with uncontrolled installations. Because these systems do not detect actual space-use patterns, they must have an override for special conditions, such as dark, rainy days and occasions when people need to work late.

Dynamic, automatic-lighting-control initiation uses an information feedback loop to respond to actual conditions that are indicated by sensors. Dynamic control systems consist of a programmable controller and field sensors plus wiring. Some systems use high-frequency signals impressed on the power wiring system to transmit control signals in a power line carrier (PLC) system. Completely wireless systems use radio frequencies and wireless transmitters and receivers.

A dimming control system permits changing seamlessly from daytime to nighttime lighting environments. Dimming also increases the lamp life for incandescent lighting. When a lighting-controls system is being specified, determining whether the system is flexible enough to expand for unanticipated needs is called for. A reliable system-controls manufacturer must be available to modify and adjust the system during the development and implementation of a project. The cost of lighting controls is always a consideration, with features balanced against competitive systems' costs. Lighting controls should be compatible with other related equipment, such as theatrical- or themed-entertainment-industry standards.

Some lighting controls allow a user to create and recall custom preset scenes for common room activities. These systems are practical for restaurants, conference and meeting rooms, offices, hotel rooms, and homes. Scenes are set by adjusting a light or group of lights controlled together in a room or space for a specific activity. Switching between scenes can be accomplished at the touch of a button.

Wireless lighting-control systems for conference and meeting rooms enable presenters to control lights, motorized window shades, and projection screens with the touch of a button. Some wireless systems use a radio frequency tabletop transmitter that can be located anywhere inside a room. Through the pressing of buttons on the transmitter, radio frequency signals are sent to controllers housed in the ceiling. These controllers then send signals to dimming ballasts to adjust the light levels and to optional motorized window shades and projection screens or other audiovisual equipment. Some systems offer control by simple slide dimmers and are designed for use in classrooms and lecture halls, where presenters may not be familiar with complex audiovisual equipment.

☑ **Simplicity of setup and use is also important. Walking into a conference room and not being able to turn on or control the lights is truly an unnecessary challenge. Too many options can be counterproductive. Sophisticated engineering allows a system to do almost anything, but making it all easy to understand and intuitive to use has eluded most major manufacturers.**

OCCUPANCY SENSORS

Between 9 AM and 5 PM, offices in commercial spaces are unoccupied only one-third to two-thirds of the time because of coffee breaks, conferences, work assignments, illness, vacations, and different work locations. Occupancy sensors can turn office lights off after 10 minutes or dim them to corridor lighting levels. Occupancy sensors can also turn off fan-coil air units, air conditioners, and fans. Relighting may be instantaneous, delayed, or manually operated by the occupant.

Passive infrared (PIR) sensors:

- They react to the motion of any heat source within their range.
- Although they are quite sensitive, they may not detect small or very small movements.
- The IR detector must "see" the heat source; it should not be blocked by furniture.
- Some units may have dead spots.

Ultrasonic sensors:

- These sensors emit energy well above the range of human hearing; they establish a pattern throughout a space.
- They detects any movement in a space, even small movements.
- Even the movement of curtains or air can trigger these sensors.
- They do not require a direct line of sight.

Hybrid (dual-technology) sensors:

- These sensors require both PIR and ultrasonic sensors to turn on lights.
- Once on, a reaction in either sensor maintains the light level.
- The sensors learn a space's occupancy patterns and react accordingly.

Occupancy sensors work best in individual rooms and workspaces. Wall-mounted sensors can be used in any small office where there is a direct line of sight between the sensor and the occupant. Private offices often use ultrasonic, wall-mounted occupancy sensors that are turned on manually and set for maximum sensitivity and a 10-minute delay. Manual-on operation prevents lights from turning on unnecessarily when triggered by corridor activity, daylight, and brief occupancy as well as when a task light is sufficient. These sensors may be wall- or ceiling-mounted or located in wall-outlet boxes in a combined sensor wall-switch configuration. The system should be tested before final installation. An IR detector can cover between 23 and 93 square meters (250–1000 sq ft.) and can save enough energy to pay for itself in six months to three years.

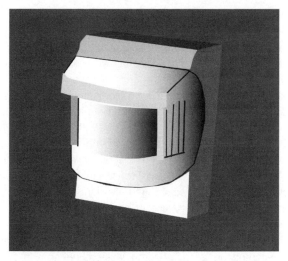

Figure 13-25 Passive infrared occupancy sensors. Although PIR sensors are not foolproof, they serve well for detecting the presence of multiple or active people in a room.

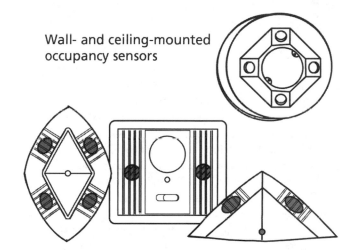

Wall- and ceiling-mounted occupancy sensors

Figure 13-26 Ultrasonic occupancy sensors. Ultrasonic occupancy sensors are more sensitive than PIRs, but they may be set off by small air movements.

In open offices, ultrasonic, ceiling-mounted occupancy sensors are set to maximum sensitivity with a 15-minute time delay so that they detect a single, quiet worker. In spaces with vertical files, partitions, or any other objects that create barriers higher than four feet, the standard coverage area given in a sensor manufacturer's literature may be too generous and more closely spaced sensors may be needed. Sensor spacing should be verified directly with the sensor manufacturer.

Some ultrasonic, ceiling-mounted sensors are specifically designed for linear corridor distribution. They are usually set to maximum sensitivity and a 15-minute time delay. The narrow, linear distribution patterns increase sensitivity at a distance, turning lights on well before a person reaches an unlighted area.

DAYLIGHT COMPENSATION

Daylight compensation is another energy-saving control system; it works by automatic dimming. Daylight compensation reduces artificial lighting in parts of a building when daylight is available for illumination needs. The system's designer establishes zone areas, usually south exposures but sometimes east or west exposures, depending on the latitude and climate. The northern exposure has only a narrow perimeter zone with adequate daylight, so it does not usually need automatic dimming. The zone size is set at the maximum room depth that will receive a minimum of one-half of its light from daylight for several hours per day. Photocells trigger dimming as required. Daylight-compensation dimming can reduce energy use in perimeter areas by up to 60 percent and will pay for itself in three months to three years. Unlike dimming, minute-by-minute changes caused by the continual switching on or off of lamp levels can annoy a space's occupants. It also damages the lamps.

Lighting System Tuning

Designing and specifying lighting is complex, and it is rare that the system functions perfectly in the field as designed. This is inevitable because of assumptions and imprecision in calculations, differences between the specified and installed equipment, and changes in equipment locations. The system is fine-tuned in the field to adjust to these changes and achieve the designer's goals.

Tuning often results in the reduction of lighting levels in nontask areas because spill light is frequently adequate for circulation, rough material handling, and other functions. Lighting system tuning can reduce energy use by 20 to 30 percent. Lighting system tuning is also required when the function of an entire space is changed or when furniture movement or changes in tasks alter a single area. It can help with glare reduction and result in improved task visibility.

During the lighting system tuning, adjustable fixtures are aimed and their positions are modified. Incandescent lamps and fluorescent tubes are replaced with lower-wattage lamps. Ballast switching and multilevel ballasts are fine-tuned for efficiency, and dimmable fixtures are adjusted. Standard wall switches are replaced with time-out units, programmable units, or dimmer units. It is a good idea to include the lighting system tuning process as part of the lighting designer's complete scope of services.

Lighting Fixtures and Codes

Building codes increasingly require energy efficient lighting. Energy restrictions commonly apply to all buildings that are more than three stories high and to all building types except low-rise housing. These are relatively new code requirements and continue to be modified and accepted in new jurisdictions. Minimum code requirements must be met to acquire a building permit. Typically, codes allow tradeoffs between energy-efficient building-envelope components and energy use by HVAC or lighting systems. Interior lighting energy use can usually be calculated either by a building area method or on a space-by-space basis. Code requirements usually apply to new construction and additions and do not require the alteration or removal of existing systems; however, some efforts at relamping existing fixtures may be required.

The process of meeting the code requirements involves extensive calculations and reporting, which are done by the electrical engineer or lighting designer using special software. Sometimes, the contractor may be accepted as the designer of record, and contractors often provide the documentation. Since the lighting energy allowance meshes with building-envelope and HVAC requirements, the entire architectural and engineering team is involved in meeting code requirements.

The energy-efficiency code requirements mandate automatic shutoff provisions for interior lighting. Incandescent lighting may effectively be eliminated for exit signs. The Energy Star® program includes lighting fixtures and lightbulbs. Some types of facilities are not included in the total energy-use calculations; these include spaces specifically for the visually impaired, enclosed retail display windows, display lighting in galleries or museums, lighting integral to advertising or directional signage, and lighting for theatrical purposes.

Lighting fixtures are marked for wall mounting, under-cabinet mounting, ceiling mounting, or covered ceiling mounting. Wall-

Figure 13-27 ADA lighting fixtures. Wall- or ceiling-mounted fixtures should not project into the space needed by a person walking close to the wall.

mounted lighting fixtures (sconces) must meet the Americans with Disabilities (ADA) maximum 4-inch projection limit where applicable. Each lighting fixture is manufactured and tested for a specific location. Those fixtures approved for damp locations are labeled "Suitable for Damp Locations." Lighting fixtures listed for a wet location can also be used in damp locations.

☑ **The NEC has strict requirements for access to electrical components. All electrical boxes must allow access for repairs and wiring changes at any time. All lighting fixtures must be placed so that both the lamp and the fixture can be replaced when needed. This is especially important when they are used with architectural elements, such as ceiling coves.**

Fire-tested and labeled lighting fixtures should be used on interior projects:

- Only certain types of fixtures are allowed in fire-rated assemblies.
- When a lighting fixture is placed in a wall or ceiling of combustible material, the mechanical part of the fixture must be fully enclosed.
- Typically, noncombustible materials must be sandwiched between the fixture and the finished surface.
- When typical 61 × 122 cm (2 × 4′) fluorescent ceiling fixtures are placed end to end, no gaps are allowed between fixtures. Side-by-side installation is not usually considered to be safe.
- Fixtures with air handling are usually allowed if they have provisions to stop air movement in the event of fire.
- The method of attachment of a fixture to the outlet box is related to its weight and the type of fixture. The outlet box can usually support fixtures up to 22.7 kilograms (50 lb.). Heavier fixtures require additional support.

Lighting System Maintenance

Maintenance is often the last consideration when a lighting fixture is selected, yet it is the one most likely to result in long-term negative feedback from building owners and facility managers. Premature failures are expensive for and annoying to building owners and tenants, tarnish lighting designers' and contractors' reputations, and may cause fire danger or other hazards. Often, the problem does not lie in the design, but in poor installation and maintenance practices. Within a short time after installation, the lighting system may be operated and maintained by a person with little training or experience with the latest equipment. An interior designer can pass on the following common problems and their cures to clients, who will welcome learning about them before problems arise.

- Circuits should be shut off before burned-out halogen lamps and lamps with screw-in bases are replaced to avoid premature burnout.
- Running incandescent lamps even slightly above their rated voltage will significantly shorten their life, sometimes by as much as half.

- Grooves or dimples on the metal end caps perpendicular to the axis of the pin connectors on fluorescent lamps are vertical when the lamp is properly rotated; a poor connection will cause electrical heating that slowly turns the lamp holders brown.
- Bad ballasts with poor soldering may cause fluorescent lamps in new fixtures to flicker a few times per second for about the first 1½ hours of use. The ballasts should be returned, and an allowance should be added to the cost for relamping labor.
- Storing fluorescent tubes on end below 10°C (50°F) can cause the mercury in the lamps to condense into small droplets and pool in the end caps of the lamps. Reduced vapor pressure can result in bands of light and dark or a complete failure to light. The lamps will usually return to normal operation over the course of a few days' use.
- Other lamping problems can result when lamps and ballasts are not carefully matched, creating poor electrical conditions for lamps. Compatibility information is listed on the ballast label.
- Lamps deteriorate over time and emit fewer lumens as they are used. Dirt, dust, and foreign matter collect on lighting fixtures and on the reflecting surfaces in a room. Some fixtures change color during use.
- Because the maximum ladder height for custodial use is around 4.6 meters (15 ft.), many fixtures may be out of reach. A lamp stick is used to reach conventional filament or mercury lamps in open reflectors up to 7.6 meters (25 ft.) high. Also used are crawl spaces above the ceiling, catwalks, and disconnecting hangers that allow fixtures to be lowered to floor level.

Emergency Lighting

Emergency lighting provides power for critical lighting systems in the event of a general power failure, the failure of a building's electrical system, an interruption of current flow to the lighting unit, and the accidental operation of a switch control or circuit disconnect. It is customary for battery-powered units to be hardwired into a building's electrical system, so that the battery can be recharged by the building power. Emergency-lighting requirements may include additional local code requirements.

- NFPA 101®: *Life Safety Code*, 2009 Edition, specifies locations that require emergency lighting and the level and duration of the lighting.
- NFPA 70: *National Electrical Code®*, mandates system arrangements for emergency light and power circuits, including exit lighting. The NEC also discusses power sources and system design.
- NFPA 99: *Standards for Health Care Facilities*, 2005 Edition, dictates special emergency light and power arrangements for these occupancies.
- Occupational Safety and Health Administration (OSHA) requirements are primarily safety oriented and cover exit and egress lighting.

- ANSI/IEEE 446-1995, *IEEE Recommended Standard Practice for Emergency and Standby Power Systems.*

Most codes required 50 lux (5 fc) on exit signs. Some exit signs are equipped with a battery and controls. Others illuminate the area beneath the sign, which is especially helpful in terms of finding the way to an exit in a smoky room. Some signs have a flasher and/or audible beeper. Nonelectrical, self-illuminating signs are considered to be part of the emergency lighting system.

Exit lighting is required at all exits as well as at any aisles, corridors, passageways, ramps, and lobbies that lead to an exit. General exit lighting and exit signs must be illuminated whenever a building is in use.

Because it takes the human eye up to five minutes to adjust to a drop in normal lighting levels, bright, spotlight-type emergency lighting heads must be very carefully arranged to prevent disabling glare and distorting shadows. It is best to provide some lighting at floor level, preferably a type that aids direction finding since people may crawl along the floor to stay below the level of smoke. Sometimes, ceiling-mounted emergency lighting fails to illuminate the floor in smoky areas or may create a bright, fog-like condition. Some codes mandate adequate egress lighting at baseboard level.

The easiest way to provide emergency lighting is to put some of the existing light fixtures on a separate circuit designed for emergency lighting and connected to a backup power source. An interior designer must make sure that if one fixture burns out, it will not leave an area in darkness. Dual-lamp lighting fixtures, fixtures with battery packs, and overlapping lighting patterns should be used.

Local emergency lighting arrangements include a rechargeable battery and charger and voltage sensing and switching equipment. For fluorescent lights, an electronic ballast is available that operates the lamp at high frequency and usually reduced output. Packaged units are available with integral incandescent lights. Equipment should be maintenance-free for up to five years.

LIGHTING DESIGN APPLICATIONS

As indicated earlier, these chapters on lighting are not intended to replace a comprehensive lighting course. The information in this chapter covers some of the basic requirements in an effort to give interior designers some insight into the way electrical engineers and lighting designers approach the design of the most common types of spaces. Lighting levels that are referenced by electrical engineers and lighting designers are given in the *IESNA Lighting Handbook*, 9th Edition, by the Illuminating Engineering Society of North America.

Recommendations for lighting levels in the United States are similar to British and CIE standards that establish a median or average requirement for a task, which is then modified for specific circumstances. Today, IESNA's illumination standards include fatigue and task familiarity in illuminance levels, set lighting power

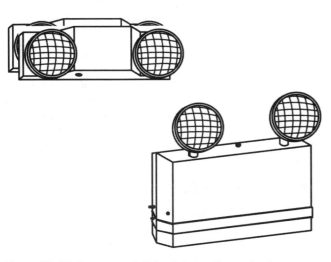

Figure 13-28 Emergency lighting fixtures. The goals of emergency lighting are to avoid distress or panic and to provide lighting for egress from the building. The level of lighting required is related to the level of normal illumination and to the degree of hazard.

TABLE 13-10. EMERGENCY LIGHTING LEVELS

Area	Lux or Footcandles (fc)
Exit areas	50 lux (5 fc)
Stairs	35 to 50 lux (3.5–5 fc)
Hazardous areas like machine rooms	20 to 50 lux (2–5 fc)
Other spaces	10 lux (1 fc)
All points along path of egress	Minimum of 1 lux (0.1 fc)
Maximum to minimum illuminances along path of egress	Must not exceed a ratio of 40 to 1
All emergency lighting (higher levels may be required where evacuation is slow)	Minimum 10-lux level for at least 90 minutes, then 60 lux (6 fc)

TABLE 13-11. LIGHTING VALUES FOR INTERIOR SPACES

Type of Activity	Interior Spaces	Characteristics	IESNA Category	Lux	Foot-candles
General lighting throughout spaces	Public spaces with dark surroundings	Little used for movement	A	20–50	2–5
	Corridors, changing rooms, bulk stores, auditoriums	Short visits; casual seeing with limited perception of detail	B	50–100	5–10
	Working spaces with occasional visual tasks	Limited perception of detail; limited risk	C	100–200	10–20
Illuminance on task	Foyers, entrances, dining rooms; monitoring automatic processes	Long occupation or visual tasks of high contrast or large size; some detail	D	200	20–50
	Libraries, sports and assembly halls, teaching and lecture spaces, packing areas	Long occupation; moderately easy tasks (large details, high contrast)		300	
	General offices, kitchens, laboratories, retail shops	Moderate-size details; medium-to-low contrast; some color	D-E	500	50–100
	Drawing and artwork; meat inspection; chain stores	Small details, low contrast; good color or well-lit, inviting interior	E	750	
Illuminance on task, obtained by general and local lighting	Inspection and electronic-assembly rooms; cabinet making; supermarkets	Very small details, low contrast; accurate color judgments or well-lit, inviting interior	F	1000	100–200
	Fine work and inspection, precision assembly, fine hand work	Extremely small, low-contrast tasks; optical aids, local lighting may help		1500	
	Assembly of minute mechanisms; finished fabric inspection	Exceptionally small, low-contrast tasks	G	2000–5000	200–500
		Very prolonged, exacting visual tasks	H	5000–10,000	500–1000
		Extremely low-contrast, small-size tasks		10,000–20,000	1000–2000

budgets, and encourage daylighting and task and ambient lighting design. Many countries, including Australia, Brazil, China, France, Germany, and Japan, have published lighting standards.

The following are some general guidelines for lighting interior spaces:

- Dark walls tend to make a space look smaller, while white walls create a sense of spaciousness.
- Bright lighting fixtures detract from walls and reduce the perceived size of a space.
- User-adjustable task lights increase comfort and sense of control.
- Feelings of relaxation and comfort are encouraged by downlighting and color highlights.
- The inability to identify the source of indirect lighting and very-low-brightness fixtures may cause discomfort.

TABLE 13-12. TASK-TO-SURFACE LUMINANCE RATIOS

Task-to-Surface Ratio	Surfaces
1 to 1/3	Adjacent surroundings
1 to 1/10	More remote darker surfaces
1 to 10	More remote lighter surfaces
20 to 1	Luminaires or fenestration and adjacent surfaces
40 to 1	Anywhere within normal field of view

LIGHTING RESIDENTIAL SPACES

Each area of a home should have multiple light levels. Through a multilayered design approach involving task, ambient, and accent lighting, a balanced, three-dimensional lighted environment is created that allows for a variety of settings or moods. The best approach is to first provide for the task lighting requirements, then determine what ambient lighting, if any, is required to supplement this layer. Finally, appropriate accenting and highlighting to enhance artwork and architectural elements should be provided. The following guidelines are helpful:

- Design for daylighting.
- Provide low-level lighting provisions in all rooms with high-low switches, dimmers, and multilevel ballasts and switching.
- Use local task lighting for demanding visual tasks.
- Provide dimming and switching for accent lighting.
- Use programmable timers with photocell override for exteriors.
- Use low-voltage or wireless control for remote control and energy savings.

Electric light sources used in the home should be in the 2700 K to 3000 K color-temperature range with CRIs of 80 or more. Residential lighting sources include:

- **Daylight supplemented by incandescent or fluorescent lighting:** used in kitchens, home offices
- **Common incandescent lighting:** used in closets, pantries, small areas with frequently switched lighting; appropriate for short-term use in bathrooms
- **Tungsten-halogen lighting:** restrict to highlighting and specialty requirements
- **Linear fluorescent lighting:** used in kitchens and other work areas and for general bathroom lighting; color temperatures between 3000 K and 3500 K offer better color rendering
- **Compact fluorescent lighting:** used in architectural coves and cornices; downlights with lower brightness when used for minimum of three hours
- **Low-wattage (9-12 W) PL fluorescent lighting:** used for extended periods of low-level lighting in corridors and stairwells
- **HID:** used for all exterior lighting

As mentioned earlier, incandescent lighting is being replaced by more energy-efficient sources. Incandescent lamps should be limited to infrequent or short-duration use and to focusing point-source fixtures. Alternatives are available for good dimming and color rendering. Although other sources may cost more per lamp, energy costs and energy conservation discourage the use of incandescent lighting.

Guidelines for Residential Kitchens

- Residential kitchens should have natural light with an area of not less than one-tenth the floor area, or a minimum of 0.9 square meters (10 sq ft.); completely artificial light may be used when daylight is not available.
- Fluorescent lights with color temperatures between 2700 K and 3000 K should be used for general lighting.
- Halogen incandescent lights should be used for energy efficiency and longer life to complement wood and natural finishes and should have dimming controls.
- Low-glare linear and nonlinear task fixtures should be mounted under wall cabinets at perimeter countertops for evenly distributed, shadow-free lighting on task surfaces.
- Pendants, downlights, or track lighting should be used over islands, peninsulas, and sinks.
- Integrated lighting should be provided in ventilation hoods over cooktops.
- Ambient lighting should be used to fill in shadows, reduce contrast, and light vertical surfaces. It should be provided by indirect lighting mounted on top of wall cabinets, suspended indirect or direct/indirect linear fluorescent fixtures, low-glare overhead surface-mounted fixtures, coves and ceiling soffits with integrated lighting, and downlights.
- Lighting should be mounted at a distance and configured so that it does not produce severe and off-center scallops on wall cabinets and appliances; lighting must be designed in three dimensions.

Guidelines for Residential Bathrooms

Good lighting should show people at their best and still provide enough light to facilitate the removal of a splinter. The quality of the light is important to complement skin tones and to help people notice when they or their children do not look well.

In most situations, a task-lighting system will also provide adequate ambient illumination, especially in small bathrooms. Downlighting, indirect coves, adjustable accents, fan/light combination fixtures, and wall sconces offer additional ambient lighting. Dimmed halogen incandescent lights should be used as a primary source for energy efficiency and color quality. The following guidelines are helpful:

- Sunlight is desirable for lighting and warmth; directing it onto an occupant's face should be avoided.
- A single overhead fixture is usually not acceptable.
- More light from one side than another will model a face in three dimensions; dimmable switches or daylight controls should be used.
- A mirror should not be located directly opposite a window in order to prevent glare; background surfaces should not be lighter than facial tones.
- Lights above a mirror may cause shadows under the eyes, and lights too close to the face can produce glare; using unprotected bulbs around a mirror is likely to cause direct glare and should be avoided.
- The use of the following is suggested: a vertically oriented linear fixture that either flanks a mirror or is integrated with the mirror, wall sconces or luminous pendants that flank the grooming position at face height, horizontally oriented fixtures over a mirror with a lensed front and enough width to illuminate a face, and architectural soffits or valances with a direct/indirect distribution.

- Downlights should not be used for grooming tasks because they tend to cast unfavorable shadows on facial features; if used, they should be placed as close as possible to a mirror, spaced on either side of the grooming position, and used with a matte white countertop for upward reflectance.
- Showers and tubs should be illuminated with a lensed downlight with a gasketed trim ring or with smaller compact fluorescent lamps.

Other Residential Lighting

Dining rooms:
- preset multiple-scene controls with variety of settings

Family rooms, great rooms, and living rooms:
- nonuniform, mostly perimeter lighting system
- ambient lighting provided by soft, indirect lighting
- downlights, wall sconces, table lamps, or other accents for higher task-lighting levels
- highlighting artwork, sculpture, and other architectural features with recessed adjustable accents, surface monopoints, a track system, or a wire/rail system for maximum flexibility.

Bedrooms:
- Small rooms up to about 12 square meters (125 sq ft.) can be adequately illuminated with a multilamped lighting fixture that provides a uniform lighting pattern throughout the space.
- Larger rooms will require additional adjustable accents on one or more walls.
- Task lighting adjacent to the bed for reading is usually best provided with table fixtures.
- Bedrooms doubling as study areas need task lighting on the desk.

Home offices and dual-purpose spaces:
- Design lighting for each use individually, with the maximum for common use.
- Fluorescent lighting for workspaces should be provided in the form of downlights, surface-mounted direct fixtures, suspended indirect fixtures, or built-in indirect coves; track lighting or other adjustable direct fixtures do not work well because of the shadows they cast.
- Task fixtures on work surfaces and accent lighting that highlights artwork help balance the space.

Home theaters:
- These areas should be lighted like a theater with a multilayer lighting system.
- General space illumination, low-level lighting for moving about in the dark, and effects lighting for fun should be incorporated into the lighting design.

Residential Lighting Controls

In most living spaces, there is a need to adjust light levels for varying tasks to provide different moods, to lower the color temperature, to increase or reduce contrasts on objects, or simply to provide a reduced level of illumination. As such, some type of dimming control is recommended. This is true not only for incandescent light sources but also for fluorescent lamps. High-quality electronic dimming ballasts are available for T8, T5, and compact fluorescent lamps for areas in which dimming these lamps is appropriate.

Lighting controls can vary from relatively low-cost, simple wallbox dimmers to remote-panel dimming systems that use one-touch preset buttons and connect to other home automation systems.

For large residences, low-voltage or wireless controls should be considered for the convenience of remote control, safety, and energy savings. Equipment can report conditions at the house to the homeowner both on-site and at a remote location. Low-wattage and wireless systems feature a wall-mounted master at each entrance in the kitchen and home office, a bedside tabletop master in the master bedroom, and radio-operated switches and dimmers in all rooms.

LIGHTING COMMERCIAL SPACES

Each type of commercial, institutional, or industrial space has its own lighting requirements. These spaces all include toilet rooms, some of which are open to the public.

Lighting Public Restrooms

Public restrooms have a high number of plumbing fixtures and high-volume use, so appropriate lighting is essential for keeping these facilities clean and pleasant. Whether an interior designer is working on the design of a restroom for an office building, where the same people will use it every day, or for a public space, creating a good impression with lighting enhances the interior design.

The lighting in a public restroom should vary from the light levels in the rest of the building. Well-lit toilet rooms encourage the maintenance staff to keep the space bright and clean and ensure users that it is safe and hygienic. The toilets, urinals, and lavatories benefit from a task-lighting approach. Other areas may be much less brightly illuminated, depending on whether the interior is in a nightclub or an office, for example. High-quality lighting near the mirrors enhances a user's appearance, which is especially important in restaurants and similar social environments. The guidelines provided under the section on residential bathrooms also apply to lighting fixtures for the mirror areas of public restrooms, with the proviso that all fixtures have to be able to withstand the potential abuse of a public (but often isolated) space.

Office Lighting

Designing lighting for an office means designing for change. Flexibility must be incorporated into both the overall layout and the degree of control that an employee has over his or her workspace. Daylighting should be included, both to serve as an energy-efficient light source and to provide the benefits of keeping in touch with nature. One way to achieve individual flexibility is with addressable ballast technology, using remote-control devices to make adjustments to the ambient light conditions in the immediate area:

- Light should be distributed relatively uniformly in a work environment, avoiding hot spots, shadows, or sharp patterns of light and dark.
- In larger offices or open-plan spaces, more than one type of light fixture, each with specific distribution characteristics, should be used.
- Fixtures specifically designed for wall washing to light walls from top to bottom should be used; locating fixtures closer than one meter (3 ft.) from walls should be avoided because if they are too close, they will create harsh patterns and dark upper walls, resulting in a cave-like appearance.
- T8 3500 K–4100 K triphosphor linear lamps or similar compact fluorescent units with high-frequency electronic ballasts offer energy conservation and good color.
- HID lamps, color-corrected HPS, and metal-halide lamps with high CRI ratings can be used for indirect lighting in spaces with high ceilings.
- Incandescent lamps may be used in storage areas, closets, and other spaces with short burning times.
- Incandescent and tungsten-halogen lamps are appropriate for illuminating displays.

ANSI/ASHRAE/IESNA Standard 90.1-2007, *Energy Standard for Buildings Except Low-Rise Residential Buildings* sets power limits for office spaces as shown in Table 13-13. The IES established recommendations for room surface reflectance levels for offices as shown in Table 13-14.

TABLE 13-13. OFFICE POWER LIMITS

Space	Watts per Square Foot
Private office	1.5
Open-plan office	1.3
Office corridors	0.7
Reception area, Lobby	1.8
Conference, Meeting	1.5
Active stairs	0.9
Active storage	1.1

TABLE 13-14. ROOM SURFACE REFLECTANCE LEVELS

Surface	Reflectance
Ceilings	80 to 92 percent; perforated ceilings about 15 percent lower than their finish
Walls and partitions	Average 40 to 60 percent
Window blinds	40 to 60 percent
Floor	20 to 40 percent
Desktops, furniture, office machines	25 to 40 percent

GLARE IN OFFICES

In an office, glare occurs when bright light sources interfere with the viewing of objects or surfaces that are less bright. The contrast between very bright and less bright may be uncomfortable or disabling, both of which are undesirable in an office environment. Fixtures located to the front or side of an employee cause direct glare. Overhead glare is caused by excessive brightness directly above. Reflected glare can also occur on glossy paper from lights directly in front. Most glare can be controlled by increasing the brightness of the surroundings, decreasing the brightness of the sources, or both. Glare on computer screens has been ameliorated by smaller, brighter, more easily adjustable screens and more flexible office arrangements.

Indirect lighting with a ceiling at least 3 meters (10 ft.) high is recommended for lighting spaces with computer monitors. Semi-indirect and direct/indirect lighting may be used in spaces with ceiling heights between 2.75 and 3.36 meters (9–11 ft.). With indirect lighting systems, ceilings and walls become the light sources in the room, and the space seems brighter and more alive. In general, indirect lighting solutions work better if an occupant has some sense of where the light is actually coming from. Very evenly illuminated spaces tend to produce a slightly eerie, unreal, or disorienting sensation in occupants. Diffusers, lenses, or perforated metal panels can provide a minimal sense of the light's origin. Some ceiling-mounted indirect fixtures are designed for easy relocation without extensive rewiring.

Ceiling-mounted indirect lighting fixtures do not work well in spaces with ceilings lower than 2.75 meters (9 ft.) because they have to be dropped below the ceiling enough to shine up on it without creating hot spots. These fixtures also do not work well in extremely long spaces, even where ceilings are high. A large array of ceiling-mounted fixtures can create the impression of a second ceiling plane below the actual ceiling and, perhaps, intensify the feeling of confinement in a low-ceilinged space.

Furniture-mounted indirect lighting, attached to the wall or to a partition system at about 168 centimeters (5½ ft.), allows plenty of room to achieve reasonable light distribution and avoid hot spots, even in very low ceiling environments. However, because codes usually require that these fixtures be hard-wired and powered at 277 volts, they cannot simply be plugged into the panels and moved easily around the space when the office is rearranged. However, some municipalities, including Chicago,

TABLE 13-15. LUMINAIRE MOUNTING HEIGHTS FOR OFFICES

Fixture Type	Distance from Ceiling
Indirect, semi-indirect	18-inch minimum, 24–36 inches preferred
Single-lamp with very wide distribution	12-inch minimum
Direct/indirect and semi-direct fluorescent fixtures	Two-lamp units: 12 inches Three- or four-lamp units: 18 inches

Illinois, require that office buildings be wired at 120 volts, which means that a truly flexible furniture-mounted lighting system is possible. A flexible furniture-mounted system may also be an option in an old building that remains wired at 120 volts.

OTHER OFFICE LIGHTING

Task lighting is often integrated with office furniture, thereby eliminating problems with changes to the furniture layout. Initial construction costs are reduced, as are energy requirements, since the light and task are close together. Each occupant has on/off control of task lighting, with the possibility of position control. Maintenance is easy because fixtures are accessible from the floor. Fixtures mounted on furniture take advantage of higher depreciation rates than fixtures on building surfaces do.

Furniture-mounted fixtures may have trouble dissipating heat and minimizing magnetic ballast noise so close to the user, so electronic ballasts should be used. Veiling reflections from reflected glare are always present because the fixtures shine on the work surface. The luminance ratios in near and far surrounding areas may exceed recommended levels. It is difficult to light a freestanding desk with furniture-mounted fixtures because most fixtures are located undercounter or are sidewall mounted. Lighting a large table or L-shaped desk areas is also difficult; the fixtures tend to concentrate light. Control by automatic switching and dimming is challenging, too. In addition, unless the light source can be repositioned, fixtures may be needed on both sides to accommodate right-handed and left-handed people.

Wall cabinets and cabinets attached to furniture partitions create disturbing shadows on the vertical surfaces they overhang. A low quantity of lighting should be provided to eliminate this shadow and maintain a balance of brightness. Undercabinet lights with opaque fronts are available commercially or are sold as part of the furniture system. In general, a single T8 lamp provides too much light, so it should be coupled with a 50-percent-output ballast, which reduces the amount of light and energy consumption and balances the brightness.

Compact fluorescent desk lights enable workers to control their own lighting to meet their individual needs. Articulated task lights, which allow adjustment in all three planes, are effective and inexpensive, and are preferable to undercabinet lights for task lighting.

Private offices need a combination of task and ambient lighting. The ambient lighting may be spill light from the task, especially if a pendant unit with an uplighting component provides it.

LIGHTING CONTROLS FOR OFFICES

Lighting controls save energy by dimming or turning off unnecessary lighting with ultrasonic occupancy sensors. By installing switching or automatic dimming for fixtures in the daylighted zone within 3.7 meters (12 ft.) from a window wall, an interior designer can reduce lighting costs when adequate daylight is available. In rooms smaller than 37 square meters (400 sq ft.), an alternative approach is to provide separate switches for the light fixtures in the daylighted zone and connect them to a separate occupancy sensor. In daylighted zones greater than 37 square meters (400 sq ft.), electronic fluorescent dimming ballasts should be considered for continuous dimming down to 20 percent or less, which is automatically controlled by photosensors. Only smooth, continuous dimming should be used for office spaces to prevent distracting employees. The smoothness of the dimming depends on the quality of the dimming ballast more than on the controls themselves.

Lighting Educational Facilities

The goal for lighting educational spaces is to conserve energy while supporting a rich learning environment through the careful selection and location of lighting fixtures and controls. Institutional and educational buildings have tight budgets and require extremely hardy, vandal-proof, and low energy consumption lighting. In general, maintenance is poor and is done on a repair rather than prevention basis, so equipment should be as maintenance free as possible.

Ideally, uniform general lighting in such workspaces as classrooms should be provided. To avoid harsh shadows, parabolic louvered or lensed fixtures should be located at least one meter (3 ft.) from walls.

For good lighting and uniformity on vertical surfaces, the center of the vertical area should not be more than twice the brightness of the edges. Lighting should be located between 0.6 and 1 meter (2–3 ft.) away from the vertical surface. Most wall washer fixtures use internal reflectors so that light reflected from the wall is not a reflected glare source for students.

The most efficient lighting source for educational buildings is daylight, followed by HPS, fluorescent, and metal-halide lighting. Long-life sources require less maintenance, so fluorescent or HID fixtures should be used in corridors, stairs, and any locations where relamping is difficult, such as high-ceilinged gyms and assembly rooms. When specific color lamps are called for, the color temperature and lamp type should be permanently stenciled in large letters on the lighting fixture to ensure proper relamping.

Most schools are not air conditioned, so there is less need to mask air noise. Ballasts and diffusers that make noise or vibrate are likely to be noticed. Electronic ballasts are better, but they may be more expensive than other ballasts.

For vandal-proof and low-maintenance fixtures, an interior designer should look for captive screws (which cannot be removed from the fixture), rust-preventive plated parts, and captive-hinged diffusers whose cleaning requires only one person.

TABLE 13-16. SCHOOL LIGHTING POWER LIMITS

Space	Watts per Square Foot
Private offices, Classrooms, Auditoriums	1.5–1.6
Dining, Cafeteria	1.4
Corridors	0.7
Active Stairs	0.9

Because ballasts should be able to be replaced without demounting fixtures, plug-in ballasts should be used. Fixtures should be made of nonyellowing plastics, with high-quality finishes and assembly.

Light levels in corridors must be adequate for seeing into lockers, viewing student displays, and providing security. Within these limits, a lower light level in corridors is not only refreshing but also necessary to meet the energy code.

Power limits for school spaces established by ANSI/ASHRAE/IESNA Standard 90.1 are listed in Table 13-16.

Retail Lighting

High-quality retail lighting can enhance a store's image, lead potential customers inside, focus their attention on products, and ultimately increase sales. Retail lighting must have good color, contrast, and balance. This can all be done with energy-efficient lighting that is energy-code compliant.

Lighting for small stores:
- Fixed location lighting using spotlights is often more effective than track lighting and floodlights.
- During planning, random fixture layouts or visual chaos should be avoided, as should an excess of both dark surfaces that reduce lighting effectiveness and shiny surfaces.
- Black ceilings will reduce indirect lighting levels, so they should be used only where this is not a problem.
- Low-level ambient lighting will allow customers to focus their attention on highlighted important elements.
- Ambient lighting must be adequate to allow customers to examine the merchandise easily.

☑ **The light source should be close to the merchandise. For ambient lighting, efficient, diffuse sources, such as fluorescent lighting, should be used. For accent lighting, narrow-beam spotlights, such as halogen PARs or low-voltage MR-16s, should be used. Using a limited number of lamp types reduces relamping mistakes and maintenance problems. Aisles should be illuminated with spill light from accented merchandising areas or displays. Light colors on the interior surfaces of shelving reflect light onto merchandise. An organized pattern of light fixtures helps customers navigate merchandise displays. High-color-rendering lamps should be used for both ambient and task lighting.**

Lighting for intermediate-sized stores:
For medium-sized stores that sell clothing, stationery, accessories, housewares, furniture, and small objects, ambient lighting is supplemented with limited accent lighting.

- The goal is illumination that is uniform enough to enable customers to see and examine products and read labels.
- Limited accent lighting is desirable to set products apart, to create highlights or enhance texture, and to attract attention to window displays.

High-end retail lighting:
Expensive or exclusive higher-end stores include those that sell jewelry, gifts, antiques, fine clothing, and accessories. Fine housewares and beauty salons are also included in this category. These stores have less activity than other retail establishments and feature the most personalized attention and assistance from sales personnel. The following lighting guidelines are helpful:

- The lighting should establish the store's image and enhance product color, sparkle, or texture.
- The lighting goal is to encourage lingering, examination of products, and impulse buying.
- High-end shops do not need to use more energy to be effective and can provide more focus and highlights by reducing ambient light levels.
- Fluorescent lighting should be used to provide ambient lighting in high-end stores.
- White-painted parabolic louvers may be preferable in small spaces or those with low ceilings.
- For the highest-end retailers, smaller diameter T5 or T2 fluorescent lamps should be considered for use in concealed applications, such as coves, valances, and shelf lighting.
- The best color-rendering lamps with CRIs above 80 and a warmer color temperature of between 3000 K and 3200 K should be used for higher-end stores.
- Since the human eye is attracted to the brightest object in the field of view and then to the next brightest object, the highest-wattage or the tightest-focus lamps should be used for the most important items or areas in the store.
- Exposed or decorative sources should be used to draw attention to specific displays or areas of the shop.

☑ **Partially concealing ambient light sources with louvers or baffles emphasizes the product. Accent lights should be located close to displays, and exposed or decorative accent lights should be used to create attention or help establish a high-end store's image.**

Proper lighting controls ensure that individual fixtures are on only when they are most effective. Display-window lights should be controlled separately from the rest of the store lights. In addition, other fixture types should be on separate circuits, controlled by an astronomical time clock that adjusts to sunrise and sunset times. This way, only the most efficient fixtures will be used outside of business hours, for such staff activities as cleaning and restocking. This not only saves energy, but also greatly reduces maintenance for burned-out accent lights.

Lighting for high-activity retailing:
Mass merchandising and discount stores, along with hardware stores, video stores, fast-food shops, and grocery stores, are identified as high-activity retail establishments. Some service establishments and stores that sell bulk or large objects, such as appliances or furniture, are also included in this category. These destination stores do not require special lighting to draw customers inside.

- The goal of the lighting design should be to light all objects uniformly, provide good visibility for reading labels, and create a bright, clean, stimulating environment.
- Exposed lighting sources help project a discount image.
- Fluorescent and metal-halide lighting sources provide the best value, supplying good color rendering and high-efficiency lighting with long life.
- Light-colored finishes should be used on wall surfaces to increase overall brightness and reflected light.

Lighting Hotel Rooms

Lighting fixtures in hotel rooms make up a significant part of overall building energy use; typically, there are five or six lights in each hotel room. IR motion sensors in guest rooms, vending machine areas, and "back of the house" areas turn on lighting only when needed. Replacing incandescent lamps with compact fluorescents uses one-fourth the energy of continuous lighting and increases lamp life tenfold.

Lighting Industrial Buildings

Industrial lighting is principally designed for cost savings. However, improved lighting has been shown to reduce the number of accidents, improve employee morale, and result in a better product.

Many industrial buildings are one story high, so roof monitors, skylights, and clerestories can provide adequate illumination via daylighting; these light sources must be accessible for cleaning. Artificial lighting sources should be highly efficient, retain their brightness over time, and offer long life. Fluorescent and HID lighting are the best choices; induction and sulfur lamps are good alternatives. HID lights are easier to maintain, store, clean, and relamp than fluorescent lighting. However, HID has a delay in restarting.

Minimal reflectances for industrial ceilings are between 75 and 85 percent. Wall reflectances range from 40 to 60 percent, with equipment reflectances ranging from 25 to 45 percent and floor reflectances are at around 20 percent.

OUTDOOR LIGHTING

Sometimes, interior designers are called on to help select lighting fixtures for a home's entry and landscaping. By lighting all exterior vertical surfaces from above—not below—whenever possible, an interior designer can reduce the light pollution that limits our ability to see the night sky. If lumenaires with shields for a sharp cutoff beyond the illuminated area are chosen, the intrusion of unwanted light onto neighbors' property and into windows can be limited. After the installation is complete, the site should be inspected at night to determine if there is a nuisance.

We have covered a great deal of information in this chapter, but there is much more to learn about lighting. New technologies and products are always becoming available. Lighting continuing-education courses are consistently popular with interior designers. In Chapter 14: Electrical Appliances and Communications Equipment, we will consider another area that sees a significant amount of change.

14

....

Electrical Appliances and Communications Equipment

Home appliances have come a long way in the last two centuries. For hundreds of years, there were no convenient local food stores, and the preservation and storage of food took a great deal of time and expertise. Cooking and washing dishes used to be the full-time jobs of cooks and scullions. Clothes were made, washed, and mended with the goal of lasting beyond the lifetime of the wearer. It is only in the last 200 years that home appliances began, as the advertisements used to say, to take the drudgery out of housework.

Today, there is a continually growing number of household appliances, designed for safe and efficient use. The "UL approved" on little tags glued quite securely onto the cords of household appliances and lighting fixtures stands for Underwriters Laboratories, an organization that provides lists of inspected and approved electrical equipment. UL approval is referenced in electrical codes as a standard for electrical-equipment safety. The UL tag ensures that the appliance is designed and manufactured for safe use.

Electrical equipment comes with several ratings that indicate wiring requirements. The voltage listing indicates the maximum voltage that can safely be applied to the unit continuously. An ordinary wall receptacle has a 250-volt (V) rating, although it usually uses only 120 volts. It is, therefore, safe to use the receptacle even if the voltage exceeds 120 volts. Some common household equipment requires 240 volts. These include household electrical ranges and clothes dryers. Electric heaters that use more than 1500 watts (W) and window air conditioners that use more than 4.4 kilowatts (kW) (1.25 tons) usually require 240 volts. These appliances must be either directly wired into a circuit or plugged into a special receptacle designed for them.

Current carrying ability, another wiring rating for appliances, is measured in amps (A). The maximum operating temperature at which components of the equipment (for example, a toaster) can operate continuously determines the number of amps. Equipment with better electrical insulation inside can carry more current safely.

In 1987, the U.S. Congress passed the National Appliance Energy Conservation Act, over the objections of the U.S. Department of Energy (DOE) but backed by utilities, appliance manufacturers, and environmental groups. This law establishes minimal efficiency criteria for heating, ventilating, and air-conditioning (HVAC) systems; refrigerators; freezers; and other appliances. When specifying any electrical equipment or appliance, an interior designer should look for the **Energy Efficiency Rating (EER)** and the estimated annual operating cost, which are listed on the yellow and black federal EnergyGuide label attached to every air conditioner, fan, dishwasher, clothes dryer, refrigerator, and freezer. The EnergyGuide label allows consumers to compare one appliance with another. Higher energy efficiency results in lower energy use and lower operating costs.

As discussed earlier, the U.S. Environmental Protection Agency (EPA) and the DOE have established the Energy Star® label in voluntary cooperation with manufacturers and retailers to identify energy efficient appliances, computers, lighting fixtures, and home entertainment equipment. Interior designers should look for the Energy Star® label when specifying refrigerators, dishwashers, and clothes washers, as well as audio equipment, computers, monitors, and other office equipment. Local electric and gas companies may offer rebates for high-efficiency refrigerators and clothes washers.

When helping a client decide what type of equipment to purchase, it is important for an interior designer to determine the most efficient solution to the problem at hand. For example, a window fan may be a more energy-efficient choice than an air

TABLE 14-1. RESIDENTIAL EQUIPMENT

Location	Appliance	Volts	Amps	Outlets on Circuit
Kitchen	Range	115/230	60	1
	Oven (built-in)	115/230	30	1
	Cooktop	115/230	30	1
	Dishwasher	115	20	1
	Garbage disposer	115	20	1
	Microwave oven	115	20	1 or more
	Refrigerator	115	20	Separate circuit recommended
	Freezer	115	20	
Laundry	Clothes washer	115	20	1
	Clothes dryer	115/230	30	1
	Hand iron	115	20	1
Living areas	Workshops	115	20	1 or more; separate circuit for heavy-duty appliances
	Portable heater	115	20	1
	Television	115	20	1 or more
	Audio center	115	20	1 or more
	Personal computer and peripherals	115; isolated ground may be required	20	1 or more, surge protection recommended
Fixed utilities	Fixed lighting	115	20	1 or more
	Window air conditioner, ¾ horsepower	115	20 or 30	1
	Central air conditioner	115/230	40	1
	Sump pump	115	20	1 or more
	Heating plant (forced-air furnace)	115	20	1
	Attic fan	115	20	1 or more

conditioner. Equipment that uses a timer, thermostat, or sensor can save energy without decreasing comfort. Photocells are available to control day and night operation. A timer on an air conditioner can turn it on or off depending on the occupant's presence or outside temperature changes, or according to a preprogrammed time schedule.

Today, manufacturers are responding to the trend to include kitchen appliances in areas other than the kitchen, including dens and master bedroom suites, by offering very compact units. One such unit resembles a big wardrobe with overall dimensions of about 1.5 m wide × 1.8 m deep x .6 m high (5 × 6 × 2 ft.) that is suited for a small city apartment or master suite. When the unit's doors are opened, a full kitchen is revealed that includes a refrigerator with freezer, a small dishwasher, a two-burner cooktop, a combination microwave/convection oven, a small sink and faucet, a recycling unit, and some storage.

KITCHEN APPLIANCES

Kitchen appliances are primarily, but not exclusively, found in the home. Interior designers who work on commercial office projects find themselves designing office kitchen and coffee areas. Even beauty salons and similar retail-oriented spaces require kitchen and laundry appliances.

As mentioned earlier, kitchen appliances and the many conveniences they provide were not always available. Before the nineteenth century, food was seasonal and had to be eaten immediately or preserved for leaner times. In England through the nineteenth century, most people who lived in small country cottages had their own pig and kept a dairy cow for milk, cheese, and butter. Before the eighteenth century, farmers did not have access to winter feed for cattle, and the animals were slaughtered in the fall. Neighborhood shops did not exist before the rise of the middle class, and isolated homesteads and manor houses relied on salting, smoking, freezing, and drying for meat, fruit, and vegetable preservation. Provisions were stored in larders, icehouses, and cellars.

☑ **Larders were rooms designed for meat to be potted into tubs and covered with lard, or salted or smoked for use through the winter. By the late nineteenth century, larders were used to store not only all kinds of meat, but also vegetables, bread, cheese, and fruit. Larders were built near the kitchen to be as cool as possible, with windows covered with screen. Thick slate or marble slabs embedded deep in the walls served as cool shelves.**

Figure 14-1 Office kitchen. Office kitchens may combine the functions of a catering kitchen, a coffee-break area, and a staff lunchroom. If not easy to maintain and share, the kitchens can become a source of employee dissatisfaction. *Photo credit: Herb Fremin*

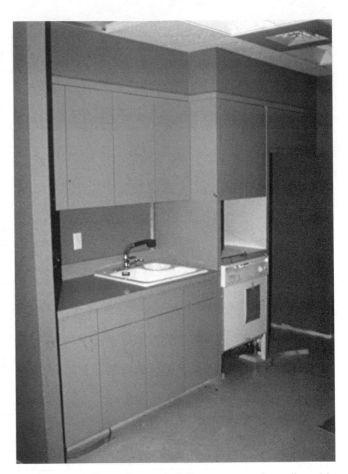

Figure 14-2 Office coffee area. Coffee areas are often adjacent to spaces that are specified for other functions. Because coffee areas tend to attract conversing employees, it is best that they be isolated from quiet areas. Space for recycling cans and bottles is a must. *Photo credit: Herb Fremin*

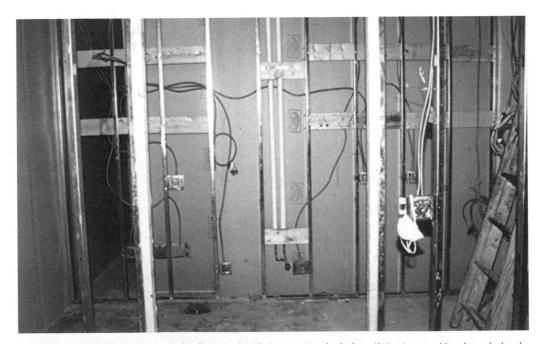

Figure 14-3 Office kitchen rough-in. Designs for kitchen spaces include outlets at several levels and plumbing for sinks and dishwashers, along with bracing for wall-hung units. *Photo credit: Herb Fremin*

Figure 14-4 Medieval kitchen. Large medieval kitchens were work centers where game and garden produce were prepared and preserved, bread was baked, and meals were prepared and cooked.

Refrigerators and Freezers

Today, most people depend on refrigerators to preserve their food. Refrigerators use a great deal of energy in order to stay cold and keep food fresh. However, there are many ways to keep food cool and fresh without the aid of electricity, which can be adapted to modern use.

Frozen food goes back at least to the fourth century BCE, when Alexander the Great had pits dug and covered with twigs and leaves to store ice and snow through the summer months. By the early seventeenth century, the French and Italians were routinely using long-term ice storage. In England, ice that was cut from ponds was stored in icehouses, where it could be kept for two years or more. By the mid-nineteenth century, small ice cellars were being built adjacent to houses, with insulated double walls and double doors to prevent cold air from escaping. Ice cellars were used to store cold water, butter, and other provisions. In 1844, Thomas Masters patented an icebox for use inside the home. Ice chests and iceboxes were often designed as pieces of furniture, with taps for draining off melted ice.

☑ **A cool closet is an insulated storage cabinet on the north exterior wall of a house. Cool air from outside enters the closet through lower vents, rises up the closet through slots in the shelves, and flows out of a top vent on the top of the house. Continuous airflow and heavy insulation lower the temperature and keep the food cold. Cool closets use no electricity, require low maintenance, and are easy to build.**

Until the early twentieth century, root cellars were used in rural areas to keep meat, milk, cream, and other goods cold. A root cellar is a hole in the ground that is minimally 3 meters (10 ft.) deep. Because the earth's temperature is always about 10°C to 13°C (50°F–55°F), the humidity and temperature remain stable inside the root cellar. These cellars can be built into a hill or in a basement that has a dirt floor. They are well insulated and have vents to circulate the air. Shelves are made from either rot-resistant or pressure-treated wood and are kept a few inches away from the walls to help increase circulation around the food. Root cellars are covered with a door, preferably made from two pieces of wood with insulation between them.

Mechanical cooling systems provided cold storage on a commercial scale long before they were adapted to home use. The first successful domestic refrigerator brand was Domelre, marketed in Chicago in 1913, followed by Kelvinator in 1916 and Frigidaire in 1917. Electric refrigerators were common by the 1930s.

Refrigerators have been greatly improved in terms of energy efficiency. Today, the average refrigerator uses about 700 kilowatt/hours (kWh) per year, one-third of the energy of a 1973 model, and is larger and has better controls as well. Newer refrigerators have more insulation, tighter door seals, a larger coil surface area, and improved compressors and motors. The purchase of a newer model can provide a quick payback through energy savings. The larger the refrigerator, the more energy it will use, but one large refrigerator will use less energy than two smaller ones with the same capacity. The most efficient refrigerators are in the 16- to 20-cubic-foot range. Side-by-side models are less energy efficient than styles with the freezer on top. Some built-in refrigerators use more energy than freestanding models. Automatic icemakers and through-door dispensers are also somewhat more energy intensive.

Energy Star® refrigerators that meeting the 2001 requirements must be 30 percent more efficient than the percentage required by 1993 standards. They accomplish this goal with more highly efficient compressors and condensers, and are available in side-to-side and freezer-on-top models.

☑ **When selecting the refrigerator style, an interior designer should consider the depth required when the door is open 90 degrees. Side-to-side models take up less space in front of the refrigerator. Typically, refrigerators use a 115-volt, 60-hertz, AC, 15-ampere grounded outlet. Some manufacturers offer counter-depth refrigerators that align smoothly with cabinets, providing maximum storage capacity without taking up a great deal of space in the kitchen.**

Special high-efficiency refrigerators are available that run on 12-volt direct-current (DC) electricity and are six times more efficient than conventional refrigerators. Their efficiency is the result of the location and design of the compressor and thick insulation. In a traditional refrigerator, the compressor is located at the bottom, and the heat it generates rises and creates a blanket of warm air around the refrigerator. With a high-efficiency refrigerator, the compressor is on top. The compressor lacks a fan and runs less often than that of a standard model, contributing to exceptionally quiet operation.

Chest-style freezers that load from the top are 10 to 25 percent more efficient than upright, front-loading freezers, the result of better insulation and the fact that air does not spill out as readily when they are opened. However, chest freezers are more difficult to organize. Manual defrosting is more common than automatic defrosting for freezers, but automatic defrost may dehydrate food and cause freezer burn.

Icemakers that produce up to 50 pounds of ice cubes every twenty-four hours are available in built-in and freestanding models. These icemakers require a water supply, and some models include a factory-installed drain pump. An icemaker's electrical requirements typically include 120-volt, 60 Hertz (Hz), 15- or 20-ampere service, with a three-wire grounded, fused electrical supply. Undercounter wine cellars are available that hold sixty bottles and require a 120-volt, 60 Hz, 15- or 20-ampere, three-wire grounded, fused electric supply.

☑ **Refrigerators and freezers should be located away from such heat sources as dishwashers and ovens, and out of direct sun. Allow a 25-millimeter (1-in.) space on each side for good air circulation. To avoid adding waste heat from a freezer to a house's cooling load, an interior designer should consider locating it in the basement or garage. Freezers do not work properly when located in spaces below 7°C (45°F).**

Stoves and Ovens

The enormous hearth typical of medieval and Tudor kitchens was a multipurpose heat source for forging, dying cloth, and other trades in between mealtimes. A large hearth might accommodate a baking oven at each end and have multiple flues. A long, horizontal bar up the chimney held pots and cauldrons, and meat was often smoked in the chimney as well. Before the advent of matches in 1831, a tinderbox and flint were used to light the fire, although once lit, glowing coals were preserved overnight to keep the fire going.

Such early kitchens had no sinks because all the washing, food preparation, and other work involving water were done in a separate scullery. Kitchen furniture was easily movable and included trestle tables and three-legged stools. Wall shelves held pottery and earthenware dishes, wooden bowls and chopping boards, and metal pots and platters.

By the early eighteenth century, kitchen fireplaces used mineral coal, thereby allowing for small, shallow grates. Set in brickwork, built-in charcoal ranges began to take up the work no longer accommodated by the smaller, more decorative fireplaces. Iron baking ovens began to replace traditional clay or brick baking ovens set in the wall of the hearth. By the 1880s, charcoal-fired ranges were beginning to replace open fires entirely.

As kitchens were freed of smoke from huge open hearths and messy tasks were diverted to adjacent sculleries, kitchen fur-

Figure 14-5 Traditional Japanese kitchen range. This illustration of a traditional Japanese kitchen range with its smoke-conducting hood was drawn by Edward S. Morse for *Japanese Homes and Their Surroundings*, originally published in 1886 by Ticknor and Company and reprinted by Dover Publications, Inc., in 1961.

nishings became more elaborate. Dressers, closets, cupboards, painted walls, and tiled floors were features of early-nineteenth-century kitchens.

The development of the kitchen range, which combined open fire, an oven, and a hot water boiler, began in the 1780s. By 1850, even working-class English homes had open ranges that were set below an open chimney; these persisted through the 1950s. The impressive-looking close range, which had a flue controlled by dampers that directed hot air around the ovens, the hot-water boiler, or the hotplate, is credited to George Bodley in 1802.

The compactness, cleanliness, and reliability of gas and, later, electric cooking stoves made it possible to reduce the size of kitchens and their adjacent spaces to accommodate the needs of twentieth-century families. Gas ranges began to replace solid fuels in the 1890s in cities where gas supplies were available.

In the early 1920s, Swedish scientist Gustav Dalen designed the Aga cooker. The thickly insulated Aga has two ovens heated by coke from an internal firebox. One oven is always very hot; the other, cool. The hot oven and hotplate are heated by radiant heat from the firebox, while the cool oven and warm plate are heated by conduction. The economical Aga could also be used to keep a large tank of water constantly hot.

The original electric cookers were expensive and slow to heat water. Electric cookers increased rapidly in popularity in the 1920s with the spread of electricity, but they still were unable to compete with the economy, convenience, and speed of gas.

Today, cooktops are available as standard ranges or as separate units and are either electric or gas. New gas ranges are required to have electric ignition rather than wasteful pilot lights.

Electric cooktops usually require single-phase, alternating current (AC), 240/208-volt, 60 Hertz, and 20- or 40-ampere grounded electrical service. Some cooktops feature a modular design, with open bays that accept halogen, radiant, or coil-element cartridges or a grill assembly.

Slide-in ranges provide a solid, streamlined impression by removing frames and crevices. Freestanding and slide-in electric ranges require three- or four-wire, single-phase, AC power. The 120/240-volt, 60-Hertz service should be on a separate 50-ampere grounded electric circuit.

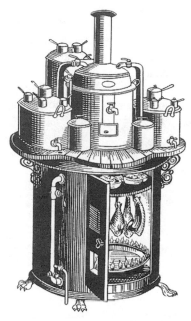

Figure 14-6 Gas cooker. This gas cooker was designed around 1850 and was intended to prepare food for 100 people at a time.

Figure 14-7 Coal range, 1895. The Grand Windsor Range was advertised in several increasingly elaborate styles in the spring and summer edition of the Montgomery Ward & Co. Catalogue of 1895. The six-burner model shown here cost less than $25 and weighed around 400 pounds.

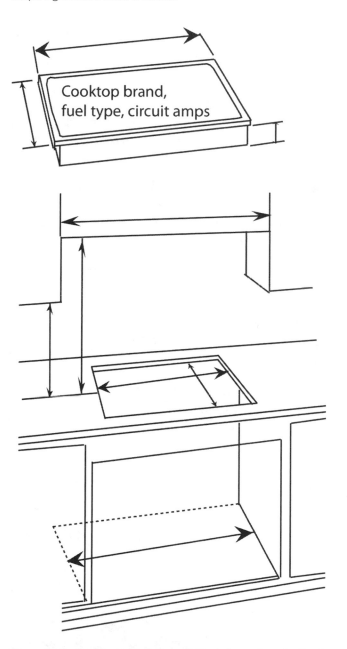

Cooktop brand, fuel type, circuit amps

Figure 14-8 Cooktop installation. Critical dimensions for the installation of a cooktop include the size and type of the cooktop itself, the horizontal dimensions between cabinets above and below the cooktop, vertical clearances above the cooktop, and the size of the counter opening required.

Electric cooktops come with a variety of heating elements, all of which require that pans have good contact with the burners, so flat pan-bottoms are a necessity. Types of electric heating elements include the following:

- Exposed coils are more difficult to keep clean than other types.
- Solid disk elements are attractive, easy to clean, and heat up slowly, increasing their energy consumption.
- Radiant elements are located under ceramic glass and are quite easy to clean. They heat up faster than solid disks, but not faster than coils; they are more energy efficient than coils or solid disks.
- Halogen elements use halogen lamps for instant heat and rapid temperature changes. They offer energy savings but have a higher purchase price. Halogen elements heat food by means of the contact of the pan on the ceramic glass surface.
- Induction elements transfer electromagnetic energy directly to the pan. They are very energy efficient but work only with ferrous-metal cookware, such as cast iron, stainless steel, or enameled iron—not with aluminum pans. When the pan is removed from the heating element, almost no heat lingers on the cooktop. These elements are very expensive.

Gas cooktops should have electric pilot lights, and they often have sealed gas burners. They typically require single-phase AC, 120-volt, 60-Hertz, 15-ampere grounded electric service. Gas cooktops are available in combination with gas grills. Those with sealed gas burners are easier to keep clean. Some manufacturers offer dual-fuel models, with sealed gas burners and an electric convection oven.

Gas cookstoves consume oxygen from room air and release carbon dioxide and water vapor. To ensure that gas-combustion products are eliminated from the house, a ventilation fan should be installed. The fan must exhaust to the outside when the stove is in use, not just recirculate air. Too large a fan should be avoided because it will waste energy and may cause backdrafting problems. Large, downdraft ventilation fans in cooktops and ranges can suck so much air that the house becomes depressurized, causing the heating system to fail to vent properly and creating a backdraft for combustion gases. Large fans need makeup air ducts, which some fan manufacturers supply.

Conventional ovens with self-cleaning features have more than the usual amount of insulation and are more energy efficient unless the self-cleaning feature is used more than once a month. A window in the door prevents energy from being wasted when the door is opened in order to look at the food being cooked. Built-in electric ovens typically require a separate 208/240-volt, 60-Hertz, 30-ampere grounded circuit. A time-delay fuse or circuit breaker is recommended. Double ovens located one above the other provide a great deal of oven in a small amount of floor space.

Convection ovens are more energy efficient than conventional ovens. Heated air continuously circulates around the food for more even heat distribution. Food can be cooked faster and at

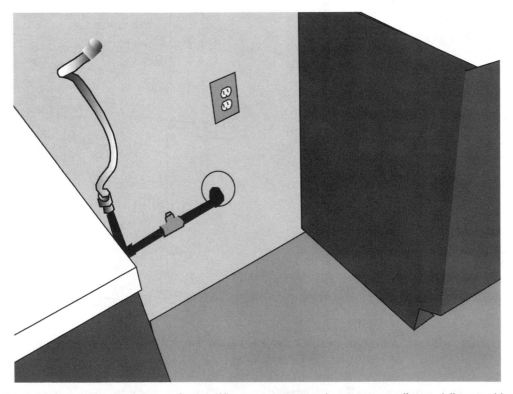

Figure 14-9 Installing gas stove and oven. When a customer purchases a gas appliance, delivery and installation must include the services of a plumber to connect the gas line.

Self cleaning | Continuous clean | Conventional

Figure 14-10 Oven efficiency. Gas ovens use less energy than electric ovens; in addition, gas may be less expensive. Self-cleaning ovens are manufactured with more insulation than other types and save energy when used. This benefit is lost, however, when the high-heat self-cleaning option is used more than once a month.

lower temperatures in convection ovens, saving about one-third of energy costs associated with conventional ovens.

A variety of accessory cooking appliances are available, but an interior designer should consider their energy consumption as well as their usefulness. Warming drawers keep contents at anywhere between 3°C and 107°C (90°F–225°F). They offer removable serving pans, and the drawer itself may be removable. The electrical service required is 120 volts, 60 Hertz. Rotisseries for residential use require electrical and gas connections as well as an exhaust hood. They are heavy, weighing about 130 kilograms (290 lb.) and must be supported adequately.

Microwave ovens use very-high-frequency radio waves to penetrate the food surface and heat water molecules in the food's interior. Using a microwave can reduce energy use and cooking times, especially for small portions and for reheating leftovers, by around two-thirds compared with those of a conventional oven. They also contribute less waste heat to the kitchen. Temperature probes, controls that shut off when the food is cooked, and variable power settings also save energy.

Microwave ovens are available in countertop, over-range, over-counter, and built-in models. Most specify a single-phase, DC 120-volt, 60-Hertz, 15-ampere, three-wire grounded circuit. Built-in

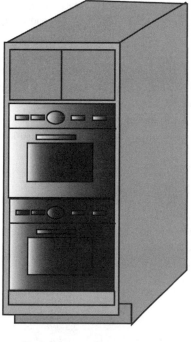

Single oven | Double oven | Oven and microwave

Figure 14-11 Oven cabinets. Cabinets for wall-mounted ovens and microwaves must be designed to accommodate the specified equipment.

Figure 14-12 Microwave mounting bracket. Wall-mounted microwaves require the support of a mounting bracket. They should not be hung directly from the cabinets above.

microwaves may offer a drop-down door and a convection hood and may require 120-volt or 240-volt, 20-ampere service. Microwave combination ovens come with a convection oven below and may require 120/240-volt, 60-Hertz, 40-ampere grounded service. Microwaves, toaster ovens, and slow-cook crock-pots, which combine an insulated ceramic pot with an electric heating element, can save energy when used to prepare smaller meals.

☑ **Professional-quality cooking equipment is sometimes specified for high-end residential projects. The allure of sleek finishes, large capacity, and added features promises that the home cook will accomplish chef-quality feats. It is important to remember that what happens in a real commercial kitchen is a world away from the experience of the home cook, and many of the features and much of the capacity of true professional equipment are beyond the scope of a residential project. Many high-end appliance manufacturers offer professional-style equipment that may be appropriate for a dedicated amateur chef, but often the issue is one of style more than substance. Brochures are replete with such comments as, "Your decorator is going to love this. A sleek, elegant six-burner cooktop." An interior designer can help clients select equipment that fits their actual needs with good design and energy savings.**

Dishwashing

The dishwasher became a necessity only when household labor was no longer cheaply available. A basic model patented in the United States in 1865 consisted of a metal cupboard that was placed on the sink drainboard and filled by a pipe from the tap. Metal plates turned by a hand crank forced water against plates in a wire rack. In 1885, a large Paris restaurant was using a machine invented by Eugene Daquin, which had eight artificial hands that gripped the plates. Plates were washed in a hot bath, vigorously brushed, then dipped in cold water. In the 1890s, Josephine Cockran of Indiana invented a dishwasher that consisted of a wooden tub with a hand-cranked set of plungers that forced water over the dishes. The tub was filled by hand, but it enjoyed some success when it was fitted with a small electric motor. The first modern dishwasher dates back to 1932, when the ancestor to the Kenwood dishwasher of the 1960s appeared. By 1951, only one million dishwashers had been sold in the United States. Dishwasher-related problems were not solved satisfactorily until the 1970s.

Heating water comprises 80 percent of the energy use of an automatic dishwasher, so using less water saves energy. Old dishwashers use 8 to 14 gallons of water per wash cycle. Since 1994, dishwashers have been designed to use between 7 and 10 gallons per cycle. With the addition of a booster heater in the dishwasher, cool water from the main water heater is raised to between 60°C and 63°C (140°F–145°F), the optimal temperature for dishwashing performance. Some dishwashers offer energy-saving wash cycles. No-heat drying circulates room air through a dishwasher by fans rather than an electric heating element. The so-called "dirt sensor" technology touted by some manufacturers has exhibited uneven performance and is generally unreliable.

Energy Star® dishwashers save both water and energy. Built-in sensors determine the length of the washing cycle and the temperature of the water necessary to clean the dishes. A speed cycle cuts wash time by 30 minutes, and a high-performance motor makes the unit run more quietly. Energy Star® dishwashers minimize the amount of water needed, thereby saving the energy required to heat the additional water. Energy Star® dishwashers exceed minimum federal efficiency standards by between 13 and 30 percent.

Dishwashers require both water supply and drain connections. Electrical connections are typically 120-volt, 60-Hertz, 15- or 20-ampere fused electrical supply with copper wire on a separate circuit. A time-delay fuse or circuit breaker is recommended. The outlet should be placed in an adjacent cabinet. Because of the heat dishwashers give off, they should not be installed near refrigerators. Unfaced fiberglass batt insulation added to the top, sides, and back of a dishwasher, if permitted by the manufacturer, results in less noise and less energy use.

Dishwashers are usually 61 centimeters (24 in.) wide with 46 cm (18 in.) wide models also sold. Portable, drawer, and EnergyStar® types are available.

LAUNDRY EQUIPMENT

Before homes had running water piped into them, laundry was frequently done outdoors. Clothing was washed more often in warm spring and summer weather than in the winter, when drying was a major problem. Before the age of inexpensive cotton, clothes were laundered as infrequently as possible. Originally, no soaps were used. Clothes were beaten clean with wooden bats on a riverbank or in a communal washing cistern, which was very hard on fine fabrics. Eventually, clothes were soaked in an alkaline solution called lye, which was made from furnace ash, bird dung, bran, or urine, all of which worked well to remove perspiration and greasy dirt that tended to rot fabrics. Soap, which was made from vegetable oils and animal fats, was expensive to buy and tedious to make.

In England in the eighteenth century, the size of a country-house laundry varied from a single washhouse separate from the main house, to a suite of rooms for bleaching, drying, ironing. and folding. Professional washerwomen in towns took care of clothing from surrounding estates as early as the fourteenth century. At the end of the eighteenth century, traveling washerwoman teams stayed for a day or two in their customers' homes. By the nineteenth century, less costly cotton clothing generated more laundry, which was sent out each week or two by middle and upper class city residents; alternatively, a professional washerwoman came to the house once a week.

The old-fashioned laundry was a sweltering, damp place, steamy from the boiling coppers, the drying closets, and the iron-heating stoves or grates. Laundry was originally washed in large wooden troughs with washboards. By the early twentieth century, these were replaced by glazed earthenware sinks. In addition, the washhouse was furnished with wooden tubs in which laundry was churned by wash-sticks. A built-in boiling copper was filled and emptied with buckets and a dipper, and heated from underneath.

Handheld agitators that were twisted or pumped up and down in a wooden tub inspired the first clothing washing machines. The earliest washing-machine patents date back to 1752, with the first practical examples produced by Harper Twelvetrees in the 1850s, although clothes tended to get knotted around the legs of the agitators. Other machines were patterned on washboards. In 1861, Thomas Bradford of Saltram, England, patented the Vowel machines (with A, E, I, O, and U models), which consisted of a hexagonal box that rocked and vibrated. Clothes rubbed against a ribbed wood lining inside. These machines were tiring to use and required constant attendance.

By the 1860s, piped hot and cold water were standard in new homes. The first electric clothes washers with motorized rotating tubs were developed around 1915 in both England and the United States. The motor under the machine lacked a protective casing, so water dripping on the motor caused short circuits, fires, and shocks. Many early machines had to be filled manually with buckets and drained by hand. Clothes were removed wet, and the machine continued to run until the plug was pulled. Later machines had a central agitator and could spin clothes almost dry. It was not until 1939 that the first washer was manufactured with automatic timing controls, variable cycles, and preset water levels.

Clothes Washers and Dryers

Today's washing machines are expected to wash clothes better with less water and less energy. Because they use less water, efficient washers also use less detergent and reduce the sewage treatment load. Heating water uses 90 percent of the energy consumed by washing machines. Appliance manufacturers met the 1993 DOE Standards by removing the option for a hot water rinse from the regular cycle and using better tub designs.

In 2007, the DOE announced new EnergyStar® standards for clothes washers. The energy and water savings to date result primarily from design innovations. More-accurate sensors lead to more efficient use of hot and cold water. Higher spin speeds that remove more water from clothes result in less drying time, thereby saving energy.

Horizontal axis machines, which are usually front-loading, are usually much more efficient than vertical axis machines. Horizontal axis machines use about one-third as much water, thus saving about two-thirds of the energy use. They also clean more thoroughly than conventional machines. Because horizontal axis machines spin faster, less water is left in the clothes, which saves time and energy in terms of clothes dryer use. Front-loading machines may allow a dryer to be stacked on top for space savings. The money saved on energy and water may add up to around $100 annually, which along with the rebates often offered by manufacturers and utilities make horizontal axis machines a wise choice.

Wash and rinse cycle options, especially cold water rinses, and water-level settings save energy, as do machines that adjust automatically to the size of the load. A washing machine should be located as close as possible to the water heater and in a heated space if possible; all of the hot water pipes should be insulated

Figure 14-13 Washer connection. Washers require hot and cold water connections as well as a drain that meets code requirements. A lever that shuts off the water supply when the machine is not in use can help prevent flooding. An electrical connection is also needed.

Figure 14-14 Dryer vent. Dryers, especially gas dryers, should be vented directly to the outside, with short, straight sections of metal duct. Flexible vinyl duct restricts airflow and can be crushed. Vinyl duct may not stand up to high temperatures. Electric dryers may be vented inside the home during the winter if the house air is dry and the vent is properly filtered. Sometimes, compact apartment or condominium dryers are vented indoors, but this may cause condensation on windows. Dryer exhausts should have a vent hood that blocks air infiltration and seals the exhaust duct very tightly when the dryer is not running. Standard dryer vent hoods use a simple flapper, which is not as effective. Tightly sealing hoods is just a little more expensive.

for further savings. Sometimes, sound protection is a valuable option, although on occasion, operating noises indicate what stage the load is in. Typically, washers require a 120-volt, 60-Hertz, AC, 15- or 20-ampere grounded electrical service.

Clothes were originally twisted dry, leading to the women's fashion for tight pleats in the eleventh century. In the late eighteenth century, mechanical wringers that squeezed clothes between rollers were attached with screws to sinks and became a standard feature of early washing machines. By 1880, rubber rollers pressed water out of clothes.

Once wrung out, clothes were spread on lawns in the sun to dry or on rosemary and lavender hedges that scented the clothes as well. Only in wet or cold weather were clothes dried indoors, on drying rods suspended from the ceiling or on airing racks hoisted overhead on pulleys. In France in 1800, M. Pochon invented a device called a ventilator. Damp, hand-wrung clothes were put in a circular metal drum pierced with holes. Cranking the handle rotated the drum above an open fire. The clothes either dried slowly or burned and smelled like soot. In the mid-nineteenth century, drying closets were constructed in large homes and institutions. Drying closets are brick enclosures built over furnaces or networks of hot pipes. Metal frames with racks were pulled out from the drying closet to load and unload laundry.

Modern clothes dryers work by heating and aerating clothes. Gas dryers are much less expensive to use than electric dryers. Automatic shut-offs save energy and are easier on clothes. The best automatic shut-offs use moisture sensors in the drum, and do not simply sense the temperature of the exhaust air. Cooldown and moisture-sensing options also reduce the energy needed for ironing. Today, electric ignition, rather than pilot lights, is required in gas dryers. Dryers should be located in heated spaces. Designing an area for air-drying delicate items protects clothes and saves energy.

Some dryer models have drop-down rather than side-opening doors, making it easier to keep loose socks from falling to the floor. Sound protection is a valuable option when a noisy dryer could be disturbing. Typically, service requirements for electric dryers are a 120/240-volt or 120/208-volt, 60-Hertz, AC, 30-ampere grounded electrical outlet. Gas dryers require a gas connection, of course, and a 120-volt, 60-Hertz, AC, 15- or 20-ampere grounded electrical outlet.

In this day of wash-and–wear clothes, people who still iron summer linens are a vanishing breed. The earliest piece of machinery used to iron sheets, tablecloths, and other flat linen was the mangle. The mangle combined pressure provided by a screw with a smoothing technique that involved wrapping linens around smooth wooden cylinders and rolling them to and fro under pressure. For other items, pairs of flat irons in different sizes were alternately used and heated on a stove. Box irons were heated internally with slugs of hot metal or charcoal. Box irons are still in use in some parts of the world where power is unreliable and expensive. Beginning in the 1890s, paraffin, oil, and petroleum irons were available. In 1882, H. W. Seeley of New Jersey patented the earliest electric iron, which dubiously featured flying sparks and weird noises. Today's irons are much safer, if less exciting. Models that turn themselves off when left unattended are preferable.

Appliance Control and Energy Conservation

A handful of companies are beginning to roll out a new generation of household appliances with Internet or network capability and a range of potential uses. Some appliances communicate

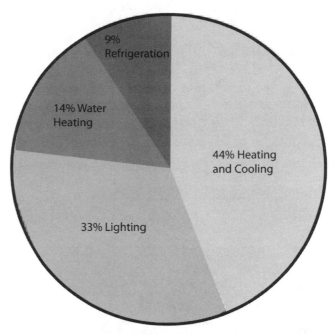

Figure 14-15 Home energy use. As this chart indicates, more than three-fourths of household energy use is devoted to heating, cooling, and lighting.

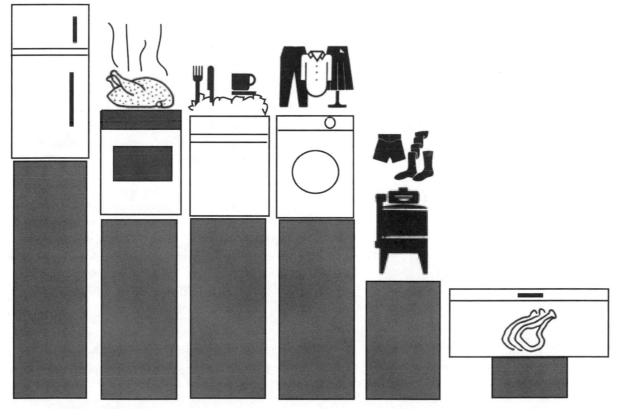

Figure 14-16 Appliance energy use. Of the energy used for various appliances, refrigerators use the most. Ovens, stoves, dishwashers, and clothes dryers also use substantial amounts of energy. Clothes washing uses somewhat less energy, and storage freezers use a modest amount of energy.

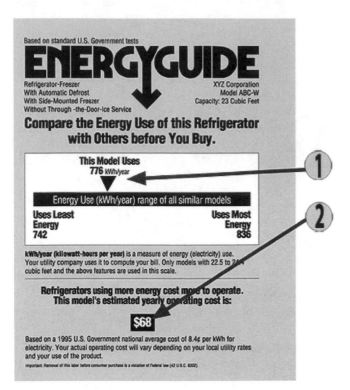

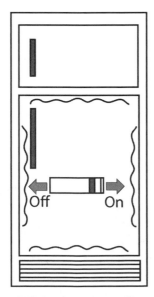

Figure 14-17 EnergyGuide label. The EnergyGuide label appears on most household appliances. The arrow at 1 indicates the model and year. The arrow at 2 shows an estimate of annual operating costs. These labels compare appliances with similar models, but the costs do not necessarily reflect current energy costs, which may rise rapidly.

Figure 14-18 Refrigerator energy-saver switch. Inside many refrigerators is an energy-saver switch that can be shut off when humidity is low. The switch activates a heater that, in turn, reduces moisture condensation. This works well in humid environments, but it uses more energy than it saves in dry climates and should be turned off.

with each other through the home electrical system, while most use the telephone line and an Internet service provider. Manufacturers are hesitant to introduce products, primarily in response to customers' concerns that the new products might not integrate with appliances from other manufacturers. Customers worry that they may need to rewire their homes or that their telephone lines will be taken over by appliances. Manufacturers are still working out industry standards.

To date, a wired refrigerator, washing machine, and microwave are available that are designed to perform intelligent tasks, such as collecting recipes from the Internet, tracking food inventory, and downloading new wash cycles from the Internet for different kinds of clothes. Each component connects to the Internet through telephone lines and built-in modems. Users may also be able to use appliance display screens to make two-way video telephone calls, watch television, or send e-mail messages.

DATA AND COMMUNICATIONS WIRING

In the first edition of this book, quite a bit of space was devoted to describing how to wire modular workstations, also called cubicles. There are still plenty of cubicles, along with vast amounts of wiring. However, wireless technologies have combined with changes in where and how people work to radically alter the planning of new offices. At the time of this writing, large office furniture companies are moving away from selling wired cubicles and are trying to refocus their product lines on furnishings that are more flexible in terms of use.

Desks are transitioning from cubicle-embedded, plastic-laminate work surfaces to something more like a table. Interior designers are free to suggest novel arrangements, such as taking over the dining-room table as a generous and rather elegant desk—and relinquishing it only for formal dinners. An almost paperless office is now possible, reducing filing cabinets to a minimum. Laptops allow people to work where and when we please, even outside on a patio or terrace.

In the interest of helping interior designers who are working with older, cubicle-based office environments, some basic information on office communications and data wiring is included here.

Interior designers are often responsible for showing the location of electrical power, data, and telephone connections, both in homes and in offices. The goals are flexibility and ease of access. Plugging in equipment should not require a user to crawl around on the floor. Rewiring for new technology should not involve ripping up walls and floors.

In the heyday of office cubicle design, standards in the United States recognized three types of communications cables. The most common is Category 5 unshielded twisted pair (UTP) cable. (There are also other Category types, such as Category 3 or Category 6.) The second type is shielded twisted pair (STP) cable. The third type, optical fiber, continues to grow in popularity and availability.

Fiber-optic cable used for communications has either a glass or a plastic filament at its core, encased in a plastic sheath. It

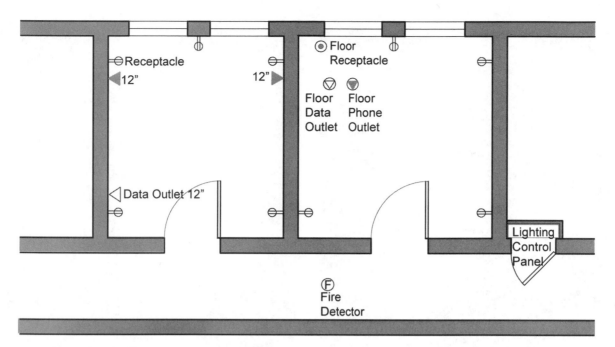

Figure 14-19 Office data and communication plan. This office plan indicates the location of electrical receptacles, data outlets, and a fire detector.

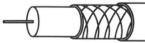

Figure 14-20 Category 5 unshielded twisted pair (UTP) cable. Category 5 UTP cable is designed to limit electronic-signal interference between adjacent pairs of copper wires, which is known as crosstalk. Although the outer jacket covering four pairs of copper wires is relatively strong and durable, it can be damaged when improperly installed.

Figure 14-21 Coaxial cable. Coaxial cable is very resistant to electronic interference or noise. It is used for cable television and radio-frequency LANs. Coaxial cable usually contains a single wire conductor surrounded by a layer of insulation, an outer shielding conductor, and a second layer of insulation.

Figure 14-22 Fiber-optic cable. Fiber-optic cable is increasingly used to carry large amounts of information with high security, low noise, and broad bandwidths. Fiber-optic cable has a core of glass or plastic filament encased in a plastic sheath.

transmits data converted to light pulses rather than electronic signals. The two major classifications of fiber optic cables are single mode and multimode.

Single-mode fiber optic cables are primarily used for distances greater than 2 kilometers (1.2 mi.), and for high-bandwidth applications. Multimode fiber-optic cables are used for distances less than 2 kilometers (1.2 mi.) and applications that have multiple-connection requirements. Multimode fiber optic cables are the most common type of cables used in commercial office buildings.

Currently, a great deal of the wiring in buildings is inactive, left over from a previous tenant or use. As wireless technology expands interior design options, more and more wiring will become obsolete.

According to Jeffrey S. Weil, senior vice president of Colliers International, a corporate real estate information resource, both tenants and landlords could be affected by a new provision announced in 2002 by the National Fire Protection Association (NFPA) that requires the removal of abandoned data and telephone cable. In buildings that are between 15 and 20 years old, there may be many abandoned wires throughout the plenum. Weil claims that used wiring does not appear to be cost-effective for recycling. Some large, institutional office-building owners are taking the lead in removing obsolete wiring as tenants move out. For many other building owners, this is a problem that will not go away anytime soon. (*2006 Telephone & Data Cable Update*, Accessed August 17, 2008)

People are surrounded by wires—even wireless equipment spends its off-duty time attached to a charger. The following are some guidelines for planning future wiring needs:

Figure 14-23 Wiring on ceiling. The design of a hair salon that included basement space necessitated the removal of a wall containing an electrical panel. Here, the wires are being rerouted across the ceiling to a new panel.

Figure 14-25 Telecommunications wiring. This spaghetti-like conglomeration is the telecommunications wiring for a 1990s office just before installation. As technology and business practices change, much of this type of wiring will be abandoned.

Figure 14-24 Wires on desk. Even with wireless and battery-powered equipment, keeping desk wiring under control is a problem. This messy reception desk was improved by rotating the placement of the equipment against the wall, leaving a clear surface facing visitors.

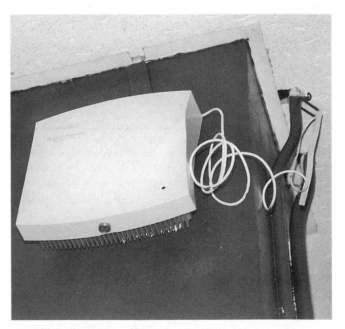

Figure 14-26 Wireless retrofit. Today, existing facilities are scrambling to become wireless. This college classroom has wireless equipment attached to a column.

Figure 14-27 Access floor data cables. A view into an access floor shows neatly bundled wires set between 4-inch (122 mm) pedestals.

- Raised-floor access to cabling and power distribution should be considered.
- Plug-and-play floor boxes for power, data, voice communications, and fiber optics should be incorporated into the plan.
- Modular and harnessed wiring and buses should be used to control cables.
- Conferencing hubs for flexibility in daily use and for reorganization should be included as needed.
- All necessary voice, cable, and data systems should be identified, and adequate equipment rooms and conduit runs should be provided, including audiovisual and speaker systems, Internet access, local area networks (LANs), wide area networks (WANs), and wireless fidelity (WiFi).
- Wireless technologies should be considered and accommodated as needed.

As fewer individuals and businesses rely on landlines for most of their telephone calls, extensive telecommunications wiring may be phased out. In the past, competing telephone service providers requested their own telephone closet in multiple-tenant buildings, duplicating wiring and space requirements.

Businesses and institutions have been racing to keep up with wireless technology. As office workers and students come to expect wireless Internet and telephone connections wherever they want them, retrofits are installed as quickly as possible. The equipment is neither invisible nor carefully designed.

As long as people continue to use wires to carry information, wires will be part of interior environments. Access flooring raised only a few inches can house wiring, yet enable it to remain easily accessible and almost invisible. The height changes must be ramped or otherwise made accessible.

The information in this chapter has ranged from archaic kitchens to wireless offices, but the book's theme is reinforced: equipment demands the attention of interior designers. These may not be life-threatening problems, but they affect people every day. In Part VI: Fire Safety, we will look at how building designers and interior designers deal with less common but much more serious threats to safety.

PART

VI

· · · · · · · · · · · · · · · ·

FIRE SAFETY

Most deaths caused by building fires occur in homes, yet the National Fire Protection Association (NFPA; www.nfpa.org; accessed September 19, 2008) reports that

> Only one-fifth to one-fourth of households (23 percent) have actually developed and practiced a home fire escape plan to ensure they could escape quickly and safely. One-third of American households who made an estimate thought they would have at least 6 minutes before a fire in their home would become life-threatening. The time available is often less. And only 8 percent said their first thought on hearing a smoke alarm would be to get out!

High-rise buildings require great numbers of persons to travel vertically down stairs in order to evacuate. The NFPA reports that "in the evacuation of the World Trade Center high-rise office tower following the first terrorist bombing in 1993, tens of thousands of building occupants successfully and safely traversed some five million person-flights of stairs.

"A portable fire extinguisher can save lives and property by putting out a small fire or containing it until the fire department arrives, but portable extinguishers have limitations. Because fire grows and spreads so rapidly, the number-one priority for residents is to get out safely."

The NFPA also says that "properly installed and maintained automatic fire sprinkler systems help save lives....What most people don't realize is that the same life-saving technology that protects [hotels, hospitals, and high-rises] is also available for homes, where 80 percent of all fire deaths occur."

Chapter 15: Basic Principles of Fire-Safety Design and Chapter 16: Fire Detection, Alarm, and Suppression cover how building interiors are designed to prevent fires and help people escape. This is, perhaps, the most valuable information that interior designers should know about building systems.

15

·················

Basic Principles of Fire-Safety Design

In 2005, the NFPA reported 511,000 building structure fires. These fires resulted in 3675 civilian deaths, 87 firefighter deaths, and 17,925 civilian injuries. Total property damage amounted to $10.7 billion.

People tend to be most aware of fires in large, high-profile buildings. However, according to the U.S. Centers for Disease Control and Prevention (CDC), four out of five fire-related deaths in the United States in 2005 occurred in homes. Fire is the primary cause of death for children under age 15 at home. In 2006, there were an estimated 396,000 reported home structure fires and 2580 associated civilian deaths in the United States. The National Disaster Education Coalition (NDEC) reports that 80 percent of all fire deaths occur where people sleep: in homes, dormitories, barracks, and hotels.

People in low-income neighborhoods are 20 times more likely to be injured or die in a house fire than people in higher-income areas, according to a study in the *New England Journal of Medicine*. A Dallas-based study by Dr. Gregory Istre revealed that children, African Americans, and the elderly are at the greatest risk in house fires. Poor residents in small, wood-framed, single-family houses are the most susceptible to fire. They are also more likely to use space heaters and less likely to have smoke detectors. Where wood-framed houses are less common in poor communities, single-family homes are less regulated than multifamily housing units and are the source of more fire problems.

When people are caught in a fire, their lungs and respiratory passages may be burned by hot air and their skin may be severely damaged by thermal radiation. Some deaths occur when panic causes people to push, crowd, and trample others. Other times, people who panic may make irrational decisions, such as running back into a burning building to retrieve their belongings.

Three times as many fire deaths result from asphyxiation due to dense smoke than from burns. Victims of fires are often suffocated by air depleted of oxygen and full of poisonous gases.

The average size of fires within buildings continues to decline. It is now rare in North America for large buildings to completely burn, thanks to automatic fire detection and fire extinguishing systems. Consequently, the focus of building fire protection is changing to minimizing water and smoke damage.

Buildings concentrate fuel that can sustain a fire. Wood building structures, wood paneling, and plastic insulating materials all will burn. Buildings often contain oil, natural gas, gasoline, paints, rubber, chemicals, and other highly flammable materials.

Buildings offer many possible sources of ignition for a fire. Defective furnaces, sparks from a fireplace, leaky chimneys, and unattended stoves can all start fires. Loose electrical connections and overloaded electrical wiring are common sources of fires. Many home fires are started by poorly maintained furnaces or stoves, cracked or rusted furnace parts, or chimneys with creosote buildup. Cooking is the primary cause of residential fires.

Smoking materials are the leading cause of preventable residential fire deaths in the United States. The U.S. Fire Administration, which is part of the Federal Emergency Management Agency (FEMA), reports that each year, around 1000 people are killed in smoking-related fires. In a press release dated January 9, 2008, U.S. Fire Administrator Greg Cade stated: "Most smoking-related home fires happen on beds, furniture, or in trash when smokers do not put cigarettes all the way out, toss hot ashes in the trash, or fall asleep while smoking."

In a study published in the August 2000 issue of *Preventive Medicine*, UC-Davis Health System reported that a worldwide study of smoking-related fire and disaster data showed that smok-

TABLE 15-1. OXYGEN CONTENT OF AIR

Oxygen Content of Air	Symptoms
21 percent	No adverse effects
15 percent	Diminished muscular skills reduce ability to escape building
10 to 14 percent	Faulty judgment, fatigue
6 to 10 percent	Physical collapse; person may be able to be revived if rescued in time

ing is the leading cause of fires and deaths from fires globally. Researchers estimated fire-related costs at $27.2 billion and deaths at 300,000 per year worldwide in 1998.

People often believe that they can heat their home more cheaply with an inexpensive portable electric space heater than by purchasing expensive home heating oil. Many people are unaware of fuel-assistance programs that could help them pay their heating bills. Even though electricity is expensive and often inefficient, the low purchase price of a space heater offers a convenient alternative. The U.S. Consumer Product Safety Commission estimates that annually, more than 25,000 residential fires and more than 300 deaths are associated with the use of space heaters.

A building is like a stove in that it contains a fire and encourages its growth. The building concentrates heat and flammable combustion gases. A fully developed room fire has a temperature that exceeds 1100°F. Vertical passages through the building that are open to the fire create strong convective drafts that fan the flames. As the fire spreads up through the building, it finds new sources of fuel.

Buildings hold dense concentrations of people and can subject them to the heat and gases from the fire. The building

design may restrict occupants' ability to escape and may also serve as a barrier to firefighters. Firefighting ladders can reach up only seven stories, so in tall buildings, firefighters must use the stairs. In addition, very broad, low buildings can put the fire beyond the reach of fire hoses. Firefighters are exposed to excessive heat, poisonous gases, and explosions. They are in danger from extreme heights, toppling walls, and collapsing roofs and floors. The loss of firefighters' lives is a tragic result of fires.

COMBUSTION

For a fire to exist, three elements are needed: fuel, oxygen, and high temperatures. Fires begin when supplies of fuel and oxygen are brought together at a sufficiently high temperature for combustion. The fire consumes fuel and oxygen as it burns and gives off gases, particles, and large quantities of heat.

Oxidation is a process in which fuel molecules are combined with oxygen molecules. The result is a mixture of gases and the release of energy. Oxidation is how the human body turns food into energy.

The process of **combustion** involves a chemical change that releases energy in the form of heat and light. A fire starts when

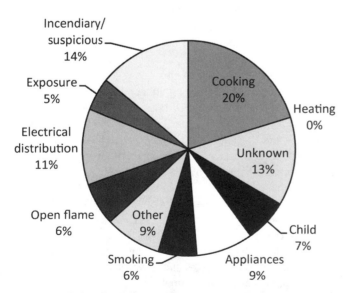

Figure 15-1 Leading causes of fires in homes. The most common identified cause of house fires is cooking. These are often small fires and are extinguished without injury to occupants.

Figure 15-2 Firefighters' ladder. Fire-truck ladders are usually 100 feet long. When used at an angle near a burning building, they reach only about seven stories.

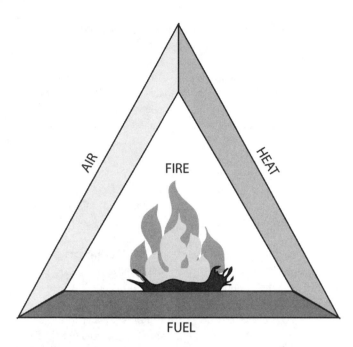

Figure 15-3 Fire triangle. The fire triangle is a graphic representation of the three elements necessary for a fire: oxygen (in air), heat, and fuel. If one element is removed, the fire will go out.

oxygen mixes with a combustible substance rapidly and continually. Smoke is produced when incompletely burned particles are suspended in the air.

The best way to avoid a tragic fire loss is to prevent fires from starting. As mentioned earlier, fires need fuel, heat, and oxygen. When this **fire triangle** is broken, a fire cannot ignite. Eliminating one element of the fire triangle prevents the fire from starting or extinguishes it. For example, fire suppression systems that cover the fuel or that displace the oxygen with another gas limit the supply of oxygen. High temperatures can be controlled by cold water from sprinkler systems. However, the primary way that building fires are prevented and controlled is by controlling the fuel: the building's structure and contents.

Building codes and zoning ordinances regulate the combustibility of materials in different areas of a city as well as the conditions for storage of flammable and explosive substances in or near buildings. Building maintenance personnel must ensure that rubbish is stored safely and removed frequently. Firefighters and **fire underwriters** (insurers) inspect buildings periodically, looking for accumulated combustible materials. Heating devices, chimneys, electrical systems, electrical devices, and hazardous industrial processes are controlled particularly stringently. Today, smoking is prohibited by law in many places, including gas stations, industrial plants, and auditoriums.

Products of Combustion

The thermal products of a fire are flame and heat. These are responsible for burns, shock, dehydration, heat exhaustion, and the blocking of the respiratory tract by fluid, and result in about one-fourth of the deaths from building fires.

Most fire-related deaths result from the nonthermal products of combustion, including smoke and other gases, which can usually be seen or smelled. Smoke is made of droplets of flammable tars and small particles of carbon that are suspended in gases. Smoke irritates the eyes and nasal passages and sometimes blinds or chokes a person.

Burning chemicals present a danger to firefighters, who must protect themselves with a breathing apparatus. In addition to displacing oxygen, the gases produced by a fire may be poisonous. Sometimes, these gases are invisible, and other times, they make up part of the smoke seen during a fire. Gases that occur without visible smoke are difficult to detect. Some of these are directly toxic and all are dangerous because they displace oxygen.

- Carbon monoxide (CO) is a deadly, invisible, odorless gas. It is often the most common product of combustion. CO makes breathing difficult and causes loss of consciousness and eventually death in building areas away from the fire itself.
- Carbon dioxide (CO_2) gas is produced in large quantities in fires. It rapidly overstimulates breathing and causes the lungs to swell.
- Other toxic gases include hydrogen sulfide, sulfur dioxide, and ammonia.
- Oxides of nitrogen, cyanide, and phosgene are also toxic.
- Burning polyvinyl chloride (PVC) produces toxic hydrogen chloride gas.

Plastic materials are found in furniture, carpet, draperies, wall coverings, plumbing systems, electrical wiring, and other prod-

TABLE 15-2. WAYS TO IGNITE A FIRE

Fire Source	Cause	Example
Chemical (spontaneous) combustion	Combustible materials saturated with chemicals rapidly produce heat and ignite.	Oily rags protected by a metal garbage can in the sun. Metal can concentrates fumes as temperature rises.
Electrical fires	Resistance-heating appliances; space-heating equipment; other electrical processes	Space heaters plugged into outlets with old, inadequate wiring; space heaters placed too close to combustible material.
Lightning	On average, 200 million volts and 30,000 amperes pass through grounded object in less than 1/1000 second.	Lightning-protection system provides continuous metallic path for high-voltage static electrical charge into solid ground.

ucts and equipment. About 10,000 new chemicals are introduced each year, and the hazards related to their behavior in a fire are unknown.

A fire with decomposing plastics can cause lung and pulmonary damage, and may cause disorientation and loss of the sense of smell. Respiratory failure can follow. Toxic chemicals at levels below lethal can be deadly in combination. Repeated exposure is especially dangerous. Some chemicals are still a danger after a fire is out.

PVC is a plastic used in electrical wiring insulation, electrical fixtures, interior plastic plumbing, and office copy machines and other equipment. Decomposition of PVC produces over 60 gases, including hydrogen chloride, phosgene, and some carcinogens. Hydrogen chloride incapacitates a person, who may then succumb to CO_2 poisoning from smoke. Phosgene gas, which has been used in chemical warfare, is produced when PVC wiring insulation is subjected to electrical arcing in transformers and control panels during fires in commercial buildings.

Urea formaldehyde foam does not combust readily unless it is subjected to the intense heat of an extensive fire. However, when it does burn, it produces hydrogen cyanide gas in large quantities.

FIRE SAFETY CODES

☑ **The work of interior designers often involves checking building codes for fire safety requirements. Whether specifying a fabric for a commercial project or checking a floor plan for the number, size, and location of exits, interior designers rely on applicable state and local code requirements. In fact, fire-safety provisions are probably the most common building code requirements that interior designers need to respect. The design professional in charge of the project is ultimately responsible for ensuring that the design meets all applicable codes. The interior designer must be familiar with the codes for each project's location and must make sure that the design complies. Failure to do so can result in costly mistakes, delays in construction, and a very unhappy client.**

Initially, modern building codes evolved as responses to devastating fires; gradually, they came to include many other health and safety issues. The goal of the code requirements is to protect the building from fire and to contain the fire long enough for people to evacuate the building safely. Building codes

- set forth height and area limits in relation to the occupancy or use of the building and the type of construction
- establish standards for structural design and for construction of walls, floors, and roofs
- detail requirements for fire protection systems and means of emergency egress
- specify minimum standards (codes cannot cover all possible aspects of a building's design because there are simply too many variables)
- require a permit before construction (plans must be submitted, checked, and approved by the building department)

- may require the architect or engineer's stamp for approval, depending on the size, type, and location of building

Fire department officials also review the plans before the building permit is granted in many communities. Inspections during construction by the building inspector verify that the construction meets the code. Fire department inspectors also visit the site. Fire-safety codes

- govern how spaces are planned and how materials are used
- dictate the location and number of fire alarms and exit signs
- include sprinkler system requirements, which affect layout of ceiling designs and lighting

The National Fire Protection Association (NFPA) is America's leading advocate of fire prevention and an authoritative source on public safety. Fire codes, authorities, and standards include the following:

- *NFPA 101: Life Safety Code 2006:* Revised every three years; dictates minimum requirements for reasonable degree of safety in buildings and structures, including means of egress, type of fire-alarm system, and type and location of fire- and smoke-detection equipment
- *NFPA 70: National Electrical Code (NEC) 2008* (an update is planned for 2010): Article 760 Fire Alarm Systems
- *NFPA 72: National Fire Alarm Code 2002:* regulations for protective signaling systems and their components
- *NFPA 80: Standard for Fire Doors and Windows*
- *NFPA 99: Health Care Facilities 2005:* fire- and life-safety issues in health-care facilities
- *NFPA 220: Standard on Types of Building Construction:* The American National Standards Institute (ANSI) reviews standards that are prepared by professional and technical societies and associations; it also approves and lists standards based on technical acceptability.
- *Council of American Building Officials (CABO)/ANSI 117.1:* **Accessible and Usable Buildings and Facilities**: Requirements for making buildings accessible and usable for people with disabilities.
- *The U.S. Department of Housing and Urban Development (HUD):* works to increase home ownership, support community development, and increase access to affordable housing free from discrimination; requirements for residential buildings and care-type facilities.
- Manufactured housing standards

Underwriters Laboratories (UL) Detection Standards: The UL has been testing products for manufacturers and government agencies for more than a century.

- Standard 38: *Manually Activated Signaling Boxes*
- Standard 217: *Smoke Detectors, Single and Multiple Stations*
- Standard 268: *Smoke Detectors for Fire Protective Signaling Systems*
- Standard 521: *Heat Detectors—Fire Protective Signaling Systems*

- Standard 539: *Single and Multiple Station Heat Detectors*
- Standard 985: *Household Fire Warning System Units*
- Standard 1730: *Smoke Detectors, Monitors and Accessories for Individual Living Units of Multiple Residences and Hotels/Motels*

Fire detection and alarm equipment are among the equipment that the UL tests.

- Standard 228: *Door Closers with/without Integral Smoke Detectors*
- Standard 464: *Audible Signal Devices*
- Standard 827: *Central Station Alarm Services*
- Standard 1480: *Speakers for Fire Protection*
- Standard 1638: *Visual Signaling Applications—private mode, emergency, and general utility signals*
- Standard 1971: *Signal Devices for Hearing Impaired*

Provisions of the International Building Code (IBC) and the International Residential Code (IRC), 2006 also address fire safety.

Building codes may differ in detail, but most are organized the same way. They begin by defining categories of use or occupancy. They also define types of construction according to the building's degree of fire resistance and combustibility. The classification of the building's construction is determined by the fire resistance of major components, including the structural frame, exterior bearing walls, and nonbearing walls. Interior bearing walls, permanent partitions, floors, ceiling and roof assemblies, stairways, and shaft enclosures are all considered.

☑ **The primary structural element that interior designers may be involved with is an interior wall, either loadbearing or nonloadbearing. The designers' work may also affect firewalls, party walls, smoke barriers, and shaft enclosures. Interior designers frequently work with columns, floor/ceiling assemblies, and roof/ceiling assemblies.**

To be classified a specific type of construction, a building must meet the minimum standards for every structural element associated with that type. The construction type comes into play when a designer changes existing interior structural elements or adds new ones:

- If the additions are not consistent with the existing building materials, they could reduce the entire building classification. This would reduce building safety and could affect building insurance and liability.
- Interiors projects that are affected by construction types and building sizes include those that involve relocating walls or adding a stairway or other structural work.
- Each construction type assigns structural elements a minimum fire protection rating. This is the number of hours that the structural element must be able to resist fire without being affected by flames, heat, or hot gases. It is, essentially, a fire endurance rating.

When construction is required to be fire resistant (FR), it must have one-hour FR construction throughout. Unprotected construction has no requirements for fire resistance, with the exception of shaft and exit enclosures or where the building code requires protection of exit walls due to the proximity to the property line.

In general, building codes are performance based, stipulating how a particular component or system must function without necessarily giving the means to be employed to achieve the required results. The codes refer to standards established by the American Society for Testing and Materials (ASTM) and ANSI as well as by various other technical societies and trade associations to indicate both the properties required in a material or component and the testing methods required to substantiate the performance of products.

Codes often relax prescriptions when an active fire-suppression system is designed for a building. Size limits may be exceeded in a building with sprinklers or in a building is divided by firewalls into separate areas, each of which does not exceed a specified size limit. A detailed computer analysis of fire spread and occupant evaluation for a given design may also allow greater distances to exits, larger open floor areas, and alternative construction methods. This performance based analysis approach to design requires close cooperation between designers and fire code enforcement officials.

There are variations among jurisdictions about the need for fire safety systems that provide redundant levels of protection. Some jurisdictions require sprinklers in almost all buildings, while others allow tradeoffs in the codes for sprinkler-equipped build-

TABLE 15-3. CODE PROVISIONS FOR EVACUATION OF LOW-RISE BUILDINGS

Egress Component	Description	Comment
Exit access	Clearly defined pathways to exits	Keep relatively clear of smoke; minimum clear wheelchair access of 32 inches (813 mm)
Vertical egress	Smokeproof towers; exterior and interior stairs and ramps; some escalators	Does not include elevators
Horizontal egress	Doors leading directly to outside; two-hour fire-rated enclosed hallways; moving walks	Special horizontal exits: internal firewalls with two fire doors swinging in opposite directions
Exit discharge	Area to outside exits leading to public way	Exit discharge provisions rarely affect interior projects.

ings. New products and more advanced tests and computer simulations may bring about more accurate representations of what would happen in an actual fire. This could streamline the types of fire protection and prevention that are possible.

FIRE SAFETY DESIGN

When a building is designed to resist the start and spread of a fire, designers protect not only the building itself and its contents, but, more important, the lives of the people who occupy the building. To react safely to a fire emergency, a building occupant needs early warning, the means to extinguish a small fire, and at least two ways out of the building. Once a fire has started in a building, people may have only a few minutes to get out safely. A fire can spread at the rate of 4.6 meters (15 ft.) per second. Smoke spreads quickly and can overcome people in moments, obscuring their vision and causing breathing difficulty. As a result, people may panic, but they need to get to a door immediately. The design of the building may help—or it may lead to a dead end, trapping them inside.

Fire Safety Objectives

In older buildings, the goal of fire-safety-design decisions was to keep the fire from spreading to other buildings. With increased fire resistant construction and control by building codes, fires are now usually confined within a single building. Today, the most common fire-safety objectives (in order of importance) are:

1. protection of life
2. protection of property
3. continuity of operation

The addition of fire suppression systems has contained most fires to one or two floors of a building. With technically advanced, automatic detection and suppression systems, fires can be contained to a single room or an even smaller area.

A single sprinkler head can extinguish many common small fires in about four minutes. Only one or two sprinkler heads are activated in the great majority of residential fires, thereby limiting damage from water as well as fire.

Fire protection requires the coordination of the architecture and interiors; the mechanical, electrical, and plumbing systems; and the signal system. The best design for fire safety is also good design for lighting, thermal, acoustic, and water systems.

Fire builds up faster in small, enclosed rooms that retain heat. Buildings without operable windows or with sunscreens that cover windows prevent firefighters from gaining access and occupants from escaping. In addition, broken windows can fall and hit people below.

Windows provide firefighting and rescue access and escape routes. They also dilute smoke with fresh air and offer daylight, ventilation, and view. Solid, noncombustible overhangs above windows discourage the vertical spread of fire over the building face, can serve as an emergency exterior refuge, and double as sun shading.

Fire safety concerns can conflict with other building design issues. High ceilings and low partitions in spaces without sprinklers can allow fire and smoke to spread.

In some buildings, continuing operations during a fire is a priority. Special fire alarm and suppression systems are available for critical operations areas, such as control rooms.

A building's heating, ventilation, and air-conditioning (HVAC) system can be designed to take in only outside air to purge it of smoke.

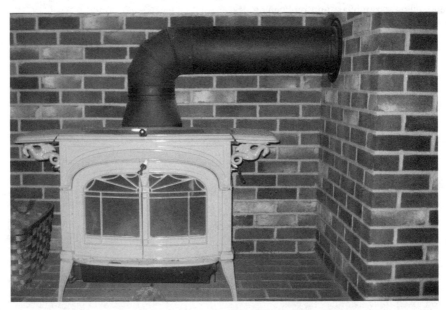

Figure 15-4 Thermal mass and fire. Most materials with high levels of thermal mass do not burn easily. Thermal mass also benefits passive heating, cooling, and acoustic isolation of airborne sound.

Figure 15-5 High ceilings and fire. High ceilings allow large quantities of smoke to collect before reaching the occupants' level and allow smoke and flames to be seen from a greater indoor distance compared with lower ceilings. High ceilings also aid daylight distribution and ventilation.

☑ **Floors should be waterproofed for the speedy removal of water dumped on the fire by the sprinkler system, but they rarely are. Waterproofing should continue up walls, columns, pipes, and other vertical elements to a level of 10 to 15 centimeters (4–6 in.).**

Creating a safe building starts with designing fire resistant exterior walls. How close a building is to its neighbors governs both the types of building materials and the extent and treatment of windows and doors.

Protection from exterior fire sources is provided by using noncombustible materials for the building exterior or by erecting firewalls between the building and its neighbors. Both exterior doors with properties that delay fire and windows with fire-rated shutters that close automatically at high temperatures also protect the building.

Wired glass, which holds together against flame for a considerable time, is usually required in windows that face nearby structures.

Protecting the Structure

A building's structure is protected in order to prevent its collapse within the time the fire runs its course or to delay the collapse of low buildings until all occupants have escaped and firefighters have had a reasonable chance to save the buildings. Buildings may survive and be salvaged rather than demolished after the fire. Protecting the structure maintains the building's value. It protects the occupants, firefighters, and neighboring buildings. Tall buildings present a significant danger if all or part of them falls.

TABLE 15-4. COMMON DESIGN ELEMENTS IN BUILDING SYSTEMS

Design Characteristic	Fire Safety	Lighting	Thermal Comfort	Acoustic Design, Water, Waste
Thermal mass	Fire barriers	Not applicable (NA)	Passive heating and cooling	Isolation of airborne sound
High ceilings	Smoke collected above occupant level; smoke or flames visible at greater distance	Daylight	Displacement ventilation	NA
Windows	Access for firefighting and rescue	Daylight and view	Ventilation	NA
Solid overhangs above windows	Help control fire spread; emergency refuge	Sun shading	Shade from sun's heat	NA
Elevated water-storage tanks	Water for firefighting	NA	NA	Water pressure for plumbing fixtures

The most important elements of a building structure to be protected are the columns. Next in importance are the girders, the beams, and, lastly, the floor slabs. Most large buildings are constructed of either reinforced concrete or protected steel. Steel does not burn but loses much of its structural strength in a fire and will sag or collapse at the sustained temperatures frequently reached by ordinary building fires. Steel reinforcing bars in concrete beams and columns are buried a specific distance within the mass of the concrete and are protected by its thermal mass and natural fire-resistant properties.

Brick, tile, and mineral fibers that are unaffected by fire can be used to protect the building structure. Brick and tile are made using the intense heat of a kiln and are not weakened by fire. However, mortar joints may disintegrate, and the construction can fail.

Concrete is more resistant to fire than steel. Because concrete and plaster are largely made up of hydrated crystals, they absorb very large quantities of heat during a fire before the water of crys-

tallization is evaporated. Consequently, concrete and plaster provide a barrier to the fire as they disintegrate slowly. If the fire lasts long enough, however, concrete or plaster will not be able to prevent serious structural damage.

Both solid brick and poured concrete are expensive and add to the structural load and the cost of the building's structure. Today, steel beams and columns are encased in lath and plaster and are surrounded with multiple layers of gypsum wallboard (drywall). Sometimes, they are also sprayed with lightweight mineral insulations in cementitious binders or have preformed slabs of mineral insulation attached to them.

Intumescent coatings, in the form of paint or a thick coating that is applied with a trowel, soften when exposed to heat and release bubbles of a gas that expands the coating to create an insulating layer.

Low industrial and commercial buildings of unprotected steel are considered to be incombustible, but there is an unlikely possibility that they may collapse rapidly in a hot fire before occupants have time to escape. Buildings constructed of heavy timber are considered to be slow-burning buildings and are permitted to be one or two stories higher than unprotected steel buildings. Plaster or plasterboard walls and ceilings offer one-half hour of protection for smaller wooden buildings.

Compartmentation and Fire Barriers

An entire building or a large space can be divided into two or more separate spaces, each completely enclosed within a fire-barrier envelope of floor-and-ceiling assemblies and walls. This **compartmentation** prevents the spread of fire, smoke, and heat beyond a restricted area of the building. Compartmentation protects the building's occupants and property by confining the fire, heat, smoke, and toxic gases to the area of their origin until the fire is extinguished or until it burns itself out completely. It also stops the spread of fire by hot combustion gases.

In row houses, fire-resistant walls separate dwellings. Compartmentation is required between different types of functions within a building. Compartmentation is also used to provide areas of refuge for occupants and firefighters.

Building codes set maximum floor areas for various types of construction and occupancies. Using sprinklers usually increases the limits on floor areas. Larger areas must be subdivided with fire-rated walls and doors.

In one-story factories and warehouses in which firewalls are not practical, incombustible curtain boards are hung from the roof to catch and contain rising hot gases. Self-opening roof vents in each compartment allow hot gases to escape before they can spread the fire. Doors of the roof vent are held closed against springs by a fusible link of a metal with a low melting point, which melts and releases the doors when heat builds up.

Fire barriers are fire-rated structural elements. They include wall, ceiling, or floor systems that prevent the spread of flame and heat through the use of fire-rated structural materials. Building codes limit the number of penetrations in a fire-rated wall. Fire barriers can be divided into three types. Firewalls, one type,

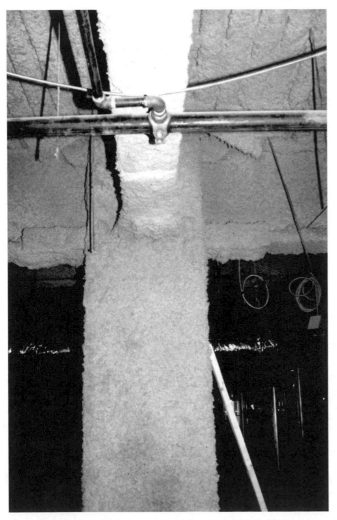

Figure 15-6 Spray-on fire protection. In the past, asbestos was used to insulate steel columns. Other forms of spray-on materials or slabs of mineral insulation are now available. *Photo credit: Herb Fremin*

have the highest fire ratings and are usually part of the building shell. Fire separation walls, another type, are used to create fire-rated compartments within a building. The fire ratings of the last category, floor-and-ceiling assemblies, depend on the walls they surround.

Firewalls, also called party walls, are used for occupancy separations. Firewalls provide continuous protection from the foundation of the building to the roof and to each exterior wall. They are built so that if one side of the wall falls, the other side will remain standing. Firewalls typically have three- to five-hour ratings. Firewalls are often used to subdivide a building into two separate types of construction. They are also used to separate one occupancy from another in a mixed-use building. In general, interior designers are not involved in designing firewalls, but their work may involve possible penetrations. All openings in a firewall are limited to a certain percentage of the wall's length and must be protected by self-closing firewalls, fire-rated window assemblies, and fire and smoke dampers in air ducts.

Fire-separation walls, which include **tenant-separation** walls (**demising** walls), corridor walls, vertical shafts, and room separations, are more likely than firewalls to be added or changed during an interior design project. Tenant separation walls create fire-rated compartments within a building that separate two tenants or dwelling units. They typically require one-hour ratings, depending on the occupancy and whether sprinklers are used. Interior designers often work with fire-separation walls.

Corridor walls must have ratings of from one to two hours depending on the way corridors are used, the occupancy, and the presence of sprinklers. Corridor walls that are used as exits usu-

Figure 15-7 Compartmentation. In 1985, this sunlit firewall saved the Palace Theater in Manchester, New Hampshire, and the rest of the street from a fire that destroyed buildings to the right.

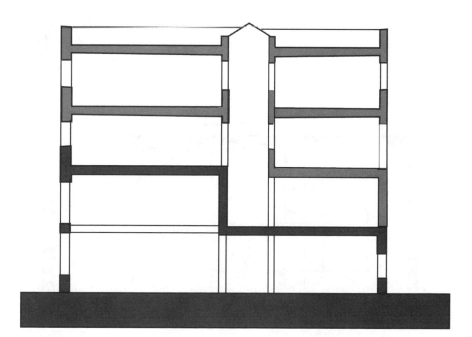

Figure 15-8 Firewalls. Firewalls combine with fire-resistant floors to contain fires both horizontally and vertically.

ally must have a two-hour fire rating, and corridors used as exit accesses usually require one-hour ratings. (All of the components of exits are discussed in more detail on page 348). Typically, codes require that corridor walls must be continuous from floor slab to floor slab and must penetrate suspended ceilings. Some corridor walls may also act as demising walls, for which stricter requirements apply.

The walls that create vertical shaft enclosures for stairwells, elevators, and dumbwaiters are usually continuous from the bottom of the building to the underside of the roof deck. Stairs used as part of an exit have requirements for fire ratings, can have only limited penetrations, and may require that the enclosure be smokeproof. Stair enclosures are required to have a one-hour fire rating for up to three stories and two-hour ratings for four or more stories. When stairs connect only two floors within a single occupancy, the space may be considered to be an atrium, and the enclosure restrictions may be less restrictive.

☑ **Most rooms within a space do not require fire-rated walls. When the contents of a room may be hazardous, codes may specify that it be separated from the rest of the building by a fire-rated wall. Construction costs are reduced when spaces with similar requirements, such as boiler rooms, furnace rooms, and large storage rooms, are located adjacent to one another.**

Fire-rated floors and ceilings are rated as either floor-and-ceiling or roof-and-ceiling assemblies. The assembly consists of everything from the bottom of the ceiling material to the top of the floor or roof above. This includes all of the ducts, piping, and wires between the finished ceiling and the finished floor above it. If a ceiling is added to a space, the ratings of the surrounding walls must be determined and must use the same rating at the ceiling.

☑ **Fire can spread quickly in concealed spaces over suspended ceilings, behind walls, within pipe chases, in attics, and under raised floors. Interior designers should specify noncombustible materials in these and similar spaces. Automatic fire detection and fire suppression systems and oxygen deprivation systems can be used in concealed spaces. Firestops and firewalls may be required to break up continuous concealed spaces.**

Areas of Refuge

Areas of refuge or refuge areas, called **areas of rescue assistance** in the Americans with Disabilities (ADA) Accessibility Guidelines for Buildings and Facilities (ADAAG), are provided in high-rise buildings and for wheelchair users in multistory buildings. In large buildings, not all occupants can evacuate easily or in a timely manner, so refuge areas provide a place for them to wait that is

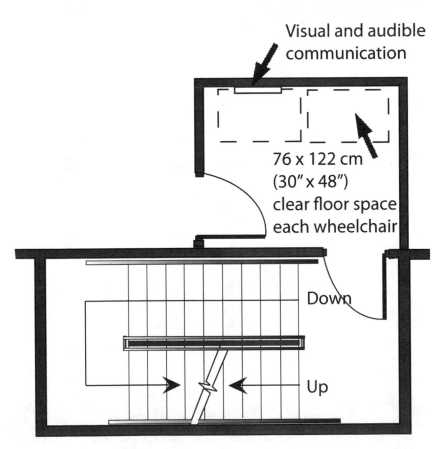

Figure 15-9 Area of refuge near stairway. This enclosed area of refuge just outside a fire stair can accommodate two wheelchairs without blocking access to the stairway.

protected from smoke. Ideally, refuge areas should remain free of smoke, gases, heat, and fire throughout a fire and until rescue. The structure of and essential services in refuge areas are intended to be maintained at all times, but these goals are almost impossible to achieve in practice.

Areas of refuge are commonly located adjacent to a protected stairway and are protected from smoke. They are provided with communications devices for people in the refuge to summon rescuers. When a stairway is used as a refuge area, it is designed to hold all of the building occupants, allowing 0.28 square meters (3 sq ft.) per person. Horizontal exits (described below) can be areas of refuge, as can smoke-protected vestibules or enlarged landings that are adjacent to exit stairways. The ADA sets minimum requirements for accessible spaces in refuge areas and mandates a specific type of two-way emergency communications system. The ADA also requires specific identifications for accessible spaces in refuge areas.

In an exit stairwell, the landings at the doors entering the stairs can be enlarged so that persons in one or more wheelchairs can wait for assistance without blocking the means of egress. An alternative arrangement provides an alcove for wheelchairs in a portion of an exit access corridor that is located immediately adjacent to the exit enclosure. Another possibility is to provide space that is immediately adjacent to an exit enclosure by creating an enclosed exit discharge, such as a vestibule or foyer.

Limited refuge areas are built from noncombustible materials around double-vestibule, pressurized stairwells. These can normally serve other functions, such as libraries, conference rooms, and restrooms. They resemble other building rooms but have direct access to stairs, self-closing fire doors, and voice-activated intercom systems that are connected to the master fire control center on the ground floor.

Enclosed exits may create some security concerns. An enclosed stair may allow an unauthorized person to gain entry to a building or provide an easy escape route for thieves. People may use enclosed stairs to travel to prohibited floors or to avoid questioning by a receptionist or security guard. While enclosed exits cannot be locked in the direction of exit travel, they can be locked from the exterior with emergency exit hardware and an alarm to deter unauthorized exits. Keeping the area that is adjacent to enclosed exit stairs easily visible to receptionists and security personnel will help control access. Glass in exit-stair doors will let people see if someone is inside.

Horizontal Exits

A **horizontal exit** does not lead to the exterior of the building. Instead, it provides a protected exit to a safe area of refuge in another part of the building or an adjoining building without a change in level. A horizontal exit uses fire-rated walls and doors to subdivide a building into separate areas, which are then treated as separate buildings. Occupants escape from a fire on one side of a building by moving horizontally through self-closing fire doors to the other side.

When people pass through the door of a horizontal exit, the whole space beyond the door is considered to be an area of refuge where they can either wait for assistance or use exit stairs to leave the building. Such areas can provide refuge for the very large building populations usually found in healthcare, detention, and educational facilities.

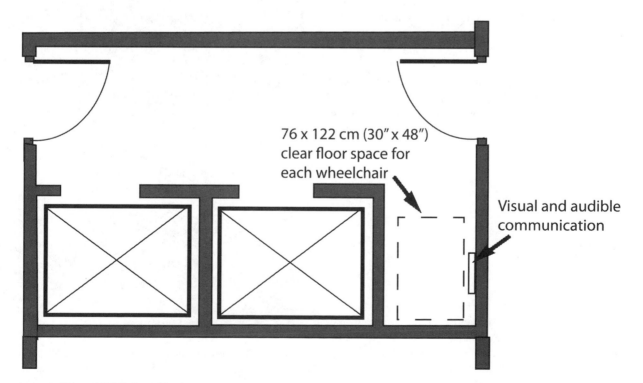

76 x 122 cm (30" x 48") clear floor space for each wheelchair

Visual and audible communication

Figure 15-10 Area of refuge near elevator lobby. In this area of refuge, the required communication panel is located next to the wheelchair space.

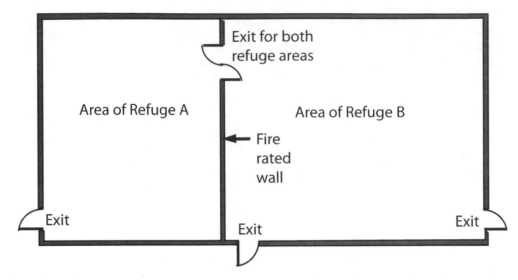

Figure 15-11 Horizontal exits. Doors in a horizontal exit must be fire-rated and swing in the direction of travel to the exit. If a horizontal exit has an area of refuge on either side, it must have two doors together, swinging in an opposite directions. This way, building occupants can push through the doorway in either direction.

Horizontal exits can be used in buildings that house any occupancy classification but are most commonly found in institutional occupancies. Hospitals use horizontal exits to divide a floor into two or more areas of refuge. This allows a patient bed to be rolled into a safe area protected by a rated firewall in a fire emergency. To reduce the danger of smoke inhalation, self-closing doors are installed on patient rooms in nursing homes and hospitals, where speedy evacuation is impossible. Prisons use horizontal exits to contain fires without having to evacuate the entire prison. These exits are also used in large factories, storage facilities, and high-rise buildings.

A horizontal exit consists of the walls that enclose the area of refuge and the doors through these walls, all of which must be fire-rated. The walls must be continuous through every floor to the ground or surrounded by both a floor and a ceiling with a fire rating.

Horizontal exits may reduce the number of other types of exits required, but codes place limits on the total number of horizontal exits that a building can have. They are allowed only when two or more exits are required and cannot be more than one-half of the total required exit widths.

Vertical Openings

Because a fire's vertical spread through a building is the most serious problem, compartmentation requirements around **vertical openings** tend to be especially strict in order to prevent the convection of fire and combustion products through the building. Open vertical shafts of any kind, including stairs, elevators, ductwork, and electrical wiring and piping chases, must be enclosed with fire-rated walls with self-closing fire-rated doors on each floor.

The only exception to the enclosure requirement for vertical shafts is a vertical atrium. An atrium is defined in many codes as

Figure 15-12 Vertical openings. The code status of complex multilevel stairways with walls of varying heights may be difficult to sort out. Determining the code status may require the expertise of an interior designer, architect, code specialist, and building official.

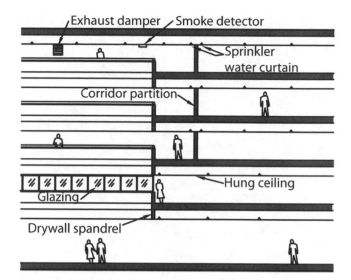

Figure 15-13 Atrium fire protection. Building codes require a 1.8-meter (6-ft.) deep curtain board (smoke barrier) at the opening to an atrium at each floor. Smoke detectors and motorized dampers in ducts are also required.

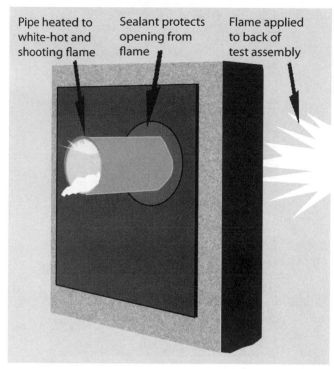

Figure 15-14 Pipe opening protection test. In this test, the sealant that protects the pipe opening is tested with intense fire.

a roofed, occupied space that includes a floor opening or a series of floor openings connecting two or more stories. Atriums are often found in shopping arcades, hotels, and office buildings. Balconies around the atrium may be open to it, but surrounding rooms must be isolated from balconies and from the atrium by fire-rated walls. An exception is made for any three floors selected by the building's designer, so that lobby spaces on several floors can be continuous with the atrium.

A building with an atrium must have sprinklers throughout. Sprinklers located 1.8 meters (6 ft.) on center at the lobby level, the atrium floor level, and on office floors that open to an atrium create a water curtain. The frames for glazing at the perimeter of the atrium should be designed for thermal expansion so that they do not break their glass when they get hot, with sprinklers on the office side of the glazing. Fire-rated frames are listed for both heat resistance and water pressure from the hose stream. The atrium must be provided with fans with dampers that open and turn on automatically in case of fire to bring fresh air into the space at ground level and exhaust smoke at the ceiling level.

Construction Assemblies

ASTM E-119 - 08a **Standard Test Methods for Fire Tests of Building Construction and Materials** gives construction assemblies one-, two-, three-, and four-hour ratings. Assemblies that are tested this way include permanent partitions, shaft enclosures for stairways and elevators, floor-and-ceiling constructions, doors, and glass openings. Doors and other opening assemblies also receive 20-, 30-, and 45-minute ratings.

Any opening that pierces the entire thickness of a construction assembly is referred to as a through-penetration. Codes require that penetrations in fire-rated assemblies be protected with fire assemblies in the form of fire doors, fire windows, firestops, and fire dampers. These opening protectives or through-penetration protection systems must have fire-protection ratings. Typically, no opening greater than 11 square meters (120 sq ft.) is permitted. The combined width of all openings must not exceed 25 percent of the length of the wall. Any assembly that passes the required tests must have a permanent label attached to it to prove that it is fire-rated.

Doors

Fire doors are actually entire door assemblies. A typical fire door includes the door itself, the frame, the hardware, and the doorway (wall opening). Fire-door assemblies are required to protect the openings in fire-rated walls. The whole assembly is tested and rated as one unit. For example, exit-access corridor enclosure walls require a one-hour construction assembly rating, and doors in those walls require at least a 20-minute rating. For a firewall with a required four-hour assembly rating, a door with a three-hour rating is required.

Many types of doors are regulated as fire doors by building codes, including swinging and vertical sliding doors as well as accordion-folding, Dutch, and bi-parting doors..

Fire doors are typically flush, either solid-core wood or metal, with mineral composition cores. A few panel doors may meet fire-door requirements, and some fire doors may have applied finishes to improve their appearance. Frames are wood, hollow metal, steel, or aluminum. The doorframe and hardware must

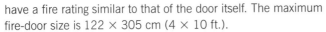

Figure 15-15 Floor door closer. Door closers located in the floor, such as this one at a glass door, are less conspicuous than overhead types. *Photo credit: Herb Fremin*

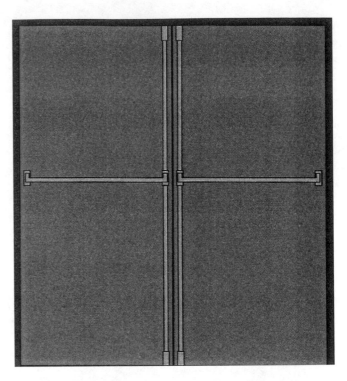

Figure 15-16 Fire-exit hardware. Fire-exit hardware may be locked for security reasons. Anyone who attempts to use the door will set off an alarm. This is not a problem during a fire, but it is very conspicuous and embarrassing otherwise.

have a fire rating similar to that of the door itself. The maximum fire-door size is 122 × 305 cm (4 × 10 ft.).

Hardware for fire doors includes hinges, latches and locksets, and pulls and closers. Hinges, latch sets, and closing devices are the most stringently regulated devices because they must hold a door closed securely during a fire and must withstand the pressure and heat that the fire generates. Hinges must be steel or stainless steel, and a specific quantity is required for each door.

Fire doors must be self-latching and equipped with a closer. Fire-rated exit doors also require a specific type of latch. The most common is called fire-exit hardware and consists of a door-latching assembly that disengages when pressure is applied on a horizontal bar spanning the interior of an emergency exit door at waist height. The push bar should extend across at least one-half the width of the door leaf on which it is installed. The term panic hardware is also used, but technically panic hardware is not tested and should not be used on fire-rated doors. On the other hand, fire-exit hardware is tested and rated. Fire-exit hardware is typically required in assembly and educational occupancies, and is often used on other exit doors. The codes also regulate the width, direction of swing, and location of required exit doors, according to a building's use and occupancy. The ADA requires that the force necessary to push open or pull open a door not exceed five pounds.

Door closers are hydraulic or pneumatic devices that automatically close doors quickly but quietly. They help reduce the shock that a large, heavy, or heavily used door would transmit upon closing to its frame, hardware, and the surrounding wall. Building codes require the use of self-latching, self-closing doors with UL-rated hardware to protect openings in firewalls and occupancy separations. For doors that are usually kept in an open position, an automatic closing device uses a fusible link that is triggered by heat or activated by the smoke detector to close the door. Other doors with lower ratings may require self-closing devices to close the doors after each use.

The doorway, including the lintel and sill, has rating requirements. Typically, fire doors are specified and sold by the manufacturer as a whole assembly. Interior designers can generally use a door with a higher rating than required, but they should check with the jurisdictional authority. The A, B, and C labels for fire-rated doors have been replaced by hourly labels. Glass entrance doors are required to have 13-millimeter or 19-millimeter (½-in. or ¾-in.) safety glazing. Building codes require the glazing for sliding glass doors to be tempered (heat-strengthened) safety glass. For energy conservation, entrance units are glazed with insulating glass.

The leaves of revolving doors must be made of tempered glass in metal frames. The revolving door enclosure must be made of metal or of tempered, wired, or laminated glass. Some building codes may credit revolving doors for up to half of the legal exit requirements, while others require adjacent hinged doors for emergency exits.

Windows

The types of windows that are covered by building-code fire regulations include casement, double-hung, hinged, pivot, and tilting windows. Stationary windows, sidelights, transom lights, view panels, borrowed lights, and glass blocks are also included.

Building codes regulate the clear opening of any operable window that serves as an emergency exit for a residential sleeping space. Typically, the minimum area permitted is 0.53 square meters (5.7 sq ft.), with a minimum clear width of 508 millimeters (20 in.), and a clear height of 610 millimeters (24 in.). The sill must be no more than 1120 millimeters (44 in.) above the floor. Codes may restrict the location of glazing.

Windows with fire ratings usually consist of a frame, wire glass, and hardware. They are used for openings in corridors, room partitions, and smoke barriers. Window ratings are similar to those of doors, with hour classifications typically not greater than one hour.

Wire glass has a wire mesh embedded in the middle of a glass sheet. The wire distributes heat and increases the strength of the glass. The codes establish size limits for wire glass. The glass product most often associated with fire rating is polished wired glass. It has provided fire protection for more than 100 years and is frequently seen in schools, hospitals, and other high-occupancy facilities. In North America, wired glass is usually rated for forty-five minutes in lite (glass pane) sizes up to 0.84 square meters (9 sq ft.). In a fire door, glazing cannot exceed 0.065 square meters (100 sq in.) of wired glass, and no single

dimension can be greater than 254 millimeters (10 in.). The primary advantage of wired glass may be its low cost. However, its relatively low-impact safety resistance and the institutional look of the wire are sometimes considered to be drawbacks.

Fire-rated glazing is available with sixty and ninety minute ratings. Fire-rated glazing must pass the appropriate tests and standards and have a permanent label etched into the glass. Once installed, this wireless product looks similar to window glass. Glass-ceramic products offer fire ratings from twenty minutes to three hours, in sizes that range up to 2.23 square meters (24 sq ft.) per lite. Like wired glass, the glass ceramics are able to withstand the thermal shock of water thrown by sprinklers or a fire hose.

Another type of fire-rated glazing is **glass ceramic**. It is made from a ceramic material or a transparent gel between several sheets of glass. This provides a heat shield and additional insulating protection. Glass-ceramic products offer great design flexibility. Products are available that provide at least four times the impact resistance of wire glass. Products can also have beveled edges and be sandblasted for artistic effect.

Glass ceramic is also available made into insulating glass units with two layers of glass with an air space between them. Depending on which components are used, they can not only provide fire protection but also comply with energy codes. They can also be used for sound-reduction applications.

European manufacturers have a glazing assembly that meets the requirements of a two hour rated wall assembly. Higher ratings allow larger sheets to be used, and these larger sizes may exceed the current maximum listings found in building codes. It is recommended that interior designers work with local code officials and the glazing manufacturer.

Another emerging category of fire-rated glass could be called **transparent wall units**. Although widely used in Europe for a number of years, they are just now becoming popular in North America. These units are special, multiproduct assemblies that block the transfer of heat. While the units appear to be regular glass, their thick composition enables them to perform similar to a way like that of a fire-rated masonry wall. With proper framing from wall to wall and floor to ceiling, these large expanses of glass have obtained fire ratings of up to two hours. They are typically used to block heat transfer through the glass while allowing visibility, light, and security. These products, like wired glass and glass ceramics, withstand thermal shock. They meet high levels of impact safety as well.

Yet another category of fire-rated glazing is **specially tempered glass**. However, these products carry ratings of only twenty or thirty minutes and cannot withstand the thermal shock of water from sprinklers or a fire hose. Such products are sometimes used in twenty minute rated doors.

Typically, glass block has a forty five minute rating, with newer types available with sixty to ninety minute ratings. Codes limit the number of square feet of glass block permitted as an interior wall. They also limit glass block used as a view panel in a rated wall, where it is required that it be installed in steel channels.

Safety glazing is required for any window that could be mistaken for an open doorway. Any window area that is greater than

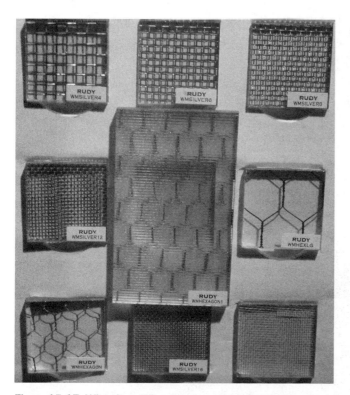

Figure 15-17 Wire glass. Wire glass is available in a variety of patterns.

Figure 15-18 Glass block. Glass block, which comes in a variety of styles, is made of two cast glass halves with a partial vacuum between them.

0.84 square meters (9 sq ft.) and located within 61 centimeters (24 in.) of a doorway or less than 152 centimeters (60 in.) above the floor must be safety-glazed with tempered glass, laminated glass, or plastic. The type and size of glazing allowed in fire-rated walls and corridors are also regulated.

Fire Dampers and Draft Stops

Fire dampers are used in HVAC ductwork. A fire damper automatically interrupts the flow of air through the duct system during an emergency. It also restricts the passage of smoke, fire, and heat. Fire dampers must be installed whenever a duct passes through a wall, ceiling, or floor that is part of a fire-rated assembly. They can be installed within a duct or on the outside as a collar fastened to the wall or ceiling. **Draft stops** are required in combustible construction to close off large, concealed spaces. They are not required to be noncombustible themselves. Draft stops are placed between the ceiling and the floor above, in attic spaces, and in other concealed spaces. They create separate spaces and prevent the movement of air.

Firestops

Firestops restrict the passage of smoke, heat, and flames in concealed spaces. They seal and protect openings for plumbing pipes, electrical conduit and wire, HVAC ducts, cables, and other

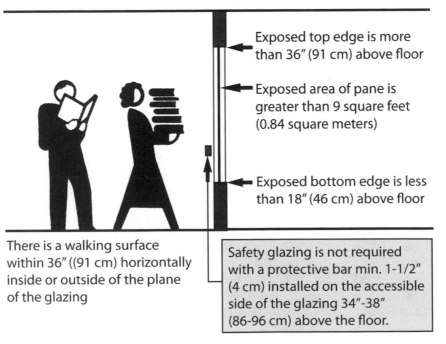

Safety glazing is required for a glazed panel meeting all of these criteria:

Exposed top edge is more than 36″ (91 cm) above floor

Exposed area of pane is greater than 9 square feet (0.84 square meters)

Exposed bottom edge is less than 18″ (46 cm) above floor

There is a walking surface within 36″ ((91 cm) horizontally inside or outside of the plane of the glazing

Safety glazing is not required with a protective bar min. 1-1/2″ (4 cm) installed on the accessible side of the glazing 34″-38″ (86-96 cm) above the floor.

Figure 15-19 Safety glazing limits.

Figure 15-20 Fire damper. A fire damper includes a fusible link on either side of the assembly the duct penetrates. This link melts during a fire, causing the fire damper to close and seal the duct.

components that pass through walls, floors, and ceilings. Firestops may also be required in concealed spaces between walls and in connections between horizontal and vertical planes. Firestops are required at through penetrations in fire and smoke barriers.

Firestops consist of silicone foam, mortar, fire-resistive board, wire mesh, collars, and clamp bands. The most common way to create a firestop system is to fill the open space with a fire-rated material and finish it with a sealant. Firestop devices are factory-built and typically are installed as part of a penetration through a wall or floor/ceiling assembly.

Designing to Help Firefighters

Firefighters often have to use the stairs to reach parts of a building above the seven-story limit of their ladders. One exit stairway in a taller building must be placed in a smokeproof enclosure. This stairway is connected to the main spaces of the building only by open-air balconies or is automatically pressurized by a fan in case of fire.

Each exit stairway in a multistory building must have a **standpipe** to connect fire hoses at any floor. A Y-shaped Siamese connection is provided at street level to enable firefighters to supply water continuously through the standpipe. One or two fire trucks can maintain pressure and volume in the standpipe if city water mains cannot keep up with demand during the fire.

Smoke Management

Smoke kills more people in building fires than heat or structural collapse. Even if a person is not killed by smoke, smoke inhalation can result in memory loss and lingering physical effects. Before a flame is visible, smoke may move more than 25 centimeters per second (50 ft. per minute) from the point of origin to kill people who are unaware of the fire. Once the flame is visible, smoke may move more than 50 centimeters per second (100 ft. per minute) before the flame starts to spread. Fires in modern buildings usually last less than 30 minutes, but smoke problems can be present for hours. As mentioned earlier, smoke inhalation leads to unclear thinking. People might claw at a doorknob instead of turning the handle. Hot smoke washing over people can cause them to panic as logic vanishes and fear overwhelms them.

The goals of smoke management are to reduce deaths and property damage and to provide continuity of building operations with minimum smoke interference. A barrier's effectiveness in limiting smoke movement depends on if and how smoke leaks through it and the pressure differences on each side of it. Pressure depends on the stack effect, the buoyancy of warm air, the presence of wind, and the operation of the HVAC system.

SMOKE BARRIERS

The heat of a fire changes the air's pressure and buoyancy, which, in turn, spreads the smoke. As the temperature increases during a fire in a low building, gases in the smoke expand and convective air motion move the smoke around. In tall buildings, these effects are compounded by the stack effect as heated air rises rapidly within vertical shafts. Wind forces outside and the forced-air system increase the stack effect.

Wall assemblies that are continuous from outside wall to outside wall and from floor slab to floor slab are effective smoke barriers. This type of construction is primarily used in institutional occupancies between areas of refuge.

In tall buildings, vertical shafts for stairs, elevators, and waste and linen chutes can be designed to be smokeproof. Smokeproof enclosures require ventilation or pressurization systems. All openings must automatically close when smoke is detected. Smokestop doors that close tightly may be required.

Vestibules that are adjacent to smokeproof stairwells or elevator hoistways and between the shaft and an exterior exit door are subject to special size requirements. Doors must be fire-rated and have closers and drop sills. The ceiling must be high enough to trap smoke and heat. Natural or mechanical ventilation is required.

When doors in stairwells that are pressurized to exclude smoke are opened to allow people to escape, they are sometimes left open. Keeping the outside air at a lower pressure than the air in the stairwell prevents smoke from getting through the open door.

Smoke-control systems are required in all buildings more than six stories high. The exit access corridors must be continually pressurized. The NFPA requires that every patient sleeping room in a hospital have an outside window operable from the inside to vent the products of combustion. An exemption is provided for buildings with an engineered smoke-control system.

SMOKE CONFINEMENT

Smoke should be confined to the area of the fire and excluded from areas of refuge. Firewalls and smoke barriers confine smoke. However, even firewalls have leaks around doors and other openings. A large, open space above dividing walls can hold a great deal of smoke while the building occupants evacuate.

Smoke dampers are similar to fire dampers but are activated by smoke. They are rarely required, except in large educational occupancies and at smoke barriers in institutional occupancies. Smoke dampers have a smoke detector located inside the duct that causes the smoke damper to close the duct.

SMOKE DILUTION

Diluting smoke with outdoor air helps people evacuate a burning building. Dilution alone is not enough to control smoke, especially when toxic fumes are present. Smoke dilution is usually combined with confinement and an early detection-and-suppression system.

Providing a large quantity of fresh air in refuge spaces creates higher pressures, which, in turn, resist smoke that enters through cracks. However, fresh air alone is not usually enough to keep smoke from entering an open door. In stairways, the fresh air should not be supplied entirely from either the top or the bottom of the stairs. Doors that open near the only fresh air source can mean that no fresh air reaches other floors.

Fans that bring in outside air must be located so that the fire does not affect their operation and their intakes remain smoke-free. Locating a fan's intake below the level of smoke accumulation keeps smoke above people's heads.

SMOKE EXHAUST SYSTEMS

Special exhaust systems that function only in fires are becoming more common. They use a combination of air velocity and air pressure to control smoke. Smoke exhaust systems work well in large-volume atriums, removing smoke at the ceiling and supplying fresh air below. These systems involve significant initial expense for special fans and smoke-exhaust shafts.

Smoke exhaust systems remove toxic gases from refuge areas. They help firefighters by providing better air quality near a fire and by creating air currents that help control the fire's direction. Exhaust systems remove unburned combustion gases and prevent backdraft or flashover smoke explosions. By creating higher pressure in refuge areas and lower pressures in fire zones, exhaust systems keep smoke out of refuge areas, even when their doors are open. These systems also prevent the stack effect from overcoming smoke-management efforts and remove smoke after the fire is over.

OTHER SMOKE CONTROLS

Automatic ventilation hatches vent heat and smoke without fans and are suitable for smaller buildings and one-story buildings, such as strip malls. When heat and smoke trigger the controls, the hatches open individually. Ventilation hatches improve conditions near the fire for firefighters, helping those on the roof locate the fire inside the building.

The coordination of the HVAC, fire detection and suppression, and smoke exhaust systems is essential to smoke management. The fire detection and suppression system activates the smoke exhaust and overrides HVAC controls. Sprinklers can conflict with a smoke-exhaust system. The curtain of water from the sprinklers can inhibit the movement of smoke. When the water cools the smoke, the resulting reduction in buoyancy causes it to descend to the level where people are. Fire suppression with oxygen replacing chemicals can conflict with fresh air from the smoke exhaust system. However, using both sprinklers and fire suppression may mean there is less need for the smoke exhaust system.

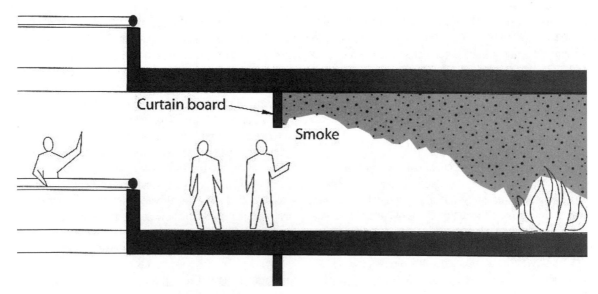

Figure 15-21 Curtain board smoke barrier. Smoke barriers, sometimes called curtain boards, are suspended from the ceiling to trap hot air and smoke. They help set off fire-detection and fire-suppression systems more rapidly. Curtain boards lose their effectiveness quickly when the smoke layer becomes too thick to contain.

ESCAPE ROUTES

In order to design safe exits from a building, interior designers must first create safe exit paths. Stairs and corridors are constructed along the paths to slow down the fire and to guide occupants out of the building. Exits are located so that they offer more than one route out and limit distances to safe exits. Finally, the number of people allowed to occupy the building at one time is limited so that the building can be emptied quickly.

At least 30 percent of fire deaths are the result of fire cutting off exit paths. Although people may panic in a fire, most of the time they initially respond to clues to the fire, such as the smell of smoke or the sounds of breaking glass, sirens, and alarm bells, more or less calmly. It is rare for people to actually see flames as the first warning of fire. Open floor plans enable more people to see signs of fire more easily. Next, occupants decide how serious the situation is. The reactions of other people influence their behavior. Without signs of fire, an entire group of people may refuse to evacuate the building in the early stages. Finally, people start to cope with the fact that the building is on fire and that they must evacuate. The fight-or-flight reaction takes over. At this point, occupants must be able to see exit paths clearly and have access to firefighting equipment, such as fire extinguishers.

A minimum of one regulated exterior exit door is required per residence, with a specified type of landing on each side. Minimum widths are specified for hallways and exit accesses. Most homes rely on exterior windows as a means of egress during an emergency, and codes restrict the size, height, and operation of windows that can be used as exits. Stairs and ramps are regulated but not as strictly as in the model building codes for commercial buildings. Smaller tread and riser sizes are allowed, and a single handrail is permitted.

In a low-rise building, the primary goal is to evacuate all occupants in the time between the detection of the fire and the arrival of the firefighters. (Some of the ways that building codes keep the route to safety clear, including stairwell enclosures and horizontal exits, were discussed earlier; see pages 337–338.)

Firefighting equipment normally reaches up to only seven stories, or around 229 meters (90ft.). In many high-rise buildings, only two exit stairways are provided. With only two exit staircases, a small, fifteen-story building with 120 people per floor can be evacuated in approximately nine minutes. By comparison, in a large, fifty-story building with 480 people per floor with two exit staircases, evacuation would take a minimum of two hours and eleven minutes. In addition, firefighters must be able to climb the stairs while occupants descend. Sometimes, occupants will try to reenter a stairway in order to rescue family members, pets, and valuables, further complicating and possibly impeding the flow.

When doors are held open on each floor to admit people to the stairwell, smoke can enter the stairs. People commonly refuse to evacuate high-rise buildings because they would rather trust the fire-extinguishing equipment than walk down many stories of stairs.

☑ **An interior designer must plan the means of egress carefully on interior projects and coordinate the means of egress requirements with fire-separation and smoke-separation requirements. Once a building occupant enters the protected portion of a means of egress, the level of protection cannot be reduced or eliminated unless code authorities allow an exemption.**

Occupant Loads

Building codes use the **occupant load** (or occupancy load) to establish the required number and width of exits for a building. The occupant load determines the maximum number of people allowed in a specific occupancy at any one time. Interior designers should be aware that the occupancy load is not the same as an occupancy classification. An **occupancy classification** indicates the use of the space, rather than the number of people. There may be more than one occupancy within a single building if there is more than one use.

The codes assign a predetermined amount of space or square feet that is required per occupant within specific occupancies and building uses. This amount of space is called the occupant-load factor. **Occupant-load factors** allow for furniture and equipment, and sometimes for corridors, closets, and other areas, in establishing the number of square feet per person for various occupancies.

The occupant load is determined by dividing the floor area assigned to a particular use by the square feet per occupant permitted in that use. It is calculated by using the area inside of the exterior walls. Some load factors are calculated in gross square feet, including interior wall thicknesses and all miscellaneous spaces in the building as a whole. Others are based on net square feet of the actual occupied space, not including corridors, restrooms, utility closets, and other unoccupied areas. Sometimes, fixed items that take up space, such as interior walls, columns, built-in counters, and shelving, are deducted from the number of square feet used in the calculations.

The minimum total **egress widths** per floor is the sum of the number of inches of width for all of the exits from a specific floor. To determine the minimum total egress width for a floor, the net or gross floor area (whichever the appropriate code calls for) is calculated, then that floor area is divided by the occupant-load factor. This gives the number of occupants per floor. Next, the number of inches of egress width required for each occupant of the floor is determined by looking in the code. Then this number of inches per person is multiplied by the number of occupants per floor to arrive at the minimum total egress width for that floor. This figure then is divided into the number of exits planned for the floor, based on each exit's clear width. The result: a minimum number of exits and their minimum sizes.

Means of Egress

A **means of egress** is a continuous and unobstructed path of travel from any point in a building to its exit or a public way. The

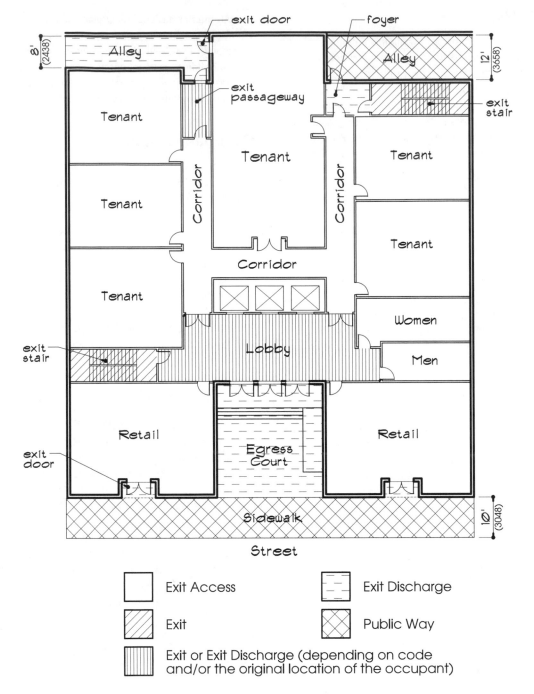

Figure 15-22 **Means of egress components.** Building codes define the specific makeup of each part of a means of egress.

means of egress is also the path of travel that an occupant uses to reach an area of refuge in the building.

Any means of egress has three components: the exit access, the exit, and the exit discharge. A means of egress comprises both vertical and horizontal passageways, including doorways, corridors, stairs, ramps, enclosures, and intervening rooms. Building codes and Life Safety Code set most egress requirements. The ADA should also be considered for related requirements.

Exit Access

The **exit access** is that portion of a means of egress that leads to an exit. An exit access leads from a room or space to the exit and can include doors, corridors, stairs, ramps, aisles, and intervening rooms. The exit access does not necessarily require a fire rating nor does it need to be fully enclosed. When a fire rating is required, it is usually one hour.

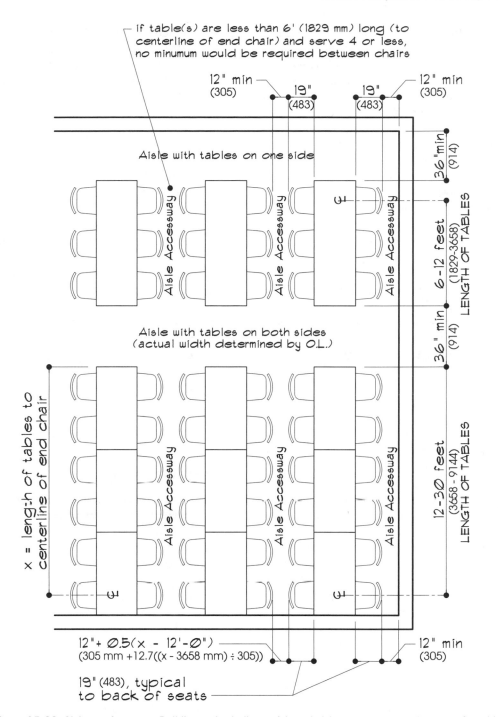

if table(s) are less than 6' (1829 mm) long (to
centerline of end chair) and serve 4 or less,
no minumum would be required between chairs

12" min
(305)

19"
(483)

19"
(483)

12" min
(305)

36"min
(914)

Aisle with tables on one side

Aisle Accessway

Aisle Accessway

3

Aisle Accessway

36" min
(914)

6-12 feet
(1829-3658)
LENGTH OF TABLES

Aisle with tables on both sides
(actual width determined by O.L.)

x = length of tables to
centerline of end chair

Aisle Accessway

Aisle Accessway

Aisle Accessway

3

3

12-30 feet
(3658 - 9144)
LENGTH OF TABLES

12"+ Ø.5(x - 12'-Ø")
(305 mm +12.7((x - 3658 mm) ÷ 305))

12" min
(305)

19" (483), typical
to back of seats

Figure 15-23 Aisle requirements. Building codes indicate aisle and aisle-accessway requirements for tables and chairs.

Doors in an exit access are regulated as to type, size, and swing direction depending on their location. Doors along a corridor must be fire-rated. Those between smaller tenant spaces or rooms do not require a rating. Typically, a minimum height of 91 meters (6 ft. 8 in.) is required. The ADAAG requires a minimum of 81 centimeters (32 in.) of clear width, but 91-centimeter (36-in.) doors are usually used to allow for the thickness of the door and its hardware. The finished floor surface on either side of a threshold must be within 13 millimeters (½ in.) of the top of the threshold; otherwise, the threshold must be beveled.

An exit-access corridor is any corridor that leads to an exit in a building. Typically, corridors are not required to be fire-rated or may require just a one hour rating. The width and length of travel of the corridor are limited by codes and by accessibility requirements. Corridors in a means of egress that must allow the passage of two wheelchairs at one point must be a minimum of 2.6 meters (8 ft. 6 in.) wide. Clearances can be smaller if a wheelchair can change direction or if passing spaces are provided in long corridors. The exit access for low-rise buildings must have at least 81 centimeters (32 in.) of clear width to permit wheelchair use. The depths of objects protruding into the corridor are limited. If possible, a horizontal or ramped route should be provided to enable people using wheelchairs to exit a building in an emergency.

An **aisle** is a pathway that is created by furniture or equipment, with a maximum wall height of 1.75 meters (5 ft.-9 in.). When the furniture or equipment is any taller, the aisle is considered to be a corridor. Tables, counters, furnishings, equipment, merchandise, and other obstructions can create aisles. Pathways between movable panel systems in offices are considered to be aisles, as are paths between tables and chairs in restaurants and display racks in retail stores. Interior designers should check the ADA for specific dimension requirements. Rules for aisles that are part of an exit access are similar to those for corridors.

Sometimes, assembly occupancies have fixed seating for large numbers of people. Codes restrict aisle widths depending on the size of the occupancy, the number of seats served by each aisle, and whether the aisle is a ramp or a stair. The minimum distances between seats and where the aisles terminate are also regulated.

An exit access should be as direct as possible. In some projects, the access path may need to pass through an adjoining room or space before reaching a corridor or exit. This may be allowed if the path is a direct, unobstructed, and obvious means of travel toward the exit. The code allows smaller rooms to empty through larger spaces to access a corridor. Reception areas, lobbies, and foyers are permitted as long as they meet code requirements. Kitchens, storerooms, restrooms, closets, bedrooms, and other spaces subject to locking are usually not allowed as part of an exit access, with the exception of a dwelling unit or a space with a limited number of occupants. Rooms with a higher susceptibility to fire are also restricted.

Elevators may not be used as part of a means of egress because of their inherent unreliability in a fire. Specially equipped elevators are required to assist firefighters in gaining quick access to upper floors of tall buildings. These special elevators must comply with elaborate precautions for reliable smoke control, secure electrical supply, and complete isolation from the effects of the fire.

Most of the stairs that interior designers deal with in buildings are exit stairs. Another category covered by codes is the exit-access stair. Exit access stairs are not as common as exit stairs; they are usually used within a space when one tenant occupies more than one floor of a building or when there is a mezzanine. Typically, exit access stairs do not call for a fire-rated enclosure unless they connect more than two floors.

No single floor should have steps or stairs within a means of egress. Ramps can be used wherever there is a change of elevation and access is required for people in wheelchairs. Ramps have width and clearance requirements similar to those of corridors. They also require landings at certain intervals and with certain dimensions that are determined by the length of the ramp and the number of changes in direction. Landings are also required at the top and bottom of the ramp. The ramp and landings require specific edge details and a rough, nonslip surface. Handrails are usually required when ramps exceed a certain angle or rise; guardrails may also be required. Code requirements for fire safety are frequently updated, so these should be verified before use.

EXITS

The **exit** is the portion of a means of egress that is separated from all of the other spaces of a building. The exit leads from the exit access to the exit discharge and must provide an enclosed, protected means of evacuation for building occupants in the event of a fire. There are specific requirements for the quantity, location, and size of exits, along with other code and accessibility requirements similar to those of the exit access. The exit must be fully enclosed and fire-rated with minimal penetrations. Typically, exits are required to have a two hour fire separation compared with the exit access and exit discharge, which usually require up to one hour.

The exit must open into another exit, into an exit discharge, or directly onto a public way. The exit may be a door opening directly to the outside from a ground-floor room or corridor. It may be an exit passageway with walls of fire-rated construction. When the exit arrives at the door from above or below grade, it is considered to be an exit stair.

Exit Passageways

An **exit passageway** is a fully enclosed, fire-rated corridor or hallway. It provides the same level of protection as an exit stair. The exit passageway consists of the surrounding walls and the doors leading into it.

An exit passageway is most commonly used to extend an exit. If an enclosed exit stairway is not located at an exterior wall, the exit passageway can connect the bottom of the exit stair to an exterior exit door. The length of the passageway is limited to the maximum dead-end corridor length permitted by the code.

An exit access, such as a corridor, can also exit into an exit passageway. This may occur on the ground floor of a building when secondary exits are required, as in malls and office buildings with center building cores. The exit passageway is created at the building perimeter between two tenants so that an exterior door can be reached off the common corridor.

An exit passageway can be used to shorten the distance to an exit by adding an enclosed, fire-rated corridor leading to a door at an exit stair. This gives a new end point for measuring the distance to the exit, and can help comply with code requirements for travel distances to an exit.

Exit Discharges

All exits must discharge to a safe place of refuge outside the building, such as an exit court or public way at ground level. An **exit discharge** may be a courtyard, patio, or exterior vestibule that

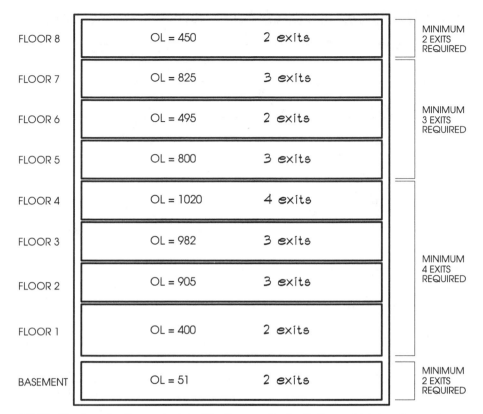

FLOOR 8	OL = 450	2 exits	MINIMUM 2 EXITS REQUIRED
FLOOR 7	OL = 825	3 exits	
FLOOR 6	OL = 495	2 exits	MINIMUM 3 EXITS REQUIRED
FLOOR 5	OL = 800	3 exits	
FLOOR 4	OL = 1020	4 exits	
FLOOR 3	OL = 982	3 exits	MINIMUM 4 EXITS REQUIRED
FLOOR 2	OL = 905	3 exits	
FLOOR 1	OL = 400	2 exits	
BASEMENT	OL = 51	2 exits	MINIMUM 2 EXITS REQUIRED

Figure 15-24 Number of exits required. In this diagram, the fourth floor, which has the most occupants, requires the highest number of exits. The corresponding code requires four exits for any occupant load over 1000. This load carries down to all of the floors below the fourth floor, which everyone must pass in order to leave the building.

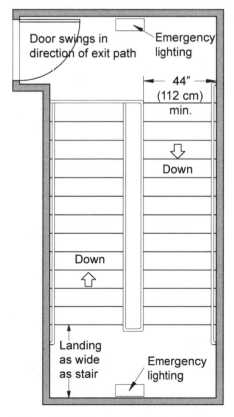

Figure 15-25 Requirements for exit stairs.

TABLE 15-5. SUMMARY OF NFPA 101 LIFE SAFETY CODE PROVISIONS FOR OCCUPANT LOAD AND EXIT CAPACITY

Occupancy		Occupant Load (N = Net, G = Gross)	
		Square Foot per Person	Square Meter per Person
Assembly	Less concentrated; not fixed seating	15 N	1.4 N
	Concentrated; not fixed seating	7 N	0.65 N
	Fixed seating	Actual Number of Seats	
Educational	Classrooms	20 N	1.9 N
	Shops; vocational	50 N	4.6 N
Care centers		35 N	3.3 N
Healthcare	Sleeping departments	120 G	11.11 G
	Treatment departments	240 G	22.3 G
Residential		200 G	18.6 G
Board and care		200 G	18.6 G
Mercantile	Street floor; sales basement	30 G	3.7 G
	Multiple street floors, each	40 G	3.7 G
	Other floors	60 G	5.6 G
	Storage; shipping	300 G	27.9 G
	Malls: See Code (conditions vary)		
Business		100 G	9.3 G
Industrial		100 G	9.3 G
Detention and correctional		120 G	11.1 G

Adapted from 1997 Fire Protection Handbook

connects the exterior exit door to the **public way**. A public way is a street, alley, or similar parcel of land that is open to the sky and permanently available for free passage and use of the general public. Small alleys or sidewalks less than 3 meters (10 ft.) wide are not considered to be public ways and become exterior exit discharges that connect the exterior exit door to a larger alley, sidewalk, or street.

The width of the exit discharge is determined by the width of the exit that it supports and the handicapped-access requirements. If more than one exit opens into an exit discharge, the width is the sum of the various exits' requirements. A minimal ceiling height of 244 centimeters (8 ft.) is typical.

In the main building lobby, the distance between the door of an exit stair and the exterior door is considered to be an exit discharge. A foyer or **vestibule**—a small enclosure on the ground floor of a building between the end of a corridor and the exterior exit door—can be part of an exit discharge. If the size of such an enclosure is kept to the minimum, the codes may not require a high fire rating. A larger enclosure may be considered to be an exit passageway, thereby requiring a higher rating.

Sometimes in older buildings, an exit stair empties into the ground floor without a fire-rated exit passageway connecting the exit stairs to the exterior door. In this case, a corridor may become an exit discharge. This is not recommended and is allowed only in a building with sprinklers.

Exit Signs

Exit signs are usually required whenever two or more exits are mandated by code. Exit signs are located at the doors of all stair enclosures, exit passageways, and horizontal exits on all floors. An exit sign is placed at an exterior exit door and at any door exiting a space or area when the direction of egress is unclear. An exit sign is usually required at a door, with directional signs at other places. Some small occupancies may not require exit signs.

Within an exit access, the maximum distance from an exit sign is limited to 30.5 meters (100 ft.). Exit signs may be required by code to be mounted 20 centimeters (8 in.) above the floor in some occupancies, in addition to ceiling or wall mounted signs.

LIMITING FUELS

The Life Safety Code has a table for finish materials. Some occupancies have additional finish restrictions or requirements. Interior designers may need to do further research in the Life Safety Code or the model building codes for the occupancy in question. Typical occupancies with special requirements include healthcare facilities, detention or correctional institutions, hotels, dormitories, and apartment buildings. Theaters, where combustible scenery and temporary electrical wiring fill the backstage area, require provision of a fire-rated curtain held rolled-up above the

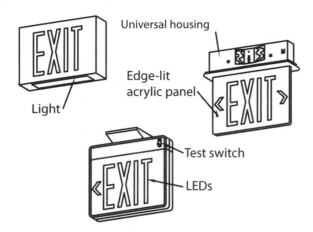

Figure 15-26 Exit signs. Today, most exit signs are made with energy-efficient light-emitting diodes (LEDs). Provisions are also made for nonelectric signs that are illuminated by other light sources.

proscenium that drops in a fire and seals the stage from the audience. Buildings with unusual structures may also have special requirements.

Stricter finish requirements usually apply when occupants are immobile or have security measures imposed on them that restrict their freedom of movement, as well as for overnight accommodations. In general, industrial and storage buildings have relaxed requirements because they have fewer occupants who tend to be alert and mobile. Sprinklers throughout a building can change the finish class ratings, so it is important for interior designers to know if a building has sprinklers and if so, where they are located.

Terminology

- By definition, **noncombustible materials** do not ignite and burn when subjected to fire. Noncombustible materials are used in a building to prevent the substantial spread of fire. Noncombustible building materials are composed of steel, iron, concrete, and masonry. Their actual performance in a fire depends on how they are used.
- **Combustible materials** ignite and continue to burn when a flame source is removed. Wood can be chemically treated for some fire resistance. It is then called fire-retardant treated wood (FRTW). Heavy timber of a large enough diameter is considered fire resistant. This includes columns that are minimally 20 centimeters square (8 sq in.) and beams that are minimally 152 × 254 mm (6 × 10 in.).
- **Flammable** and **inflammable** have the same meaning: tending to ignite easily and burn rapidly. Both words are the equivalent of highly combustible. Codes sometimes use the term "flammable."
- The term **flameproof** should not be used because very few materials are truly completely resistant to flame. The proper terms are **flame-retardant** and **flame-resistant** or **fire-resistant**. Fire resistant materials include gypsum wallboard, gypsum concrete, plaster, and mineral-fiber products.

- **Fire rated** means that a product has been tested to obtain an hourly fire rating. Manufacturers must label tested products to ensure that they have passed the tests. Most manufacturers usually test products before putting them on the market. Manufacturers know that products must meet code requirements to be specified. Interior designers must know how to find and obtain the required test results. Many manufacturers list test results on samples and products or can provide the information on request.

☑ **Interior designers need to keep current on testing and code requirements. Even where the jurisdiction may have lower standards, it is advisable to specify the most advanced tests and materials. If ever held legally liable, an interior designer must substantiate use of the most advanced requirements at the time of the project design.**

☑ **An interior designer would be wise to determine which tests are required for each area before selecting finishes and furniture for a project. Making copies of the information in manufacturers' labels is recommended. When fabric is treated for fire retardance, an interior designer should keep copies for future reference and follow up with the fire-retardant treatment company to make sure it sends certificates to the client. Designers should also double-check requirements for spaces where people will be seated for extended periods as well as for areas that permit smoking. These include transport terminals, cocktail lounges, restaurants, and the lounge areas of public buildings.**

Various organizations publish lists of tested assemblies for walls and partitions, floor-and-ceiling systems, and roof-and-ceiling systems. They set standards for protection of beams, girders and trusses, columns, and window assemblies. The following organizations publish such lists:

- UL: *Fire Resistance Directory* covers beams, columns, floors, roofs, and partitions in Volume I and through-penetration firestop systems in Volume II.
- Gypsum Association: *Fire Resistance Design Manual* illustrates wall constructions.

To rate an assembly in an existing building, interior designers must determine the fire rating required by the building code, then use these publications to find a fire-rated assembly that is most similar to the existing condition. The file number of this assembly should be used in the specifications for new construction in the building. Building materials with the correct fire rating for interior partitions must be specified: too low a rating can reclassify the whole building into a lower category.

Test results and ratings of materials and assemblies can become invalid if the products are not used and maintained properly. Then the product or assembly must be retested or have added fire protection. If the construction of joints between each assembly, such as wall to wall, wall to ceiling, or wall to floor, is substandard, fire and smoke can penetrate regardless of the quality of the assembly. Some assemblies are tested with conventional openings, but some are not. Wall electrical switches and outlets, electric raceways, or pull boxes in the floor or ceiling can affect a system's endurance. Fire can impair the stability of a structural assembly. If an assembly is exposed to flame and heat, the strength and structural integrity of the building materials can be adversely affected. Consequently, the original fire rating may not be accurate after a fire.

☑ **Interior designers should ask suppliers how materials have performed in real fires. Modern polymer materials have a complex response to fire: while, they may have good fire retardance, they may have high toxicity and smoke. A wall covering that is not flame resistant can spread a fire down the length of a corridor in seconds, igniting other flammable materials and producing smoke, heat, and toxic fumes. Interiors designers should be cautious if a manufacturer is unresponsive or cannot provide answers to their questions.**

Using Materials Safely

☑ **Many finishes and furnishings that an interior designer will specify are subject to fire code restrictions. Interior wall finishes include exposed interior surfaces applied over fixed or movable walls, partitions, columns, and other constructions. Interior ceiling finishes include exposed interior surfaces, such as suspended ceiling grids and coverings applied to fixed or movable ceilings, soffits, and space frames. Fire code provisions regulate exposed interior surfaces, including coverings applied over finished or unfinished floors, stairs (including risers), and ramps.**

Until recently, codes regulated only interior wall, ceiling, and floor finishes, with the exception of the strictest jurisdictions, and did not establish requirements for furnishings or their finishes. Requirements continue to grow stricter and to spread to more jurisdictions. It is an interior designer's responsibility to check requirements and to select furnishings with full knowledge of codes and standards. Codes that affect furnishings cover exposed finishes found in furniture and window treatments, such as fabrics, wood veneers, and laminates. The codes also include non-exposed finishes, such as the foam in seating and the linings in draperies. The term "furniture" includes whole pieces of furniture and upholstered seating as well as panel systems.

Many jurisdictions share a number of rules for determining what is covered, although some localities use older code editions with less restrictive rules. The 10-percent rule for trims and decorative finishes that usually have low fire ratings states that they must make up less than 10 percent of the surface and be evenly distributed (eg, not concentrated in one area). This means that crown molding or wainscoting distributed throughout a project and amounting to less than 10 percent of the wall surface may be allowed, but paneling concentrated wall to wall and ceiling to floor in a law office may not be up to code.

The ⅛-inch rule states that most interior finishes, such as paint and wallpapers applied to noncombustible building materials (e.g., gypsum wallboard, brick, concrete) do not have to be rated if they are less than 0.9 millimeters (⅛ in.) thick. This rule does not apply when finishes are layered on top of each other.

Vinyl wall covering is regulated in all thicknesses because of its burning characteristics and high smoke density. When a finish is applied to furring strips rather than directly on a noncombustible material, the total thickness is permitted to be a maximum of 44 millimeters (1¾ in.) thick. Spaces between the strips must be filled with a fire-rated material or fire-blocked at 2.4-meter (8-ft.) intervals.

In some jurisdictions, the presence of sprinklers may lower the permissible fire rating enough to allow finishes without ratings. This may not be permitted by some building codes, and it is not acceptable for new healthcare facilities.

All exits and paths of travel to and from exits must be clear of furnishings, decorations, and other objects. No drapes or mirrors are allowed to obscure exit doors, and mirrors are prohibited next to exit doors. Attention must not be drawn away from the exit sign.

Typically, wood columns, heavy timber beams, and girders are allowed to remain exposed because they are spaced relatively far apart and do not provide a continuous surface for flame spread. This is specified in the structural sections of the building code.

Foam plastics and cellular materials may not be used as wall or ceiling finishes unless they pass a test or comply with the 10-percent rule, although there may be some small exceptions to this requirement.

☑ **Interior designers are encouraged to specify office furniture that is as noncombustible as possible, along with steel filing cabinets. Wall coverings should be either noncombustible or low hazard. Everything in a plenum should be noncombustible or encased in noncombustible materials. In many major fires, combustible materials in hidden spaces result in injuries, deaths, and property losses. The way a material or system is oriented in relation to the environment also affects how readily it will burn.**

As mentioned earlier, deaths occur more often in residential fires, but the codes are much stricter for commercial projects. An interior designer has the option of choosing to design a residential project to the higher commercial standard. All wall and ceiling finishes for a residence, with the exception of trims and materials less than 0.9 millimeters (⅛ in.) thick, are required to meet ASTM-E84 testing requirements. Some finishes, such as wood veneer and hardboard paneling, must conform to other standards as well. Finishes in showers and bath areas are also regulated and must be smooth, hard, and nonabsorbent; they include fiberglass and vinyl or ceramic tile.

☑ **It is important for interior designers to determine if they are selecting a finish or a furnishing. The same items take on different meanings depending on the jurisdiction and the project. For example, carpet may be considered to be a furnishing when it is installed over a finished floor. Movable walls and panel partitions may be considered to be furnishings or temporary walls, depending on the jurisdiction. Most window treatments are not regulated by codes unless they cover large portions of a wall. Codes consider draperies and tapestries to be finishes only when they cover more than five to ten percent of the wall area. Some jurisdictions do have requirements for draperies and wall hangings.**

Many jurisdictions consider built-in cabinetry and seating with continuous expanses of plastic laminates and wood veneers to be interior finishes. High-back, upholstered restaurant booths can be restricted in certain jurisdictions.

Finish Classes and Test Ratings

Fire resistance classes become stricter as you move closer to the exit, with the strictest ratings at the exit itself.

Classes A, B, and C are wall- and ceiling-finish classifications based on the Steiner tunnel tests interior floor finish classes I and II are based on the radiant panel tests.

As mentioned earlier, flame spread is the speed at which fire may spread across the surface of a material. Smoke development ratings indicate the amount of visibility in a given access route when a material is on fire and creating smoke.

SMOKE DEVELOPMENT RATINGS
- **Class A** is the strictest rating and includes any material classed at a flame-spread rating of less than 25 with a smoke-development rating below 450.
- **Class B** includes materials with flame-spread ratings between 25 and 75 and smoke-development ratings below 450.
- **Class C** includes flame spreads between 76 and 200 but still limits smoke-development ratings to below 450.

MATTRESS TESTS
Currently, there are three tests that apply only to mattresses, although they are also tested with small-scale upholstered-furnishings tests.

- ASTM E1590, *Standard Test Method for Fire Testing of Mattresses*
- CAL 129, *Flammability Test Procedure for Mattresses Used in Public Buildings*
- DOC FF4 -72 (or CFR 1632), *Standard for Flammability of Mattresses*

The first two tests listed above measure heat release, smoke density, toxic gases (e.g., CO), and weight loss when exposed to flame. These tests use full-scale mattresses and are used for bedding in hotels, dormitories, hospitals, prisons, and other public occupancies, but not for residential mattresses.

DOC FF4-72 applies to mattresses used in single-family dwellings and for commercial projects. It is a cigarette ignition test required by the federal government for most mattresses and mattress pads sold in the United States. Cigarette ignition tests are also called smolder-resistance tests and are described below (see page 354).

PILL TEST
All carpets manufactured for sale in the United States are required to meet the Federal Flammability Standard, also known as the pill test. This is a pass/fail test that regulates the ease of surface ignition and surface flammability.

Figure 15-27 Pill test. For this pill test, a test sample of carpet is placed in a draft-protected cube and held in place by a metal plate with a hole with a 20-centimeter (8-in.) diameter. A timed methenamine pill is placed in the center of the hole and lighted. If the sample burns to within one inch of the metal plate, the carpet will fail the test.

TABLE 15-6. INTERIOR FINISHES AND TESTS

Type of Material	Finishes	Tests
Ceiling treatments	Ceiling tiles; fabric or vinyl coverings; special finishes	Steiner tunnel test; Room-corner test
Floor coverings	Carpets and pads; hard-surface flooring; resilient flooring; rugs	Pill test; Radiant-panel test
Furniture	Mattresses; panel systems; seating	Mattress test; Smolder-resistance test; Upholstered-seating test
Trim and decorative materials	Baseboards; chair and picture rails; decorative moldings; wainscoting	Room-corner test; Steiner tunnel test
Upholstery	Battings; fabrics; fillings; foams; interliners; vinyls; welt cords	Smoke-density test; Smolder-resistance test; Steiner tunnel test
Wall coverings	Fabric wallcoverings; vinyl wallcoverings; expanded vinyl wallcoverings; wood paneling; wood veneers	Room-corner test; Steiner tunnel test
Window treatments and vertical hangings	Acoustical fabrics; blinds; draperies; liners; panel fabrics; wall hangings; wood shutters	Vertical flame test

The Life Safety Code rates interior floor finishes as either Class I or Class II. Class I requires a minimum critical radiant flux of 0.45 watts per square centimeter, and Class II requires a rating of 0.22 watts per square centimeter.

RADIANT PANEL TEST

The Flooring Radiant Panel Test (NFPA 253, ASTM E-648, or NBS IR75-950) is used to rate interior floor finishes, including carpet, resilient flooring, and hardwood floor assemblies. There are also two more recent standard tests available, both of which are named the *Standard Method of Test for Critical Radiant Flux of Floor Covering Systems Using a Radiant Heat Energy Source* (one is NFPA 253, and the other is ASTM E648). Flooring tests of this type address the concern that heat radiating through the walls of a burning room could ignite the flooring materials in exit-access corridors.

ROOM CORNER TESTS

A room corner test is used for such vertical treatments as curtains, draperies, window shades, and large wall hangings or tapestries. Any vertical finish exposed to air on both sides may be covered. When vertical treatments cover a large area, they may also be required to pass the Steiner tunnel test. When napped, tufted, or looped textiles or carpets are used on walls and ceilings, a corner test (or a similar test under another name) is used. This is a pass/fail test for flame spread, burning drops, flashover, and net peak heat. The following are three vertical flame tests:

- NFPA 701, *Standard Methods of Fire Tests for Flame Propagation of Textiles and Films*
- ASTM D6413, *Standard Test Method for Flame Resistance of Textiles (Vertical Test)*
- UL 214, *Test for Flame-Propagation of Fabrics and Films*

SMOLDER RESISTANCE TESTS

Smolder resistance tests are also called cigarette ignition tests. These tests are also used to measure the reaction of upholstered furniture components to a smoldering cigarette. This nonflame test uses a lit cigarette to see how a product will smolder before either flaming or extinguishing. The test is used to check individual samples and mockups and is especially important for seating using padding or foam.

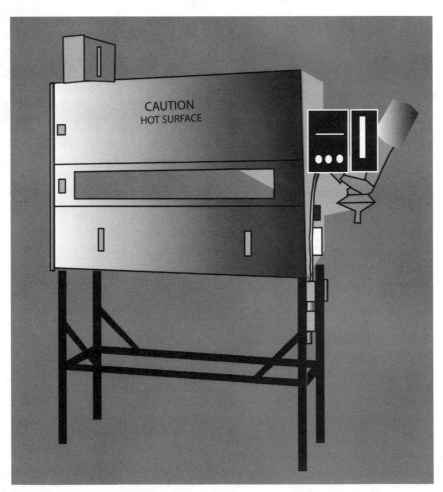

Figure 15-28 Flooring radiant panel test. A flooring radiant panel test measures a floor covering's tendency to spread a fire.

Figure 15-29 Room corner test. NFPA 701 encompasses two separate pass/fail tests. A small-scale test is used for straight hanging pieces. A large-scale test applies to fabrics used in folds, such as gathered drapery.

Figure 15-30 Cigarette ignition test. In a cigarette ignition test, a lit cigarette is placed on a sample and covered with a layer of sheeting material. The cigarette is allowed to burn its full length. Then the char length is measured. If it exceeds test limits, the sample will not pass. If the sample ignites, it will automatically fail the test.

Pass/fail smolder-resistance tests for individual finishes or textiles include the following:

- NFPA 260, *Standard Methods of Tests and Classification System for Cigarette Ignition Resistance of Components of Upholstered Furniture*
- ASTM E1353, *Standard Test Methods for Cigarette Ignition Resistance of Components of Upholstered Furniture*
- CAL 116, *Requirements, Test Procedure and Apparatus for Testing the Flame Retardance of Upholstered Furniture*

Another type of smolder-resistance test was developed for furniture mockups that consist of multiple components used in realistic combinations. The following are three such tests:

- NFPA 261, *Standard Method for Determining Resistance of Mock-up Upholstered Furniture Material Assemblies to Ignition by Smoldering Cigarettes*

- ASTM E1352, *Standard Test Method for Cigarette Ignition Resistance of Mock-up Upholstered Furniture Material Assemblies to Ignition by Smoldering Cigarettes*
- CAL 117, *Requirements, Test Procedures and Apparatus for Testing the Flame Retardance of Resilient Filling Materials Used in Upholstered Furniture*

SMOKE DENSITY TESTS

Smoke density tests determine whether a solid material will hold a flame or smolder, and how much smoke it will emit during a fire. The tests measure how thick and dark the smoke is to determine the amount of visibility during a fire and provide a rating based on the results. The two best-known smoke density tests are NFPA 258 and ASTM E662. The smoke density chamber test, NFPA 258, measures the optical density of the smoke on a scale of 0 to 800. Many codes require a smoke development rating of 450 or less for finish materials.

STEINER TUNNEL TEST

ASTM E-84, the Steiner tunnel test, determines both the flame-spread and the smoke development ratings for materials applied to walls, the ceiling, and other structural elements, including columns. ASTM E-84 rates the surface burning characteristics of interior finishes and other building materials. During the test, a sample piece is placed in a tunnel test chamber that has a controlled flame at one end.

TOXICITY TESTS

Toxicity tests are fairly new and are not currently required by the International Code Council (ICC) or NFPA codes. The test was originally known as the Pitts Test or LC50. It is now known by the following two names:

- NFPA 269, *Standard Test Method for Developing Toxic Potency Data for Use in Fire Hazard Modeling*
- ASTM E1678, *Standard Test Method for Measuring Smoke Toxicity for Use in Fire Hazard Analysis*

This test measures the amount of toxicity that a material emits when burned, and tests wall, ceiling and floor finishes. Upholstered furniture, mattresses and mattress pads, electrical wire and conduit, mechanical ductwork, thermal insulation, and plumbing pipes are also tested. The higher the LC50 rating, the less toxic are the emissions.

UPHOLSTERED SEATING TESTS

There are two general types of upholstered seating tests. Full-scale tests use an actual piece of furniture or a large mockup of that piece; small-scale tests uses smaller mockups made of multiple components of a piece of furniture. The results of these tests can be greatly affected by the actual configuration of an upholstered piece of furniture, so full-scale tests are considered to provide the most reliable results.

Full-scale upholstered-seating tests include:

- ASTM E1537, *Standard Test Method for Fire Testing of Upholstered Furniture*
- UL 1056, *Standard for Safety for Fire Test of Upholstered Furniture*
- CAL 133, *Flammability Test Procedure for Seating Furniture for Use in Public Occupancies*

These full-scale flame-resistance tests were developed to eliminate the flashover that occurs in the second phase of a fire. The tests do not approve individual materials; the entire piece of furniture must be tested and approved.

These tests measure the CO, heat generation, smoke, temperature, and weight loss of an entire piece of furniture. A burner is held just above the upholstered seat, ignited for eighty seconds, then turned off. Combustion is allowed to continue for up to thirty minutes as products of combustion are collected by an exhaust hood above.

The small-scale tests identified below are intended for upholstered furniture and mattresses that are destined for commer-cial, institutional, and high-risk occupancies. These tests measure the speed with which materials will ignite and the rate of heat release. Small-scale tests measure a sample's ignitability, heat release, smoke obscuration, mass loss, and toxicity.

- NFPA 272, *Standard Method of Test for Heat and Visible Smoke Release Rates for Upholstered Furniture Components or Composites and Mattresses Using an Oxygen Consumption Calorimeter*
- ASTM E1474, *Standard Test Method for Determining the Heat Release Rate of Upholstered Furniture and Mattress Components or Composites Using a Bench Scale Oxygen Consumption Calorimeter*

Tests are performed on small, block-shaped samples made of fabric and padding material plus any layers in between, such as liners, polyester fiber, and other fillers. A test apparatus exposes the sample first to a radiant-heat source and then to a spark ignition source. The igniter is turned off after a sustained flame occurs, and a duct system above collects data.

Finish and furnishing tests are constantly changing, and codes have improved older tests and added new tests. It is critical for interior designers to keep abreast of changes so that the specified finishes and furnishings can pass the correct tests.

Nontested Finishes

Sometimes, finishes that are geared to residential use or are made by small manufacturers with specialty items have not been tested. In these situations, an interior designer must have the finish tested or make sure that it is properly treated in order to meet code requirements. Depending on the situation, testing companies can be very costly to use because they may have to simulate actual installations.

It is often more cost-effective to have a finish treated for fire retardance. Flame resistant finishes add fire retardant coatings to materials that have not passed tests. Local manufacturers' representatives know the local requirements and companies that treat materials. Treatment may be applied to the material's surface or as a fire resistant coating used as a backing. The treatment delays the ignition of the material and slows the flame spread without changing the basic nature of the material. It may also lower the smoke development value.

An interior designer sends the fabric or other finish to the treatment company and explains which tests the finish must pass. Then the treatment company adds the appropriate fire retardant coating. Treatments can usually upgrade nonclassed finishes and may even improve the performance of some rated materials to a higher class. Next, the treatment company sends the interior designer a Certificate of Flame Resistance (CFR), which indicates which tests the fabric will pass.

Some fabrics are not suitable for treatment. Flame retardant treatments can alter finishes and furnishings and cause a variety of potential problems when added to fabric. For example, the fabric may shrink or decrease in strength so that it tears more easily. The hand or feel of the fabric may become stiffer. If the fabric has a texture, it may flatten or distort. The treatment itself may cause the fabric to give off toxic fumes, especially in the presence of fire. If the fabric received a wet treatment, the dye in the fabric may bleed or possibly fade or otherwise change color in the future.

An interior designer should check with the company doing the treatment, and submit a sample for testing prior to purchasing or treating the entire amount of fabric. The results of the treatment will depend on the content of the fabric and the type of treatment. It is best to have the fabric treated before applying it to the surface or furniture where it will be used.

Interior designers use their knowledge of these basic principles and tests regularly when designing and specifying interior finishes and furnishings. These are the keys to fire prevention. Another aspect of fire safety, how to deal with a fire once it has started, is addressed in Chapter 16: Fire Detection, Alarm, and Suppression.

Fire Detection, Alarm, and Suppression

FIRE SUPPRESSION

In high-rise buildings and buildings with large areas, there are places that cannot be reached by firefighters' ladders and hoses. While most fire deaths occur in smaller, often residential buildings, larger commercial, industrial, and institutional buildings have the potential for many deaths and injuries from a single fire. High-rise buildings require an inordinate amount of time to evacuate. Stack effects can be created in high-rise buildings that are more than 23 meters (75 ft.) tall. Such buildings must have their own firefighting system, which usually takes the form of an automatic sprinkler system.

Automatic sprinkler systems extinguish incipient fires before they have a chance to get out of control. Sprinkler heads are so efficient that one or two heads can usually put out a fire.

Although water cools, smothers, emulsifies, and dilutes a fire, it also damages building contents and can conduct electricity when used as a stream (less so as a spray). Water will not put out burning oil; the flammable oils will float and burn on the water's surface. When water hits a hot fire, the steam can harm firefighters. Despite these disadvantages, water remains one of the main ways to suppress a fire.

Building codes commonly allow buildings with a sprinkler system to have greater distances between exits, thereby eliminating one or more stairways in a large building. Because codes permit larger floor areas between fire separations, some fire resistant walls and doors may be eliminated. Buildings may also be allowed to have greater overall areas and heights. Some structural elements may need less fire protection, and the building may be able to contain larger amounts of combustible building materials.

OCCUPANCY HAZARD CLASSIFICATIONS

Building codes classify various occupancies according to fire hazard. These classifications are used to determine the design of sprinkler systems. In general, sprinkler systems are required for factory, hazardous, and storage occupancies as well as those in which large groups of people are present, such as assembly, institutional, and large mercantile and residential occupancies. The requirements are based on the number and mobility of the occupants, along with the types of hazards present.

Sprinkler systems are commonly used in basements, windowless buildings, and high-rise buildings. Sprinklers are often found in furnace and boiler rooms; at incinerator, trash, and laundry collection areas; and at the tops of chutes. They are required in kitchen exhaust systems and at spray-painting shops or booths. Sprinklers are used in vertical openings, duct systems that exhaust hazardous materials, drying rooms, and atriums.

Residential sprinklers are designed for fast response and are tested and listed for the protection of dwelling units. The sprinklers are sensitive to both smoldering and rapidly developing fires. They are designed in such a way that one or two heads open quickly to prevent smoke and toxic gases from filling small rooms.

Today, many codes require sprinklers in all residential occupancies. Residences do not ordinarily have a sufficient water supply capacity for standard sprinkler systems. Most codes that require residential sprinkler systems exempt the following spaces:

• Bathrooms up to 5.1 square meters (55 sq ft.)
• Closets whose smallest dimension is up to 0.9 meters (3 ft.)

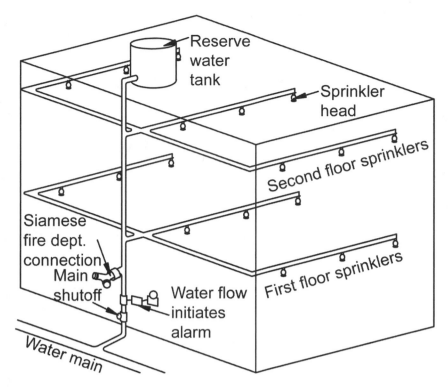

Figure 16-1 Sprinkler system. A sprinkler system consists of a network of pipes in or below the ceiling. The pipes are connected to a water supply and have valves or sprinkler heads that are made to open automatically at a certain temperature. Each sprinkler head is controlled by a plug or link of fusible metal that melts at approximately 66°C (150°F).

- Open porches, garages, and carports
- Uninhabitable attics and crawl spaces not used for storage
- Entrance foyers that are not sole means of egress

Residential sprinklers are designed to deliver water high enough on walls and ceilings to prevent a fire from extending above the sprinklers. By cooling the ceiling, they reduce the number of sprinklers that open.

DESIGNING FIRE SUPPRESSION SYSTEMS

A plumbing engineer or a sprinkler system specialist usually details the requirements for spacing sprinklers and references the appropriate codes. The design of the system takes into account the degree of hazard to the occupants. The maximum floor areas per head are set by the hazard level. The areas covered by various

TABLE 16-1. OCCUPANCY HAZARD CLASSIFICATIONS

Classification	Contents	Examples	Maximum Sprinkler Spacing
Light Hazard	Low quantity, combustibility, heat–release rate	Apartments, auditoriums, churches, hospitals, hotels, libraries, museums, nursing homes, office buildings, restaurants, schools, theaters	15 feet
Ordinary Hazard	Moderate to high quantity, heat-release rate; relatively low combustibility	Automobile showrooms, bakeries, beverage and dairy plants, canneries, electronic and glass manufacturing, laundries and dry cleaners, libraries, mercantile, post offices, restaurant service areas, stages, wood machining and assembly	15 feet
Extra Hazard (severe)	Very high quantity, combustibility; rapid fire development; high heat-release rates	Where volatile combustible materials are processed, mixed, or dispensed, such as aircraft hangars, die casting and metal extruding, particle-board and plywood manufacturing, textile processing, upholstering	12 Feet

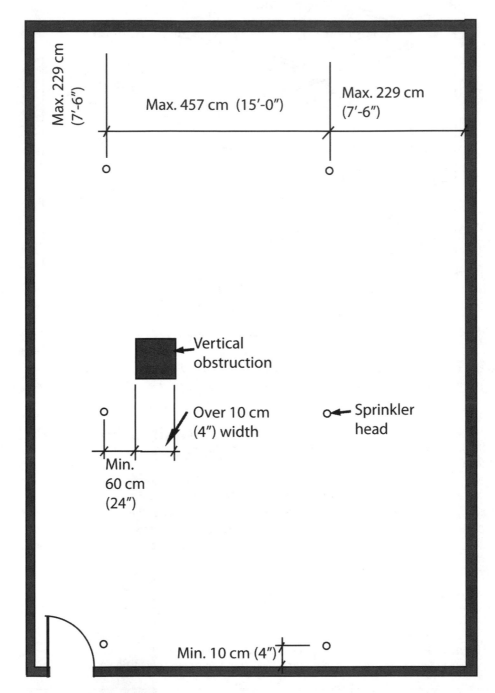

Figure 16-2 Sprinkler clearances. An interior designer should work closely with the sprinkler system designer to verify sprinkler head locations and provide adequate clearance at each sprinkler. Typically, a minimum of 46 centimeters (18 in.) must be left open below the sprinkler-head deflector. The interior designer should be especially observant of this requirement in areas where wall cabinets or shelving are used, such as storage rooms, kitchens, and libraries.

types of sprinkler heads determine their approximate locations. Heads are located in such a way that they detect fire readily and discharge water over the greatest area. The sprinkler system designer considers such obstacles as joists, beams, and partial height partitions. The design of the hydraulic piping that supplies the sprinklers is a complex process.

Sprinkler System Components

Sprinkler systems need both an adequate water supply and standby power for water pumping. Sprinkler systems require very large supply pipes, valves, and fire pumps. Valves shut off the system for maintenance, system modification, or replacement of heads that have operated after a fire. An improperly closed valve is the primary reason for sprinkler system failure. Fire pumps provide the required water pressure in a standpipe or sprinkler system when the pressure in the system drops below a predetermined value.

SPRINKLER HEADS

The sprinkler head keeps the water in the system by a plug or cap held tightly against the orifice (opening) by levers or other restraining devices. The levers are held in place by the arms of the

sprinkler body. In the past, the restraining device was usually a fusible metal link that melted at a predetermined temperature.

Currently, quick response sprinkler heads are required in light hazard occupancies, including office buildings, hotels, motels, and other buildings. Because they are more sensitive to heat than ordinary sprinkler heads, even fewer heads are needed to fight a fire. Their thermal sensitivity may cause them to open when exposed to high heat that is not fire related.

The deflector on the sprinkler head converts the solid stream to a spray. Directing the spray down and horizontally rather than up is more efficient, and produces better water distribution near the head and more effective coverage below.

Sprinkler head finishes are available in plain or polished brass, satin or polished chrome, stainless steel, and gold. A manufacturer may be able to coat ornamental pendants to match a desired décor. Sprinkler heads are never permitted to be field coated.

According to a National Fire Protection Association (NFPA) code, NFPA 13: *Standard for the Installation of Sprinkler Systems*, 2007 Edition, early suppression fast response (ESFR) sprinklers are used for specific challenging fire hazards, such as storage that is piled high. The sprinkler's higher pressure and flow penetrate a fire's base faster.

Figure 16-3 Interior siamese connection. Siamese connections allow fire engines to pump water into the system from outside the building. They are installed close to the ground on the exterior of a building and provide two or more connections through which firefighters can pump water to a standpipe or sprinkler system.

Figure 16-4 Sprinkler supply pipes. Supply pipes for sprinkler systems are large and are distributed throughout a building.

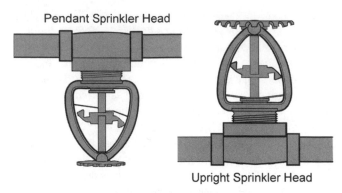

Figure 16-5 **Pendant and upright sprinkler heads.** Upright sprinkler heads sit on top of exposed supply piping. Pendant heads hang below piping. Pendant heads may be recessed, with part of the sprinkler body concealed above suspended ceilings and the deflector located below the ceiling. Flush heads have only the heat-detecting element below a ceiling. Concealed heads are located entirely above a ceiling, with a cover plate that falls away in a fire.

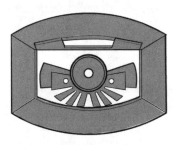

Figure 16-6 **Sidewall sprinkler head.** Sidewall sprinkler heads are usually located adjacent to one wall of small rooms, as in hotels or apartments. They throw a spray of water across the room, enabling an entire small room to be covered by one sprinkler head.

Extended-coverage sprinklers are used for unobstructed construction with flat, smooth ceilings and without projecting lighting fixtures or grilles. These sprinklers are also available listed for other ceiling constructions. Details are included in NFPA 13, which is scheduled to be updated in 2009.

SPRINKLER SYSTEM PIPING

Wet-pipe systems are the most commonly used type of sprinkler-system piping. The pipes contain water under enough pressure to discharge immediately and continuously through sprinkler heads.

Wet-pipe sprinkler systems are used in spaces with air temperatures that exceed 4°C (40°F), where frozen pipes are not a problem. Wet-pipe systems must be drained in order to change the location of a sprinkler head, adding expense and inconvenience to the project.

A **dry-pipe system** contains pressurized air or nitrogen that is released when a sprinkler head opens, allowing water to flow through the piping and out the opened nozzle. Dry-pipe systems are used in unheated areas where wet-pipe systems might freeze, such as loading docks, cold-storage areas, and unoccupied

buildings. Dry-pipe systems require compressed air, heated main-control valve housing, and pitched piping to allow drainage after use.

A **preaction system** is a dry-pipe system with air in the pipes, and with water flow controlled by a valve operated by separate heat or smoke detection devices that are more sensitive than those in the sprinkler heads. The preaction valve holds water back until heat or smoke opens it, sounding an alarm and filling the pipes with water. Preaction systems are used in buildings whose contents are sensitive to water damage. The early alarm enables the fire to be extinguished manually without using the sprinklers in computer rooms, retail stores, and museums. However, the delay can allow the fire to grow rapidly, by as much as 30 percent within sixty seconds, requiring 30 percent more water to extinguish it.

A **deluge sprinkler system** uses open sprinklers on dry pipes. Deluge systems are used for areas with a risk of extremely rapid fire spread, such as aircraft hangars and places where flammable liquids are stored or used.

When a heat and smoke detection system opens the deluge valve, the sprinkler system floods with water and all heads emit water. This releases a huge quantity of water.

A **circulating closed-loop system** is a wet-pipe system with larger sprinkler piping. The system circulates water for water-source heat pumps. Temperatures must stay between 4°C (40°F) and 49°C (120°F).

Sprinkler System Damage Control

A space with sprinklers should have adequate water drainage during and after a fire. When fire hoses and sprinklers overshoot the fire area, the building and its contents sustain water damage, even in areas where there is no fire. The water drains to lower building levels; floor drains safely carry this water away from the building. Salvage covers can protect sensitive objects and direct water toward drainage points. A readily accessible outside valve that controls all of the normal sources of supply to the system can cut off water promptly when it is no longer needed.

Standpipes and Hoses

Standpipe and hose systems help fight fires in buildings. They are classified by their intended use. System components may include standard hose racks or hose racks and fire extinguishers in cabinets.

Standpipes and hoses are supplied by a separate water reserve, upfeed pumping, or fire department connections. Standpipes are water pipes that extend vertically through a building to supply fire hoses on every floor. Wet standpipes contain water under pressure and are fitted with fire hoses for emergency use by building occupants. Dry standpipes do not contain water; they are used by firefighters to connect fire hoses to a fire hydrant or pumper truck.

Other Fire Suppression Systems

Sometimes, when the use of significant quantities of water threatens a building's structure or contents as much as a fire would, other means are used to smother the fire without substantial prop-

Figure 16-7 Standpipe access panel. Firefighters need instant access to equipment when they arrive at the site of a fire. This standpipe is located immediately inside the entrance to a municipal building and is identified clearly on building fire safety plans. It is discreetly hidden behind an unlocked access door.

erty damage. These include intumescent materials, clean-agent gases, and foams.

HALON

Hydrogenated hydrocarbons, of which the best known was Halon 1301, were used for commercial aircraft, computer and electronic equipment rooms, museums, libraries, and kitchens as well as other locations where harm to people or equipment was a major issue. The production of Halon 1301 was phased out in 1994 when it was identified as a long-lasting and significant threat to the earth's protective ozone layer.

Intumescent materials that expand rapidly when touched by fire create air pockets to insulate surfaces from the fire or swell ma-

terials to block openings through which fire and smoke could travel. Intumescent paints, caulks, and putties are available, as are 6-millimeter (¼-in.) thick sheets with a variety of facing materials.

CLEAN-AGENT GASES AND FOAMS

Clean-agent gases continue to be developed to replace Halon 1301. These products are designed for enclosed areas in which people may be present. They offer quick response and low levels of damage, and they are marketed as being environmentally friendly and people-safe. For example, the Inergen® fire suppression system by Ansul®, a mixture of 52-percent hydrogen, 40-percent argon, and 8-percent carbon dioxide (CO_2), claims to cause no ozone depletion or global warming and to not linger in the atmosphere.

Firefighting foams float on the surfaces of burning liquids. They smother and cool the fire while sealing in vapors. Many types of foam firefighting agents are available.

COMMERCIAL KITCHEN FIRE SUPPRESSION SYSTEMS

Commercial kitchens use liquid agents or dry-chemical systems for grease fires. The exhaust plenum and duct system becomes coated in grease, and the kitchen's high operating temperatures create a fire hazard. A flash fire in a cooking appliance can ignite grease in the duct. A chemical sprayed into the plenum chamber and ducts extinguishes the fire in seconds.

Restaurant fire suppression systems automatically cut the supply of heat to the stove or appliance, whether it is gas or electric. Grease fires can distort a duct, allowing grease to spill into concealed spaces in walls and ceilings. As a result, fire suppression nozzles are located in hoods over cooking areas and in ducts.

MIST SYSTEMS

Mist systems were originally used for fires on ships. Their faster alarm initiation and more rapid response to water, as well as the smaller volumes of water they use, have brought them into consideration for other applications. Mist systems offer an alternative to Halon and other clean-agent gases; they pose no threat to firefighter safety and offer many other advantages. They are covered by NFPA 750: *Standard on Water Mist Fire Protection Systems*, 2006 Edition.

A mist system allows a speedier initiation of the alarm and a quicker response to the fire than a sprinkler system. By using smaller volumes of water, mist systems reduce property damage.

TABLE 16-2. STANDPIPE AND HOSE CLASSIFICATIONS

Class	Used by	Use
Class I	Trained firefighters	Full-scale firefighting in buildings with and without sprinklers more than three stories high and in malls; most commonly used class
Class II	Building occupants	First-aid fire fighting before fire trucks arrive. Difficult for untrained users to operate, although still found in large unsprinklered buildings and special hazard areas such as stages.
Class III	Building occupants, trained firefighters	Difficult for untrained users to operate; use is declining

The mist poses no safety threat to firefighters and allows more building ventilation during a fire. It also eliminates residues from clean-agent gases and can be returned to service faster after use.

CARBON DIOXIDE

Carbon dioxide prevents the ignition of potentially flammable mixtures and extinguishes fires that involve flammable liquids or gases. It absorbs combustion energy and reduces the temperature of the flame and vapor mixture below the level necessary to sustain combustion.

Carbon dioxide smothers fires by displacing oxygen, and is limited to use in tightly confined spaces without people or animals. It is appropriate for use in display cases, mechanical and electrical chases, and unventilated areas above suspended ceilings or below raised floors. CO_2 is used in data centers, telecommunications equipment spaces, and electrical-equipment rooms where water would damage the contents.

Carbon dioxide is stored as a liquid in cylinders under great pressure. It is noncombustible, and will not react with most substances. In addition, it does not conduct electricity and usually does not damage sensitive electronic equipment. There is no residue to clean up after use.

After use, CO_2 gas escapes to the atmosphere at levels that pose a significant danger to building occupants and firefighters. Smoldering embers may ignite again after being suppressed by CO_2. Furthermore, accumulation of CO_2 in the atmosphere is a major cause of global climate change.

Portable Fire Extinguishers

Portable fire extinguishers are used to extinguish fires at an early stage. These extinguishers are movable and do not require access to plumbing lines. They are rated for the class of fire they are designed to fight. The number of portable fire extinguishers required and their locations depend on the hazard classification of the occupancy. They must be located in conspicuous places along ordinary paths of egress.

A typical home fire extinguisher is not designed to fight large or spreading fires and may run out in eight or fewer seconds. Fire extinguishers are rated for the type of fire that they can put out. The extinguisher must have adequate force to fully extinguish the fire. Extinguishers are located where it is both quick and safe to reach in case of fire. The person who operates the fire extinguisher must have the strength and knowledge to use it properly and without hesitation.

Building codes specify which occupancies and types of building use require fire extinguishers. Most occupancies do require extinguishers, and some specific areas within buildings have special requirements. Commercial kitchens and smaller kitchens and break rooms in commercial spaces require extinguishers. NFPA 10: *Portable Fire Extinguishers* provides guidelines for types and locations of extinguishers. In general, no occupant may be more than 22.9 meters (75 ft.) from a fire extinguisher in places where they are required.

Figure 16-8 Fire safety equipment mounting. Fire extinguishers may be surface-mounted or recessed within a wall, using a special cabinet with a vision panel. The extinguisher must be visible at all times, must be tested regularly, and must have an approved label. This presents a challenge to interior designers since fire extinguishers and related equipment are bright red and are in highly visible locations. Showing this equipment on interior elevations helps interior designers and their clients become aware of a room's final appearance.

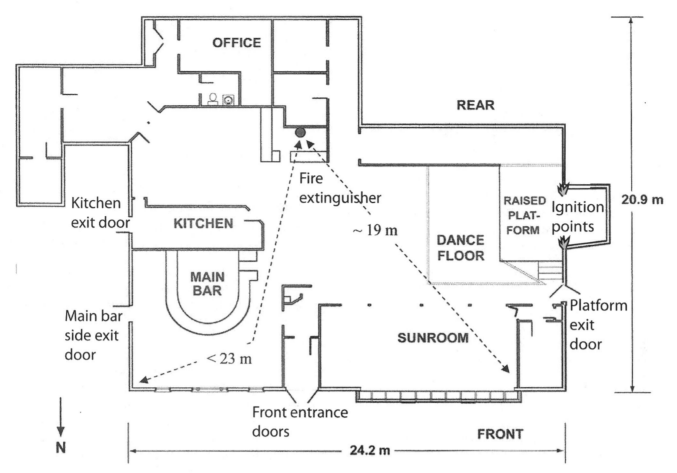

Figure 16-9 Station Nightclub fire extinguisher location. In 2003, one hundred people died in a fire at the Station Nightclub in Warwick, Rhode Island. The building had just one fire extinguisher, which was located behind the counter near the front entrance.

TABLE 16-3. PORTABLE FIRE EXTINGUISHERS

Type/Class	Contents	Used On	Effect
Type A 1A to 40A	Water, aqueous film-forming foam (AFFF), film-forming fluoroprotein foam (FFPP), multipurpose dry chemical (ammonium-phosphate base)	Ordinary combustibles, such as wood, cloth, paper, rubber, many plastics	Water: heat-absorbing, cooling; dry chemicals: coating, interruption of combustion chain reaction
Type B 5B to 40B	CO_2, dry chemicals, AFFF, FFFP	Flammable or combustible liquids, flammable gases, greases and similar materials	Exclude oxygen; inhibit release of combustible vapors; interrupt combustion chain reaction
Type C	CO_2, dry chemicals	Fires in live electrical equipment	Do not conduct electricity
Type A, B, C	Dry chemicals (primarily ammonium phosphate)	Multipurpose	Ammonium phosphate leaves very hard residue if not thoroughly cleaned up as soon as fire is extinguished
Type D	Dry powders (graphite, sodium chloride)	Combustible metals	Designed and labeled for specific metal

Fire extinguishers are classified by types that are represented by letters. They also have force ratings indicated by numbers. The higher the rating number, the more extinguishing agent the unit contains and, therefore, the larger the fire the extinguisher should be able to put out. A higher force number also means a heavier extinguisher.

☑ **Interior designers need to be familiar with the codes and Americans with Disabilities Act (ADA) requirements for portable fire extinguishers. If a fire suppression system will be used by a building's occupants, it must be mounted at accessible heights and located within accessible reaches from a front or side wheelchair approach. Fire suppression equipment may not protrude more than 102 millimeters (4 in.) into the path of travel. This requirement may eliminate the use of bracket-mounted fire extinguishers and surface-mounted fire protection cabinets in some areas.**

FIRE DETECTION AND ALARMS

Sprinkler systems are designed to simultaneously start to extinguish a fire and send out an alarm. When water flows through a sprinkler head, an alarm goes off outside the building. The alarm alerts people outside the building to the fire and allows building occupants to make additional firefighting arrangements in order to both minimize loss and speed the end of the fire and limit water damage.

Fire alarms are often connected to private, regional supervisory offices that call the municipal fire department. All public buildings and some other buildings are required to have fire-detection and fire alarm systems with an indicator that shows the location of the fire in the custodian's office.

Fire Detection

A fire progresses through four stages: incipient, smoldering, flame, and heat. Different types of fire and smoke detectors are designed to indicate problems at each stage.

Incipient-stage detectors include the following:

Ionization-type detectors:
- Early-warning type; instantaneous response once particles are detected
- Used indoors with low airflow, large particles
- Not used in areas where warm air collects or particles are usually expected
- Require periodic cleaning and recalibration

Gas-sensing fire detectors:
- Early-warning type
- Often used with particulate detector
- Detect combustion gases

Wilson cloud-chamber detectors (see page 367):
- Early-warning type; very sensitive
- Used in museums, data-processing spaces, libraries, clean rooms, facility control rooms
- Detect microscopic particles with few false alarms
- Require piping; quite costly in small installations

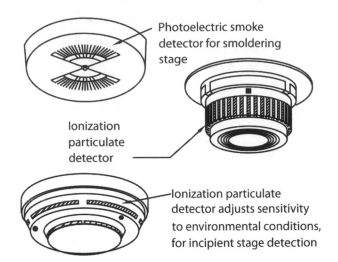

Figure 16-10 Fire detector types. Incipient-stage detectors (right and bottom) are the most sensitive smoke detectors—and are too sensitive for many interior spaces. Most detectors indicate fires at the smoldering stage (upper left).

Smoldering-stage detectors include the following:

Projected-beam photoelectric smoke detectors:
- A beam transmitter and beam receiver on opposite sides of a space detect when the beam is obscured.
- Response is slower than with early-warning detectors.
- They are used in high-ceiling areas, such as atriums, churches, malls, and auditoriums; spaces with medium- to high-velocity airflow; and closed areas with little airflow.
- They can be shielded against dirty, corrosive, humid, very hot, and very cold conditions.
- They are more expensive than other systems.
- They require an unobstructed view.

Scattered-light photoelectric smoke detectors (Tyndall-effect detectors):
- A pulsed light-emitting diode (LED) light beam is reflected from smoke particles and strikes the alarm cell.
- They are used in commercial and high-quality residential applications.
- Low sensitivity to normal dust and dirt accumulation or lamp aging necessitates less maintenance than other smoke detectors.

Laser-beam photoelectric smoke detectors:
- A very high sensitivity laser-diode source gives early warnings.
- These smoke detectors react to light scattered by particles and differentiate between smoke and dust particles.
- They are used in clean environments.

Air-sampling detection systems:
- Piping and fans sample air throughout a space and bring it to a detector for testing.
- Multizone control units reduce the number of false alarms when larger areas are divided into zones.

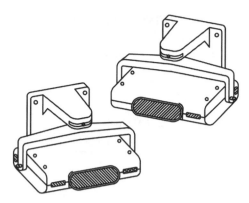

Figure 16-11 Projected beam smoke detectors. Projected beam smoke detectors work in pairs in order to cover the long distances commonly found in atriums, churches, malls, and auditoriums.

Flame-stage detectors include the following:

Ultraviolet (UV)-radiation detectors:
- Long-range, very sensitive; detectors react in milliseconds and respond to most types of fires.
- They are effective at detecting fires of organic materials.
- They are used in highly flammable or explosive storage and work areas.
- UV detectors require rapid fire suppression and building evacuation.
- They can detect reflected UV radiation from walls and ceilings.
- They can be blinded by thick black smoke.

Infrared (IR)-radiation detectors:
- These detectors are used in enclosed spaces, such as sealed storage vaults.
- They detect rapid flaming combustion and CO_2 production and react in seconds.
- IR detectors have less range and lower sensitivity than UV detectors.

Combined UV/IR-radiation detectors:
- They are used in aircraft hangars, fueling stations, and flammable storage areas.
- Combined data reduces the number of false alarms.

Heat-stage detectors include heat-actuated, thermal, thermostatic, or temperature detectors. They are available as spot or linear units:

Spot units:
- are mounted in center of protected area
- respond to hot air convection from fire

Linear units:
- sense heat along entire length of unit
- are used in cable trays and bundles and for large, long equipment
- respond to hot air convection from fire
- detect overheating of surface without presence of fire

Wilson cloud-chamber detectors are sensitive to microscopic particles in the early stages of a fire but are insensitive to dust. They use continuous air sampling and give few false alarms. These detectors require piping and are expensive in small installations. Their price becomes competitive when more than thirty detection points are needed. They are used in such high-value installations as museums, data-processing spaces, libraries, clean rooms, and facility control rooms.

A basic, residential smoke detection system places a listed smoke detector outside and adjacent to each sleeping area, in each sleeping room, and at the head of every stair, with at least one on every level, including the basement. Combined smoke and heat detectors are recommended in the boiler room, kitchen, garage, and attic. An alarm in any smoke detector should set off a fire alarm in all audible and visible units.

Smoke detectors are usually placed 15 to 30 centimeters (6–12 in.) from the ceiling when mounted on a wall. If the alarm is too close to the intersection of the wall and ceiling or too close to a doorway, the air currents may carry smoke and heat past the unit. If unsure, an interior designer should check the proper placement of a smoke detector with the manufacturer or with code officials.

Codes specify which occupancies require smoke detectors but do not always provide specific locations, so an interior designer must determine the best placement. Smoke detectors are subject to false alarms from moisture and particles in the air; in general, the higher the sensitivity of the detector, the higher the number of false alarms. Choosing the appropriate type and avoiding placement where conditions cause problems will limit the number of false alarms. If a smoke alarm must be located in a less-than-ideal location, more than one type of detector should be used, with provisions for extra maintenance and for verification of alarms.

Problems areas for smoke detectors include the following:

- Kitchens, laundries, boiler rooms, shower rooms, and other spaces with high humidity and steam create problems for smoke detectors.
- Repair shops and laboratories with open flames used in their work as well as garages and engine test facilities with exhaust gases affect sensors.
- Smoking rooms and areas near designated smoking areas can be problematic, as can areas with heavy accumulations of dust and dirt.
- High volumes of air movement near loading docks, exit doors, and discharging ducts and registers also pose problems for smoke detectors.
- Locating smoke detectors in areas where normal cooking processes will activate the alarm in kitchens should be avoided.

Most jurisdictions require installation and hard wiring of smoke detectors in residential occupancies and hotel or motel units. Interconnected detectors tied into a building electrical system and with a battery backup are required in many new homes and homes with new additions or alterations. Other homes are required to have at

TABLE 16-4. RESIDENTIAL FIRE DETECTION SYSTEM AND FIRE ALARM SYSTEM COMPONENTS

Component	Description	Location
Detectors	Listed smoke detectors	Outside and adjacent to each sleeping area; in each sleeping room; at head of every stair with at least one on every level, including basement
	Combined smoke and heat detectors	Boiler room, kitchen, garage, attic
	Listed heat detectors	Attic, kitchen, boiler room set at 185°F (85°C); others set at 135°F (57°C)
Alarms	Found in any detector	Alarm produced in all audible and visual units; exterior bell or alarm
Control unit (central panel)	Shuts off oil and gas lines, attic fan; turns on interior and exterior lights, phones in alarm	Annunciated to show location of alarmed device
Backup power	Supervised storage battery with trickle charger	
Wiring	Supervised circuits with trouble alarm that is distinct from fire alarm	

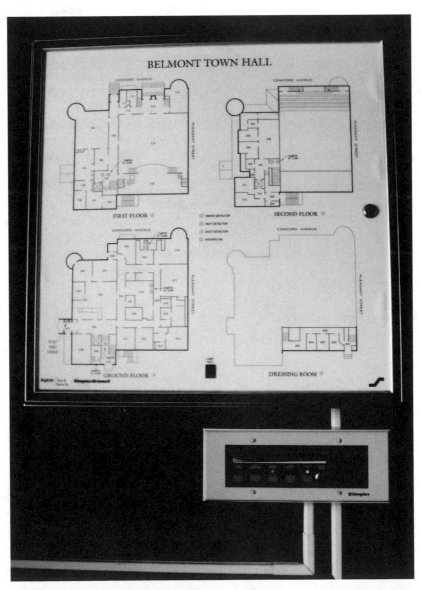

Figure 16-12 Fire alarm control panel. Located immediately inside the main entrance, this set of plans lights up to show the location of activated smoke detectors, heat detectors, duct detectors, and water flow in an emergency. The control box is located directly below.

least battery-operated units. Residences are usually required to have smoke detectors outside each sleeping area and on all habitable floors. Townhouses have even stricter requirements.

Smoke detectors in apartment houses, dormitories, hotels, motels, and rooming houses are governed by NFPA 101 and NFPA 72. Alarm systems are designed to provide early warning and orderly egress at times when building occupants may be asleep. Audible and visual alarms are positioned so that all sleeping persons, including those with vision or hearing impairments, will be wakened. Interior designers should keep in mind that living rooms may be regularly used as sleeping areas. There should be an alarm light over the door of each apartment or suite to indicate the alarm location, especially if the central panel shows only a zone location. In high-rise residential buildings, an emergency voice alarm communication system should be provided.

Smoke detectors should be located in the corridors of multiple-dwelling buildings as well as in service spaces and utility and storage rooms. Battery-powered detectors are not permitted in multiple dwellings. All fire-alarm circuits should have standby power.

All alarms must be identifiable by addressing or annunciation, which indicate the location of the alarm. Annunciator panels that have a map and lights can be located at a system control panel in a building management office or at the lobby desk of a hotel or dormitory. Lobby annunciators are helpful to firefighters.

In apartments, false alarms that result from kitchen smoke and excessive dust are common. Some apartment-building alarm systems provide only a local alarm signaling that the apartment should be evacuated. A separate central heat-detector system sounds a remote alarm. This reduces the number of false alarms but increases the risk of a fire growing before activation of the fire-suppression system or before firefighters are dispatched. Detectors that combine UV and IR radiation are available to lower the risk of false alarms.

Fire Alarm Systems

The goals of a fire alarm system are first to protect life and second to prevent property loss. Systems are tailored to specific building types and uses. A fire alarm system includes equipment that signals a problem, processes the signal, and alerts people to the situation. A fire alarm system can initiate fan controls, smoke venting, smoke-door closers, rolling shutters, and elevator controls as part of an overall fire protection plan.

SIGNALING THE FIRE

Sometimes, an automatic fire detector first detects the fire, discussed directly above. At other times, a person is the first to notice the fire and set off the alarm by using a pull station or telephone.

☑ **New handicapped-accessible types of pull boxes are available that are actually pushed and that take minimal effort to operate. Both regular pull boxes and the newer accessible boxes must be red.**

TABLE 16-5. FIRE PROTECTION EQUIPMENT FOR MULTIPLE DWELLINGS

Component	Description	Location
Alarms	Audible and visual alarms; should be addressable or annunciated	Positioned to waken all sleeping persons (including vision- or hearing-impaired people); living rooms may be regularly used as sleeping areas
Smoke detection	Battery-operated detectors not permitted	Corridors, service spaces, utility and storage rooms
Standby power		In all fire alarm circuits
Annunciators	Identify location of alarm	System control panel in building management office or lobby desk in hotel or dormitory; lobby annunciator for firefighters' use
Alarm light	Indicates location of alarm	Desirable over door of each apartment or suite
Emergency voice-and -alarm communication system	Communicates emergency instructions to occupants	High-rise buildings

TABLE 16-6. PROBLEM AREAS FOR FIRE DETECTION EQUIPMENT

Problem	Areas
High humidity and steam	Kitchens, laundries, boiler rooms, shower rooms
Open flames used in normal work	Repair shops, laboratories
Exhaust gases	Garages, engine testing facilities
Cigarette smoke	Smoking areas and adjacent areas
Heavy dust and dirt accumulation	Manufacturing and construction areas
High air movement	Loading docks, exit doors, areas near discharge from diffusers or registers

Figure 16-13 Manual pull station. Manual fire alarm initiation stations must be placed in the normal path of egress to be used by people as they exit a building. Manual stations must be well marked and easily found. Designers should never specify painting over smoke detectors or other fire-safety equipment because this may hamper their effectiveness by keeping fusible links from melting.

The architect or designer of the fire alarm system must ascertain the current regulations of the jurisdiction before designing the system. In general, the codes specify where manual or automatic fire signaling systems or fire alarm systems are required. The codes specify required systems and provide testing data. An electrical engineer is involved in the design of an extensive fire alarm system.

PROCESSING THE ALARM SIGNAL

In a conventional fire alarm system, detectors and manual stations transmit alarm signals only. All signals are identical, so people have no way to determine if a signal is a false alarm or an alarm malfunction. False alarms occur with all types of detectors. In such places as hospitals, theaters, office buildings, and large dining facilities, false alarms can cause serious disruption, property loss, personal injury, and even death. Continual maintenance checks are required in order to verify that all alarms are working properly; however, they are expensive and time-consuming.

For a residential building, the central panel should show the location of the alarmed device and be designed to shut off the oil and gas lines as well as the attic fan to prevent spread of smoke. The central panel should also turn on the lights inside and outside the residence and automatically ring a neighbor's or a commercial central station's telephone and give a distinctive alarm sound when answered. An outside bell to transmit the alarm is an important feature. A supervised storage battery can provide backup power. Wiring should be on supervised circuits with a trouble alarm to indicate faults that is distinct from the fire alarm.

Because large facilities are difficult and dangerous to evacuate, most of them have fire and evacuation plans that include some type of alarm verification before a general evacuation alarm sounds. Some fire codes permit or even mandate alarm verification. Verification systems require the activation of a minimum of two detectors in a single area. The detector on a remotely set alarm must repeat its alarm after being reset. By requiring a minimal alarm time, false alarms that result from smoke puffs are eliminated. A physical inspection of the site may be required to eliminate the possibility of a false alarm. This requires knowing the exact location of detectors, so they need to be grouped in zones with an annunciator that indicates the location

Fire alarm signal processing uses a control panel to start the audible and visible alarm circuits, illuminate the annunciator panels, and control fans and door releases. Control panels can be

TABLE 16-7. FIRE ALARM DEFINITIONS AND TERMS

Term	Definition
Addressable detector	Smoke or fire detector that identifies location when communicating alarm and indicates "OK," "Trouble," or "Alarm" when tested
Alarm signal	Audible and/or visual signal indicating fire emergency and, usually, need to evacuate building
Alarm verification	Such techniques as minimum alarm time or repeat alarm after reset intended to reduce number of false alarms
Control unit (fire alarm panel)	Controls and related equipment necessary to furnish power to fire alarm system, receive and process signals, and electrically supervise system's circuitry.
Listed or listing	Inclusion of device in list published by testing organization, such as UL; indicates that device meets referenced standard's requirements
Manual system	Alarm-initiating device operated manually to produce alarm signal
Private mode	Alarm system that relies on specifically trained personnel to react to alarm signal
Public mode	Alarm system that alerts all protected spaces and occupants audibly and/or visually
Station fire alarm	Manually operated alarm-initiated device that emits either continuous (noncoded) signal or series of coded pulses

TABLE 16-8 TYPES OF FIRE ALARM SYSTEMS

Classification	Type	Description	Uses
Household fire warning systems			Residential
Protected premises systems (local alarm)		Sounds alarm only locally; notification to fire department manually; may automatically initiate fire-suppression system	Privately owned facilities
Off-premises systems with local alarms	Auxiliary fire-alarm system	Local system with direct connection to municipal fire-alarm box	Public buildings including schools, government offices, museums
	Remote-station protective signaling system	Similar to auxiliary system, with telephone line to police or staffed answering service	Private buildings, such as stores and offices that are unoccupied for extended periods
	Proprietary fire-alarm system	Manned, on-site central supervisory station receives signals from all buildings	Large multiple-building facilities, including universities and manufacturing facilities
	Central-station fire-alarm system	Similar to proprietary, but equipment is owned and operated by service company	Supervises many unrelated local systems for fee

both simple and reliable. However, with system growth, they can become heavy, complex, and expensive. Panels can become large and bulky, and changes may be difficult. Troubleshooting is often faulty and time-consuming, and false alarms may be difficult to locate quickly. Because of these problems, addressable control systems were developed.

With an addressable fire alarm system, each detector is a separate zone that can be identified centrally, with up to 100 detectors on one line. The detectors are continually checked from a central panel to determine whether they are working and on standby, are signaling an alarm, or are experiencing trouble. It is easy to confirm an alarm with an addressable system, so false alarms are reduced. The system records any decrease in detector sensitivity or malfunction. The initial hardware costs of such systems are higher than those of a conventional control panel, but maintenance costs are lower.

A firefighters' command post, which is usually in the building lobby, should have two-way active communication access to a minimum of one fire station per floor, all mechanical equipment rooms, elevator machine rooms, and air-handling fan rooms. The system should include a visual display of all fire alarm devices, including sprinkler valves, fire pump status, emergency generator status, and water-flow indicators. The control center houses controls for any automatic stair door locking system that provides security access. The location indicators and operation and capture controls for the elevators and controls for smoke doors and dampers should also be included. In addition, the system should provide a means to test circuits and devices.

Firefighters' communication systems that provide verbal contact between the fire command center and firefighters are usually required for high-rise construction. They are also required in large structures in which a portable radio carried by a firefighter may not reliably penetrate the building. The communications system is a simple intercom system at all stair-tower doors and at each elevator lobby, and may include a telephone jack for the firefighters' telephones.

INDICATING THE ALARM

Each required exit must have a fire alarm that is not more than 1.5 meters (5 ft.) from the entrance to the exit in order to help occupants locate the exit during an emergency. Water-flow switches in sprinklers can be used to set off an alarm and can show up on a sprinkler alarm panel.

Audible signals have minimum sound levels for public and private spaces. Setting these levels is a highly technical process and requires an acoustic analysis of the space, the occupancy,

Figure 16-14 Audible and visual fire alarm. The ADA requires handicapped-accessible warning systems to be both audible and visual and establishes requirements for the type of system and specific locations. When required, alarms must be provided in each restroom, hallway, and lobby as well as in other common-use areas, such as meeting rooms, break rooms, examination rooms and classrooms. In occupancies with multiple sleeping units, a predetermined percentage of the units must be equipped with both a visible and an audible alarm.

and the characteristics of various devices. Alarm bells must not be placed inside a suspended ceiling.

Visible signals are required primarily for hearing-impaired people. These may be lighted signs that flash "FIRE" above alarm bells or rotating beacons or strobe lights. Manufacturers use a variety of names for visible fire alarms, including visible alarm signals, visible signal devices, visible signaling appliances, and visual-notification appliances. Strobe lights are usually xenon flashtubes that flash at an interval that minimizes problems for people with photosensitive epilepsy. Careful placement of visual signals also helps prevent problems. These signals must be visible from any point in a space regardless of the viewer's orientation. The maximum distance between strobes is 30 meters (100 ft.). When visible alarms are required, they must be placed in more locations than audible alarms because they require direct sight lines.

Because fire truck ladders cannot reach the upper floors of tall buildings and walking down stairs filled with many people is very difficult, voice alarm systems are required by almost all major cities for high-rise construction. A voice alarm issues specific instructions to occupants of each part of a building about areas of refuge and the progress of rescue efforts. Voice alarms are also very good in any large building where people may not be familiar with the building, evacuation procedures, or the alarm system. This includes hotels and convention centers, where visitors often ignore or misunderstand bells and horns.

High-rise office buildings require emergency voice alarm communication systems. Such systems should allow full control of transmission and building-wide distribution of all tones, alarm signals, and voice announcements on a selective or all-call basis. Alert tones, signals, and prerecorded messages on independent channels should be distributed to selected areas over a building-wide system of loudspeakers. A voice-alarm system either can use a standard public-address (PA) system independent of the fire alarm system or can be electronically supervised and an integral part of the fire alarm system. Messages may be prerecorded or live. The system must have adequate sound quality for clarity.

In schools, particularly elementary schools, rapid, orderly evacuation is essential. Fire gongs should not sound similar to program gongs, and the system must be arranged to facilitate fire drills.

In factories, large storage facilities, and other hazardous occupancies, fire alarm systems are tied to an audio system. This intercom system directs occupants out of the building and may also indicate the location of the emergency. Industrial facilities have manually controlled alarm stations at points of egress and horns instead of bells or gongs because of the high noise level.

Integrating fire safety into a building requires coordination among the architect, engineers, interior designer, and other members of the design team. In Part VII: Acoustics, a variety of building conditions that are directly affected by an interior designer's decisions will be discussed.

PART
VII

....

ACOUSTICS

The quality of the sound in a building depends on many factors, some of which originate in the building's siting and architectural design. According to *Mechanical and Electrical Equipment for Buildings* (Benjamin Stein et al., John Wiley & Sons, Hoboken, NJ, 2006, p. 729):

> Achieving good acoustics, however, has become increasingly difficult for a variety of reasons. To lower construction costs, the weight of various materials used in many of today's buildings has been reduced from those prevalent 25–50–100 years ago. Since light structures generally transmit sound more readily than heavy ones, lightweight buildings bring the potential for major acoustical problems. Population density in office spaces has steadily increased, thus raising the amount of noise generated. Worse yet—from the acoustics point of view—many offices today are designed as open areas with, at best, only thin partial-height dividers (cubicles) separating workers. Forty percent or more of a building budget may be allocated for mechanical systems—most of which generate noise. Outside noise sources, such as cars, trucks, trains, and airplanes, can also present problems and require isolation of interior spaces from exterior sounds.

Interior designers are in an excellent position to deal with some of these problems. As designers of office spaces, they must have an awareness of acoustic principles and remedies. Even noises propagated by a building's structure and mechanical systems as well as noises from the outside can be ameliorated by effective acoustic design.

17

Acoustic Design Principles

Interior designers develop an intense awareness of the visual qualities of the spaces they occupy. They notice and comment on the colors, materials, lines, forms, and patterns they see. Their work involves selecting and manipulating materials for the visual effect. Interior designers also design beauty for the eye of the beholder.

Although interior designers' experience the world in a strongly visual way, they are often deeply affected by messages received by their other senses as well. Perhaps the most critical of these is the sense of hearing. Sound in a well-designed space reinforces the function of the space and supports the occupants' experience. A poorly designed acoustic environment hinders both the function and the enjoyment of the space, and it can even damage the health of the user.

Acoustics is the branch of physics that involves the production, control, transmission, reception, and effects of sound. **Acoustical design** is the planning, shaping, finishing, and furnishing of an enclosed space to establish an acoustic environment that is necessary for the distinct hearing of speech or musical sounds. Understanding how people hear sound and how sound interacts with the built environment helps interior designers create spaces that are as acoustically pleasing as they are visually rich.

Sound can be defined as a physical wave, a mechanical vibration, or a series of pressure variations in an elastic medium. Perhaps the best definition of sound for our purposes is an audible pressure variation.

Sound is induced through the ear by means of waves of varying air pressure emanating from a vibrating source. In order for sound to exist, there must be a source, a transmission path, and a receiver. So, technically, when a tree falls in a forest and no one is there to hear it, there is no sound.

ACOUSTIC DESIGN

The history of modern acoustics began with the design of the Fogg Art Museum Lecture Hall at Harvard University in Cambridge, Massachusetts. When the building was erected in 1895, the acoustics of the main lecture hall space were a disaster, and the space could not be used for lectures. Wallace Clement Sabine, a 27-year-old new assistant professor in the physics department, was asked to find a solution. He started by considering the age-old problem of why the acoustics of some rooms were good, while others were mediocre or impossible.

Sabine isolated himself from his colleagues in the physics department and worked with two lab assistants late in the evening and early in the morning to avoid the impact of street noise and the vibrations from the newly constructed Harvard Square subway line. He had promised the university authorities to return everything to normal each morning by class time, so he and his assistants dragged hundreds of upholstered seat cushions from the nearby Sanders Theater to the lecture hall after midnight each night and back again at dawn. Sabine studied and measured the sound quality of similar spaces. He used his ears and a stopwatch to measure the length of reverberations from organ pipes.

Through his efforts, Sabine was able to develop **reverberation** equations and **absorption coefficients** for many common building materials. He discovered that the reverberation time of a room is directly proportional to the cubic volume of the room and inversely proportional to the **sound absorption** provided at the room's boundary surfaces and by the room's furnishings. His equation uses the simple dimensions of the room and absorption coefficients of materials to determine the acoustic effect of the space, offering a simple method for architects to determine favorable room proportions and treatments.

Thanks to Sabine's recommendations, the Fogg Lecture Hall was reopened in 1898. Sabine then went on to work as acoustic consultant for Boston Symphony Hall. His input resulted in one of the world's best concert halls.

Incidentally, the Fogg Lecture Hall satisfied Sabine but remained unpopular with the faculty who lectured there. In 1912, the hall was reduced in size from around 400 to 200 seats and redesigned with a semicircular wall and flat floor. By World War II, much of the curved wall was covered with hair felt (felt made of animal hair) and perforated asbestos board. In the 1960s, the floor was carpeted, but students complained of a whispering-gallery effect and difficulty hearing at some locations. In 1972, the wall was covered with highly absorbent glass fiberboard, and a large canopy was added at the front, which finally improved intelligibility. Ironically, the space was demolished in 1973. However, it was tested first, and the curved wall and domed ceiling were found to be the cause of the intelligibility problems.

The Fogg Lecture Hall is a lesson not only in the development of the art and science of acoustics, but also is a reminder of both how difficult it can be to remedy a space that is initially built with poor proportions and how inexact the process of acoustic design can be. It is much, much easier to design a well-proportioned and properly finished space than to remedy a bad design once the building is complete. It is difficult if not impossible to retrofit a proper acoustic design without substantial structural alterations. Solutions to acoustic problems depend on experienced judgment and common sense, along with at least a conceptual understanding of the basic properties of sound, how it is propagated throughout building spaces, and how various building materials and construction systems influence it.

WAVELENGTHS AND FREQUENCIES

A vibrating object radiates sound waves outward from the source equally in all directions until they hit a surface that either reflects or absorbs them. Sound waves have peaks and valleys, similar to ocean waves. The distance between the peak of one sound wave and the peak of the next is called the **wavelength**.

Perceiving a sound as high or low depends on its **frequency**. The peaks in sound waves will pass a stationary point at different rates. A high-pitched sound has peaks that pass at a higher frequency (more frequently), while the peaks of a lower-pitched sound pass at a lower frequency (less frequently). The frequency with which these peaks pass a given point is measured as the number of **cycles** completed per second, in **Hertz (Hz)**. One Hertz equals one cycle per second, so a wave whose peaks pass at 50 cycles per second has a frequency of 50 Hertz.

High-pitched sounds have higher frequencies than low-pitched sounds. High frequency corresponds to a short wavelength. Bass notes have lower frequencies; low frequency and long wavelengths go together. Frequency is an important variable in how a sound is transmitted or absorbed and must be taken into account when designing the acoustics of a building.

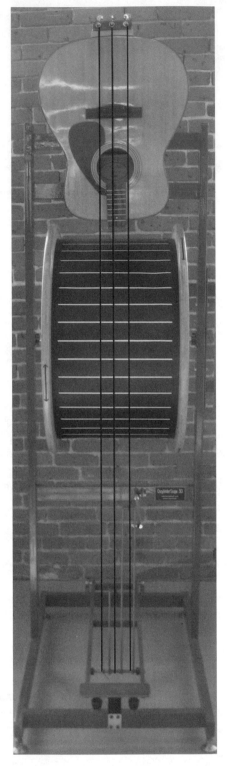

Figure 17-1 Guitar string sound waves. This educational display at the SEE Science Center in Manchester, New Hampshire, illustrates how linear sources radiate sound waves. The museum visitor strums the strings, which makes them vibrate and simultaneously sets the drum spinning. When the drum spins, a wave pattern appears; the visitor's eye momentarily retains the vibrating string images and their brain combines a series of images into the illusion of a wave pattern. Changing the thickness or length of the strings changes the frequency of the vibration.

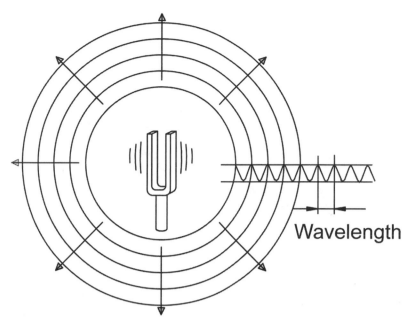

Figure 17-2 Wavelength. People can hear wavelengths of sounds that vary from more than 15.25 meters (50 ft.) for very low pitches to less than 25 millimeters (1 in.) for very high pitches.

THE EAR

If you have ever tried to draw someone's ear, you will have noticed that people's ears are as individual as their fingerprints. They are small and large, simple and convoluted, smooth and fuzzy—and even hairy, but all healthy ears have the same parts.

The structures of the human ear enable people to collect sound waves, which are then converted into nerve impulses. The outer ear is an efficient sound-gathering funnel but lacks the collecting and focusing capacity of a cat's ear.

In the middle ear, sound waves set the eardrum (tympanic membrane) in motion. At the threshold of hearing, the displacement of air molecules on the eardrum and the eardrum movement are approximately equal to the diameter of an atom. If the human ear were one order of magnitude more sensitive, we would be able to hear thermal noise, the noise generated by the agitation of electrons in a conductor. The sensitivity of our ears is close to the practical limit for sound reception. The average human ear can withstand the loudest sounds of nature, yet be able to detect the tiny pressures of barely audible sounds.

The middle ear is an air-filled space surrounded by bone and bounded by two membranes: the eardrum on the outer side and a flexible membrane that separates it from the inner ear on the inner side. The primary function of the middle ear is amplification. The vibrations from the eardrum are transmitted across the middle-ear space by three tiny levers of bone to the extraordinarily sensitive inner-ear mechanism (**cochlea**). The three bones, called the ossicles, are the malleus (hammer), incus (anvil), and stapes (stirrup). The movement of each bone increases the amplification of sound. The footplate of the stirrup bone is attached to a flexible membrane that covers an opening into the inner ear called the oval window. Moving back and forth like a piston, the stirrup

bone sets in motion the fluids of the inner ear. In the short but intricate journey from the eardrum to the inner ear, the sound wave is amplified as much as 25 times.

In the inner ear, sound vibrations are converted to electrical nerve impulses for interpretation by the brain. The rhythmic waves in the inner-ear fluid are set in motion by the stirrup bone's pressure on the oval window. They excite a highly delicate organ that is at the heart of sound reception. Coiled like a snail shell (its name, cochlea, is from the Latin word for snail), it is sometimes described as a spiral piano keyboard. Hair cells at one end of the keyboard respond to sounds at high frequencies, up to 20,000 cycles per second; those at the opposite end respond to lower frequencies, down to 16 cycles per second. The receptors for low tones are at the innermost turn of the spiral. The basilar membrane in the cochlea resonates at one end at a frequency of 20 Hertz and at the other end at 20 kiloHertz (kHz). This range of 20 Hertz to 20 kiloHertz establishes the range of frequencies that the human ear can hear.

As the vibrations of the hammer shake the hair cells of the cochlea, anvil, and stirrup, they initiate an electrical impulse that is transmitted to the nerve fibers, which then merge into the auditory nerve. These impulses are carried to the central auditory pathways of the brain and ultimately to the cerebral cortex, where their pattern is interpreted as sound.

Young people whose ears are in excellent physical condition can hear sounds in the 20 to 20,000-Hertz range; they will be most sensitive to frequencies in the 3000 to 4000-Hertz range. Very high frequencies may be uncomfortable for young listeners, who may be very sensitive to the sound of, for example, high-speed dental drills. A person's ability to hear higher frequencies decreases with age. By middle age, the typical upper limit is around 10 to 12 kHz. Upper-range hearing loss is usually more pronounced in men than in women.

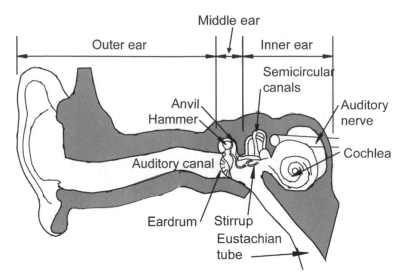

Figure 17-3 Structures of the ear. Sound travels from the outer ear through the auditory canal, which is also called the external ear canal, and into the middle ear.

The human ear can pick out specific sounds to which a person wants to pay attention, but more frequently, it combines sounds that are distinct from each other in frequency and phase, such as musical chords. Most sounds are actually complex combinations of frequencies. Musical tones combine fundamental frequencies with **harmonics** (overtones). A trained conductor can distinguish a single instrument in a 120-piece orchestra. Amazingly, people have the ability to pick out one voice in background noise much louder than that voice, a phenomenon that is known as the cocktail party effect.

Speech is composed of sounds in the 125- to 8000-Hertz range, with most spoken sound in the 200- to 5000-Hertz range. Most of the information in speech is carried in the higher frequencies, which is why people tend to listen most attentively to higher pitches. However, most of the acoustic energy is in the lower frequencies (think of the way you can feel the beat of a bass drum in your stomach). For sounds of equal energy, the human ear is less sensitive to low frequencies than to middle and high frequencies. The human voice consists of a fundamental frequency in the range of 100 to 600 Hertz, plus harmonics up to 7500 Hertz.

Telephone and radio signals use lower-frequency bands than the human ear can hear. The loss of information in the limited-frequency range results in loss of voice quality and intelligibility.

SPEECH

The vibration of people's vocal cords produces human speech. These vibrations are modified through the throat, nose, and mouth. Each sound that makes up speech lasts only one-fiftieth to one-thirtieth of a second.

Most of the sounds in speech fall in the range of 100 to 600 Hertz. Many consonants, however, have the most energy at much higher frequencies and must be heard clearly for maximum intelligibility. In English, most information is carried in the conso-

nants, not the vowels. The sounds "s" and "sh" have their greatest energy above 2 kHz, and both are important in conveying information. Male voices center around 500 Hertz, while female voices are usually around 900 Hertz. High frequencies carry sound with a greater sense of direction and can be heard around a barrier more easily than lower frequencies. In addition, high frequencies are the most easily absorbed.

LOUDNESS

The human ear is sensitive to a very large range of sound power, which is measured in acoustical watts. A source's acoustical magnitude is a measure of the power of sound and may be called sound power, sound pressure, and sound intensity, depending on the type of power that is being measured. Although there are technical differences between these terms, the term **sound power** will be used here.

The way people experience a change in loudness is subjective; it is not related in a linear way to sound power. A sound that people perceive as twice as loud as another sound is actually much more than twice as powerful.

The loudness of sounds is measured in a way that relates actual sound intensity to the way humans experience sound. Loudness is measured according to a mathematical logarithmic scale of **decibels (db)**. A decibel is a unit for expressing the relative pressure or intensity of sounds on a uniform scale from zero decibels for the least perceptible sound, to around 130 decibels for the average threshold of pain. People hear a doubling of sound pressure and intensity not as twice as loud, but as a barely perceptible change.

A person's perception of a sound's loudness depends both on the power of the sound and on the distance from the source of the sound to the ear. Every time the sound power is doubled, the actual sound-intensity level changes 3 decibels. When the distance from the source of the sound is doubled, the sound-intensity level changes 6 decibels. Decibel levels from two sound sources cannot be added mathematically; the decibel scale is logarithm. For example, 60 decibels plus 60 decibels equals 63 decibels, not 120 decibels.

A **sone** is an alternative unit of perceived loudness that lacks the high precision needed for scientific work, but which is sometimes used to rate building equipment. A doubling of sones sounds to the human ear like a doubling of sound pressure.

Because people are not equally sensitive to all frequencies within the human audible range, they can hear only certain frequencies at the lowest levels of loudness. In the range of 3000 to 4000 Hertz, people can hear sounds even at minus 5 decibels. The most information in human speech is found between 3000 Hertz and 4000 Hertz, so people are adept at listening for very quiet speech. Sensitivity drops off at low decibel levels, especially at low frequencies. This is why most amplifiers provide a boost for bass sounds at lower volumes. At the **threshold of hearing** at zero decibels, people can hear only at 1000 Hertz.

The upper limit for loudness is between 120 decibels and 130 decibels. This level of sound intensity is high enough to produce the sensation of pain in the human ear that is called the **threshold of pain**. At this level, people experience pain at all frequencies.

140 dB
Threshold of pain
Jet engine at 75 feet

120 dB
Jet takeoff at 300 feet
Loudest rock band

105 dB
Tree chipper

95 dB
Popular music group

80 dB
Heavy truck
Average street traffic

70 dB
Conversational speech maximums

60 dB
Active business office

30 dB
Quiet living room
Empty concert hall

15 dB
Rustle of leaves

0 dB
Threshold of hearing

Figure 17-4 Decibel levels. The decibel scale uses whole numbers to measure the increase of sound levels. Ten decibel units equal a doubling of loudness, so 30 decibels are twice as loud as 20 decibels, and 70 decibels are twice as loud as 60 decibels. When the change in decibels is 20 decibels, the loudness is doubled twice, so 30 decibels are four times as loud as 10 decibels.

SOUND WAVES

Sound waves travel at different velocities depending on the medium they are traveling through. Sound travels through air at around 0.3 kilometers (km) (1087 ft.) per second at sea level. Sound travels through water more rapidly than it does through air, at around 1.4 kilometers (4500 ft.) per second. Through wood, sound moves at about 3.6 kilometers (11,700 ft.) per second; sound moves through steel at around 5.5 kilometers (18,000 ft.) per second.

Sound waves radiate spherically from a point source. A point source, like a tuning fork, is relatively small compared with the wavelength produced. A line source, such as the string of a violin, creates cylindrical waves. Large, vibrating surfaces, such as the heads of large drums, create plane waves. When sound originates from a source like the human voice, it radiates more strongly in some directions than in others.

Sound energy, like heat energy, can be absorbed or reflected by objects. The ground, building surfaces, and other objects interact with sound waves with which they come in contact. Because of the complexity of these interactions, sound fields in the real world cannot be described by simple mathematical expressions.

How much sound energy is absorbed or reflected by a surface has a significant effect on what a person hears within a space. When little sound is absorbed and a great deal is reflected, sounds are mixed together. When steady sounds are mixed together, they accumulate in a **reverberant field** and produce a noisy space. In a reverberant space, speech becomes less intelligible, but music may sound better. Conversely, when much of the sound energy is absorbed and little is reflected, the room sounds quiet for speech but may sound dead to music.

Reflected Sound

The lengths of sound waves for audible frequencies vary from 15 meters (50 ft.) for very low pitches to less than a few millimeters (less than 1 in.) for very high pitches. When a sound wave strikes a surface that is large in comparison to the wavelength, a portion of the sound energy is reflected (like light from a mirror) and a portion is absorbed. The harder and more rigid a surface the sound wave strikes, the more sound is reflected. **Reflected sound** leaves a surface at an angle equal to the angle at which it strikes it.

Figure 17-5 Piano strings. Piano strings, like guitar strings, are linear sound sources that create cylindrical waves. The harp of the piano interweaves these waves, which, in turn, vibrate the piano's large surface to create plane waves that spread throughout the listening area.

REVERBERATION

Reverberation is the persistence of sound after the source of the sound has ceased; this is the result of repeated reflections. Reverberation affects both the intelligibility of speech and the quality of music. The **reverberation time** of a space is the amount of time that sound bounces around a room before dying out to an inaudible level. It is also defined as the time required for sound energy to decay 60 decibels, or to one millionth of its initial intensity.

The reverberation time of a room should be appropriate to the use of the space. For speech in offices and small rooms, a reverberation time of between 0.3 and 0.6 seconds is desirable. The reverberation time for auditoriums ranges from 1.5 to 1.8 seconds. The quality of the sound can be controlled by modifying the amount of absorptive or reflective finishes in a space.

The reverberation of sounds in lecture halls, theaters, houses of worship, and concert halls sustains and blends sounds, making them much smoother and richer than they would be in open air. Short reverberation times are best for speech because they allow clarity for consonant sounds. However, some reverberation enriches a speaker's voice and gives the speaker some sense of how well his or her voice is carrying to the audience.

Music benefits from longer reverberation times that extend and blend the sounds of instruments and voices. Music sounds dead and brittle with too short a reverberation time, but it loses clarity and definition when the reverberation time is too long.

ATTENUATION

Sound energy lessens in intensity as it disperses over a wide area. **Attenuation** is the decrease in energy or pressure for each unit area of a sound wave. Attenuation occurs when the distance from the source increases as a result of absorption, scattering, or spreading in three dimensions.

SOUND REINFORCEMENT

Natural (as opposed to electronic) **sound reinforcement** is the amplification of a sound being heard from various reflections as well as directly from the source. Covering the ceilings of meeting rooms, classrooms, and auditoriums completely with sound-absorbing material eliminates the potential for sound-reinforcing reflections off the ceiling and may result in inadequate sound levels in the rear of the room. Having to install an electronic **sound-reinforcing system** can be avoided by leaving the center of the room as a reflecting surface.

ECHOES

In very large halls, the delay in receiving the sound from multiple reflections causes echoes and produces confusing sound. **Echoes** result when repetitions of a sound are produced by the reflection of sound waves from a surface that are loud enough and received late enough to be perceived as distinct from the source.

A clear echo is caused when reflected sound reaches a listener from 50 to 80 milliseconds after the listener has heard the

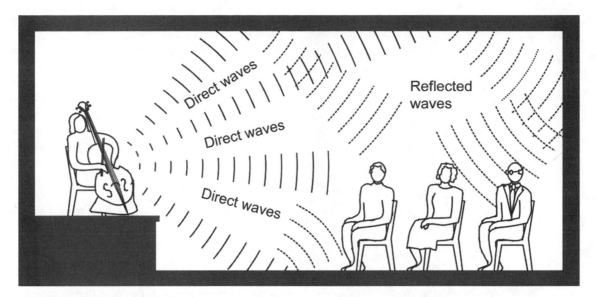

Figure 17-6 Reverberation. The sound in a room is a combination of direct sound from the source and reflected sound from walls and other obstructions. The human ear senses reverberation as a mixture of previous and more recent sounds. The reverberation time is longer in a room with a larger volume, as the distances between reflections are longer. When sound-absorbing materials are added to a space, the reverberation time decreases as sounds are absorbed.

direct sound. Echoes are undesirable even if they are not distinct because they make speech less intelligible and cause music to sound muddled. Frequently, auditoriums produce echoes between the back wall and the ceiling above the proscenium. Echoes may occur when parallel surfaces are more than 18 meters (60 ft.) apart.

☑ **Echoes can be avoided through the careful planning of a room's geometry or the selective use of absorptive surfaces. Absorbing the sound energy in echoes wastes energy that can be redirected to places where it becomes useful reinforcement. It is useful to allow natural sound reinforcement along short paths and to absorb sound at excessive distances.**

FLUTTER

When sound waves are rapidly reflected back and forth between two parallel flat or concave surfaces, an effect called flutter can result. **Flutter** is a rapid succession of echoes with sufficient time between each reflection for a listener to be aware of separate, discrete signals. People perceive flutter as a buzzing or clicking sound.

Flutter often occurs between shallow domes and hard flat floors. The remedy for flutter is to change either the shape of the reflecting surfaces or their parallel relationship. An alternative solution is to add absorptive materials to the space. The best solution depends on the reverberant requirements of the space, the cost of corrections, and the aesthetics of the result.

STANDING WAVES

Standing waves operate on the same principle and are caused the same way that flutters are, but they are heard differently.

Standing waves are perceived as points of quiet and of maximum sound in a room. Certain frequencies of voice or music are exaggerated as they bounce back and forth repeatedly between opposite parallel walls. When the walls are exactly half a wavelength apart, the tone is very loud near the walls and very quiet halfway between them because the waves cancel each other out in the center of the space.

Standing waves must be avoided in rooms for music performance, but the problem presents only an annoyance for speech. Standing-wave problems in rooms with parallel walls are improved by slightly tilting or skewing two of the walls or by adding acoustic absorptive material to one wall. Rooms for music rehearsals and broadcast studios often have nonparallel walls, and undulating ceilings are also used. The proportions of a room can minimize the effect, which is especially noticeable for bass frequencies.

FOCUSING AND CREEP

When sounds are reflected from a concave surface, they may converge at a single point. This is called **focusing**. The sound is greatly reinforced at the focal point and is less loud elsewhere.

A space with concave surfaces can become a **whispering gallery**. This is a room in which two people can stand at two related focal points of curved surfaces and hear each other's whispers with startling loudness and clarity while remaining unheard by other people in the space.

DIFFUSION AND DIFFRACTION

Convex surfaces scatter sound, reinforcing sound levels in all parts of a room. **Diffusion** occurs when sound is reflected from a

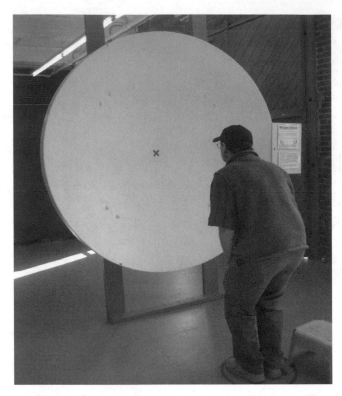

Figure 17-7 Whisper dish: focusing. A person speaking quietly and directly into the center of this disc from a designated spot can be heard clearly in front of a second concave surface across the room. Spaces with concave domes, vaults, or walls focus reflected sound into certain areas of rooms. Focusing deprives some listeners of useful sound reflections and causes intense sound spots at other positions.

convex surface. Flat horizontal and inclined reflectors produce some diffusion as well. Diffusion produces a sound level that remains fairly constant throughout a space, which is a very desirable quality for music performance.

When a sound wave strikes an object that is smaller than or similar in dimension to its wavelength, it is diffracted, and the wave is scattered around the object. **Diffraction**, the ability to be heard beyond a barrier, is measured by the amount that airborne sound waves are bent by moving around an obstacle in their path.

Absorbed Sound

Materials do not reflect or absorb sound perfectly; there is always at least an insignificant amount absorbed by any reflecting material or reflected by an absorbent one.

☑ **Absorbed sound is one of the chief acoustic techniques used by interior designers. Soft, porous materials absorb a large proportion of the sound energy that strikes them. When sound is absorbed, the sound energy flows through the material as heat. Greater thicknesses of porous materials are required to absorb lower frequencies. Thin-fabric wall coverings absorb only frequencies near or above the top of the audible range of the human ear. Padded carpet and thick drapery absorb the majority of sound waves in a higher proportion of the audible range.**

Sound Masking

Studies confirm that poor office acoustics in open-plan offices is the most common barrier to the productive use of office space.

Figure 17-8 Creep. The reflection of sound along a curved surface from a source near the surface is called creep. The sound can be heard at points along the surface but is inaudible away from the surface.

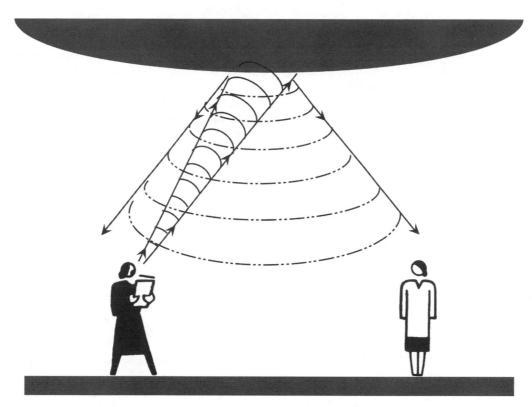

Figure 17-9 Diffusion. A convex surface overhead helps distribute a speaker's voice clearly over a larger area than would otherwise be possible.

Figure 17-10 Water sound masking. The sound of water flowing changes with the amount of turbulence it encounters along the way. Here, the smooth sheet (on the right) is much quieter and calmer than the rapids-like flow (on the left).

People are sensitive to sounds that are louder than the background sound, and they are especially aware of speech that is intelligible over the rest of the sounds in a room.

When two separate sound sources are perceived simultaneously, they tend to obscure each other. This phenomenon is called **sound masking**. Sound masking introduces a nonintrusive, ambient background sound into the environment that renders speech unintelligible, so that it does not call undue attention to itself. Sound masking helps ensure speech privacy, reduces stress and absenteeism, and creates a better work environment.

Masking is most effective when two sounds are close in frequency; in this situation, it is harder for the human ear to tell them apart. Background noise that is used for masking unwanted sounds is **broadband** (containing many frequencies), continuous, and without intelligible information. This helps cover both lower- and higher-frequency sounds.

Musical Sounds

Musical sounds are usually of longer duration than speech sounds. They encompass a much broader range of frequencies and sound pressures than other sounds; this is particularly true of instrumental music.

Musical instruments often produce very high frequencies in high-pitched overtones. Some large pipe organs produce pitches with frequencies near the extreme lower end of the hearing range.

Musical sound often depends on **resonance**. Sometimes, a vibration in one object produces sympathetic vibrations of exactly the same period in a neighboring body. Resonance occurs when sound is intensified and prolonged by sympathetic vibration.

Noise

Noise is simply defined as any unwanted sound. This is a subjective judgment; one person's noise is another person's music. Children yelling while they play and run around the yard is reassuring and welcome to the parent who is keeping track of their whereabouts, but it may be a disturbing noise to a neighbor who is trying to get some sleep before working the night shift.

The amount of annoyance produced by unwanted sound is subjective, psychological, and proportional to the loudness of the noise. The most annoying sounds are high-frequency rather than low-frequency sounds as well as intermittent rather than continuous noise. Pure tones are more conspicuous than broadband sounds. A sound that is moving and without a fixed location tends to be distracting. Finally, sounds bearing information are harder to ignore than nonsense noise.

The types of sound that can constitute noise are extremely varied. Speech or music may sometimes be considered noise. Natural sounds, such as wind and rain, may be pleasant or disturbing. Mechanical sounds, such as engines, gears, fans, tires on pavement, squealing brakes, buzzing electronic equipment, and banging pipes, are commonly considered to be noise.

Engineers use **noise-criteria (NC) curves** to represent the amount of sound pressure at various frequencies that is acceptable for background noises in various environments. Higher noise levels are permitted at lower frequencies since the human ear is less sensitive to sounds in lower frequencies. Outside the United States, a similar measurement is called **noise-rating (NR) curves**.

NC curves are not well defined in very low and very high frequencies. The American Society of Heating, Refrigerating and Air-Conditioning Engineers (ASHRAE) has developed similar curves called **room-criteria (RC) curves**. These curves are used to evaluate the acceptability of background mechanical system noise for typical space types.

The Designer's Role

When designing a building, an architect and interior designer must recognize potential noise problems and take steps to solve them. The acoustic design of the building should be integrated with other architectural requirements. By carefully planning the building's siting and structure, the architect can reduce noise penetration into the building. The overall building design and function should be reviewed in terms of desirable acoustic qualities. Noise sources should be placed as far as possible from quiet areas. The internal acoustics of individual rooms must be reviewed. For special acoustic issues, an acoustic consultant should be brought into the process as early as possible.

The amount of necessary acoustic treatment can be reduced by limiting sources of noise. When designing for an existing building, the architect and interior designer must first define the character of the sound problem. For new buildings, they have to imagine what noise sources can be anticipated. All parts of the building and its surfaces are potential paths for sound travel. The design team can compare the costs and coordinate the work of the construction trades to get the most cost-effective combination of modified sound sources and acoustic treatments.

Acoustic consultants are most commonly called in for buildings where loud noise is a special problem or where the quality of interior sound is critical. Opera houses and concert halls, as well as theaters and places of worship, have essential acoustic criteria. Classrooms, lecture halls, libraries, and music-practice rooms greatly benefit from effective acoustic design. All types of residential structures, including apartment buildings, hotels, and multiple-family and single-family residences are improved by sensitivity to acoustic problems. Airports and other transportation structures need to block noise from the outside, and athletic buildings and sports stadiums should control the noise produced within. Other commercial and industrial buildings also benefit from the expertise of an acoustic designer.

Acoustic consultants play a role in selection of materials and the details of construction components. They also influence the selection and use of interior surface materials. Their work has direct implications for interior designers. Acoustic consultants also design and specify sound and communications systems, and they detail components for noise and vibration controls in mechanical systems.

Ongoing interdisciplinary research in architecture, neuroscience, psychology, music, theater, engineering, speech, and other fields is developing methods to evaluate, model, predict, and simulate the acoustic qualities of a building. These methods are expected to be available for evaluating specific rooms in a building through **acoustic modeling** and aural simulation. New materials are being developed to diffuse sound in predictable ways.

Modern instrumentation and extensive testing of building materials and construction details provide information on their ability to block **sound transmission**. New methods for testing noise from impacts on flooring systems are also being developed. Studies on how to reduce plumbing system noise are underway. Duct linings, which reduce heating, ventilation, and air conditioning-(HVAC) system noise, are being studied for their effect on health. The acoustic qualities of air conditioning noise are being studied to refine the design criteria for acceptable equipment noise. Advances in sound system components and design continue to improve quality while, in many cases, reduce the size of equipment.

BLOCKING EXTERIOR NOISE

The sounds of cars, trucks, airplanes, and trains outside a building vary with the time of day and volume of traffic. Traffic noise ranges from high-pitched horns and squealing brakes to low-frequency truck motors. Other noise sources coming from a building's neighborhood include construction noise, playgrounds, industrial plants, and sports arenas. On-site noises include children's play areas, refuse collection, and delivery or garage areas. Sound can also be reflected from other buildings.

Sound energy lessens in intensity as it disperses over a wide area, so outdoor sound control starts with siting the building as far from the noise source as possible. Locating physical mass, such as earth berms or the irregularities of the natural terrain, between a noise source (for example, a highway) and the building blocks unwanted sound. Heavy walls of concrete or masonry can block noise along direct sight lines between a quiet space and the noise source if they are high and wide enough. To avoid sound that is diffracted around the edges of the barrier, it must be close enough to the noise source or to the protected room. Light wood fencing does not help much. Dense planting of trees and shrubs diffuse and scatter sound, but single trees do not make much difference. Planting grass or other ground covers provides more sound absorption than hard, reflective surfaces.

☑ **A building interior can be screened from outside noise sources by using mechanical, service, and utility areas as sound buffers. Activities with higher noise levels should be located on the noisier side of the building. It is best to locate quieter rooms as far as possible from noise sources, such as busy streets. Building configurations with a central court or U-shaped buildings can create an echo chamber, in which noise bounces from one wall to another.**

Building materials and construction assemblies designed to reduce the transmission of **airborne** and **structure-borne sound** help control both exterior and interior noise sources. The walls, floor, and ceiling of the protected room should be heavy and airtight. Window and door openings can be oriented away from the sources of undesirable noise. Multiple glazing of windows can also help.

ADDRESSING INTERIOR ACOUSTIC DESIGN ISSUES

"**Acoustic attenuation**" is the term used for the reduction of the magnitude of a sound signal by a variety of means. This reduction may be the result of separating a sound source from a listener, enclosing the source to isolate the sound, absorbing the sound with materials that change the sound energy to heat, or canceling sound waves by electronic means.

Changes in the ways buildings are designed and constructed have had an effect on the amount of noise produced and transmitted indoors. Over the years, the weight of building materials has been reduced to lower construction costs, but lighter materials allow sound to be transmitted more easily through a structure. Offices are becoming smaller and more densely packed with people, thereby increasing the human and equipment noise levels. Open office plans eliminate barriers to sound and create challenges for speech privacy. Mechanical systems also add to the noise.

How sound behaves in a given room depends on the shape, size, and proportions of the room. The amounts of sound of various frequencies that are absorbed, reflected, and diffracted from the room's surfaces and contents also determine acoustic effects. The room's shape determines the geometry of the paths along which sound is reflected and can alter the sound quality, sometimes in unexpected ways.

What people hear at any point in a room is a combination of sound that travels from the source directly to their ears and sound reflected from the walls and other obstructions. When the reflections are so large that the sound level becomes uniform throughout the room, the result is a diffuse acoustic field.

Most rooms have a variety of acoustic fields. The area within one wavelength of the lowest frequency of sound produced in the room is called the **near field**. For the male human voice, that distance would be about 3.36 meters (11 ft.). The **reverberant field** is the area close to large obstructions such as walls, where conditions approach a diffuse acoustic field. The **free, or far, field** falls between the near and reverberant fields.

Ideally, every listener in a lecture hall, theater, or concert hall should hear the speaker or performer with the same degree of loudness and clarity. This is not possible using only direct sound paths from the source to the listeners, so the acoustic designer reinforces desirable reflections and attempts to minimize and control undesirable ones to even out the sound in the space. Designers usually consider only the first acoustic reflection because the second and third times that the sound bounces are less noticeable. When sound reflects off a hard, polished surface, the result is called a **specular reflection** (as it is with light reflected off such a surface). Acoustic designers sometimes place a reflecting panel above theater seats, sized to a minimum of one wavelength at the lowest frequency they are considering, in order to bounce the sound from the stage to the audience.

The design of a space, such as a concert hall, to obtain good listening conditions starts with developing a room shape that distributes and reinforces sound evenly throughout the audience. The distribution of sound is predicted by plotting the paths of the

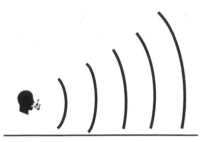

Sound outdoors: free field

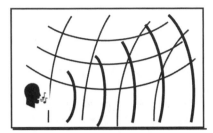

Sound indoors: reverberant field

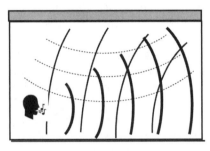

Sound indoors with boundary surface absorption: reverberant field

Figure 17-11 Acoustic fields. Sound produced in a free field attenuates as it spreads out without interruption. In a reverberant field, sound waves are multiplied and interwoven. Applying absorptive materials to the boundaries of a reverberant field decreases the loudness of reverberated sound waves.

sound rays and their reflections on plan and section drawings or with computer graphics. The process can also involve electronically testing a scale model of the hall.

When rehabilitating an existing building for a new use, an interior designer will not be able to achieve the optimal configuration and proportions for the space. **Electronic acoustics**, which consist of a system of speakers and amplifiers, can remedy the problems with the natural acoustic conditions. Electronic acoustics can focus additional sound into acoustically dead areas by adding a fraction of a second of reverberation time. Computer software can predict what the acoustic properties of a space will be as well as model it with electronic equipment to simulate what

music will sound like from any location in the hall. This enables the designer to try out the hall before construction, propose changes that address problems, and then hear the results.

Acoustics and Building Codes

City and town regulations or zoning by-laws set standards, regulations, criteria, and ordinances for noise. Agencies also set standards for specific industries, including limits on sound produced by a source. Building codes have recently added limits on noise as well. The U.S. Occupational Safety and Health Administration (OSHA) regulations require hearing protection for workers from high noise levels. Continual exposure to high noise levels results in a degree of temporary deafness in most people. Long periods of exposure, such as an eight-hour workday, result in permanent hearing impairment. OSHA sets the safe upper limit at 85 decibels. A continual 75-decibel to 85-decibel level produces or contributes to physical and psychological ailments, such as headache, digestive problems, cardiovascular problems, anxiety, and nervousness.

Several organizations set standards for building industry acoustic analysis and test methods. The American Society for Testing and Materials (ASTM) has established methods for measuring, analyzing, and quantifying noise. The American National Standards Institute (ANSI) has set scientific parameters and criteria used in acoustic analysis. ASHRAE has determined sound levels for mechanical systems in buildings.

Noise Reduction

The noise inside a building comes from the activities of the building's occupants and the operation of building services. As discussed earlier, additional sound comes in from outside the building.

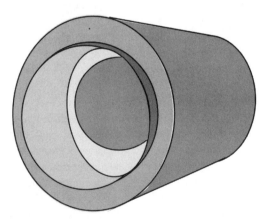

Figure 17-12 Duct silencer. To keep mechanical-system noise out of inhabited spaces, engineers may use duct silencers, which are sound traps designed to fit round or rectangular ducts of various sizes. Duct silencers contain fiberglass baffles to absorb sound and attenuate duct-borne noise and perform like duct lining but are more efficient. They offer fair performance at low frequencies, are best for mid-frequency sounds, and are quite effective at high frequencies.

The first principle of noise reduction in a building is to reduce the noise at its source. Typically, this involves the proper selection and installation of mechanical equipment. The second step is to reduce noise transmission from point to point along the transmission path by selecting appropriate construction materials and construction techniques. Finally, noise can be reduced at the listener's end by acoustic treatment of the space.

The acoustic design of variable-air-volume (VAV) ceiling diffusers can be coordinated with the expected air velocities and any requirements for masking noise in the space. Partially closing dampers on ceiling diffusers produces very high noise levels.

MASSIVE MATERIALS

Brick has substantial mass and effectively attenuates sound. When a wall is made of two layers of brick used side by side but without connection, the level of sound attenuation is very high. Brick walls absorb very little sound and reflect sound at all frequencies.

Normal-weight concrete is one of the best materials for attenuating sound. Lightweight concrete is less effective. Concrete absorbs almost no sound; however, it carries and transmits impact sounds. Aerated concretes are porous and absorb sound fairly effectively.

Concrete masonry units (CMUs) with hollow cores can attenuate sound quite well, especially when the CMU is made of normal-weight concrete and when the hollow cores are filled with concrete, sand, or grout. Walls of two unconnected CMU layers have exceptionally high attenuation. Unless painted or sealed, CMUs, especially cinder blocks, are slightly porous. If sealed, CMUs can reflect all frequencies well. Other forms of masonry vary, but they are similar to brick, concrete, and CMUs.

Stone, including such reconstituted materials as terrazzo, can be used for massive, loadbearing walls, stone veneer facing, or paving. Thick, well-sealed stone walls attenuate sound very well. Marble is among the most acoustically reflective materials. Some stone is naturally porous and, therefore, less reflective.

Plywood has a modest amount of mass and is relatively ineffective for attenuating sound. Thin plywood furred out from a solid wall effectively absorbs low frequencies. Plywood is quite reflective at high frequencies.

REFLECTIVE MATERIALS

A smooth, dense wall of painted concrete or plaster absorbs less than 5 percent of the sound striking it, thereby serving as an almost perfect sound reflector. Applying a skim coat of plaster does very little to improve masonry's ability to absorb sound, except for absorption of low frequencies when suspended or furred out from the solid surface. Concrete is a massive material that reflects sound. Resilient flooring, such as vinyl, cork, asphalt, and rubber sheet or tile, also reflect sound, although it is acoustically useful to cushion impact noises.

Glass is massive but thin, so its ability to attenuate sound is marginal. Well-separated double-glazing offers superior sound attenuation, as do some types of laminated glass. Laminated glass consists of two or more sheets of glass with plastic interlayer sheets that provide damping when the glass sandwich is flexed. Some types of laminated glass have substantially better attenuation than equal thicknesses of glass alone. Glass reflects higher frequencies almost completely. Because glass resonates, it absorbs significant amounts of low frequencies.

Figure 17-13 Interior brick and concrete. Acoustically massive materials, such as concrete and brick, reflect sound while resisting vibrations that could allow the sound to continue in adjacent spaces. This dramatic interior wall is in the Stata Center at the Massachusetts of Technology in Cambridge, Massachusetts.

Figure 17-14 Gypsum wallboard partition. A gypsum wallboard partition reflects most of the sound waves that hit it. The openings in this partition allow sound to pass through. *Photo credit: Herb Fremin*

Figure 17-15 Open-weave fabric. Most sound waves pass through open-weave fabric. If open-weave fabric is backed with a sound-absorbent material, the energy of the sound waves will enter and not be reflected.

Figure 17-16 Vinyl wall covering. Applying vinyl wall covering to a wall does little to reduce the amount of sound reflected. A very resilient wall covering with substantial thickness lowers the noise generated by an impact on its surface.

☑ **When designing interior glazing, an interior designer must keep in mind that glass lights with laminated glass set in resilient framing have more mass and offer better damping than plain glass in rigid frames.**

Acoustically Transparent Surfaces

Soft, porous, acoustically absorbent materials are often covered with perforated metal or other materials to provide protection and stiffness. These coverings are designed to be acoustically transparent, except at higher frequencies. With even smaller holes, the higher frequencies can also pass through. Staggering the holes improves absorption. Open-weave fabric is almost completely transparent.

When a thin layer of wall covering is applied to a sound-reflective material, such as gypsum wallboard, it makes little difference in the amount of sound reflected. This is true whether the covering material is an open-weave fabric (see Fig. 17-15) or a vinyl wall covering (see Fig. 17-16).

This chapter has introduced the basic principles of acoustic design without getting into complex mathematical calculations. In Chapter 18: Sound Absorption Within a Space, we will explore how interior designers can control the sound absorption levels of an interior space.

Sound Absorption Within a Space

Both this chapter and Chapter 19: Sound Transmission Between Spaces will examine how sound in one space can be reduced within that space as well as what determines how much sound that travels to an adjoining space will be heard. The following factors relate to three major interior sound issues:

- Sound absorption within a space
- Sound transmission loss as it travels to an adjoining space
- Ways to limit the disturbance caused by unwanted sound

If a noise problem does not come from outside a room but is a result of the sound inside the room bouncing around, an interior designer needs to address noise reduction within the space. The acoustical treatment of a space starts with reducing the noise source as much as possible, followed by control of unwanted sound reflections. Speech privacy is another major acoustic concern for the interior designer. Sometimes, it is also necessary to decrease or increase reverberation time for sound clarity and quality.

Noise is reduced in a building through the interception of sound energy before it reaches a person's ears. This is accomplished by changing acoustic energy into heat energy. The amount of heat energy produced by sound is miniscule; 130 decibels (db) of sound, which is loud enough to cause pain, produce only one one-thousandth watt (W) of heat. Most of this heat can easily be absorbed by the room contents and wall coverings and by the structure of the building itself.

The contents of the space control the noise levels in the space, while the building structure controls the transmission of noise between spaces. In a normally constructed room without acoustical treatment, sound waves strike walls or the ceiling, which then transmit a small portion of the sound. The walls or ceiling absorb another small amount, while most of the sound is reflected back into the room. The amount of transmission to an adjoining space is determined primarily by the mass of the solid, airtight barrier between the spaces, not by the surface treatment. However, the amount of sound that is reflected off the surfaces back into the room is greatly decreased by absorptive materials. When acoustical material is applied to a wall or ceiling, some of the energy in the sound wave is dissipated before the sound reaches the wall and the portion that is transmitted is reduced slightly.

SOUND ABSORPTION

Adding absorptive materials to a room changes the room's reverberation characteristics. This is helpful in spaces with distributed noise sources, such as offices, schools, and restaurants. The acoustics of a space with hard surfaces can be improved by adding absorptive materials. In spaces with concentrated noise sources, the noisy equipment should be enclosed; this is preferable to trying to treat the entire space.

Coefficient of Absorption

Materials are neither perfect reflectors nor absorbers of sound. The **coefficient of absorption** measures how efficiently a material absorbs sound. When all of the sound energy striking the material is absorbed and none of it is reflected, the absorption coefficient is 1.0. This is what happens when sound flies out an open window: the window opening is said to absorb (not reflect) all the sound.

Rooms are constructed and furnished with a mixture of materials, each with a different absorption coefficient. With most common materials, the ability to absorb sound varies with the

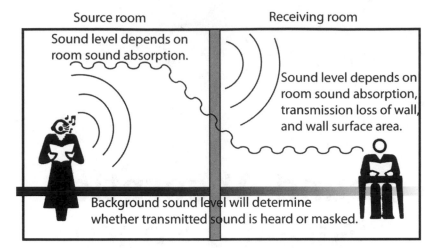

Figure 18-1 How interior sound travels. In the room on the left, the loudness of the singer's voice will be tempered by how much absorptive material it encounters in the room and by how much of it can be distinctly heard above any background noise. Any sound that passes through the wall and into the room on the right also can be obscured by absorption and background sound.

frequency of the sound. In order to provide a useful and general idea of a material's ability to absorb sound at a variety of frequencies, the absorption coefficients at 250 Hertz (Hz), 500 Hertz, 1000 Hertz, and 2000 Hertz are averaged together for the **noise-reduction coefficient (NRC)**. The NRC is useful as a single-number criterion for measuring the effectiveness of a porous sound absorber at midrange frequencies. It does not accurately indicate a material's performance at high or low frequencies. Because it is an average, two materials with the same NRC may perform differently.

INSTALLATION OF ABSORPTIVE MATERIALS

"Noise reduction is essentially the science of converting acoustical energy into another, less disturbing form of energy—heat. Since the amounts of energy involved are minute... the heat produced is completely negligible." (*Mechanical and Electrical Equipment for Buildings*, Benjamin Stein et al., John Wiley & Sons, 2006, p. 787)

It is the tiny frictional drag of air moving between the fibers of fibrous materials that makes them effective sound absorbers. The fibers themselves do not usually absorb any sound energy. The amount of absorption depends on a material's thickness, density, porosity, and resistance to airflow. For effective absorption, air paths must extend from one side of the material to the other. The following are observations about absorbent materials:

- Sealing or painting a material can ruin its ability to absorb sound.
- Most materials are better at absorbing high frequencies than low ones.
- The thickness of a material does not increase its absorbency, except at very low frequencies.

- Installation methods are very important in determining the effectiveness of an absorptive material.
- A layer of air between an absorptive material and a rigid surface works almost as well in mid-range frequencies as it would if the same cumulative thickness of absorptive material were used, which is helpful to know because air is cheaper than other materials.
- To obtain the best low-frequency absorption, a deep air space on the ceiling is needed and the walls should be treated as well. A suspended ceiling 41 centimeters (cm) (16 in.) below the structural slab is too shallow to even absorb mid-range frequencies well.
- The best way to install acoustically absorbent material is to hang cubes or tetrahedrons from the ceiling. When very thick blocks are installed at a distance from each other, the edge absorption is very large, especially in the high frequencies. However, these objects become major architectural elements in the space.
- Although louvers and baffles may not be appropriate for all uses, they offer a somewhat less effective but simpler option.

☑ **For best results, the ceiling, the floor, and the wall opposite the sound source should be treated approximately equally. Treating the ceiling alone may miss highly directive high-frequency waves, which may not reach the ceiling until the third reflection off a surface.**

Materials absorb high frequencies better than they do lower frequencies. The amount of absorption is not always proportional to the thickness of the material but depends on the material and its method of installation. Beyond a certain point, added thickness does little to increase absorption, with the exception of very low frequencies. The lowest musical frequencies cannot be absorbed efficiently by ordinary thicknesses of porous material.

TABLE 18-1. NOISE-REDUCTION COEFFICIENTS

Material Category	Material	Description	NRC
Building materials	Brick	Unglazed	0.005
		Painted	0.00
	Concrete	Coarse block	0.35
		Painted block	0.05
		Floor	0.00
	Door	Hollow core (slightly vibrating)	0.03
	Glass	Large panes of heavy plate glass	0.05
		Ordinary window glass	0.15
	Gypsum board	½ in. on 2 × 4s at 16 in. on center (o.c.)	0.05
	Plaster	On lath or brick	0.05
	Ventilating grilles	In opening	0.15-0.50
Finish materials	Carpet	Heavy, on concrete	0.29
		Heavy, on carpet pad	0.55
	Fabric	Light velour hung straight, in contact with wall	0.15
		Medium velour draped to half area	0.55
		Heavy velour, draped to half area	0.60
	Flooring	Terrazzo	0.00
		Linoleum, rubber, or cork on concrete	0.05
		Wood	0.10
	Paneling	Plywood ⅜ in. thick	0.15
		Rough wood (tongue-and-groove cedar)	0.14
		Thin wood, vibrating (on 16 in. o.c. studs)	0.05
	Tile	Marble or glazed	0.00
Acoustic absorptive materials	High-performance, vinyl-faced, fiberglass ceiling panels	1 in. thick	0.09
		1.5 in. thick	0.95
	Painted, nubby grass cloth panels	.75 in. thick	0.85
		1 in. thick	0.95
	Random fissured panels	¾ in. thick	0.70
	Perforated metal panels	Infill 1 in. thick	0.85
	Mineral fiber tiles and panels, typical averages	¾ in. fissured	0.65
		¾ in. textured	0.70
		⅝ in. fissured	0.60
		⅝ in. textured	0.50
		⅝ in. perforated	0.60

Fibrous Materials

Materials absorb acoustic energy via the friction of air being moved in the tiny spaces between fibers. A material's sound-absorption capacity depends on its thickness, density, porosity, and resistance to airflow. Paths must extend from one side of the material to the other, so that air passes through. Sealed pores do not work for sound absorption, and painting may ruin a porous absorber, such as an acoustical tile ceiling. If smoke can pass through a porous, fibrous, thick material, the material should make a good sound absorber.

Fibrous batts and **blankets** improve attenuation when used either between the two faces of a partition in a stud space or above a suspended ceiling between the ceiling and the floor above. These materials absorb sound as it passes through the partition's cavity. Their ability to absorb sound is limited when the wall is tied rigidly together with wood studs, but they improve sound transmission loss significantly with light-gauge steel studs. The performance of fibrous batts and blankets is determined by their thickness. Fibrous batts and blankets should never completely fill a cavity.

Fiberglass comes as batts, blankets, and boards with excellent sound absorption. The manufacturing process for fiberglass

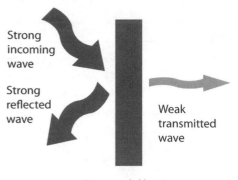

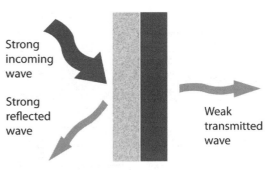

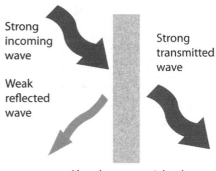

Figure 18-2 Sound waves striking barriers. Absorptive material primarily affects the amount of sound reflected. The amount of sound energy transmitted depends mostly on the mass of the solid, airtight barrier.

creates consistent, very fine sound-absorbing pores. Fiberglass is used for many applications, including insulation in stud walls and ducts and industrial noise control. Compressed blocks or sheets are used to form resilient supports or hangers or as joint fillers instead of rigid ties. The absorption of fiberglass depends on the airflow resistance and is affected by the material's thickness and density and the fibers' diameter. The thickness of the board or blanket is usually the most important element.

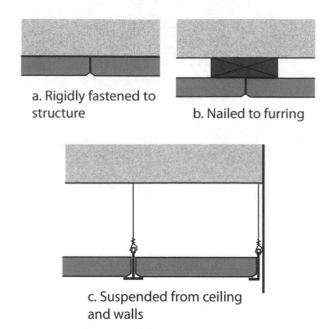

Figure 18-3 Installation of absorptive materials. The way materials are installed affects their ability to absorb sound. Here, the least effective sound-absorption method is shown in (a), a somewhat better method is shown in (b), and a far superior method is shown in (c).

Loose acoustical insulation is similar to fibrous batts and blankets, but it is blown or dumped in place. Loose insulation reduces sound transmission through the partition. Cellulose fiber is a sound-absorbing material that is the basis of acoustical tile, wood wool, fibrous sprays and other acoustical products.

Acoustical Ceiling Materials

The ceiling is the most important surface to treat for sound absorption. Some of the fibrous materials discussed earlier are used for ceilings, either openly or covered with acoustically transparent fabrics or perforated panels. There are also products designed specifically for the acoustical treatment of ceilings, the most common of which are acoustical ceiling tiles.

ACOUSTICAL CEILING TILES

Acoustical ceiling tiles are excellent absorbers of sound in a room, where they help lower noise levels by absorbing some of the sound energy. Their extreme porosity and low density, however, offer no reduction in the passage of noise from room to room through a ceiling or wall. To improve resistance to humidity, impact, or abrasion, these tiles are available factory-painted or with ceramic, plastic, steel or aluminum facing.

Acoustical tile is made of mineral or cellulose fibers or fiberglass. Mineral fiber tiles have NRC ratings between 0.45 and 0.75. Faced fiberglass tiles are rated up to NRC 0.95. Acoustical tiles are both lightweight and low density and can be easily damaged by contact. Consequently, they are not recommended for walls and other surfaces within reach. The main purpose of

TABLE 18-2. FIBROUS MATERIALS

Acoustical Product	Description	NRC Rating	Installation/Use
Structural acoustical deck of perforated steel backed with absorptive material, usually fiberglass	Acoustical panels available in widths up to 1.22 m (4 ft.) and lengths up to 3 m (10 ft.)	Around 0.50 to 0.90 when used exposed	Acoustical deck can greatly reduce noise, reverberation in gyms, factories, workshops
Fibrous plank acoustical deck	Rigid material usually made of coarse wood fibers embedded in cementitious mix; fibrous surface absorbs sound, with performance depending on thickness forms; usually made of polyurethane cells	25 mm (1 in.) plank around 0.40; up to 0.65 for 76 mm (3 in.) thick planks	If surface is exposed to room, fibrous planks will reduce noise, reverberation in room; Some planks can be used as structural roof decking
Acoustical foam	Air can be blown into and through open cell acoustical foam; Each cell in closed cell acoustical foam is sealed, material is airtight; Excellent sound absorber if thick enough	6 mm (¼ in.) thick has NRC of 0.25; 51 mm (2 in.) thick foam has NRC of up to 0.90	Padding for upholstered theater seats
Fibrous batts, blankets	Fiberglass or mineral fiber; Absorb sound to reduce noise and reverberation in room; performance depends on their thickness, facing properties	As high as 0.90	Acoustical or thermal insulation; Exposed to room as wall finish behind fabric or open grille or as ceiling finish behind perforated pans or spaced slats
Fibrous board	Works like batts or blankets, but has higher density; Rigid or semi-rigid boards, especially those made of fiberglass, offer excellent absorption	25 mm (1 in.) around NRC 0.75; around NRC 0.90 for 51 mm (2 in.)	Available with variety of sound-transparent facings, including many fabrics; Used as wall or ceiling panels
Fibrous sprays	Include variety of spray-on insulation materials; Inherently porous and, therefore, absorptive; performance depends on their thickness, application technique used	Well-applied 25 mm (1 in.) thick coat can achieve NRC of 0.60 or higher	Often specified for fire resistance, instead of asbestos fibers

Figure 18-4 Acoustical batt insulation. These packaged sound attenuation batts are waiting to be installed in a wall. *Photo credit: Herb Fremin*

acoustical ceiling tiles is sound absorption. Membrane-faced tiles absorb less high-frequency sound than porous-faced tiles.

Acoustical ceiling tiles are available in the following sizes:

- modular sizes between around 31 centimeters (12 in.) square and 61 centimeters (24 in.) square
- rectangular tiles 61 x 122 centimeters (24 × 48 in.)
- based on 51-centimeter (20-in.), 76-centimeter (30-in.), 122-centimeter (48-in.), and 153-centimeter (60-in.) dimensions
- thicknesses of 13 millimeters (½ in.), 16 millimeters (⅝ in.), and 19 millimeters (¾ in.)

The thicker the tile, the better the absorption. Edges may be square, beveled, rabbeted (cut or grooved edge), or tongue-and-groove. Acoustical tiles come in perforated, patterned, textured, or fissured faces. Some tiles are fire-rated, and others are rated for use in high-humidity areas.

Acoustical tiles are usually suspended from a metal grid, but they can also be glued or otherwise attached to solid surfaces.

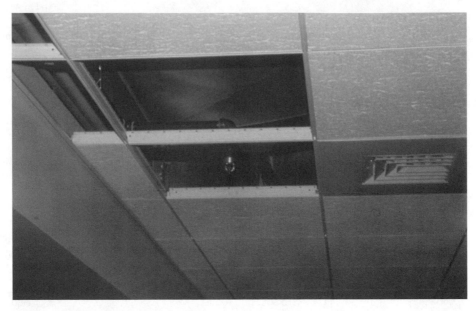

Figure 18-5 Acoustical tiles. Acoustical tiles are usually installed in metal ceiling grids that allow them to be removed for access to the plenum above. *Photo credit: Herb Fremin*

Figure 18-6 Suspended ceiling grid. Grids for suspended ceilings are made with longer runners and shorter cross pieces. The grids are suspended from the building structure by flexible wire hangers. *Photo credit: Herb Fremin*

Suspended applications absorb more low-frequency sound than glued-on tiles. Suspended grids create space for ductwork, electrical conduit, and plumbing lines. They allow lighting fixtures, sprinkler heads, fire detection devices, and sound systems to be recessed. The grid consists of channels or runners, cross tees, and splines suspended from the overhead floor or roof structure. The main runners are sheet-metal tees or channels suspended by hanger wires from the overhead structure and are the principal supporting members of the system. The cross tees are secondary sheet-metal supporting members, carried by the main runners. The grid may be exposed, recessed, or fully concealed. Most systems allow acoustical ceiling tiles to be removed for replacement or access.

In addition to absorbing sound in a room, many acoustical tiles also attenuate sound passing through to adjacent rooms. This can be critical when partitions stop against or just above the ceiling to create a continuous plenum. Tiles for sound attenuation in this use are usually made of mineral fiber with a sealed coating or foil backing.

An integrated suspended ceiling system includes acoustical, lighting, and air-handling components. Typically, the grid is 152 centimeters (60 in.) square, with flat or coffered acoustical panels. Air-handling can be integrated into the modular luminaires to disperse conditioned air along the edges of the lighting fixtures; alternately, it may be part of the suspension system and diffuse air through long, narrow slots between ceiling panels.

PERFORATED METAL PANS AND PANELS

Perforated metal pans backed by fibrous batts are an alternative to acoustical tile ceilings. Similar panels may be used on walls to absorb sound. Perforated metal-faced units are available for use with suspended ceilings. The metal panels have wrapped mineral

Figure 18-7 Plenum air return. Suspended ceiling systems readily accommodate air returns and other equipment. *Photo credit: Herb Fremin*

wool or fiberglass fill and receive somewhat lower NRC ratings than acoustical tiles. They are available in sizes from 31 × 61 centimeters (12 × 24 in.) to 61 × 244 centimeters (24 × 96 in.). Baked-enamel finishes are available in a variety of colors. Metal panels are easy to keep clean, have a high luminous reflectivity, and are incombustible. With the acoustical backing removed, a perforated unit can be used for an air return.

The size and spacing of the perforation—not just the percentage of openness—affect the performance. Depending on the perforation pattern and type and thickness of batt, the NRC of perforated metal pans can reach 0.50 to 0.95. If the batts are en-

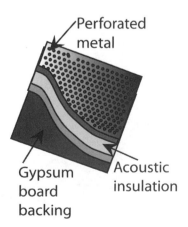

Figure 18-8 Perforated metal pan ceiling tile. Perforated metal pans backed by fibrous batts look hard and reflective, but they effectively absorb sound.

cased in plastic, as is required in some states, the high-frequency absorption is impaired. Metal pans do not reduce sound transmission unless they have a solid backing.

Perforated steel or aluminum panels with finished edges provide both absorptive and reflective surfaces for environments in which a variable reverberation time is desirable, such as music rooms, concert halls, performing-arts centers, and restaurants. The units are 61 centimeters (24 in.) wide closed and hinge-open to 122 centimeters (48 in.) wide for additional absorption.

Perforated galvanized steel or aluminum panels that can be individually attached to ceilings or walls offer an economical sound-absorbing and fire-resistant approach to acoustical control. The panels are hung on metal brackets and backed with high-performance acoustical fill. Panels can be cleaned in place without removing the acoustical fill. Optional protective plastic or fiberglass wraps are available. Perforated metal panels are appropriate for gymnasiums, swimming pools, weight rooms, and similar facilities. They can also be used in auditoriums, theaters, libraries, and food-service operations in which noise is a problem and cost is an issue. They are also appropriate for industrial applications.

LINEAR METAL CEILINGS

Linear metal ceilings consist of narrow, anodized aluminum, painted steel, or stainless steel strips. Slots between the strips may be open or closed. When they are open, a backing of batt insulation in the ceiling space permits sound absorption. Linear metal ceilings are usually used as part of a modular lighting and air-handling system.

Figure 18-9 Linear metal ceiling. Linear metal ceiling panels can be cut for lighting fixtures. The spaces between the strips accommodate acoustic materials or allow airflow.

SLATS AND GRILLES

Wood or metal slats or grilles in the ceiling are often believed to have acoustical value, but they serve only to protect the material behind them, typically absorbent fiberglass. The absorption value is maintained when the grilles or slats are small and widely spaced. Increasing the size of the dividers or reducing the space between them will cause high frequencies to be reflected.

ACOUSTICAL CEILING PANELS

Acoustical ceiling panels or boards of treated wood fibers bonded with an cementitious binder are available from 31 × 61 centimeters (12 × 24 in.) to 122 × 305 centimeters (48 × 120 in.). They are available from 25 millimeters to 76 millimeters (1–3 in.) thick, with a smooth or shredded finish. Acoustical ceiling panels are installed in ceiling suspension systems or nailed or glued to walls and structural ceilings. They receive NRC ratings from 0.40 to 0.70.

Acoustical ceiling panels have high structural strength and are abuse resistant. They have an excellent flame spread rating. Panels can be used across the full span of corridor ceilings or as a long-span finish directly attached to the ceiling. They are appropriate for wall finishes in school gymnasiums and corridors. Although they are usually resistant to humidity, check high-humidity use with the manufacturer, especially for panels with reveal edges.

Acoustical lay-in panels are fabricated of steel or aluminum with textured and embossed facings to provide a cloth-like appearance. With acoustical fiber fill, the panels offer sound absorption as high as 1.10 NRC and meet fire safety standards.

Figure 18-10 Perforated acoustical panel. Architect Frank Gehry's design for the Stata Center at the Massachusetts Institute of Technology in Cambridge, Massachusetts, includes Douglas fir perforated acoustical panels over sound-absorbing backing. The effect is visually warm and textured.

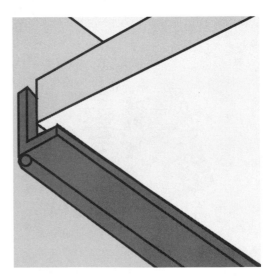

Figure 18-11 Acoustical ceiling panel. This edge-support detail shows how an acoustical ceiling panel is free to move, further helping to absorb sound vibrations.

Acoustical ceiling backer is available in 61 centimeters (2 ft.) square or 61 × 122 centimeters (2 × 4 ft.) sizes. Ceiling backer can easily be placed on top of an existing ceiling-tile system that does not provide enough sound attenuation. The barrier material is a reinforced-aluminum and fiberglass construction.

ACOUSTIC BAFFLES

Acoustic baffles are available in 51-millimeter (2-in.) fiberglass and a variety of standard heights and widths. These panels are designed to acoustically upgrade existing spaces, such as cafeterias, auditoriums, pool areas, and any area in which high ceilings and poor acoustics require more sound absorption. The facing of the baffles is stretched to provide a smooth surface free from wrinkles or other distortion.

CLOUD PANELS AND ACOUSTICAL CANOPIES

Cloud panels are used when ceiling heights are too low for traditional baffle installations and perform the same acoustical functions without sprinkler or lighting interference. A 25-millimeter (1-in.) or 51-millimeter (2-in.) fiberglass core acts as an absorber and is contained within an extruded aluminum frame. The panels are available up to 122 centimeters (48 in.) square and are finished with fabric.

Acoustical canopies are available filled with standard acoustical ceiling tile set in a grid. These can be configured into interesting patterns and suspended over areas that call for more sound absorption.

Manufactured curved panels are another variation on acoustical canopies. An additional option is custom-designed, stretched, open-weave fabric suspended on frames and backed with an acoustical absorbing material.

Wall Panels

Acoustical wall panels are used in offices, conference rooms, auditoriums, theaters, teleconferencing centers, and educational facilities. Wall panels have wood or metal backing and mineral-fiber or fiberglass substrates. Fabric coverings are usually fire rated. Wall panels are available in various styles and sizes:

- Fabric-covered panels are available from 25 millimeters to 51 millimeters (1–2 in.) thick.
- NRC ratings vary from 0.5 for direct-mounted, 25-millimeter mineral-fiber panels to 0.85 for strip-mounted 38-millimeter (1½ -in.) fiberglass panels.
- Panels are available from between 46 centimeters (18 in.) and 122 centimeters (48 in.) wide and up to 305 centimeters (120 in.) long.
- Reveals at the ceiling and base help ensure a good fit.
- Openings for wall plates and thermostats can be field cut.

Acoustical wall-panel systems can also include tack boards that are used as accessory panels in cubicles, conference rooms, break rooms, reception areas, and lobbies. Tack boards may be attached using hook-and-loop attachments.

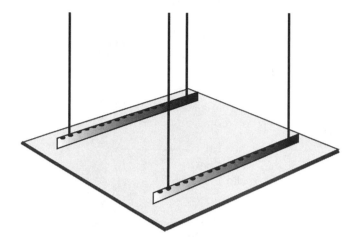

Figure 18-12 Acoustical cloud installation. Spaces with exposed structural ceilings do not need to be loud. Acoustical cloud panels can be suspended from the structure's noisier areas.

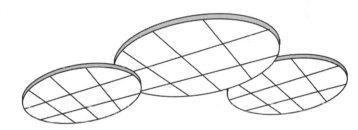

Figure 18-13 Oval acoustical canopies. Today, manufacturers of acoustical ceiling materials offer acoustical canopies in a variety of shapes and sizes.

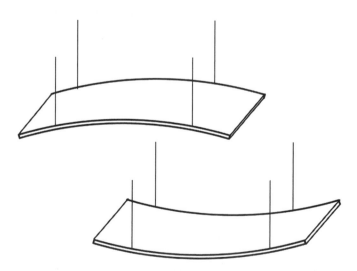

Figure 18-14 Curved acoustical canopies. Another variation on acoustical canopies consists of suspended curved panels, which can be hung with either concave or convex curves toward the sound source.

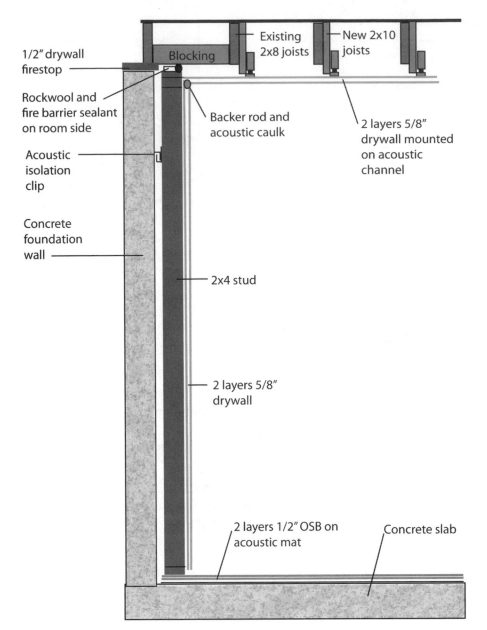

Figure 18-15 Basement acoustical finish. Today, manufacturers of acoustical materials supply entire systems for finishing and acoustically conditioning basement spaces. It is essential to ensure that the basement is secure and dry before these systems are installed.

Carpet

Carpet is the only floor finish that absorbs sound. In almost any degree of density, looping, and depth (especially when used with additional padding depth), carpets produce a high degree of absorption in the mid- to high-frequency range. Carpet can be glued to a floor or installed over an underlayment of hair felt or foam rubber. Its absorption is proportional to the pile height and density; and carpet absorption increases with the thickness of a fibrous pad, unless the carpet has an airtight backing. Carpet earns an NRC of between 0.20 and 0.55, primarily for high frequencies.

Sometimes, carpet is installed on walls where drapery is not feasible and wall panels are impractical. It should be installed on furring strips with an enclosed air space behind to increase absorption over the entire acoustical spectrum, especially in the low frequencies where glue-down application performs poorly. Carpet on walls may have different fire-rating requirements than carpet on floors.

Carpet does not reduce the passage of sound from room to room, but it can prevent noise that originates when an object makes hard contact with the floor. Using a thick carpet with a pad, along with a resilient layer within the floor construction, reduces impact noise.

Draperies, Fabrics, and Upholstery

Curtains absorb sound if reasonable heavy—at least 500 grams (gm) per square meter (15 ounces. per square yd.)—and, more important, if the airflow resistance is sufficiently high. The curtain fabric must severely impede but not stop the airflow through the material.

The NRC of drapery fabrics depend on their fullness and the tightness of their weave. Sound absorption at all frequencies is increased when drapery encloses an air space between the wall and the drape. Curtains do not reduce the passage of noise from room to room through a ceiling or wall. Interior designers should keep the following in mind when choosing draperies:

- Drapery fabrics at 100-percent fullness vary between 0.10 and 0.65 NRC.
- A light curtain has an NRC of around 0.20.
- Heavy, flow-resistant drapery covering up to one-half of the area can achieve an NRC greater than 0.70.
- Venetian blinds, by comparison, have an NRC rating of 0.10.

Fabrics attached directly to hard surfaces do not absorb sound. Fabric that is not airtight and is stretched over fiberglass or other

Figure 18-16 Sound absorbing window treatment. Some of the same window treatments that provide thermal insulation also absorb sound. This custom-made window panel has translucent quilt batting inside.

absorbent materials creates an excellent finish that fully preserves the absorption of the underlying material. Deep, porous upholstery absorbs most sounds from mid-range frequencies upward.

Acoustical Properties of Other Finish Materials

Acoustical plaster is a less-well-known, porous, plaster-like product that originally contained asbestos. It was intended to create surfaces without joints that absorb sound. It consists of a plaster-type base with fibrous or light aggregate material on top. Acoustical plaster is useful for curved or nonlinear surfaces, can be applied up to 38 millimeters (1.5 in.) thick, and is fire-rated.

Unfortunately, the performance of acoustical plaster depends on correct mixing and application techniques. Under controlled conditions, acoustical plaster can achieve an NRC of 0.60. Field installations are usually much less effective, so acoustical plaster cannot be relied upon as a sound absorber. Acoustical plaster is very easy to abuse and is not resistant to humidity.

As mentioned earlier, resilient tile made of vinyl, asphalt, rubber, cork, or similar materials is almost as sound reflective as concrete. If it is foam-backed, resilient flooring can attenuate high frequencies.

Relatively thin finishes of wood boards or panels, usually attached to furring, are, in general, not much better than a basic wall. Wood paneling absorbs low frequencies by resonance and can result in a serious bass deficiency in music rooms unless it is thick or attached directly to the wall without an airspace.

SOUND ABSORBERS

Sound can create a resonance in hollow constructions whose natural frequencies match that of the sound. Air in the hollow acts as a spring, oscillating at a related frequency. Because a resonating body absorbs energy from the sound waves that excite it, resonating devices can absorb sound energy. Resonators are easiest to construct for lower frequencies. They are often used in modern concert halls and are constructed as concealed hollows in the walls.

Volume or **cavity resonators**, also known as **Helmholtz resonators**, consist of an air cavity within a massive enclosure that is connected to its surroundings by a narrow neck opening. Sound causes the air in the neck to vibrate and the air mass behind causes the entire construction to resonate at a particular frequency. The result is almost total absorption at that frequency. These resonators are sometimes used to cancel out electrical hums.

Cavity resonators can be tuned to different frequencies, for example, to 120 Hertz for an electrical transformer hum. Concrete blocks can be used as cavity resonators by tuning their openings and adding absorptive materials. The use of a fibrous filler in the block increases high-frequency absorption.

Resonator sound absorbers come in a wide variety of shapes and sizes. Some are manufactured in standard sizes, but most are tailored to a specific job using standard designs. They are usually large and must be integrated into the architectural design of the space.

Panel resonators consist of a membrane of thin plywood or linoleum in front of a sealed air space that usually contains an absorbent material. The panel is set in motion by the alternating pressure of the sound wave. Then the sound energy is converted to heat. Panel resonators are used for efficient low-frequency absorption as well as when mid- to high-frequency absorption is not sought or is provided for by another acoustical treatment. These resonators are often used in recording studios.

Space units are blocks of fibrous and porous material made of mineral fibers or fiberglass. They look much like acoustical tiles and are typically 50 millimeters (2 in.) thick. Space units are applied to hard wall and ceiling surfaces. They absorb sound efficiently, helped by the exposure of their thick sides.

Functional absorbers are free-hanging cylinders used in industrial applications. They employ both surface absorption and tuned resonances to absorb sound and help reduce noise and reverberation in a room.

Quadratic residue diffusers consist of a series of narrow wells of unequal depth separated by even narrower plates. Typical depths are between 10 centimeters (4 in.) and 41 centimeters (16 in.) or more. This results in an attractive ribbed appearance. Quadratic residue diffusers work by spreading the sound reflections over a wide arc at an angle to their wells. They are used in broadcast and recording studios, control rooms, and wherever specular reflections off plain surfaces should be avoided. They can be made of any hard material and may be engineered to work over a wide range of frequencies.

Armed with all of this information about how to absorb sound within a space, an interior designer will be able to tackle sound that is transmitted from a source room to other spaces, which will be explored in Chapter 19.

....

19

Sound Transmission Between Spaces

Sound travels through other materials in addition to air. These include steel, wood, concrete, masonry, and other rigid construction materials. The sound of a person walking is readily transmitted through a concrete floor slab into the air of the room below. A metal pipe carries plumbing noise throughout a building. A structural beam can carry both the vibrations of a vacuum cleaner to an adjacent room or the rumble of an electric motor throughout a building.

Buildings generate their own sounds. Rain and sleet pound and clatter on building surfaces. Doors slam, and old wood floors creak. Heating and plumbing systems, elevator machinery, and such machines as garbage disposers produce mechanical noises. When a building structure is pushed and pulled by the wind, heat, or humidity, the building creaks, groans, and crackles.

CONTROLLING BUILDING SYSTEM NOISE

Much of the noise in a building comes from mechanical systems. Machines cause noise by vibration. Enclosing the noise at its source with materials that reduce noise by absorption and block airborne sound minimizes the problem. Often, an equipment supplier can provide prefabricated partial and full enclosures. Curtains and panels may also help isolate the machinery.

Laundry machines, mixers, bins, chutes, polishing drums, and other machinery with sheet-metal enclosures that vibrate can create a great deal of noise. The vibration can be dampened by permanently attaching a layer of foam to the vibrating metal, which converts the noise energy to heat. Adding a heavy, limp barrier material to the outside of the foam creates a composite damping barrier material and further reduces the noise.

The first step in quieting machine noise is to select quiet equipment and install it away from inhabited parts of a building. Equipment should be mounted with resilient fittings to eliminate structure-borne noise, and noisy equipment should be housed in sound-isolating enclosures to cut down on airborne noise transmission. Damping is accomplished by rigidly coupling a machine to a large mass called an inertia block.

Decoupling the vibration from connections that would carry it throughout the building can reduce airborne machine noise. Breaking the connection from the vibration source to the building structure will also keep noise from spreading. To accomplish his, flexible joints should be used in all pipes and ducts connected to the noisy machine. Flexible conduit connections should be used for all motors, transformers, and lighting fixtures with magnetic ballasts.

Elevators, including freight elevators, and escalators are localized sources of noise, and generally run at fairly low speeds. If the spaces around them are located judiciously, their noise should not be a significant problem. However, the motors and controls can be noisy.

Higher-priced upper floors in a building may be near noisy elevator machine rooms, mechanical equipment rooms, and cooling towers. An acoustical expert should be called in during the equipment design phase because these problems are almost impossible to solve later.

Plumbing and Mechanical System Noise

The piping for a building's plumbing system can also be a source of noise, including both the normal sounds of water rushing through uninsulated pipes and those from water hammer in im-

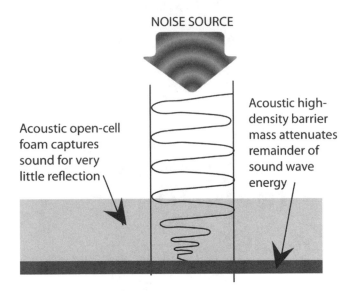

Figure 19-1 **Quieting equipment.** Capturing the vibration of noisy equipment with very absorbent material and a high-mass barrier prevents it from spreading throughout a building.

Figure 19-2 **Modular acoustical screens.** Temporary noise sources can be screened with quilted acoustical panels hung from tubing supports.

properly designed systems. Pipes and flushing toilets should be kept away from quiet areas.

In many buildings, 40 percent of the construction budget is spent on the mechanical system. Mechanical equipment in a building has many noise-producing components. The air-handling system includes fans, compressors, cooling towers, condensers, ductwork, dampers, mixing boxes, induction units, and diffusers, all of which can either generate noise or carry it to other

locations. For example, in one hotel on the East Coast, the roof-mounted chiller causes clearly audible vibration in the meeting-room chandeliers below. Mechanical systems also include pumps and liquid flowing through piping.

Roof-mounted heating, ventilation, and air-conditioning (HVAC) units are very economical but very noisy. The vibrating equipment, short duct runs, and sound reflections lead to acoustical problems. The use of vibration isolators, sound mufflers, and careful location of equipment all help.

Electrical System Noise

Most noisy electrical equipment produces a low-frequency 120 Hertz (Hz) hum that is difficult to reduce. However, mounting a transformer on vibration isolators, hanging it from a wall with resilient hangers, or placing it on a massive slab can minimize electric transformer noise. When transformers are located near acoustically reflective surfaces, the sound can be amplified. Sound-absorbent material behind the unit is not useful at 120 Hertz; only cavity resonators will work at that low frequency. Flexible conduit connections should be used. Interior designers must be aware of transformer locations so that they do not end up adjacent to or immediately outside quiet areas or directly below a window.

Magnetic lighting-fixture ballasts for fluorescent and high intensity discharge (HID) sources also produce a 120-Hertz hum. Magnetic ballasts have been replaced by electronic ballasts in fluorescent sources, and more recently in HID fixtures. When a ballast is attached to a lighting fixture, the sound is amplified. A large number of fixtures in a plenum can lead to a serious noise problem. Absorbent materials in plenums, flexible conduit, and resilient fixture hangers can minimize the noise. Ballasts can be remotely mounted if necessary.

Weatherstripping on windows and doors reduces wind noises, and cuts the transmission of outdoor noises into the building. Weatherstripping also reduces heat loss. Rain and sleet noises can be reduced with heavier roof and window construction.

Structural noises in a building caused by building components slipping past each other during sporadic releases of built-up stress may be inevitable and are difficult to remedy. If a noise source can be precisely located, the component can be nailed or bolted tighter. Sometimes, blowing graphite particles into a moving joint as a lubricant helps to remedy the problem.

AIRBORNE AND STRUCTURE-BORNE SOUND

Airborne sound originates in a space with any sound-producing source and changes to **structure-borne sound** when the sound waves strike the room boundaries, but this sound is still considered to be airborne because it originated in the air. Structure-borne sound is energy delivered by a source that directly vibrates or hits the structure. In practice, all sound transmission involves both airborne and structure-borne sound.

When airborne sound hits a partition, it makes the partition vibrate, generating sound on the other side. The sound will not pass through the partition unless an air path exists. If the partition is airtight, then the sound energy causes the structure itself to become a sound source by vibrating the partition. While the partition vibrates primarily in the vertical plane, it also causes some energy to pass into the floor and ceiling, resulting in structure-borne sound.

When a mechanical contact vibrates or hits a structure, the sound travels along the structure and causes vibrations, which then become airborne sound. Rigid wall-to-floor connections result in sounds that can be he clearly through the building structure. A rigid structure with rigid connections offers a good sound path, even in a massive concrete structure with masonry walls. In this situation, the approach then becomes one of absorbing impacts with heavy carpet and resilient floor-wall connections.

When there is no air cushion between a noise source and a building's structure, high-intensity energy is introduced into the structure, where it travels at great speed with minimal attenuation. The sound in the structure is attenuated only by breaks in the structure. The structure must have structural integrity to carry loads, so breaking the structure to stop noise is complex and expensive.

With structure-borne sound, the entire structure becomes a network of parallel paths for the sound. Partial solutions do not work because sound finds **flanking paths**. The entire building structure must be soundproofed. Adding mass usually does not block structure-borne sound, especially in buildings with long spans. The floor becomes a diaphragm, improving structure-to-air noise transfer efficiency, similar to the way a drumhead does. Exposed structural ceilings further reduce the attenuation that would occur in a plenum. Since most structure-borne sound is carried by floor structures, the sound radiates up and down into the rooms above and below.

Airborne sound is usually considered to be less disturbing than structure-borne sound. The initial energy is usually very small and attenuates rapidly at the room's boundaries. Airborne sound changes directions (diffracts; see page 404) easily. Low-frequency sounds are the most flexible and can get around barriers.

TABLE 19-1. SOUND PATHS

Sound Path	Cause	Desired Use	Problems	Comments
Specular reflection	Sound reflecting off hard, polished surface	Sound reflected off surface above theater seats to minimize attenuation	Sound reflected off glass diminishes acoustical privacy in open office	Minimizes attenuation by shortening sound path
Echoes	Reflected sound at sufficient intensity reaches listener more than 50 milliseconds after direct sound	Almost always undesirable	Make speech less intelligible; make music lose brilliance	Produced in auditoriums by back wall and ceiling above proscenium; energy can be redirected as useful reinforcement
Flutter	Buzzing or clicking sound produced by repeated echoes traversing back and forth between two nonabsorbing parallel flat or concave surfaces	Almost always undesirable	May require changing shape of reflecting surfaces or their parallel relationship; absorbent materials may help	Sharp sound, such as handclap, causes flutter to occur between shallow domes and hard, flat floors
Diffusion	Sound level remains relatively constant throughout space	Very desirable for musical performance		Sound is reflected from convex surfaces; to lesser degree from horizontal, inclined reflectors
Focusing	Concave domes, vaults, or walls focus reflected sound into certain areas of rooms	Can create novel effects when sounds are not audible	Deprives some listeners of useful sound reflections; causes hot spots at other positions	Change shape of reflective spaces; add absorbent materials
Creep	Reflection of sound along curved surface from source near surface	Sound can be heard at points along surface; is inaudible away from surface		Move source away from surface
Standing waves	Steady, pure tone produces repeated sound paths between two parallel walls spaced apart at certain distances	In large rooms and high frequencies, many standing waves occur; total effect is less disturbing, frequently hardly noticeable	Can produce resonance, which is accentuation of particular frequency—problem for musical-performance spaces	Important only in rooms that are small in proportion to length of wavelength generated

Figure 19-3 Structure-borne sound. In this situation, the easiest way to reduce sound carried through the building structure would be to install padded carpeting upstairs.

Structured-borne sound has a higher initial energy level than airborne sound and attenuates slowly through the structure, thereby disturbing large sections of the building. Structure-borne sound is magnified by the sounding-board effect, such as when the handle of a tuning fork is placed on a table. The sound appears to be amplified, although it actually is a case of a more efficient energy transfer from the tuning fork to the human ear. Similarly, a vibrating pump may make little sound but will transfer a large amount of energy to the structure, resulting in audible sound at each partition, floor, or wall rigidly coupled to the structure. Soft or damping connections prevent energy transfer, so less energy is transferred into the connecting efficient radiation surfaces.

Structure-borne sound travels much more rapidly than airborne sound. Sound that travels along a massive structure will radiate outward from the structure only minimally—but enough to be quite annoying. The large mass minimizes vibration in the outward direction while focusing the speed along the direction of the structural members.

Diffraction

Although much of a sound wave is blocked by a small opening, the portion that is able to get through establishes a new wave front. The wavelength of the source wave and the size of the opening affect the amplitude of the diffracted wave. For a small hole, short wavelengths (high frequencies) are attenuated less than long wavelengths (low frequencies).

Diffraction is the physical process by which sound passes around obstructions and through very small openings. Any point on a sound wave can establish a new wave when it passes an obstacle. When most of the wave is blocked, the portion that gets through a small opening starts a new wave. A small hole, therefore, can block long wavelengths more than short ones.

Sound diffracts around or over a barrier. The ideal location for a barrier is either very close to the source or close to the receiver. The least desirable position is halfway between a source and a listener. A massively thick barrier is only slightly better than a moderately thick one, so there is a practical limit to thickness. Absorptive material on the source side of a barrier reduces the amount of noise reflected back to the source, but it does not help the receiver much.

Flanking Paths

Sound will find parallel or **flanking paths**, which are something like an acoustical short circuit. It is important to avoid locating doors and windows where they will allow shortcuts for sound. The most common flanking path is a plenum with ductwork, registers, and grilles. A plenum makes an excellent intercom unless it is completely lined with sound-absorbent material. Even then, low-frequency sound will get through.

Air turbulence in HVAC ductwork creates noise, which increases with increasing velocity and at sharp bends. Sound travels as easily against the airflow in an HVAC duct system as with the airflow. Both supply and return ducts should be lined with absorbent duct lining to control the transmission of fan noise.

DUCT LINING

Duct lining is acoustical insulation that is usually made of fiberglass impregnated with rubber or neoprene compound to prevent fibers from coming loose in the air current. Duct lining is available in thicknesses between 13 millimeters (½ in.) and 51 millimeters (2 in.) thick. In high-velocity ducts, the duct lining may be faced with perforated metal to prevent deterioration of the lining.

Typically, duct lining is installed only in rectangular ducts. Round ductwork requires an internal, perforated screen to hold the lining in place. There are proprietary products that mechanically fasten the lining to the interior surfaces of round ducts, saving effort and money.

Duct linings should not be used in such areas as humidifiers or cooling coils, where the air may be very moist. Moisture can condense on linings from cool air moving through the ducts, creating environments for the growth of mold, spores, and bacteria that can then be blown throughout a building. The mechanical engineer must provide adequate air movement and control the

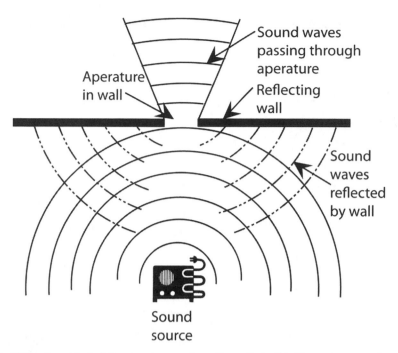

Figure 19-4 Diffraction. Most of the sound waves from the radio in this illustration are reflected back into the room. Those that pass through the wall continue to spread out beyond the opening. This is how a small gap can let more than a tiny stream of sound pass into the next room.

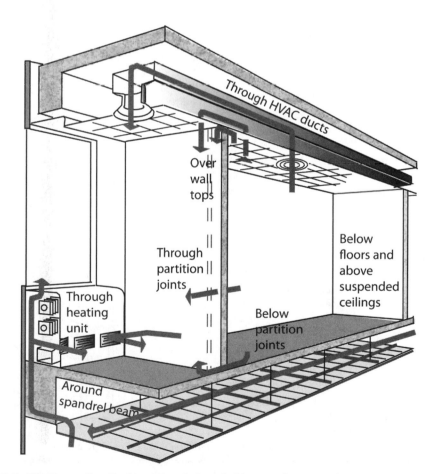

Figure 19-5 Flanking paths. Flanking transmission of airborne noise occurs in many ways: over, above, around, and through building components.

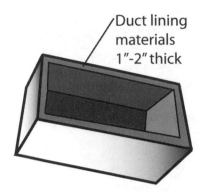

Duct lining
materials
1"-2" thick

Figure 19-6 Duct lining. Fiberglass was formerly used for acoustical duct lining, but would break down and release fibers when exposed to high-velocity air and emit small glass particles into the airstream. Newer duct-lining designs eliminate this problem.

air's moisture content. Duct linings should be avoided when the airflow is contaminated by laboratory hood exhausts or in some types of industrial or laboratory environments. Duct linings also should not be used in such healthcare areas as burn units, where bacteria present a significant problem; the only exception is when air is filtered before it enters the room.

Duct lining absorbs sound and attenuates noise as it moves along the ducts. Duct lining does not work as well for low frequencies as it does for high frequencies. When the ducts themselves are made of fiberglass, the attenuation is similar, but the lightweight construction allows sound to escape into the surrounding space. Duct lining is inexpensive and takes up little room.

Designing smooth transitions between ducts of different sizes is another way to reduce noise. Keeping adjacent ducts as far apart as possible can also minimize cross talk between rooms and between ducts. Gluing damping material on the outside prevents thin, metal duct walls from resonating. Mufflers and silencers on fans can reduce high-frequency noise, but they do not help much with lower frequencies.

TRANSMISSION LOSS

The most important measurement in defining the actual amount of sound loss provided by a barrier is **noise reduction (NR)**. Noise reduction is defined as the difference between the sound intensity levels in two rooms. NR should not be confused with an unrelated but similar term, noise-reduction coefficient (NRC).

Transmission loss (TL) is a measure of the performance of a building material or construction assembly in preventing the transmission of airborne sound. It is equal to the reduction in sound intensity as it passes through the material or assembly when tested in a laboratory at one-third octave band center frequencies between 125 Hertz and 4000 Hertz. In Europe, TL is referred to as sound reduction index (R).

The TL indicates the sound-insulating quality of a wall and is related to the wall's physical characteristics, mass, rigidity, materials of construction, and method of construction and attachment.

The **sound-transmission class (STC)** is a single-number rating of the performance of a building material or construction assembly in preventing the transmission of airborne sound. The STC is derived by comparing the laboratory TL test curve for a material or assembly to a standard frequency curve. The higher the STC rating, the greater the sound-isolation value. An open doorway has an STC value of 10. Normal construction has STC ratings between 30 and 60. Special construction is required to achieve an STC rating over 60.

Stiffness and Resonance

The stiffer a barrier, the more it will be set in motion by sound energy. The stiffness of a barrier is determined by its material and the rigidity of its mounting. In a stiff material, the sound-energy motion is passed from molecule to molecule, conducting sound very efficiently. Less stiffness results in high internal damping because the motion of the molecules is not transmitted well. Consequently, less stiff materials are good sound insulators. The rigidity of a mounting is like a drumhead: the tighter it is, the more sound it transmits. Stiff barriers transmit the most sound at low frequencies.

Lead sheet is sheet metal made of lead or a lead alloy. It is available combined with other materials, such as in leaded vinyl. Lead sheet is used to close off a plenum above a room where the partitions extend only to the suspended ceiling. Lead sheet effectively cuts down sound transmission because it is both heavy and limp. It easily conforms to irregularities and tightly seals barriers.

Steel joists and trusses are structural members used to support floors and roofs. They do not aid in sound attenuation, but their spacing and rigidity can affect vibration isolation. In general, steel structural components do not absorb sound, but they may help diffuse sound if they are exposed.

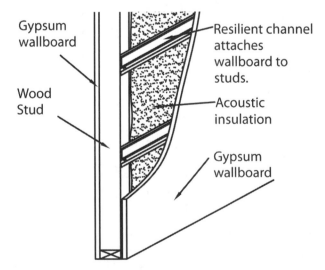

Gypsum wallboard

Wood Stud

Resilient channel attaches wallboard to studs.

Acoustic insulation

Gypsum wallboard

Figure 19-7 Resilient channels. Resilient channels separate a wall's structure from its surface material, in this case, gypsum wallboard. They make the wall a less stiff barrier, inhibiting vibrations from passing through to the other side.

Compound Barriers

The transmission loss of a sound barrier can be improved by constructing it as two separate layers that are not rigidly interconnected. The air in the cavity between the layers reduces the stiffness of the barrier and improves its ability to block sound.

The transmission loss for an entire cavity wall increases with the width of the air space at the rate of approximately 5 decibels (db) per doubling. Performance can be improved even more by filling the void with porous, sound-absorbent material. This acts to further decrease the stiffness of the compound structure and to absorb sound energy that reflects back and forth between the two inside surfaces.

Most partitions are built of light, upright framing members with plaster or gypsum-wallboard surfaces attached to both sides. This construction does not provide a very good sound barrier. Adding layers of gypsum wallboard to one or both sides increases the wall's mass and improves acoustical performance.

Gypsum wallboard consists of fire rated sheets of gypsum that has been heated to a high temperature, plus additives. These are then sandwiched between sheets of special paper. Gypsum wallboard is not very heavy or thick but provides fair sound attenuation. The best construction detail for blocking sound uses multiple layers of gypsum wallboard with a resilient separation between the two faces of the partition, and with absorptive material in the stud space. The wallboard joints must be perfectly sealed. Gypsum wallboard will resonate unless it is attached directly to a solid substrate without an air space; this enables gypsum wallboard to absorb low-frequency sounds. It is highly reflective at higher frequencies.

Compound barriers or cavity walls improve transmission loss when the void between the two sides of a wall is filled with porous, sound-absorbent material. This decreases the stiffness of the compound structure and absorbs the sound energy reflecting back and forth between the inside wall surfaces. Steel channel studs are used to frame partitions and are covered with gypsum wallboard. Light-gauge steel studs are lightly resilient, which helps the wall attenuate sound. Heavy-gauge steel studs and wood studs are stiffer and offer less sound attenuation. Steel or wood studs do not add significantly to a wall's sound absorption.

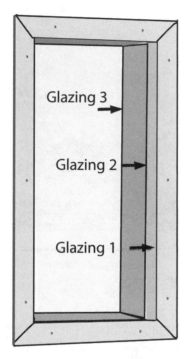

Figure 19-8 Acoustical window. The more layers of rigid but flexibly installed material separated by airspaces, the less sound will pass through an opening.

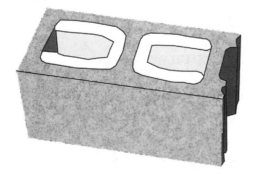

Figure 19-9 Acoustical insulation in concrete masonry unit. Special acoustical liners are produced to fit inside the openings in concrete blocks, significantly increasing a concrete masonry unit (CMU) wall's acoustical transmission loss.

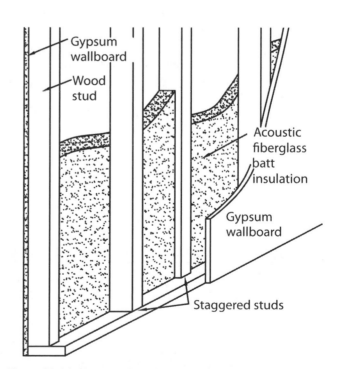

Figure 19-10 Staggered-stud partition. One of the best ways to block sound from one room to another is to stagger the wall studs and fill the spaces with acoustical insulation. This produces a wider wall that effectively blocks sound.

When one layer of gypsum wallboard is attached to the framing with resilient metal clips instead of tight screws, the structure-borne transmission of sound through the partition is reduced substantially. Resilient clips and channels are usually made of light-gauge sheet metal and are used between studs or joists and the finished gypsum-wallboard or plaster surface. They are highly effective with wood joists and studs. By breaking the rigid connection between the two faces of the partition, resilient channels and clips permit room surfaces to vibrate normally without transmitting vibrating motions and their associated noise to the supporting structure. They also decrease the sound transmission through the partition or ceiling.

When the studs are used in two unconnected rows, their stiffness is not an issue. Staggered-stud partitions for reducing sound transmission between rooms are framed with two separate rows of studs arranged in a zigzag fashion and supporting opposite faces of the partition. This type of wall is often used in recording studios. A fiberglass blanket is usually inserted between the rows of studs. A stud wall with staggered studs is better than a single-material or common stud wall.

Sound Transmission Between Rooms

Wherever an opening exists—even a keyhole, a slot at the bottom of a door, or a crack between a partition and the ceiling—sound will move from one room to another. Weatherstripping cracks around ill-fitting windows and doors and closing all other cracks and openings with airtight sealants eliminate this problem. The use of telephones with mechanical ringers or wall-hung phones with electronic ringers that vibrate through to the adjacent unit should be avoided. Mounting sound-system speakers on resilient padding can minimize the transmission of low-frequency noise. Installing closers on all cabinetry decreases impact vibration that reradiates as sound to an adjacent space.

A small, sealed air space improves thermal insulation better than a large one, which could permit convection currents to transfer heat. However, a narrow air gap does not work acoustically: it acts as a stiff spring between the panes and does an excellent job of transmitting sound. On the other hand, a large space traps acoustical energy and provides a noise barrier.

Partitions from the top of a floor slab to the underside of the next floor provide maximum sound isolation. For best results,

Figure 19-11 Acoustical insulation in interior wall. This is the acoustical batt insulation shown in its bags earlier installed in a wall. *Photo credit: Herb Fremin*

partitions should be built in as massive and airtight a manner as possible. **Acoustical mass** resists the transmission of sound by the inertia and elasticity of the transmitting medium. In general, the heavier and denser a body, the greater is its resistance to sound transmission.

Thick brick walls provide a good sound barrier between rooms. A partition of concrete blocks is not as effective because it is somewhat porous and allows sound to penetrate. Adding plaster on one or both surfaces results in a better, airtight wall.

TABLE 19-2. IMPROVING SOUND-TRANSMISSION-CLASS RATINGS IN STUD WALLS

Partition Condition	Description	STC
Basic partition	Single wood studs, 16 in. on centers, ½ in. gypsum board on both sides, air cavity	35
Add to basic partition	Double gypsum board, one side	+2
	Double gypsum board, both sides	+4
	Single-thickness absorbent material in air cavity	+3
	Double-thickness insulation	+6
	Resilient channel supports for gypsum board	+5
	Staggered studs	+9
	Double studs	+13

However, as discussed earlier in this chapter in the section on structure-borne sound (see page 402), an impact on a massive wall can be transmitted throughout a building if the structure is rigid.

The overall acoustical performance of **composite walls**—those walls with a window, door, vent, or other opening—is strongly affected by the element with the highest sound transmission. The acoustical quality is harmed less if the poor-performing element is much smaller than the better-performing parts of the wall. Even a very small opening seriously degrades the ability to keep sound within the room.

Doors

The acoustical performance of a door depends on its core construction (hollow or solid), its thickness, any openings through or around the door, and whether the door is constructed singly, as a sequenced pair of doors, or as part of a special acoustical construction.

TABLE 19-3. TYPICAL SOUND TRANSMISSION CLASS VALUES FOR DOORS

Door Construction	STC
Louvered door	15
Any door with 2 in. undercut	17
1 ½ in. hollow-core door; no gasketing	22
1½ in. hollow-core door; gaskets; drop closure	25
1¾ in. solid-wood door; no gasketing	30
1¾ in. solid-wood door; gaskets; drop closure	35
Two hollow-core doors; gasketed all around; sound lock	45
Two solid-core doors; gasketed all around; sound lock	55
Special commercial construction; lead lining; full sealing	45–65

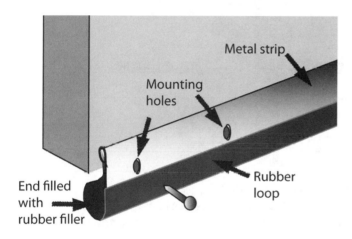

Figure 19-12 Acoustical door sweep. Doors undercut to permit air movement are useless as sound barriers. An acoustical door sweep is a simple way to block the gap when necessary.

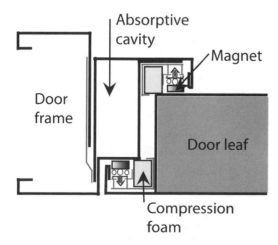

Figure 19-13 Acoustical door seal with magnet. Here, compression foam is held in place with magnets. The door, of course, must be steel.

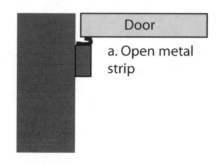

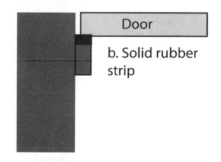

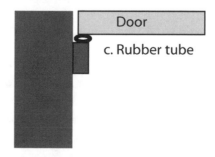

Figure 19-14 Acoustical door jamb seals. An open metal strip is compressed when the door is closed (a), while compressible rubber serves as a seal, as shown in (b) and (c).

The most important step in soundproofing doors is completely sealing around the opening. A door in the closed position should exert pressure on gaskets, thereby making the joints airtight. Louvered and undercut doors are useless as sound barriers.

There are many kinds of door seals. All of them block the gap at the door jamb with a compressible material.

Special sound-insulated wood flush doors have their faces separated by a void or a damping compound. They are installed with special stops, gaskets, and thresholds.

Windows

Exterior walls usually have a high STC, but windows are the weakest part. Sound leaks through cracks in operable windows are more critical than the type of glazing in terms of keeping sound out. Weatherstripping for thermal reasons helps acoustical performance. The manner of opening and the window placement also affect transmission loss.

Plate glass that is 13 millimeters (½ in.) thick has an STC in the low 30s, while laminated glass of the same thickness may approach an STC of 40.

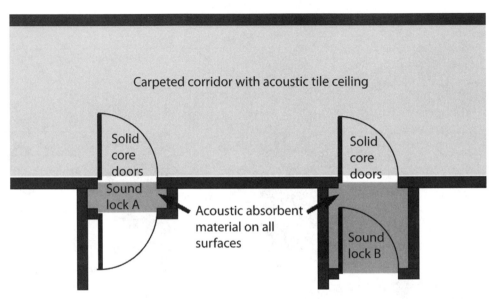

Figure 19-15 Two-door sound locks. Two gasketed doors, preferably with enough space between them for a door swing, are used to create a sound lock. All surfaces in the sound lock are completely covered with absorbent materials, and the floor is carpeted. A sound lock increases attenuation by a minimum of 10 decibels and by as much as 20 decibels at some frequencies.

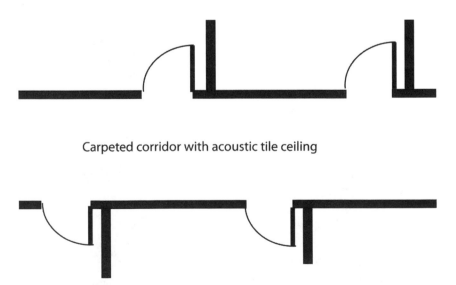

Figure 19-16 Arrangement of doors on corridor. In order to keep sound from passing easily from one space to another, doors in residential buildings, including private homes, apartments, dormitories, and hotels, and in commercial offices should not be located directly across from each other.

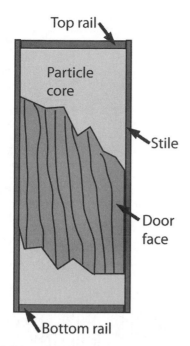

Figure 19-17 Solid-core door. Solid-core doors are superior to hollow-core doors as barriers to sound. The construction and installation of the frame also make a difference.

STEEL DECKING

Steel decking is sheet steel that is corrugated for strength. It is highly sound-reflective unless it is free to vibrate, when it will absorb low frequencies. Steel decking is used for noise barriers along highways. It is often used as a base for other materials, but the combined mass of the deck and the concrete topping are not much better at reducing sound transmission than the concrete by itself.

Operable and Demountable Partition Systems

Lightweight operable and demountable partition systems have many panel joints, floor and ceiling tracks, and side wall intersections where sound can escape. It is relatively easy to seal a fixed partition, but the seals for operable or demountable partitions must also be operable and durable enough to last the life of

the installation with minimal maintenance. The details of the materials, system, and specifications must ensure that panel joint seals will last.

None of the designs for operable partitions completely eliminate the transmission of sound between the spaces they separate. It is not advisable to have a noisy function, such as a wedding reception, on one side of an operable partition while a quiet meeting takes place on the other. Although operable partitions are installed with jamb and bottom seals, deflection of the end wall where the operable panel partition is installed can allow sound leakage. Heavy-duty bottom seals may be required to prevent noise from passing through a textured floor covering, such as a loop pile carpet.

Demountable partitions are available as either gypsum panel systems or unitized panel partitions. The framing for the thicker gypsum panels is erected separately with concealed fasteners and pressure-fit members.

CUSHIONING IMPACTS

Impact noise is often the most serious acoustical problem in buildings with multiple residents. Reducing the sound of footfalls and other impacts on the floor can be done in a variety of ways. Kitchens and bathrooms should be stacked and not located over living rooms or bedrooms. Interior designers should specify felt sliders for chairs and other movable furniture.

Cushioning the initial impact that produces a noise will frequently eliminate all but severe problems. The impact isolation class (IIC) is a rating for floor construction, similar to STC ratings for walls. The IIC is based on tests of actual construction using a

TABLE 19-5. IMPACT ISOLATION CLASS RATINGS AND RESILIENT FLOORING

Type	Add Resilient Material	IIC Rating
Tile	1/16-in. vinyl	0
	1/8-in. linoleum, rubber tile	3–5
	1/4-in. cork	8–12
Carpet	Low pile: fiber pad	10–14
	Low pile: foam-rubber pad	15–21
	High pile: foam-rubber pad	21–27

TABLE 19-4. TYPICAL SOUND-TRANSMISSION-CLASS VALUES FOR WINDOWS

Window Construction	Description	STC
Operable wood sash	1/8 in. glass; unsealed	23
	1/4 in. glass; unsealed	25
	1/4 in. glass; gasketed	30
	Laminated glass; unsealed	28
	Double-glazed, 1/8 in. panes; 3/8 in. air space; gasketed	29
Fixed sash	Double 1/8 in. panes; 3 in. air space; gasketed	44
	Double 1/8 in. panes; 3 in. air space; gasketed	48

TABLE 19-6. CONTROLLING IMPACT NOISE

Solution	Strategy	Material or Product	Conditions	Avoid
Cushion impact	Resilient cushioning materials	Carpeting with pad	Direct impact force reduced	Hard materials attached directly to structure
		Floor tile: rubber, cork		
Float floor	Separate impacted floor from structural floor by using resilient element	Rubber or mineral wool pads or blankets	Load spread evenly over large area; airtight construction, especially where partition rests on floating floor	Short-circuits at walls of by penetrations; mixed construction types that invite flanking noise paths
		Spring-metal sleepers		
Suspend ceiling	Suspended ceiling with acoustical absorbent layer	Resilient separators	Floor slab above must be decoupled from walls below	Avoid flanking paths into walls, then into space below
Isolate piping	All rigid structures isolated	Resilient sealant	Penetrations by piping caulked	Avoid flanking and air-sound leakage paths

tapping machine, and the results are compared to a standard. The IIC rating is influenced by the weights of the floor system and the suspended ceiling below, the sound absorption in the cavity between the floor and ceiling, whether the floor is carpeted or not, and the type of building structural system. Wood structural components and wood bearing walls lower the IIC when compared with post-and-slab steel buildings.

Floor finishes can increase IIC ratings. Resilient tile has little effect on the sound attenuation of the floor construction, but it will help reduce the sound generated by high-frequency impacts, especially if it is foam backed. Vinyl tile 1.6 millimeters (¹⁄₁₆ in.) thick has an IIC rating of zero. Linoleum or rubber tile 3 millimeters (¹⁄₈ in.) thick is rated between 3 and 5. Cork tile 6.4 millimeters (¹⁄₄ in.) thick is rated between 8 and 12.

Floor/ceiling assemblies with relatively low STC ratings may have high IIC ratings, especially if the floor is carpeted. This means that sound may be transmitted through the wall from an airborne source, yet direct impact on the floor will be muted.

☑ **Living units above other occupied living units should probably be carpeted. Carpet with padding provides excellent impact isolation. It is most useful when the floor structure is exposed to the space below as well as in buildings with wood bearing wall construction. Often, condominium rules require carpets in hallways and foyers and over half of the other living areas to minimize most of the objectionable footfall noise.**

Isolating Sound in Floor and Ceiling Spaces

Another approach to controlling impact noise is to suspend the ceiling and use an absorber in the resulting cavity. The most disturbing noise tends to be that which radiates down from the ceiling. A flexibly suspended ceiling with an acoustically absorbent layer suspended in it is effective when paths leading into walls and reradiating into the space below do not flank it. The insulation is usually 76 to 152 millimeters (3–6) thick and not packed

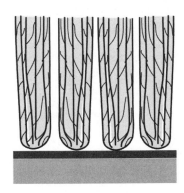

Figure 19-18 Carpet pad. Low-pile carpet on a fiber pad has IIC ratings between 10 and 14. With a foam-rubber pad, the IIC rating increases to 15 to 21. High-pile carpet with a foam-rubber pad earns IIC ratings between 21 and 27.

into the space. Insulation may lie on the ceiling or be attached to the underside of the floor. When blown-in insulation is used, it must evenly cover the area and not be packed into the cavity.

Two or more layers of gypsum wallboard on a metal channel frame suspended from vibration-isolation hangers can replace or be added to an existing ceiling. A double-layer gypsum wallboard ceiling can also be installed on resilient channels or clips, with fiberglass insulation in the cavity.

Installing a resilient layer between the structural floor and a hard-finish floor treatment like marble, ceramic tile, or wood will help cushion impacts. Resilient products are often installed beneath lightweight gypsum concrete or other lightweight leveling materials. Floor underlayments are used to control sound transmission of both impact and airborne noise in floor systems and consist of precompressed molded glass fibers. The sound mat is installed between a plywood subfloor and the floor's finish material. They provide a system that is stiff enough to prevent grout cracking in tile floors while being resilient enough to greatly reduce noise.

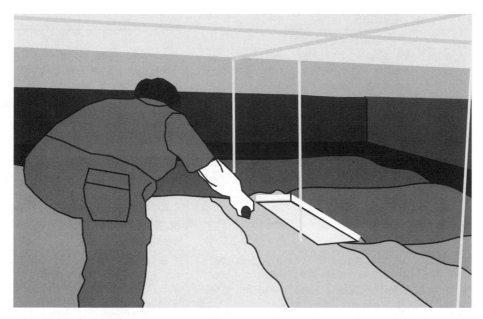

Figure 19-19 Insulating above suspended ceiling. Low ceilings and limited, safe walking space can make adding insulation to an existing ceiling difficult.

Wood decking supported by beams or trusses to form a floor or roof are often used for exposed ceilings. Wood decking has a relatively low mass and does not attenuate sound well unless it is ballasted with heavier materials. Wood decks are acoustically reflective, but cracks between boards absorb a fair amount of sound. Increasing the weight of the structural floor may help, but this is often not feasible and requires a significant increase in mass to be effective.

FLOATING FLOORS

Floating floors reduce transmission of impact noise and increase the acoustical TL rating of a structure. These floors are used in condominiums, apartments, and commercial buildings to control the impact noise produced by footfalls or other impacts. Floating

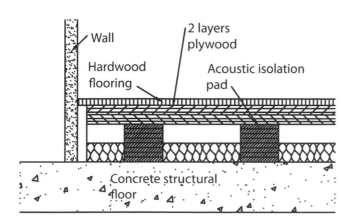

Figure 19-20 Floating floor. A floating floor can be an effective way to isolate impact noise.

floors reduce the transmission of external noise into recording studios, sound rooms, and television and movie studios. Floating wood floors are used for dance and exercise floors with resiliency requirements.

A floating floor can be separated from the structural floor by a resilient element, such as rubber or mineral wool pads, blankets, or special spring metal sleepers. The effectiveness of such a system depends on the mass of the floating floor, the compliance of the resilient support, and most important, the degree of isolation of the floating floor, avoiding flanking paths at the borders.

The mass of the floating floor must be large enough to spread loads properly; otherwise, the padding underneath will compress, deform, and transmit impacts. The total construction must be airtight and, consequently, sound tight. When partitions rest on a floating floor, they must not compress it. Flanking paths that allow sound to escape at walls or penetrations should be avoided. The construction should be consistent throughout because mixed construction types create flanking paths.

First, isolation pads are placed on the floor, separated by low-density acoustical fiberglass. Then, continuous wood nailers or steel channels are installed, and a plywood subfloor is constructed. Depending on the design requirements, multiple layers of plywood or a combination of plywood and gypsum board may be specified. A floating wood floor is completed with the installation of parquet, hardwood, vinyl tile, or other finish flooring.

Roll-out floating, concrete floor systems consist of 51-millimeter (2 in.) thick, high-density precompressed molded fiberglass isolation pads, separated by low-density acoustical fiberglass. Mechanical equipment noise, loud musical instruments, and industrial noise can all be significantly attenuated with floating concrete floors. The floating floor material is laid over the structural concrete floor and topped with a floating layer of concrete.

TABLE 19-7. ACOUSTICAL DEVICES

Device	Description	Use
Air springs	Work by trapping volume of air in inflexible jacket. Spring is installed to eliminate any mechanical ties between building structure and what is to be isolated. Compressible air provides spring. Air pressure plus jacket provide stiffness.	Vibration isolation; custom designed for critical applications where only extremely low levels of vibration can be tolerated
Resilient hangers (vibration isolators)	Steel springs, pieces of rubber-like materials, or compressed fiberglass; resilient ceiling hangers improve attenuation even better than resilient clips	Spring-like devices designed to support suspended ceilings or to suspend pieces of mechanical equipment or ducts or pipes connected to equipment
Resilient mounts	Similar to resilient hangers, for floors; double floors with structural slab and floating slab provide exceptionally good sound attenuation	Used as vibration-isolating supports for mechanical equipment; also used to support floating floors, where they are typically 51 mm (2 in.) tall and made of solid neoprene or neoprene-covered fiberglass
Flexible connections	Flexible inserts of canvas or leaded vinyl that are located between two pieces of metal duct; flexible conduit or flexible hose are also considered flexible connections	Offer resilient breaks in ducts, pipes to attenuate vibrations; essential in all duct, pipe, and conduit runs between piece of vibration-isolated equipment and building structure
Sway braces	Neoprene or fiberglass insulating material attached to steel clips or angles; small angle braces lend stability to masonry walls whose tops must be kept free of slab above for sound-isolation reasons	Allow structure to be supported without any rigid ties; construction of freestanding walls in double-wall construction where rigid braces would reduce sound attenuation
Gaskets	Airtight seals of pliable neoprene or vinyl designed for acoustical doors and sound-rated partition systems	Eliminate air leaks; perfect fit required to provide maximum attenuation in sound locks

Another type of floating device for a concrete floor is used for areas with regular perimeters and light or uniform loads. Isolation mounts are placed up to 122 centimeters (4 ft.) on center each way on top of polyethylene that has been laid on the structural floor. Then, reinforcing bars are installed across rows of isolators, and the concrete is poured. After curing, the slab is raised to operating height using built-in jack screws or spring-lift slabs.

Special Acoustical Devices

When a building design calls for the placement of quiet spaces, such as executive offices, conference rooms, theaters, and recording studios next to, under, or over noisy mechanical equipment rooms, kitchens, or manufacturing spaces, additional measures must be taken to ensure that quiet spaces will remain quiet. Double partitions and high mass ceiling materials are used to create a room within a room with a floating floor. Acoustical product manufacturers have developed systems for gypsum wallboard that isolate the partitions from the structure while providing lateral restraint to prevent toppling or collapse. The systems include resilient, loadbearing underlayment, vertical joint isolation material, sway braces, and top wall brackets.

In Chapter 20: Acoustical Applications, we will review common acoustical problems in different types of spaces and explore their solutions.

....

20

Acoustical Applications

Interior designers can have a profound effect on the acoustical quality of an interior environment. Each of the types of interior spaces discussed below has its own acoustical requirements and recommended treatments.

SPEECH PRIVACY

When interior designers want to keep the sounds of conversation contained within an office, a good place to start is with the use of absorbent materials, which reduce sound levels within a room. This lowers the level of sound that is available to pass to adjacent spaces. Next, designing barriers between spaces with heavy, airtight construction cuts down on the amount of sound transmitted to adjoining rooms. Providing masking noise in neighboring spaces helps disguise the information carried by speech and makes it less intrusive.

RELATIVE QUALITY OF SOUND ISOLATION

Designers identify a number of levels of acoustical separation, related to the amount of acoustical privacy that is needed.

Total privacy:
- Barrier sound-transmission class (STC) 46–50
- Shouting barely audible
- Music room, practice room, sound studio, bedrooms adjacent to noisy areas

Excellent sound isolation:
- Barrier STC 42–45
- Normal voice levels inaudible; raised voices barely audible but not intelligible
- For dividing noisy and quiet areas; party wall between apartments

Very good sound isolation:
- Barrier STC 35
- Normal voice levels barely audible
- Raised voices audible but largely unintelligible
- Suitable for offices next to quiet spaces

Good sound isolation:
- Normal voice levels audible but generally unintelligible
- Raised voices partially intelligible
- Room divider where concentration is not essential

Fair sound isolation:
- Barrier STC 30
- Normal voice levels audible and intelligible some of the time
- Raised voices generally intelligible
- Space divider

Poor sound isolation:
- Normal voice audible and intelligible most of the time

No sound isolation:
- Normal voice levels always intelligible

Enclosed Offices

Some offices require more intense efforts to ensure speech privacy than others. The level of acoustical treatment in the room where the sound originates depends on the loudness of the speech, the effect of the room's sound absorption on the speech level, and the degree of privacy required.

The amount of privacy is also affected by the acoustical isolation of the receiving room. This depends on the STC rating of the

TABLE 20-1. PARTITION SOUND-TRANSMISSION-CLASS RATINGS

Type of Partition	Description	STC
Demountable partition	Up to acoustical ceiling	20–30
Drywall partition	Up to acoustical ceiling	30
	Extending 12 inches above acoustical ceiling-tile system into ceiling plenum	35
	With cavity insulation, full height to underside of slab above	40–45
	Two layers with insulation, full height to underside of slab above	50

barrier between the rooms, the noise-reduction (NR) factor, and the background noise level in the receiving room. Greater sound absorption in the receiving room reduces the reverberation build-up of sound for a listener, lowering the speech level and intelligibility. The larger the size of the listener's room as compared with the source room, the lower the speech level will be in the receiving room.

Acoustical consultants use a speech privacy analysis method that quantifies the principal acoustical factors into a single privacy rating number. This method is used both to analyze existing spaces and to design new spaces.

RECOMMENDED STCS FOR PARTITIONS IN OFFICES

Executive office, physician's suite, confidential privacy adjacent to:
- Another office STC 45–50
- General office area STC 45–48

- Public corridor STC 42–45
- Washroom, toilet room STC 47–50

Normal office areas adjacent to:
- Other offices, public corridors STC 38–40
- Washroom, kitchen, dining area STC 40–42

Conference rooms adjacent to:
- Corridor, lobby STC 35–38
- Kitchen, dining area, data processing STC 38–40

Open Offices

Open offices create a multitude of problems for achieving speech privacy. Open-office spaces are more densely populated with office workers, with fewer buffering spaces, such as storerooms, between people. The trend toward more employees working at computers or desks results in open-office plans with increasingly smaller cubicles for one or two people.

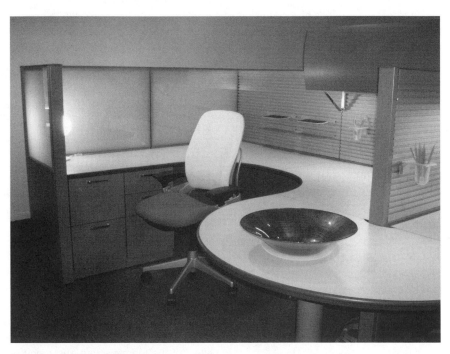

Figure 20-1 Modular office cubicle. In recent years, office systems manufacturers and distributors have lightened the look of their products. In doing so, they have effectively given up trying to achieve speech privacy with cubicle walls.

LEVELS OF SPEECH PRIVACY

The amount of speech privacy required in an open office varies. Acoustical consultants identify three levels of speech privacy: normal, confidential, and transitional.

Normal speech privacy:

- This level allows normal voice levels from an adjacent cubicle to be heard, but without easy intelligibility.
- Raised voices will generally be intelligible.
- Where overall noise levels are low, background-noise levels should remain within 6 decibels (db) of the intruding sound to obscure speech.

Confidential speech privacy:

- This level requires that normal voice levels are audible, but in general, they are unintelligible.
- Raised voices may be partially intelligible.
- The background noise level should be no more than 2 decibels less than the intruding sound and a maximum of 3 decibels more.

Figure 20-2 Sound in open office. Sound in open offices can travel directly from the source to the listener; it may also be diffracted by objects in its path or reflected off ceilings or walls. The architectural arrangement of a space has a great impact on speech privacy. When an open-office plan is designed, spaces should be grouped according to their speech-privacy requirements. Confidential areas should be at the edge of open areas that serve as a buffer zone, with low overall sound levels, including any background noise.

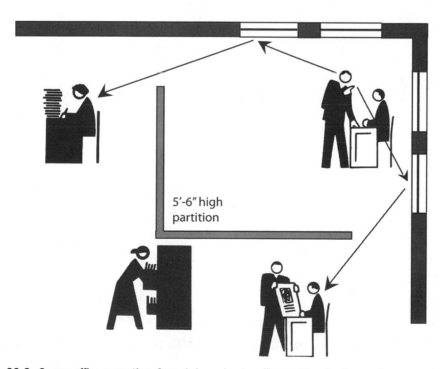

5'-6" high partition

Figure 20-3 Corner office acoustics. Speech in perimeter offices with reflective surfaces may bounce out into areas occupied by other workers. High noise production areas should be grouped and placed on the perimeter at a maximum distance from confidential areas.

- In such a space, 95 percent of the people do not sense sound as intrusive and disturbing, and are able to concentrate on most types of work.

Transitional speech privacy (minimal or marginal privacy):
- This level is considered to be intolerable by around 40 percent of people, and the number of people whose productivity would suffer is even higher.
- Speech at normal voice levels in adjoining open offices is readily understood most of the time, and the overall noise level is average.
- Intruding speech levels may be 10 decibels or more than the background noise level.
- Offices with two occupants or one office receiving noise from three adjacent offices have transitional levels of speech privacy.
- It is almost impossible to have adequate speech privacy in a cubicle shared by two people.

Open areas within an open-office plan should be as large as possible with acoustical insulation on the perimeter walls. Ceiling height should be no lower than 2.75 meters (9 ft.), with a 914 centimeter (3-ft.) plenum above. Ductwork should be acoustically treated.

Individual office cubicles should be as enclosed as possible, with the maximum partition height possible. Occupants should be at least 3 meters (10 ft.) apart, which increases to 3.7 meters (12 ft.) for normal privacy and 4.9 meters (16 ft.) for confidential privacy.

The absorption characteristics of the ceiling are the most important factor in designing open-office speech privacy. Metal air pan diffusers and flat lighting fixtures provide strongly reflective speech paths, which bounce sound rising from one cubicle down into another. Highly absorptive baffle strips on equipment perimeters help block sound paths.

RATINGS FOR CEILING FINISHES

Absorption coefficients are used with all sorts of materials to measure how well they absorb sound. A perfect absorption score would theoretically be one, so most acoustically absorbent materials have ratings in decimals less than one, although a few highly absorptive materials are rated higher.

As mentioned earlier, in open-office design, the ceiling's absorption characteristics are the critical factors in speech privacy. Speech sounds strike the ceiling between 30 and 60 degrees, with most of the sound striking above 45 degrees.

Articulation class (AC) ratings are designed for open-office conditions. They indicate how well ceiling materials absorb speech sound striking between 45 and 55 degrees. AC ratings usually range between 210 and 180; the higher the number, the less sound bounces off the ceiling into adjacent cubicles.

Ceiling attenuation class (CAC) ratings measure how well a ceiling structure attenuates airborne sound between two closed rooms over the range of speech frequencies.

Noise reduction coefficients (NRCs) measure the average percentage of noise that a material absorbs in the mid-frequency range. Refer to Table 18.1 in Chapter 18 (see page 391).

The Public Building Service of the U.S. General Services Administration (GSA) sets criteria and standards for the design, specification, and evaluation of systems and components for open-office spaces in federal buildings. The GSA's **speech privacy potential (SPP) rating** is a summary of background-sound level and attenuation between typical source and listener locations. Interior designers may encounter this rating when doing work in federally owned buildings as well as when specifying materials that are marketed to government agencies.

In terms of selecting the most efficient ceiling tile for speech privacy, the best choice is the tile with the best absorption at voice frequencies; AC ratings indicate this capacity. For general sound at a variety of levels, the absorption coefficients are the best indicators. Although the CAC rating indicates how much sound passes through to the space above the ceiling, this is, in general, less important because it can be readily dissipated and absorbed within this space.

Table 20-2 provides a hypothetical example for comparison. Note that although the CAC rating for the mineral tiles is higher, both the NRC and AC ratings make light fiberglass a better choice.

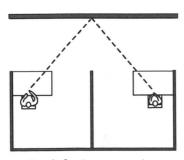 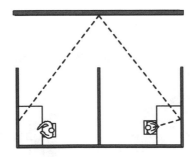 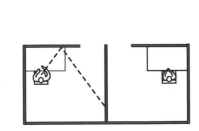

a. Desk facing opening　　b. Desks facing partition　　c. Desk surrounded by partitions

Figure 20-4 Cubicle desk orientations. Desk orientations do not need to be the same in all cubicles. When furniture arrangements alternate, more speech sound is blocked.

TABLE 20-2. COMPARISON OF CEILING TILES

Material	NRC Rating	AC Rating	CAC Rating
Light fiberglass ceiling tiles	0.95 at voice frequencies	200	26
Mineral-fiber tiles	0.8–0.85	180	40

☑ **If flat-bottom lighting fixtures are placed directly over low office partitions, they provide a speech path between the offices. From an acoustical standpoint, the best fixture has deep reflector cells with parabolic bottom surfaces (which are what reflects both light and sound) in a 31 x 122 cm (1 x 4 ft.) or 61 x 122 m (2 x 4 ft.) format.**

Because sound always finds the path of least resistance, very little sound actually passes through low office partitions; it usually goes over the top of the partitions. When a speaker's mouth is between 112 centimeters and 122 centimeters (44–48 in.) high and about a meter (3 ft.) away from the partition, the partition should have an STC of 25 to 26. With greater distance and height, an STC of 20 to 22 is permissible. AC ratings should be in the 200–220 range. Joints between partitions should be carefully sealed because even small openings lower efficiency. For acoustical isolation, partitions should reach the floor, although lower areas do not have to be insulated in low speech-privacy areas.

Partitions must be high enough to block direct line-of-sight voice transmissions. The median height of the mouth of a standing American man is 160 centimeters (63 in.), so partitions should not be lower than 165 centimeters (65 in.), and preferably between 168 centimeters and 183 centimeters (66–72) when located between cubicles. Because the greater 183-centimeter height also blocks vision, tall partitions are typically used only between departments, with 160–168-centimeter high partitions between cubicles.

☑ **Teamwork areas should either be located away from normal working spaces or be completely enclosed in full-height fixed or demountable partitions. Areas with raised voice levels, such as videoconferencing rooms, telecommunications spaces, and areas with speaker phones or voice-activated computers, should be sited carefully or completely enclosed.**

GLASS SURFACES

Windows often are located in managers' offices, where confidential discussions routinely take place. Windows and walls that lack absorptive treatment will reflect sound out of the space at an angle. To preserve privacy in these offices, full-height partitions and fixed glass vision panels should be used, with doors in openings. If windows are present, heavy drapes can be used to eliminate reflections. Such confidential spaces should be located in groups and buffered from open-office spaces with unoccupied storage areas.

Floors in open offices do not affect the overall sound absorption very much. However, cushioned floors greatly reduce the noise of chair movements and footfalls. For this reason, all floors

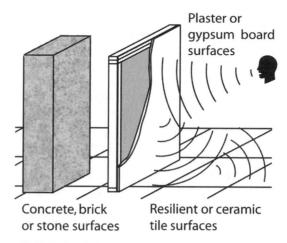

Figure 20-5 Reflective surfaces. Many common interior finish and building materials reflect sound.

in open-office areas should be carpeted, but pile depth makes only a minimal difference. Using a polyurethane pad rather than jute provides the same positive difference as a thicker pile.

Masking Sound

Background sound that is close to the frequency of speech reduces the intelligibility of speech. In a busy room full of people, so much noise is generated in the frequency range of human speech that only the closest, most attentive listeners can understand what people standing right next to them say. For the same reason, a spy will turn up the radio before holding a conversation in a room that may be bugged.

Noise that carries information reduces the productivity of office workers. What people hear depends on how much attention they are paying to what they are doing and to the intrusiveness of the outside sound. In a very quiet space with no background noise, any sound is distracting. With a constant ambient sound level in the listener's room, sound transmitted from another room is masked, becoming inaudible or simply less annoying.

When it is too costly or too difficult to treat a building for a persistent or distracting noise source, low-level **masking noise** may help. Masking sounds are also useful in rooms that are so quiet that heartbeats, respiration, and body movement sounds are annoying, such as in a bedroom where small noises disturb would-be sleepers.

The heating, ventilation, and air-conditioning (HVAC) system background-sound levels rarely provide the spatial uniformity necessary for speech privacy. Practically all open-plan office installations use carefully designed electronic masking systems to provide uniform background sound at the proper level and with good tonal characteristics. Such masking systems are usually operated at or near the upper limits of acceptability for average building occupants, which is around 50 decibels. Higher sound levels make the masking sounds themselves a source of annoyance.

For use in offices, **sound-masking units** are hung above the ceiling, where they are completely out of sight. The sound masking fills the plenum area, then gently filters down through the ceiling tiles into the office space below to unobtrusively raise the background sound level. The speakers can be adjusted to the individual acoustical comfort requirement in any given area.

Masking-system loudspeakers should not be visible because they attract interest and eventually become annoying. They can be placed face-up in a plenum to increase dispersion and improve uniformity, but should not be mounted face-down in the ceiling. Most ceiling tiles will allow masking sound to penetrate to the office area below.

Suspended ceiling systems are available that not only incorporate wireless systems for office communication, but also include sound systems that deliver sound masking, paging, and music simultaneously, without shutting off the masking sound. All three modes are delivered through the same set of speakers that blend invisibly into the ceiling plane. This eliminates the need for redundant systems.

SPACES FOR MUSIC AND PERFORMANCE

The design of spaces for musical and other performances is both an art and a science. For concert halls and other important music spaces, the services of an acoustical consultant are essential.

Although the architectural character of a performance space is usually worked out well before the interior designer becomes involved in the project, the finishes and details of the hall's interior are critical to its acoustical success. A relatively long reverberation time is needed for music, so the amount of sound reflection and the liveliness of the space matter a great deal. Because brilliance of musical tone is primarily a function of high-frequency content, spaces that are too absorbent will dull musical sounds. A good sound path for musical tone is equivalent to a good visual path, which means that a seat that provides a good view of the performers is likely to also be a good seat acoustically.

Figure 20-6 Sound masking equipment. The number of sound-masking units required depends on the size of the area to be masked. On average, one unit can cover approximately 21 to 23 square meters (225–250 square ft.). The units are easy to install and maintenance free, and have negligible operating costs.

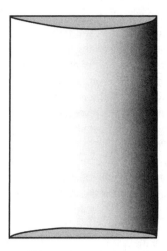

Figure 20-7 Convex diffuser. Acoustical-device manufacturers offer products that address specific needs. This convex diffuser is designed to spread sound evenly.

When people listen to music, they want a sense of the direction of the source. This sense, called **directivity**, declines if a reinforced signal is excessively delayed by too many reflective surfaces.

Diffusion is desirable for musical performances because it spreads the sound evenly over a wide seating area. Sound reflected from convex (outward-curving) surfaces is diffuse, producing a constant sound level throughout the space.

The acoustical design of a space for the performance of music, theater, or other presentations starts with control of all undesired sounds from exterior sources, adjacent spaces within the building, the HVAC system, and other noise sources. Next, all sounds that the audience has come to hear are controlled so that they are adequately loud and properly distributed without echo or distortion throughout the space. Typical paths from the sound source to the receiver are studied, usually using computer-aided design (CAD) and analysis procedures.

In order to ensure that the sound source is loud enough, major room surfaces can be reinforced naturally to direct reflected sound to the audience. Sound reinforcement is coordinated with the basic acoustics of the room. Electronic reinforcement systems are used in large rooms or for weak sources (see page 427). Very large auditoriums and sports arenas use electronic amplification systems.

Concert Halls

The traditional European shoebox-shaped hall developed along with Western classical music, and the two influenced each other. During the fourth century under Constantine, churches were modeled after the Roman civic basilica. The very long reverberation times of these buildings literally turned speech into music. This had a profound effect on the development of European music. Monophonic chant developed from speech, and the rhythm was provided by the Latin text. Eventually, harmony and

polyphony were added. The evolution of the organ for religious music occurred along with the architecture of the cathedrals it fills with sound. Traditional European concert music was developed from this environment.

Through the Renaissance, secular music evolved in rooms that were not designed specifically for musical performance. Music was performed in small oratories with a rectangular shape and in rectangular palace ballrooms. Eventually, with the evolution of a middle class with leisure time and money, concerts moved out of oratories into new concert halls with the same rectangular shape. The construction methods, aesthetics, and the ability of patrons to see and be seen influenced the design. Composers wrote music for the acoustical qualities of these specific spaces.

Traditional shoebox-shaped concert halls were successful due to their narrow tall shape with plenty of lateral reflections. Understanding how **lateral sound reflections** work has been a catalyst for radical designs of concert halls, particularly in the 1970s and 1980s. Some of the major work on the importance of lateral reflections was done by British acoustician Michael Barron.

It is important for an architect to spend time with the acoustical consultant early in the design of a concert hall, to incorporate acoustical qualities into the architectural design. The shape of the building is critical to the quality of the music heard there. The design should proceed from the outside in, then the materials should be selected. The interior designer must work closely with both the architect and the acoustical designer to create a design that will accommodate a variety of musical styles and instrumentations.

After researching fifty-four concert halls, acoustical expert Leo Beranek developed a list of essential acoustical attributes of a concert hall. They include:

- Reverberance
- Loudness
- Spaciousness: affects ambiance
- Clarity: intelligibility, articulation, definition
- Intimacy
- Warmth
- Ability to hear on stage

Good sight lines, which often are also good listening paths, are critical as well. The hardest place to get good sound is in the center middle seats, which, ironically, are the most expensive seats in a concert hall.

The sense of being enveloped by the music, especially when listening to large groups playing symphonic music, depends largely on lateral reflections that are received from the side. When an audience sits in a fan-shaped area, side reflections are limited. A saw-tooth–shaped wall or reflector panels along the wall help create the desired reflections. Non-horizontal ceiling reflector panels also produce some lateral reflections, especially for people who sit in the balcony.

During outdoor concerts, people receive sound straight from the orchestra, there are no reflections from walls, and the sound appears distant. When music is played inside, reflections from the walls, ceiling, and floor embellish the sound. When sound reaches the listener from the stage, the same sound signal is received at both ears. This is because the human head is symmetrical and the sound to both ears travels an identical path. When reflections come from the side, the sound received at each ear is different. Sound to the farther ear has to get around the head. This means the sound arrives later and is significantly altered. The brain senses that it is in a room, and a feeling of being enveloped by the music occurs.

Halls that are too wide and low lack these important lateral reflections. The basic shoebox shape works well for up to 2000 people. The surfaces of these shoebox-shaped spaces are not smooth or slick in either older or new halls, with side and rear balconies breaking up the geometry. Details, such as niches and statues in older buildings or deliberate architectural manipulations in the ceilings and walls of new concert halls, create diffusion. Chandeliers, however, do not enhance diffusion.

High stage ceilings can create on-stage communication problems by absorbing sound directly above the performers. The configuration of the performance area has both functional and acoustical implications. A large sound-reflecting surface suspended over the performing area improves the ability of musicians on stage to hear one another.

Sound-reflecting panels were first used to cure focusing effects and improve sound distribution in domed auditoriums. They have also been used to improve the distribution of reflected sound in concert halls. A clear space above the panels adds to the reverberant volume. In-the-round stages have problems since musical instruments and the human voice are directional sound sources, and most classical music was written for performance in conventional rectangular spaces. Circular and elliptical shapes risk focusing sound on hot spots.

☑ **The acoustics of concert halls are designed to work best with the audience seating at least 80 percent full. Performers like a nearly full hall, so the size of the hall should not be over-designed. However, it can be difficult to rehearse in an empty hall, so spaces sometimes use movable curtains and banners to minimize this problem during rehearsals.**

When audiences are seated behind the performers, nondirectional trombones, percussion, and some other instruments are clearly heard. Even directional instruments like horns can be heard from behind, and seats behind the stage are usually good seats; exceptions are oratorios, cello concertos, or piano pieces because the directionality of the source prevents good acoustics in all directions.

Music continues to evolve to take advantage of the acoustics of new types of concerts. The combination of electronic and acoustical sources for live music performance adds a whole new layer to the acoustical complexity of concert spaces.

Opera Houses

Opera houses, with singers onstage and the orchestra in the pit, require both reverberation and clarity for speech and song. Both acoustics and visibility necessitate good sight lines from all seats to the stage. In addition, the proscenium arch that separates the performers from the audience and the tall stage tower behind the proscenium for rapid scene changes make it harder for people on stage to be heard. The design of an opera house is further complicated by the fact that the pit may be raised for events that do not call for an orchestra, so more seating can be added. Finally, there are concerns about the reverberant and absorbent qualities of finish materials and the details of the design that determine lateral sound reflections.

In the 1920s, almost all opera houses were designed to double as concert halls. Although the stage tower can do double duty as a concert shell and part of the tower can be used to add to the reverberation, it is better to design a separate space for concert performances because the sound is otherwise compromised for economy. Many of these halls have been redesigned in response to an increased awareness of quality concert-hall sound.

Recital Halls

Small halls for the performance of chamber music are often also used for a wide range of other activities. Adjustable absorption, such as draperies on tracks, allows flexible control of reverberation time and loudness. Stage areas can be adjusted for various sizes of performances using movable stage wall elements and batten-hung ceiling elements.

Other Listening Spaces

In addition to concert halls, recital halls, and opera houses, many other types of rooms have acoustical requirements for the performance of music, such as the following.

- Alternative listening spaces include large rehearsal rooms, ensemble rooms, faculty studios, music classrooms, practice rooms, and recording facilities.
- Prefabricated and pre-engineered sound isolation rooms are available for use as music practice rooms and for laboratory testing.
- Medical facilities use sound isolation rooms for diagnosing hearing problems.
- Industrial spaces use hearing protection booths to isolate workers from extremely loud processes.

Musical instruments can sound uncomfortably loud in a small room, so sound-absorbing materials are necessary. Instrumental rooms need more acoustical treatment than choral rooms because the music is louder. Adjustable absorption devices allow the treatment to change to fit the use.

Spaciousness is desirable in ensemble and rehearsal rooms, which are usually 1½ stories but are, ideally, 2 stories for larger rooms. Ensemble and rehearsal rooms often use suspended sound-reflecting panels. They should have sound-absorbing materials for reverberation control and loudness reduction, as well as to prevent the possible flutter-echo paths between parallel walls.

Evenly dispersed sound reflections are critical for optimal sound quality and consistency. **Geometric sound diffusers** are

Figure 20-8 Musical practice room. Absorptive material should be installed on the walls, at least between sitting and standing height. This minimal amount is appropriate for small practice rooms, but larger or high-ceilinged rooms require more coverage. Absorption should take place in all three dimensions.

used for band and choral rehearsal rooms, where the shaped surfaces of the diffusers break up direct sound reflections and disperse them evenly throughout the listening space. Made of heat-molded plastic and available in two standard shapes, geometric diffusers are commonly used in conjunction with acoustical wall panels for a combination of sound diffusion and absorption that improves overall room acoustics.

AUDITORIUMS

Interior designers are often involved in the design or renovation of spaces that do double duty. Auditoriums and theaters are often used by multiple and diverse community groups with varying levels of acoustical sophistication. Lecture rooms in schools, colleges, and other institutions often combine unamplified verbal presentations with electronic visual presentations. Churches, synagogues, mosques, and other worship spaces vary in size, function, and the combination of music and voice.

Auditoriums must accommodate many activities, including concerts, with varying acoustical requirements. Their acoustical

quality depends on the design concept, the budget, and the availability of auditorium staffing to adjust movable acoustical treatments. Solutions, therefore, must either be a compromise between the disparate needs or be adjustable to accommodate varied circumstances. The acoustical design of an auditorium involves room acoustics, noise control, and sound-system design.

Changing the volume of the space, moving reflective surfaces, or adding or subtracting sound-absorbing treatments can alter the acoustical environment of an auditorium. The size of the audience, range of performance activities, and sophistication of the intended audience influence the acoustical design. Once the basic floor area is determined by the size of the audience, the volume of the space is determined by the reverberation requirements.

The ceiling and side walls at the front of the auditorium distribute sound to the audience. They must be close enough to the performers to minimize time delays between direct and reflected sound. The ceiling and side walls also provide diffusion.

To allow adjustments to the acoustics for different events, large areas of tracked sound-absorbing curtains can be installed along the room's boundaries. The curtains can retract into storage pockets to maximize the reverberation time. For movies and lectures without music, permanent sound absorption on the ceiling, rear, and side walls results in a low reverberation time.

When the orchestra is enclosed by special movable surfaces, less sound is lost backstage and full-range sound is efficiently transferred and distributed to the audience. Orchestra-enclosure surfaces offer a good balance between parts of the orchestra and enhance on-stage communication between the musicians. The simplest, most economical modular surfaces allow leakage and reflect sound imperfectly at lower frequencies. Custom designs are heavier, more complex, and more expensive, but they work better.

Fully upholstered seating minimizes the difference in sound between the times when the room is full of people and when it is almost empty, such as during a rehearsal. Upholstery covered with an open-weave material is particularly effective.

Reflector panels are used on the ceilings of auditoriums, performing-arts centers, lecture halls, and churches. They are designed for large spaces that require improved sound reinforcement and timing of sound reflections to enhance listening quality. The sound-reflective and -diffusive surface of the flat panel is bowed and positioned in the field to the architect or acoustical consultant's specifications. The panels are made of a plywood core faced with a fiberglass gel-coat finish and are available in widths up to 30.5 meters (10 ft.) and lengths up to 12.2 meters (40 ft.). Panels are mounted with wire rope or cables.

THEATERS

In a theater, the effortless perception of speech is the most important acoustic goal. Sound reinforcement is essential in large theaters that seat more than 1000 people, and in theaters in the round that seat more than 600 people. A moderate fan-shaped plan enables a larger number of people to sit close to the stage than a rectangular plan. Balconies also bring people closer to the performers.

Monumental, high-ceiling spaces do not work well for theaters because they have long reverberation times and require strong reinforcement for speech. All wall and ceiling surfaces that do not produce quick reflections should be treated with efficient sound-absorbing material to control echo and reverberation.

LECTURE ROOMS

Lecture rooms are similar acoustically to small theaters. Their boundaries, especially the ceiling, should be shaped for effective natural reinforcement of speaking voices. Applied sound-absorbent treatments control reverberation, echo, and flutter.

The rear wall, the perimeter of the ceiling, and the side wall areas—especially where parallel—between seating and standing height are the most important to treat. Acoustical tile ceilings with hard walls are not an adequate solution for a lecture room. Classrooms linked through interactive video networks for distance learning are treated in a similar way to that used for teleconferencing rooms.

WORSHIP SPACES

Houses of worship combine speech and music during the same service, so changing draperies to accommodate either is not an option. The type of music varies from amplified gospel choruses that favor shorter reverberation times, to traditional boys' choirs and organs that benefit from longer reverberations. Liturgical music from medieval times to the present has depended on long, echoing interiors for much of its emotional effect. To accommodate this complexity, the acoustics are usually designed for music, with special assistance for speakers.

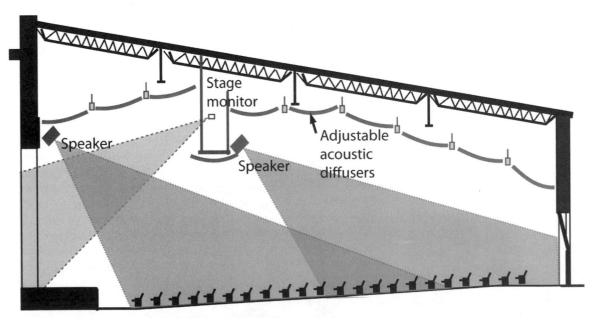

Figure 20-9 Auditorium adjustable sound treatments. Auditoriums must frequently accommodate a wide variety of performance events. Adjustable drapes and ceiling panels can facilitate this.

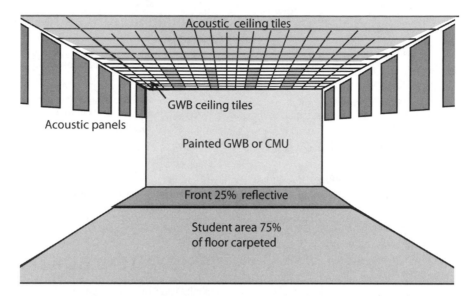

Figure 20-10 Classroom acoustical treatment. In a space used primarily for lectures, it is important to have good sound reflection in the teacher's area at the front of the room.

When preaching is the most important element of a service, the space should be designed for short reverberation times. A sound-reflecting canopy over the pulpit directs the speaker's voice to the congregation. A loudspeaker may be added over the canopy. Chanted liturgy may have derived from the need for clarity in early religious buildings with enormously long reverberation times.

The materials in worship spaces are often hard and reflect sound, like those in concert halls. Wood paneling absorbs low-frequency energy unless it is very thick or bonded to a massive surface. Brick, stone, and concrete reflect sound well, as does thick plaster.

Carpet is not widely used in worship places, with the exception of large evangelical churches. No sound-absorbing materials are used on the ceiling. Sometimes, pew cushions are needed to compensate for missing sound absorption in empty pews.

In the past, too much sound-absorbing material in large cathedral spaces resulted in acoustically dead spaces that were very poor for music and not very good for speech. The remedy was often the addition of an expensive sound system. The contemporary approach to acoustical design for churches is to design a spacious room with hard, sound-reflecting surfaces that effectively distribute the sound of music through the room, allowing the members of the congregation to hear themselves sing and producing ample reverberation. This is coupled with a sophisticated sound-amplification system to place amplified speech energy into the sound-absorbing seating area without directing large amounts of amplified energy at wall and ceiling surfaces. The process requires careful coordination among the architect, interior designer, acoustical consultant, and sound-system contractor.

Small, low, meetinghouse-type churches may have a medium-sized pipe organ or an electronic instrument. The style of architecture eliminates a long reverberation time, and favors the more intimate types of music. Speech will probably be clear without amplification.

Medium-sized churches and many synagogues and mosques can have good concert-hall acoustics. Typically, the church will have a moderate- to large-sized pipe organ. They often have hard, sound-reflecting surfaces. There is usually a relatively simple sound system with a central cluster of speakers.

Large evangelical churches are like large auditoriums with an amplified chorus, electric instruments, and television. Carpet is used in large evangelical churches, especially near the choir and organ. Pew cushions are always called for with amplified music.

Because of the need for a high level of intelligibility in a space with a long reverberation time, some houses of worship use speakers distributed in the backs of the pews. Wireless microphones accommodate mobility, with automatic microphone mixers for simplicity of operation.

SCHOOLS

Schools have a variety of spaces as well as a variety of acoustical environments. Auditoriums require sound systems for some activities. Some schools use a modified gym or cafeteria for musical and theatrical presentations. If the space includes large areas of sound-absorbing materials, it will not work well as an auditorium. Integrating loudspeakers into the design without creating large obstructions can be architecturally difficult, and they should be designed early in the process.

Classrooms are usually around 9 meters (30 ft.) square with ceilings that are 3 meters (10 ft.) high. The following are important elements of classroom design:

- Sound-absorbing materials should be used in order to reduce noise levels.
- The ceiling tile should have an NRC rating of at least 0.7.
- Walls should be designed to provide adequate privacy between classroom spaces, with sound blocked from leaking through doors between classrooms.
- Partitions should be full height from floor to ceiling slab or roof construction.
- The air-handling system and ductwork should avoid excessive noise.
- Unit ventilators in a room can provide adequate background noise, but they do so only when they are operating.

School dining areas are especially noisy. The kitchen and serving areas should be kept separate from the eating area so that kitchen noise does not add to the clamor of hundreds of children and teenagers. The ceiling and walls should have sound-absorbing materials, and the ceiling tile should have a minimum NRC rating of 0.8.

Nothing will quiet the excessive noise in a gymnasium, but noise is expected. The ceiling should be sound-absorbing, with an NRC rating of 0.7. If there is a sound-amplification system, the walls should also have sound absorption to prevent echoes.

Swimming pools are chaotically noisy. Special moisture-resistant acoustical materials are available for such wet areas as swimming pools and shower rooms.

Workshops have noisy machines and manual tools that produce airborne and structure-borne sound. These noisy functions should be isolated from quiet areas. Ceiling and wall treatments with an NRC rating of 0.75 should be used.

Recommended STCs for Partitions in Schools

School classroom walls adjacent to:
- Corridor, public area STC 38–40
- Another classroom STC 40–42
- Recreation area, toilet room STC 42–45
- Mechanical room STC 45–50
- Kitchen, dining area, shop STC 47–50
- Music room STC 50–55

School music-practice room adjacent to:
- Other practice room STC 50–55
- Public corridor STC 42–45

RESIDENTIAL BUILDINGS

Acoustical considerations for residential buildings include single- and multiple-family dwellings may also apply to other spaces where people sleep, such as dormitories, hotels and motels, and even healthcare facilities.

☑ **Understanding how to control noise in a residential building is a critical part of an interior designer's work. Whether an interior designer is trying to separate a home office from a blaring radio in a teenager's bedroom or to isolate the sound of a toddler's almost constant footfalls from the retired couple's apartment on the floor below, his or her sensitivity to acoustical design issues will help keep the peace among family members and neighbors.**

TABLE 20-3. SOUND TRANSMISSION CLASS AND IMPACT ISOLATION CLASS RATINGS FOR CEILINGS AND FLOORS

Rooms	Ceiling Below	STC	IIC	Floor Above	STC	IIC
Bedroom	Bedroom	52	52	Bedroom	52	52
	Living room	54	52	Living room	54	52
	Kitchen	55	50	Kitchen	55	50
	Family room	52	58	Family room	56	48
Living room	Bedroom	54	57	Bedroom	54	52
	Living room	52	52	Living room	52	52
	Kitchen	52	52	Kitchen	52	57
	Family room	54	50	Family room	54	50
Kitchen	Bedroom	55	62	Bedroom	55	50
	Living room	52	57	Living room	52	52
	Kitchen	50	52	Kitchen	50	52
	Family room	52	58	Family room	52	58
Family room	Bedroom	56	62	Bedroom	56	48
	Living room	54	50	Living room	54	60
	Kitchen	52	58	Kitchen	52	52
Bathroom	Bathroom	50	50	Bathroom	50	50
Corridor	Corridor	48	48	Corridor	48	48

TABLE 20-4. ACOUSTICAL GUIDELINES FOR HOUSING

Grade	Noise Environment	Wall STC Rating	Floor/Ceiling IIC Rating
I	Suburban quiet environment	3 points higher	3 points higher
II	Residential urban and suburban areas with average noise environments	Greater than 52	Greater than 52
III	Noisy environments	4 points lower	4 points lower

The guidelines below for acoustical design of apartment buildings and other buildings with multiple residents strive to protect privacy and reduce annoyance:

- Plan the locations of convenience outlets, medicine cabinets, mechanical services, and direct exhaust duct connections between apartments carefully.
- Use rugs or carpets with pads to limit footfall noise.
- Group quiet spaces together and away from noisy activities.
- Bedroom ceilings should have ceiling-mounted absorptive materials with an NRC rating of at least 0.6.
- A mechanical system with a continually operating fan can help mask sound from adjacent residential units.

Both the U.S. Department of Housing and Urban Development (HUD) and the Federal Housing Administration (FHA) issue acoustical design standards that supplement model building code requirements for residential buildings in the United States.

The FHA and HUD publish *A Guide to Airborne, Impact and Structure-Borne Noise Control* and other publications for multiple-residency buildings. They also set grades based on building location for STC and impact isolation class (IIC) levels.

RECOMMENDED STCS FOR PARTITIONS IN RESIDENTIAL SPACES

Motel, hotel, hospital, or dormitory sleeping rooms adjacent to:
- Other bedroom STC 50–52
- Bathroom STC 45–50
- Living room, dining area, corridor, lobby, public spaces STC 42–45

RESIDENTIAL BATHROOMS

Residential bathrooms are inherently reverberant spaces (which is why people sound so good when they sing in the shower) that demand acoustical privacy. The sounds of flushing toilets, spraying showers, running water, and whirring fans can be difficult to isolate inside a bathroom. In addition, people prefer to keep bathroom activities acoustically private and separate from adjacent spaces. The following are some ways to accomplish acoustical privacy:

- Separating the bathroom from bedrooms through the use of intervening closets and hallways isolates the sound.
- The construction of doors, walls, ceilings, and floors can be modified to reduce the passage of sound.

- Eliminating undercut or louvered doors (which are often used to improve ventilation) and providing acoustical treatment around the door frame keep sound within the bathroom.
- Back-to-back electrical outlets between the bathroom and bedroom should be avoided.
- Air grilles should not open into ducts and then out into a bedroom.
- Another operable window should not be located near a bathroom window.

The sound of water in pipes can travel from the bathroom throughout the house and end up next to the dining table, so pipes should be wrapped and resiliently mounted. When the layout of a house is first planned, the fixtures should be located in such a way that piping is inside walls that are less acoustically critical.

PUBLIC TOILET ROOMS

People should not be able to hear the noises from toilet rooms in adjacent spaces. When toilet rooms within service cores are designed, they should be surrounded with corridors and mechanical spaces. Seating people adjacent to a wall with plumbing, where they will hear the rush of water through the pipes, should be avoided.

Ventilation openings and access ways carry sound to other spaces. Interior designers should discuss this with the mechanical engineer or contractor.

Within a public restroom, a lack of acoustical privacy results in repeated flushing, which is wasteful and noisy. A steady masking sound should be used to obscure sounds. A higher-sound-level ventilating system, such as a noisy fan, solves this problem and is less expensive; however, it can carry through ductwork to other spaces. Music can disguise sounds very well. Another option is a recirculating fountain. The very clever owner of an Italian restaurant played the soundtracks to Italian soap operas in the restrooms!

ELECTRONIC SOUND SYSTEMS

The goals of sound reinforcement are to adjust acoustical problems and to ensure that everyone in the listening space can hear well. The ideal sound reinforcement system would give every listener the same loudness, quality, directivity, and intelligibility. Speech would be as clear as if the speaker were between 61 centimeters and 91 centimeters (2–3 ft.) away, with a longer distance acceptable for music. Sound reinforcement systems should be designed to provide adequate sound levels without distortion. Loudspeakers cannot completely correct poor acoustics, but they can improve a bad situation.

Design of Sound Reinforcement Systems

The designer of a sound reinforcement system needs a clear understanding of the functions that the system is intended to perform. These include the following:

- The size and placement of loudspeakers strongly influence interior design.
- The controls should be located where they are accessible but unobtrusive.
- Signal-processing and amplification equipment requires adequate space and ventilation as well as an adequate electrical supply.
- Loudspeaker placement should be coordinated with other interior features.
- Wiring for the sound system should be run discretely, preferably within walls.
- If sound wiring is not shielded from interference in metal conduits, the sound system may hum.
- The design of the sound system should be coordinated early in the design process

Specialists in sound-system design are sometimes certified members of the National Council of Acoustical Consultants. Others may operate independently, so it is always wise to check sound-system consultants' experience and previous work.

In a well-designed, carefully installed, and properly operated sound system, the pleasant, natural quality of the sound is not disturbed by distortion or coloration. The quality of the frequency response should bear the same relationship between frequencies as the original sound. **Distortion** occurs when a system changes the shape of the acoustical signal that it receives; some stages of the amplification are overloaded, and some frequencies are incorrectly amplified. Distortion usually results from a mismatch between the size of the signal and the size of the equipment that is processing it. If a system was designed for a single person giving a speech and is used for a rock band, the undersized equipment will probably distort the excessive signal. If the equipment that was purchased and installed was inadequate for the designated use, distortion will again result.

Sound coloration occurs when a reproduced sound loses its naturalness and acquires an unpleasant, ringing quality. Coloration may be caused by certain frequencies being amplified more than others. When this situation is extreme, typically because the system is turned up too loud, acoustical feedback or howling will result. Both problems can be corrected, but they may require changes in or adjustments to the equipment or system design.

The sound should appear to be coming from the original source, so that the loudspeakers are not identifiable by location. Speakers are placed in such a way that the reinforced sound arrives at a listener's ears with a slight delay following the sound directly from the natural source. This enables the listener to localize the sound as arriving from the direction of the source, not the loudspeaker.

A sound reinforcement system is usually required for spaces larger than 1400 cubic meters (50,000 cubic ft.). This is approximately the space occupied by 550 people in a lecture room with a 4.6-meter (15-ft.) high ceiling or a 325-person theater with an average 6-meter (20-ft.) ceiling height. The normal speaking voice can maintain a volume of 55 to 60 decibels in a room this size. With limited background noise, the speaker will be heard, but in a noisier space the speaker's voice will be less intelligible. Strong speakers will be heard clearly in smaller rooms that hold about 100 people, but people with weaker voices will require sound reinforcement. The voice level should be a minimum of 25 decibels above the background noise. Amplification of speech sounds at frequencies greater than 500 Hertz (Hz) restores intelligibility, but the result does not sound natural. To create a more natural effect, a high-quality sound system starts amplification around 125 Hertz. The intelligibility of sound in rooms with a long reverberation time is improved with a sound system that directs sound at the listeners' position.

Sound System Components

A sound reinforcement system consists of three parts: the input, the amplifier and controls, and the loudspeakers. The input can be a microphone, any of a variety of types of commercial broadcast signals, or one of many means of reproducing recorded material in common commercial formats, including compact discs. In sophisticated systems, the input is connected to local computers and computer networks.

Microphones convert sound waves into electrical signals, which are further amplified, transmitted, and processed as required in the sound system. Microphones may be handheld or on stands or may be miniature lavaliere types. Small, wireless transmitters are available for any type of microphone; these are especially helpful for theatrical plays.

Preamplifiers reinforce the signal of the microphone for additional processing and feed it to the other components of the sound system. A control console and mixer do the same job as a preamplifier; these options are more complex but allow for more flexible control of the sound.

Power amplifiers provide a signal output with sufficient power (voltage and electrical-current output) to feed the loudspeakers connected to the system. In situations where the background sound level is 60 decibels, an amplifier is rated to deliver sufficient power to produce between 85 decibels and 90 decibels for speech, 95 decibels for light music, and between 100 decibels and 105 decibels for symphonic music. Systems for rock bands produce sound-pressure levels that exceed 110 decibels, and exposure to this level of loudness for extended periods will damage hearing. An amplifier's power can be reduced in quiet spaces. An acoustical specialist or a sound engineer usually specifies the amplifier. Amplifiers have controls for volume, tone mixing, and input-output selection.

Signal-processing equipment includes equalizers, limiters, electronic delays, feedback suppressors, and distribution amplifiers.

Loudspeaker Systems

Loudspeakers convert an electrical signal supplied from the power amplifier into air vibrations that the human ear perceives as sound. Loudspeakers must be the same high quality as the rest of the sound system.

The design and placement of the loudspeaker system must be coordinated with the architectural design. The speaker placement of conventional distributed loudspeaker systems has to be coordinated with the locations of lights, sprinklers, and air-handling system diffusers. Central loudspeaker systems require architectural enclosures and adequate supports.

Depending on the application, loudspeakers are arrayed in either a centralized system or a distributed pattern. Centralized systems are used in large spaces with high ceilings to project sound with strong directionality from a focal point, such as a stage or pulpit. Distributed loudspeaker patterns are used in spaces with lower ceilings where the sound is distributed evenly and without a strong sense of source through many smaller speakers, as in offices or restaurants.

Central loudspeaker systems provide directional realism for medium- to large-sized auditoriums. In places where the audience is deep, the coverage of the front and distant parts of the audience is likely to be uneven, so supplemental speakers are used. Deep balconies and areas under balconies as well as wide first rows often call for supplemental speaker coverage. Delayed signals help preserve the sense of direction of the sound.

Distributed loudspeaker systems use a series of small low-level speakers that are between 10 centimeters and 31 centimeters (4–12 in.) in diameter located throughout the space. These are often ceiling-mounted or recessed in the ceiling and send sound directly down, so that each speaker covers a small area. Speakers may also be located in the backs of seats or pews. Distributed loudspeaker systems are used in areas with low ceilings where a central loudspeaker cluster cannot provide the proper coverage. These systems are also used for public-address (PA) functions when directional realism is not essential, as in exhibition areas, airline terminals, and offices. In public areas with highly reflective surfaces, careful speaker positioning and volume levels are critical; otherwise, the result is extremely loud but unintelligible speech.

Individual loudspeakers in a distributed system can be easily switched on or off for proper coverage. Ideally, a listener's position receives sound from only one loudspeaker. If the speakers overlap, loudness and garbled speech results. Another significant advantage of a distributed system is that the speakers closest to the microphone can be switched off, which is important in deep rooms with low ceilings. Speakers should not be placed on each side of a proscenium opening, and rows of speakers should not be located on one or both sides of a room.

Whatever the loudspeaker arrangement, the sound-system operator should be within the covering pattern of the speakers. This means that space must be provided within the audience-seating area or in a control room with a large opening located at the rear of the space. The best location for the sound-control room

Figure 20-11 Audio equipment. Loudspeakers come in many sizes and configurations. Current tendencies are toward miniaturization, although large speakers are still used for live performances and public-address (PA) systems.

or position is in the rear of an auditorium, where the operator can directly hear the sound and follow activity. The sound-control room should either be fully open to the volume of the space, which is practical only for small systems without much equipment, or in a separate sound-control room with a large, operable sound-control window. Using a monitor loudspeaker or working from a remote-location control room produces unsatisfactory results for live performances. Many performing arts sound reinforcement systems use control facilities located entirely within the audience area.

Interior designers are routinely involved in coordinating the many details of an installation, and this sometimes includes the sound system. There is a tendency to think of the sound-reinforcement system for a smaller project as an add-on and to leave it to the end of the design and construction process. However, doing so risks last-minute crises when sound wiring, speaker locations, and space and wiring for control equipment has to be retrofitted into locations for which it was not planned. Running wires within walls is much easier before the walls are closed in and finished. Although sound-reinforcement design may not technically be a part of an interior designer's work, ignoring these details creates difficulties that adversely affect the appearance of the project and the smoothness of the construction process. A familiarity with the equipment required for specific types of spaces will help interior designers anticipate conflicts with the details of the interior design and prevent last-minute problems.

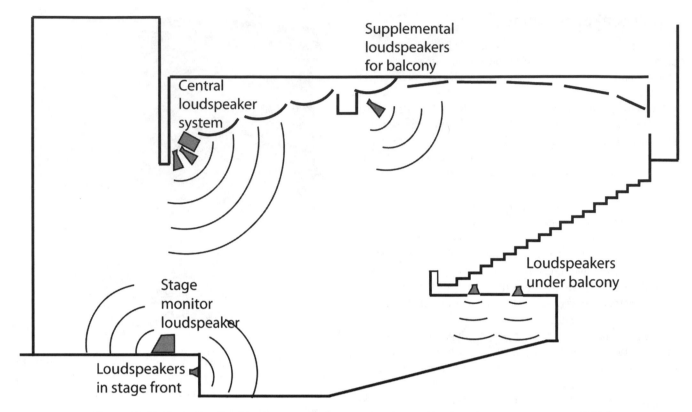

Figure 20-12 Centralized loudspeaker system. A conventional central loudspeaker system uses a carefully designed, central speaker array of high-quality, sectional (multicell), directional, high-frequency horns, and less directional, low-frequency large-cone woofers to provide directional realism with a relatively simple design. The array is placed either slightly in front of the primary speaking position or above the source of the live sound. In most theaters, this is directly above the proscenium arch on the centerline of the room. These components are very large, and the architect and interior designer must be aware of the dimensions to be accommodated. Smaller units are available with folded horns, but they are less responsive in low frequencies, which makes them acceptable for speech but inappropriate for music. Supplemental speakers may be added for coverage of the balcony and under-balcony areas.

Figure 20-13 Distributed loudspeaker system. In large meeting, convention, and exhibition halls, distributed loudspeaker systems offer flexibility in seating arrangements and reinforce sound from any position in the room, even when the room is divided by movable partitions. Distributed systems allow flexibility in spaces where the source and the listener locations vary according to the use of the space. These systems do not provide directional realism, but they offer very good clarity and intelligibility. Distributed systems are not appropriate for rooms with very high ceilings.

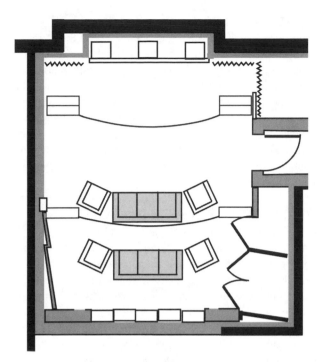

Figure 20-14 Home listening room acoustical design. This home listening room acoustical design incorporates buffer areas, angled walls, and rear-wall sound reinforcement.

Home listening Rooms:

- These rooms experience significant coloration and poor spatial imaging of reproduced sound when they are not extensively and uniformly treated with broadband sound-absorbing materials.
- The goal in these rooms is to suppress the sound of the room itself, but not to completely deaden it; this requires large areas of sound-absorbing and sound-diffusing treatments on all surfaces.
- Treat paired surfaces in the same manner. The treatment must be completely symmetrical on the left and right sides of the main listening axis, so that sound-transmission paths for left and right playback channels are identical. Surround-sound channels have special placement considerations that should be coordinated with the equipment supplier.

Office spaces:

- Sound reinforcement may be limited to announcements or background music.
- Distributed loudspeakers should be either recessed in ceilings or concealed in the ceiling plenum behind acoustically transparent ceiling panels.
- Open offices usually have masking-sound systems for speech privacy.
- High-rise office towers may include a sound system that is designed for life-safety announcements and the transmission of warning signals.
- Emergency sound systems are usually separate from other systems and use fire rated equipment, wiring, and installation materials.

Auditoriums and lecture halls:

- In medium- to large-sized auditoriums, sound systems have a sense of directional realism
- In auditoriums and lecture halls, the controls for sound, projection, and lighting are frequently located in the listening room.
- Typically, these spaces have a provision for remote controls for projection, volume control of the sound, and dimming of lights at the lecturer's position.
- Large assembly halls may have central or distributed loudspeakers.
- In spaces in which the audience or delegates participate from the floor, microphone arrangements vary from simple to very complex.
- Assembly halls for multinational conferences must have a system for simultaneous translation.

Concert halls:

- High quality, full-range sound reinforcement systems are used in concert halls with multiple functions.
- Typically, a central loudspeaker system with high directivity is suspended in free space or integrated into the architecture.
- Sound reflectors or canopies are located above the orchestral platform.
- Backstage performance monitoring as well as intercom and paging systems may be used.

Theaters and opera houses:

- These spaces may reinforce vocals over orchestral sounds, but some music fans prefer the sound without amplification.
- Amplification is more of a necessity in larger theaters.
- A central loudspeaker system is usually located at the proscenium to provide directional realism; there may also be supplemental speakers.
- Microphone receptacles are located in the footlights at stage front and may also be in the wings.
- Program monitoring and stage-manager paging systems for the cast may be located offstage.
- Production communication systems are provided for light and sound technicians, projection rooms, and similar functions; these may be special intercom systems with mobile wireless remote stations.
- The normal frequency range for a high quality sound reinforcement system is between 40 and 12,000 Hertz.

EXHIBITION HALLS

Exhibition halls use sound reinforcement for announcements and for background music. If a hall includes a permanent or demountable platform for stage presentations, it will typically include a central loudspeaker system located above the front of the platform in order to provide sound reinforcement with directional realism.

HOTEL BALLROOMS AND BANQUET HALLS

Hotel ballrooms and banquet halls are often divided for smaller groups of people, and microphone pickup may be required from any location on the floor. Overhead speakers are distributed throughout the rooms. If a room contains a stage platform or projection screen, it should also include a central loudspeaker system.

Hotel banquet rooms are used for many types of activities, from medical conferences to bar mitzvahs and fashion shows. The sound designer should consider including production communication facilities for lighting, projection, and sound-control technicians. Typically, the controls for these functions are located in wall-mounted boxes, which should be integrated into the room design rather than being attached to the walls during construction.

☑ **During renovation projects, it is a good idea to check whether existing wall-mounted equipment is actually in use. In one hotel, microphone antennas that had not been used for 12 years would have been given special treatment when the wallpaper was installed if an alert technician had not noticed and alerted the interior designer.**

SPORTS FACILITIES

Indoor sports arenas that contain a maximum of 15,000 seats use a directional loudspeaker system located in their center. If there are additional performance stages, each platform needs its own system. Multipurpose arenas have a performance monitoring and paging system as well as an intercom system for stage management, lighting, and sound. Arenas require a great deal of acoustical treatment for low-frequency sound; otherwise the noise becomes uninterrupted and speech clarity and intelligibility suffer. Systems can limit the signal to exclude the lowest frequencies without harming the quality of speech.

Sports facilities with more than 5000 seats are also used for large public events and popular-music concerts. The surfaces are too far from the performers and listeners for sound reinforcement from reflected sound energy without the problem of echoing. Massive applications of acoustical treatments with high absorption coefficients in the speech-frequency range, especially those between 250 Hertz and 4000 Hertz, are used to make the boundary surfaces sound absorbent.

In concrete structures, thick sound-absorbing foam boards can be left in place on the underside of the concrete. Steel surfaces can be made of perforated-metal roof decks with glass fiber in the middle. Inflatable domes use a special sound-absorbing fabric that sags below the dome fabric.

☑ **Wall and ceiling surfaces should be acoustically treated. Seats should be upholstered if possible; otherwise, perforated-metal seat bottoms with an absorbent material should be used inside the seats. Sound-absorbing material also helps control crowd noise and allows the sound system to communicate emergency information over the noise.**

MOVIE THEATERS

Movie theaters use amplified sound and cushion the space with highly absorbent materials, so the shape of the theater is not acoustically important. The most critical consideration is the reflectivity of the room boundary. A large quantity of wall- and ceiling-mounted broadband sound-absorbing material should be used to control reverberation. A minimum of half of the walls and between half of and the entire ceiling should be treated. Loudspeakers are located in the front of the theater behind a perforated screen. Baffling is used to capture the sound radiating to the rear of the screen.

SPECIAL SOUND-SYSTEM INSTALLATIONS

Paging and voice-alarm systems are used in power plants and other industrial facilities, in which high levels of ambient noise and long reverberation times overwhelm PA systems. Paging and voice-alarm systems also cost less and are smaller than PA systems. Lights or sirens are used for simple messages, and headsets can be used with earmuffs.

The Americans with Disabilities Act (ADA) requires assistive listening systems in some assembly areas and specifies the types and placement of systems. Listening devices are often provided at selected seats in auditoriums by an outlet jack that accommodates both a headset and an individual volume control under the chair's armrest. Wireless systems can cover all auditorium areas. In transient-lodging accommodations, such as hotels and motels, a certain number of rooms must be accessible to people with hearing impairments.

☑ **Interior designers need to be aware of acoustical concerns that affect the health, safety, and enjoyment of the public; this is an important part of their role as a member of the building design team. Their knowledge of all of the systems that make a building work will enhance the quality of their work, the value of the building to those who use it, and their own enjoyment of their professional work.**

I wrote this second edition of *Building Systems for Interior Designers* to enlighten interior design students and others about some of the less glamorous—though not less important—aspects of building design. This book is also intended as a refresher course for interior designers who are preparing for the National Council for Interior Design Qualification (NCIDQ) exam as well as a desk reference for anyone who needs to know how buildings work.

INDEX